# ISLAND TO EMPIRE

## 300 Years of British Art

### 1550–1850

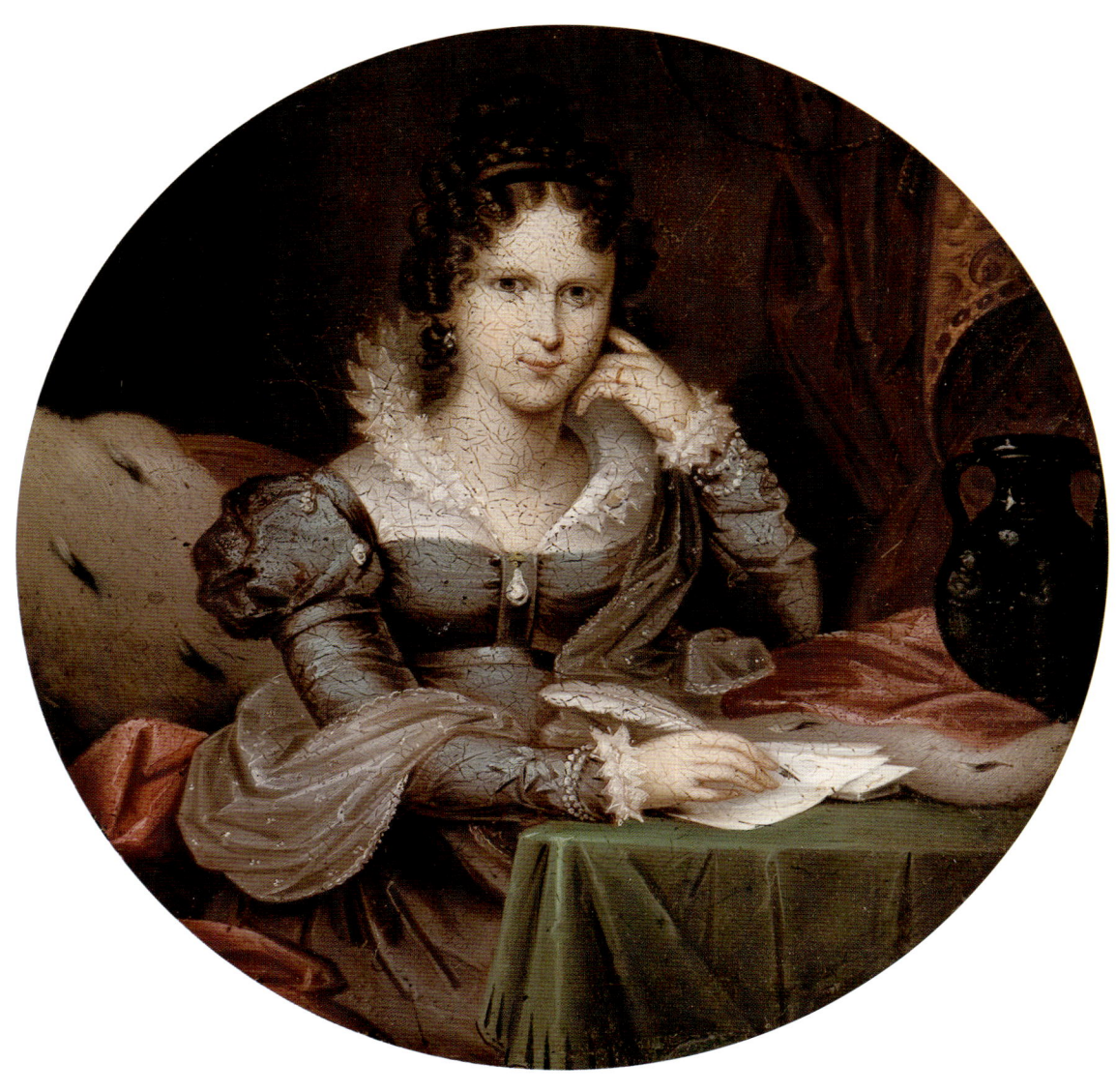

This portrait is of Queen Adelaide, after whom the City of Adelaide was named. She was the consort of William IV who was king when the province of South Australia was founded. It was given to the Gallery by Queen Mary consort of George V who had opened the Art Gallery of South Australia when a young prince in 1881.

Samuel Raven, 1775–1847, after Mary Green (née Byrne), *Queen Adelaide as Princess Adelaide*, c.1818, oil on papier mâché, 13.7 cm diam. Gift of Her Majesty Queen Mary 1946

# ISLAND TO EMPIRE
## 300 Years of British Art
### 1550–1850

PAINTINGS   WATERCOLOURS   DRAWINGS   SCULPTURES

from the collection of the

## Art Gallery of South Australia • Adelaide

Ron Radford

THIS BOOK IS GENEROUSLY SPONSORED BY THE GORDON DARLING FOUNDATION

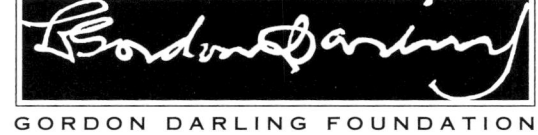

GORDON DARLING FOUNDATION

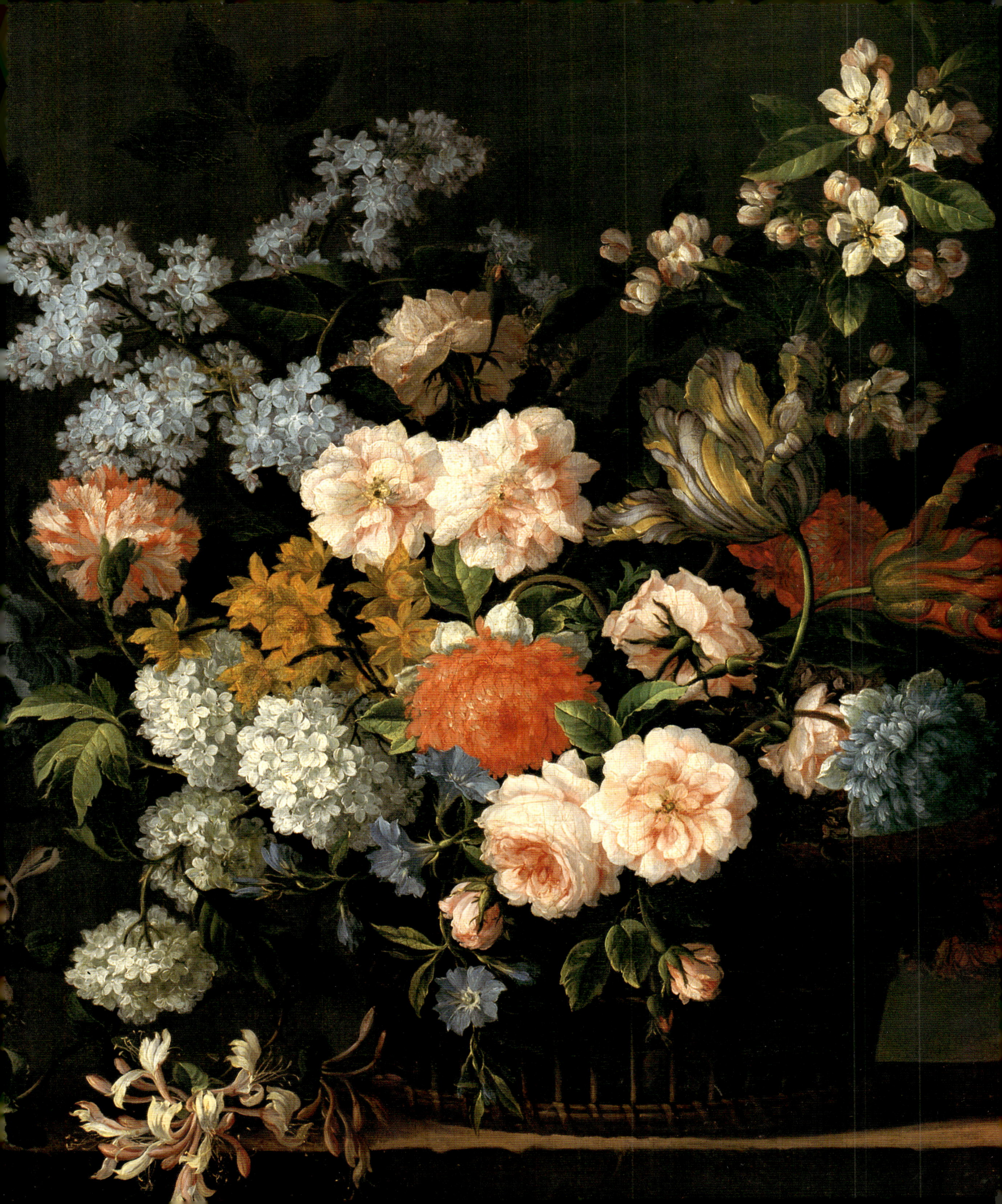

# Acknowledgements

In working on this book over a period of many years there are numerous people whose assistance I would like to acknowledge. Scholars in Britain who have been extremely helpful include Hugh Belsey, Kenneth Garlick; Karen Hearn and Tabitha Barber both of the Tate, London; Elizabeth Einberg, Andrew Wilton, formerly of the Tate; Malcolm Rogers, formerly of the National Portrait Gallery, London; Michael Jaffé, Sir Roy Strong, and the staff of the Witt Library of the Courtauld Institute, London. Of those in the United States I would like to thank Scott Wilcox of the Yale Center for British Art, New Haven, and Shelley Bennett of the Huntington Library & Art Collections, San Marino, California.

Acknowledgement must be made to the dealers who have supplied information on the works including Julian Agnew, Donald Garstang, Nicholas Hall, Robert Crompton Jones, Frank McDonald and Mark Weiss.

I wish to thank many members of my staff at the Art Gallery of South Australia: Julie Robinson, Curator of Prints, Drawings & Photographs; Jane Messenger, Associate Curator, Prints, Drawings & Photographs; Adam Free and Angus Trumble, former Curators of European Art; Christopher Menz, former Curator of European & Australian Decorative Arts; Tracey Lock-Weir, Curator of Australian Art; Sarah Thomas, former Curator of Australian Art; Barbara Fargher, Curatorial Assistant; Cherie Prosser, Acting Assistant Curator of Australian Art; and especially Jin Whittington, Librarian. They have all recently helped with so many details.

I would also like to thank a number of volunteers who undertook certain research for me, the late Necia Gilbert, Lesley Lynn and especially Jenny Kalionis.

Most of the fine photography of the Gallery works has been taken by Saul Steed and I thank him.

I have received much assistance in Britain, America and Australia on specific works and I have acknowledged this help within the texts on the individual works.

The first drafts of the first chapter, "The Britishness of British Art", and last chapter, "Collecting British Art in Adelaide", were written in the peaceful township of Robe in South Australia, under the generous hospitality of Belinda Morgan. For this I am greatly indebted to her.

Much of my initial research was undertaken in Britain and America in 1990 as a result of being awarded a Churchill Fellowship (used mainly to do research at the Courtauld Institute), a Fellowship in British Art at the Yale Center for British Art, and a Huntington Research Fellowship at the Huntington Library & Art Collections. I am grateful for the opportunities for research these scholarships afforded me and I am particularly grateful for the access to documents and the other research resources at Yale and Huntington.

I also thank my editor, Daniel Thomas who has gone well beyond the usual scope of editing and made extremely useful suggestions, checked a great number of facts and corrected much else. I must take full responsibility if there are any other mistakes or inconsistencies.

The Gallery's Publications Manager, Antonietta Itropico, has been endlessly patient in designing this very complex and beautiful book and seeing it through production.

My full appreciation must be recorded for the long-suffering, ever faithful, and always patient Lindsay Brookes who typed and retyped my lengthy handwritten manuscripts.

The Gordon Darling Foundation has given a very generous grant towards the publication enabling us to produce an elaborately illustrated and affordable catalogue book.

Above all, of course, I must thank the great number of individual private donors, many recent, who have helped build this unusually balanced collection of British art dating from 1550 to 1850 into a major part of the European art collection within the Art Galley of South Australia. They are individually acknowledged within the texts.

**Ron Radford** AM
Director, Art Gallery of South Australia

p. 5 detail:
Jean-Baptiste Monnoyer, 1636–1699
*Still-life with basket of flowers*, 1690s
oil on canvas, 73.0 x 103.5 cm
Gift of Anne Clemens 1985

p. 7 and p. 8 detail:
Pompeo Batoni, 1708–1797
*Edward Weld*, c.1761
oil on canvas, 75.0 x 62.0 cm
James & Diana Ramsay Fund 2004

pp. 10–11 detail:
J. M. W. Turner, 1775–1851
*Scarborough town and castle: morning: boys catching crabs*, c.1810
watercolour on paper
68.5 x 101.5 cm (sheet)
On long-term loan to the Art Gallery of South Australia since 1987

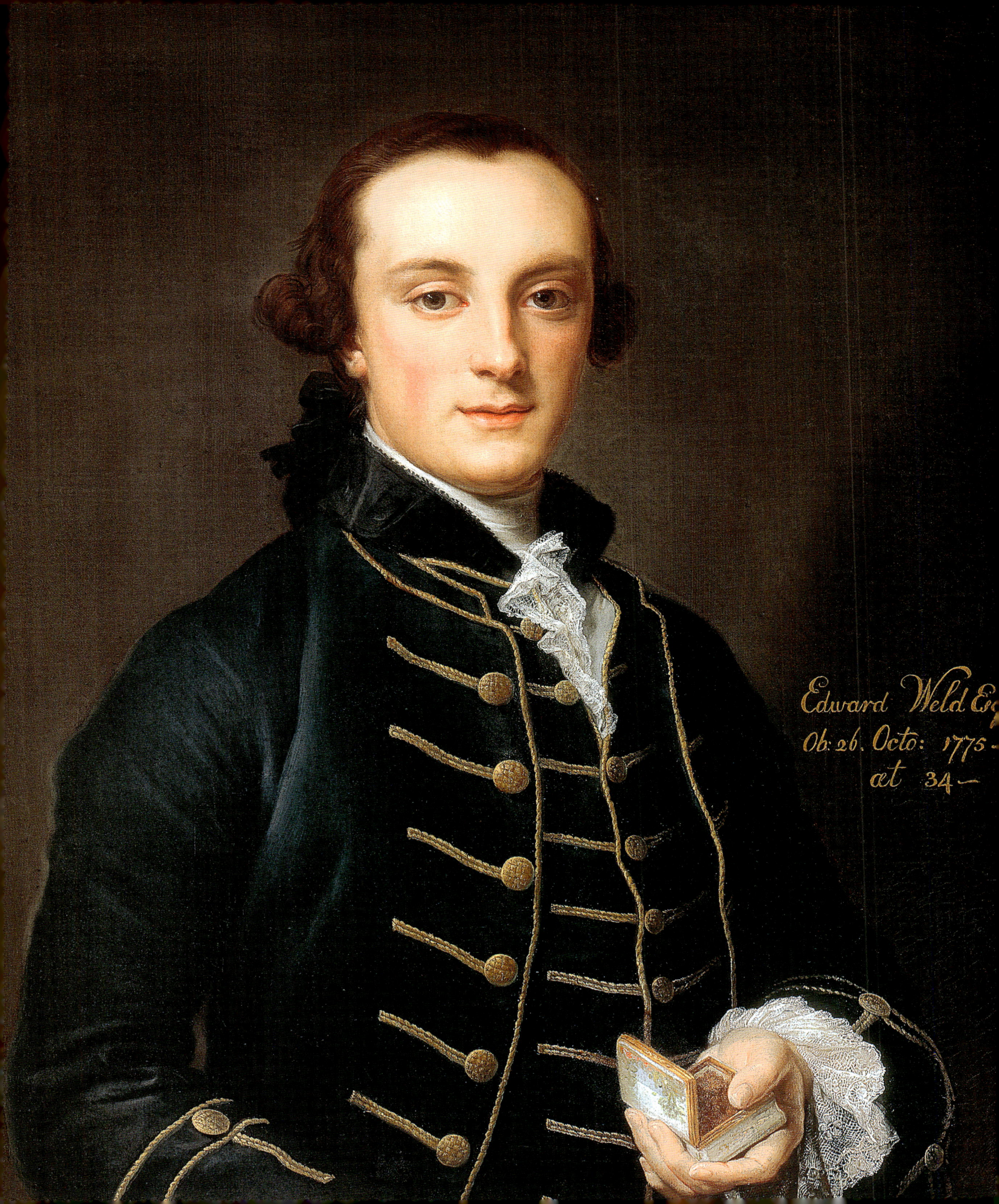

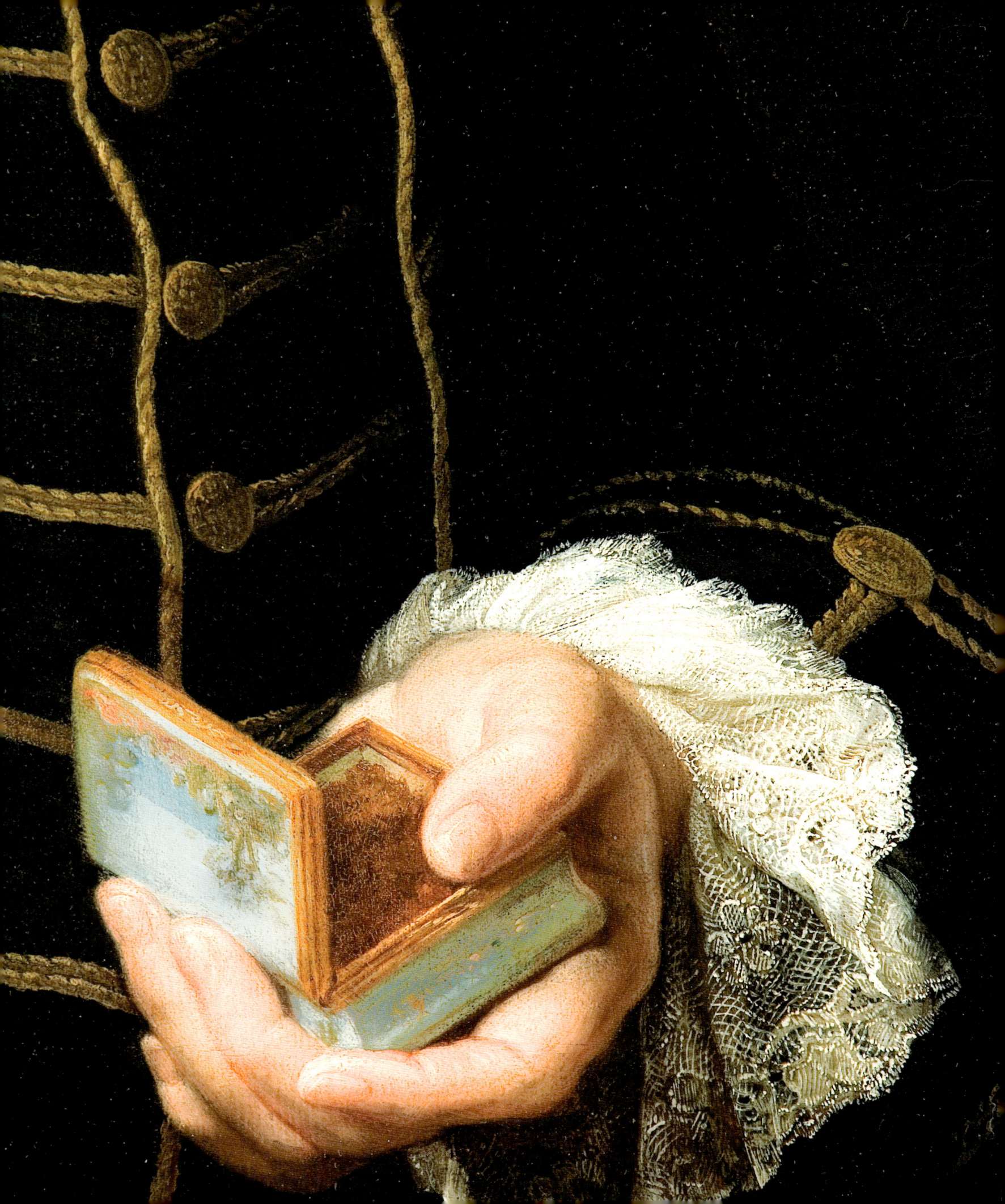

# Contents

The Britishness of British Art: 10
   From the heritage of Hans Holbein to Holman Hunt

Cataloguing the Collection 32

Catalogue Essays 35

End Notes 277

Collecting British Art in Adelaide 289

Catalogue 297

Select Bibliography 328

Index 331

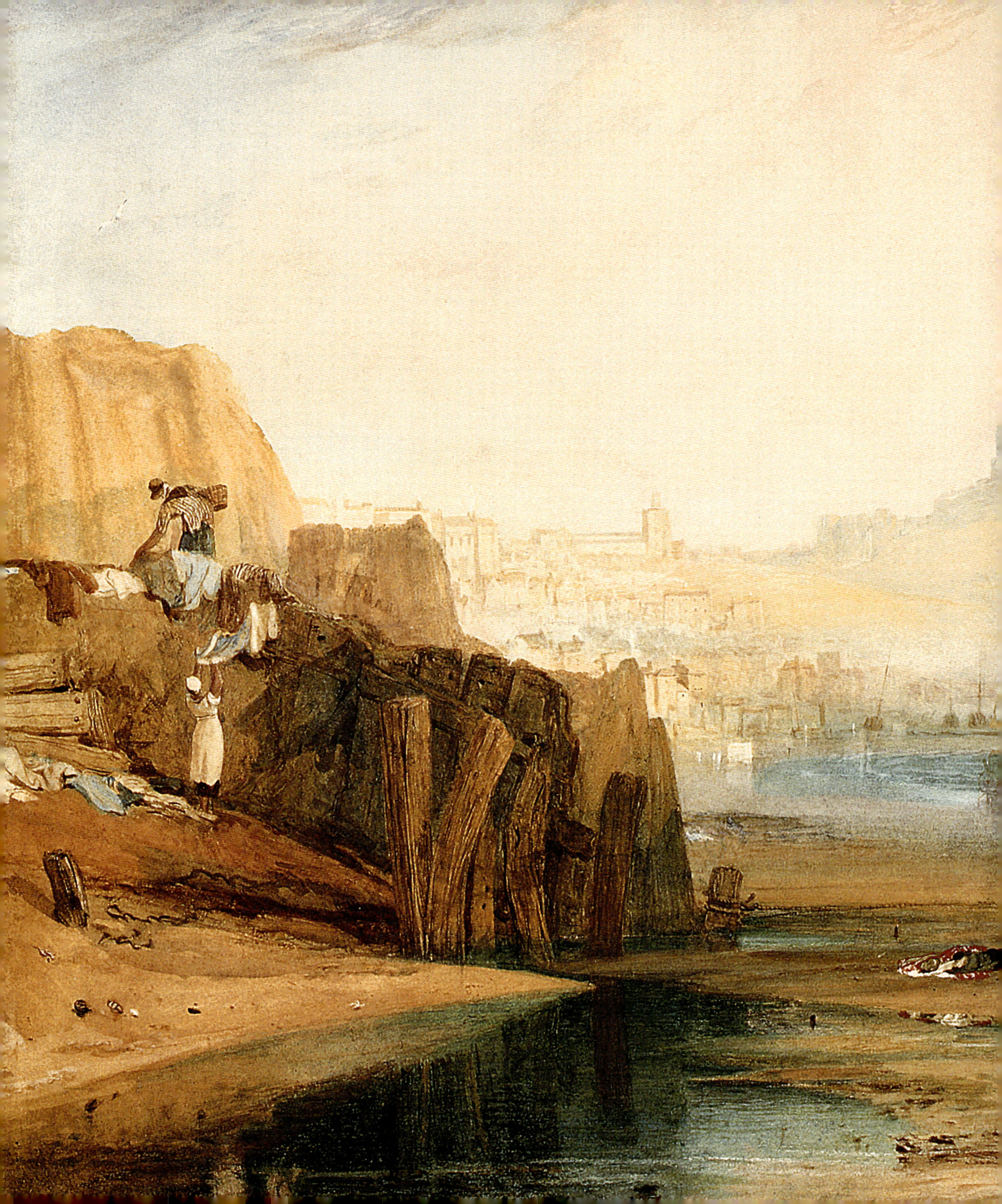

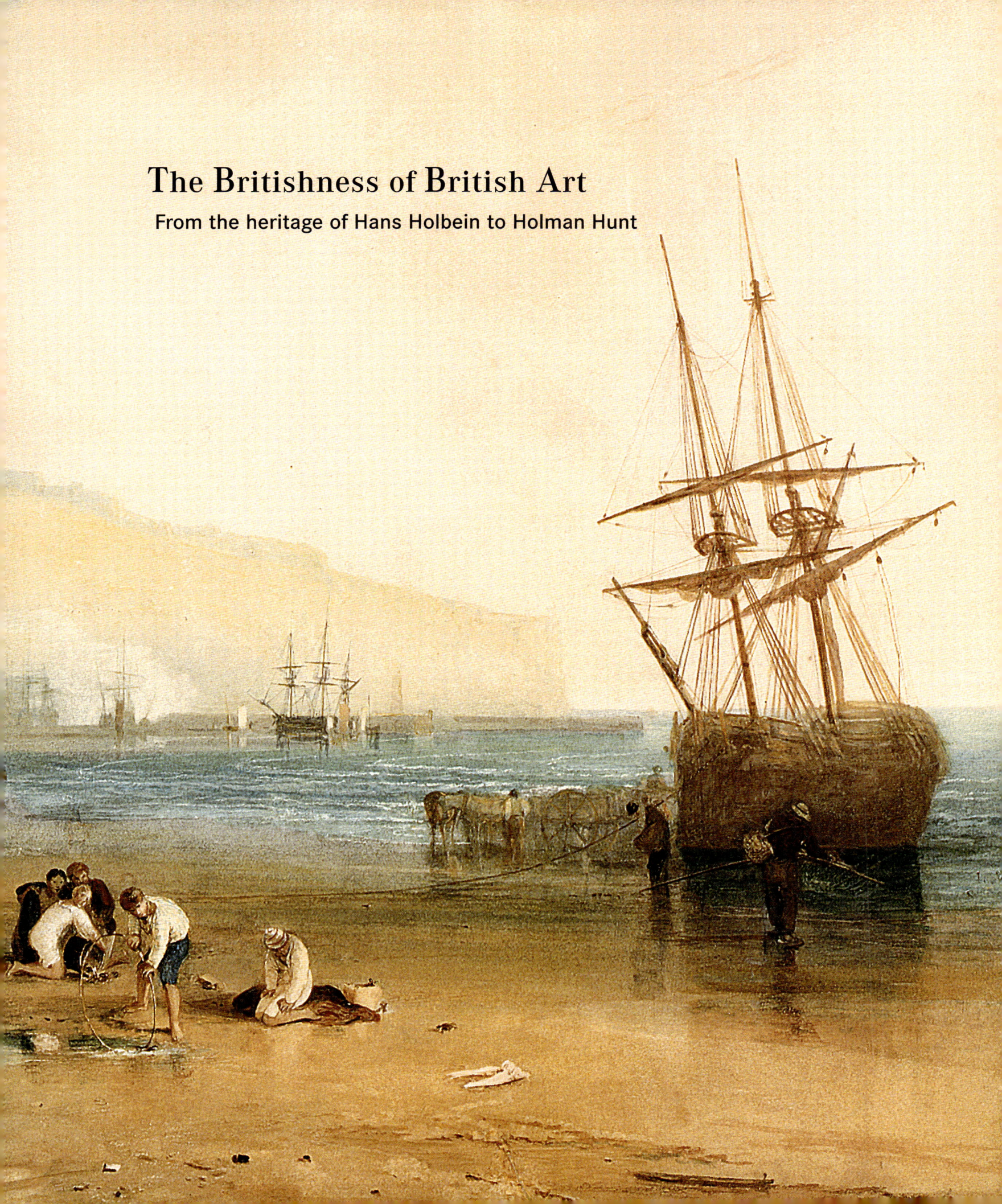

# The Britishness of British Art
From the heritage of Hans Holbein to Holman Hunt

# The Britishness of British Art: From the heritage of Hans Holbein to Holman Hunt

Traversing the essays on individual works that cover the period from about 1550 to 1850, a reader will follow an outline of the development and themes of British art as well as the contributions of individual artists. This chapter sums up the characteristics and achievements of British art as seen largely through the collection of the Art Gallery of South Australia in Adelaide.

We will analyse what distinguishes British art from its influential sources in the art of continental Europe. The distinctive subjects found in British art will be an important consideration. And we will see how fully the Gallery's collection reflects British art of the period. This is not an attempt to write a short history of British art from 1550 to 1850. That would require a larger collection and more chapters. Instead some of the broad trends are outlined here. To accompany the discussion there are illustrations of British prints from the Gallery's extensive collection, amassed in complementary parallel with the catalogued paintings, drawings and sculptures. British traditions of course constituted the beginnings of Australian colonial art in the first half of the nineteenth century, and their impact in Australia enters the story.

The first and most obvious observation is the almost overwhelming presence of portraiture. Portraits dominate British art from the sixteenth century onwards to the early nineteenth century. Landscape painting struggled to the fore only in the late eighteenth century, triumphed by the 1810s and 1820s, and finally confirmed its prestige after the death in 1830 of Sir Thomas Lawrence, President of the Royal Academy and in his time probably the most esteemed portrait painter in the world. The Gallery's collection well reflects the development of the self-regarding British preoccupation with portraiture. It includes most of the major and some of the minor portrait painters over the three-hundred-year period.

From the first arrival in Renaissance Britain in 1526 of Hans Holbein the Younger, the most important northern Renaissance portrait artist, British art was wholeheartedly devoted to portraiture. Henry VIII, to whom Holbein later became official portrait painter, dismantled the Roman Catholic Church and its monasteries in Britain, declaring himself head of a new Church of England. Religious imagery, the main subject of European art, was declared to be idolatry and later banned in Britain. Religious works of art were destroyed. What was regarded in the sixteenth century as the whimsy of classical mythological subjects never really interested the British, who regarded themselves as down-to-earth and practical. Even after the establishment of the Royal Academy two hundred years later, its classical principles and training failed to generate a substantial body of elevated history painting. A constant characteristic of British art is its close contact with reality. So portraiture became the most appealing option for artists; it suited not only the newly found individualism of the Renaissance but also the confident independence of the British people from the older culture of the Continent. Holbein's portraits raised the standard of Renaissance realism. His astonishing technique mesmerised the British ruling class, and the court and leading families followed the King's dynastic uses of portraiture. This could be seen clearly in Holbein's 1537 life-size mural, in Whitehall Palace, of Henry VIII and his queen Jane Seymour (who had given birth to their son and heir to the throne) standing in front of his father Henry VII and his mother, Elizabeth of York. The mural is now destroyed but the Holbein School portrait image in the South Australian collection

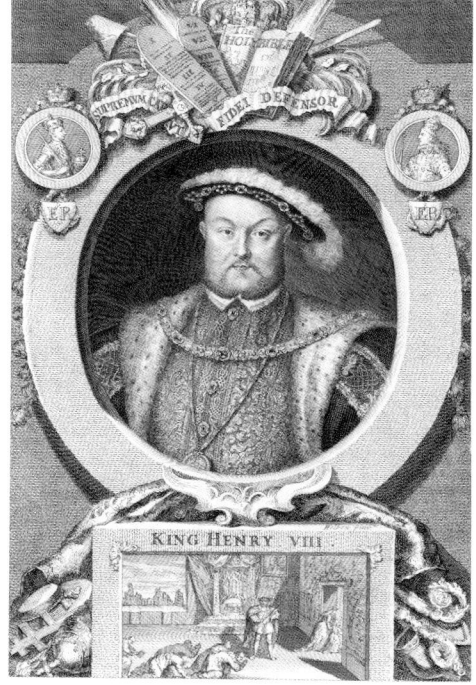

George Vertue, 1684–1756
after Hans Holbein the Younger, 1497–1543
*King Henry VIII*, 1732
engraving, etching & stipple on paper
29.6 x 18.8 cm (plate)
Bequest of David Murray 1908

ultimately derives from it. To emphasise dynasty, heraldic family coats of arms were often painted onto the background of the portraits (as in our *Richard Goodricke*), particularly those of the new class of landowners that Henry VIII helped to create or support by his grants of property once owned by the dissolved monasteries. Holbein's individualistic portraits of the King and his land-enriched court set the model and established the dominant tradition for art in Tudor England. In the great Elizabethan and Jacobean houses a new architectural fashion demanded a Long Gallery, a side-lit corridor hall for reception and indoor strolling, and for a pictorial display of ancestry. To this day in Britain and countries of her former Empire we understand the term 'gallery' to be a place in which to hang paintings.

It is interesting to note here, though it should not be surprising, that in the nineteenth century the British were the first to develop National Portrait Galleries, in London (1856) and Edinburgh (1889). The United States also has a popular portrait gallery. In 1998 Australia established its own National Portrait Gallery in Canberra, and two other former British colonies, Canada and New Zealand, have more recently laid foundations. The idea of portraiture has long been and still is especially admired in English-speaking countries.

A speciality within British portraiture, developed in Holbein's time, was that of the portrait miniature. Although miniature painting did not originate in and was not unique to Britain, it was the British who took to portrait miniatures with the greatest and longest-lasting enthusiasm. The tradition began with King Henry's miniature painter Lucas Horenbout. Miniatures could be encased in jewellery and worn or carried when travelling, or easily sent long distances to relatives and friends. The fashion grew in popularity in the reign of Henry VIII's daughter Elizabeth I and remained a distinct and precious part of British art-making until the invention of photography in the mid nineteenth century. Miniature painting in Britain reached a high point of achievement in the late Elizabethan and Jacobean periods, particularly in the work of Nicholas Hilliard and Isaac Oliver. The Gallery demonstrates the importance of miniature painting in Britain with a jewel-like portrait by Oliver and a few later seventeenth- and eighteenth-century miniatures, the finest of which is an enamel by Nathaniel Hone. However, most of the Gallery's miniatures date from the Regency period. The Gallery also holds examples of the tradition as transferred to the Australian colonies, where miniatures were a significant component of local portraiture in the first half of the nineteenth century. They began with Australia's first professionally trained portrait painter, Richard Read senior, a convict transported to New South Wales in 1813, and continued in the work of his free-settler son Richard Read junior, who arrived in Sydney in 1819. A little later in Tasmania the convict artist Thomas Bock and Australia's first female artist Mary Morton Allport were major colonial exponents of miniature painting. In the 1830s and 1840s South Australia's first professional artist was Martha Berkeley who painted miniatures of the first settlers of Adelaide.

Miniature painting in late-sixteenth-century Britain had some effect on the style of life-size portraiture, particularly in the second half of the long reign of Elizabeth I. The ageing queen instructed her miniature-painter Nicholas Hilliard to avoid painting shadows when recording her artificially whitened face. This emphasised a flattening

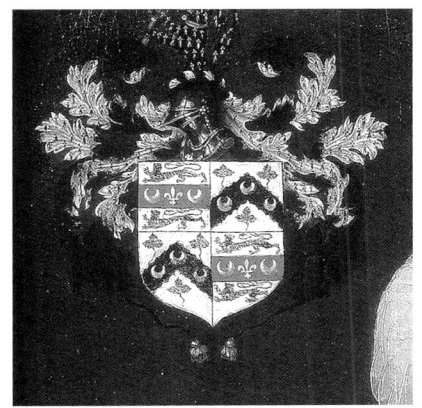

detail: Cornelius Ketel, 1548–1616
*Richard Goodricke of Ribston, Yorkshire*, c.1578
oil on oak panel, 106.0 x 81.0 cm
Roy & Marjory Edwards Bequest Fund 2004

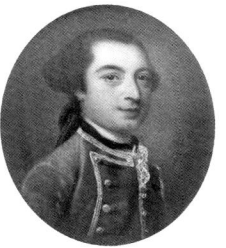

Nathaniel Hone, 1717–1784
*Naval Officer*, 1758
enamel on copper, 3.5 x 3.0 cm
Helen Bowden Gift Fund 2004

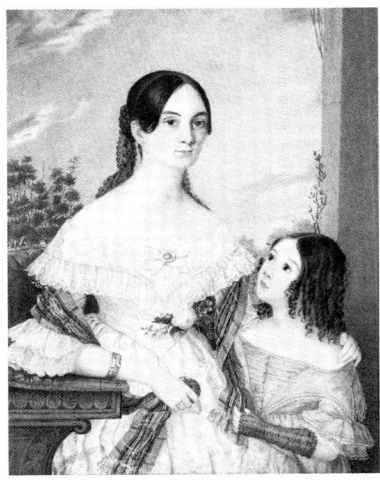

Martha Berkeley, 1813–1899
*Anne Eliza Duff with her daughter Jessie*, c.1847
watercolour on paper, 16.5 x 13.3 cm
Purchased 1994

Crispijn de Passe the Elder, 1564–1637
after Isaac Oliver, based on Nicholas Hilliard
*Elizabeth, Queen of England*
1603/04, Cologne, Germany
engraving on paper, 34.8 x 22.5 cm (sheet)
David Murray Bequest Fund 1949

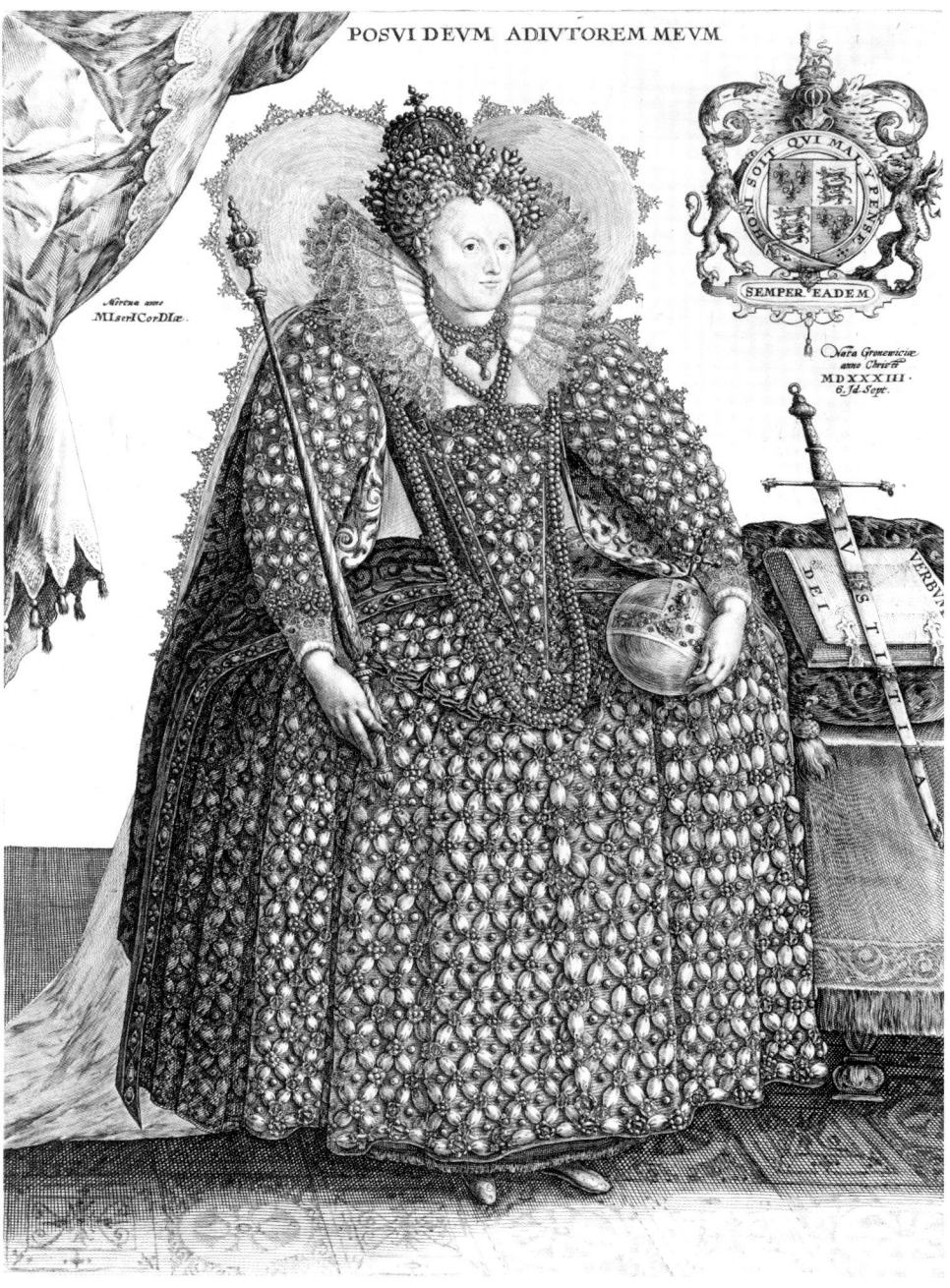

of the form while still recording the detail of her heavily-bejewelled costumes. Such characteristics were translated into life-size portraits of Elizabeth and her courtiers and became the notable stylistic feature of portraiture in the later part of her reign. This decorative and emblematic quality can be seen in the Gallery's stiffly dignified portraits by the Queen's painter George Gower (*Portrait of a lady*, c.1590) and by Robert Peake (*Frances, Lady Reynell*, c.1595). The decorative portraits of Elizabeth herself became increasingly iconic as the mystique of her persona was promoted, especially after her navy's defeat of the Spanish Armada. Her status in these portraits became as if sanctified or deified. In Protestant Tudor England, icons of the Virgin, the Queen of Heaven, were replaced by icons of the 'Virgin Queen' of England.

The iconic and decorative quality of Elizabethan portraiture continued well into the reign of James I, who died in 1625, and in provincial England even beyond the mid seventeenth century. It was a Medievalising style that defined a class rather than individuals. British portraiture could not have evolved further from the realism of Renaissance and early Baroque portraits produced in Italy or the Low Countries. However, within the more sophisticated court circles of James I the influence of Dutch realism gradually began to change the distinctive nature of English portraiture. Marcus Gheeraerts had painted Queen Elizabeth at the beginning of the 1590s but about 1620, when he painted the stiff melancholic portrait of *Magdalen Poultney, later Lady Aston*, the style had become old fashioned by court standards. Gheeraerts was superseded by both Paul van Somer and Jan Mytens who arrived from the Low Countries in 1616 and 1618 respectively to be court painters. It is thought they were at least partially trained for a time by the major Dutch artist Michiel van Miereveld. Miereveld, regarded as a prolific modern equivalent to Holbein, as early as 1610 had painted realistic portraits of English sitters who visited The Hague. In 1612 the Jacobean court tried but failed to attract Miereveld to London. The Gallery's 1625 portrait of the great Duke of Buckingham is a splendid example of a British subject painted by this Dutch artist. Miereveld's portraits held in Britain may have affected a number of local painters, among them Gheeraerts's student Cornelius Johnson whose half-lengths, characterised by intimate realism, began by 1620 to be fashionable among the upper and middle classes. The Gallery's head-and-shoulders portrait by Johnson is typical of his quest for individuality over emblematic class stereotypes.

At the end of 1620 Rubens's young and prodigiously talented Flemish assistant Anthony van Dyck was persuaded by art-loving noblemen to come and paint in Britain. Van Dyck was already a rare master of the double portrait as seen in the Gallery's *A married couple* (c.1620), a picture influenced by the relaxed realism of the great Venetian painter Titian. However, Van Dyck's advanced style of animated Baroque realism was then to have little effect on English portraiture as he stayed less than five months, painting for only a few patrons such as the Earls of Arundel and Buckingham. His impact on British art came when he returned, eleven years later as a mature artist, to be King Charles I's Principal Painter, whereupon he was immediately knighted. Sir Anthony's flamboyant style thereafter radically changed British portraiture. His informal naturalism swept away any archaic stiffness that had lingered into the earlier years of the Caroline court; British portraiture would never be the same again. Van Dyck's aristocratic swagger style held uninterrupted sway over the local tradition of grand portraiture for the next two hundred years.

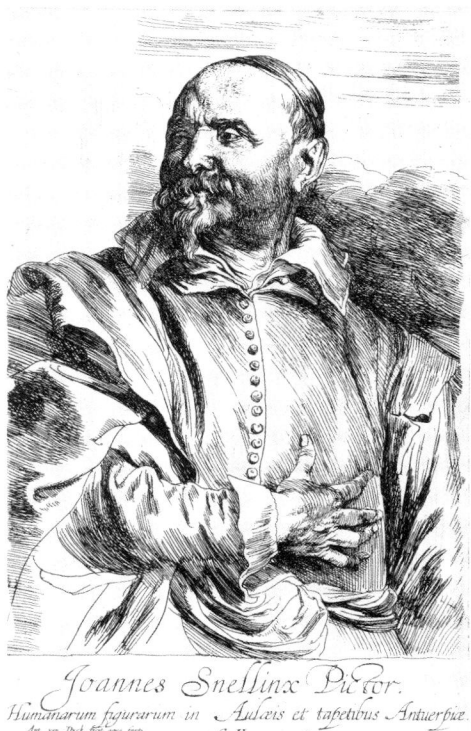

Anthony van Dyck, 1599–1641
*Jan Snellinx* from the set *The Iconography*, c.1628–32
etching on paper, 24.4 x 15.7 cm (plate)
David Murray Bequest Fund 1949

As will have been obvious thus far, British art was heavily reliant on Continental artists who settled in Britain, and most of them were Flemish or Dutch. While it is true that the style of these émigré portrait painters was modified to some extent by the conditions and demands of their British patrons, they invariably had a greater impact on the art of their new country. The German Holbein and the Flemish Van Dyck both returned to London to become the King's painter, in 1532 and 1632 respectively. Both artists enjoyed international reputations before they finally migrated to Britain, where they settled and died. Exactly one hundred years apart, their different styles – Holbein's solid Renaissance realism and Van Dyck's animated Baroque realism

detail: Anthony van Dyck, 1599–1641
*A married couple*, c.1620
oil on canvas, 120.0 x 154.0 cm
Gift of James Fairfax assisted by the
Art Gallery of South Australia Foundation 1993

– changed the nature of British portraiture and greatly raised its standard.

Other notable artists arrived in Britain from the Continent during those hundred years, some of them already mentioned. In the early Tudor period there were the miniaturist Lucas Horenbout, who arrived from Flanders by 1531, and fourteen years later his compatriot Hans Eworth; Cornelius Ketel followed them in 1573, in the first part of Elizabeth's reign. Besides Van Dyck in the early Stuart period there were Paul van Somer from Antwerp and Daniel Mytens from The Hague, and in 1636 Wenceslaus Hollar from Germany. The significant locally born or locally trained artists included Queen Elizabeth's Sergeant Painter George Gower, the miniature painters Nicholas Hilliard and Isaac Oliver, and the painters of larger portraits Robert Peake, Marcus Gheeraerts the Younger, John de Critz, William Larkin, Cornelius Johnson and, later, William Dobson. It was during the latter half of Elizabeth's and the first half of James I's reign – from the 1580s up to about 1615 – that locally trained artists flourished. England was then artistically very isolated. The lack of patronage from Elizabeth resulted in few major foreign artists being attracted to her court and none stayed. The artists sometimes emulated their foreign counterparts but mostly made individual contributions to the archaic local style, flat and decorative, a peculiar form of provincial late Mannerism. None of them enjoyed the exceptionally high status that Van Dyck gained in Britain.

The steady stream into Britain of foreign portrait painters, beginning in the second half of James I's reign, did not end with Van Dyck. Peter Lely arrived in London from the Netherlands about 1641, shortly after Van Dyck's death, but well before the execution of Charles I, whom he painted. Lely was profoundly affected by Van Dyck's grand style, especially after the restoration of the monarchy in 1660. As Principal Painter to Charles II for twenty years until his own death in 1680, Lely played a similar role to that of Van Dyck at Charles I's court; they set the styles of their different times. We cannot think of those reigns and courts without thinking of the distinctive and potent images the two artists forged.

The straightforward style seen in the Gallery's sober yet elegant portrait, thought to be of Lord Delamere, painted by Lely at the end of the austere republican Commonwealth period, bloomed into a more flamboyant mode after the restoration of the monarchy. Lely's full-blown Restoration style is epitomised in the series of 'Windsor Beauties', voluptuous portraits of women of the court, commissioned by the Duchess of York. These sensuously painted women exude a quality that reappears only in the mid nineteenth century – namely sex. Except for Lely's ladies, and often his gentlemen as well, British art during the three centuries under discussion is very respectable. This is especially obvious when one compares British art with Italian, French, Flemish and Dutch art of the same time. The sexless quality of British art is certainly reflected in the Gallery's collection of serious and distinguished portraits, and even the few seventeenth- and eighteenth-century nudes produced in Britain were relatively sexless. The restrained decorum is arguably a reflection of Protestant Puritanism.

Lely's role as the leading painter at Charles II's court was taken by yet another foreign artist, this time Godfrey Kneller from Germany. He had trained in the Dutch Netherlands and Italy before arriving in London in 1676, quick to absorb much of Van

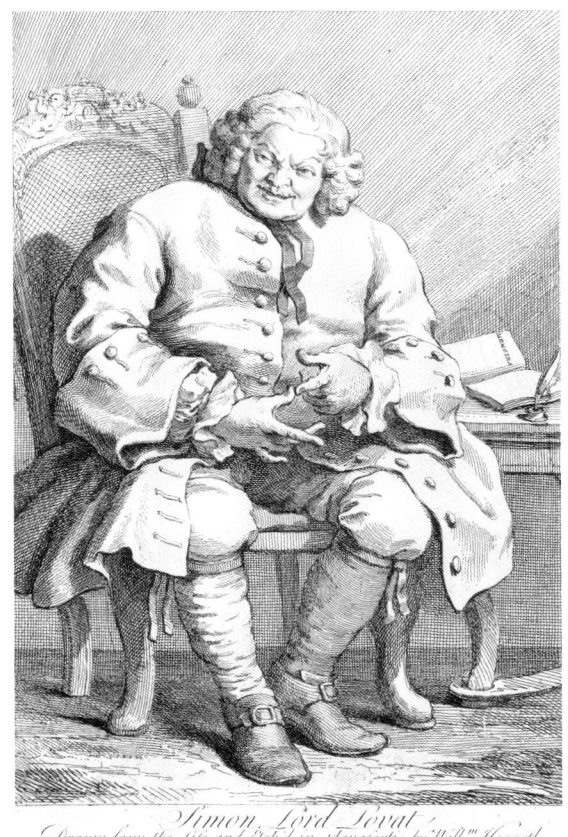

Simon Lord Lovat
Drawn from the Life and Etch'd in Aquafortis by Will:m Hogarth.

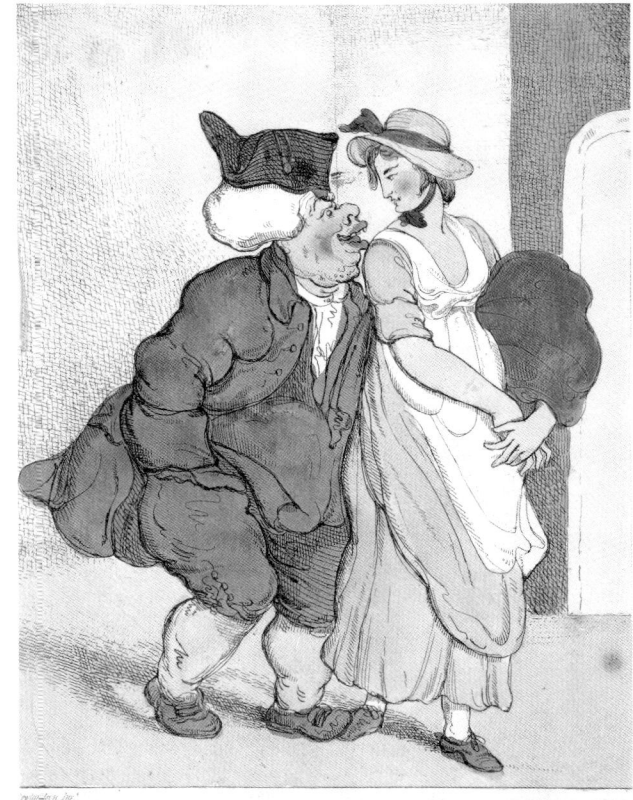

COME LIVE WITH ME AND BE MY LOVE.

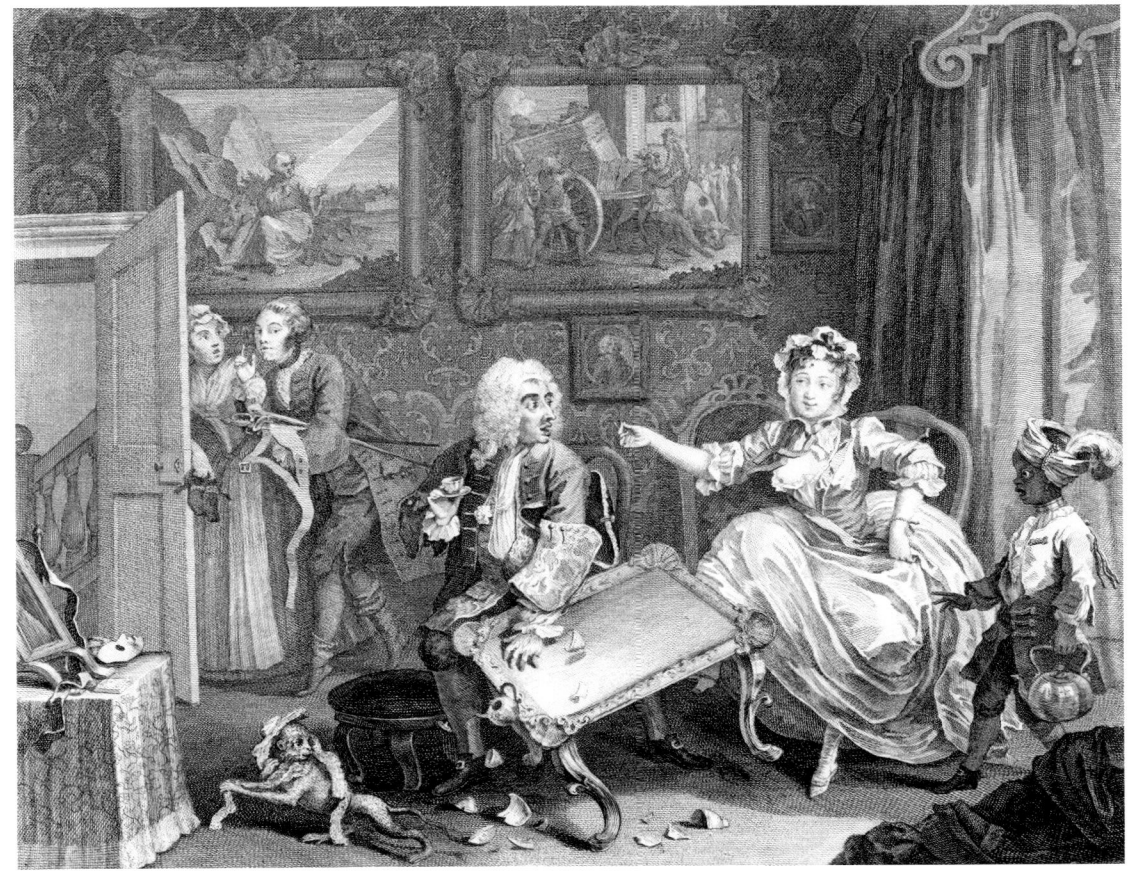

19

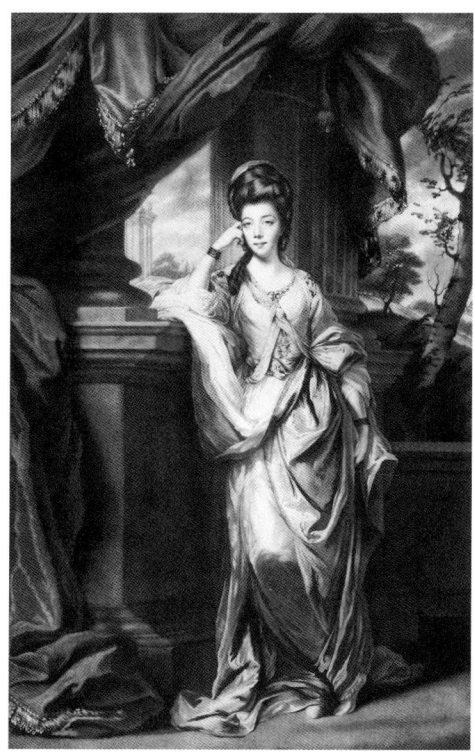

James Watson, c.1740–1790
after Joshua Reynolds, 1723–1792
*Anne, Duchess of Cumberland*, 1773
published by James Watson, London
mezzotint on paper, 62.4 x 38.0 cm (plate)
David Murray Bequest Fund 1954

mid 1760s Ramsay was succeeded in fame and success by Joshua Reynolds, whose style was even grander and more ennobling. In Rome the British on the Grand Tour patronised a slightly older portraitist, Pompeo Batoni, and the many paintings of his to be seen in England, much finer than those by local artists, must have influenced British painting in the same way that Miereveld's had over a century earlier. The Art Gallery of South Australia's small portrait by Batoni of *Edward Weld* (c.1761) is included in the present book.

Reynolds, who was born in 1723, the year of Kneller's death, initiated the eagerly-welcomed Royal Academy in 1768 and became its first President. (It was the year after he painted the Gallery's intimate portrait of his friend Dr Armstrong.) The Royal Academy trained successive generations of British artists in the full academic manner but also promoted their work, and the status of artists, by presenting high-prestige exhibitions in prominent venues. British art would no longer need protection against foreign competition. This coming of age of British art included portrait painters like Francis Cotes, Tilly Kettle and George Romney, all well represented in Adelaide's collection. However, Thomas Gainsborough outshines them; his shimmering glamour, which owes a great debt to Van Dyck, made him one of the greatest portrait painters in Europe at the time. Gainsborough's late style, seen in his rendering of the opera singer *Madam Lebrun* (1780) in unusually expressive and abbreviated painterliness, represents a high point in British portraiture. The golden age concludes in the Regency period of the early nineteenth century with stylish portraits by Thomas Lawrence, famed in his lifetime throughout Europe and America, and emulated in the Australian colonies long after his death. Lawrence's portrait of *Caroline Matilda Sotheron* (c.1808) is a characteristically elegant and dashing example of his style.

Portraiture prevailed as the dominant vehicle of British art for three centuries, and it included the peculiarly British speciality of animal portraiture. The British sometimes liked to be known for their love of pets, their obsession with horses and their strong interest in the special breeding of farm animals, and these qualities are reflected in their art. From the second half of the eighteenth century they commissioned portraits of favourite pets and prize animals, especially horses, as enthusiastically as they did members of their families. Thomas Barlow in the late seventeenth century can be considered the first English animal (and bird) painter, but George Stubbs in the second half of the eighteenth century raised animal painting to great art with his magnificent and sensitive portraits particularly of horses and dogs. He was the first British artist carefully and scientifically to study the anatomy of animals. His animal portraits show an accuracy and individuality much treasured by his patrons and by us today. He also painted dramatically romantic images of wild animals such as *A lion devouring a horse.*

The Agricultural Revolution in Britain ran parallel with broader patronage of the natural sciences. Sir Joseph Banks, a typical great landowner, commissioned a portrait of himself from Reynolds and wrote tracts on mildew in wheat, and on wool-growing with merino sheep. Less typically, when young, instead of a Grand Tour of Italy he led a scientific party to the South Seas on a voyage instigated by the Royal Society (for promotion of science) and captained by James Cook. Banks's

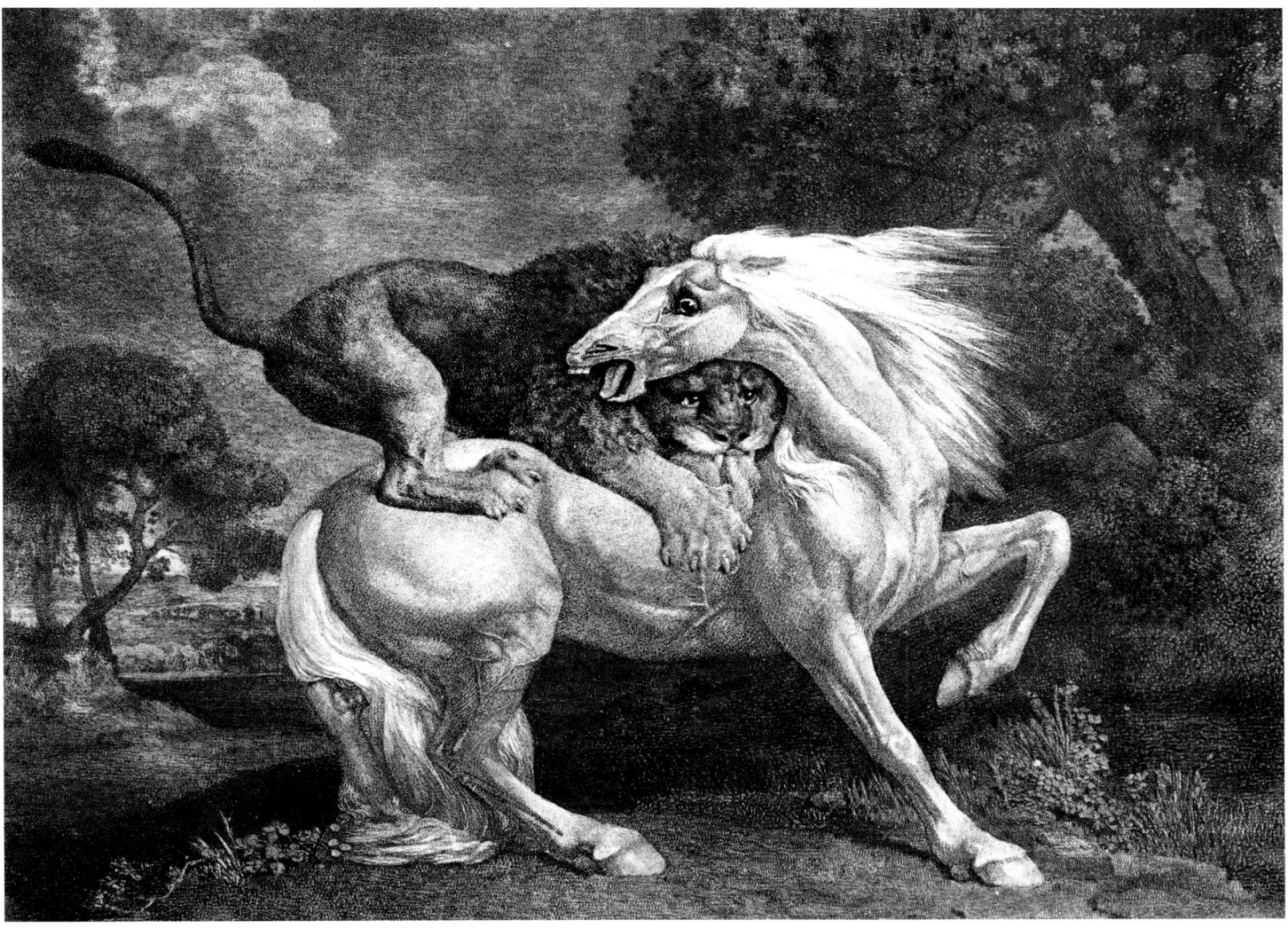

George Stubbs, 1724–1806
*A lion devouring a horse*, 1788
soft-ground etching with roulette work on paper
27.3 x 35.3 cm (plate)
David Murray Bequest Fund 1954

recommendation that a colony be founded at Botany Bay, a place near Sydney that had greatly excited the naturalists in 1770, made him in effect the founder of the nation now known as Australia. On his return home he was immediately at the centre of scientific enquiry. King George sought his advice on the development of the Royal Botanic Gardens at Kew and in 1778 he was elected president of the Royal Society. In 1801 he made sure that Matthew Flinders's hydrographic survey of the Australian coasts included another high-powered party of botanists and the outstanding botanical artist Ferdinand Bauer.

A number of major and many more minor artists made a living from the patronage of animal breeders and animal lovers. James Ward in the early nineteenth century was a significant animal painter as can be seen in his portrayal of the handsome spaniel Dash painted in 1819 in the manner of Titian and proudly and successfully exhibited at the Royal Academy that year. Towards the mid nineteenth century J. F. Herring painted many fine equestrian portraits and occasionally dogs. His set of four paintings of the seasons, promptly translated into popular prints, was really an excuse for horse painting as can be seen in the Gallery's *Autumn*. Queen Victoria's favourite painter Edwin Landseer made a fortune in the mid nineteenth century with paintings in which dogs were shamelessly imbued with sentimental human qualities.

Portraits of pets and prize racehorses are linked to another English speciality, that of hunting and field-sports pictures. They hung in upper- and middle-class British houses, generally in gentlemen's studies and games rooms or hallways: portraits of horses and bulls, sheep, pigs and other farm animals cohabited with genre scenes of hunting, shooting and fishing field-sports. Inns were another place for the display of sporting pictures. The British agricultural revolution and its interest in special breeding stock at the beginning of the nineteenth century was accompanied by portraits of outstanding or unusual specimens like Robert Hills's painting of the curious and ancient Soay sheep. John Glover, a farmer's son, cashed in on animals. His *Cattle: The last Gleam of the Setting Sun* (1816), a giant painting of almost life-size cows, combined connoisseurship of farmers' livestock with awareness of art-history traditions; he follows the style of Aelbert Cuyp's Dutch seventeenth-century cattle landscapes. T. S. Cooper devoted his long career of nearly seventy years to painting cows, one of his earliest and finest being the Gallery's *Fording a brook, suburbs of Canterbury* (1834). Only in Britain was there such a serious and lucrative tradition of animal painting, one that lasted into the twentieth century. It was also adopted in the Australian colonies, particularly in Victoria after the 1850s gold rush, and flourished for a further fifty years.

Although portraiture prevailed in British art it was not the only specialised practice. There was also a lively marine-painting tradition. Genre painting, the term for scenes of everyday life, included satirical art, as mentioned. And finally and belatedly there was the triumph of landscape painting.

In the British Isles marine painting developed long before landscape painting – indeed nearly two centuries before. Maritime paintings (and tapestries) from the later Elizabethan period include nationalistic battlepieces of the defeat of the Spanish Armada. It is logical that maritime art should develop in an island nation and a growing maritime power. It was likewise a strong presence in Dutch art, especially in the early to mid seventeenth century when the Dutch were at the height of their global trading and sea-going power. The defection in 1672 from the Netherlands to Britain of Willem van de Velde the Elder and his more influential son Willem van de Velde the Younger reflects the decline of Dutch maritime power and consequently marine art, and the steady rise of the latter in Britain. They had a retainer from Charles II for pictures of sea fights. The Van de Veldes' atmospheric realism profoundly affected marine painting in Britain. Throughout the eighteenth century there was a significant and growing practice of sea and ship paintings from followers of Van de Velde the Younger, including Peter Monamy, Charles Brooking, Francis Swaine and Dominic Serres (who became a founding member of the Royal Academy). In the Gallery's collection a major mid-eighteenth-century work by Swaine illustrates the movement, and later one by Serres. In the nineteenth century there are works by artists like Thomas Butterworth, Clarkson Stanfield, and above all J. M. W. Turner who uplifts and transforms the practice from descriptive ship and coastal painting to sublime seascapes. He became the greatest marine painter in

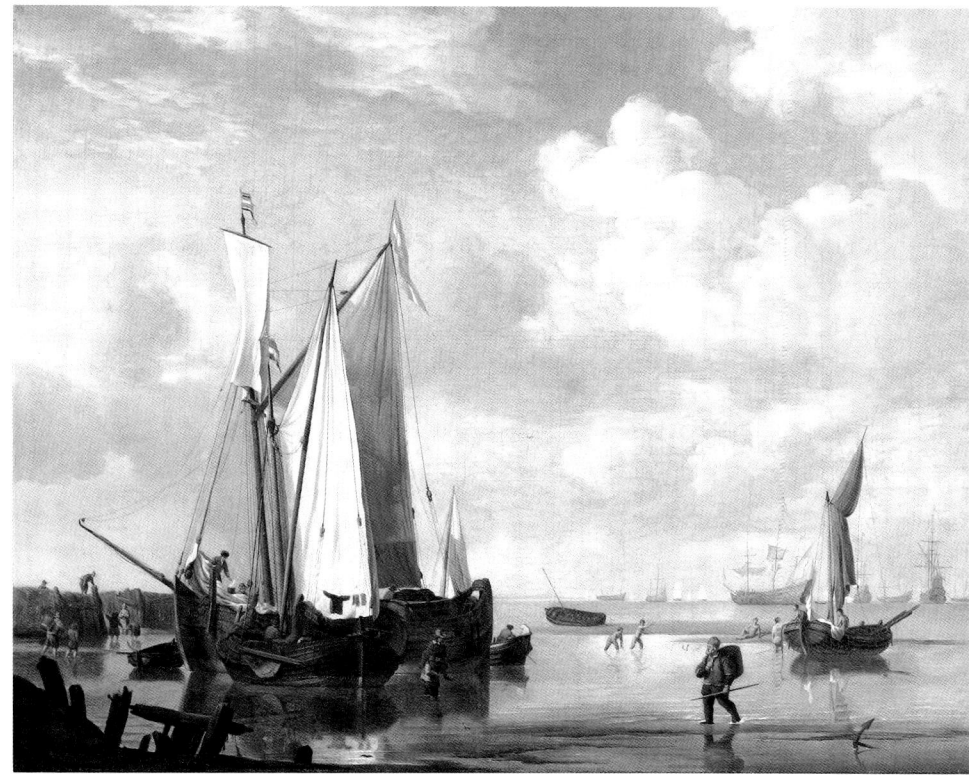

Willem van de Velde the Younger, 1633–1707
*Coast scene*, c.1661
oil on canvas, 60.0 x 70.0 cm
Gift of Ethel Brookman Kirkpatrick 1959

Britain and remains probably the greatest marine painter of all time. Turner, however, cannot be categorised easily. At the height of the Romantic period he was at the zenith of both seascape and landscape painting in Europe; his genius is not defined by or confined to any one kind of seascape or landscape.

Only in Britain did marine painting long precede landscape painting. The latter developed very slowly in the second half of the eighteenth century. A seventeenth-century precursor of landscape painting was the topographical tradition of country-house views – often bird's-eye views – mainly by artists from the Low Countries. They can be termed country-house portraits, an extension of British portraiture and a symbol of ownership. British art and patronage reflected a sense of self-absorption and a preoccupation with possessions: portraits of themselves, their wives and children, their pets and livestock, their houses and property and agricultural improvements. Country-house portraits continued throughout the eighteenth century and into the early nineteenth century. They are forerunners of the homestead pictures that flourished in Australia from the 1820s to the 1870s, first seen in watercolours that Joseph Lycett painted back in Britain from Australian drawings.

There were only minor landscape painters in early-eighteenth-century Britain. Then in the late 1740s and 1750s we see the emergence of Gainsborough's early landscapes, heavily influenced by the seventeenth-century Dutch and Flemish paintings that were entering British collections under the leadership of the connoisseur Prime Minister Sir Robert Walpole. Some of Gainsborough's early portraits, and Arthur Devis's, had extensive landscape backgrounds. The Gallery's Gainsborough drawings reflect Italian as well as Dutch influence. But it was Richard

Wilson who fully absorbed the classical landscape tradition of Claude Lorrain and Gaspard Dughet while working in Rome in the 1750s, and home again translated those conventions into grandly conceived English and Welsh landscapes. He raised the status of British landscape by aspiring to the then accepted Roman canon of classical landscape, just as Ramsay and Reynolds demonstrated a learned awareness of classical culture in their modern grand-manner portraits. The Gallery's *Dinas Bran from Llangollen* (c.1772–75) is an example of a British landscape painted by Wilson in the Roman manner. Yet such works are also very British in their mood. In the 1760s and 1770s local landscape art was at last taken seriously by artists and patrons in Britain, one hundred and fifty years after the development of the Classical landscape tradition in Rome or the Realist tradition in Haarlem in the Netherlands.

For all the learned grandeur of Wilson's British landscapes and his patrons, most of whom had been on the educational Grand Tour that culminated in Rome, by the end of his career in the late 1780s he could neither sell his landscapes nor gain commissions. He died almost destitute in 1782. The Scottish landscape painter Jacob More, himself initially influenced by Wilson, arrived in Rome in the early 1770s and found that patronage there was better than at home. He died in Rome in 1793 after a very prosperous twenty-year career as an expatriate. His *A distant view of Rome across the Tiber* (c.1774) is an example of the popular landscape paintings that earned him fame throughout Europe.

Throughout most of the eighteenth century the British did not really come to terms with their own landscape. They much preferred to see a Roman scene by Claude Lorrain or Gaspard Dughet and also increasingly enjoyed the realism of Dutch seventeenth-century landscapes. British collectors had acquired most of Claude's œuvre by the end of the century. Times were changing in the 1790s, the beginning of the careers of young Turner and John Constable who would become leaders of the new Romantic landscape painting. A popular school of landscape in watercolour emerged at the same time. Dr Thomas Monro, an enthusiastic collector and promoter of watercolours, conducted a salon at his house where younger artists could study and patrons could meet, admire and discuss watercolour painting. Turner and Thomas Girtin were the most influential of Monro's new 1790s generation of landscape watercolourists who especially admired picturesque and romantic scenery in Scotland, Wales and the Lake District of north-western England.

Like portrait miniatures in the sixteenth century, landscape watercolours were not invented by the British, but were most ardently embraced by them. At the end of the eighteenth century and beginning of the nineteenth century they were perceived on the Continent as a peculiarly English phenomenon. Paul Sandby in the 1760s and 1770s had begun to raise watercolour painting above mere topographical recording. He did this with the support of distinguished patrons and especially by the exhibition of large watercolours and gouaches in the Royal Academy, of which he was a prominent foundation member. By the time of Sandby's death in 1809 landscape watercolours were the most flourishing part of the British art scene.

Continental travel was limited during the Napoleonic wars, which encouraged the British to travel at home and admire their own scenery. The intimate art of watercolour

David Lucas, 1802–1881
after John Constable, 1776–1837
*A summerland*, 1829-1831
mezzotint on paper, 17.9 x 25.2 cm (plate)
David Murray Bequest Fund 1952

David Lucas, 1802–1881
after John Constable, 1776–1837
*Hadleigh Castle near the Nore*, 1831 / 1832
published 1832
mezzotint on paper, 17.9 x 25.0 cm (plate)
David Murray Bequest Fund 1974

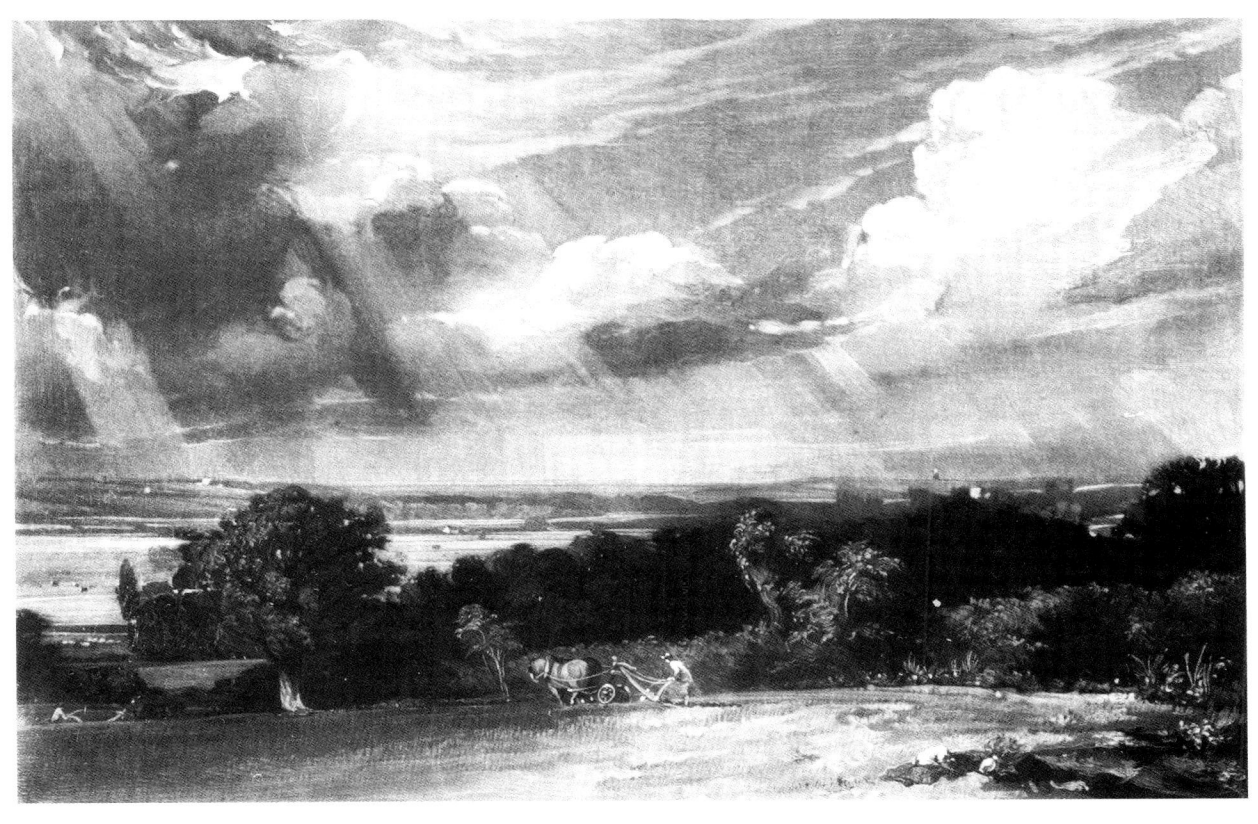

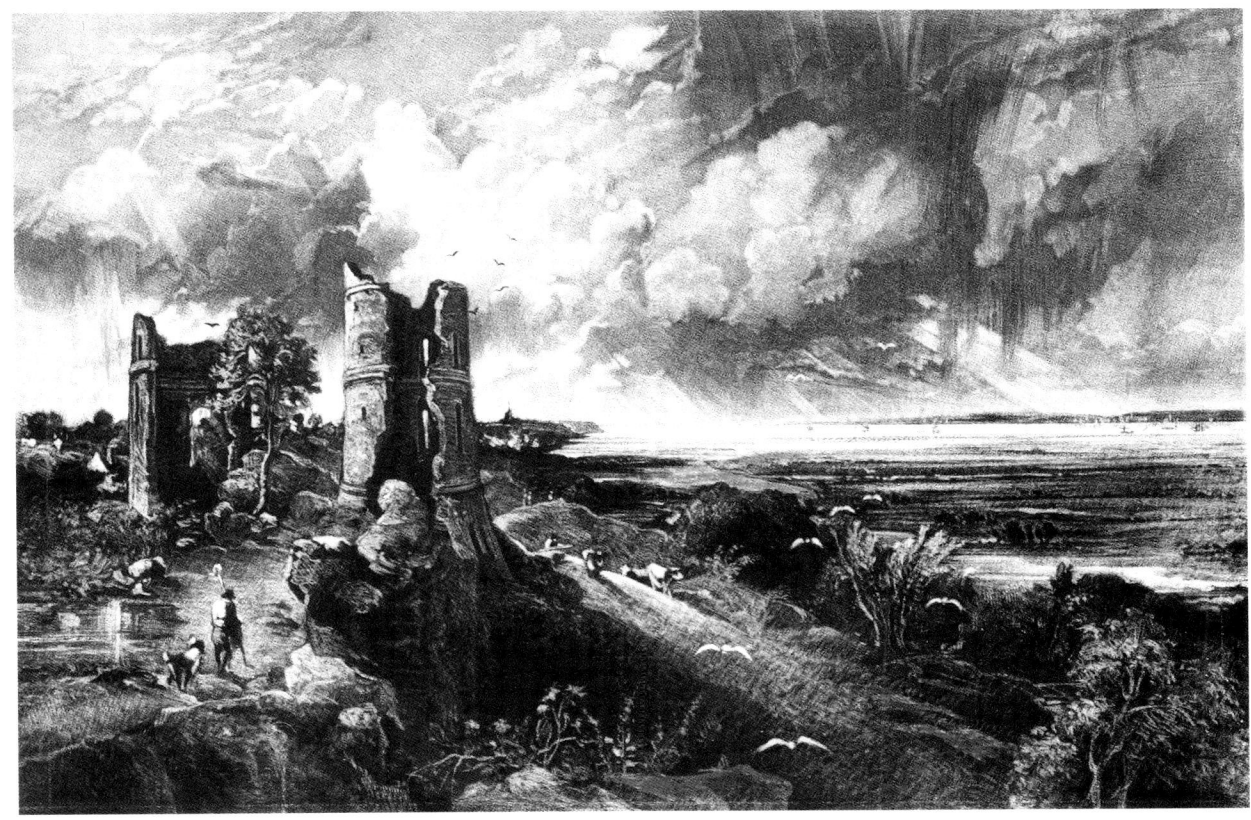

painting fostered widespread appreciation of British countryside and wilderness; larger oils became generally acceptable rather later. John Glover, who painted the first outstanding Australian landscapes after his arrival in Tasmania in 1831, had helped promote British watercolour painting at the beginning of the nineteenth century. He was a founder of artists' associations for the exhibition of watercolours.

Although landscape watercolours were more numerous, and made the greatest impact on British art, by the 1790s watercolours were also used in popular human-interest genre. In the Gallery's collection this can be seen in Francis Wheatley's *The blind pedlar* (1794), Richard Westall's *The birds' nest* (1794) and Thomas Rowlandson's *The Brilliants* (c.1801). Sentimental or humorous works like these were often the basis for engravings that could be hand-coloured with watercolour and printed in large editions. A strong demand for British prints of the kind developed throughout Europe.

However, there were also the supreme high-art illustrations in watercolour and in prints by the artist-poet William Blake. His entirely imaginary world contrasted sharply with the watercolours of sentimental and satirical figure compositions or of the natural world. At the beginning of this chapter we suggested that British art always kept in touch with observation and reality. Yet nothing could be further removed from this than the strange imagination of Blake, who stated: "Inspiration and Vision…will always Remain, my Element, my Eternal Dwelling place." His basic classical figuration, and fiery inner vision, interpreted Biblical and other texts, of which an example is the Gallery's *St Paul before Felix and Drusilla* (c.1803). In British art his visionary watercolours seem to stand alone, but in his own lifetime he influenced others such as John Flaxman (see his illustrations to *Arcana Cœlestia*) or the young Samuel Palmer.

Partly because of the excessive flooding of the British art market with watercolours and partly because of economic difficulties at the end of the Napoleonic wars, the huge and uniquely British watercolour boom subsided in the 1810s. It had lasted less than fifteen years but it remained an inventive and prominent part of British art to the middle of the century and was still popular at the end of Queen Victoria's reign. The Gallery's splendid examples of early-nineteenth-century Romantic watercolour landscapes include Peter De Wint's evocative *Kenilworth Castle* (c.1827), Samuel Palmer's atmospheric *Summer storm near Pulborough, Sussex* (c.1851), and above all Turner's tranquil *Scarborough town and castle* (c.1810) and haunting *Alnwick Castle* (c.1829). Turner's exhibition pieces, such as these brilliant but contrasting atmospheric works, represent the highest achievements of watercolour painting.

Not surprisingly, in the British colonies in Australia landscape painting in watercolour flourished in the 1830s and 1840s among emigrant artists. Watercolour was an ideally portable medium with which to record and interpret a newly colonised continent. Except for John Glover's oils, early-colonial landscape consisted largely of watercolours. Landscape painting expanded only after the 1820s when the settlers felt they had a safe hold on pastoral land. Before that the inland was seen as an unapproachable wilderness unworthy of depiction and views of the coast-hugging settlements were preferred as signs of progress and success. As landscape art took on, pictures were sent back to a curious Britain. Watercolourists such as Conrad

William Blake, 1757–1827
*The Destruction of Job's sons*
plate 3 from *Illustrations of the Book of Job*, 1823–26
published 1874 by John Linnell (2nd edition)
engraving on chine collé on paper
21.9 x 17.1 cm (plate)
David Murray Bequest Fund 1954

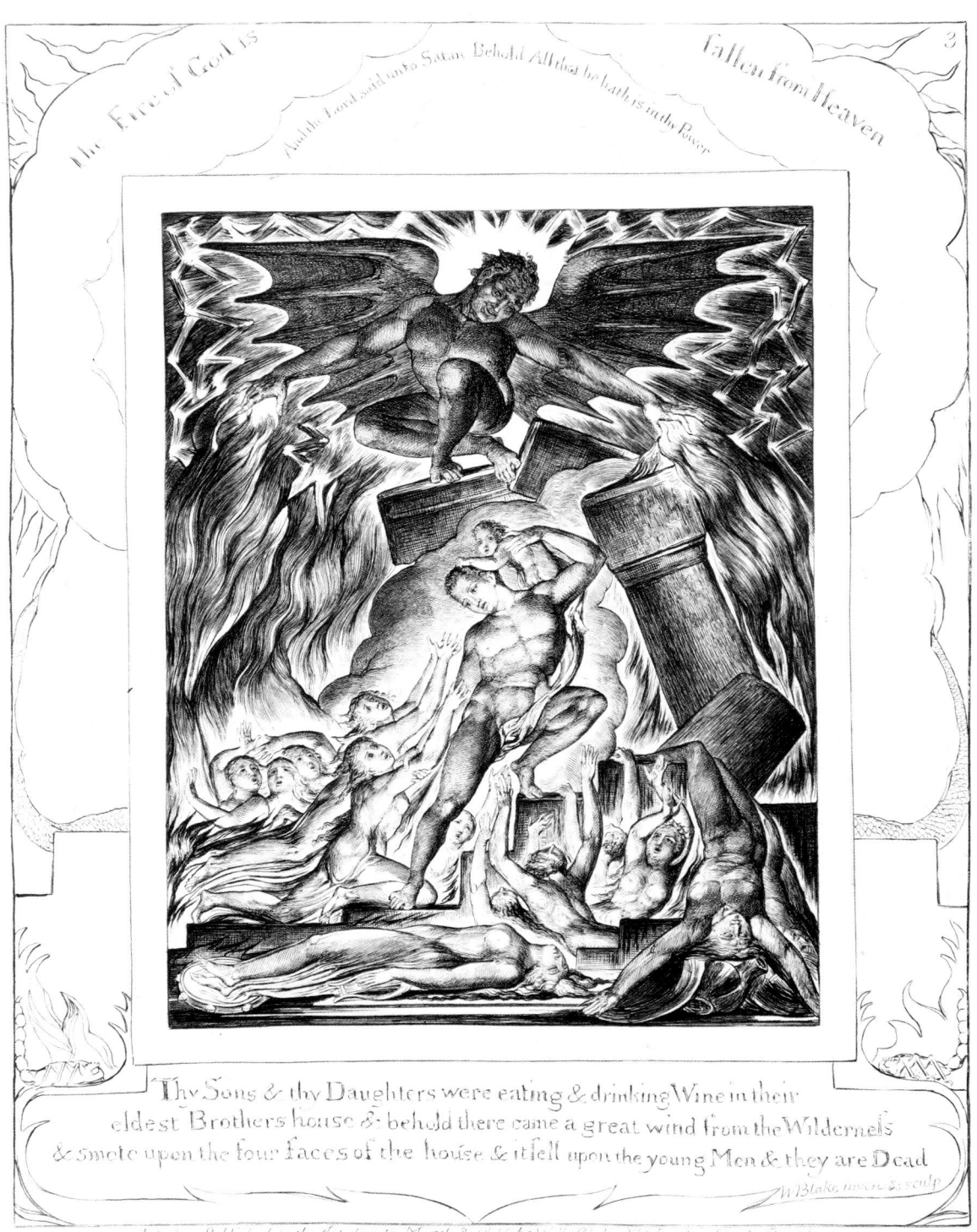

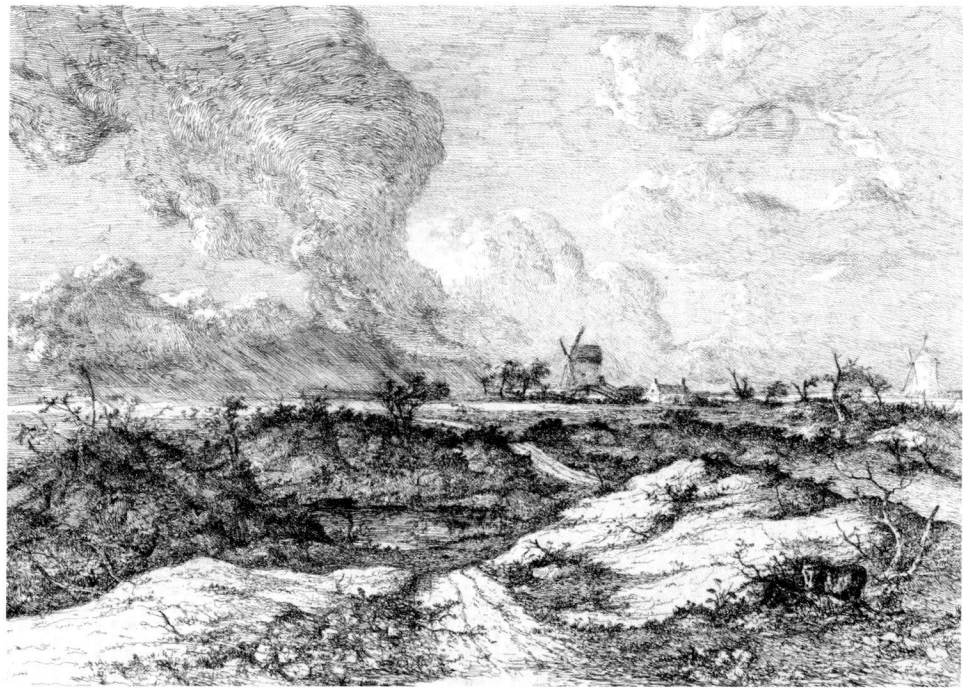

John Crome, 1768–1821
*Mousehold Heath*, c.1816
etching on chine collé on paper
20.7 x 28.3 cm (image)
David Murray Bequest Fund 1954

right: John Glover, 1767–1849
*View of Mills' Plains*, c.1833
oil on canvas, 76.2 x 114.6 cm
Morgan Thomas Bequest Fund 1951

Martens, John Skinner Prout, S. T. Gill and George French Angas interpreted the unique but varying Australian landscape with enthusiasm. Until the 1860s landscape watercolours remained a major part of nineteenth-century Australian art.

In Britain by the 1810s and 1820s landscape painting at last surpassed portraiture as the most dynamic and important form of art-making and began to contribute most to the prestige of British art. As mentioned, the shift was led by Turner and Constable but other major landscape artists included Samuel Palmer, John Sell Cotman, John Crome, Peter De Wint, Samuel Prout, John Glover and others well represented in the Gallery's collection. A distinctive English realism emerged, fresh and more advanced than elsewhere. These landscape painters rejected eighteenth-century classical rationalism and believed instead that landscape art should be more an expression of personal involvement with nature. The changing moods of a beloved countryside should be captured with feeling. The romantic sensibility in landscape art was recognised outside Britain, particularly by progressive French artists of the Romantic movement. After the death of Sir Thomas Lawrence in 1830 Britain did not again produce or patronise an internationally recognised portrait painter until the very end of the century.

Britain in the nineteenth century grew to become the world's richest and most powerful country, with the largest Empire, still expanding, that the world had ever known. Depictions of land and sea, both at home and across the Empire, therefore became crucial subjects for paintings. In this wider context, Glover's vital Tasmanian landscapes of the 1830s are part of Britain's land-claiming, land-loving art. Glover sent sizeable canvases across the world to be exhibited and admired in London, the centre of the Empire.

Turner's death in 1851 marked both the climax of Romantic landscape art and the end of Britain's pre-eminence in it. We end this survey at a time when the French

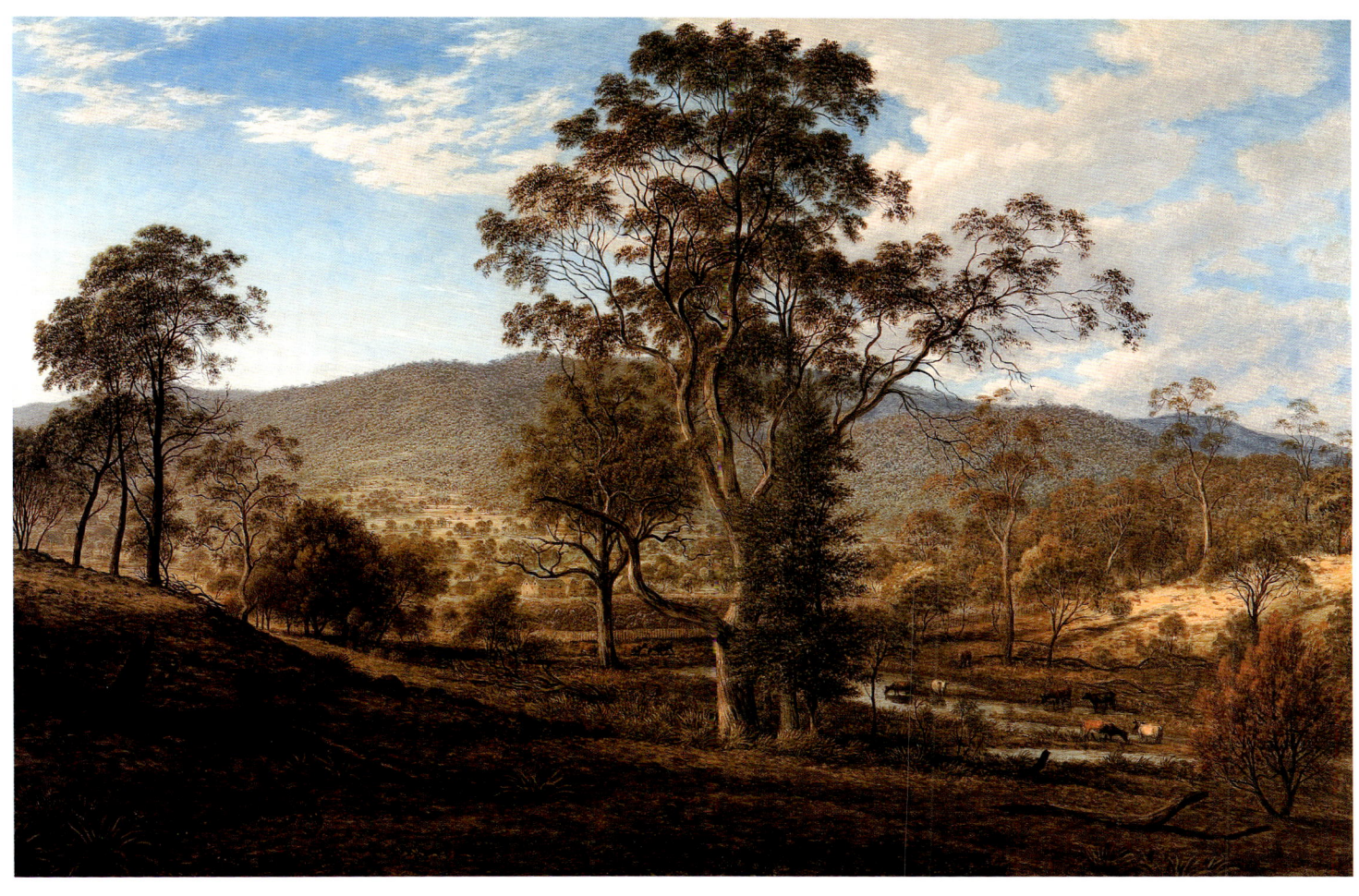

began to take over advanced landscape art through pre-Impressionist painters like Corot and Courbet in the 1850s, soon followed by the outdoor Impressionists. However, in the late 1840s a group of young British artists had started to breathe new life into their nation's painting through highly detailed landscapes but mostly through narrative, especially in religious subjects that had scarcely entered British art since the Reformation. As part of romantic revivalism they looked back to the supposed sincerity of Medieval and early Renaissance art from before the time of Raphael. Hence they named themselves the Pre-Raphaelites. Their passionate zeal, intense realism and emotional extremity are epitomised by William Holman Hunt's *Christ and the Two Marys*, which could be the first Pre-Raphaelite painting and a beginning to a uniquely British alternative to mainstream nineteenth-century visualities – an art, instead, of inwardness, of the spirit and the body. Commenced in 1847 even before the group had found a name, Hunt's painting was not finished until half a century later but it opened a new chapter in British art, and is an appropriate end to this book.

The Art Gallery of South Australia's collection provides a rare glimpse outside Britain of the outlines of British art onwards from the mid-sixteenth-century arrival of Renaissance humanism. This book ends at the mid nineteenth century just as the Australian colonies were claiming independent self-government but before they began to build their own public art collections – their so-called 'National Galleries' – which all began in the second half of the nineteenth century largely as collections of British contemporary art.

The three hundred years of British art as seen through the single collection of the Art Gallery of South Australia is a simplification of a more complex historical picture but is nevertheless unusually suggestive. And it also gives some insight into the basis for Australian early art.

detail: William Holman Hunt, 1827–1910
*Christ and the Two Marys*, 1847 & 1897
oil on canvas over wood panel, 117.5 x 94.0 cm
d'Auvergne Boxall Bequest Fund 1964

Nottingham workshops
*Two Apostles, St Simon and St Jude*
mid to late 15th century
Nottingham alabaster with traces of paint
42.0 x 24.5 x 5.0 cm (irreg.)
South Australian Government Grant 1952

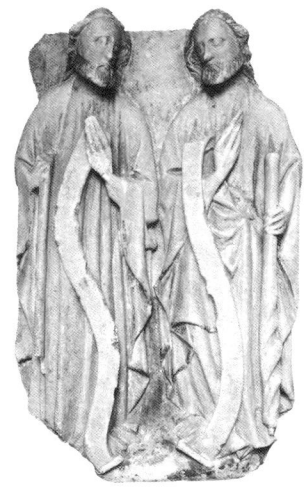

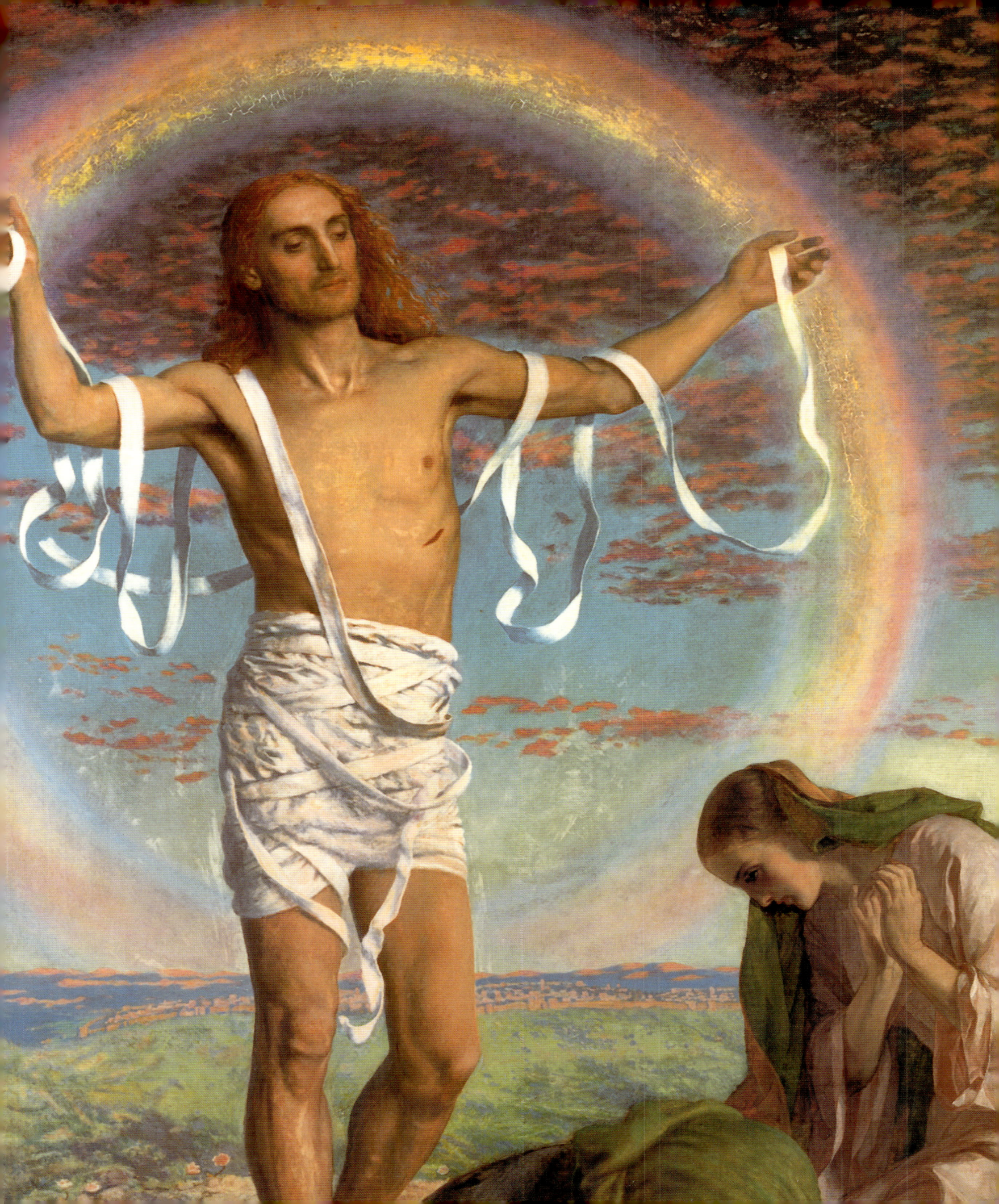

# Cataloguing the Collection

The detailed cataloguing of Adelaide's large and long-established collections has never been easy. For one thing the Gallery has employed curators only since the mid 1960s, and when curators were appointed their curatorial areas were almost impossibly broad. When I began at the Gallery at the end of 1980 it was as curator of both European and Australian paintings and sculptures of all periods. In 1982 a large collection of pictorial South Australiana – paintings and watercolours collected as regional history rather than art – were added to the responsibilities and at the end of 1983 the important and complex area of Aboriginal art was also added. There was no curatorial assistant. Australian and European paintings (and sculptures) have since been divided into separate curatorial areas and there is also now an Associate Curator of Australian Art. A separate Curator of European Art was appointed as recently as 1996. A very small staff for a sizeable, broad-ranging collection has often meant that research and record-keeping (particularly of provenances) could never be a priority.

From the 1970s curators at the Art Gallery of South Australia have been involved with, and inevitably overwhelmed by, the constant stream of exhibitions that audiences had come to expect. Opportunities for detailed cataloguing of and research into the collections were therefore even more limited. Furthermore, the Gallery's research library until 1979 was merely a cupboard room and in spite of the large British collection there were few books and catalogues on the subject, particularly of the earlier periods. A full-time Senior Librarian was appointed only in the mid 1990s. I am pleased to say that the much-expanded Gallery Library and its staff are now an invaluable support to the collection and its research.

The most obvious disadvantage for research into international collections in Adelaide is being so far removed from research papers, primary records, institutions, colleagues and comparable collections. Therefore most of the early British and other European paintings had not been thoroughly catalogued before the present publication.

In addition there was no professionally trained Paintings Conservator until 1982, soon after which, in 1985, the conservation staff from the Art Gallery of South Australia, the South Australian Museum and the State Library of South Australia were brought together and expanded into a separate and efficient State Conservation Laboratory now known as Artlab Australia, Adelaide. After a Conservator of Paintings was appointed I took the opportunity to begin what I referred to in-house throughout the rest of the 1980s as the "RE-Program" for the rehabilitation of many early European paintings. Apart from the numerous Old Master paintings then on display and which needed cleaning, I was shocked yet also excited by discovery of the Gallery's then mostly evacuated off-site store for undisplayed works, in city-centre Kingston Street. It was given up in 1981; during 1978–79 most of the undisplayed paintings and other collections had already been transferred to what was then a new state-of-the-art storage facility in an inner suburb. Among the neglected paintings still at the Kingston Street 'graveyard' in 1980–81 were many unattributed European pictures badly needing conservation and research. With the appointment of the Paintings Conservator in 1982 a steady program of conservation began. The commencement of the RE-Program was under way. Paintings were carefully RE-stored, then RE-searched, then RE-attributed, then RE-framed and finally RE-displayed.

Among the early British works reattributed after revelatory cleaning and restoration were Simon Verelst's *Portrait of an Ambassador* (c.1686), Nicolas de Largillierre's *Portrait of a Frenchman* (c.1678) and Matthew Dixon's *Portrait of a man* (1670s). Hitherto unrecorded signatures were found on a number of pictures including Michiel van Miereveld's *George Villiers, Duke of Buckingham* (c.1626), Dominic Serres's *Foudroyant and Pégase entering Portsmouth Harbour, 1782* (1782) and, much more recently, the inscription and date on Francis Swaine's *The Landing of the Sailor Prince at Spithead* (1765).

In April–May 1989 an exhibition was held of the results of the RE-Program of conservation and research (including photography before and during conservation). As the climax of the program, the exhibition was titled *Hidden Treasures: South Australia's European Old Master paintings: Restoration and Reattributions* and it proved to be very popular with the public. A less dramatic but steady stream of early European works has continued through the conservation laboratory up to the time this book went to print.

Late in 1989 I was awarded three overseas research fellowships to catalogue the Gallery's European Old Master collections. A Churchill Fellowship was awarded for research, in Britain and on the Continent, into the full European collection. Much of the time was spent in the Witt Library at the Courtauld Institute, London, where it was alarming to find on some Witt Library mounts photographs of Adelaide's pictures with the annotations "now lost", "whereabouts unknown" and, worst of all, "thought destroyed in the war". The other two fellowships, from the Yale Center for British Art and the Huntington Library & Art Collections, were for research confined to British art. That invaluable study trip also made it possible to see variant versions of works in the collection, and works that were related. The planned seven-month research trip in 1990, however, was slightly curtailed by an early return to Adelaide for interviews for the directorship of the Art Gallery of South Australia, a position for which I was reluctantly persuaded to apply. Having taken up the appointment of Director at the beginning of 1991, research into and cataloguing of the European collections proceeded slowly, and virtually stopped in 1994 when the pressures of planning and supervising the West Wing extensions to the Gallery took over. Not till the second half of 2003 was I able to return to systematic cataloguing of the British works dating from 1550 to 1850.

Formerly insecure attributions to artists have been verified. Unknown or misidentified sitters for many portraits have been identified. Unknown landscape subjects are now mostly located. Versions of Gallery works and related works are now recorded.

The extended period of research and its long suspension have had both disadvantages and advantages. It was difficult to pick up all the threads, to remember sources of information and maintain consistency. On the other hand, much has been published on British art since 1990 and I have had the benefit of recent scholarship by others. There has been the opportunity for much self-editing. And most of the Gallery's British paintings have now been conserved. Most importantly, the Gallery's collection has grown considerably in the past decade, making it a more balanced and a more complete chronological survey of British art of the period, and therefore ever more interesting and worthy of publication.

I must again acknowledge here the devoted editing by Daniel Thomas, who has picked up many inconsistencies and corrected much else about these works, with many of which he has long been familiar. For any omissions and mistakes, of course, I must take full responsibility.

# Notes to the Catalogue

Essays on individual oil paintings, watercolours, drawings and sculptures are arranged largely chronologically. The full catalogue of all works 1550–1850 at the back of the book is arranged alphabetically according to artists' names.

*Attributed to*: Probably by the named artist according to the weight of available evidence, although the available evidence stops short of reasonable certainty.

*Studio of*: Produced in the named artist's studio by assistants, possibly with some participation by the named artist. It is an important criterion that the creative concept is by the named artist and that the work was meant to leave the studio as his.

*Style of*: Produced by an unknown artist working more or less specifically in the style of the named artist, and who may or may not have assisted or been trained by the named artist.

*Follower of*: Produced by an unknown artist specifically based on known works by the named artist.

*After*: A copy of any date.

**DATING:** The following conventions for dates are used:

| | |
|---|---|
| 1790 | Executed in 1790 |
| c.1790 | Executed sometime around 1790 |
| 1790–1795 | Begun in 1790, finished in 1795 |
| 1790/1795 | Executed sometime between 1790 and 1795 |
| c.1790/1795 | Executed sometime around the period 1790–1795 |
| 1790 & 1795 | Executed in 1790 and also in 1795 |

**MEASUREMENTS:** Dimensions are given in centimetres, height before width.

**INSCRIPTIONS:** Primary inscriptions (including artist's signature and date) on the face of the work are included. Secondary inscriptions elsewhere have been included only occasionally, and only when vital to the attribution, dating or the title of the work.

**PROVENANCE:** By whom and where the work was previously owned.

**EXHIBITIONS:** Where and when the work is known to have been exhibited.

**LITERATURE:** Where the work has been mentioned in texts and/or illustrated.

**CONSERVATION:** Where and when the work was last conserved is recorded if known.
The condition of works has been restricted to four categories:

Excellent: Very fine condition for its age, similar to when it was executed.

Good: Fine condition for its age with some changes since execution.

Fair: Passable condition for its age, but evidence of deterioration.

Poor: Obvious deterioration such as paint loss or colour fading.

Extra conservation information has been mentioned only where necessary, and also given in the body of the texts or footnotes where especially relevant. Most of the oil paintings have been conserved during the past twenty years, largely by Artlab Australia, Adelaide, the state of South Australia's joint museums conservation centre.

**FRAMING:** Original frames are identified.
Nearly all the sixteenth- and seventeenth-century oil paintings have lost their original frames, but appropriate period-style frames now surround most of the paintings. The majority of the eighteenth- and early-nineteenth-century oil paintings retain their original frames. However, only one work on paper, the watercolour by Turner, *Scarborough*, c.1810, retains its original frame. And only one other work on paper, William Blake's *St Paul before Felix and Drusilla*, c.1803, retains its original (inscribed) mount.

detail: Samuel Hieronymous Grimm, 1733–1794
*The Grange Hall, Horne Farm and Woolley Wood*, 1781
watercolour on cream paper
38.0 x 54.6 cm (sheet)
South Australian Government Grant 1956

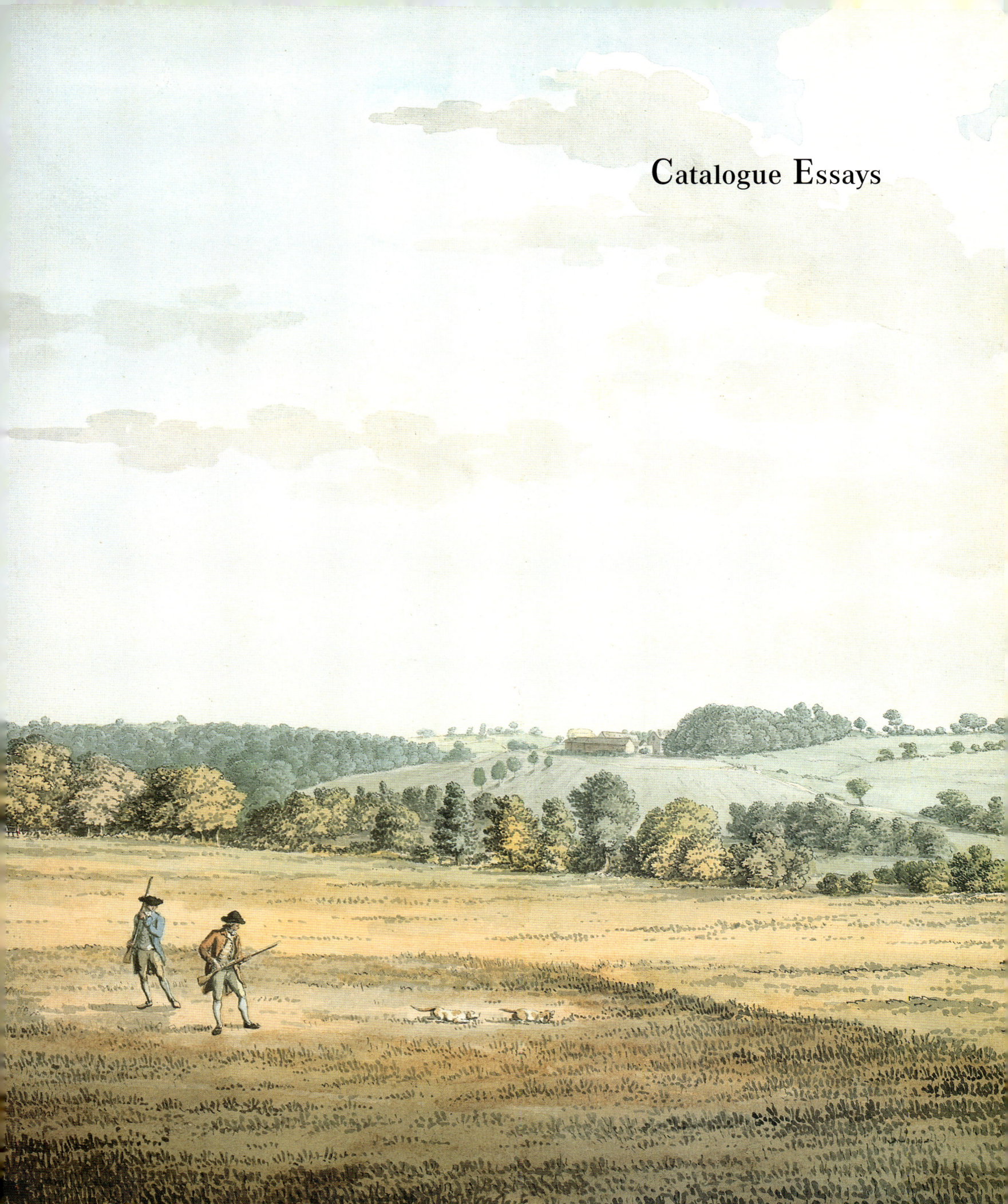

# Catalogue Essays

# Hans Holbein the Younger 1497/98–1543

Hans Holbein the Younger, principal court painter to King Henry VIII, introduced Renaissance realism and confidence to the art of portrait painting in England. The greatest portrait painter in northern Europe, he changed the course of British art which henceforth, until the beginning of the nineteenth century, was dominated by portraiture.

He was born in 1497 or 1498 in Augsburg, where he was trained by his father Hans Holbein the Elder, a painter of altarpieces who worked principally in Switzerland. By 1515 the son was in Basle, at first working principally as a designer for print publishers; in 1519 he became Master in the Basle Guild of Painters. Based chiefly in that Swiss city, he painted religious works and portraits, and continued to make designs for prints, until his first visit to Britain.

He arrived in London in 1526. The celebrated Dutch humanist Erasmus had given him a letter of introduction to fellow humanist Sir Thomas More whose family portraits Holbein painted. After eighteen months he returned to Basle but, finding that fanatic Protestant extremism severely reduced the number of commissions, he settled in England in 1532. There, about 1535, he became the King's principal painter and thereafter received numerous commissions from royalty. Outside the royal circle Holbein's patrons included at least a quarter of the English peerage and many of the most influential politicians of the day.

Holbein was the most outstanding artist to have been appointed to the royal service or to have worked hitherto in England. He died in London in 1543. His impact had been considerable and his influence would continue long after his death.

## Follower of Hans Holbein the Younger
### King Henry VIII, 1540s?
oil on wood panel, 65.0 x 57.5 cm
A. M. & A. R. Ragless Bequest Funds 1965

This portrait is by one of Hans Holbein's close followers, as yet unidentified, but possibly painted while Holbein was still alive, and is based on his iconic image of King Henry VIII.[1]

Henry VIII (1491–1547) is the best known to posterity of all early English monarchs and was an outstanding ruler. He was the son of Henry VII who, as Duke of Richmond, defeated the last Plantagenet king, Richard III, at the battle of Bosworth Field in 1485 and thus established the Tudor dynasty. As the second Tudor monarch, Henry VIII firmly ruled a prosperous Renaissance England for nearly forty years from 1509 to 1547. He was highly educated, talented, fair and an accomplished Renaissance man. His early rule was enlightened and full of promise, but history has judged him on his later rule as a tyrant. Henry VIII broke with the Roman Catholic Church, dissolved the monasteries and established the Church of England of which he made himself head. He is notorious for having six wives two of whom he divorced and two he had beheaded. The last three Tudor monarchs, the young Edward VI, Mary I and Elizabeth I, were fathered by Henry VIII.

The painting is based on a Holbein image that became the approved prototype portrait of the King. It ultimately derives from the dynastic group portrait mural painted by Holbein in 1537 for the Privy Chamber in the King's principal palace at Whitehall. The mural, destroyed by fire in 1698, is known to us by Remiguis van Leemput's two small copies of 1667 and 1669 (Royal Collection, Hampton Court, and Petworth House, West Sussex), and also by Holbein's surviving preparatory cartoon for the left side of the composition (National Portrait Gallery, London), which includes the principal standing image of the King. The figures in the cartoon are life-size.

The complete composition of the mural consisted of four standing figures, two either side of a large plinth with a Latin inscription about rightful Tudor rule. In the left foreground was the dominant frontal figure of Henry VIII and, on a step behind him, his father Henry VII. In the right foreground was Henry's third and favourite wife Jane Seymour who had just died giving birth to the Tudor heir, Prince Edward, later Edward VI. On the step behind Jane Seymour is Henry VII's Queen, Elizabeth of York, mother of Henry VIII. The composition aimed not only to reinforce the Tudor dynasty and legitimise any succession but also, from the inscription on the central plinth, Henry's supremacy over the English Church.

The life-size group portrait for Whitehall Palace, dominated by what has become the stereotype image of Henry VIII, was preceded the year before by a small half-length portrait of the King (Thyssen-Bornemisza Collection, Madrid), the only extant portrait painting of Henry by Holbein's own hand. It is the forerunner to, and anticipates, the Whitehall image but is not as powerful, showing the head facing left, as does the drawing in the cartoon for the Whitehall mural. Holbein made a decisive change when he composed the mural: the King now squarely faces the viewer and thus appears more confronting and powerful.

Holbein's forthright image of the King in his elaborate

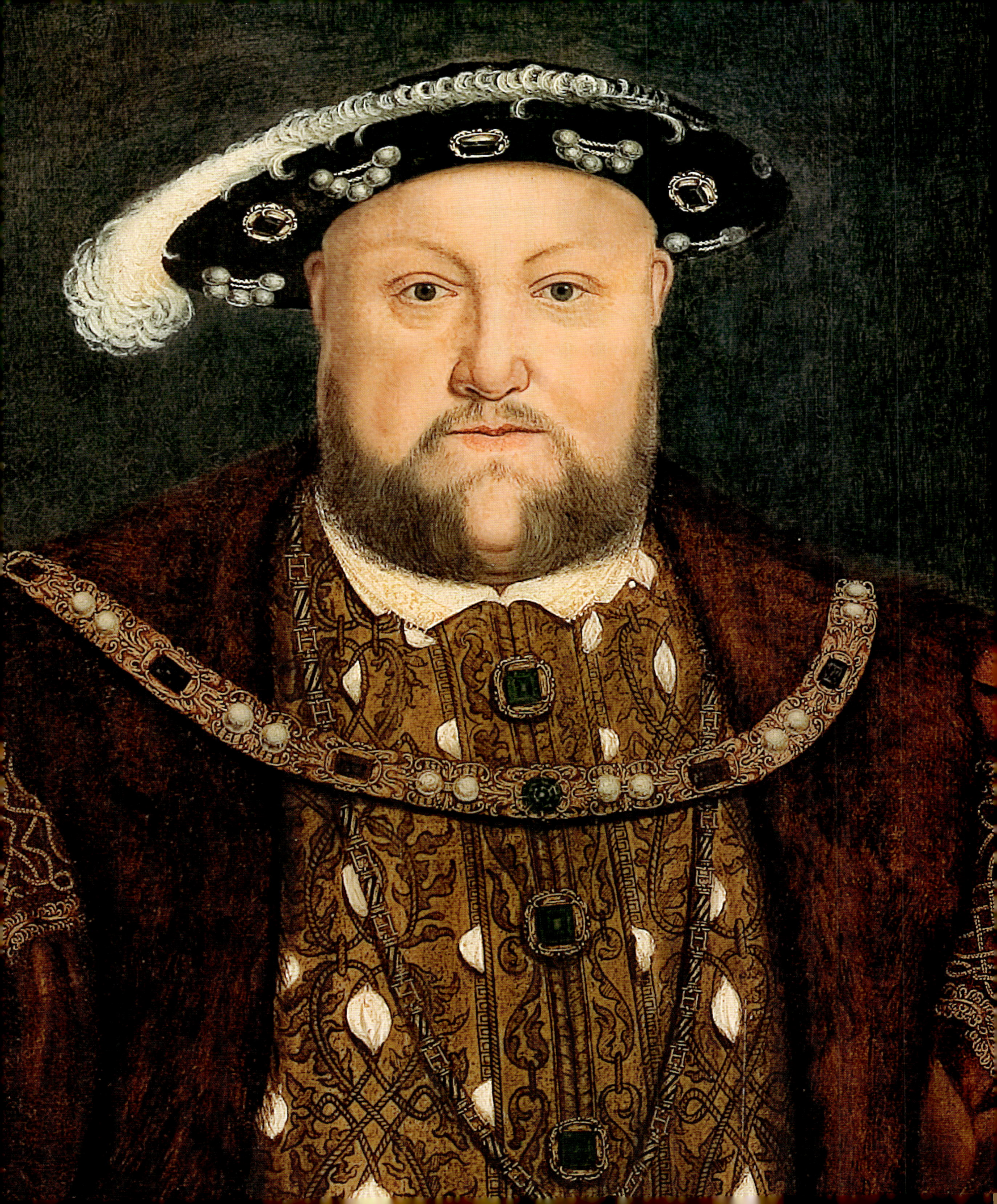

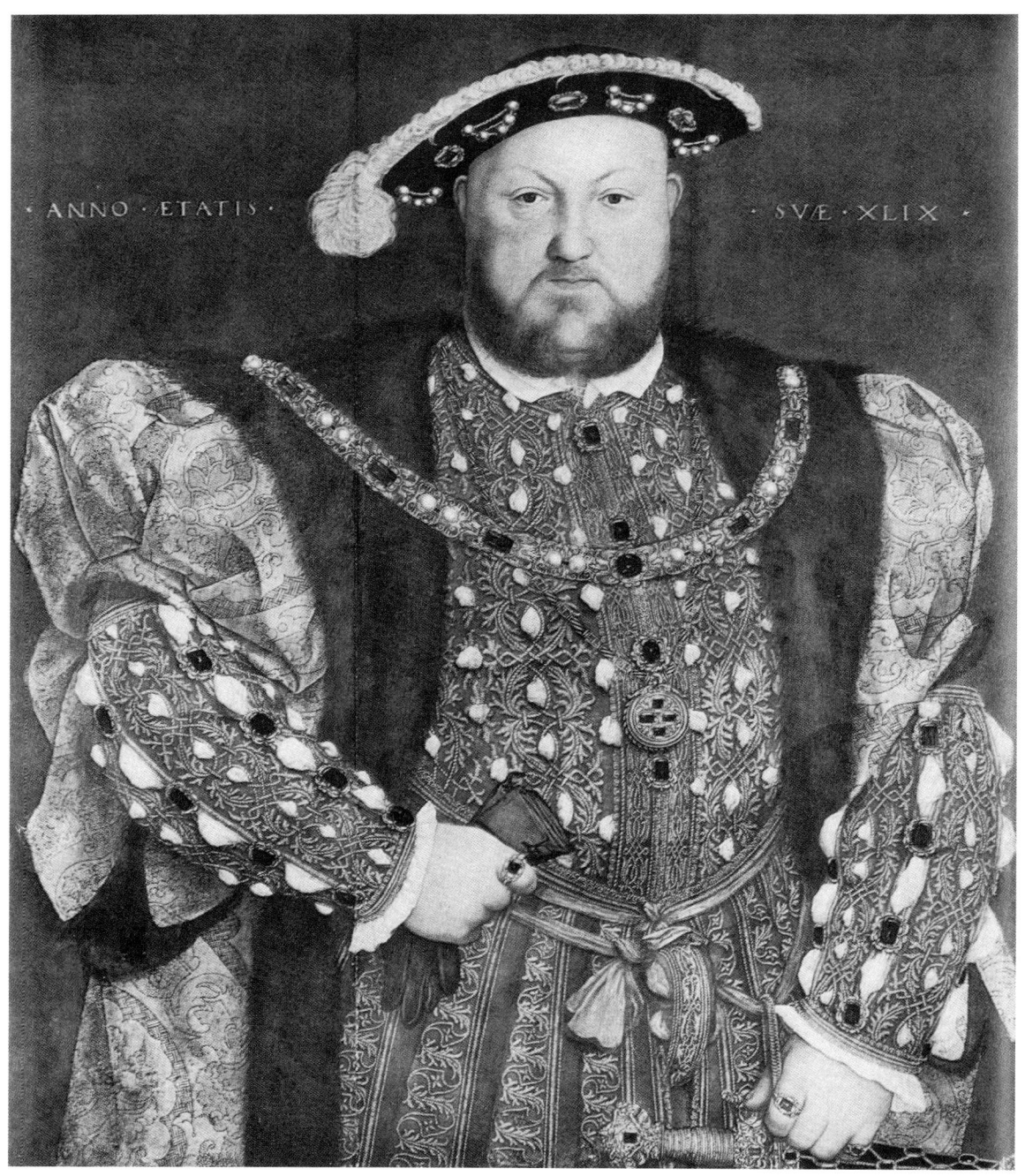

after Hans Holbein the Younger, *Henry VIII*, 1540. Galleria Nazionale d'Arte Antica, Palazzo Barberini, Rome

opposite: Follower of Hans Holbein the Younger, 1497/98–1543, *King Henry VIII*, 1540s?, oil on wood panel, 65.0 x 57.5 cm.
A. M. & A. R. Ragless Bequest Funds 1965

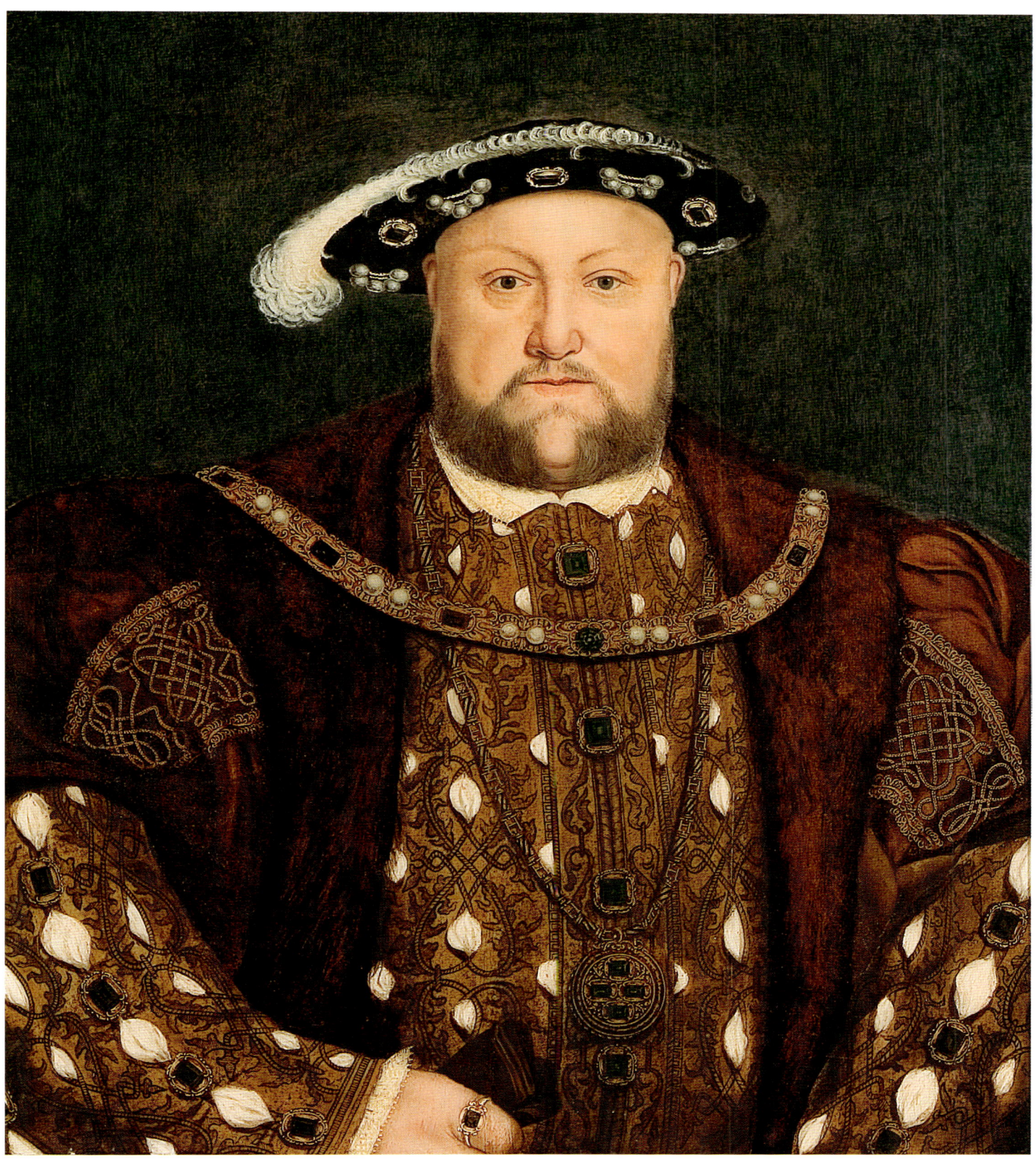

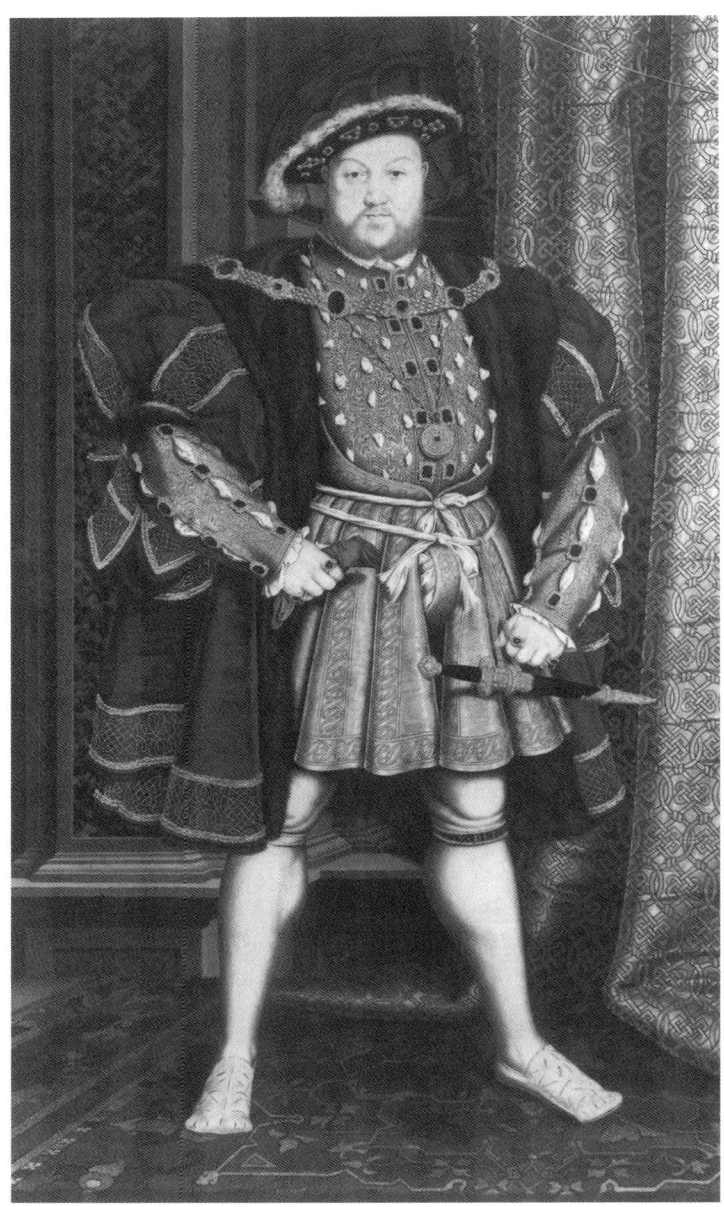

after Hans Holbein, *Henry VIII*, 1540s? National Museums Liverpool (The Walker), Liverpool

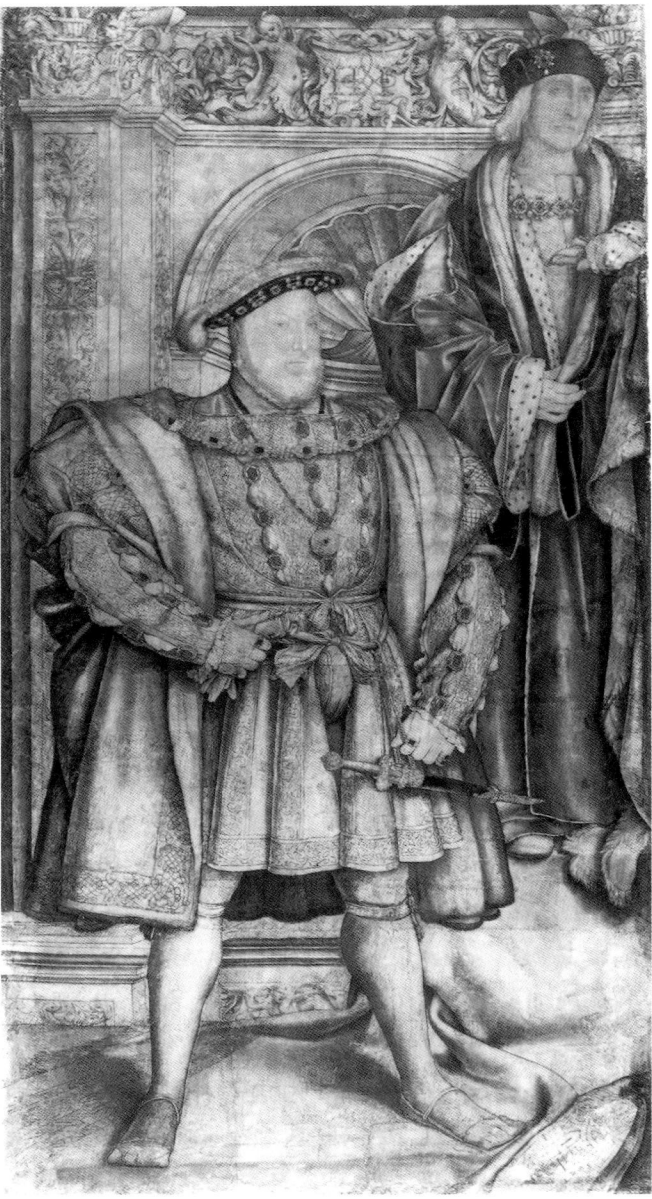

Hans Holbein the Younger, *Henry VII and Henry VIII*, 1537. National Portrait Gallery, London

attire of rich browns, russets and golds is the one by which we know Henry VIII today. It is an image of the square-faced and robust forty-six-year-old monarch in full charge of his kingdom and his church. It is the reason we think of Henry VIII not as a young Renaissance prince or as an ailing older man. We are familiar only with this indomitable, eternally middle-aged iconic image of the King at the height of his powers.

The image commands; a king gazes out at us, requires submission. Sumptuous clothing, exaggerated shoulders, give immovable and expansive presence and authority. A heavily brocaded and bejewelled doublet, and a russet surcoat trimmed and lined with ermine, envelop the royal bulk; the doublet is slashed to disclose puffs of white undershirt. A gold collar studded with pearls and stones rests across the massive chest over a longer chain and jewelled gold pendant. Pearls and stones also decorate the halo brim of the King's bonnet, which is trimmed with ostrich feathers and worn at a jaunty angle. His right hand with ringed finger clutches leather gloves.

The use of underlying gold leaf, gleaming through the transparent colour glazes that represent the gold brocade,

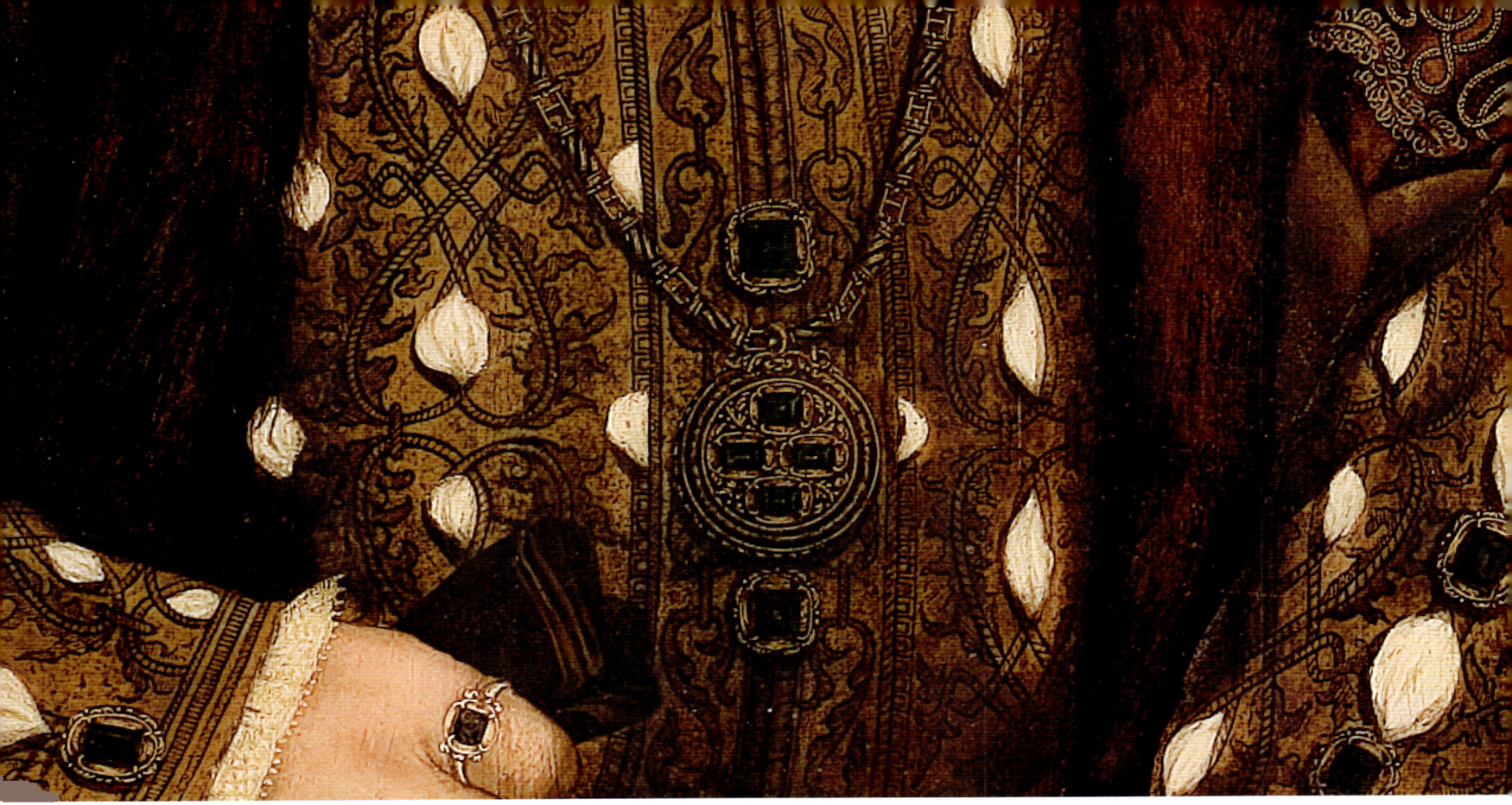

chains and gems, was a traditional practice familiar to Holbein from medieval panel paintings. It was also a common miniaturists' practice certainly used by the King's miniature-painter Lucas Horenbout. Unusually in this version of the portrait there is silver leaf as well, underlying the russet surcoat. The combination of underlying gold and silver leaf is unique in the known portraits of Henry VIII. This may confirm that our version is early, and possibly painted during the time of Holbein.[2]

There exist seven full-length portraits that follow the Holbein model of Henry VIII. Recent conservation research by Xanthe Brooke and David Crombie and the Conservation Centre of the National Museums Liverpool, has shown that two of these, at Liverpool and Petworth, were painted after Holbein and possibly in Holbein's or Henry VIII's lifetime. Another two, at Trinity College, Cambridge and Chatsworth House, were painted a quarter of a century after Holbein's death by Hans Eworth (*fl.* 1540–1573). The other three versions (Belvoir Castle, Leicestershire, Parham House, West Sussex, and St James's Palace), seem to be later still, from the late Elizabethan or early Jacobean periods.[3]

Of the Holbeinesque half-length portraits of Henry VIII the closest to this Gallery's is the slightly larger version (83.0 x 74.0 cm), dated 1540, which includes his left-hand and dagger and the full shoulders (Galleria Nazionale d'Arte Antica, Palazzo Barberini, Rome). The modelling in our painting is not as fine as this version in Rome[4], nor is the brocade as elaborate, but the russet velvet and gold-braided shoulder puffs in our portrait are closer to those in the original Whitehall mural. But unlike the Whitehall image and the Liverpool full-length ours shows what is probably the reverse side of the hanging medallion; it displays four jewels, not one. The same four jewels appear in the Rome half-length and Petworth's full-length, and in a half-length at Christ Church, Oxford, a painting believed to have been given to the college in 1546 by the King himself.

The public collections of the former British colonies of Australasia are rich in British art and this striking mid-sixteenth-century portrait of Henry VIII is the earliest British painting in the region. Here in Adelaide it is an appropriate beginning for the Art Gallery of South Australia's remarkably extended survey of British art.

Provenance: Possibly 4th Earl of Pembroke [Philip Herbert] (1584–1650); Captain de Voeux; Milligan collection, Caldwell Hall, Derbyshire; Lady Sophie de Voeux by 1866; Leggatt's by 1964; secured by Sir Alexander Downer for Art Gallery of South Australia, 1964.

Exhibitions: *National Portrait Exhibition*, 1866, London, (as *Holbein*). *Art Treasures from Adelaide: From the Collection of the Art Gallery of South Australia*, Art Gallery of New South Wales, Sydney, 1977. *Island to Empire: 300 Years of British Art 1550–1850*, AGSA, Adelaide, 2005.

Literature: *NGSA Bulletin*, April 1965. Hugh Paget, *Lucas Hornebolt, Court Painter to Henry VIII*, Art Galleries Association of Australia, 1970, pp. 8–18. *Picture Book*, Adelaide: AGSA, 1972, p. 13 (illus.).

Condition: Good; last conserved in London prior to acquisition in 1964.

Frame: Not original.

# Cornelius Ketel 1548–1616

Cornelius Ketel was the most significant and best trained painter of life-size portraits in England in the 1570s. He was also one of the few during the Elizabethan period to produce large-scale allegorical pictures in the Mannerist style.

Ketel was born in Gouda, Holland, in 1548 and first trained as an artist with his uncle Cornelis Jacobsz Ketel (died 1568). In 1565 he worked with Anthonie Blocklandt (1532–1585) in Delft followed by further training in France, both in Paris and Fontainebleau. He intended to study in Italy but was prevented from doing so by a French decree of 1567 that forced all visitors from Spanish territories to return home. (The Netherlands were then part of the Hapsburg Empire.) In 1573, a time when the Dutch revolt had flared up, he moved to London where he first stayed with a friend of his uncle's, the sculptor William Cure.

His earliest English patrons were merchants of the German Steelyard. In 1577 he was commissioned to paint some nineteen portraits for the Cathay Company, including a full-length of Sir Martin Frobisher now in the Bodleian Library, Oxford. He evidently gained a reputation for painting sets of portraits for the mercantile classes. A remarkable surviving group of three portraits depicts the family of Thomas Smythe, the collector of customs duties in the Port of London (private collection, Britain). He later painted the nobility, including the Earl of Oxford, and is said to have painted Queen Elizabeth in 1578 but the picture has not been firmly identified.[1] His earlier portraits in Britain showed the influence of the solid realism of Hans Holbein who had died in London thirty years earlier. His later English portraits appear to be freer in style, which may not have had general appeal and perhaps lowered his prospects for a long-term stay in England.

Despite his success as a portrait painter, Ketel's desire was to be known as a painter of grand allegorical and historical subjects. Few patrons requested such subjects in Elizabethan England, or in the following three centuries in Britain. Only one of his Mannerist allegorical compositions has survived from his British period (Delman Collection, San Francisco). In 1604, Karel van Mander, his artist friend and biographer, remarked on Ketel's period in Britain and stated that he "obtained many portrait commissions but none for histories towards which his spirit still ever inclined".[2] It is possible, too, that he expected royal patronage. In 1581, the same year that a rival portrait painter, the less talented but locally-born George Gower, was appointed Sergeant Painter to Queen Elizabeth, 'Cornelius Kettil' (his English signature) left London for Amsterdam.

In Holland he introduced life-size, full-length and group portraits to the Dutch. These were often of middle-class burghers who apparently also appreciated his complex allegorical figure compositions. He was paralysed by a stroke in 1613 and died in Amsterdam three years later.

## Richard Goodricke of Ribston, Yorkshire, c.1578

oil on oak panel, 106.0 x 81.0 cm

Roy & Marjory Edwards Bequest Fund 2004

The proud young Richard Goodricke of Ribston Hall, near Knaresborough in Yorkshire, was born in 1560, at the beginning of the reign of Queen Elizabeth I. Here he is fully launched into the adult world, aged eighteen, probably about two years after he matriculated from Christ College, Cambridge.[4] His father, also Richard, had married a Yorkshire heiress Clare Norton, daughter of Richard Norton of Norton Conyers; Norton's wealth helped Goodricke senior attain the position of High Sheriff of Yorkshire in 1579, which was about the time his son's portrait was painted. On 4 November 1578 their eighteen-year-old son and heir, the subject of this portrait, married Muriel, daughter of William, 2nd Lord Eure. Muriel could claim descent from numerous former kings of England, among them Alfred the Great, William the Conqueror, Henry III, Edward I, and Edward III.[3] In the year he was married, Richard Goodricke junior was admitted to Gray's Inn, to study law like his father before him. He was only twenty-two when he inherited his father's estates on the latter's death in 1582. In 1591 he too became High Sheriff of Yorkshire. He died at Ribston at the age of forty-one on 21 September 1601. He fathered seven sons and two daughters and his son Henry, aged twenty-one, succeeded to the estates.[5]

This impressive portrait shows the self-satisfied young man dressed in great style but in sober black, a taste more prevalent in Spain and Holland than in this period in England. His padded satin jacket is highlighted by gold buttons and discreetly embroidered horizontal bands of gold braid. Enamelled gold jewels surround the brim of a black velvet hat as if hinting at a coronet for his head. With a highly fashionable 'millstone' neck ruff, a black velvet cloak over his left shoulder, his right hand on his hip and the other on his sword, Richard Goodricke junior is swashbuckling smart.

The portrait was perhaps painted in 1578, the young heir's momentous year of marriage and admission to the study of law. Very significantly, the upper right corner of the painting shows a small image of a fiery comet. In November 1577 the spectacular Great Comet appeared over Europe and remained visible until January 1578.[6] For a year or so it featured in many paintings and prints. With its great tail, the comet was one of the brightest recorded in history, its brilliance outshining

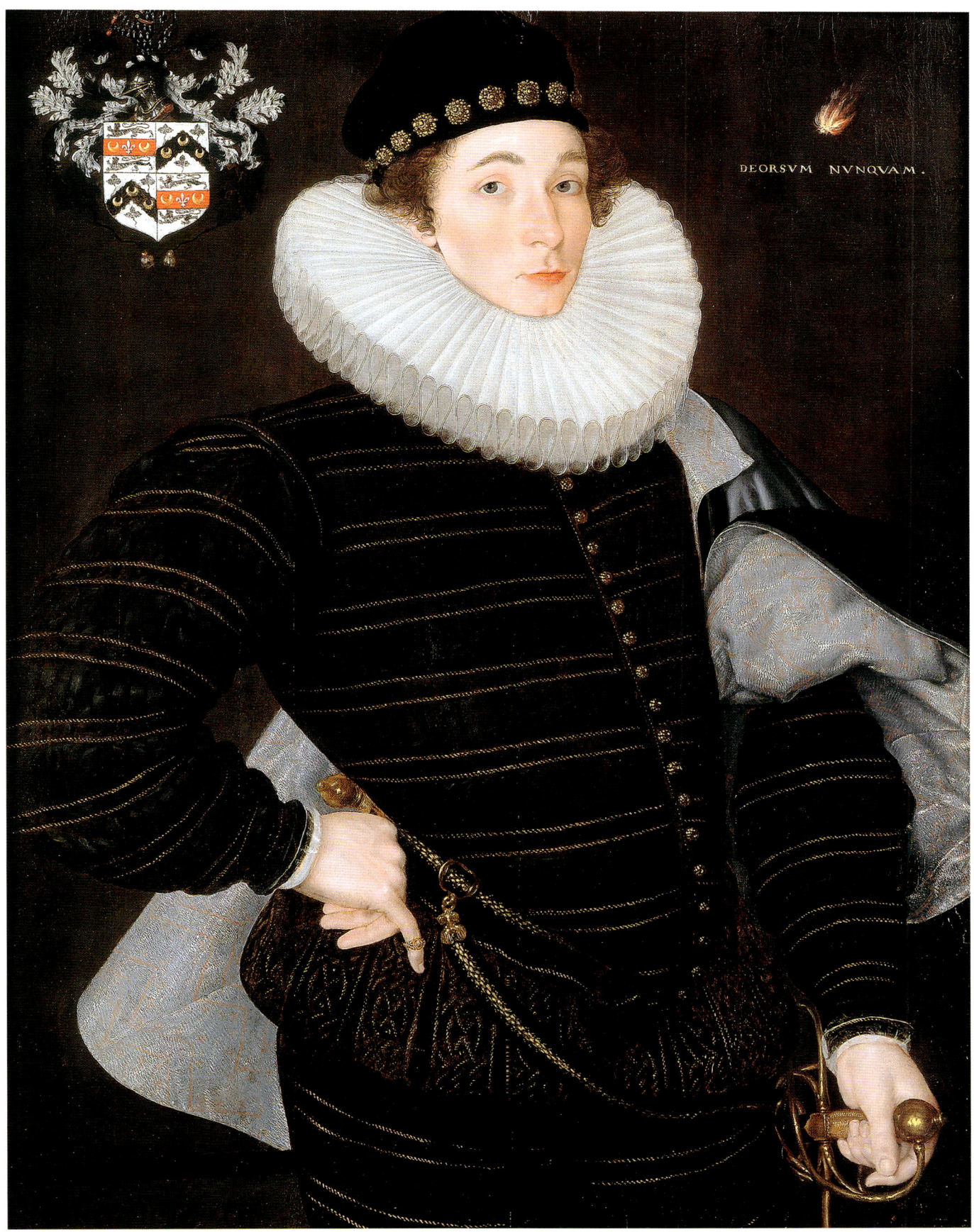

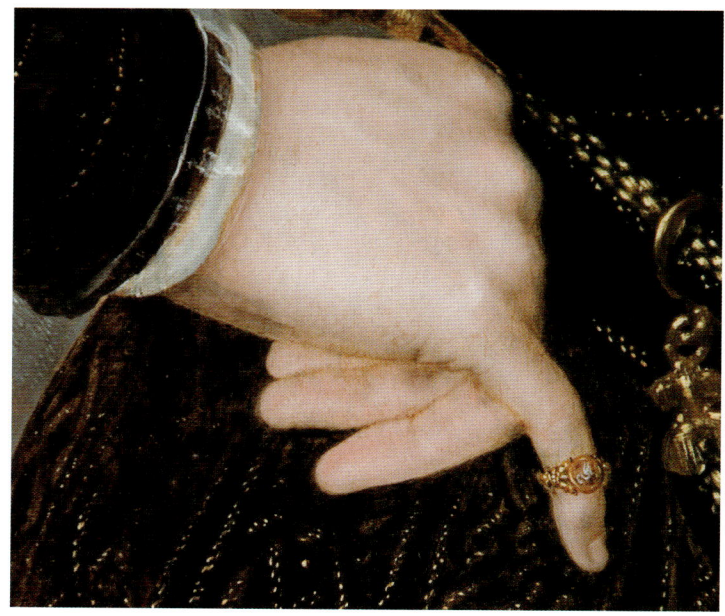
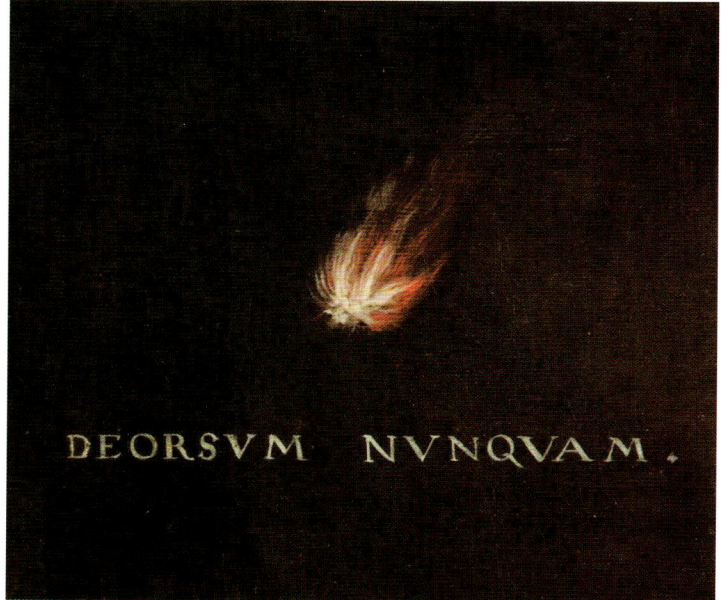

even Venus. Here, below the astronomical emblem is the Latin inscription DEORSVM NVNQVAM which means "never downwards" – apt for the upwardly mobile heir who married Lord Eure's daughter in the year of the wondrous comet.

A majority of British portraits from the Tudor period onwards are marriage portraits, as this may be. The visual prominence of the ring with a swan design on Richard's little finger could indicate a betrothal ring: its small size suggests that it was originally made for a woman, and so could be a ring exchanged with his wife-to-be.[7] However, the ruff may suggest a slightly later date for the painting. The earliest known portrait showing such a huge ruff is of 1579, and if this is earlier it might be the first portrait to show the large millstone style.[8]

The inclusion of a coat of arms in the upper left corner of the picture was not unusual for Elizabethan and Jacobean portraits. It emphasised the dynastic purposes of British portraiture. And for our art-historical purposes the coat of arms of the family of Goodricke of Ribston has helped confirm the identity of the sitter.

Because Ketel was a painter of allegories we should entertain the possibility that he conceived the portrait around the idea of the Great Comet. He has made the sitter's star-crowned head appear almost to float, and the white ruff to radiate like flames around a luminous face. The black clothing, relieved only by gold tracks, merges into a dark background and almost dissolves into limitless night-sky space. The cloak, with zigzag embroidery glowing pink on its silver lining, flows behind him and suggests the burning tail of a comet.

Ketel's typically dexterous modelling of the face and hands is superior to the work of his English contemporaries of the 1570s and 1580s. But there is also some deliberate flatness of the forms, a distinctive style in English sixteenth-century portraiture, already evident as early as the end of the 1530s in Holbein's last portraits, and to be taken to emblematic extremes, after Ketel's departure, in the final two decades of Queen Elizabeth's reign.

Ketel's surviving portraits are rare enough but in the early Elizabethan period it is exceptionally rare to have a portrait that is not only signed but also of an identified sitter. It is the only such sixteenth-century British portrait in Australia.

**Inscription:** Signed l.r., oil: "Cornelius Kettil Fecit". Inscribed u.r., oil: "DEORSVM NVNQAM." below image of the Great Comet of 1577–78.

**Provenance:** By descent at Ribston Hall, Yorkshire, to Sir Harry James Goodricke, 7th Bt (1798–1833), who died unmarried; thence to Sir Francis Lyttleton Holyoake, who assumed the name Goodricke, until c.1863; Mark Kynaston Mainwaring, Oteley, Ellesmere, Shropshire; Christie's, London, 5 April 1946, lot 143 (as by Zuccaro); private collection, England, 1960s; Weiss Gallery, London, 2004.

**Exhibitions:** *Icons of Splendour: Early portraiture 1530–1700*, Weiss Gallery, London, 2004, no. 4. *Island to Empire: 300 Years of British Art 1550–1850*, AGSA, Adelaide, 2005.

**Literature:** Karel van Mander, *Lives of the Illustrious Netherlandish and German Painters* (from his *Book of Painting*, 1604), Hessel Miedema (ed.), 1994, p. 358. Mark Weiss, *Icons of Splendour: Early portraiture 1530–1700*, London: Weiss Gallery, 2004, no. 4.

**Condition:** Good; conserved in 2004 in London prior to acquisition.

**Frame:** Probably not original to the painting but nonetheless an original Sansovino-style frame from the sixteenth century.

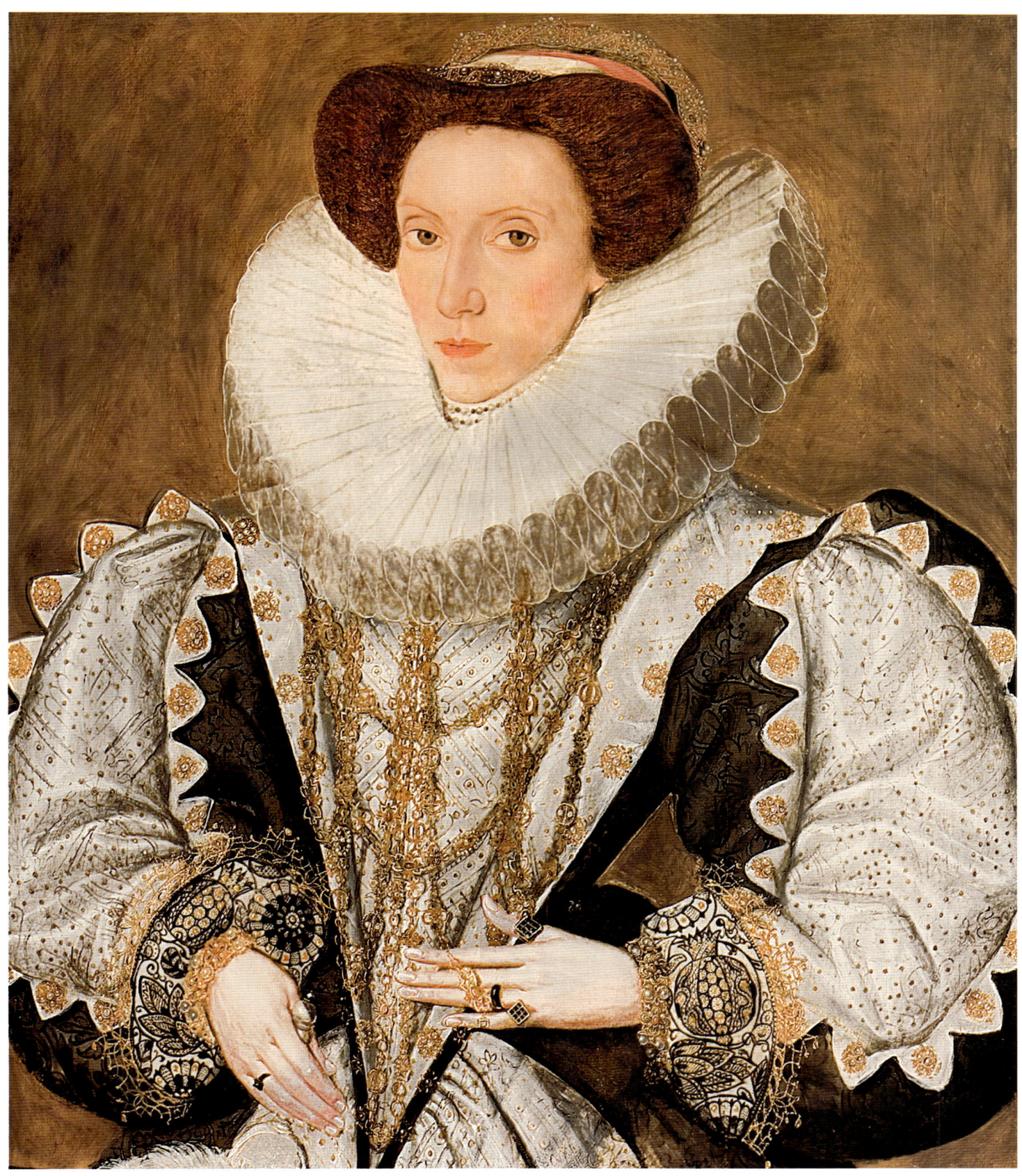

heavy-lidded deep-set eyes, with eyeballs sharply turned to the corners of the eyes while looking out, are all very characteristic of Gower's distinctive style. The lady here is less an individual than a representative of a certain class. That class had come into being largely through Henry VIII's dissolution of the monasteries and abbeys and his distribution of the former church lands to those who had supported his claim as head of the independent English Church; the new class was intensely interested in property and status.

This portrait admirably demonstrates the rigid neo-medievalism of Elizabethan portraiture, retrogressive compared with the naturalism of Italian, Flemish and German Renaissance portraiture. Mid-sixteenth-century Protestant England saw the destruction of 'Popish' religious icons only to see them reappear in another form, ironically, as portraits of English iconoclasts. Stereotype medieval images of God were replaced by stereotype neo-medieval images of man. Jewel-encrusted icons of the Virgin were destroyed only to be replaced by jewel-encrusted icons of the Virgin Queen. The royal images set the pattern for court portraiture which followed. The emphasis on decoration and patterning of the bejewelled costumes in the portraits of both the women and the men became more important than accurate likenesses. As well demonstrated in this portrait, pale mask-like faces float within flat but brilliant patterning of lace, brocade and jewels. Although heraldic and backward-looking, in a broader sense, these elaborate late-Elizabethan portraits could also be interpreted as a late provincial flowering of European Mannerism.

This portrait is a splendid example of the high Elizabethan style and it is the latest in date of the thirty or so portraits ascribed to Gower.[3]

**Provenance:** Ivor and Joan Weiss Gallery, Essex, England.
**Exhibition:** *Island to Empire: 300 Years of British Art 1550–1850*, AGSA, Adelaide, 2005.
**Literature:** *Apollo*, June 1984, p. 39 (illus.).
**Condition:** Good, but thin paint through age has become translucent. Last conserved in 1983 in London before acquisition. Split panel repaired in London, 1998.
**Frame:** Not original.

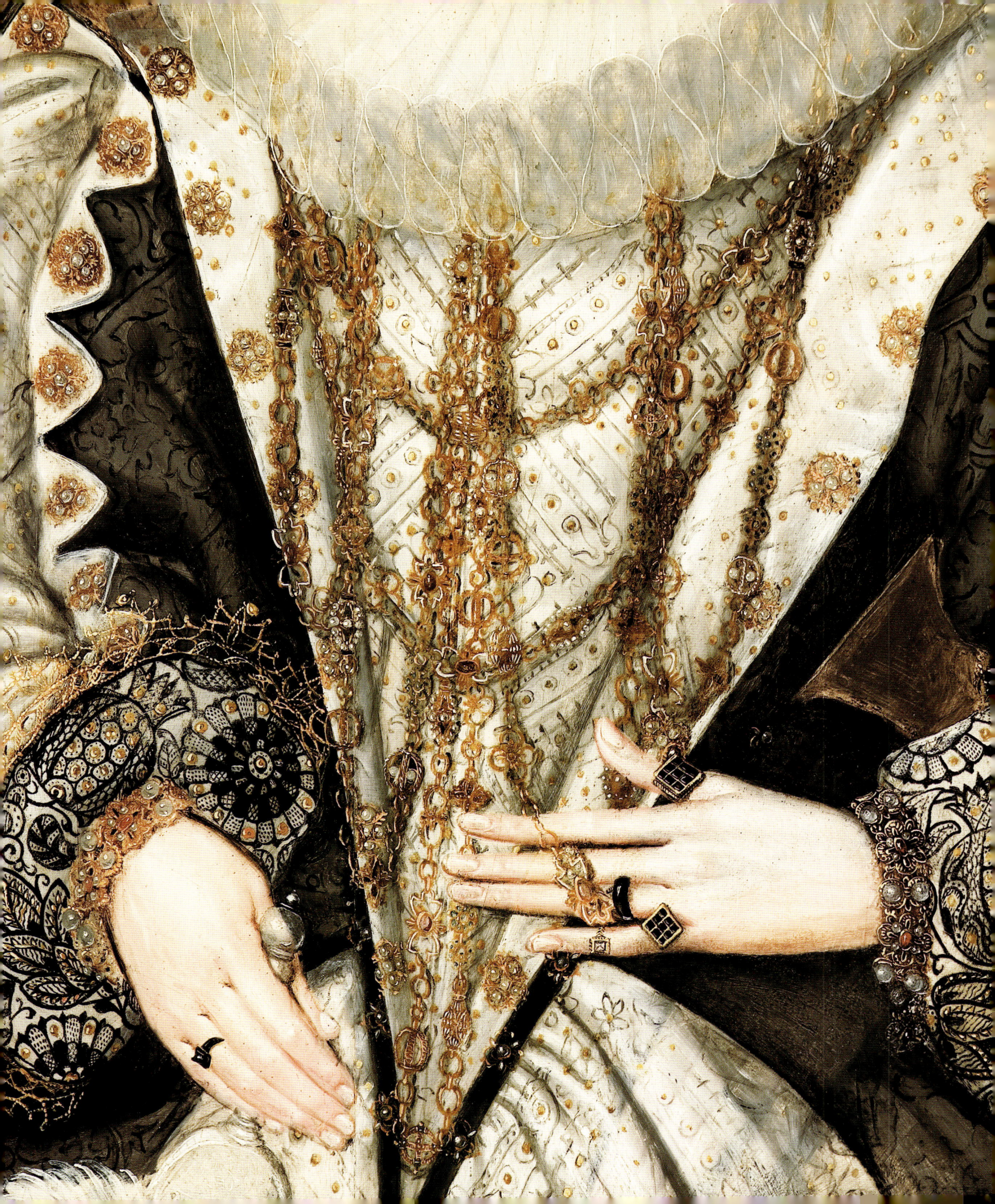

# Isaac Oliver c.1565–1617

Isaac Oliver is often linked with his teacher and mentor Nicholas Hilliard (1547–1619) as the most important miniature painter of the late Elizabethan and early Jacobean period. Miniature portrait painting, although not invented by the British, became known as a peculiarly British practice in the Elizabethan period and remained a British obsession until the rise of photography in the mid nineteenth century. Portrait miniatures were more highly prized than full-scale portraits in the Elizabethan and Jacobean age and are among the most notable artistic achievements of the time. Miniatures of loved ones were worn, sent to relatives and friends and carried with ease by their owners while travelling; the production of several versions of the same portrait miniature was common.

Isaac Oliver was born in France, at Rouen, probably about 1565. In 1571 Isaac's father Pierre, a Huguenot goldsmith, brought his family to England to escape religious persecution. In London, Oliver trained as a limner, that is a painter of miniature portraits, and probably in the late 1570s became the pupil of Elizabeth I's most esteemed miniature painter, Nicholas Hilliard. Isaac Oliver's earliest dated portrait miniature is 1587. His first works show a full understanding of the engravings of the Dutch artist Hendrick Goltzius whom Hilliard extolled as second only to Albrecht Dürer as a model from whom a limner should learn hatching. Oliver used a restricted light source and often produced more contrasting shadows than Hilliard. Oliver's works of the late 1580s and early 1590s are stylistically close to Netherlandish art, leading to speculation that he travelled to study for a time in the Low Countries – possibly with Marcus Gheeraerts the Younger who later became his brother-in-law. Although there is no firm documentary evidence for it he could have also had some training in his homeland France. In the mid 1590s, however, he certainly visited Venice, and the influence of Venetian art led to his use of softer hatching and more vibrant colours.

From 1596 one of Oliver's important and influential sitters was Queen Elizabeth's favourite, Robert Devereux, 2nd Earl of Essex (an example is in the collection of the Yale Center for British Art) whose patronage led to further commissions from the nobility. In 1602 he married the sister of the leading full-scale portrait painter Marcus Gheeraerts the Younger. Oliver came fully into his own during the early reign of James I. He was appointed a Court Painter to James's consort, Queen Anne, in 1605 and he was drawn into the circle of the young and precociously-cultivated Henry Prince of Wales, whose portraits he also painted. Although his art is often linked to Hilliard's, Oliver was far more responsive to continental European influences and more in touch with the tastes of the Jacobean court; this is particularly reflected in his small Mannerist style figure compositions.

He had a son Peter Oliver (c.1594–1647) whom he taught and who also became a prominent miniature painter in Britain.

## Man with fair hair and beard, c.1590
watercolour on vellum backed with ivory, 5.1 x 4.2 cm
Mary Overton Bequest Fund assisted by the Art Gallery of South Australia Foundation 2004

This portrait is of an unknown sitter with greying fair hair and beard. The sitter's costume can be dated to about 1590 so unless this ageing gentleman is out of fashion this is an early portrait by the artist. About thirty miniatures are known from before Oliver's trip to Venice but it is just possible that this work was painted after the mid-1590s Venetian visit. The modelling of the features is softer and more painterly than most early works and there is a vibrant sense of light.

The striking blue background is an example of the use of blue bice, the most precious and valuable of all artists' colours at the time, made from crushed and powdered azurite. The rich blue provided a perfect contrast to delicate skin tones and its use is characteristic of miniatures painted for the Elizabethan and early Jacobean courts.

As was the practice for Elizabethan miniatures, the sitter would probably have had three sittings with the artist, each of a few hours duration. The intricate details of the costume and the stippling of the face are executed with the exquisite virtuosity characteristic of Oliver's work. The oval format derives from Hilliard who changed from the previously current circular format, usual in Britain since Horenbout's miniatures of the mid 1520s. During a visit to France in 1576–78 Hilliard saw oval miniatures by François Clouet (c.1516–1572), and adopted the format. Thenceforth nearly all British miniature portraits were oval.[1]

The miniature was once attributed to Nicholas Hilliard.[2] Authorities on miniature painting of the period, including Sir Roy Strong, Katherine Coombs and Alan Derbyshire (the latter two of the Victoria & Albert Museum), are now convinced it is by Hilliard's pupil Isaac Oliver.[3]

This portrait is the only Elizabethan miniature in an Australian public collection. It forms an important part of the nation's only collection, albeit small, of Elizabethan and Jacobean paintings.

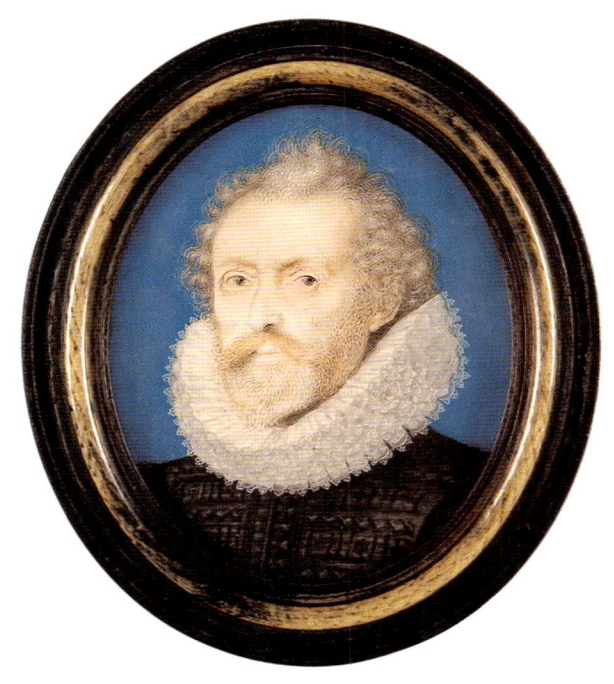

Provenance: 17th century house of the Blofeld family, Hoveton House, Norfolk; 1989 to D. S. Lavender (Antiques) Ltd, London; from 1989 Albion Collection, Albion House, London; Bonham's, London, 22 April 2004, lot 3; D. S. Lavender (Antiques) Ltd.

Exhibitions: *Secret Passion to Noble Fashion: The world of the portrait miniature*, Holburne Museum of Art, Bath, April 1999, no. 1, later at Scottish National Portrait Gallery, Edinburgh. *Island to Empire: 300 Years of British Art 1550–1850*, AGSA, Adelaide, 2005.

Literature: Ann Sumner and Richard Walker, *Secret Passion to Noble Fashion: The world of the portrait miniature*, Bath: Holburne Museum of Art, 1999, pp. 46–47 (illus.). *The Albion Collection of Fine Portrait Miniatures*, London: Bonham's, 22 April 2004, lot 3.

Condition: Good; evidence of some fading.

Frame: Possibly original.

# Robert Peake the Elder c.1551–1619

Robert Peake was one of the most prominent portrait painters in the reigns of Elizabeth I and her Stuart successor James I. He held two important positions at the Stuart court, first as principal Picture Maker to the short-lived Henry, Prince of Wales (1594–1612), then as Sergeant Painter to King James from 1607, an office he held jointly with John de Critz (1551/52–1642). In both situations, Peake's work reveals the influence of the bright colouring, elaborate patterns and general warmth of Elizabethan miniature-painting, specifically the work of Nicholas Hilliard.

Peake was born of a Lincolnshire family about 1551, and according to tradition was apprenticed to a goldsmith in Cheapside. He was apprenticed in London in 1565 becoming a Freeman of the Goldsmith's Company in 1576, and is first documented in the same year as an employee of the Office of the Revels whose artists provided stage-sets, decorations, banners and other ephemera for masques and ceremonies. Peake's positions as a court artist continued until his death in 1619, an unusually long career of over forty years. His earliest known portraits date from the mid 1580s, and his workshop became exclusively devoted to this lucrative genre.

Shortly after the 1603 accession of King James, Peake was commissioned to paint portraits of the royal family, and later especially Henry, Prince of Wales. As many as eighteen of his works are royal portraits, ten of them representing Prince Henry, most notably the life-size equestrian portrait now at Parham House, West Sussex. He also painted numerous members of the Jacobean court, among them the King's young favourite George Villiers, later Duke of Buckingham (see p. 73).

## Frances, Lady Reynell of West Ogwell, Devon, c.1595
oil on oak panel, 113.5 x 88.5 cm
Gift of the Art Gallery of South Australia Foundation 1998

The Gallery's magnificent three-quarter-length portrait by Robert Peake of Frances Reynell is from near the end of Elizabeth I's long reign. Lady Reynell is formally presented with solemn dignity in the elegant restraint of black and white. The stiff, iconic formality of this picture reflects the complex, rigid conventions that radiated from images of Queen Elizabeth herself. The formulaic stiffness and flat patterning of those conventions, and the Elizabethan love of rich decoration, are apparent in the tight, boned corsetry, funnel-shaped sleeves, heavy skirt and many jewel ornaments with which the lady is adorned. The delicacy of the pale face and hands, however, and the schematic handling of sumptuous decoration are here closer to the techniques used by the prominent miniature painters Nicholas Hilliard and Isaac Oliver.

The identity of the sitter is established by family tradition as that of Frances, the first wife of Sir Thomas Reynell (1555–1621), the senior member of an ancient and distinguished family of Devon gentry. He rebuilt the manor house of West Ogwell in 1589, purchased by his father, reputedly employing Spanish prisoners from the defeated Armada. Frances, who was the daughter of John Aylworth of Polsbow, Devon, had married Sir Thomas in about 1580 and by him had nine children from 1581, three sons and six daughters; she died in 1605. Sir Thomas's brother, Sir Carew Reynell, was cup bearer to Queen Elizabeth. A portrait of another brother, Sir Richard Reynell, a lawyer who amassed a fortune through his office at the Exchequer, was consigned with this picture of his sister-in-law Frances to the same Christie's sale in London in 1922 and went to the same buyer. In 2002 Sir Richard's portrait was exhibited in *The Courtly Image: early portraiture 1550–1680*, at the Weiss Gallery, London.[1]

Our portrait may be dated with reasonable certainty to around 1595 on the basis of costume details which in the study of late Elizabethan paintings offer particularly reliable information. A very great deal is known about Elizabeth's own taste in costume, partly a result of the extraordinary cult of the 'Virgin Queen' which she permitted to flourish throughout her long and eventful reign. Lady Reynell's 'bombasted' sleeves are finely slashed and pulled, then covered with an embroidered scale pattern of pearls suspended from looped threads. Her enormous skirt or 'wheel farthingale' is made from an extremely expensive, heavy black-and-white silk brocade, decorated with oak-leaf and pomegranate motifs, which are common costume decorations of the time. The upper edge is draped with a gathered frill of the same material. The hem of her black coat or gown is composed of scallops decorated with many identical dress jewels of pearls and gold. Similar jewels are stitched to the V-shaped hem of the bodice. The lower edge of her bodice is finished with 'pickadils', or squared scallops. She wears a long chain consisting of gold and enamel links and a large matching brooch with three drop pearls is attached by a knotted thread to her sleeve. Finally, her hair is raised over a high wire support or 'palisadoe'. All of these details are consistent with the taste for extravagant, highly ornate formal dress in the mid 1590s.[2]

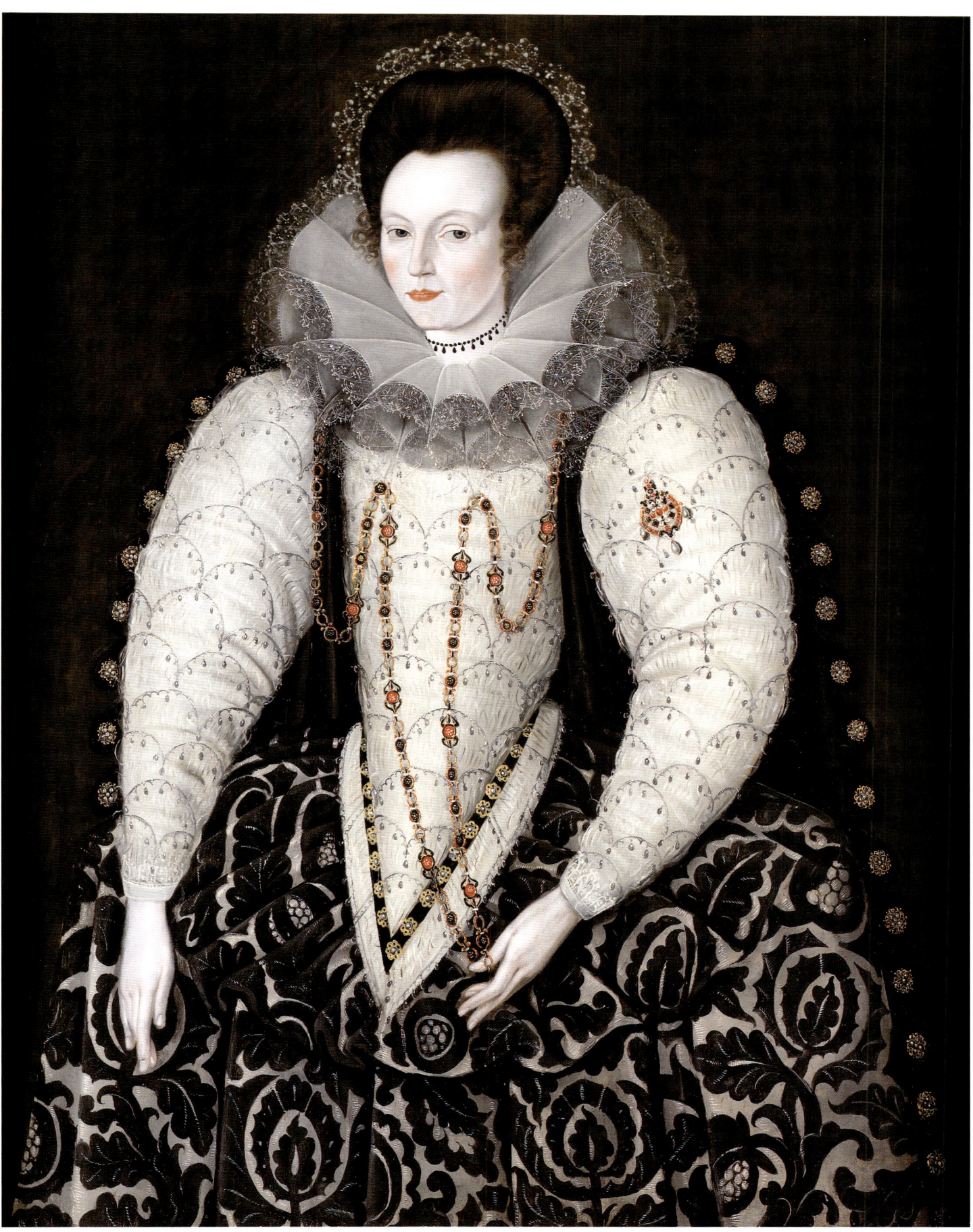

# Robert Peake the Elder

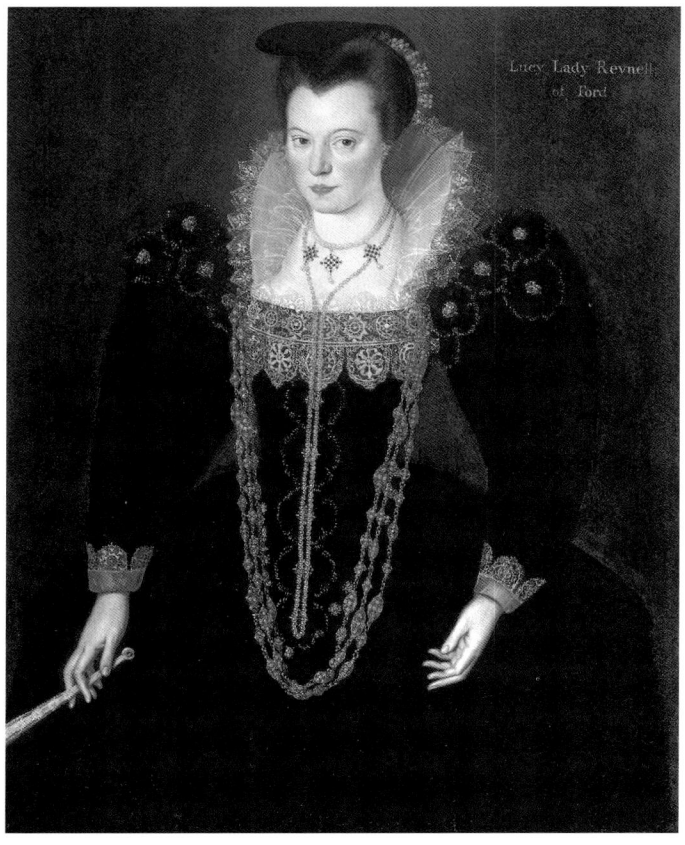

Marcus Gheeraerts, *Lady Lucy Reynell*, c.1600. Private collection

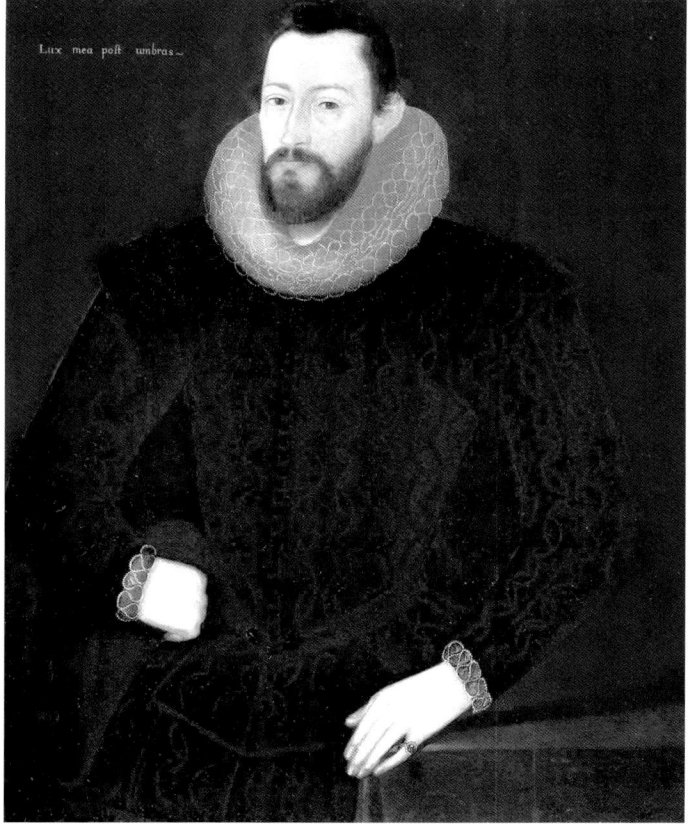

Unknown English School, *Sir Richard Reynell*, 1602. Private collection

The painting might be precisely dated to 1597, when Sir Thomas was knighted  It was frequently thought appropriate to commission a pair of commemorative portraits in formal attire on such an occasion. If so, the portrait of Sir Thomas is lost.

Like the Gallery's portrait by Gower, the elongation and flat heraldic patterning of this figure represent the height of Elizabethan style. It was a distinctive, provincial English version of Italian and French Mannerism, which is sometimes described as "the stylish style".

The painting has a tangential link to South Australia. The Reynell brothers' uncle, John Reynell, established a branch of the family from which – after nine generations – descended the South Australian pioneer John Reynell (1809–1873). The first Australian Reynell arrived in Adelaide in October 1838 and established the Reynella Winery, the nation's earliest commercial wine-growing venture. Reynella is now an outer suburb of Adelaide, and contains an Ogwell Street. The pioneer John Reynell's grand-daughter, Gladys Reynell (1881–1956), became an important modernist painter and significant pioneer of Australian studio pottery. The Art Gallery of South Australia owns a large collection of Gladys Reynell's drawings, paintings and pottery, as well as her friend and fellow-student Bessie Davidson's stiff grey portrait of Gladys dated 1906, a distant echo of the ancestral portrait of Frances Reynell from a little over 300 years earlier.

**Provenance:** By descent from Thomas Reynell (1555–1621) of West Ogwell, Devon, to Colonel Pierce Taylor (1840–1921) of Newton Priory, Tetbury, Gloucestershire; at Christie's, London, 28 July 1922 (as *Frances Lady Reynell in white bodice embroidered skirt and white lace ruff and jewelled rope*, assigned to Nicholas Hilliard), bt Grissell; thence by family descent; Weiss Gallery, London, 1997.

**Exhibitions:** *Tudor and Stuart Portraits 1530–1660*, Rex Irwin Gallery, Sydney, 1997. *Island to Empire: 300 Years of British Art 1550–1850*, AGSA, Adelaide, 2005.

**Literature:** *Art Prices Current*, vol. 1, 1921/22, pp. 495–6. Mark Weiss, *Tudor and Stuart Portraits, 1530–1660*, Sydney: 1997, pp. 1–2. Ron Radford, *Treasures*, Adelaide: AGSA, 1998, p. 27. Mark Weiss, *A Noble Visage: Early portraiture 1545–1660*, London: Weiss Gallery, 2001, no. 10 (illus.). Mark Weiss, *The Courtly Image: Early portraiture 1550–1680*, London: Weiss Gallery, 2002, no. 10. "Recent Acquisitions at the Art Gallery of South Australia", *The Burlington Magazine*, London, April 2003, p. 328.

**Condition:** Excellent; last conserved in London in 1997 before acquisition.

**Frame:** Not original.

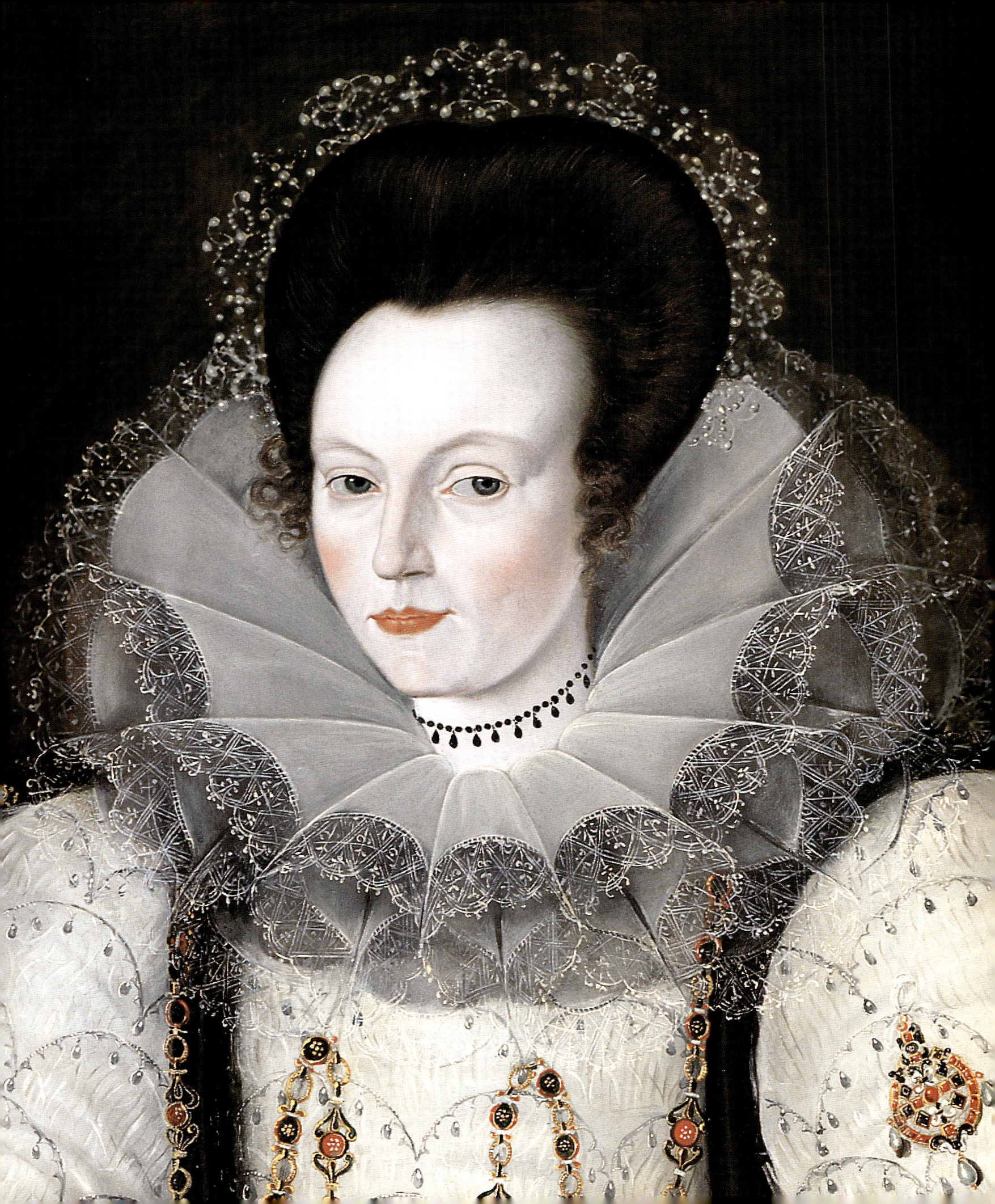

# Anthony van Dyck 1599–1641

Anthony van Dyck is one of the greatest portrait painters in European art. His aristocratic, elegant style appealed to patrons in the seventeenth century, especially in Italy, Britain and his native Flanders. He lived in London for the prolific final third of his career.

His move from Flanders in 1632 to become court painter to King Charles I was momentous for British art, causing a radical change to the style and direction of portraiture, which was and would long remain the primary concern of the nation's painting. A relaxed Baroque naturalism superseded the decorative, stiffly archaic Elizabethan and Jacobean style, characterised in the Gallery's collection by the work of George Gower, Robert Peake and Marcus Gheeraerts. Van Dyck's dynamic realism and flamboyant grace held uninterrupted sway for a full two centuries. Then after fading in the mid nineteenth century the style was revived again in the 'swagger' portraits of early-twentieth-century Britain, the United States and Australia.

Born in 1599, he was a child of a merchant in Antwerp, the commercial centre of the Flemish Netherlands. In 1609 he became a student of the painter Hendrik van Balen. By 1612 – a child prodigy – he had painted his first professional portraits and by 1618 he was accepted into the artists' Guild of Saint Luke. Flanders was in the Catholic part of the Netherlands, so at Antwerp he painted religious and mythological subjects as well as portraits. There, too, he was a familiar presence in the palatial studio of Peter Paul Rubens, Europe's most celebrated contemporary artist, and he became Rubens's principal assistant in 1618. Van Dyck absorbed his master's famously accomplished rendering of flesh, and complex compositional skills, but the refinement, the nervous line, the sensitive touch and animated, shimmering surfaces were qualities of his own. It was in Rubens's studio, with its collection of many master paintings and drawings, that he first encountered works by sixteenth-century Venetian artists.

In October 1620, sponsored by three connoisseur patrons, the Earl of Arundel, Sir Dudley Carleton and King James's favourite George Villiers (recently created Earl of Buckingham and soon to be raised to Duke), the young Van Dyck made his first visit to Britain. He received the patronage of James I who paid him an annual pension of £100. After less than five months in London he was granted leave to travel to Italy.

Departing Britain in March 1621 for Antwerp, in October he proceeded onwards and spent over five years visiting Padua, Venice, Florence, Milan, Mantua, Bologna, Turin, Rome and Palermo. However, for most of his Italian period Van Dyck was based in Genoa, where he received many portrait commissions from the local nobility. During the Italian years he became even more strongly influenced by the rich colour, painterly textures, sumptuousness and grandeur of Venetian painting, especially that of Titian and Veronese, first seen in Rubens's studio and then more notably in London in the Arundel and Buckingham collections, formed by noblemen for whom he had worked in 1620–21. Van Dyck was so obsessed by Venetian painting that he began systematically to build a large collection of works by Titian. By the time of his death he owned no fewer than nineteen paintings by that master (most of which were portraits) and had arranged them in a special gallery attached to his studio. He also painted copies after Titian.

Van Dyck left Italy in 1627 and returned to Antwerp to set up a studio in his and Rubens's home town. Nearly five years later he was at last induced to move to London where he was appointed "Principal Painter in Ordinary to their Majesties" and simultaneously knighted by King Charles I. During this influential and very productive second period in Britain Sir Anthony twice returned to Antwerp to paint portraits, in 1634 and again in 1640. In 1641, nine years after making it his base, Van Dyck died in London, aged forty-two.

## A married couple, c.1620
oil on canvas, 120.0 x 154.0 cm
Gift of James Fairfax assisted by the Art Gallery of South Australia Foundation 1993

This splendid early work by Van Dyck, a double portrait of a seated Flemish couple, dates from around 1620, just before or during his brief first period in Britain. In the nineteenth and early twentieth centuries it was thought to be by Cornelis de Vos but in 1922 the art historian W. R. Valentiner corrected the attribution.[2]

It is probably a betrothal portrait. The sitters are shown half-length with, as was customary in such double portraits, the man on the left (the heraldic right) and his wife on the right (the heraldic left). Of the middle class, in Flemish dress, they look directly out to the viewer and appear consciously to be posing for us; we are the witnesses to their mutual life-commitment. She is possibly no more than twenty years old whereas he is probably in his thirties. Although he does not have handsome features, Van Dyck has made the husband distinguished by using his characteristic arabesque brushstrokes. She appears nervous and shy, her head slightly lowered; he is more open and confident. His chin up and as if reassuring her, one arm is around her shoulders, the other takes her right hand in his, as if in sudden linkage. Clasped right hands, a gesture known as *dextrarum iunctio*, had been a symbol of marital fidelity since ancient Roman times and here allude to the joining of the bride and groom's right hands in a marriage service. Van Dyck – a painter as young as the bride – has deftly captured their role-playing, in facial expression and in hand gesture. It is both sensitive and intimate yet at the same time a public statement. Van Dyck records their togetherness, but also their individuality.

Van Dyck was masterly in this format, but this was one of his earliest double marriage portraits and one of the few painted in the first decades of the seventeenth century.[3] Susan J. Barnes, co-curator in 1990 of the Anthony van Dyck exhibition at the National Gallery of Art, Washington, and co-author of the 2004 complete catalogue of his paintings,

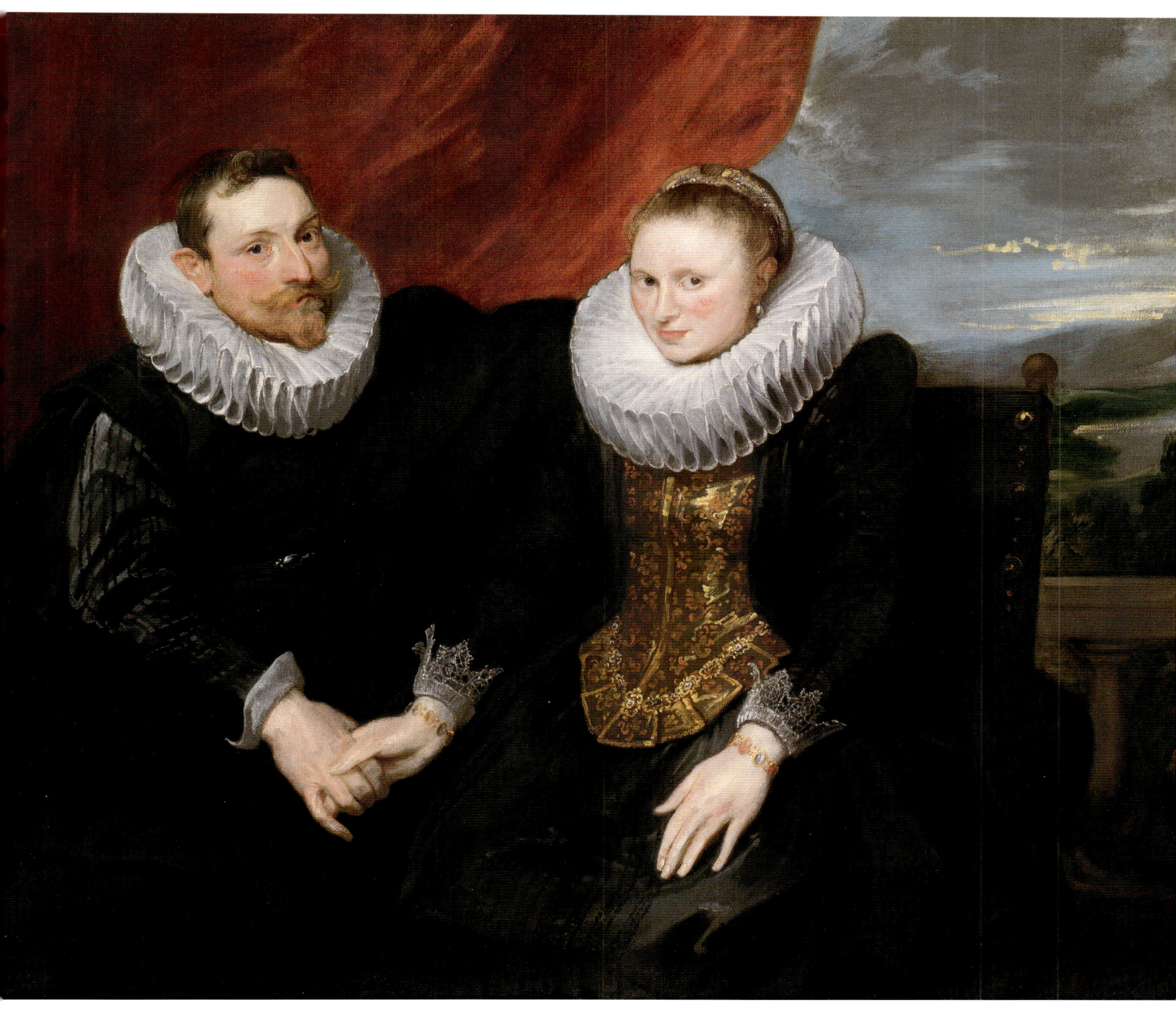

assesses the work as "…an early, ambitious essay in the double portrait – the form that Van Dyck continued to develop throughout his career and the one for which he is perhaps most famous of all".[4] The late Michael Jaffé, a senior Van Dyck and Rubens scholar, praised the portrait: "The handling of the brushwork…superbly fluent and deft. The compositional relation of the sitters to each other…is most sensitive."[5]

The portrait follows a 200-year-old Flemish tradition seen as early as Jan van Eyck's (1385–1441) *The Betrothal of the Arnolfini*, 1434 (National Gallery, London). A more immediate precedent was Rubens's own betrothal self-portrait of 1609 (Alte Pinakothek, Munich), well known to the teenage Van Dyck when he worked in Rubens's studio. (Young Anthony's admiration for his master's wife is revealed in his own portrait of her, painted on the eve of departure for Italy, his final break from the high cultural stimulus of life in the Rubens studio.) Van Dyck's own prototype composition for our *A married couple* seems to be the smaller *A married couple* (Szépmüvészeti Múseum, Budapest) which has been dated about 1618 but is probably a little later (see below).[6]

The identities of our Flemish couple remain unknown. In the nineteenth century the portrait was thought to be of the animal painter Frans Snyders and his wife Margaretha de Vos.[7] Later it was thought to be of the landscape painter Jan Wildens and his wife Maria Stappart.[8] Nearly all scholars now reject those identifications.

They are seated on what appears to be a balcony with a classical balustrade overlooking an expansive landscape. It is a romantic, dusky suggestion of middle-distance foliage, a winding river, distant grey-blue hills and cloud-filled sky. Vigorously painted, the land and sky have an impressionistic spontaneity and the free Venetian brushwork found in Tintoretto's late paintings. The sitters' fine Flemish garments, black with white ruffs and cuffs, are relieved only by the woman's golden brocaded bodice. The colour scheme is enriched by red drapery behind them, a curtain as a schematic and compositional backing device for the faces, which are not at all schematic but most subtly modelled, with summary brushwork. Van Dyck's characteristically sensual, elegant renderings of hands are also brushed with great subtlety.

There has been some disagreement on the date and place of execution of the picture. Once assigned various dates between 1618 and 1621, recent opinion has concentrated on 1620. Most Van Dyck scholars, including Susan Barnes and Michael Jaffé, believe it to have been painted immediately before the artist's first visit to Britain, that is before October 1620. Another Van Dyck authority, Professor Egbert Haverkamp-Begemann, has instead declared it to be one of the few surviving works painted in Britain on the first visit. Haverkamp-Begemann's reasons are its close relationship to *The Continence of Scipio* (Christ Church, Oxford) and particularly to the portrait *The Earl of Arundel* (J. Paul Getty Museum, Los Angeles), both firmly documented to the time in Britain from October 1620 to March 1621. Professor Haverkamp-Begemann argues that those two paintings and our double portrait "…share the broad manner of painting, with rapid brushstrokes that often remain transparent. The face of Thomas Howard (Earl of Arundel), his hands, and the landscape behind are remarkably similar to the same

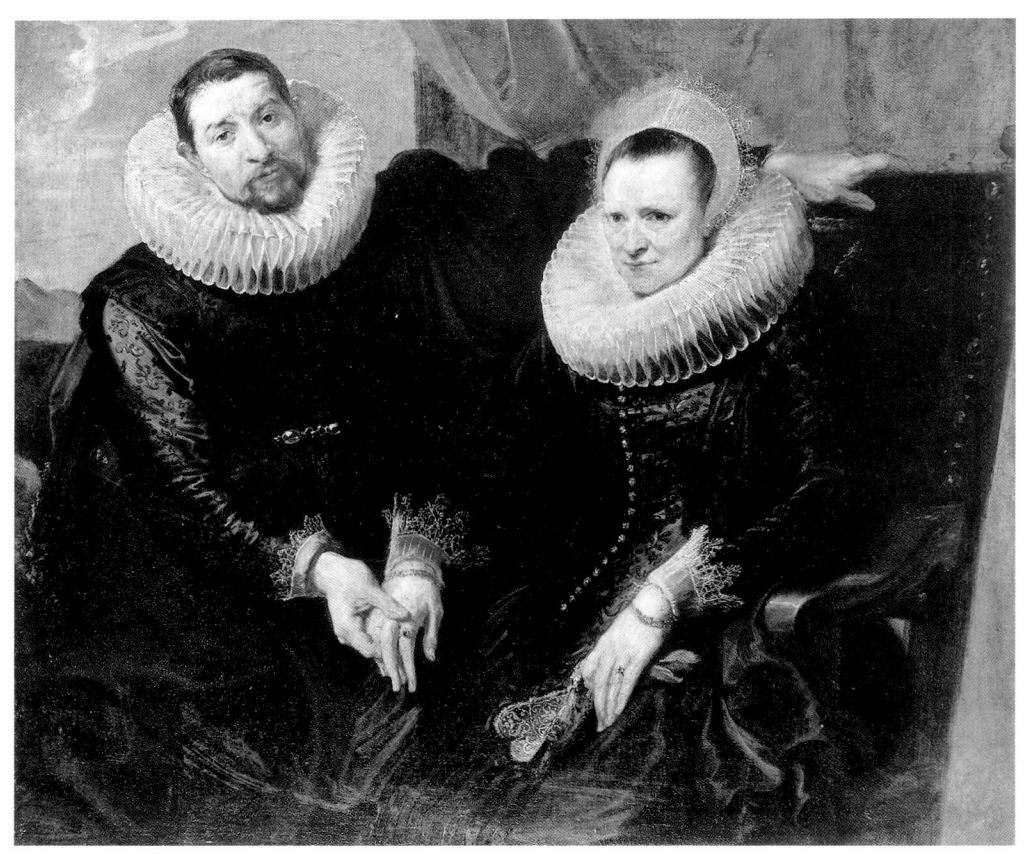

Anthony van Dyck, *A married couple*, c.1618. Szépmüvészeti Múseum, Budapest

motifs in the double portrait". He notes that *The Continence of Scipio* and this double portrait are both painted on heavily-woven canvas primed with a distinctive grey ground. He supposes the sitters could be Flemish émigrés in England.[9] To strengthen the opinion, exactly the same style of chair, with a wooden knob finial and large and smaller alternating metal studs supporting the upholstery, is present in both the Getty and Adelaide portraits, the former upholstered in red, the latter in black.

The technique of the portrait echoes the dry distinctive brushstrokes evident in the works of the Venetian painters Titian, Veronese and Tintoretto which, as mentioned, Van Dyck saw in the collections of his English patrons Arundel and Buckingham and also the Royal Collection. The mountainous landscape background is much closer to a British than a flat Flemish landscape and closely resembles the background of the portrait of the Earl of Arundel.[10] Further, the balustrade device is similar to that used in Van Dyck's *The Continence of Scipio*, commissioned by Buckingham. It must be said, too, that Van Dyck, a fairly rapid painter, surely would have executed more than the three paintings hitherto assigned to his first English period of nearly five months duration.

It is also possible to argue that Van Dyck painted *A married couple* during his months back in Antwerp in 1621. It can be related to the Venetian-style portrait of Rubens's wife *Isabella Brant* (National Gallery of Art, Washington), painted in Flanders just before his departure for Italy. The English appearance of the landscape in our portrait could be merely a Titianesque invention. However, this third option is less likely than the earlier Antwerp or London periods, for after them his modelling became subtly but perceptibly firmer. Jewellery presents interesting observations: the distinctive three-colour stone bracelets worn on both wrists of the female in our portrait are very like a bracelet of alternating red, black and clear stones worn by Isabella Brant in Rubens's 1609 betrothal portrait. Such distinctive bracelets have not been noted in other portraits of the time and could indicate a connection between the sitters in the two portraits. As to evidence of date and place, this bracelet type is also used as an upper armband of the female figure (thought to be an allegorical representation of Buckingham's wife Katherine Villiers) in Van Dyck's 1620/21 London composition *The Continence of Scipio* commissioned by Buckingham.

We can conclude that the picture is certainly an immediate stylistic precursor to the artist's Italian portraits and most likely painted immediately before his first arrival in Britain. The body of recent scholarly opinion, though differing, is in general agreement on an origin either in Antwerp or London, about 1620, but at a crucial time in the development of Van Dyck's career.

The robust painterly handling and relaxed, convincing naturalism are in marked contrast with the Gallery's smoothly modelled formal portraits by Michiel van Miereveld, Cornelius Johnson and Marcus Gheeraerts. (The Miereveld portrait is of Van Dyck's patron the Duke of Buckingham.) Those three portraits were all painted by 1625, at roughly the same time as the double portrait by Van Dyck, but these Dutch and British artists still followed the tight realism of a Northern Renaissance tradition. This painting by the great Flemish artist illustrates a turning point not only in Van Dyck's art and, especially, in British portraiture but also a shift to the influence of Venetian art on Baroque portraiture throughout northern Europe.[11]

**Provenance:** Prince Esterhazy [possibly Paul Anton III] (1786–1866); Henry Nugent Banks, London; James E. Scripps by whom given to the Detroit Institute of Arts in 1889 (as *Portrait of Frans Snyders and his wife Margaretha de Vos* by Cornelis de Vos); Detroit Institute of Arts until 1992; Sotheby's, New York, 15 January 1993, lot 259, bt Colnaghi, New York.

**Exhibitions:** Detroit Institute of Arts, 1889 (as *Portrait of Frans Snyders and his wife Margaretha de Vos* by Cornelis de Vos). *Loan Exhibition of Paintings by Van Dyck*, Detroit Institute of Arts, 1929 (as *Portrait of Jan Wildens and his wife Maria Stappart*). *A Celebration: Recent acquisitions of heritage and contemporary art*, AGSA, Adelaide, 1996. *Island to Empire: 300 Years of British Art 1550–1850*, AGSA, Adelaide, 2005.

**Literature:** *Catalogue of the Scripps Collection of Old Masters*, Detroit, 1889, no. 33, as Cornelis de Vos and as representing Frans Snyders and his wife. W. R. Valentiner, "Rubens and Van Dyck in the Detroit Museum", *Art in America*, August 1922, pp. 204, 208, fig. 4. W. R. Valentiner, *Bulletin of the Detroit Institute of Arts*, August 1922, pp. 11–12. *Paintings and Sculptures Illustrated*, Detroit Institute of Arts, 1927, p. 91. Henrich Rosenbaum, *Der junge Van Dyck (1615–21)*, Ph.D. diss., Ludwig-Maximilian University, Munich, 1928. W. R. Valentiner, "Die Van Dyck Ausstellung in Detroit", *Zeitschrift für bildende Kunst*, 1929, vol. 63, pp. 105–11. *Eighth Loan Exhibition of Old Masters, Paintings by Anthony van Dyck*, The Detroit Institute of Arts, 1929, no. 7. *Catalogue of Paintings*, Detroit Institute of Arts, 1930, no. 65. Gustav Glück, *Van Dyck, des Meisters Gemälde, Klassiker der Kunst*, no. 13, 2nd rev. ed., Stuttgart/New York/London, 1931, as representing Wildens and his wife. *Detroit Institute of Arts, Catalogue of Paintings*, Detroit Institute of Arts, 1944, p. 42, no. 65. W. Adler, *Jan Wildens: Der Landschaftsmitarbeiter des Rubens*, Munich, 1980, pp. 13–14, 77, no. 52. *The Collections of the Detroit Institute of Arts: Flemish and German paintings of the 17th century*, Detroit Institute of Arts, 1982, pp. 27–29. E. Larsen, *The Paintings of Anthony van Dyck*, Freren, 1988, p. 41, no. 71. *Antique Fair: Orangerie*, 1993, Berlin: Schloss Charlottenburg, 1993. Donald Garstang, *Master Paintings 1400–1800*, London: Colnaghi, 1993, p. 28. Ron Radford, *Van Dyck: Portrait of a seated couple 1620/21*, Adelaide: AGSA, 1993. Philip Mould, *Sleepers: In search of lost Old Masters*, London, 1995, pp. 18–23. Ron Radford et al., *Treasures*, Adelaide: AGSA, 1998, p. 29. Christopher Brown and Hans Vlieghe, *Anthony van Dyck 1599–1641*, London: Frans Baudoin, 1999, pp. 102–3. "Recent Acquisitions at the Art Gallery of South Australia", *Burlington Magazine*, April 2003, p. 328. Susan J. Barnes, Nora de Poorter, Oliver Millar and Horst Vey, *Van Dyck: A Complete Catalogue of the Paintings*, New Haven, 2004, I.115, p. 109 (illus.).

**Condition:** Good; last restored London in 1993.[1]

**Frame:** Not original but English, second half of the eighteenth century.

# Anthony van Dyck

## A wooded ridge, mid 1630s?
pen & brown ink, brown ink wash on paper, 20.6 x 29.8 cm
V. B. F. Young Bequest Fund 1989

This is one of only twenty-nine surviving on-the-spot landscape drawings and watercolours by Van Dyck and, like most of them, it was probably executed in Britain.[1] Its naturalism, distant viewpoint and ink technique derive partly from the Flemish tradition of pen-and-ink landscape drawing that can be seen, for instance, in sketches by Pieter and Jan Bruegel, and partly from Italian influences in the work of Titian and among Van Dyck's contemporaries in Rome. But unlike the landscape drawings of his Flemish predecessors this, like his other known landscape drawings, is more spontaneous, loosely composed and shows the use of vigorous wash. Such qualities are also present in the landscape drawings of his mentor Rubens who absorbed similar Flemish and Italian influences.

The subject, a small tree-covered knoll, is likely to have been in the English countryside. Fine pen-work outlines the foliage and a broad ink wash gives mass and shadow to the trees and bushes. The stronger foreground and lighter middleground tones of the wash help suggest distance, where hills are faintly outlined on the right. Wisps of cloud in the sky are indicated by only a few hastily-scratched pen strokes, and in the immediate foreground there seems to be a brushed-in suggestion of a fence line. The most notable quality for a landscape drawing of this early date is the remarkable sense of light. Bright sunshine caresses the trees, casts deep shadows and gives substantial volume.

Martin Royalton-Kisch suggested in his *The Light of Nature: Landscape drawings and watercolours by Van Dyck and his contemporaries* that the Gallery's drawing may have been done in Italy. He noted a similarity with the foliage in the upper left of a drawing (Royal Collection) inscribed "fuori de Genua / quarto", which would therefore be dated between 1621 and 1627.[2] The trees do have the appearance of Italian pines, perhaps stone pines or Aleppo pines rather than English oaks or other distinctively British vegetation. However, the Gallery's drawing has greater stylistic affinity to a signed English watercolour sketch from the mid 1630s, *A hilly landscape with trees and a distant tower*, held at Chatsworth, and similarly of hillside trees in sunlight. Trees on a slope are also the subject of a major signed English pen drawing *Trees on a hillside* (British Museum) from the same period. Furthermore, three other English landscape drawings of about the same date are on the same kind of paper and the exact same width of sheet as the Gallery's landscape, namely 29.8 cm. One, *A wooded slope with farm buildings* (British Museum), is again of a similar subject. The remaining same-width sheets are landscapes with a castle on the Sussex coast: *The Ypres Tower at Rye* (Museum Boymans–Van Beuningen, Rotterdam) and *View of the coast with the Ypres Tower* (Fitzwilliam Museum, Cambridge). The sheets could all come from the same English sketchbook and thereby offer further evidence that they might be of similar date.

It appears that though Van Dyck occasionally executed landscape drawings and watercolours for relaxation most were intended for backgrounds to figure compositions and portraits. Unusually for on-the-spot landscape drawings of the time, some are signed and dated by the artist; he regarded them highly. Traces of oil paint on this drawing may indicate that it was once present in the artist's painting studio, intended as a basis for a landscape background. An example of an English-looking landscape background to a portrait can be seen in the Gallery's *A married couple*. In his landscape backgrounds Van Dyck very much followed Titian's Venetian style. This drawing was obviously not intended to become a fully developed landscape composition but was merely a rough jotting from nature, an on-the-spot sketch of a tree-covered outcrop.

Van Dyck's relatively few landscape drawings and watercolours are distant forerunners of the important watercolour landscape movement that emerged in England in the second half of the eighteenth century. They are also particular forerunners of Gainsborough's landscape studies in watercolour or chalk. If indeed executed in Britain, this rare landscape drawing by Van Dyck is not only the earliest British drawing in the Art Gallery of South Australia but also the earliest British landscape held in an Australasian collection.

Provenance: Christie's, London, 6 December 1988, lot 170.

Exhibitions: *Hidden Treasures: South Australia's European Old Master paintings, Restorations and Re-attributions and South Australia's European Old Master drawings*, AGSA, Adelaide, 1989. *Island to Empire: 300 Years of British Art 1550–1850*, AGSA, Adelaide, 2005.

Literature: *Old Master Drawings*, London: Christie's 6 December 1988, p. 106 (illus.). Ron Radford, *Hidden Treasures*, Adelaide: AGSA, 1989, pp. 9–10 (illus.). Martin Royalton-Kisch, *The Light of Nature: Landscape drawings and watercolours by Van Dyck and his contemporaries*, London: British Museum, 1999, pp. 22–23 (illus. 56).

Condition: Fair.

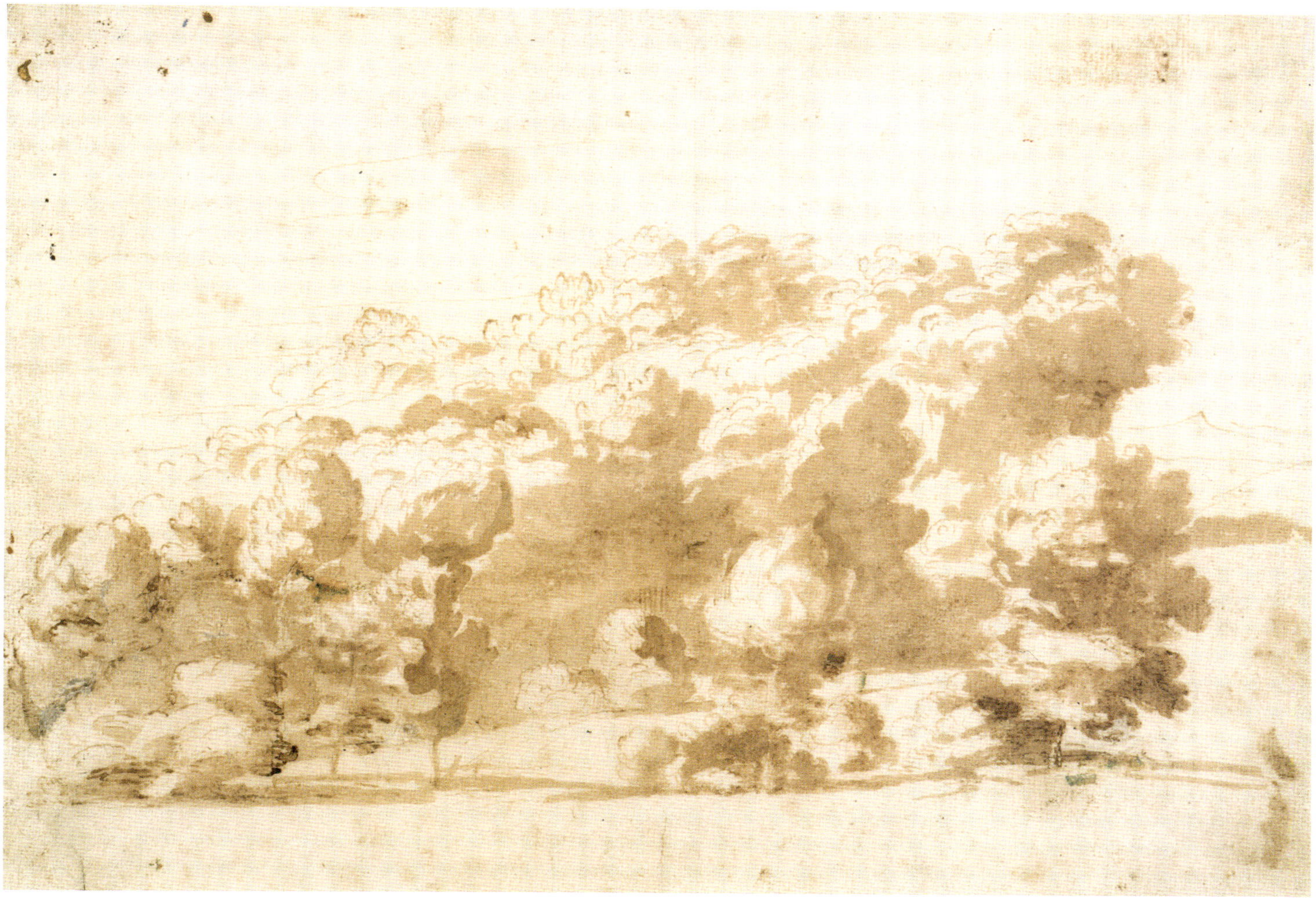

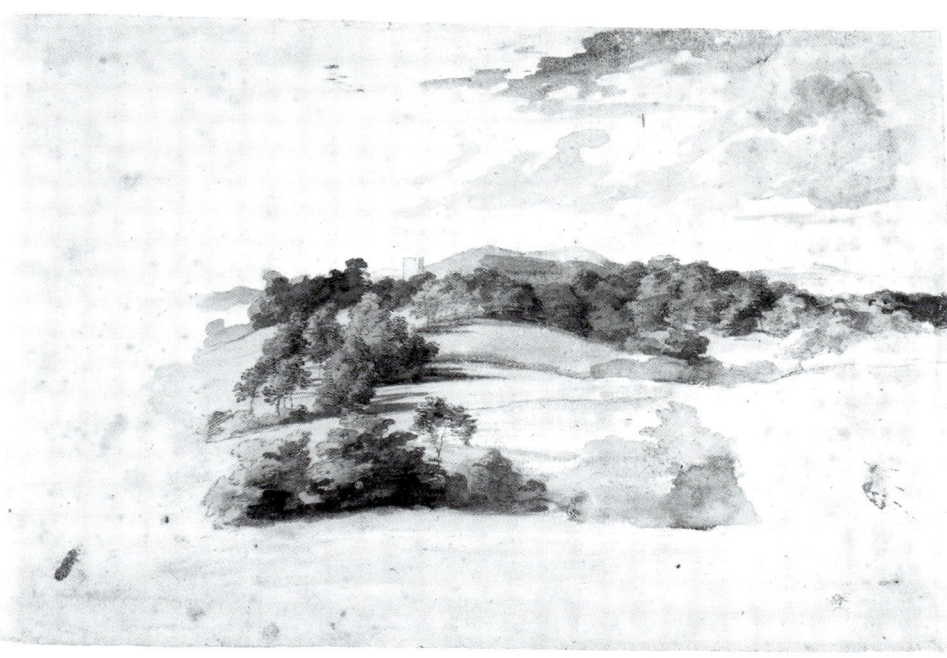

Anthony van Dyck, *A hilly landscape with trees and a distant tower*, mid 1630s. Chatsworth House Trust, Derbyshire

# Marcus Gheeraerts the Younger 1561/62–1636

Marcus Gheeraerts the Younger was the most significant painter of full-length portraits working in England between the 1550s, the time of Hans Holbein's follower Hans Eworth, and the arrival of Anthony van Dyck in the 1630s. From the 1590s Gheeraerts popularised the life-size portrait on canvas. Such portraits were usually intended for display in a dynastic hang in a 'Long Gallery', the broad side-lit hallway which was a distinctive feature of large Elizabethan and Jacobean houses. A leading painter with an extensive workshop, Gheeraerts enjoyed royal patronage and his long career spanned the reigns of Elizabeth I, James I and Charles I. His famous 'Ditchley Portrait' of Elizabeth, c.1592 (National Portrait Gallery, London) shows the Queen standing on a map of England.

Born in Bruges in 1561 or 1562, Gheeraerts was brought as a seven-year-old child from Flanders to England in 1568 by his Protestant father, the painter and engraver Marcus Gheeraerts the Elder (1520/21–1600?), to escape religious persecution in the Catholic Netherlands. Marcus the Younger was probably first trained by his father and possibly by other Netherlandish artists in London such as Lucas de Heere (c.1554–1584). Like a number of British artists of the period he may also have studied for a time in the Low Countries.

The Gheeraerts family dominated art production in late-Elizabethan and Jacobean England. In 1590 Gheeraerts the Younger married Magdalena, the sister of portrait painter John de Critz. Gheeraerts the Elder married Suzanna de Critz as his second wife. As Magdalena and Suzanna were sisters, Marcus the Younger became his stepmother's brother-in-law.

The artistic connections were strengthened further when Sarah, the daughter of Marcus Gheeraerts the Younger married Isaac Oliver, who with Nicholas Hilliard was the leading miniature-painter of the time. It is possible that Isaac Oliver and Gheeraerts the Younger both visited Antwerp in the late 1580s and were influenced by the portrait style of Frans Pourbus I (1545–1581).

Roy Strong has written: "Gheeraerts's success lay in his ability to subdue the bourgeois robustness of Flemish painting and fuse it with the melancholic, aristocratic, courtly fantasy of late Elizabethan England."[1] Nevertheless, by about 1620, the date of this portrait of Magdalen Poultney, the formal, stiff style was regarded as rather archaic and Gheeraerts no longer painted for the fashionable court. He was superseded by Paul van Somer, Daniel Mytens, his own student Cornelius Johnson and later most emphatically by the Baroque flourish and naturalism of Anthony van Dyck.

## attributed to Marcus Gheeraerts the Younger and Studio

### Magdalen Poultney, later Lady Aston, c.1620

oil on canvas, 231.7 x 136.0 cm

Morgan Thomas Bequest Fund 1948

Magdalen Poultney was born in 1600, the second daughter and co-heir of Sir John Poultney of Poultney and Misterton, Leicestershire, and Margery Fortescue, daughter of Sir John and Dame Alice Fortescue. Magdalen and her three sisters Alice, Mary and Jane and her brother John were orphaned in 1615 when their father died, their mother having died earlier in 1613.[2] The administration of the estate of Sir John Poultney was granted in 1617 to Dame Alice Fortescue, his mother-in-law and the children's grandmother. On 4 July 1627, six or seven years after this portrait was painted, Magdalen became the first wife of Thomas Aston (1600–1645) of Aston, Cheshire. He was a wealthy landholder who was created a baronet in 1628, became High Sheriff of Chester in 1635 and the Member for Cheshire in the Short Parliament of 1640. In the English Civil War he was devoted to the Royalist cause, raising 300 horses at his own expense and command. He died in the service of King Charles I in 1645. Magdalen had died in childbirth a decade earlier, in 1635.

In the painting the stiff conical form of the elaborately costumed Magdalen Poultney is self-consciously posed – as if about to perform in a Jacobean masque. The setting, with its props, is like a small stage with a backdrop of rich red and gold. She stands uneasily on a turkey carpet over woven rush matting and is flanked by looped red velvet curtains with gold-braid fringes. To her left is a red velvet chair with a gold-braid fringe and a matching cushion. This dignified, melancholic and stage-like portrayal is characteristic of Gheeraerts's portraits and of Jacobean art (and literature) in general. The twenty-year-old Magdalen is cast in a role that is serious and sad.

The distinctive costume helps date the painting to 1620, just after the British court finally abandoned the cumbersome farthingale form of dress. (The farthingale was like a padded platform around the waist and King James's consort Anne of Denmark, in spite of the King's extreme dislike of the late-Elizabethan affectation, had maintained it at court until near the time of her death in 1619.) Magdalen Poultney's silver-with-red brocade dress hangs like a corrugated metallic cone from a high V-waist and is trimmed with wide silver braid with silver spangles along the hemline, shoulders, the edge of the split in the upper sleeves, and the hanging sleeves. Her 'standing-

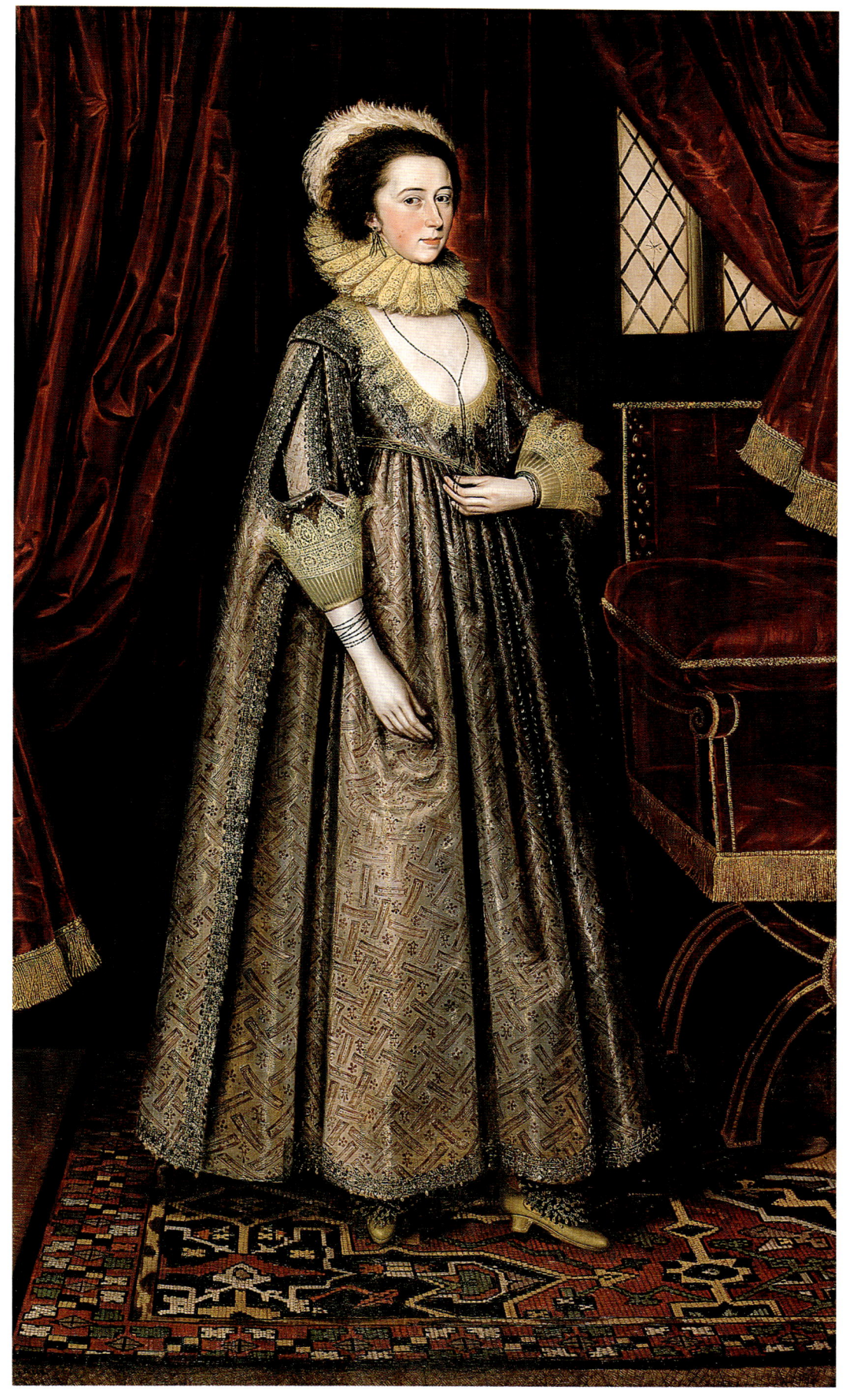

# Marcus Gheeraerts the Younger

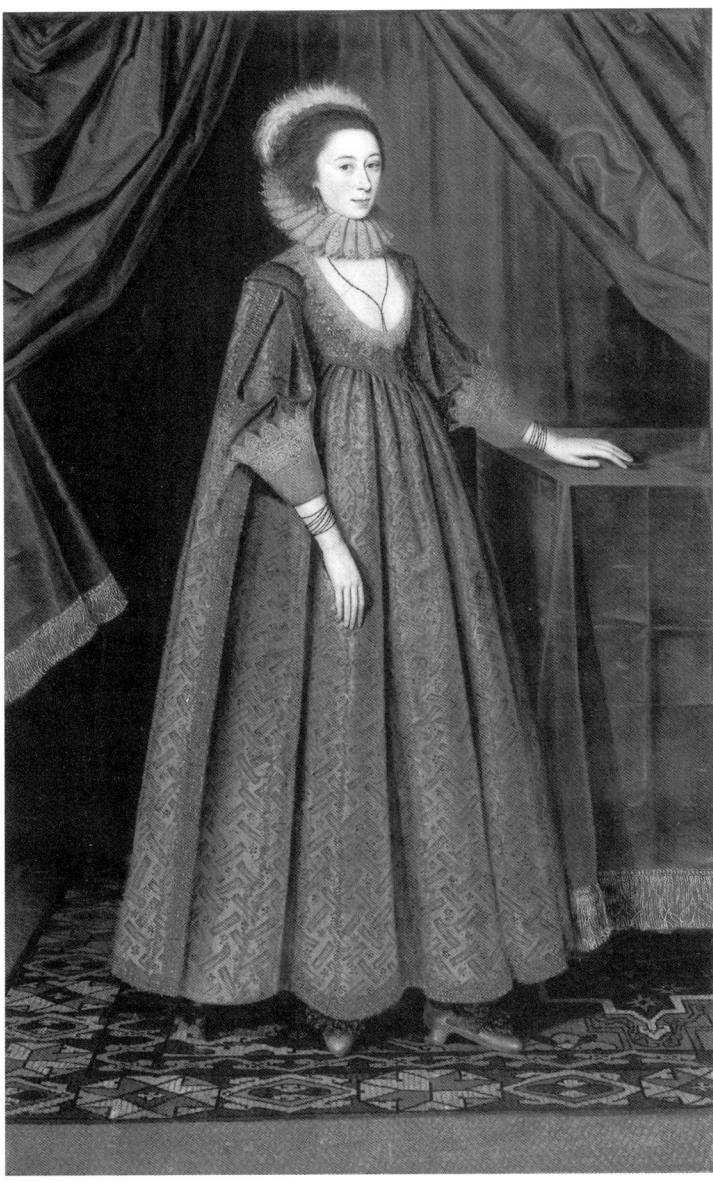

British School c.1620, *Magdalen Poultney, later Lady Aston*, formerly known as *Gertrude Sadler*, c.1620. © Tate, London 2004

This portrait of Magdalen Poultney has long been attributed to Marcus Gheeraerts the Younger. Tate Britain, London, holds a full-length variant in the same dress, possibly by Gheeraerts's studio.[5] The Tate version is simpler, appears less well executed, includes a table with a red cloth and gold fringe instead of the chair, and does not have the background window; Magdalen stands on a differently patterned turkey carpet (see left) and wears different earrings in each portrait. In the Tate version, she wears a green stocking on her right foot but in our portrait this is covered by the spangled rosette pom-pom. The Tate, however, no longer ascribes its painting directly to Marcus Gheeraerts.[6]

The two portraits may have been intended as pre-marriage pictures created for both families,[7] the Tate's painted later, based on our version, at the time of the Poultney–Aston marriage in 1627. Alternatively, it is possible that when Magdalen reached the very marriageable age of twenty or twenty-one the two portraits were commissioned by her perhaps anxious guardian grandmother, Dame Alice Fortescue, for tactful negotiation with prospective distant suitors and families.[8] Magdalen's young son Thomas Aston became the heir of Magdalen's brother John Poultney who died in 1637 and Poultney properties – perhaps including portraits – passed to the Aston family. Indeed at least one of the two portraits may have come from Dame Alice Fortescue who had died by 1621 when her will was proved. The portraits of Magdalen, united at Aston Hall, were mistaken in a mid-nineteenth-century inventory as "Twin sisters of the Time of Queen Elizabeth".[9]

When Magdalen died aged thirty-five, in childbirth, on 2 June 1635, her death and that of her infant were movingly recorded in a symbolic family portrait commissioned by her distraught widower from the Cheshire artist John Souch (c.1593–1643). The commission was completed in September, several months after her death. In Souch's painting (Manchester Art Gallery, see p. 66) the posthumous images of Lady Aston depicted both on her deathbed and as in life are almost certainly based on the two earlier Gheeraerts paintings of her which Souch must have seen together at Aston in 1635. Souch made a mirror image of the face of the live Magdalen in the corner on the right, updated her costume and made her left hand a mirror image of the right hand in the Tate's version. Conversely, Souch adopted a reverse image of the left hand in Adelaide's Gheeraerts for the deathbed figure.[10]

In the Adelaide version of the Magdalen Poultney portrait, it is possible that the otherwise inexplicable cracks in the diamond-shaped windowpanes (and perhaps, too, the windows themselves) were painted in later, perhaps even by Souch

falling' ruff is of pale yellow Italian cutwork and geometric needle lace that matches the lace worn on the bodice and cuffs. Her accessories are satin high-heeled shoes with silver braid and spangled rosette pom-poms, a bonnet with white ostrich-feather trimming and tiny jet seed beads which circle the wrists and neck and are looped from her ears.[3] She does not yet wear a marriage ring.

Conservation of the painting in 1997 removed over-painting on the sitter's face, revealing two distinct moles on her right cheek.[4] This is unusual in portraits of the period. Gheeraerts painted Magdalen 'warts and all' but the blemishes were unacceptable to later viewers and painted over.

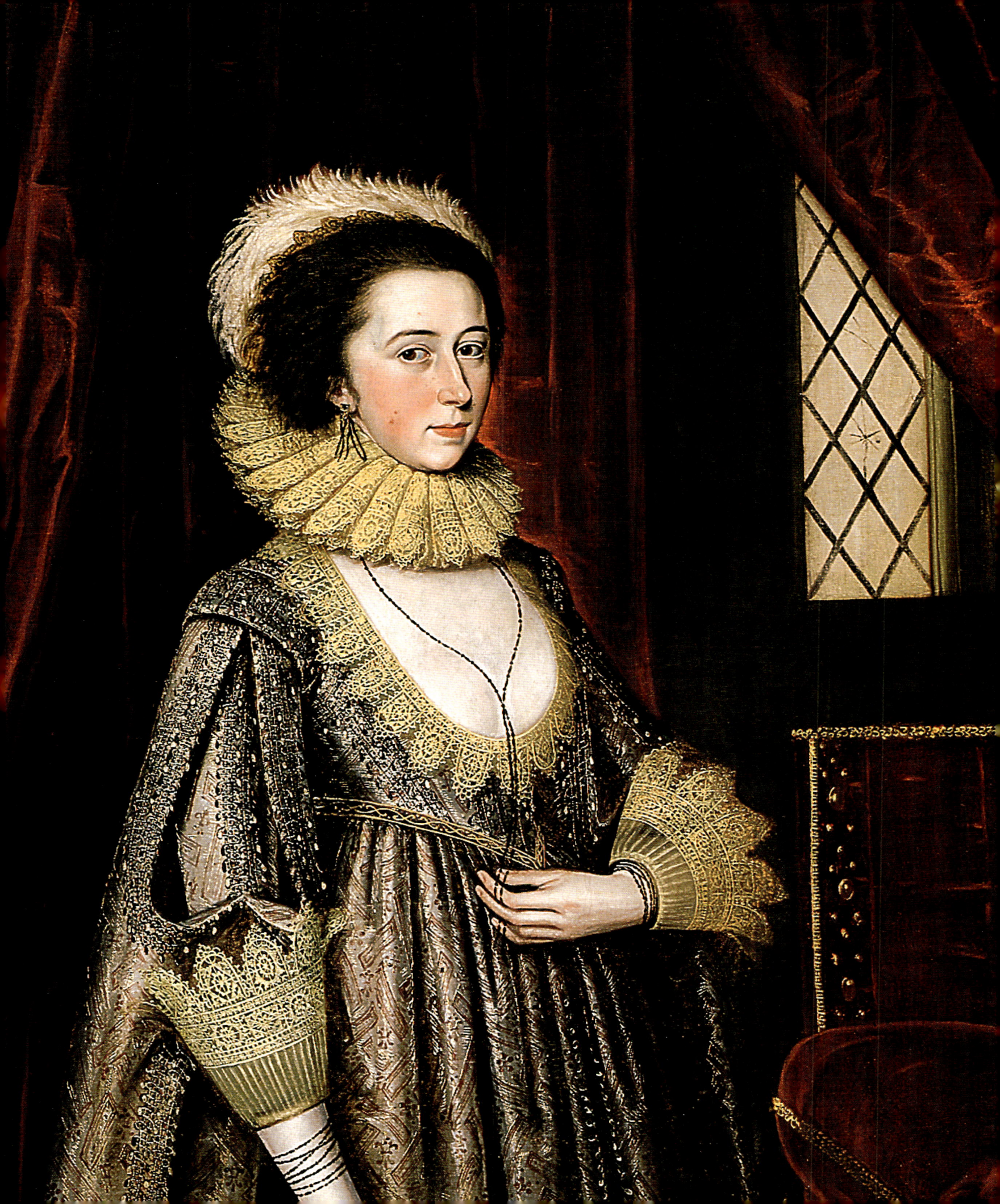

# Marcus Gheeraerts the Younger

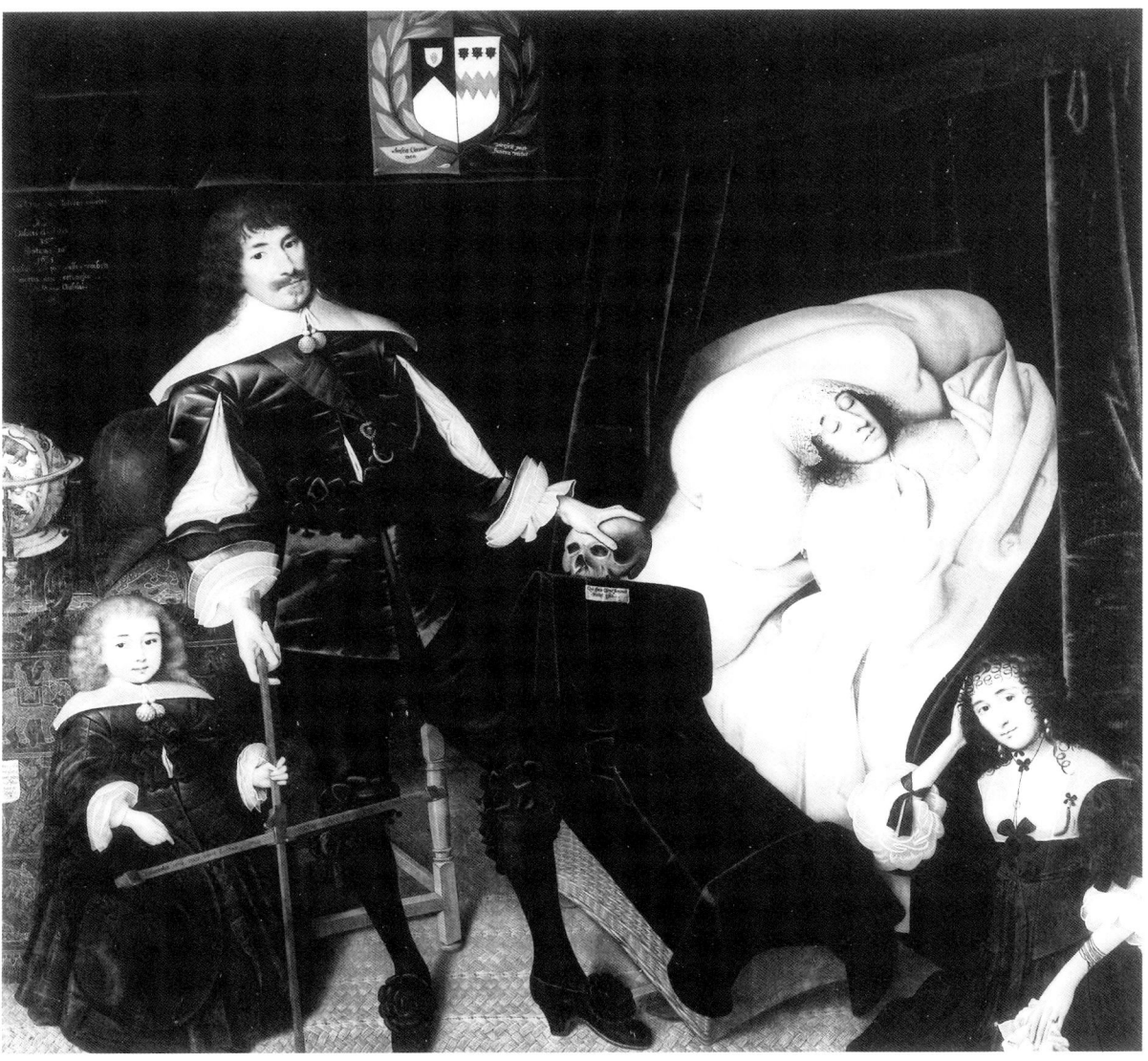

John Souch, *Sir Thomas Aston at the deathbed of his wife*, 1635. Manchester Art Gallery

after Magdalen's death. The shattered panes could symbolise her early death and Sir Thomas's broken heart, for such melancholic allusions were then characteristic of English literature and painting.[11] Posthumously published in 1633 only two years before Magdalen's death, the metaphysical poet John Donne (1571–1631) wrote in his sonnet *The Broken Heart*, "…but Love, alas, / At one first blow did shiver it as glass".[12] Sir Thomas Aston, an Oxford graduate and author, erected a memorial tablet in the Aston chapel with his composed heart-felt epitaph dedicated to his dear wife; he called it his "sacred amoris ergo".[13]

**Provenance:** Possibly commissioned by the sitter's grandmother Lady Alice Fortescue, c.1620; to Magdalen, Lady Aston; Sir Thomas Aston in 1635; Aston family by descent, Aston Hall, Cheshire; Brigadier-General Hervey Talbot sale, Aston Lodge, April 1927; Mrs Otto Herman Kahn, New York; Christie's, New York, 27 May 1938, lot 141; bought by Agnew's, London; purchased by the Art Gallery of South Australia on the recommendation of Harold Wright, 1947.

**Exhibitions:** *Autumn Show 1947*, Thomas Agnew & Sons, London, no. 54. *The Morgan Thomas Bequest Centenary Exhibition*, AGSA, Adelaide, 2003. *Island to Empire: 300 Years of British Art 1550–1850*, AGSA, Adelaide 2005.

**Literature:** *Autumn Show 1947*, London: Thomas Agnew & Sons, no. 54. *NGSA Bulletin*, Adelaide, vol. 10, no. 3, January 1949. Roy Strong, *The English Icon: Elizabethan & Jacobean portraiture*, London, 1969, p. 303, no. 312. *Picture Book*, Adelaide: AGSA 1972, p. 8 (illus.). National Art Collections Fund, Annual Report, London, 1979, p. 33. *Art Gallery of South Australia 1881–1981*, Adelaide: AGSA, p. 64. Elizabeth Einberg, *Tate Gallery 1978–80: Illustrated catalogue of acquisitions*, London: Tate Gallery, 1981, p. 27. Peter Tomory and Robert Gaston, *European Paintings before 1800 in Australian and New Zealand Public Collections*, Sydney: 1989, p. 24, no. 44 (illus.). Ron Radford et al., *Treasures*, Adelaide: AGSA, 1998, p. 28 (illus.).

**Condition:** Good; last conserved in 1997 by Artlab Australia, Adelaide.

**Frame:** Not original, but early eighteenth century.

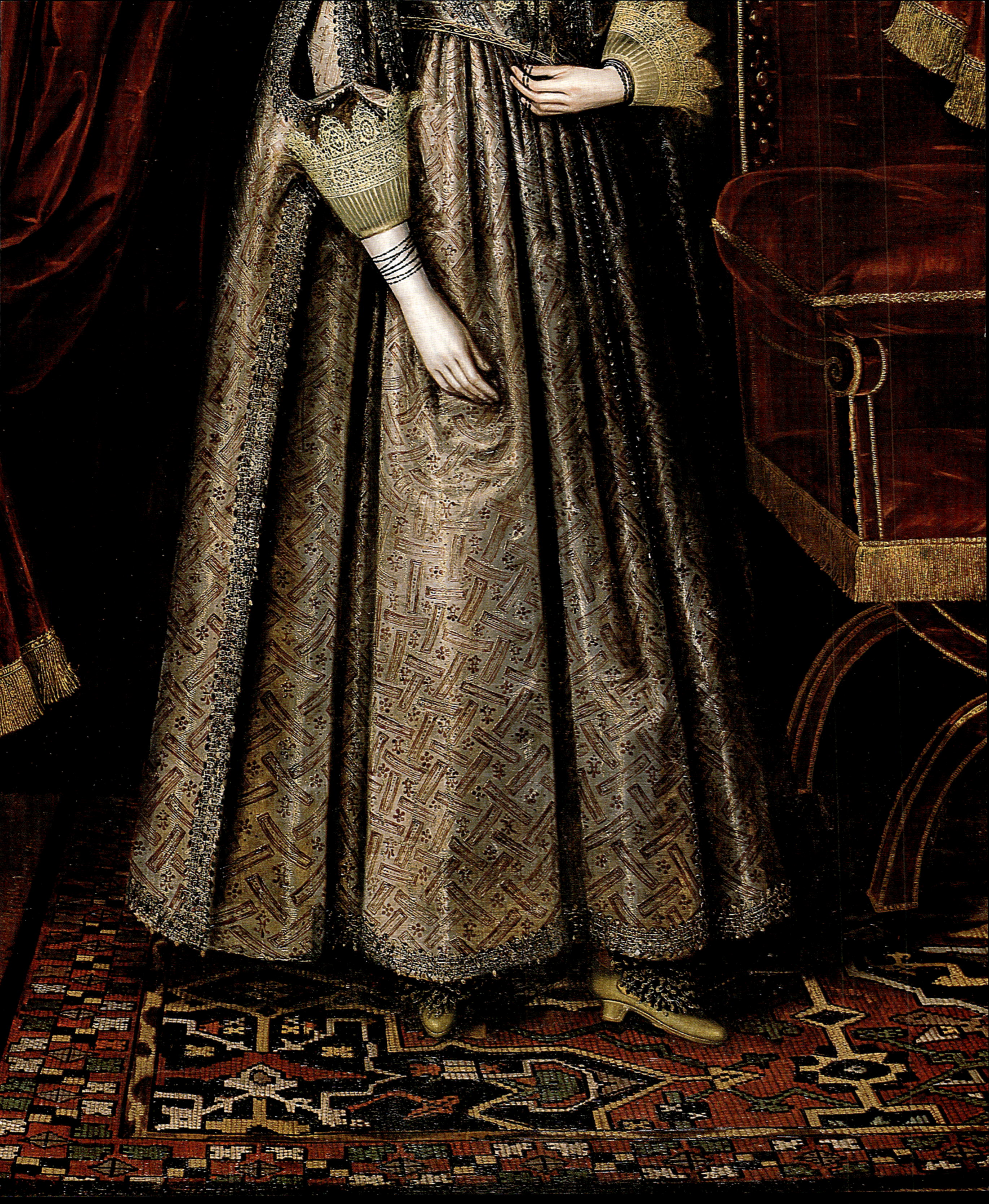

# Cornelius Johnson 1593–1661

Cornelius Johnson's portraits show the beginning of change away from the stiff, flat and emblematic tradition of the late-Elizabethan and Jacobean periods. He offers more realistic, three-dimensional and personal images, usually in the intimacy of single half-lengths. One of the few major English-born and trained artists of the first half of the seventeenth century, Johnson is believed to have been taught in London by Marcus Gheeraerts the Younger, whose style Johnson's resembles but which he developed into a more informal naturalism. However, he rarely, and then only later in his career, tackled the full-length format that was Gheeraerts's speciality. Johnson's outstanding quality was his sensitivity to individual character. The head-and-shoulders format allowed him to concentrate on the carefully modelled features that some claim as the first to represent typical English faces and reticent manners.

He was born Cornelis Janssens, in London in 1593, of Netherlandish parents who had been refugees from Antwerp, but the family originally came from Cologne. His earliest dated works are from 1619 and he continued his straightforward realism until the beginning of the 1630s. Although in December 1632 Johnson was appointed as "His Majesty's servant in ye quality of Picture Drawer" to King Charles I, the arrival of Anthony van Dyck earlier that year clearly had an impact on his patronage and to some extent on his own compositions. He attempted, with some success, to emulate Van Dyck's fashionably Baroque style that so impressed the court of Charles I. Yet Van Dyck himself appears to have looked at Johnson's unpretentious 'English' style when the court painter wished to paint a straightforward head and shoulders. It may have been Van Dyck who also inspired Johnson to attempt, with less success, a few full-length portraits and family groups.

Johnson's sober realism also suggests that he was aware of the portraits of the much-esteemed Dutch painter Michiel van Miereveld (1567–1641) who from the 1610s was commissioned by English aristocrats and diplomats visiting the Dutch Netherlands, and whose work Johnson would surely have seen in British collections. Miereveld is believed to have taught Paul van Somer who arrived in Britain in 1616 and Daniel Mytens who arrived in 1618, just prior to the time that Johnson began to date his work. Since his style resembles Dutch portraiture there remains the further possibility that Johnson trained for a while on the Continent.

In 1641 Johnson was still among the King's "servants in ordinary of the chamber" but in 1643, after the outbreak of the Civil War, he escaped troubled England to work in the Netherlands at Middelburg, where he continued to paint portraits. He settled in Utrecht in 1652, and died there in 1661, but also worked from time to time in Amsterdam and The Hague. His artist son, also named Cornelius, was born in London in 1634 and it is possible he assisted his father in his later years.

## A lady, thought to be Catherine Fenn, 1623
oil on wood panel, 77.0 x 60.0 cm
South Australian Government Grant 1984

This was once thought to be a portrait of Susan, Countess Montgomery, the first wife of Philip Herbert, Earl of Montgomery and later 4th Earl of Pembroke, Lord Chamberlain, Chancellor of Oxford University and a great patron of the arts.[1] However, the Countess, who was born in 1587 and married in 1604, would have been about thirty-seven years old in 1623, too old for a painting dated to that year. The sitter is a much younger woman.

A much more likely candidate is Catherine Fenn, a portrait of whom by Johnson, dated 1624 and therefore painted only a year later than the Gallery's picture, is at Parham Park, West Sussex. There is a remarkable facial likeness between the two works, and since Johnson was known for his grasp of individuality our portrait is therefore likely to be of the same sitter, possibly painted at the time of Catherine Fenn's first marriage.[2]

Catherine, the beautiful daughter of Hugh Fenn of Wotton-under-Edge, Gloucestershire, was born about 1605. She apparently had four successful marriages. The first, about 1623, was to Hugh Perry, an Alderman of London who died in January 1634/5. In August 1635 she married Lord Barrett of Newburgh, Fife, who died in 1644. In 1653 she married William Morgan, her steward, with whom she was still living in 1664. Her fourth husband was a Frenchman named Bussy. She died in 1674. There is no record of any children to Catherine Fenn, later Mrs Perry, Lady Barrett, Mrs Morgan and Madame Bussy. Widowed for the first time, as Mrs Hugh Perry, she was said to be worth the then princely sum of £10,000 and that she "useth to be a little mad sometimes".[3]

The Gallery's portrait is of a very attractive woman, expensively dressed and no more than about twenty years old. Her abundant hair is held in place by a plaited hairpiece incorporating a ribbon. The flowing hair indicates that this was probably a pre-marriage likeness. A large proportion of Elizabethan and Jacobean and later British portraits were painted because of a marriage. Here Johnson follows a convention that called for the flowing and loose arrangement of a bride's hair, hence the expression "she was married in her hair".[4] If this is a pre-marriage portrait perhaps commissioned by her father, the one from the following year, at Parham Park, surely looks like that of an established married lady, wife of a successful alderman of London.

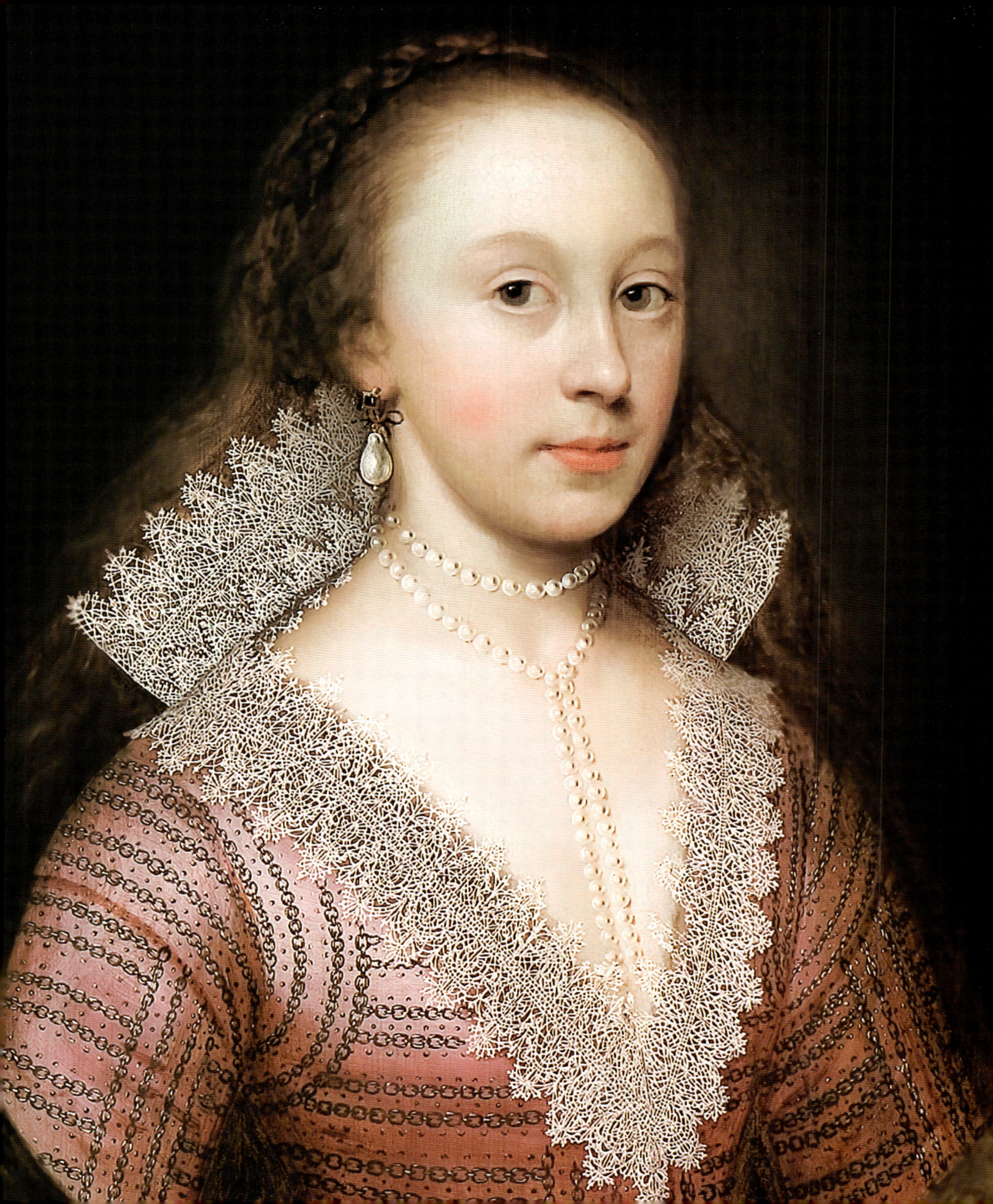

# Cornelius Johnson

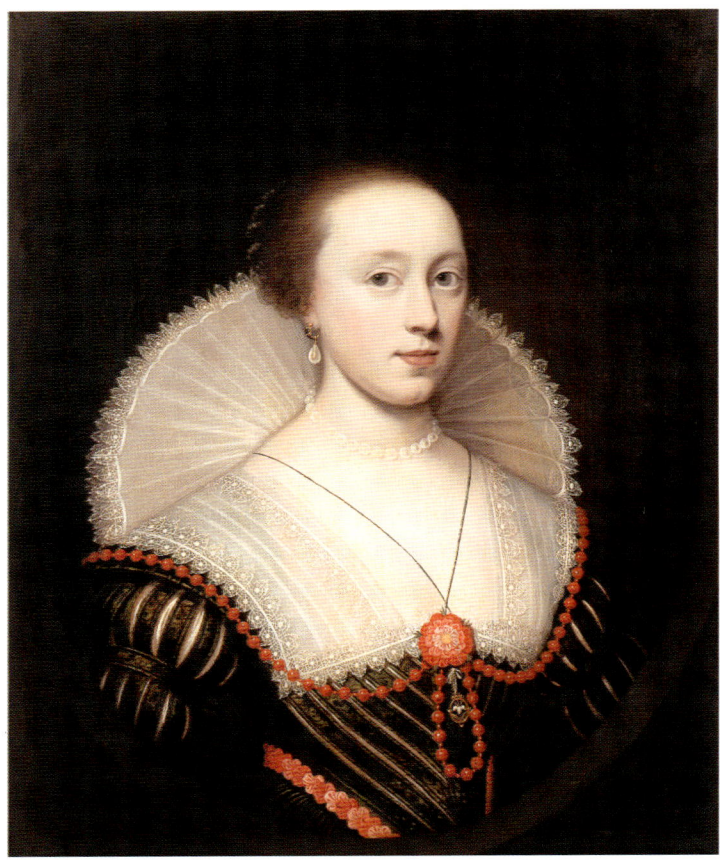

Cornelius Johnson, *Catherine Fenn,* 1624. Collection at Parham House & Gardens, West Sussex

The picture shows Johnson in his early stylistic maturity two years after Van Dyck's first stay in London but nine years before the celebrated artist's permanent move to England, where he changed the style of British portraiture. Typical of Johnson's work, this portrait displays the artist's firm but sensitive, realistic and translucent modelling, his glossy enamel-like surface and his characteristic feigned-marble surround for the image, a device that he continued to use until the beginning of the 1630s for his half-lengths and busts. It is painted on a wood panel, another characteristic of his portraits until the 1630s. The image of the sitter is placed low in an oval, which is typical of Johnson, and therefore settles perfectly into a setting that echoes her oval face. His use of the oval in a rectangle derives from the English miniature tradition, and is a format for half-lengths that continued to be used by a number of British painters throughout the seventeenth and first half of the eighteenth centuries. Again typical of Johnson's works, the surround depicts grey marble, as if incorporated into an architectural setting. From the mid 1620s Johnson also painted oval miniatures, and his supposed teacher, Marcus Gheeraerts, continued to paint half-length portraits in oval settings. The format helps to concentrate the viewer's attention on the individual face rather than the elaborate costume. In this Johnson moves away from the English late-sixteenth-century and early-seventeenth-century fashion, seen in works by earlier painters George Gower and Robert Peake where the decorative patterning of extravagantly rich costume is emphasised at the expense of individuality. Their faces appear almost mask-like; by contrast, Johnson emphasises the young woman's personality and introverted character.

Nonetheless, the costume with its intricate lacework is articulated in full detail. The sitter wears a low-necked bodice with matching skirt of pink silk, embroidered with fine silver chains and sequins. The style of the bodice with its tight sleeves and plain epaulettes at the shoulder is typical for the period. A double layer of standing strips of Flemish bobbin lace with castellated edging forms a fan-like collar and lace of a similar pattern borders the plunging neckline. A ruffled band of fine lawn or gauze trims the waist.[5] She is richly attired but compared with the previous Elizabethan and early-Jacobean generation the costume in this late Jacobean portrait is relatively restrained. Restraint continues in the artist's subtle and restricted palette of translucent cool greys and warm pinks.

Catherine Fenn's fair and pearly complexion is matched by her winding pearl necklace and large pearl drop-earrings. Pearls were an emblem of the purity that young Miss Fenn embodies here, and probably adhered to at this early stage of her life.[6]

**Inscription:** Signed and dated l.r. corner, oil: "C. J. / fecit / 1623".
**Provenance:** Sotheby's, London, 11 July 1984, lot 24.
**Exhibition:** *Island to Empire: 300 Years of British Art 1550–1850*, AGSA, Adelaide, 2005.
**Literature:** *British Paintings 1500–1850*, London: Sotheby's, 11 July 1984, p. 33 (illus.). Ron Radford et al., *Selected Works*, Adelaide, AGSA, 1991, p. 8 (illus.). Jeremy Black, *History of England*, London, 1993, p. 78 (illus.).
**Condition:** Good; last conserved in 2004 by Artlab Australia, Adelaide.
**Frame:** Not original.

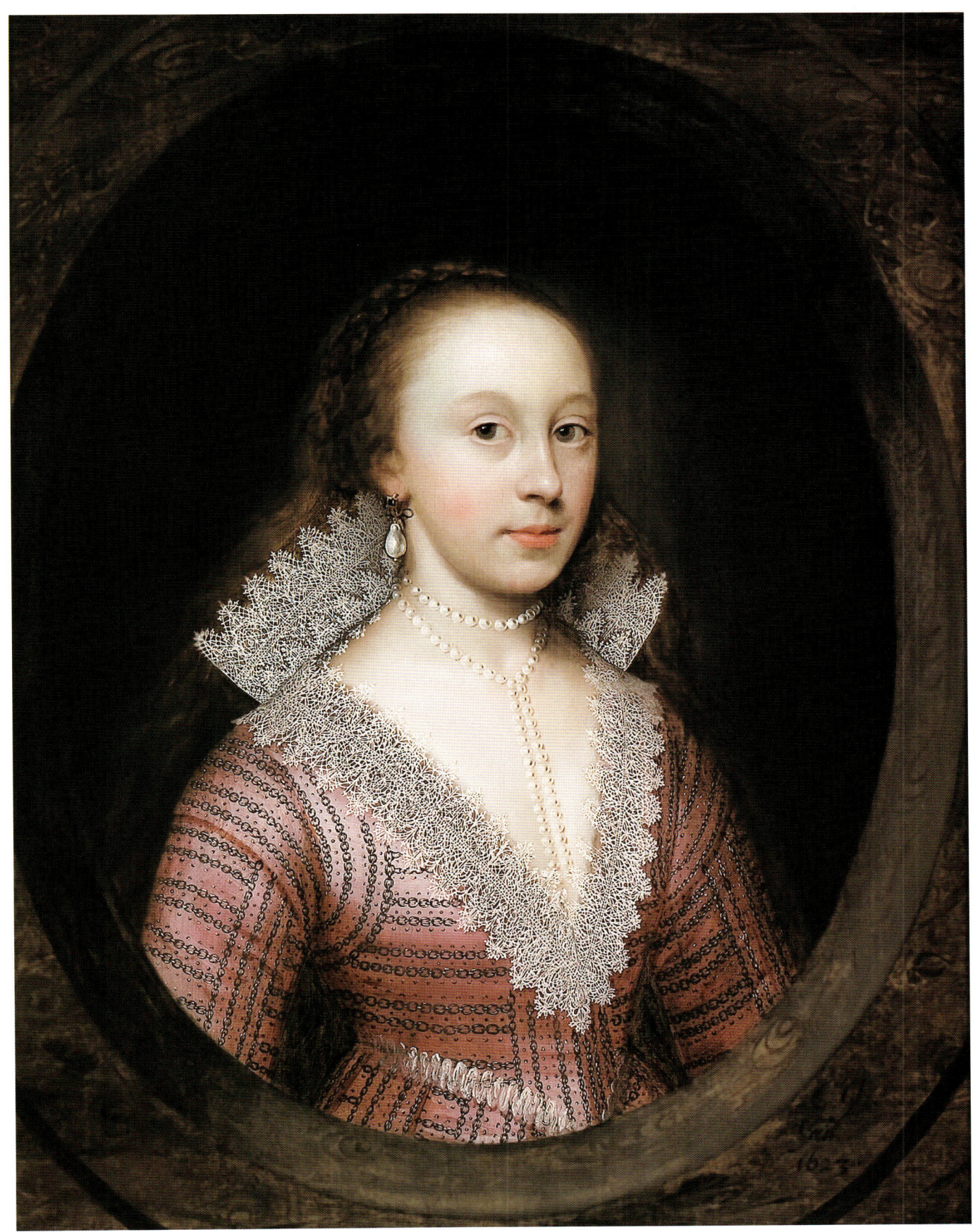

# Michiel van Miereveld 1567–1641

Michiel van Miereveld was the leading Dutch portrait painter during the first decades of the seventeenth century. British royalty tried to entice him to London to be a court painter but he never made the journey. Nevertheless, his work is included in this catalogue of British art because of the pre-eminence of the particular sitter, the Duke of Buckingham, because the artist also painted many other British sitters and because his work probably influenced British portraiture. From 1610 onwards Miereveld painted many of the English officials, diplomats and soldiers who passed through The Hague either to visit the court of Elizabeth of Bohemia, daughter of James I, or on military campaigns. His straightforwardly realistic but dignified style appealed to the Dutch and British nobility. It was the young Prince Henry, Prince of Wales, who attempted to bring him into the royal service in Britain, the first time as early as January 1611,[1] when he spoke of the artist as "the most excellent Painter of all the Low-Countries".[2]

Miereveld was born in Delft in 1567, and studied there with Willem Willemsz. He later studied with Anthonie van Blocklandt at Utrecht before returning in 1583 to Delft where he set up as a portrait painter. He joined the Delft painters' guild in 1587 and served as headman in 1589–90 and again in 1611–12. He spent the rest of his life in Delft but he frequently took sittings at The Hague nearby. In 1607 he became court painter to Prince Maurice of Nassau and began a career as the favoured artist of the House of Orange-Nassau and the leading portraitist of aristocratic and patrician families in The Hague as well as in Delft. Miereveld became a prolific later counterpart to Holbein in northern Europe, for he and his workshop often produced multiple versions of his portraits of important sitters. Among the many artists he influenced and trained were Paul van Somer and Daniel Mytens both of whom went to England in 1616 and 1618 respectively to become court portrait painters. His style may have influenced the English-born Cornelius Johnson. Miereveld died in Delft in 1641, the same year that Van Dyck – whose Baroque style had eclipsed his own – died in London.

### George Villiers, Duke of Buckingham, 1625/26
oil on wood panel, 69.5 x 57.5 cm
South Australian Government Grant 1967

George Villiers, the subject of this painting, was born in 1592, the son of Sir George Villiers of Brockesley, Leicestershire. In 1609, when sixteen, his widowed mother sent him and his elder brother to France where he developed the equestrian and other skills such as dancing and fencing regarded as indispensable for anyone aspiring to a career at court. The sitter's good looks, good nature and charm attracted King James I when he was introduced in 1614 and he quickly became the king's favourite, given the pet name of 'Steenie' which was an allusion to St Stephen "who had the face of an angel". Under James's favour he rose rapidly, was appointed Cup Bearer in 1614, Master of the Horse in 1616, Earl of Buckingham in 1618, Lord High Admiral in 1619, and in 1623 he was raised to be the first Duke of Buckingham.[3] In 1620 with the encouragement of James I he married Lady Katherine Manners, daughter and heiress of the sixth Earl of Rutland.

Buckingham became the most powerful man in Britain, influential during both the reign of James I and the early reign of James's impressionable son Charles I. History was quick to judge Villiers harshly as highly ambitious, corrupt and lacking the stature to hold high office. He travelled with Prince Charles to negotiate the latter's marriage to the Spanish Infanta and when this failed he was said to have impetuously hurried James I into war with Spain. As Lord High Admiral he was blamed for the bungled expeditions to Cadiz and La Rochelle that became the House of Commons' "grievance of grievances" and thereby impaired Charles I's relationship with Parliament. The Duke was accused of being capricious and arrogant, and was unpopular. He was assassinated by a certain disaffected John Felton at Portsmouth in 1628. Distraught at the loss of a beloved friend, Charles I adopted the Duke's family into the royal household and brought up the Villiers children with his own. He also paid off Buckingham's considerable debts.[4]

More recent historians have been kinder.[5] They note that Buckingham's enemies, including many parliamentarians, were jealous and resentful of his rapid rise to power and suspicious of his apparent leniency towards, and association with, Catholics. The hard-working Duke was the scapegoat for many policies and decisions that were in fact made by Kings James and Charles.

During his short lifetime he became one of the greatest art patrons and collectors in British history. His paintings were surpassed only by those of Charles I, whose collection was the finest ever personally assembled in Europe. The Duke, who had some hand in forming Charles's collection, gathered into his London residence, York House, a spectacular profusion of 330 pictures. They included works by the greatest Italian masters such as Leonardo, Michelangelo, Raphael, Correggio,

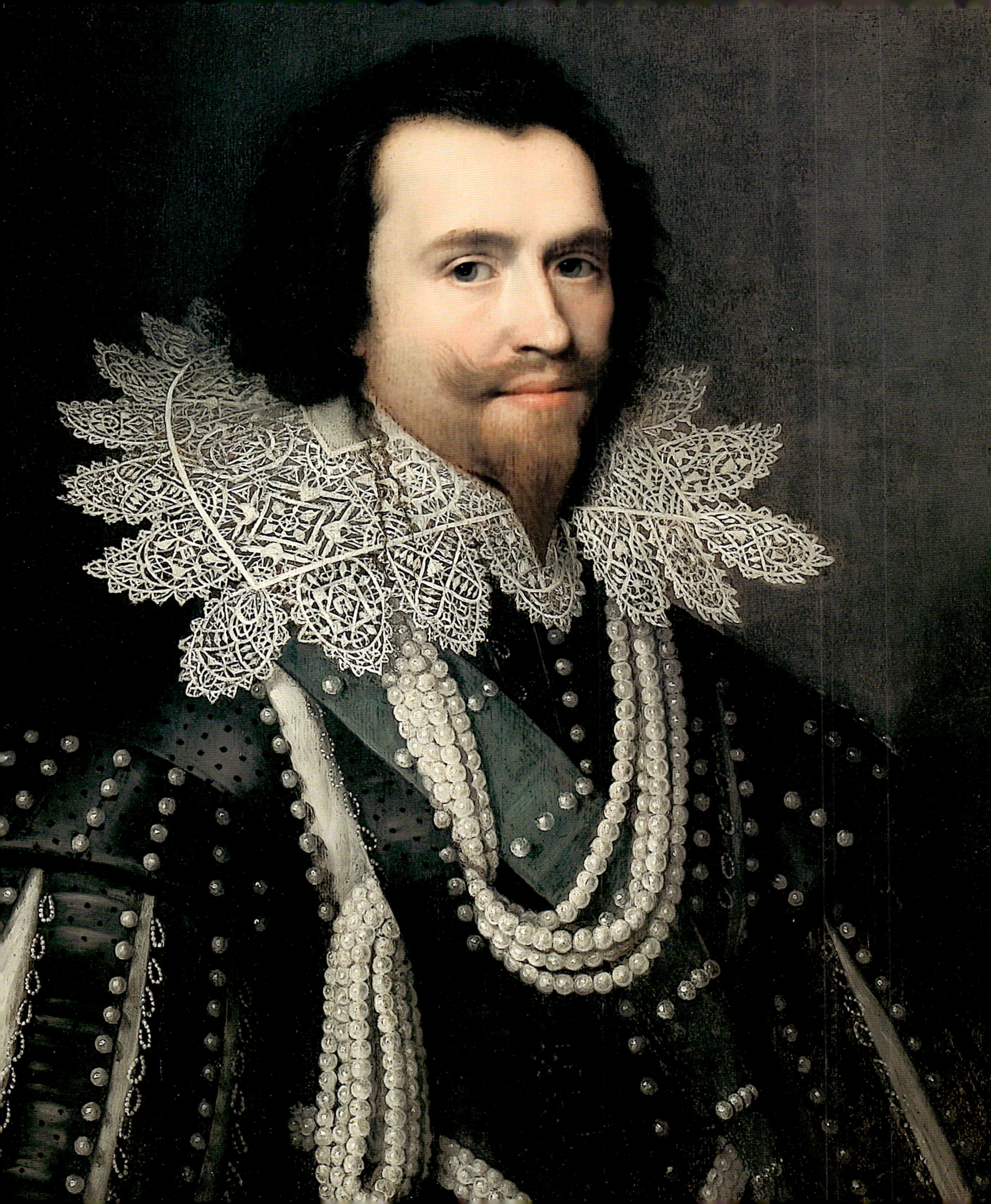

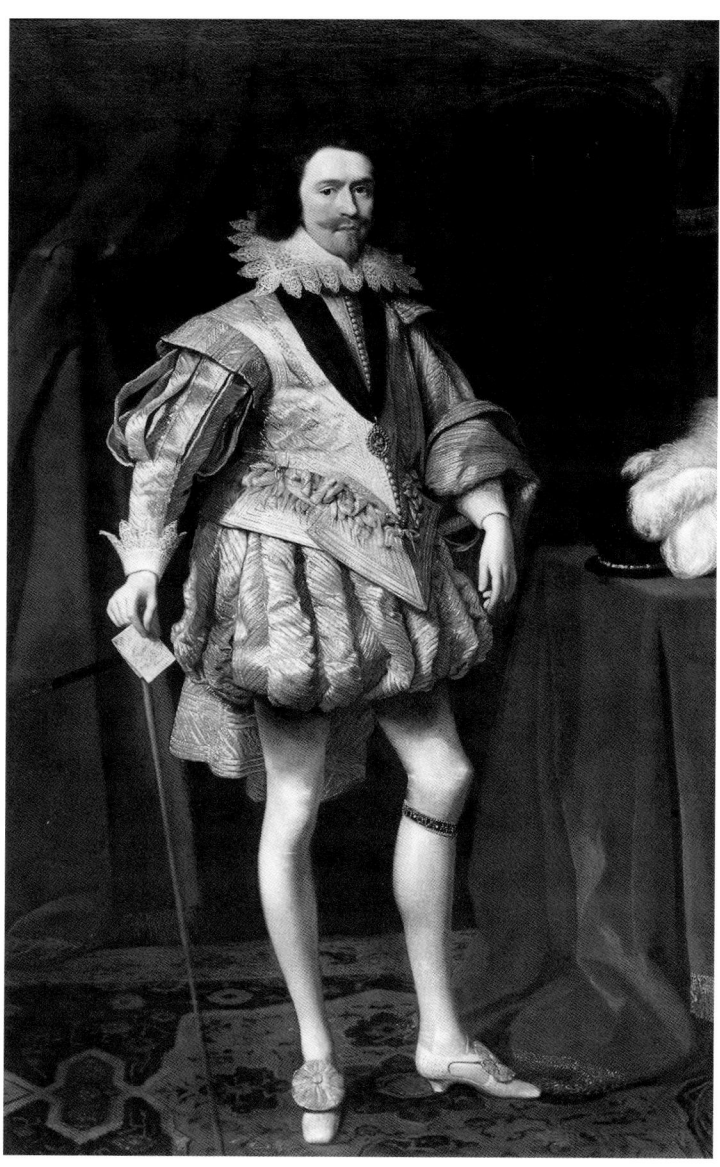

Daniel Mytens, *George Villiers, Duke of Buckingham*, c.1626. Duke of Grafton, Grafton Estate, Suffolk

Caravaggio and the sculptor Giovanni Bologna, but especially favouring the Venetian school – Giorgione, Veronese, Bassano, Tintoretto and above all Titian – of whose paintings he owned twenty. In 1627 Buckingham managed to purchase most of Rubens's famous collection of master paintings and sculptures. When Rubens was in England in 1629, the year after Villiers's death, he wrote: "When it comes to fine pictures by the hands of first class masters, I have never seen such a large number in one place as in the royal palace and in the gallery of the late Duke of Buckingham."[6] Buckingham also collected and commissioned works by contemporary artists such as Rubens himself, Van Dyck, Bartolommeo Manfredi, Guido Reni and Orazio Gentileschi, the last of whom he lured in 1625 to Britain from the French court. The Duke was assisted in building up his collection by the artist Balthasar Gerbier, who flattered him in 1625 that "sometimes when I am contemplating the treasure of rarities which Your Excellency has in so short a time amassed, I cannot but feel astonishment in the midst of my joy; for out of all the amateurs and princes and kings there is not one who has collected in forty years as many pictures as Your Excellency has collected in five".[7]

Sir Dudley Carleton, Ambassador to The Hague from 1616 to 1629, also assisted the Duke. There are portraits by Miereveld of Carleton dated 1620, 1625 and 1628 and it is possible that Carleton recommended Miereveld to Buckingham. It is also possible that the recommendation came from Charles I himself; the King had long owned works by Miereveld, including one, of Prince Maurice of Nassau, inherited from his brother Prince Henry in 1612, considerably before Villiers's ascendancy.

Since he was an exceptionally handsome and powerful figure, nearly all the major portrait painters of the age both on the Continent and in Britain were engaged to paint Villiers's portrait. These included Rubens, Van Dyck, Gerrit van Honthorst, Paul van Somer, Robert Peake, William Larkin, Isaac Oliver and Daniel Mytens as well as Miereveld.

This image displays Villiers in his amazing pearl suit. The carcanets of great pearls are unusually extravagant even at a time when men's clothing was often elaborate and bejewelled. Giant pearls are also encrusted in lines over his grey- and black-spotted satin doublet; the sash of deep green satin is decorated with further rows of pearls; the sleeves are split in contrived ribbons and large pearls form imitation buttons with eyelets of loops of small seed pearls as if intended to secure the split sleeves. Around his head is a linen collar of Italian cutwork and geometric needle lace with boldly castellated edges. The Duke's excessive opulence contrasts with the restrained appearance of Miereveld's Dutch male sitters of similar date (and earlier British sitters) who are often shown in austere black with plain ruffs as can be seen in the Gallery's other portrait by Miereveld, a 1614 three-quarter-length of a Dutch gentleman.

In February 1627 it was probably from this encrusted apparel that the Duke had the pearls removed, thus raising £1500 (amongst the sale of much of his other jewellery), "for the use of His Majesty's Navy" which was in dire need of finances.[8] For the Lord High Admiral, as in his other lofty positions, personal and public expenditures were inextricably entwined.

Here in 1625 Villiers is thirty-three and at the height of his power; in less than three years he would be assassinated. It is the year Charles I ascended the throne and the pearl suit may have been made especially to wear at the King's coronation. The Duke sat for Miereveld at The Hague some time between early November and early December 1625 during an embassy to the Low Countries; his accounts include a payment of £60 "To the picture drawer" who was almost certainly Miereveld.[9] The artist became a member of the Guild of St Luke at The Hague in 1625, the year the Duke sat for him, though he continued to live in nearby Delft. Like most celebrity portraits of the time Miereveld's image exists in several versions. This one is signed by the artist, and at least one other is dated 1625.[10] The suit was possibly sent separately to the Netherlands for the sittings and left at Miereveld's studio to complete the rendering of the dress, a common practice at the time. In England the Miereveld-trained court painter Daniel Mytens and his studio used this half-length by Miereveld, or a version of it, as a model for Mytens's own standing full-length portraits of the Duke of Buckingham.[11]

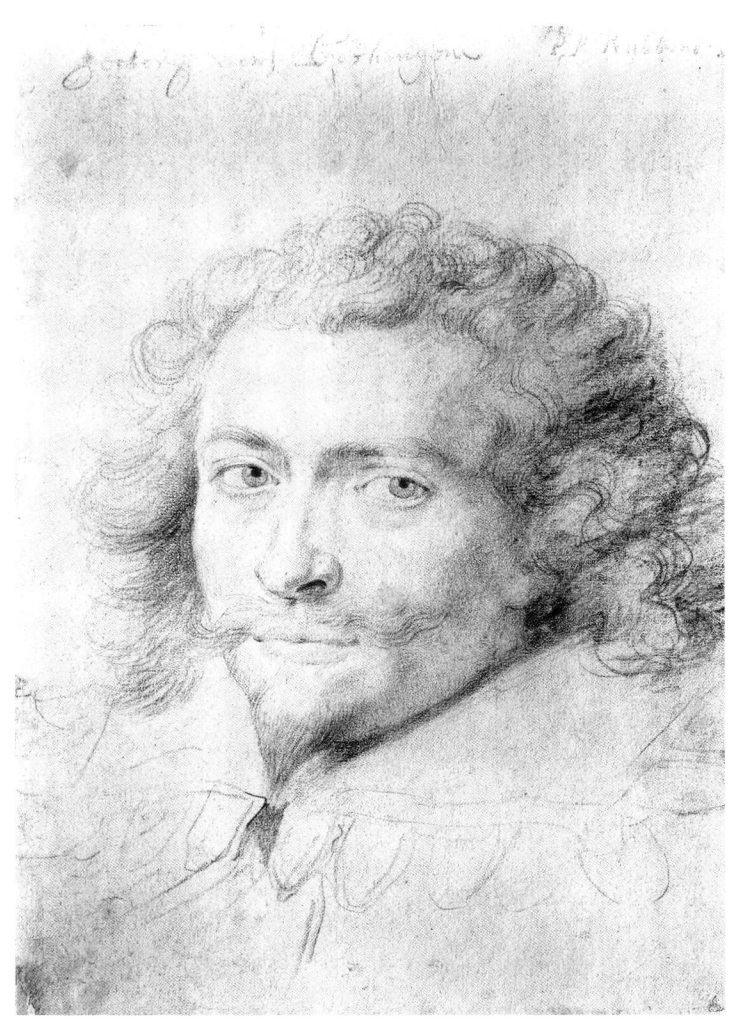

Peter Paul Rubens, *George Villiers, Duke of Buckingham*, 1625. Albertina Museum, Vienna

**Inscription:** Signed c.l., brown paint: "M. Miere…[d]t sui ipsius / principale depinxit".

**Provenance:** Christie's, London, 13 April 1951, lot 20 (as C. Jonson); Captain Edward George Spencer Churchill (1876–1964) of Northwick Park, Gloucestershire, until 1953; purchased from Mr G. S. Ingram, Melbourne, 1967.

**Exhibitions:** *Elizabeth and the Royal House of Tudor*, Cheltenham Art Gallery, Gloucestershire, May–July 1953, no. 8. *Island to Empire: 300 Years of British Art 1550–1850*, AGSA, Adelaide, 2005.

**Literature:** *Picture Book*, Adelaide: AGSA, 1972, p. 17 (illus.). Jeremy Black, *History of England*, London, 1993, p. 78 illus.

**Condition:** Good; last conserved in 1999 by Artlab Australia, Adelaide.

**Frame:** Probably not original but late seventeenth century.

# Peter Lely 1618–1680

Lely's opulent portraits are mostly associated with the ostentatious Restoration period of King Charles II, for whom the artist became Principal Painter in 1661. However, he was already working in England before the 1649 execution of Charles I and had painted the previous king and the royal children. His career continued through the Commonwealth republic that Oliver Cromwell led. For the thirty years until his death in 1680 Lely dominated British portraiture, and set a fashion for countless contemporaries and followers.

Peter Lely was born Pieter van der Faes of Dutch parents in Soest, Westphalia, Germany, in 1618. He studied in Haarlem in the studio of Frans and Pieter de Grebber and became a master in 1637. His first known works are neo-Venetian arcadian figure compositions larger than but similar to those by Cornelis van Poelenburgh. He left the Netherlands for London soon after Van Dyck's death in 1641, and continued to paint arcadias. However, the sensuous figure compositions met with little favour among English patrons during the austere Commonwealth. Lely then confined himself to portraiture, in which he was already closely following the aristocratic style of Van Dyck.

He followed not only the Baroque illusionism of Van Dyck's manner, he also followed him as a great art collector. Lely assembled the finest collection of paintings and drawings of his day and at his death owned twenty-five portraits by Van Dyck. As early as about 1650 Lely had established a workshop; his first patrons were the Earls of Northumberland, Leicester and Pembroke who had been Van Dyck's patrons. During the Commonwealth he lent his services to Parliament and in 1653 painted a renowned portrait of Cromwell (Birmingham Museum & Art Gallery).

After the restoration of the Stuart monarchy in 1660 and his appointment soon after as court painter to Charles II, Lely ran a very large studio, turning out hundreds of portraits. His most famous series, "a gallery of the fairest persons at Court", painted between 1662 and 1665 and known as the Windsor Beauties but now held at Hampton Court palace, was commissioned by the Duchess of York, first wife of Prince James, later James II. The ladies' loose, provocative languor has come to epitomise our perceptions of Restoration society.

Lely taught many artists and over the years his studio grew to include such painters as John Greenhill, John Baptiste Gaspers, Thomas Hawker, Willem Wissing, Mary Beale and others. He was knighted by Charles II in 1680, the year of his death.

## Portrait of a man, thought to be George Booth, Lord Delamere, c.1660
oil on canvas, 91.2 x 76.2 cm
A. M. & A. R. Ragless Bequest Funds 1957

The supposed sitter, George Booth, 1st Lord Delamere (1622–1684) was the son of William Booth, member of an old family at Dunham Massey, Cheshire. He became the member of parliament for Cheshire many times between 1645 and 1660. An active early supporter of the Parliamentary cause in the Civil War he was nevertheless imprisoned in the Tower of London in 1659 because his appointment as Commander-in-Chief of all forces in Cheshire, Lancashire and North Wales had been made by the exiled King Charles II. He was soon liberated, took his seat in parliament and was one of the twelve members deputed to carry the message of the House of Commons inviting Charles II, exiled at The Hague, to take up the British throne. On the occasion of Charles II's coronation in 1661 George Booth was created Baron Delamere.

As portraits were usually commissioned to celebrate significant events, it is possible that this one celebrates the creation of the barony and that the depiction holding a document could be intended to represent him as one of the twelve petitioners inviting the restoration of a monarchy in Britain. This supposition fits the probable date of the painting, the age of George Booth at the time, which was thirty-eight, as well as the conspicuous presentation of a sheet of paper.

An earlier portrait by Lely, painted in 1647, is also believed to be of George Booth (Bodleian Library, Oxford) but although there is a resemblance it does not appear to be the same man, even given that he would be younger by fourteen years. However, it cannot be confirmed conclusively that Booth is the subject of either portrait.[1]

The sitter's clothes and Lely's painting style date this half-length to about 1660 and perhaps reflect the austerity of the Commonwealth period (1649–1660). It is more assured than his portraits from the 1640s and early 1650s, indeed painted at the height of his artistic powers. On the other hand it is sober in colour and avoids the stereotype flamboyance that mars many of Lely's later works. The man is very much an individual, and dressed in elegant but restrained apparel.

His handsome, fine features are sensitively but firmly modelled, as is the graceful hand. Long golden-brown hair, lightly tousled, complements the rich brown of slashed satin coat-sleeves. Dark tones contrast with the white of a satin shirt and the white of the important document. The mood is serious, the sitter is intent and looks firmly to our left as if to the recipient of his petition. It is a highly accomplished painting and unlike much of Lely's later work appears to have little or no studio assistance.

Although Lely is the best-known English seventeenth-century painter after Van Dyck, and one of the most influential and prolific, this fine example of his portraiture is the only authenticated work by the artist in an Australian public collection.

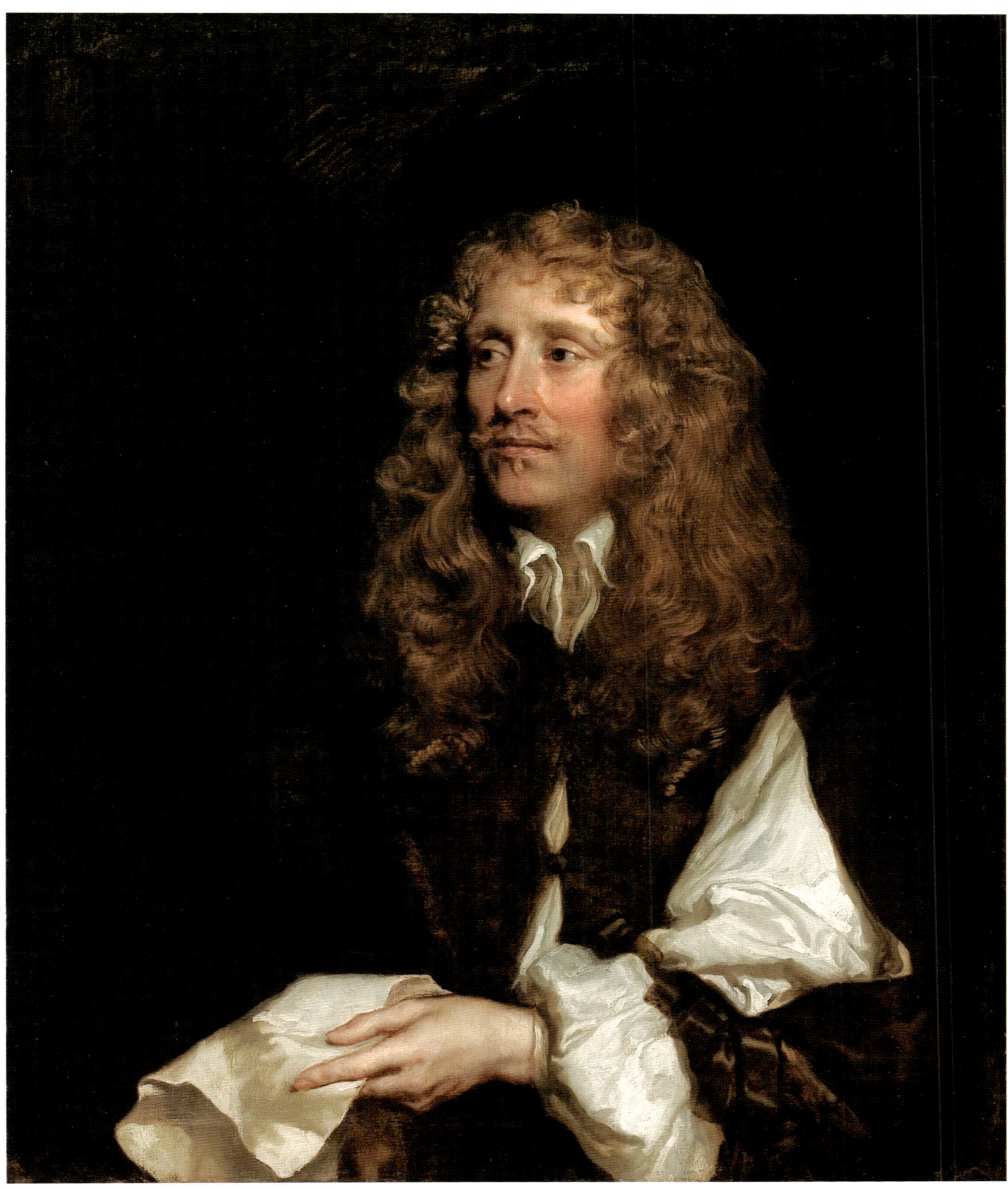

**Provenance:** Sir John Foley by 1928; Grey sale, Christie's, London, 15 June 1928; Leonard Law Collection; Purchased from Mrs W. G. McBeath, Toorak, Melbourne, 1957.
**Exhibitions:** *Art Treasures*, Manchester, 1857. *Island to Empire: 300 Years of British Art 1550–1850*, AGSA, Adelaide, 2005.
**Literature:** *NGSA Bulletin*, vol. 18, no. 4, April 1960. *Picture Book*, Adelaide: AGSA, 1972, p. 16 (illus.). Peter Tomory and Robert Gaston, *European Paintings before 1800 in Australian and New Zealand Public Collections*, Sydney, 1989, p. 33, no. 76 (illus.). Jeremy Black, *History of England*, London, 1993, p. 87 (illus.).
**Condition:** Excellent; conserved in 1999 by Artlab Australia, Adelaide.
**Frame:** Not original.

# Matthew Dixon 1640s?–1710

Matthew Dixon, a portrait artist in crayons, oils and miniatures, worked in London in the late seventeenth century. He followed the court portrait tradition of Peter Lely, principal painter to Charles II. However, unlike many followers and contemporaries of Lely, Dixon's portraits show not merely a representation of a class but also something of the sitter's distinct individuality. The few known works by Dixon display a rather nervous and personal manner.

Biographical and professional details are scant. He was born probably in the late 1640s, his career began probably in the 1660s, and continued until about 1690. When he retired from painting he bought a farm at Thwaite, a small Norfolk village by the Suffolk border near Bungay, where he married in 1691 and had six children. He died in Thwaite in 1710.

George Vertue writes in a notebook that Dixon had been a "Scholar of S[r]. P. Lelly [and] drew in crayons the Duchess Cleveland, Portsmouth".[1] Dixon owned a painting by Lely. Because he drew portraits of the king's rival favourites, the Duchesses of Cleveland and Portsmouth, it might be assumed that Dixon was a reasonably fashionable portrait painter. However, those two mistresses of the king were celebrities of their day, influential at court, and most British artists of the period painted them – not always from life – knowing the 'pin-ups' were likely sales. It is highly unlikely that the duchesses sat for Dixon.

His style can be recognised from five portraits of the Sotheby family of Ecton Hall, Northampton, the earliest of which is firmly documented and dated 1671. Receipts paid to the artist in 1679 and 1680[2] confirm these as being by Dixon. The narrowing of the eyes, slight elongation of the face, flattening of the drapery and dryness of the thin paint application are all qualities seen in the Sotheby family portraits and also found in the Gallery's painting.

attributed to Matthew Dixon

## Portrait of a man, 1670s

oil on canvas, 76.2 x 63.5 cm

Gift of Mr A. Cowell 1952

This distinctive portrait attributed to Matthew Dixon[3] takes on some of the fashionable mannerisms found in Lely's work but it is much more idiosyncratic and individual. The costume dates the painting to the 1670s.

The painted oval framing is a typical seventeenth-century device said to derive originally from the English miniature tradition of the sixteenth century, and it is believed that Dixon painted miniatures. In this highly mannered head-and-shoulders portrait bust the artist has made particular use of the oval. The sweep of the sitter's arm within a brown damask cloak, and the hand clasping the cloak, echo the curve of the bottom of the oval; the voluminous frizzy hair of the wig of similar brown repeats the oval at the top. The wig and the fine Venetian lace of the neckerchief frame the elongated oval face and form another complete inner oval. The resulting rhythmically circling composition is admirably self-contained, like the mood of the sitter himself.

There is a certain flattening of the forms, rather like an enlarged miniature or pastel drawing, and indeed the rendering of the drapery gives an illusion of being drawn in pastel rather than painted in oils. Since Dixon executed portraits in crayon this no doubt inspired the technique demonstrated here. The sitter's expression of gentle gravity is emphasised by a restricted palette of subtle richness with unifying browns, greys and cream.

| | |
|---|---|
| Provenance: | Gift of Mr A. Cowell, Eden Bridge, Kent, 1952. |
| Exhibitions: | *Hidden Treasures: South Australia's European Old Master paintings, Restorations and Re-attributions and South Australia's European Old Master drawings*, AGSA, Adelaide, 1989. *Island to Empire: 300 Years of British Art 1550–1850*, AGSA, Adelaide, 2005. |
| Literature: | *NGSA Bulletin*, vol. 14, January 1953, no. 3 (illus.). Ron Radford, *Hidden Treasures*, Adelaide: AGSA, 1989. |
| Condition: | Good to fair; last conserved in the Gallery's Conservation Laboratory in 1983. |
| Frame: | Not original. |

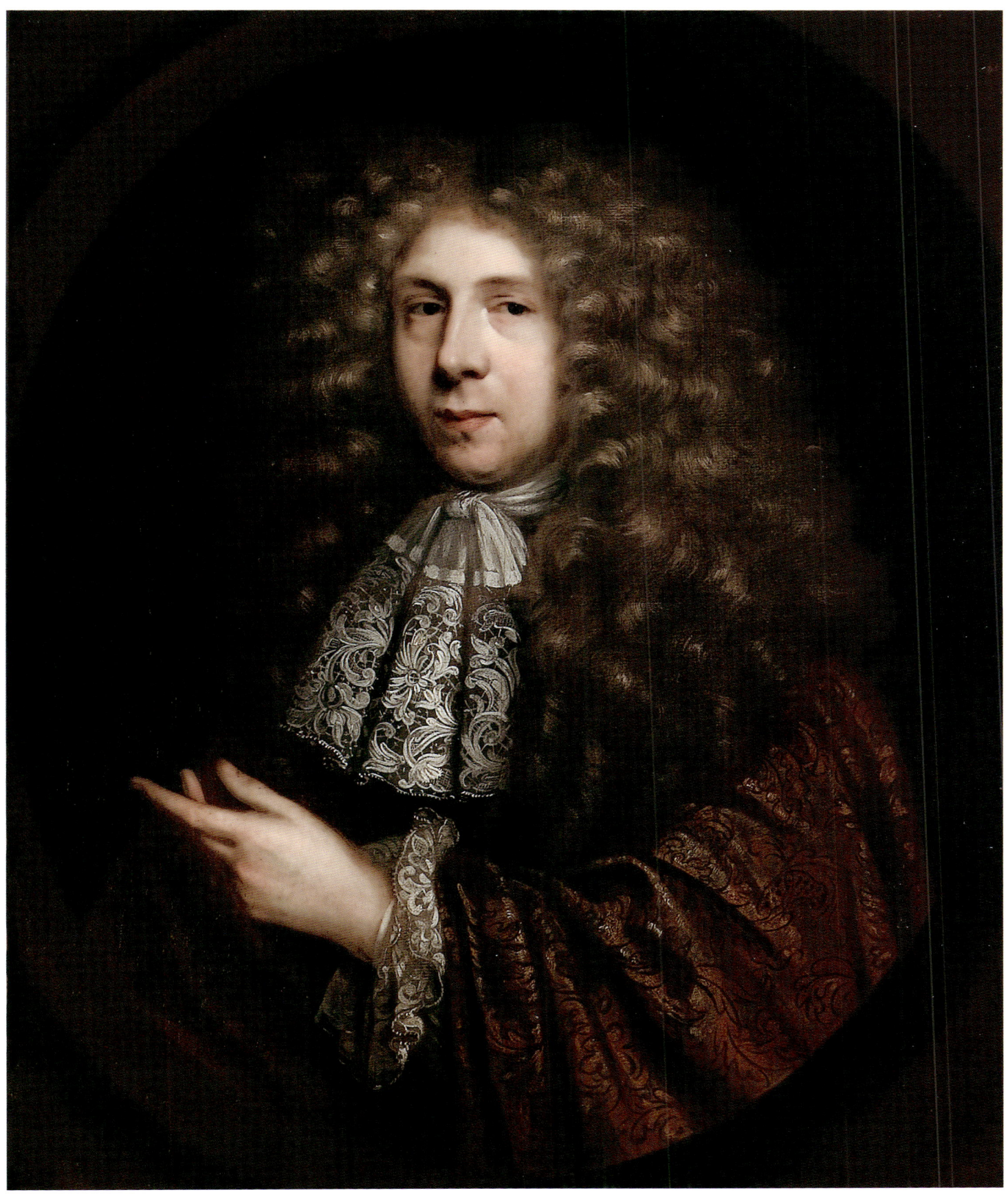

# Mary Beale 1633–1699

Mary Beale was the first major British-born professional female painter. With the support of her husband Charles Beale (1631–1705) she set up a prominent London studio where she produced portraits in the style of Peter Lely.

Born Mary Craddock in Barrow, Suffolk in 1633, she was the first child of the Reverend John Craddock, the rector of Barrow and an amateur still-life painter. It is most likely that he gave Mary her first encouragement and lessons in art. She probably studied with Robert Walker (1607–1658), a portrait painter favoured by Richard Cromwell and the Puritans. Her father sat for a portrait with Walker; later Walker also painted portraits of Mary and her husband. The Beales married in 1652 in Barrow and enjoyed a very happy union in which their shared interests included art, paint technology and religion. Charles was also a serious art collector. His most significant act of devotion was to become, eventually, his wife's studio assistant and manager.

They moved to Covent Garden, London in 1656 and set up a painting room where the young mother painted portraits for a pastime. Their two sons, Bartholomew born in 1656 and Charles born in 1660, both became, around 1675, their mother's studio assistants, painting draperies and ovals. Charles Beale, senior, had a lucrative position at the Patents' Office until the family fled in 1665 to the small village of Albrook, Hampshire as the Great Plague swept through London. It was not until 1670, when they returned to London and established her studio in Pall Mall, that Mary Beale became a full-time professional portrait painter and the family's principal income earner.

The Beales earned the friendship and support of Peter Lely, who had been appointed Principal Painter to Charles II in 1661. Mary emulated Lely's style of fashionable portraiture based on Anthony van Dyck's model. Mary and Charles commissioned portraits from Lely, the progress of which Mary received permission to observe. Lely's support undoubtedly assisted Beale's career and she was often commissioned to copy his portraits. She maintained a friendship with him over many years, and actively participated in artistic and religious circles. In 1667 she sent Elizabeth Tillotson, wife of the Reverend John Tillotson, later Archbishop of Canterbury, her manuscript *Discourse on Friendship* which she warmly dedicated to the friend. Throughout her artistic life, Beale painted close friends and such works from before her professional period are among the finest and most intimate of her portraits.

The Beales' son Charles studied under Thomas Flatman (1637–1688) and became a professional miniature painter. She had other pupils including Sarah Curtis, later Mrs Hoadley. At Lely's death in 1680 Beale's practice was already in decline and by the time of the Bloodless Revolution that deposed James II in 1688 her style had fallen out of favour for major commissions.

Mary Beale died in London in 1699, the same year as the French/British flower painter Jean-Baptiste Monnoyer (1636–1699) and like him was buried at St James's Church, Piccadilly. The exceptional documentation of her life and career provides a remarkable and unique record of the British art world of the Stuart Restoration.

## Mary Wither of Andwell, early 1670s

oil on canvas, 73.0 x 60.0 cm

Gift of Helen & John Bowden in memory of Mary Overton 2003

Mary Wither, the sitter for this stylish Restoration period portrait, was the daughter of Thomas Faulkes of Oxford. Mary Faulkes, probably born around 1656, married Thomas Wither of Andwell, Hampshire (1652–1700). The date of the marriage is unknown, but it was probably 1674 or 1675 as in the years from 1676 to 1682 Mary Wither had six children.

The Withers's eldest son and heir William, who was born in 1676, married the daughter of Thomas Biffin of Basingstoke but died childless, as did their other male offspring, so the Wither family line came to an end. It is probable that Mary Wither died as a result of complications arising from the arrival of her sixth child, John; she passed away at the end of February 1682 just after the time of his birth. Mrs Wither and her husband, who died in 1700, were both buried in the grounds of the family church at Wotton, near Basingstoke in Hampshire.[1]

This portrait of a young and attractive Mary Wither would have been commissioned in the early or mid 1670s, not long after Mary Beale commenced her full-time professional career. For such half-lengths Beale charged £5,[2] which compares with the £20 that Lely then charged for a half-length portrait.

The *faux* cartouche, a painted oval surround that imitates Baroque plasterwork or carved and painted wood, is a device derived from early-seventeenth-century decorated encasements of portrait miniatures. It may have been painted by one of her sons Bartholomew or Charles who had become their mother's assistants when this portrait was executed. Similar decorative cartouches occur in some of Lely's paintings of the time, among them Lely's portrait of the Beales' friend the Reverend John Tillotson, then the Dean of Canterbury (Elton Hall Collection, Peterborough, Cambridgeshire). That very portrait was commissioned by and for the Beales in 1672,[3] probably a couple of years before Beale painted the portrait of Mary Wither. Lely permitted Mary Beale to observe him paint his Tillotson portrait. In both Beale's and Lely's portraits the *faux* moulding looks as if it is part of an interior decorative scheme. The portrait of Mary Wither may have been part of a marriage pair to be hung

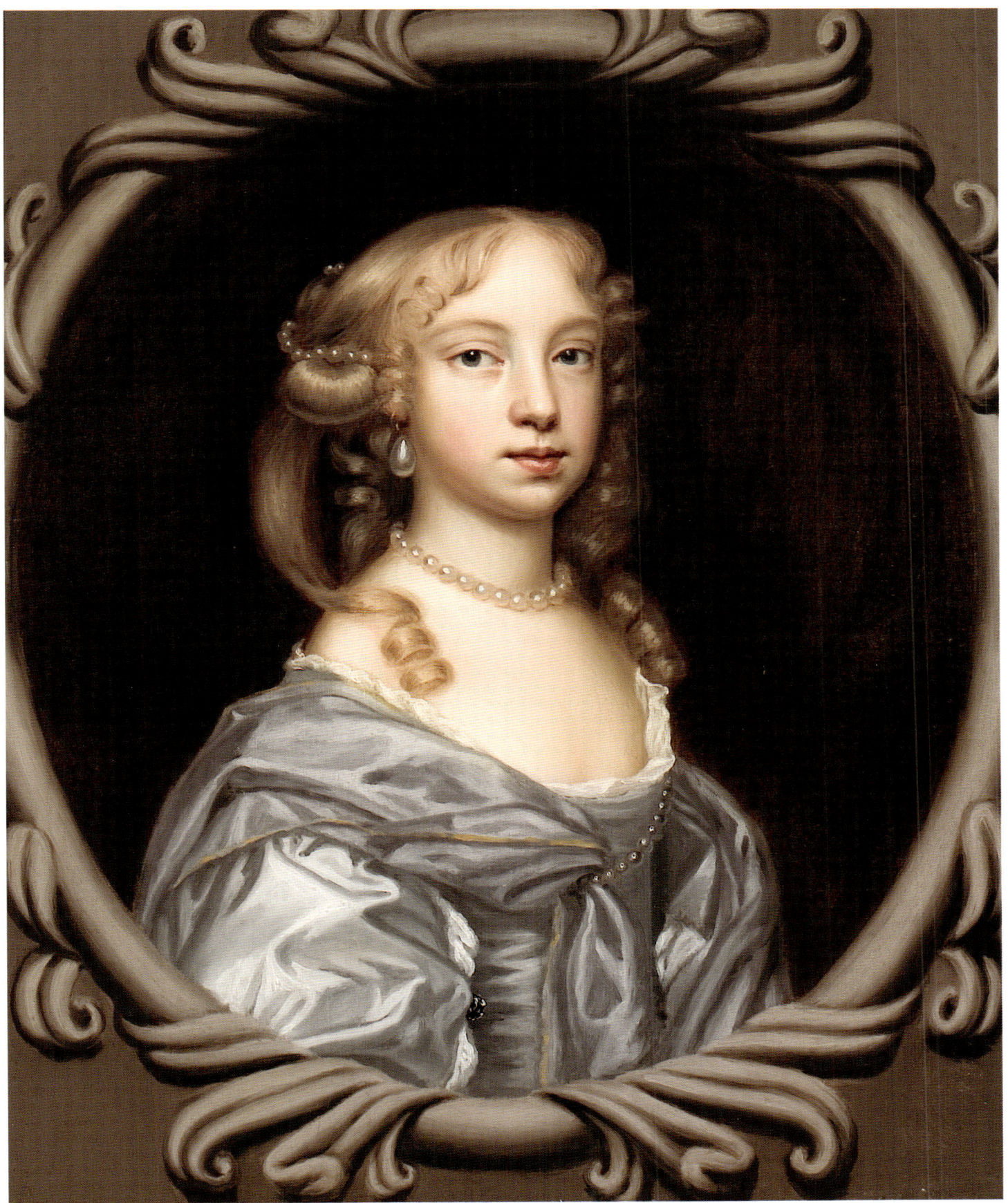

either side of a fireplace, or a doorway or window. Since the sitter married Thomas Wither about 1674 this is possible, but no Beale portrait of Thomas Wither is known.

Here the distinctive oval surround is an integral part of the decorative composition. The sitter's cascading hair-style of loops and loose curls intertwined with a string of pearls is consciously echoed in the intertwining tendrils of the cartouche and also in the complex folds of her shimmering silk dress. Mary Wither's hair and costume are similar in cool tones and restricted colour to the feigned frame. The scheme is one of restrained subtle greys–grey browns, grey mauves and cream. Its refined and decorative qualities prefigure later eighteenth-century portraits.

Mrs Wither appears less an individual than a representative of a certain class, even perhaps as a decorative possession. She has the fashionable appearance of one of Lely's court ladies, especially his famous 'Windsor Beauties' of the 1660s. Although it is tempting to interpret this painting of a woman by a woman artist as possessing a feminine sensibility, it is more likely that here a female artist is trying to paint as competently and professionally as the leading male artist of the day, her friend Peter Lely. However, Mary Wither as painted by Beale shows much more modesty and decorum than the court ladies painted by the male Court Painter.

The picture is now a memorial to Mary Overton, whose nephew John Bowden and his wife Helen (Mrs Overton's close confidante and secretary) gave funds for an acquisition in memory of the Gallery's great benefactor. She especially favoured European Old Master paintings. It is pleasing and apt that this fine British Old Master portrait by a Mary, of a Mary, is a memorial to another Mary.

**Provenance:** Major Vigor, Cheshire; thence by descent.

**Exhibitions:** *The Courtly Image: Early portraiture 1550–1680*, Weiss Gallery, London, 2002, no. 24. *Island to Empire: 300 Years of British Art 1550–1850*, AGSA, Adelaide, 2005.

**Literature:** Mark Weiss, *The Courtly Image: Early portraiture 1550–1680*, London: Weiss Gallery, 2002, no. 24.

**Condition:** Excellent; last conserved in 2002 in London before acquisition.

**Frame:** Probably original.

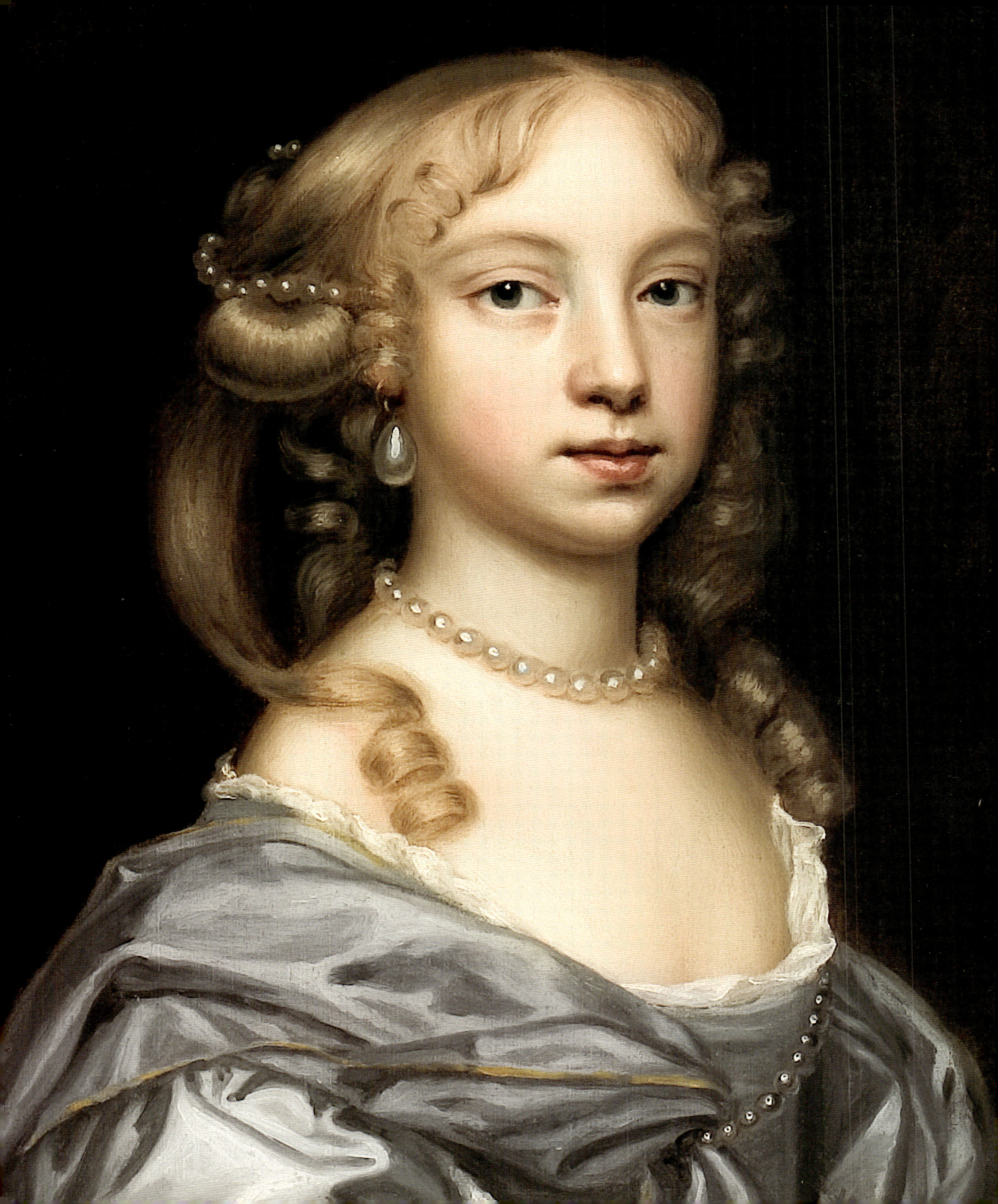

# Simon Verelst 1644–1721?

Simon Verelst was a Dutch-born and -trained painter of still-life compositions, especially flowers. After his arrival in Britain in 1669 he continued to paint flowers but also turned to portraits. He emulated to some degree the portrait mannerisms of his fellow Dutch-born artist Peter Lely and when Lely died in 1680 Verelst was favoured for a few years by the Stuarts, especially at the court of James II.

Simon Pietersz Verelst was born at The Hague in 1644 and, like his elder brother Herman who followed him to London, was first trained by his father Pieter Verelst. In 1666 he joined the Guild of St Luke at The Hague. Simon Verelst arrived in London in 1669 in the reign of Charles II who bought six of his flower pieces and later commissioned him to paint his portrait (Royal Collection, formerly collection of Her Majesty Queen Elizabeth the Queen Mother). He became the first artist in Britain to make a successful career as a flower painter – two decades before Jean Baptiste Monnoyer's arrival in London from Paris with a more sophisticated French style. It is thought that it was George Villiers, second Duke of Buckingham (son of the first Duke for whose portrait see p. 73), who first encouraged Verelst, probably in the late 1670s, to turn to portraiture, the traditional mainstay for British artists. Verelst painted the second Duke's portrait about 1680 (Collection Earl of Jersey).

Verelst also produced decorative portraits that incorporated flowers. He painted several mistresses of Charles II including the influential Duchess of Portsmouth (Private collection) and the actress Nell Gwynn (National Portrait Gallery, London). About 1680 he painted a pair of portraits of the future James II and his consort, Mary of Modena, when they were Duke and Duchess of York (Collections of Bolton Hall and Her Majesty the Queen respectively). Another very decorative portrait, believed to be of Mary of Modena by Verelst, is at the Yale Center for British Art, New Haven.

Towards the end of his life Verelst suffered a period of mental instability and was confined to an asylum. Horace Walpole commented on the excessive vanity of the artist, who referred to himself as "The God of Flowers" and "The King of Painters". He charged far higher prices for portraits than any artist in London in the seventeenth or early eighteenth century.[1] He died in London in 1721.

## Portrait of an Ambassador, c.1686
oil on canvas, 125.1 x 100.9 cm
South Australian Colonial Government Grant 1896

The Gallery's portrait by Verelst was once thought to be of Jean Baptiste Colbert, Marquis de Torcy, who was French ambassador to the Court of King James II in 1687.[2] He was the son of the Marquis de Croissy and nephew of the Jean Baptiste Colbert who was chief minister to Louis XIV. However, the portrait cannot be of de Torcy as he was born in 1665 and would have been only twenty-two when he became ambassador to London. Our portrait is of a much older man most probably in his fifties or sixties.

A Latin inscription on the paper held by the sitter reads: "*Serenissimo et potentis/ simo Principi, Fratri Consan/ guinis Amies et foederato/ nostro clarissimo Domino/ IACOBO ejus nominis secundo/ Magnae Britanniae Franciae/ et Hyberniae Regi/ Fidei Defensor.*" (Translated: "To the most serene and powerful Prince, our beloved brother ally the glorious Lord James, second of that name, King of Great Britain, France and Ireland, Defender of the Faith".) The missive confirms a date in the 1685–88 reign of James II and suggests the bearer was an ambassador to London, and therefore a likely subject for Verelst. "Defender of the Faith" is a conventional title of the British sovereigns, but here perhaps refers particularly to James's Catholicism. The envoy therefore could be from a Catholic state, possibly Rome or Venice, though not France as the English claim to part of France would not be acknowledged in writing. Since James had married an Italian Catholic, a d'Este from Modena, perhaps the sitter was a Modenese relative of the Queen as indicated by the message to "our beloved brother ally".

Most known portraits by Verelst of notables at the late-seventeenth-century Stuart court are three-quarter-lengths like this characteristic example. The pose is similar to that in Verelst's portraits of Charles II, James II and his Queen, and the second Duke of Buckingham. Those portraits show the same dignified, almost arrogant pose and proud tilt of the head: chin up, facing left but eyes looking imperiously down at the viewer. They all show the left hand on the hip with the right holding some attribute. In the case of the Gallery's painting the sitter is holding his rolled petition to the King. The pose was previously one of Lely's but Verelst made it more mannered and the sitters more obviously haughty, almost characterising French portraiture of the period.

This sitter is wearing a cravat and cuffs of distinctive Venetian point lace. His coat, vest and cloak are of sumptuous satin in browns and greys that blend with his cascading wig.

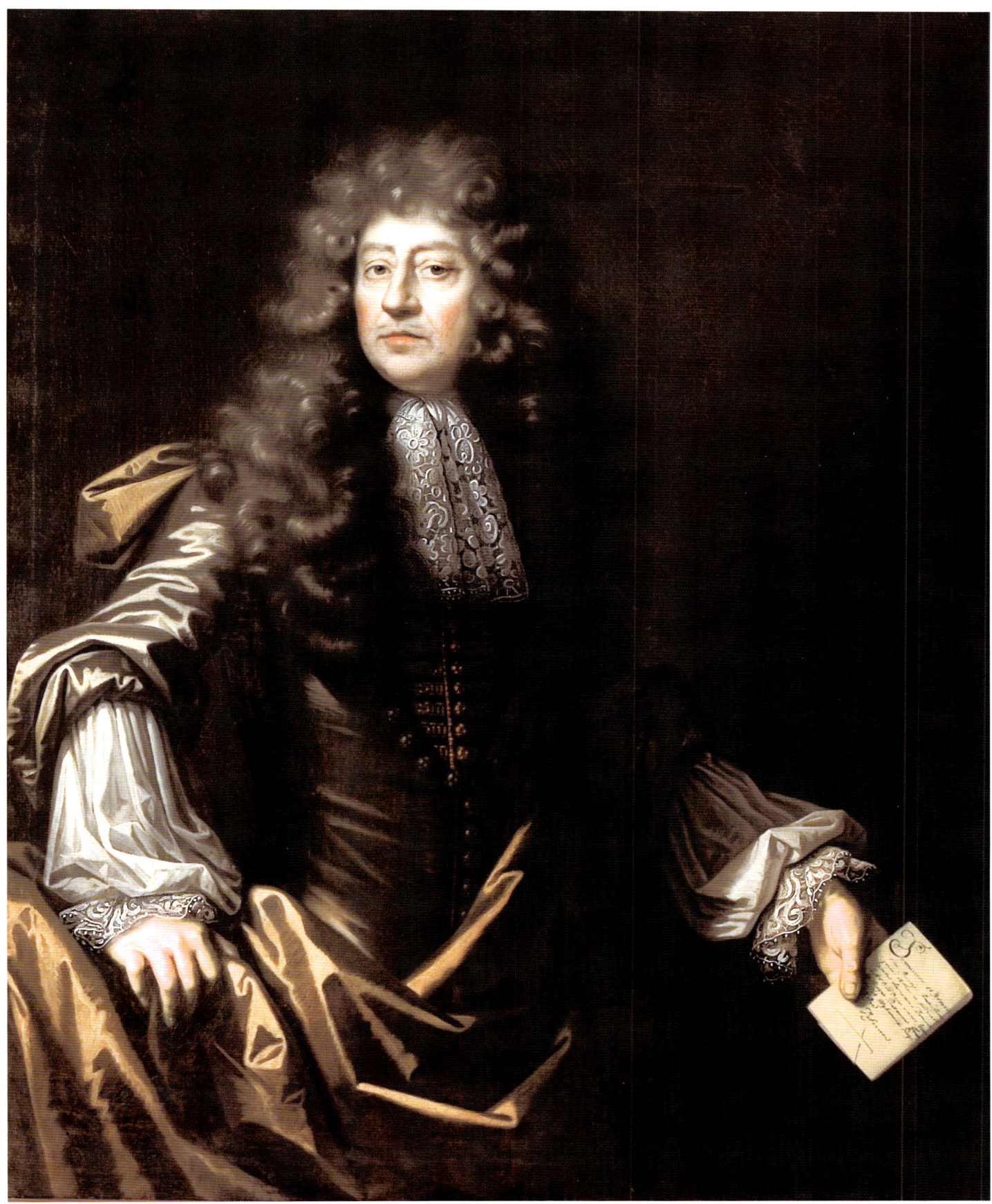

The portrait shows Verelst's characteristic acid colouring against a black background. The artist's distinctive modelling of the satin drapery takes on the appearance of crumpled sheet-metal. However, at least part of this effect, which can be seen in many of his works, is probably the result of fading and poor conservation over the past 300 years. The middle tones appear to have partly sunk into the dark background, creating a somewhat ghostly appearance. This is a characteristic problem in many of Verelst's portraits.

By way of local distinction it was the first Old Master painting bought by the Art Gallery of South Australia. Its acquisition, in 1896 from an Adelaide collection, was due to the supposed royal sitter, not for its artistic qualities or because it was by a significant artist. It was bought as a portrait of James II, by an unknown artist. By the 1940s the identification of the sitter had shifted from the King to the now disproved Marquis de Torcy[3], and it was almost a century before an attribution settled on the artist Simon Verelst.[4]

**Provenance:** Purchased from Mr W. H. Selway, Adelaide, 1896.

**Exhibitions:** *Hidden Treasures: South Australia's European Old Master paintings, Restorations and Re-attributions, and South Australia's European Old Master drawings*, AGSA, Adelaide, 1989. *Island to Empire: 300 Years of British Art 1550–1850*, AGSA, Adelaide, 2005.

**References:** *NGSA Bulletin*, vol. 6, no. 2, October 1944; Ron Radford, *Hidden Treasures*, Adelaide: AGSA, 1989.

**Condition:** Fair; as in many of the artist's surviving portraits the middle tones have sunk and the colours faded. Last conserved in 1988 by Artlab Australia, Adelaide.

**Frame:** Not original.

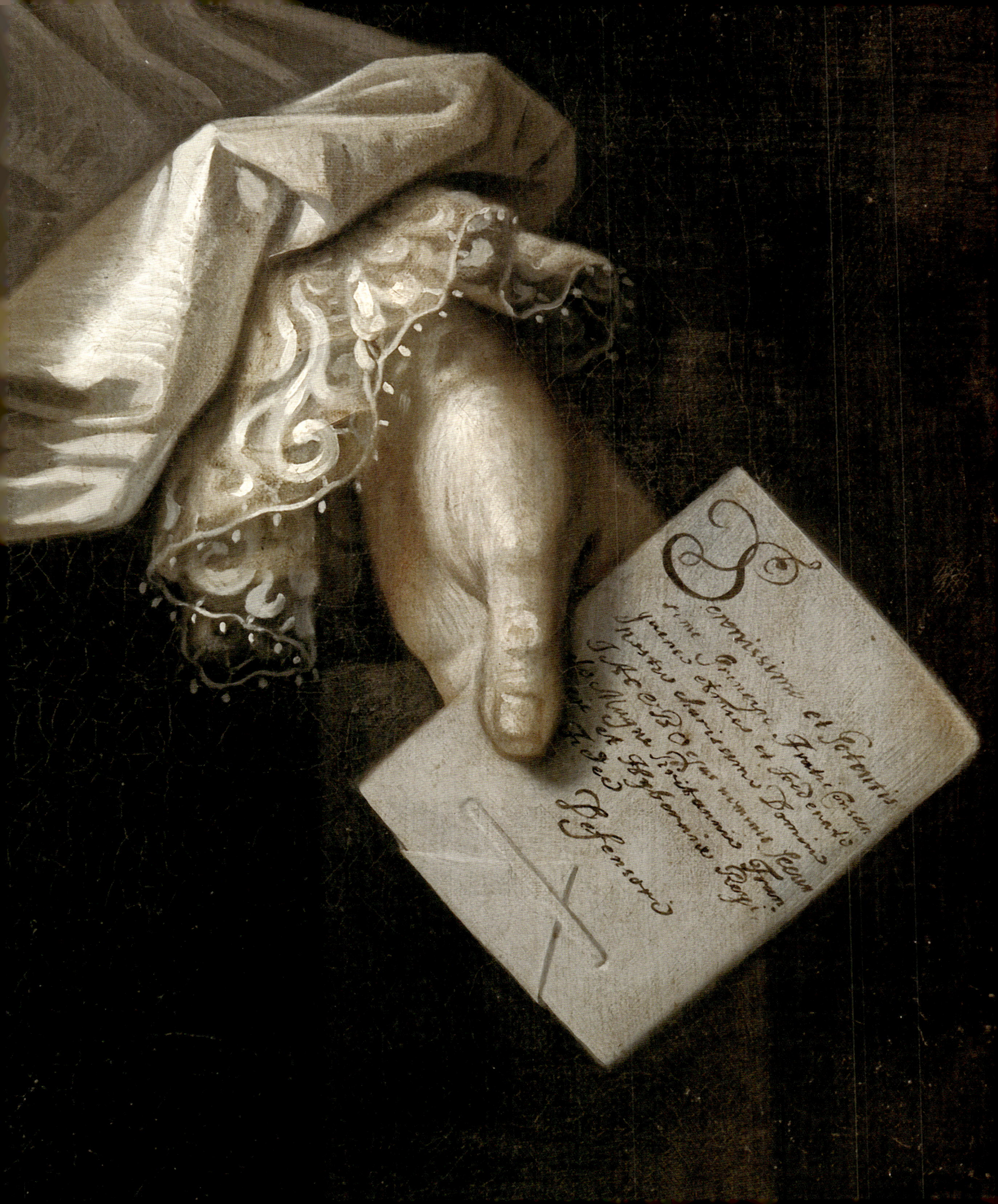

# Nicolas de Largillierre 1656–1746

Nicolas de Largillierre was one of the two most accomplished and significant French portrait artists of the late seventeenth century and the early eighteenth century. A crucial part of his training and early career was in England.

He was born in Paris but spent most of his childhood and youth in Antwerp, where his family moved in 1659. He also spent a twenty-month period in London where he was sent by his father in 1665 at the age of nine. Back in Antwerp he was apprenticed in 1668 to a little-known Flemish painter of market scenes and landscapes, Antoni Goubau (1616–1698), and in 1673–74 he became a Master of the Antwerp Guild of St Luke. Trained in the Flemish genre and still-life traditions, he returned to London in 1675 and was there apprenticed to Antonio Verrio (1639–1707), a Neapolitan mural painter of allegories who had worked in France from 1666 before arriving in England in 1672. Verrio painted compositions such as *Sea Triumph of Charles II*, 1675, for Whitehall Palace and in 1675 began, for Hampton Court, a decorative ceiling cycle dedicated to the history of British monarchy, which again featured Charles II. Largillierre would have assisted Verrio in these works and learned the principles of the allegorical court portrait.

In London the apprentice artist painted still-lives independently of Verrio and became friendly with Peter Lely, the court portrait painter. Lely owned a still-life painted in England by Largillierre. The Gallery's oval portrait of an unknown man now attributed to Largillierre possibly emanates from this period.[1] As a French-born Catholic in England, the artist encountered difficulties in 1678 when a French Catholic plot against Charles II was discovered, and in the following year the artist is believed to have left for Paris. He lived there for the rest of his life but returned to Britain in 1686–87 and painted portraits of the Catholic King James II (who had come to the throne in 1685) and his consort Mary of Modena. After the king's exile in 1688 Largillierre continued to paint the Stuarts and their supporters in Paris.

His early portraits, before 1700, show a strong dependence on the English portraits of Van Dyck. Throughout his long and prolific French career Largillierre specialised in portraits of the wealthy bourgeois but he also painted aristocrats and courtiers, vying with those of Hyacinthe Rigaud (1659–1743), the other leading portraitist in France. Largillierre was Rigaud's rival in the aesthetic domain as well. Whereas Rigaud preferred cool hues, straight lines and rigorous clarity of composition, Largillierre's Flemish training inclined him towards warm hues, bold, thick brushwork and the curved lines which gave his canvases their interesting dynamism.

From the end of the seventeenth century Largillierre was a dominant personality in the Académie Royale serving as its Chancellor in 1733, Director in 1734–35, Rector in 1735, and again was finally elected Director from 1738 to 1742.

### attributed to Nicolas de Largillierre

## Portrait of a Frenchman, c.1678?

oil on canvas, 61.0 x 50.8 cm

Bequest of V. K. Burmeister 1957

This picture of an unknown Frenchman is probably from Largillierre's early period in England, but it is difficult to confirm a date as no portraits by him from those years are known for firm comparison.

There are only four indisputable signed and dated works by Largillierre from his formative stay in England during 1675 to 1679. All are still-lives that reflect the Flemish-Dutch tradition of his earlier training in Antwerp, and another three still-lives have been attributed to Largillierre at this period. He must have executed portraits during the time in England, for his earliest securely dated portrait, that of *Jean-Baptiste Tavernier*, 1679, was painted in France in the year of his departure from London, and its great technical proficiency makes earlier portrait experience seem a certainty.[2]

The oval shape is consistent with most of Largillierre's earliest known oil and engraved portraits of the 1680s and 1690s. By contrast, British portraiture of the period sometimes uses an oval format but nearly always (except for miniatures) within a rectangular canvas. Here the thinly painted hair, the background and parts of the face allow the canvas grain to show through and this is consistent with his English still-lives like the *Two bunches of grapes*, 1677 (Fondation Custodia Institut Néerlandais, Paris). The painting of the white lace cravat is also characteristic of Largillierre's rendering of such fabrics.

However, the lace cravat and red ribboned knot is more in keeping with French fashion of the earlier 1680s; in the 1670s ribbons were simpler but by the middle of the 1680s the loops in the bows became increasingly numerous. It is closer to the cravat and tie worn by James II in Largillierre's portrait of 1686 (National Maritime Museum, Greenwich). This could mean that the Gallery's portrait was painted in Largillierre's third English period of 1686–87 rather than between 1675 and 1679. It could also indicate that the painting was executed in Paris in the early 1680s. The costume is certainly French not English and, though James II dressed close to French fashion, the portrait could be of a Frenchman, perhaps a diplomat in London.

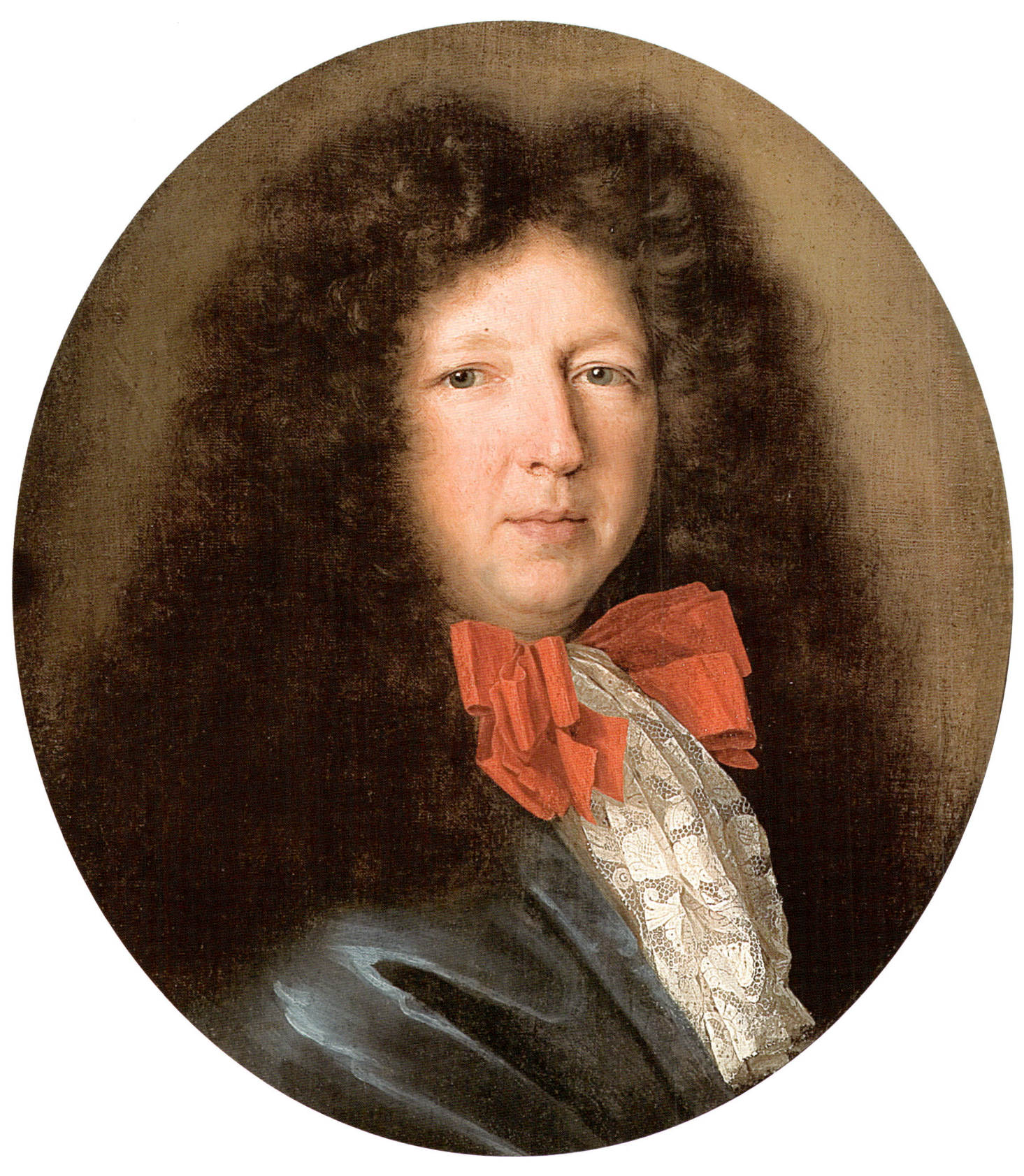

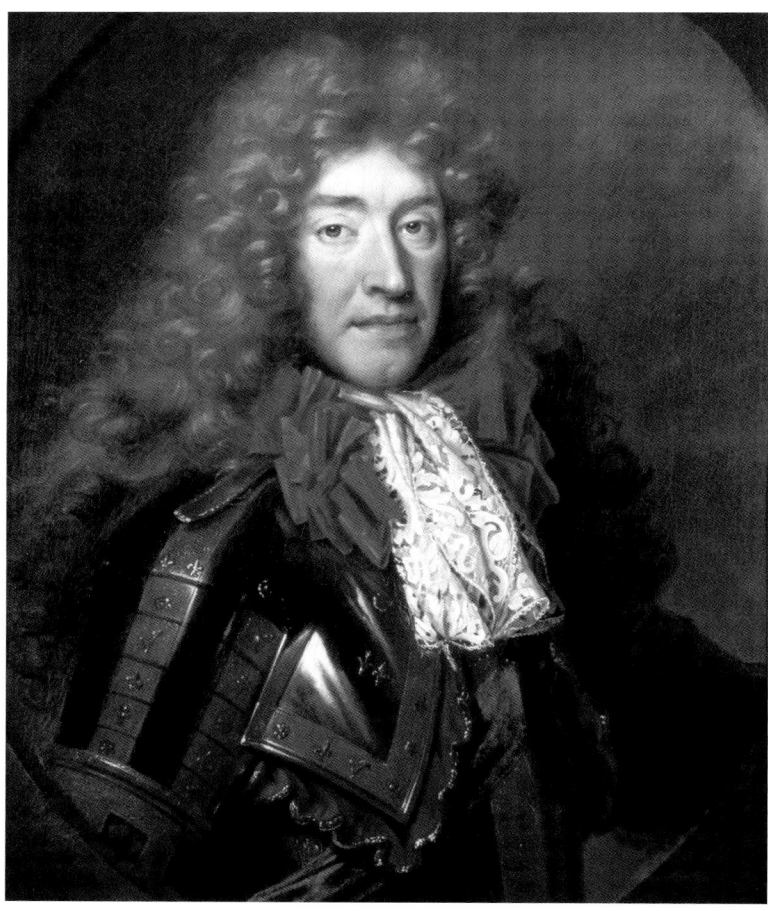

Nicolas de Largillierre, *James II*, c.1686. © National Maritime Museum, London

The meticulously rendered ribbons and lace are like a still-life, an echo of Largillierre's training in Antwerp. The rich warmth of the flesh tones is also a Flemish quality that he never lost. It is possible that this portrait was intended only as a study, for the hair, the blue cloak and parts of the face remain sketchy. It was not uncommon for Largillierre in his earlier career to paint smaller oval sketch-portraits as a preparation for larger oval portraits or more elaborate full-lengths. Several other male portraits from the 1780s and 1790s are of the same size and oval format and show equally detailed treatment of lace alongside sketchiness of hair and flesh.[3]

Until firmly dated English portraits of the late 1670s and further French works of the early 1680s are securely identified, the attribution to Largillierre and to his principal English period must remain speculative.

| | |
|---|---|
| Provenance: | Acquired in London by V. K. Burmeister, Adelaide, before 1956. |
| Exhibitions: | *Hidden Treasures: South Australia's European Old Master paintings, Restorations and Re-attributions and South Australia's European Old Master drawings*, AGSA, Adelaide, 1989. *Island to Empire: 300 Years of British Art 1550–1850*, AGSA, Adelaide, 2005. |
| Literature: | Ron Radford, *Hidden Treasures*, Adelaide: AGSA, 1989, p. 4. |
| Condition: | Good; last conserved in 1988 by Artlab Australia, Adelaide. |
| Frame: | Not original. |

# Nicolas de Largillierre

## Frances Wollascot, an Augustinian nun, 1729
oil on canvas, 80.6 x 65.4 cm
Gift of William Bowmore AO OBE through the Art Gallery of South Australia Foundation 1991

Painted in France by a French artist, this portrait of Frances Wollascot is included in the catalogue of the Gallery's early British collection because of the British sitter and also because crucial parts of Largillierre's early life, training and career were in London. The painting is about half a century later than the Gallery's earlier portrait attributed to Largillierre and displays the artist's mature and sophisticated French style at the summit of his long career.

The portrait is from a group of four that were commissioned in Paris in 1729. The others are of Frances Wollascot's maternal relations, members of the Throckmorton family, two of them also in the Augustinian nuns' habit.[1]

The Throckmortons maintained tenacious allegiance to the Catholic cause, and Frances Wollascot followed her aunt Ann Throckmorton and her cousin Elizabeth Throckmorton into the Augustinian order in Paris. On a visit there in 1729 Sir Robert Throckmorton, 4th baronet (Frances's cousin, Elizabeth's brother and Ann's nephew) commissioned portraits of the three nuns along with a portrait of himself, almost certainly on behalf of his uncle George Throckmorton. The portraits were to be sent home to family in England and were already there when George Vertue saw them at Weston House, Northamptonshire, the home of George Throckmorton; in 1749 they were recorded hanging in the dining room.[1] By 1855 all four portraits were hanging in Coughton Court, Alcester, Warwickshire, a Throckmorton house. In 1964 the National Gallery of Art, Washington, acquired the portrait of Elizabeth Throckmorton. The pictures of Ann Throckmorton and Sir Robert Throckmorton remain at Coughton Court, which now belongs to the National Trust and houses Jacobite relics.

The Augustinian convent had been founded in 1634 by the Englishwoman Lady Mary Tredway. Driven out of her native land by religious strife she first created a refuge in Flanders and later, in France, gained the support of Cardinal Richelieu to establish a community in Paris. The convent sheltered many nuns from well-connected English families. It was moved in 1911 to Ealing near London, where it remains.

The sitter is Sister Mary Ann Frances Wollascot, born in England in 1708, the daughter of Martin Wollascot. In 1727 she took vows as a member of the Order of Blue Nuns at the Augustinian Convent, Paris; she died in Paris in 1751 in her forty-third year.[2] When Largillierre painted her in 1729 she was twenty-one years old. The artist, a French Catholic who had trained and worked in England – where he painted the Catholic King James II, a cousin of the French King Louis XIV – was an obvious choice for the Throckmorton commission.

The tempering of Largillierre's usual flamboyance with the severity of the Augustinian white-and-black habit has resulted in an extremely sensitive, penetrating and powerful portrait. This decorous portrayal contrasts with the artist's ornamental Baroque style, as seen for example in the worldly portrait of Frances's cousin, Sir Robert Throckmorton. The nun's mood is quiet and contemplative, yet the painter has captured her winning countenance and shapely form, and made her strangely alluring. The restraint of the costume encourages us to concentrate on her gaze and her rosy-cheeked face. Largillierre has rendered exquisitely the beautiful hands with which she holds a needle and orange woollen yarn and embroiders a canvas in tent-stitch or petit point. This embroidery was typical of the work commonly done by religious communities in France at the time.[3] The needlework would have been used for upholstery, perhaps for a stool or cushion, maybe a cushion for a prayer stool.[4] In the three portraits of the women Largillierre distinguished the interests and the status of Frances from that of her aunt Ann, the Abbess of the convent, who holds its seal, and her cousin Elizabeth, who holds a book, probably a Bible or book of prayers. If Frances was known as the embroiderer, the books on the background shelf indicate that she was also learned. One of the books is entitled *Pensée Crétienne* which translates as *Christian Thought*.[5]

The portrait shows Largillierre's brilliance as a colourist and illustrates his theory of colour harmony, in particular the lesson he gave to Jean Baptiste Oudry (1686–1755) on how to paint a bouquet of white flowers.[6] The nun's white robe, the key to the subtle colour scheme, is modelled with touches of silver, beige and gold; these touches are picked up strongly in the sitter's flesh, the embroidery and in the more neutral background. Largillierre has grouped the dark tones, the browns and blacks, in the background to highlight the central scheme of light tones of white, beige and pink. To this gentle combination he adds piquancy with the rose-coloured lips, cheeks, embroidered canvas, thread and suggestion of a chair. Largillierre's ravishing colour scheme and his subtle

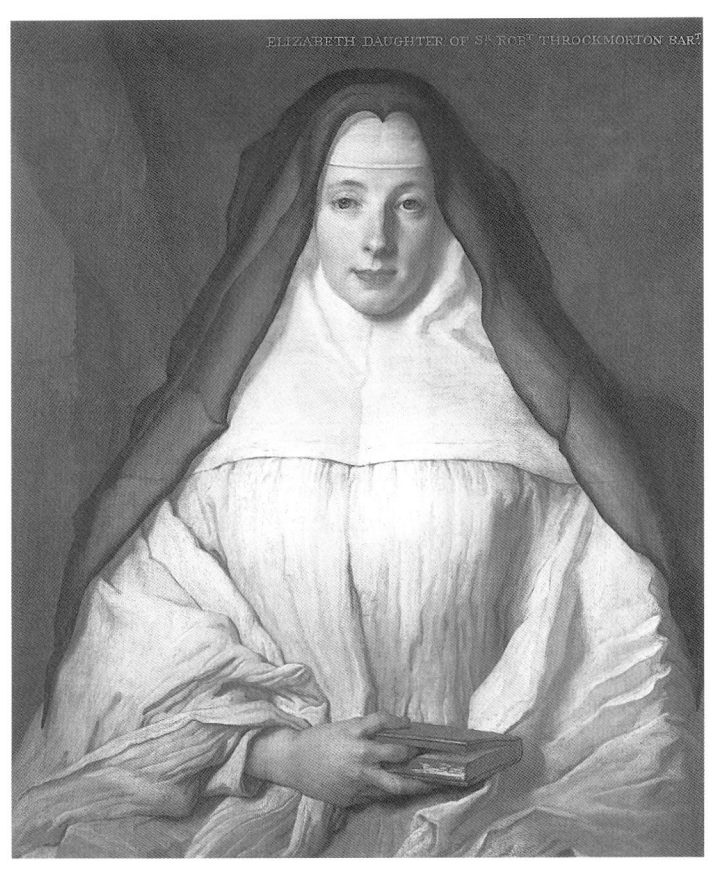

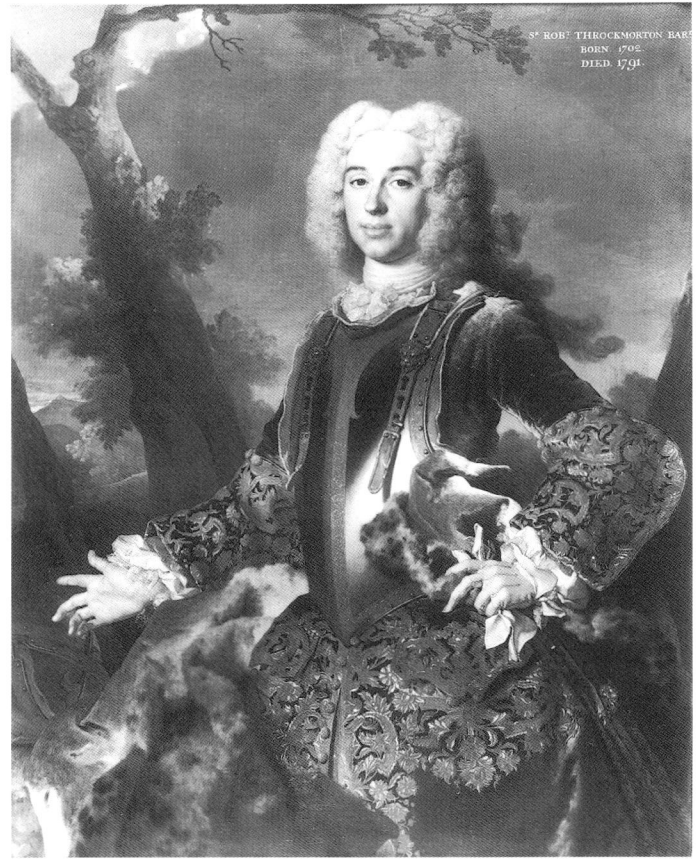

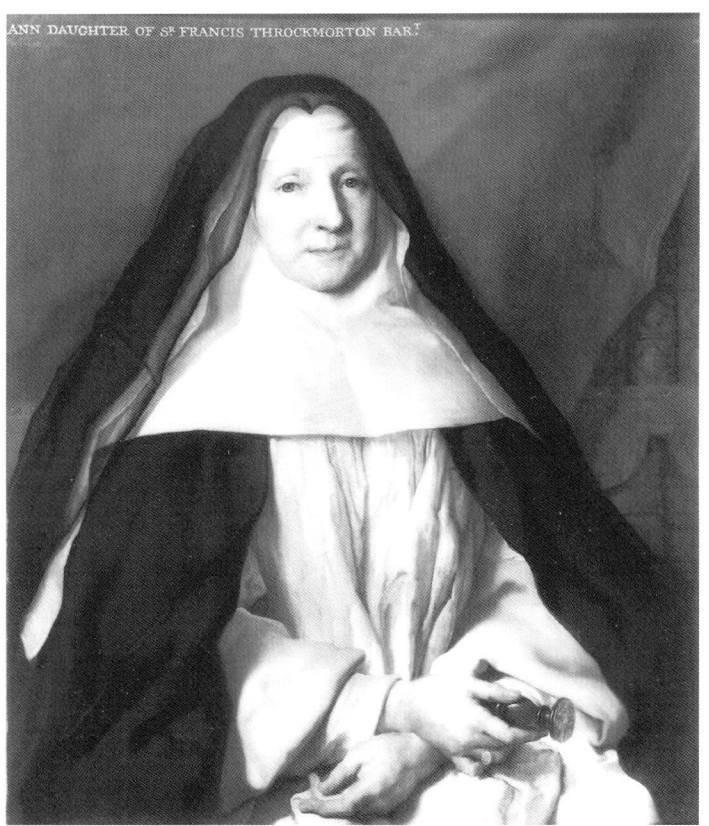

above: Nicolas de Largillierre, *Sir Robert Throckmorton*, 1729. Coughton Court, The Throckmorton Collection, The National Trust. Photograph: Photographic Survey, Courtauld Institute of Art

top: Nicolas de Largillierre, *Elizabeth Throckmorton*, 1729. Ailsa Mellon Bruce Fund, Board of Trustees, National Gallery of Art, Washington, Image © 2004

bottom: Nicolas de Largillierre, *Ann Throckmorton*, 1729. Coughton Court, The Throckmorton Collection, The National Trust. Photograph: Photographic Survey, Courtauld Institute of Art

opposite: Nicolas de Largillierre, *Frances Wollascot, an Augustinian nun*, 1729, oil on canvas, 80.6 x 65.4 cm. Gift of William Bowmore AO OBE through the Art Gallery of South Australia Foundation 1991

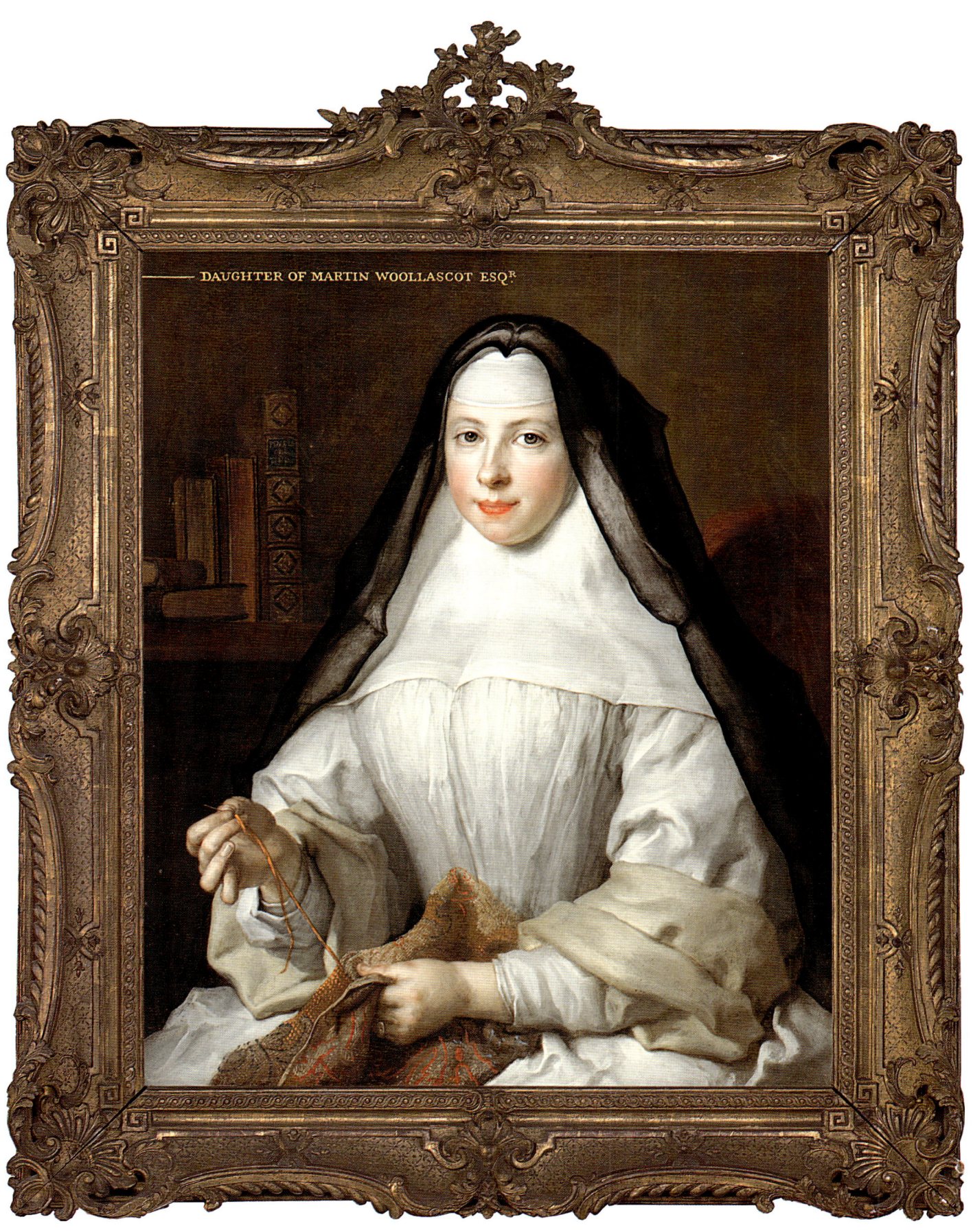

modelling in translucent layers create an immaculate paint surface. His polished technique contrasts with the coarser paint handling and more stereotyped depictions of most British portraiture of the same time.

Largillierre's simple but powerful triangular composition of a half-length veiled woman was repeated in the three portraits of nuns. It is an arrangement ultimately derived from fifteenth-century Flemish madonnas and the white-veiled female portraits with which he would have been familiar since his student days in Antwerp. He may also have been aware, through engravings or copies, of Raphael's beautiful white-veiled portrait of *La Donna Velata* (Pitti Palace, Florence). Closer precursors include Van Dyck's portrait of *Isabella Clara Eugenia of Austria in the habit of a nun* (Louvre, Paris) and nuns in white habits by Largillierre's predecessor Philippe de Champaigne, for example *Portrait of Mother Angelique Arnauld*, 1654 (Louvre, Paris).

This extremely attractive portrait must rate amongst the artist's finest works and as a masterpiece of early-eighteenth-century French portraiture.

Inscription: Inscribed u.l., oil: "–DAUGHTER OF MARTIN WOOLLASCOT ESQ.ᴿ" (a later inscription and not by artist). Inscribed on the back of canvas in what is probably an eighteenth-century hand: "Peint par N. de Largillière 1729".

Provenance: George Throckmorton, Weston House, Northamptonshire, by 1749; by descent in Throckmorton family at Coughton Court, Warwickshire since 1855; Christie's, London, 7 July 1972, no. 30; Thomas Agnew & Sons Ltd, London, *Master Paintings*, May–June 1976, no. 15; William Bowmore, Newcastle, New South Wales, 1976 to 1991.

Exhibitions: *French Art in the Eighteenth Century*, Royal Academy, London, 1968, no. 441. *A Celebration: Recent acquisitions of heritage and contemporary art*, AGSA, Adelaide, 1996. *The Fine Art of Giving: 90 masterpieces from the William Bowmore Collection*, AGSA, Adelaide, 1999, no. 8. *Island to Empire: 300 Years of British Art 1550–1850*, AGSA, Adelaide, 2005.

Literature: George Vertue notebooks (V), *The Walpole Society*, vol. 26, 1938, p. 109. E. K. Waterhouse, "The Manchester Exhibition, 1957", *Burlington Magazine*, vol. 99, 1957, p. 415. Sacheverell Sitwell, "The Pleasures of the Senses", *Apollo*, vol. 87, 1968, p. 132. *French Art in the Eighteenth Century*, Royal Academy, p. 411, fig. 45. *Largillierre and the Eighteenth Century Portrait*, Montreal: Museum of Fine Arts, 1982, pp. 274–276 (illus.). Ron Radford et al., *Treasures*, Adelaide: AGSA, 1998, p. 45. Angus Trumble in Ron Radford, *The Fine Art of Giving*, Adelaide: AGSA, 1999, p. 42–43. Pauline Johnstone, *High Fashion in the Church*, Leeds, 2002, p. 98 (illus. plate XXIA). "Recent Acquisitions at the Art Gallery of South Australia", *Burlington Magazine*, London, April 2003, p. 329.

Condition: Excellent; believed to have been last conserved in London in the early 1970s before coming to Australia.

Frame: Original, identical with the other three portraits in the set.

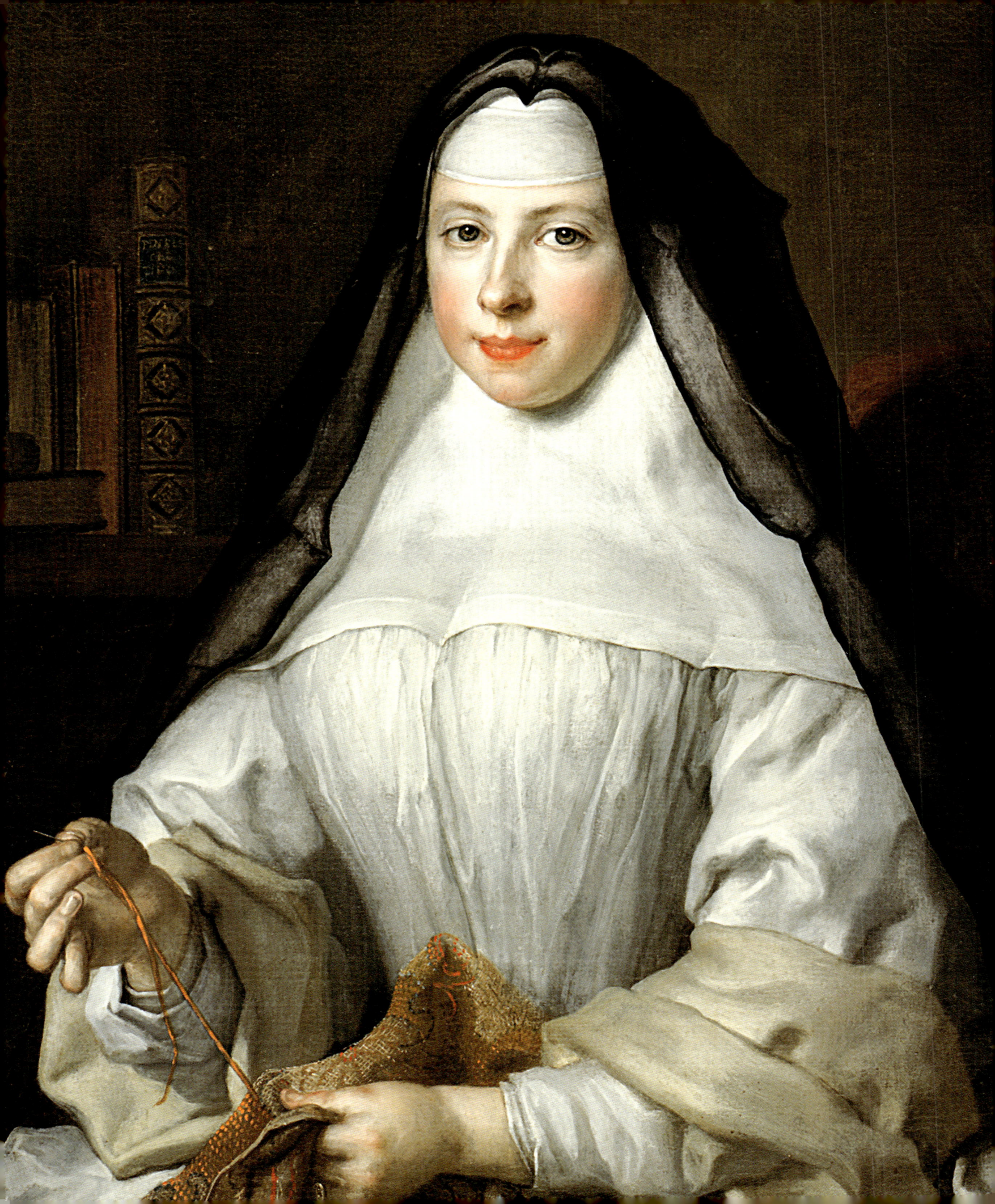

# Jean-Baptiste Monnoyer 1636–1699

Jean-Baptiste Monnoyer was the leading French still-life painter of flowers in the late seventeenth century. He spent much of the last decade of his life in England, and died there. Following Simon Verelst, who was less accomplished, he helped establish flower painting as a worthy subject in British art and decoration for interiors. His manner epitomises French aristocratic taste of the time, combining Flemish realism and detail with the more monumental form of Italian still-lives. His work is naturalistic, yet broad in style and sumptuously decorative. Monnoyer's painterly application has none of the enamel hardness and crystalline precision found in much seventeenth-century and early-eighteenth-century Dutch flower painting, which accommodated bourgeois taste in the Low Countries.

Monnoyer was born in 1634 in Lille which was then part of the Spanish-controlled Netherlands but was ceded to France in 1667. He trained in Antwerp, then a centre for flower painting, but as well as flower painting he is believed to have studied more elevated figure compositions. Some time between 1652 and 1655, soon after his training, he was lured by the artistic magnetism of Paris. It was the beginning of a great period of French patronage under Louis XIV who took up the reins of government in 1660. Monnoyer became involved in many royal schemes of decoration, collaborating with and working under Charles le Brun (1619–1690) who became the principal painter to the king, and in charge of all royal patronage. Louis XIV acquired no fewer than sixty of Monnoyer's pictures and the artist helped decorate various royal residences, among them the Louvre, the Châteaux of Vincennes, Marly, Meudon and Saint-Germain-en-Laye, and at Versailles the Grand Trianon and the Menagerie.

Monnoyer was accepted by the French Academy in 1663 and was highly visible in its exhibitions and those at the Salon from the 1660s to 1680s. He also worked at the Gobelins tapestry workshops from 1662 and the Savonnerie from 1665. In 1690 Monnoyer moved to London having been summoned by the Duke of Montagu, British Ambassador to France, to decorate Montagu House, now the site of the British Museum. He was later commissioned to decorate Hampton Court, Burlington House, Windsor Castle and Kensington Palace.

As well as floral decorations and floral canvases, it is believed that Monnoyer collaborated with portrait painters such as Hyacinthe Rigaud and Nicolas de Largillierre in France, and later in England with Godfrey Kneller, to paint flowers into their portraits. (Kneller painted Monnoyer's portrait in the late 1690s.) Monnoyer returned to Paris probably in early 1693 but was in London again at least by 1698, and died there in February 1699 and was buried at St James's Church, Piccadilly.[1]

In France and England Monnoyer's elegant and decorative style, so different from that of the more austere French still-life painters of the first half of the seventeenth century, was continued by his son Antoine, who painted in England from 1717 to 1747, and by his son-in-law, Blain de Fontenay. Monnoyer was generally known as Baptiste, and in his later years in Britain as Old Baptiste to distinguish him from his son.

## Still-life with basket of flowers, 1690s

oil on canvas, 73.0 x 103.5 cm

Gift of Anne Clemens 1985

This is an extremely fine example of Monnoyer's late painting on canvas. Much of his British work was done between 1690 and 1693 and the painterly qualities and mature style here are typical of late work executed in England. The painting's British provenance is possible evidence.[2] All the species of spring flowers in the painting were available in Britain by the 1690s. However, it is very difficult to ascribe precise dates to his works or distinguish his late French paintings from his British ones.

The fragrant blossoms in a large wicker basket include lilacs, roses, guelder roses, tulips, carnations, honeysuckle, apple blossom, peonies, jonquils and blue convolvulus. They are all flowers that bloom in the English spring around April. Jonquils normally flower earlier and peonies a little later. It was not unusual for flower painters to include combinations of flowers of different seasons by working from drawings, engravings and other paintings. Here the fragile apple blossom, for instance, would not endure the length of time needed to paint it.

The basket is set on a ledge in a graded light against an indigo-coloured background in a tangible space. The satisfyingly decorative qualities of the composition have not been sacrificed to mechanical naturalism. While the formal arrangement of the flowers has a balanced classical stability, the subtle arrangement of colour is complex, rich and Baroque. Light-coloured blooms emerge from the darkness. Here Monnoyer has produced a very stylish flowerpiece of rare and refined taste.

Near-pastel colours and luscious paint quality make Monnoyer's work, in spite of its shadowy Baroque background, a precursor of the lighter French eighteenth-century style of Rococo flower canvases and decorations. The decorative possibilities first suggested by Monnoyer can be seen fully expressed in the Gallery's collection in French works like Jean-Jacques Bachelier's high-keyed *Still-life with flowers and a violin* of 1750.

Monnoyer's floral masterpiece is the only painting by the artist in a public collection in Australasia.

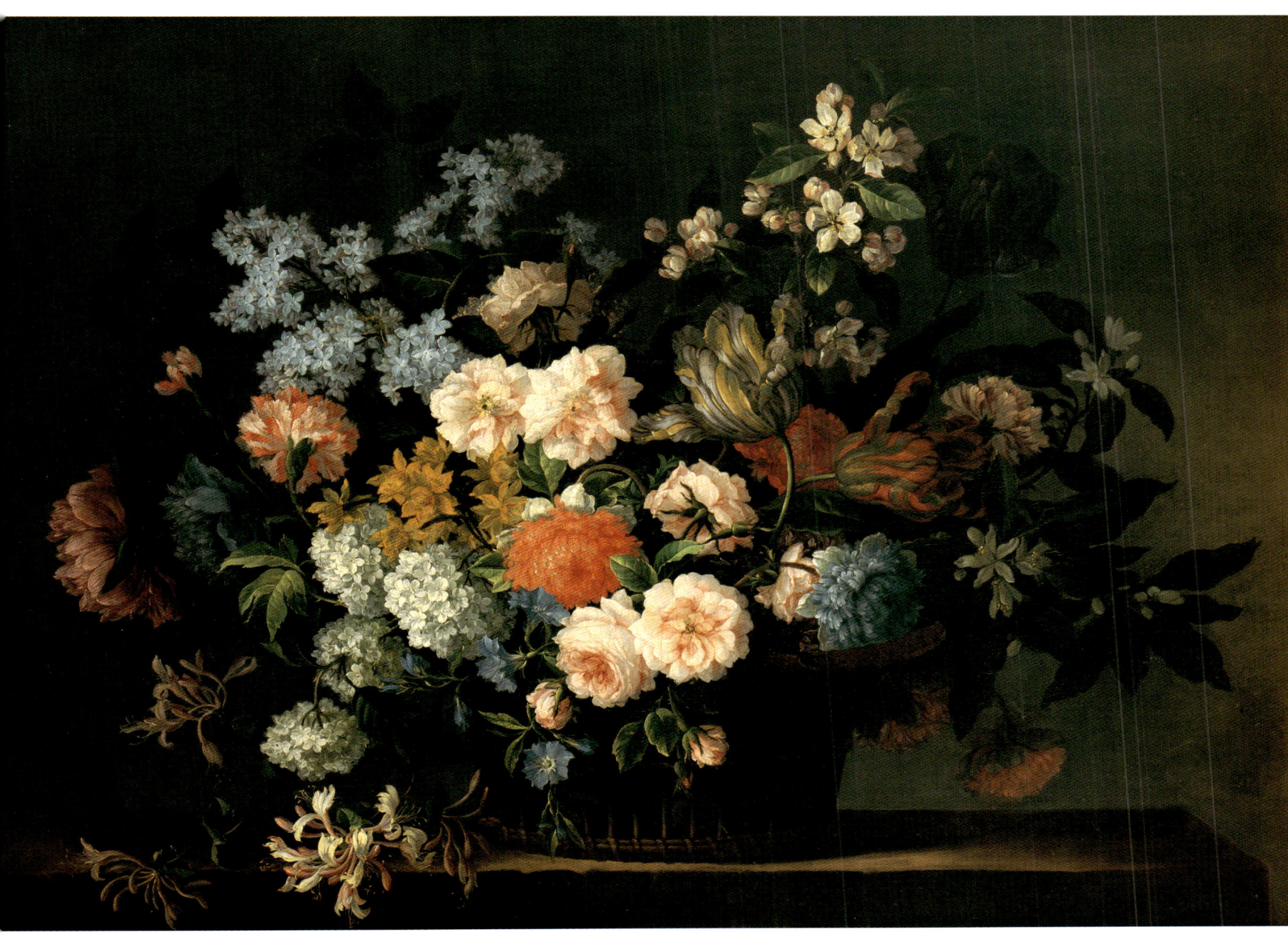

| | |
|---|---|
| **Inscription:** | Signed l.r. corner, oil: "JBaptiste" (J and B in monogram). |
| **Provenance:** | Lewis & Simmons, London, bt 1927 by Miss Jane C. Turnbull of Melbourne (d. June 1963); her estate auction, Joel's, Melbourne, 1964, bt by her niece Anne Clemens, Melbourne. |
| **Exhibitions:** | *Still-life still lives*, AGSA, Adelaide, 1997. *Island to Empire: 300 Years of British Art 1550–1850*, AGSA, Adelaide, 2005. |
| **Literature:** | Ron Radford et al., *Selected Works*, Adelaide: AGSA, 1991, p. 17. Ron Radford et al., *Treasures*, Adelaide: AGSA, 1998, p. 50 (illus.). Terry Ingram, "Saleroom", *Australian Financial Review*, 29 January 1987, p. 20. Ron Radford, Angus Trumble and Christopher Chapman, *Still-life still lives*, Adelaide: AGSA, 1997, pp. 10, 18 (illus. p. 13). |
| **Condition:** | Excellent; it is not known when it was last conserved. |
| **Frame:** | Not original, but English late seventeenth century. |

# Francis Barlow c.1626–1704

Francis Barlow is notable for introducing animals, birds and hunting into British painting and illustration, subjects that are now regarded as characteristically British. He was also the first of the long line of native-born book illustrators and the first professional British-born etcher.

Barlow was born in Lincolnshire about 1626 and on arriving in London was apprenticed to the portrait painter William Sheppard. In 1650 he was elected a member of the Painter-Stainers' Company. In 1652 his first illustrated book, Edward Benlowes's metaphysical epic *Theophila, or Love's Sacrifice*, included numerous human figures. However, by then Barlow was known as "the famous painter of Fowle, Beasts and Birds". Birds remained a speciality, as can be seen in mural decorations at Clandon Park, Surrey.

His etching studies might have been under Francis Cleyn in the mid 1640s. His technique in the medium resembles that of Anthony van Dyck whose *Iconography*, a series of etched portraits of illustrious men, would have been familiar. Barlow would also have known the outstanding English etchings made by Wenceslaus Hollar who came from Germany in the mid sixteenth century. Barlow's very fine etchings for illustrated books included *Æsop's Fables* in 1666 and 1687, John Ogilby's narrative *Androcles, the Roman Slave* in 1668, and many others.

Barlow's successful career further included numerous decorative scenes for painted ceilings and over-doors, but his many canvases of birds and animals in landscape settings are best known. A fish painting, noted in 1653, is the first recorded in the history of British art, and therefore a forerunner to the Gallery's painting by J. W. Lewin (1770–1819) of *Fish catch and Dawes Point, Sydney Harbour*, c.1813, the earliest extant oil painting executed in Australia.

## A lion attacked by hounds, 1694
pen & brown ink, grey wash on paper, 14.8 x 20.3 cm (image)
V. M. Stuart Bequest Fund 1991

In this spirited drawing executed towards the end of Barlow's career, the lion is in heraldic *passant* mode (in reverse) and also a dynamically living creature. Savagely attacked by six dogs, the magnificent beast has already killed two of them and has a third in its powerful jaws. A more than interested eagle hovers low in the sky. (Eagles and lions regularly appear in Barlow's illustrations to *Æsop's Fables*.) Barely evident behind the oak-covered mound to the right, two terrified men hide and witness the violent animal fight. This lion in his own territory shows no sense of distress or fear as he eliminates the attackers one by one. The lion conquers all. The presentation hints at heraldry so this might therefore be a symbolic British lion, perhaps alluding to Britain's growing economic and mercantile power against the 'dogs' of continental Europe. The specific meaning or purpose of the drawing is not known.

The earliest signed and dated work by Barlow is a 1648 drawing of the biblical David single-handedly slaying the lion. Lions continued to appear in his illustrations throughout his long career. Barlow always represents the lion, the king of the beasts, in a noble manner, almost emblematically. He may have originally based them on studies made of the lions kept at the Tower of London, or seen with other wild animals and birds that were on show in London taverns and country estates at the time.

Barlow was a prolific draughtsman who usually used brown ink applied with a quill pen and strengthened with grey wash, as in this highly finished drawing. The carefully executed outlines of the forms were meant to aid the easy transfer to a copper plate for engraving or etching, but no resulting print is known. The lion *passant* in reverse indicates that this may have been intended for an engraving in which the image is reversed. The drawing shows some influence of the Flemish-Italian artist Jan van der Straet called Stradanus (1523–1605), whose hunting scenes executed over a century earlier were famous and would have been known to Barlow through engravings. This drawing by Barlow can be compared, for example, with the Gallery's two drawings by Stradanus, one of which shows dogs attacking deer, the other dogs attacking badgers.

This is the only example of Barlow's original work held in an Australasian collection and is the earliest British animal image in the Art Gallery of South Australia.

**Inscription:** Signed and dated l.r., pen & brown ink: "F. Barlow 1694".
**Provenance:** W. M. A. Moseley, Britain (d. 1976), his sale, Christie's, London, 2 March 1976, lot 7; Colin Hunter 1976–91; Sotheby's, London, 11 July 1991, lot 26.
**Exhibition:** *Island to Empire: 300 Years of British Art 1550–1850*, AGSA, Adelaide, 2005.
**Literature:** *Important English Drawings and Watercolours*, London: Christie's, Manson & Woods Ltd, 2 March 1976, p. 9 (illus.). Edward Hodnett, *Francis Barlow: First Master of English Book Illustration*, London, 1978. *Early British Drawings from the Collection of Colin Hunter*, London: Sotheby's, 11 July 1991, p. 42 (illus.).
**Condition:** Good.

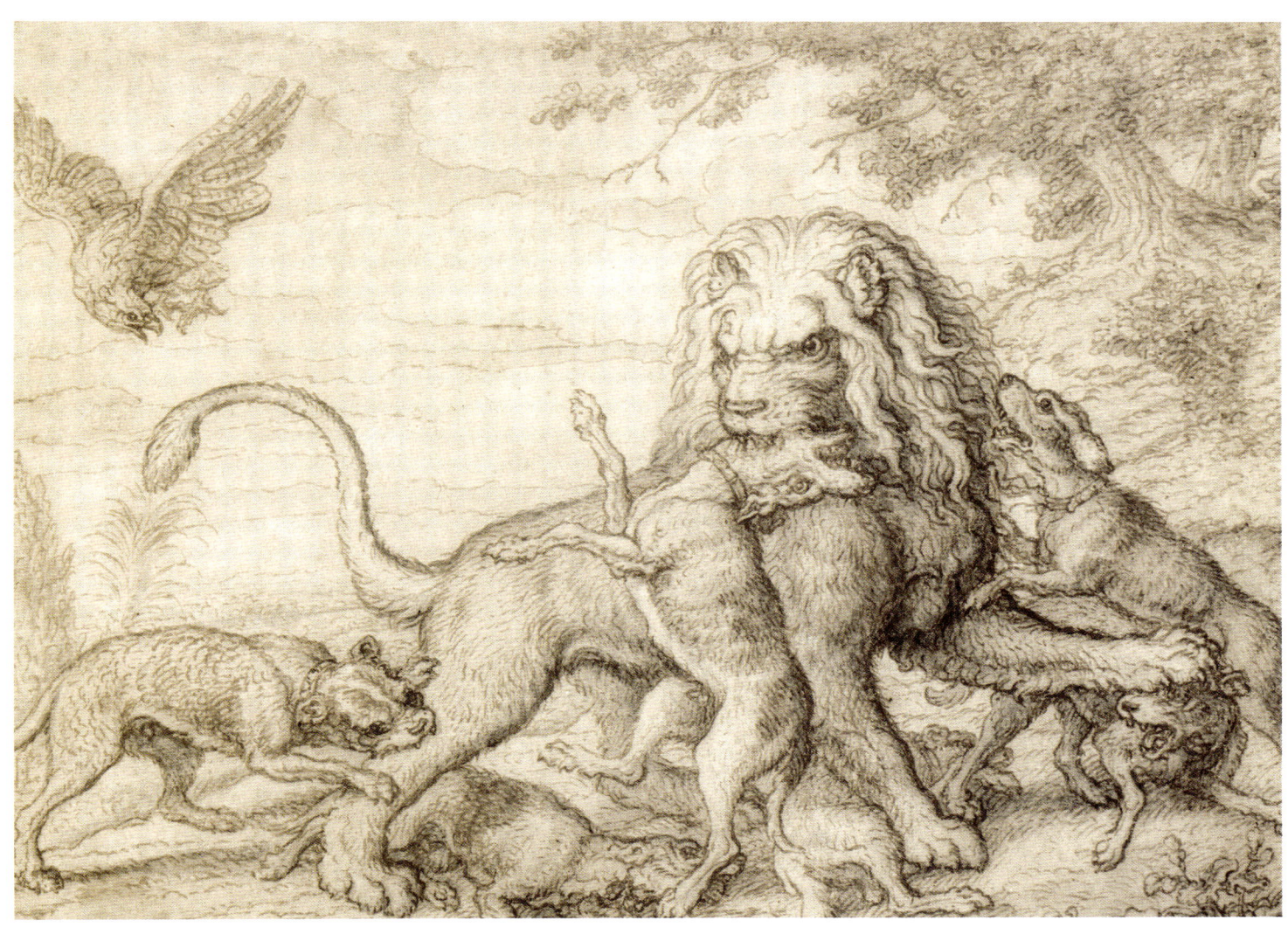

# Edward Collier c.1640–1710?

The Dutch-born Edward Collier (Edwaert Colyer in the Netherlands) was one of the first artists to introduce still-life and trompe l'œil painting into British art. When portraiture, long the dominant genre in British art, was at a low ebb at the end of the seventeenth century Collier's work, and Monnoyer's, constituted a refreshing alternative.

Collier was born in Breda in the northern Netherlands about 1640; his family might have been of English descent. Very little is known about his life but he may have trained and worked at Haarlem before he was admitted into the Guild of St Luke at Leiden in 1673. He was registered at Leiden until 1681 and working in Amsterdam in 1686. One might speculate that he followed his countryman William of Orange to London hoping for special patronage from the new king after the English revolution in 1688. He was certainly in London by 1693.

The latest known date of a British work by Collier is December 1706. It is believed he died in 1710. It is likely that he returned several times to the Netherlands after his first arrival in London.

Although still-life flourished in Holland throughout the seventeenth century and later, it was something of a novelty in British art. A minor painter Alexander Marshal is known to have painted flower pieces in the 1660s and another, Parry Walter painted a few still-lives in the mid seventeenth century. The much better-known Dutch-trained painter Simon Verelst (see p. 84) painted flower pictures (and portraits) in Britain from the 1670s. Nicolas de Largillierre, French but trained in Flanders, painted still-lives in London in the 1670s and Jean-Baptiste Monnoyer, the French master of flowers (see p. 96), came to London in 1690 possibly just before Collier. It seems that no painter could make a sustained living in London exclusively from still-life painting until the arrival of Collier and Monnoyer.

Many of Collier's Dutch and English paintings are vanitas still-lives, that is, still-life subjects that include objects such as a human skull, an hour-glass or a snuffed candle as allusions to the transience of life and the passing of time. Dutch vanitas painting was developed in Leiden where Collier had trained and worked. That city remained the centre for the genre until the end of the seventeenth century. In Britain, however, Collier is remembered for his trompe l'œil. His still-lives frequently include trompe l'œil printed books, hand-written documents, newspapers, globes and maps. His letter-rack subjects always contain written matter and many such paintings survive in British collections. They clearly appealed to literal and literary British tastes. Trompe l'œil painting became a specialised though minor genre in Britain and France in the eighteenth and early nineteenth centuries and was exported to the United States. There it became an important art form, reaching its height of popularity near the end of the nineteenth century.

## Letter rack, c.1698
oil on canvas, 48.5 x 61.5 cm
Gift of James & Diana Ramsay and the James & Diana Ramsay Fund
through the Art Gallery of South Australia Foundation 1991

This is a typical example of Collier's London work of the 1690s. In Britain the artist's straightforward letter racks are often more successful than his combinations of still-life with trompe l'œil literary matter. In the latter there is sometimes an unresolved and less convincing sense of real space between objects and written documents. In his letter racks, and also in his trompe l'œil paintings of engravings pinned to walls, two-dimensional objects are held by pins, tacks or leather straps onto flat panels and there is no ambiguity in the illusion of space.

Here a flageolet – a recorder-like instrument – and a music score appear among other objects more commonly found on his letter racks. They include a letter addressed with the artist's characteristic hand-written name, profession and city, a folded copy of the *London Gazette* dated to 5 April in an illegible year 168[…], a sealed letter, a seal, a stick of sealing wax, a rolled document bearing a partly obscured number (probably a date), a quill pen, scissors, a letter-opener, two wig combs as well as the bound music score, which is open and displaying a minuet. All are meticulously rendered to give the illusion that they are held in by leather straps tacked onto the letter-rack board. The only exception is the flageolet which is suspended from one of the tacks. The mainly masculine objects can be seen as part of a social history of middle-class London city life at the end of the seventeenth century. The painting would probably have hung in a hallway or study.

Collier's still-lives and trompe l'œils often had symbolic or esoteric meanings that can be difficult for us to decipher though they were clear to the audiences of his day. For instance the partly illegible date of 5 April 168[…] could refer to the artist's date of first arrival in London or to an event in the Glorious ("Bloodless") Revolution that began in June 1688 and continued through 1689. The partly obscured number on the rolled document could be interpreted as 1698, which is a likely date for the painting.

Collier's letter racks and his trompe l'œil still-lives usually include a folded paper, presumably an addressed letter, with his name and city (in this case London) provided as if in self-advertisement. He might have placed such paintings in shop windows or inns to attract attention for commissions. We can assume that a patron could dictate the objects of his fancy for inclusion in a still-life or letter rack. This painting was likely produced for an amateur musician or music lover. The music score is of a playable but not masterful minuet, doubtless for the adjacent flageolet, and either a favourite piece of music or even composed by the patron.

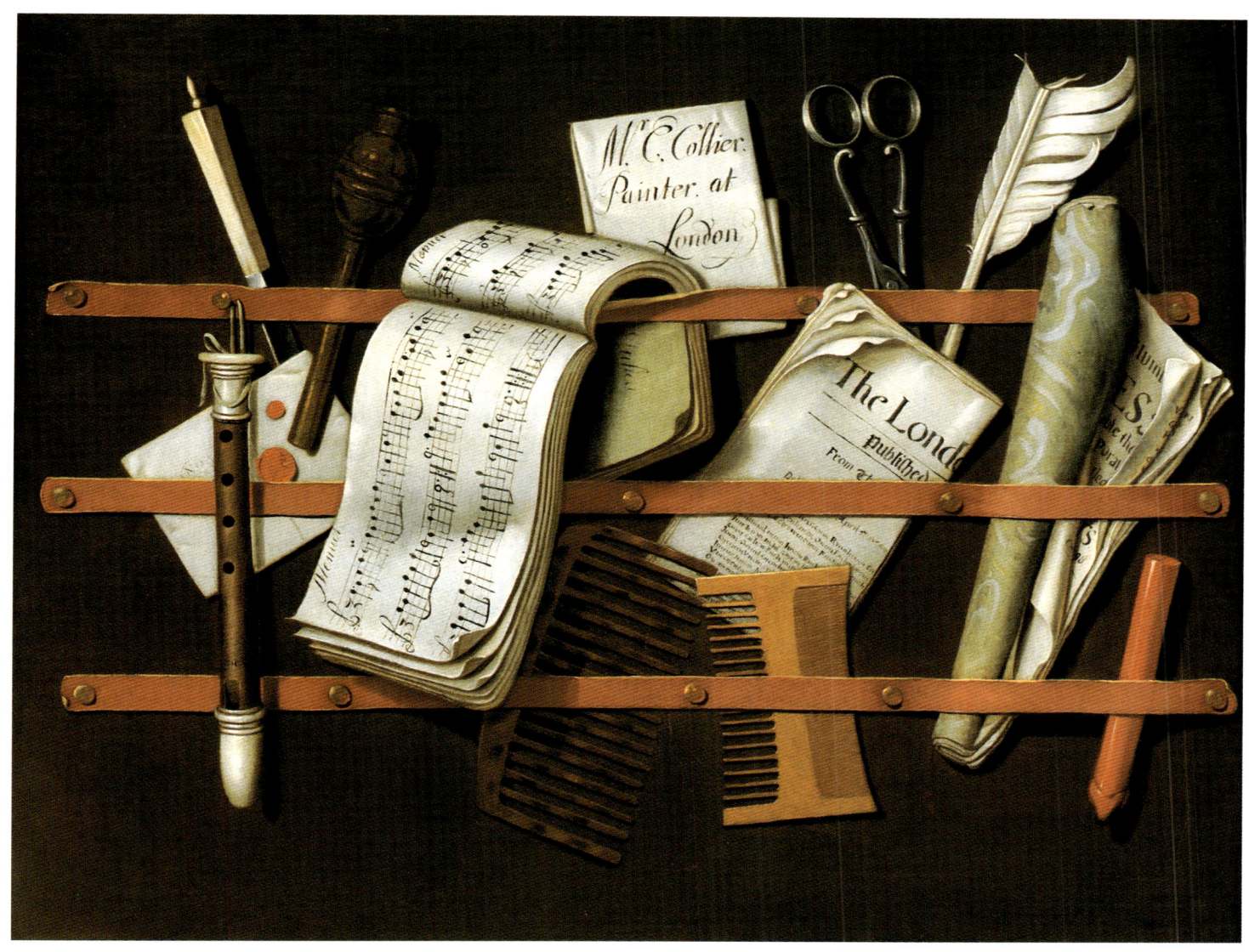

| Inscription: | Signed, top c., oil (on folded paper depicted in letter rack): "M<sup>r</sup> E. Collier. / Painter. at / London". |
| --- | --- |
| Provenance: | From Peter H. Tillou Works of Art, London. |
| Exhibitions: | *A Celebration: Recent acquisitions of heritage and contemporary art*, AGSA, Adelaide, 1996. *Still-life still lives*, AGSA, Adelaide, 1997. *Island to Empire: 300 Years of British Art 1550–1850*, AGSA, Adelaide, 2005. |
| Literature: | Ron Radford, Angus Trumble and Christopher Chapman, *Still-life still lives*, Adelaide: AGSA, 1997, p. 16 (illus. p. 17). |
| Condition: | Excellent; probably conserved in London just prior to acquisition. |
| Frame: | Not original. |

# James Thornhill 1675–1734

James Thornhill was the only major British-born exponent of Baroque mural painting. The practice was of continental, especially Italian origins. Trained in England in the 1690s, Thornhill's independent career commenced at the start of the eighteenth century. He was influenced directly by Antonio Verrio (1639–1707) and Louis Laguerre (1663–1721), the leading continental practitioners in Britain of a style in which crowds of swarming figures decorated ambitious architectural interiors, both secular and sacred. Pietro da Cortona (1596–1669) and Luca Giordano (1634–1705) were their main Italian sources.

Born at Woolland in Dorset in 1675, Thornhill was apprenticed in 1689 for seven years to his distant relative, the now forgotten artist Thomas Highmore (1660–1720), who was Sergeant Painter successively to William III, Queen Anne and George I. In 1702 Thornhill worked as an assistant to Verrio on wall decorations at Hampton Court palace. He was made a freeman of the Painters-Stainers Company in 1704 and the following year received his first known commission, which was to decorate Stoke Edith, a grand house in Herefordshire. Subsequent important commissions followed, for Greenwich Hospital 1707–14 and 1718–25, Chatsworth 1709, Hampton Court 1714–15, Queens College, Oxford, 1716, and – his most famous work – St Paul's Cathedral 1718–21.

In 1711, following the example of Sir Godfrey Kneller, he set up a teaching academy for young artists and then in 1716 took over Kneller's Academy. William Hogarth (1697–1764), who would become the finest British artist of the first half of the eighteenth century, in 1729 married Thornhill's daughter Jane. In 1720 when Thornhill became Sergeant Painter to George I he was knighted, the first British-born artist so honoured. With his death in 1734 Baroque decoration in Britain came to an end, superseded by the classical Palladian taste of Lord Burlington and his circle.

Thornhill's first ideas for commissioned schemes were sketched in pen-and-wash drawings like the Gallery's fine example. He was a prolific draughtsman; some 400 such drawings survive, most of them now housed in the British Museum and the Victoria & Albert Museum, London. The sketches on paper were then developed into modellos, larger oil sketches on canvas, to be presented for final approval. Once approved, scaffolding would be erected and the artist would begin to cover the walls and ceilings. Thornhill, like Verrio and Laguerre, worked with oil paint on dry plaster rather than the fresco method used in Italy, where water-mixed pigments were applied to wet plaster. Fresco was unsuitable for the colder and damper climate of Britain.

## Minerva and the Gods of Olympus: A design for the hall ceiling at Easton Neston, c.1712
pen & brown ink, grey wash, black chalk on paper, 25.3 x 46.1 cm
V. B. F. Young Bequest Fund 1992

*Minerva and the Gods of Olympus* is typical of Thornhill's design sketches. It was for a ceiling in the great country house Easton Neston in Northamptonshire. The architect at Easton Neston was Nicholas Hawksmoor, developing a concept by Christopher Wren, and the building was completed in 1702. Ten years later, probably about 1711, Lord Leominster, who had built the house, commissioned mural and ceiling designs to decorate the entrance hall and grand staircase. Thornhill's wall decorations at Easton Neston, still extant, are monochrome so this sketch in grey wash gives an accurate tonal impression of how the ceiling was intended to look. The lack of colour hinted at marble or plaster relief sculpture and reflected a new taste for the austere classical over the sumptuous Baroque.

This subject is an allegory of civilising force, a morally uplifting theme considered appropriate for an impressive entrance hall. It is an illusionistic opening up into a sky that teems with ancient Greco-Roman gods reclining on clouds high above the painted architecture. Minerva, goddess of wisdom and patron of the arts and sciences, presides on the highest cloud. She was the daughter of Zeus, the supreme deity (seen immediately below with an eagle at his feet) and his wife Hera. Minerva here appears as a figure in armour with a spear, shield and helmet; she is the defender of civilisation and hence her symbolic importance in the eighteenth century, the Age of Reason. Lower down from Minerva and Zeus we can identify other denizens of Mount Olympus. They include Hera, Aphrodite, Poseidon, Dionysus, Cronus and Hermes, the last depicted flying into the cloudy space. The theme and composition are very similar to a number of works by Verrio, upon whose compositions and subjects Thornhill at times made recognisable variations. On the reverse of the drawing are very faint pencil inscriptions written in what appears to be an early-eighteenth-century hand, possibly by Thornhill himself.[1] They could refer to Pallas Athene who was the Greek equivalent of the Roman Minerva – and who in Thornhill's world also had an equivalent in the warrior goddess Britannia. In the eighteenth century there was a cheerful muddling of the use of Greek and Roman antiquity.

The figures are drawn with vivacity and exuberance but the composition is well contained in an architectural framework that is in turn surrounded by emblems. The sketch offers alternative designs for the spandrels, including Lord

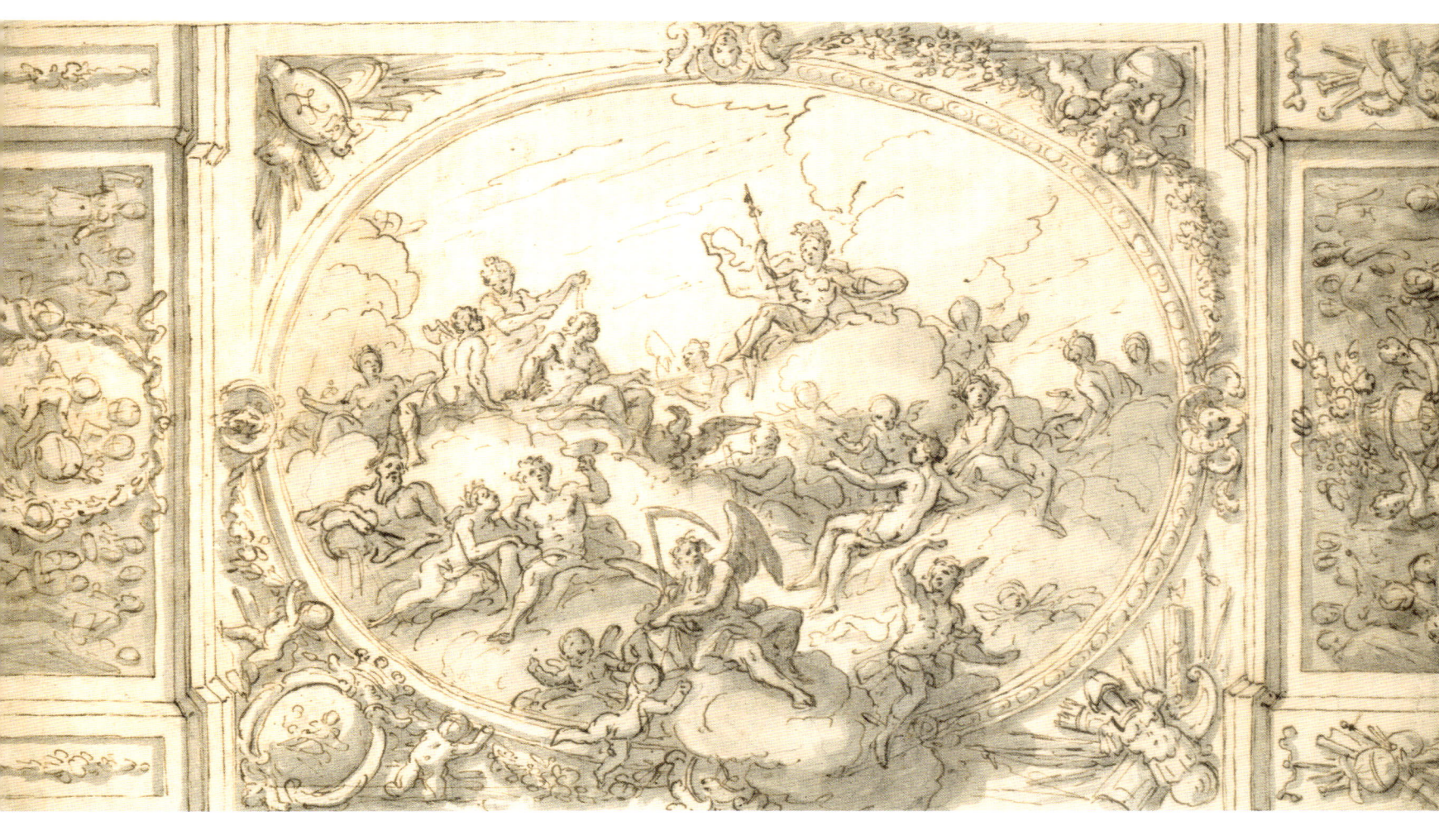

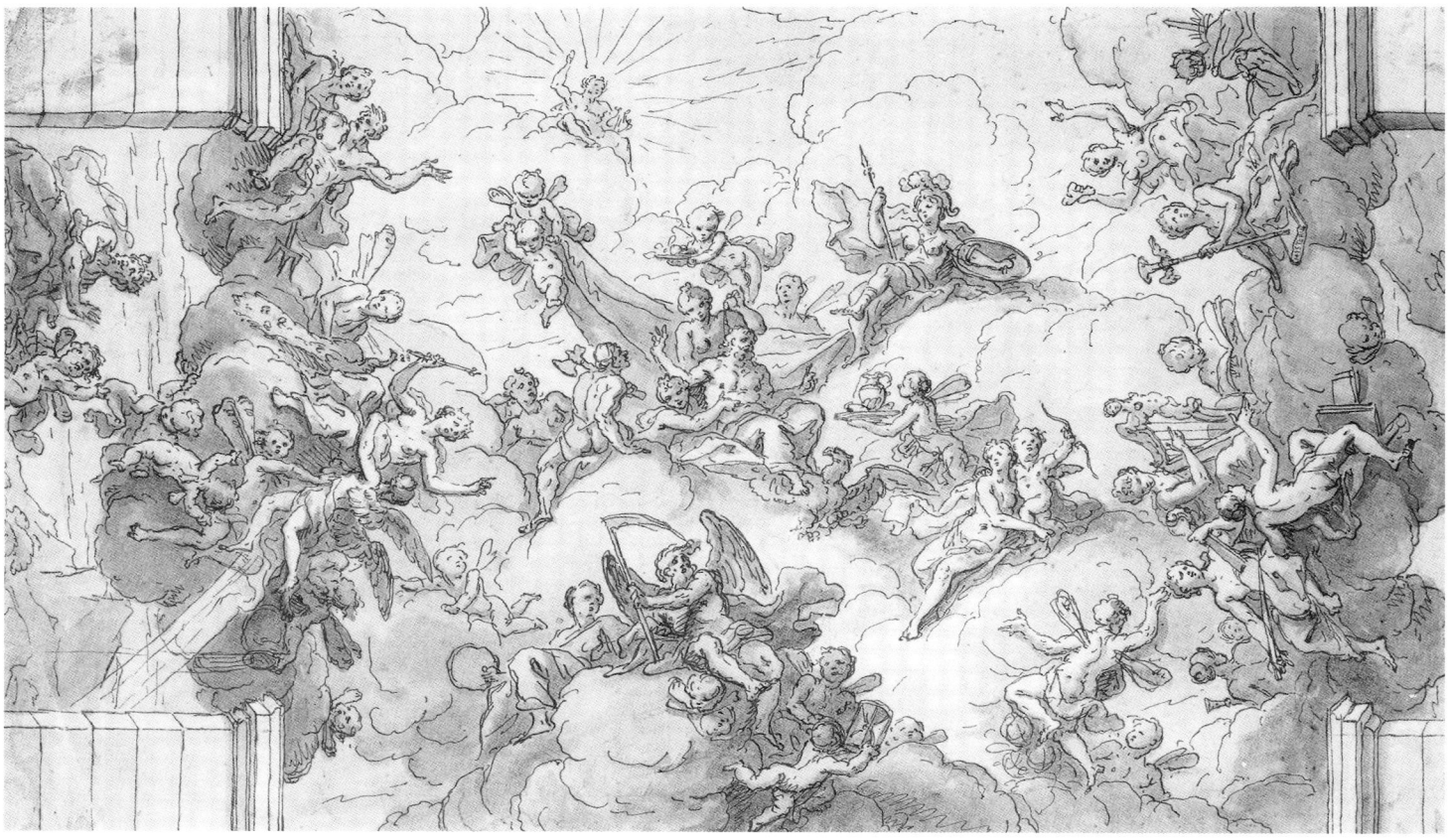

James Thornhill, *Marriage of Jupiter and Juno*. © Copyright The Trustees of The British Museum, London

Leominster's intertwined initials and his coronet. Like most of Thornhill's drawings, this very fine example is livelier and more animated than his finished murals.

The ceiling decoration at Easton Neston was never realised. Thornhill worked on the monochrome grey murals that surround the staircase but Lord Leominster died in 1713 and work was probably then stopped. His son and heir was only a minor when Leominster died.

We can date the drawing to just after the completion of Thornhill's work at Greenwich in 1712. It is based on designs he made for an upper hall ceiling there that was abandoned. The British Museum holds another version of the composition, without the oval surround, under the title of *Marriage of Jupiter and Juno*.

There exists another sketch design for the hall ceiling at Easton Neston. It depicts *Queen Anne as Britannia promoting the Arts*, the attributes of Britannia being similar to those of Minerva, on whom she is based. That sketch had the same provenance as the Gallery's drawing, both held until 1990 by Thornhill's descendants. A sketch for the entrance-hall walls at Easton Neston is in the Thornhill Sketch Book in the British Museum.

*Minerva and the Gods of Olympus* is the only work by Thornhill in Australia.

Inscription: Inscribed verso, pencil (very faint, with some words illeg.): bot.c. "sacrif to Pall-/ muse"; c.r. "Troph of .../ Arch ... Geog .../ War ... peace"; l.r. "Pallas/ Fame .../ who is...Acts of Vc/... / nine muses 7 lib. Arts"; l.r. "virtuous acts/ Love of her country/ Archt/ Geom/ Perspect/ Unity/ Painting".

Provenance: The artist and by descent in his family until 1990; private collection; purchased from Hazlitt, Gooden & Fox, London, January 1992.

Exhibitions: *English Drawings*, Hazlitt, Gooden & Fox, London, 1990, no. 15. *Island to Empire: 300 Years of British Art 1550–1850*, AGSA, Adelaide, 2005.

Literature: *English Drawings*, London: Hazlitt, Gooden & Fox, 1990, p. 33 (illus.).

Condition: Excellent.

# Godfrey Kneller 1646–1723

Godfrey Kneller – and his conventional style – dominated English portraiture for half a century, from the death of Peter Lely in 1680 until the rise of William Hogarth in the 1730s. He was enormously prolific and through the reigns of six sovereigns everyone of note sat to him: monarchs, aristocrats, gentry, intellectuals, artists, soldiers, politicians and beauties.

Born in Lübeck, Kneller studied in Amsterdam from about 1665 under Ferdinand Bol (1616–1680) and Rembrandt. In 1672, in Rome, he came in contact with the leading Baroque sculptor Gianlorenzo Bernini (1598–1680) and the painter Carlo Maratta (1625–1713). A year later, in Venice, he was influenced by the contemporary painter Sebastiano Bombelli (1635–1719) and the great works of Titian from the past. He returned from Venice to Germany in 1675.

On his arrival in England in 1676, aged thirty, Kneller was the most cosmopolitan of the many foreign artists to work there since the death of Anthony van Dyck. In England influences from the portraits of Van Dyck, Lely, the resident French artists and the native English school combined with his earlier continental experiences to form his mature style. This was a distinctive, more solidly modelled and broader variant of Van Dyck's grand Baroque manner, a style that persisted throughout the early eighteenth century in Britain, North America and to some extent in Europe.

In 1688 Kneller and John Riley were jointly appointed Principal Painters to the crown and from Riley's death in 1691 Kneller was sole occupant of the position for a further thirty-two years. In 1711 he became the first Governor of the 'Kneller Academy of Painting and Drawing', the first such institution to be set up in London and the training ground for a number of artists including Joseph Highmore. Kneller was knighted in 1692 and in 1715 George I acknowledged his prominent social position and his services to so many sovereigns by granting him a baronetcy, the only artist to receive one. He died in 1723, the birth year of Joshua Reynolds, who would follow Kneller's tradition.

## Lady Henrietta Crofts, Duchess of Bolton, c.1715

oil on canvas, 127.0 x 102.0 cm

Elder Bequest Fund 1991

This portrait is an excellent example of Kneller's mature style, painted towards the end of his extraordinarily long career. His recent baronetcy, granted in 1715, is appended to the signature on the lower left of the painting.[1]

The sitter, Lady Henrietta Crofts, was born in 1683, the natural daughter of the first Duke of Monmouth (died 1685), and Eleanor, daughter of Sir Robert Needham; Monmouth, acknowledged by Charles II as a son by a mistress, had changed his name from James Crofts to James Scott on his marriage to the Countess of Buccleuch. In 1697 Henrietta, the sister of Jane Myddelton, a famous beauty, married, as his third wife, Charles Paulet (1661–1722), soon to be second Duke of Bolton. She had one son, Lord Nassau Paulet. She was appointed a Lady of the Bedchamber to the Princess of Wales in 1714, just before our portrait was painted; it may have been commissioned to commemorate the occasion though not completed until later. Kneller had earlier, in about 1700, painted a full-length portrait of the Duchess standing holding flowers, now known only from a 1703 mezzotint engraving made by John Smith.[2] The full-length could have been commissioned to mark the occasion when she became Duchess of Bolton upon her husband's succession to the dukedom in 1699. The Duchess of Bolton died in 1730 aged forty-seven.[3]

Our three-quarter-length portrait depicts the attractive thirty-two-year-old duchess seated in a silver-white satin dress and, as in Kneller's earlier portrait of her, she holds a small basket of flowers. The flowers include roses, narcissus, primulas, lime blossom and lime leaves and fruit. The fragrant spring blooms are a conventional symbolic reference to the sitter's beauty and virtue. The flowers are also a decorative touch that enlivens the somewhat stoic mood of the painting without resorting to the extreme floral embellishment used in much French portraiture of the eighteenth century.[4] But Kneller was fundamentally a seventeenth-century artist and the vanitas theme is seldom far from the surface of seventeenth-century art. The plucked flowers, many in full bloom, are a symbol not only of beauty but also of the brevity of life, since they pass so quickly from bloom to decay.

The Duchess is seated, her left arm resting on a wall fountain formed by a classical dolphin spouting water and housed in a scallop-arched niche, with a curved basin below. On the left of the painting is a stone pier decorated with a bas-relief, bearing Kneller's signature at the base, and between this pier and the sitter is the glimpse of a cool Italianate garden with tall cypress trees. Fountains and flowing water have long been associated with women in Western literature and art and here probably symbolise, in a general way, the flow of life and love. More particularly, from antiquity the dolphin was an attribute of Venus and an emblem of love. The attributes of Neoplatonic virtue were not uncommon in Kneller's female portraits. Indeed Kneller's most famous group of female portraits, the 'Hampton Court Beauties', all contain references to Neoplatonic Renaissance doctrines of virtuous love and beauty as does Lely's famous

# Godfrey Kneller

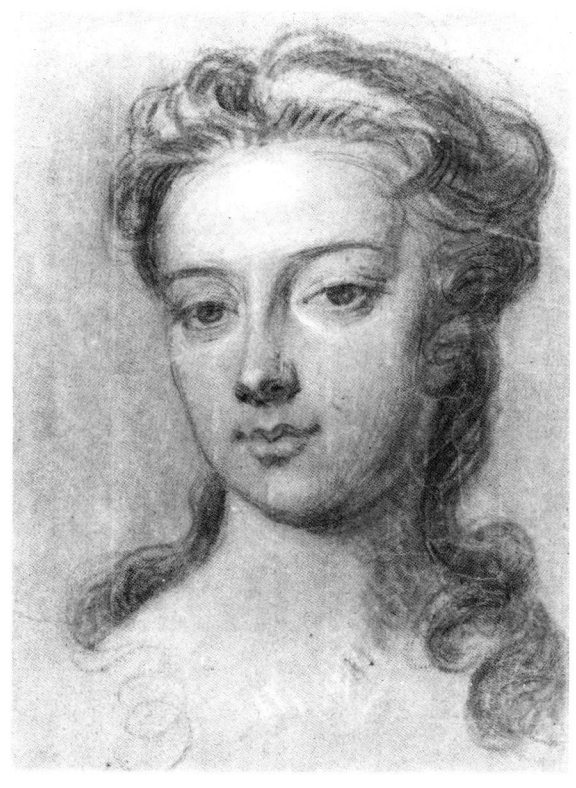

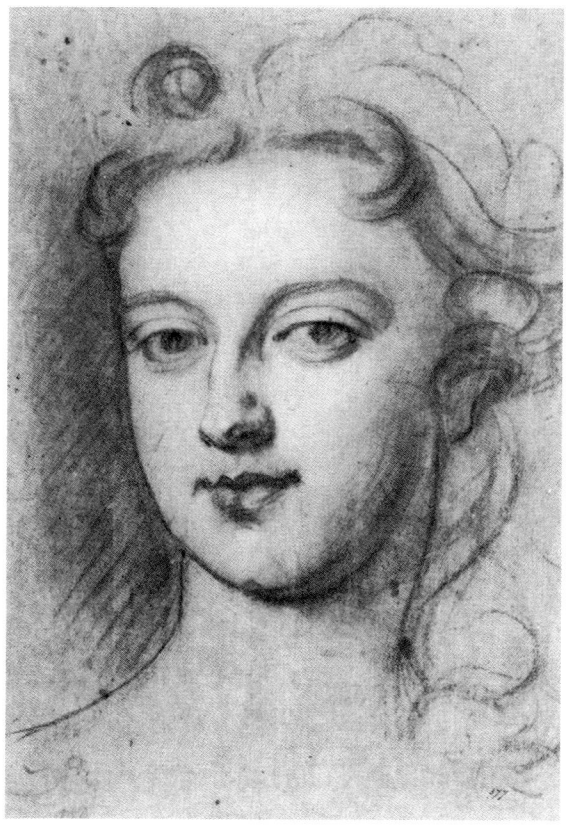

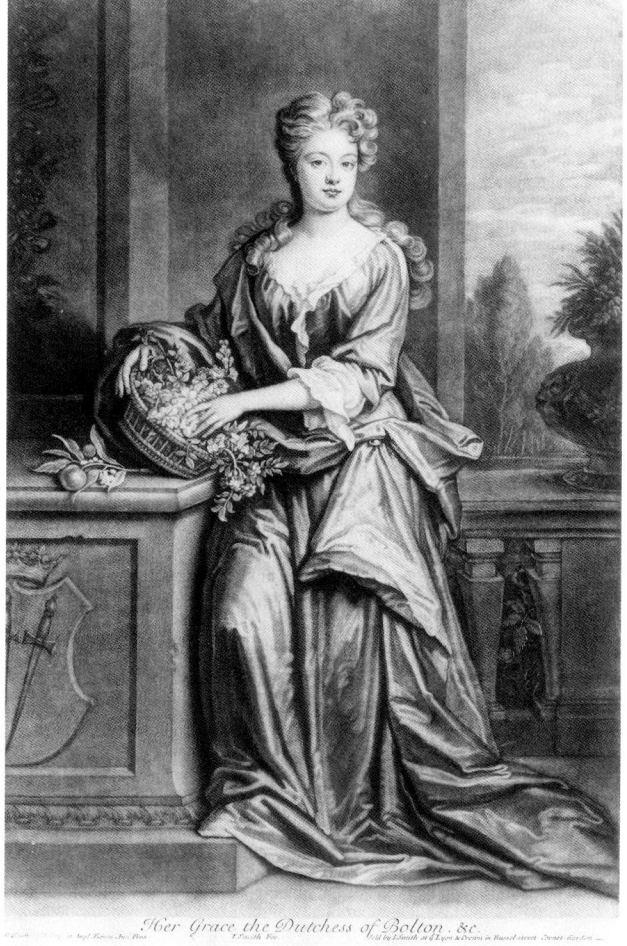

above: John Smith after Godfrey Kneller, *Lady Henrietta Crofts, Duchess of Bolton*, 1703. © Copyright The Trustees of The British Museum, London

top left: Godfrey Kneller, *Women's head*, c.1715. © Copyright The Trustees of The British Museum, London

left: Godfrey Kneller, *Women's head*, c.1715. V & A Images/ Victoria & Albert Museum, London

opposite: Godfrey Kneller, *Lady Henrietta Crofts, Duchess of Bolton*, c.1715, oil on canvas, 127.0 x 102.0 cm. Elder Bequest Fund 1991

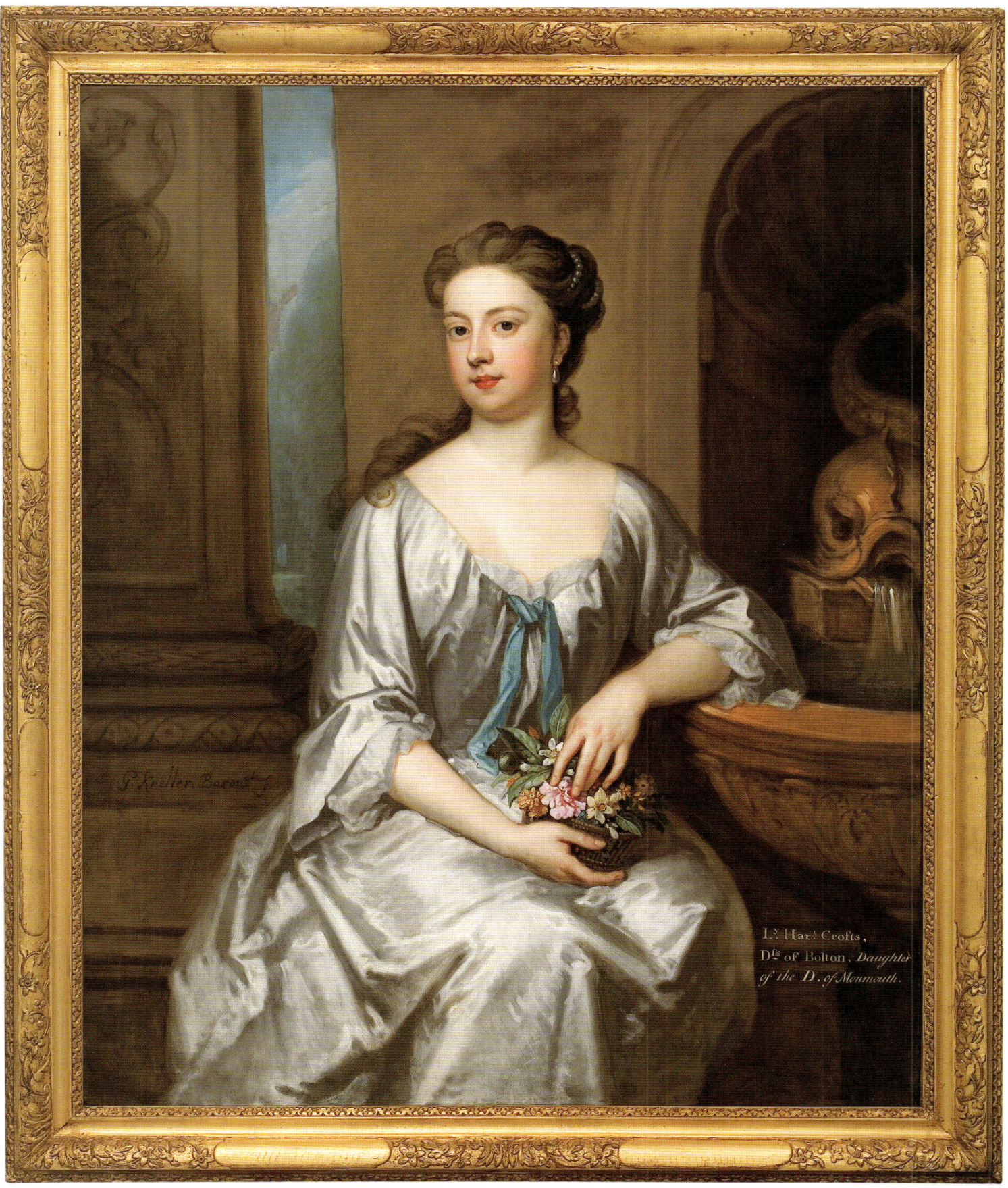

series of 'Windsor Beauties', which is Kneller's precedent. It is interesting to note that the Duchess of Bolton's aunt, Mrs Myddelton, was one of Lely's Windsor Beauties and she too was depicted beside a dolphin fountain. In an earlier Neoplatonic allusion, Kneller's *The Duchess of Grafton*, 1690, one of his Hampton Court Beauties, associates with a dolphin fountain.

The Duchess of Bolton's half-turned head, her regular features and deep-grey eyes directed at the viewer are characteristic of Kneller's formalised female portrait type. Although his manner ultimately derives from Van Dyck, his female faces from the second half of his British career have much more in common with Van Dyck's teacher Rubens. The modelling of the features and turn of the head in this portrait are, for instance, reminiscent of the well-known painting by Rubens, *Toilet of Venus*, 1613 (Liechtenstein Collection, Vaduz). In 1697 Kneller visited Brussels where he studied numerous works by Rubens and thenceforth stereotype faces typical of Rubens can be seen in most of his female portraits. They became frozen into what has been called the 'Kneller mask', a type that dominated British (and American) portraiture until overtaken by Hogarth, Highmore and early work by Allan Ramsay. This portrait's 'Kneller mask' is possibly based on two preparatory drawings, one held by the British Museum and the other by the Victoria & Albert Museum.[5]

Kneller's last period, exemplified here, was a phase that revealed his taste for a more austere and classical form. The Duchess is solidly and firmly modelled and wears a white gown that hints at a Roman robe, almost suggesting that she could be carved from marble. The background, including the fountain, suggests ancient architecture. She is calm and grave and possesses a sense of decorum lacking in the recent past in Lely's work and in late Baroque or Rococo portraiture in France in Kneller's time. There is no sentiment, there are no flamboyant frills or garlands and the palette is restrained. Kneller's gradual shift in the early eighteenth century from the Baroque to a style based more on antiquity is parallelled in the sculpture and architecture in England of the same period and shares the contemporary classical qualities of English Augustan prose.

**Inscription:** Signed l.l. near base of pillar, oil: "G. Kneller. Baron.<sup>t</sup> F". Not dated. Inscribed l.r., oil: "L<sup>y</sup>. Har.<sup>t</sup> [*sic*] Crofts, / D<sup>ss</sup> of Bolton. Daughter / of the D. of Monmouth.".

**Provenance:** Lord Northesk, anonymous sale, Christie's, London, 16 February 1951, lot 148, sold to Ron Appleby; Martin Crabbe, Esq., Stanton Manor House, anonymous sale, Christie's, London, 23 November 1984, lot 70; bought for the Art Gallery of South Australia from Christie's, London, 12 April 1991.

**Exhibitions:** *A Celebration: Recent acquisitions of heritage and contemporary art*, AGSA, Adelaide, 1996. *Island to Empire: 300 Years of British Art 1550–1850*, AGSA, Adelaide, 2005.

**Literature:** J. Douglas Stewart, *Sir Godfrey Kneller and the English Baroque Portrait*, New York, 1983, p. 95, no. 101A.

**Condition:** Excellent; last conserved in 1998 by Artlab Australia, Adelaide.

**Frame:** Probably original.

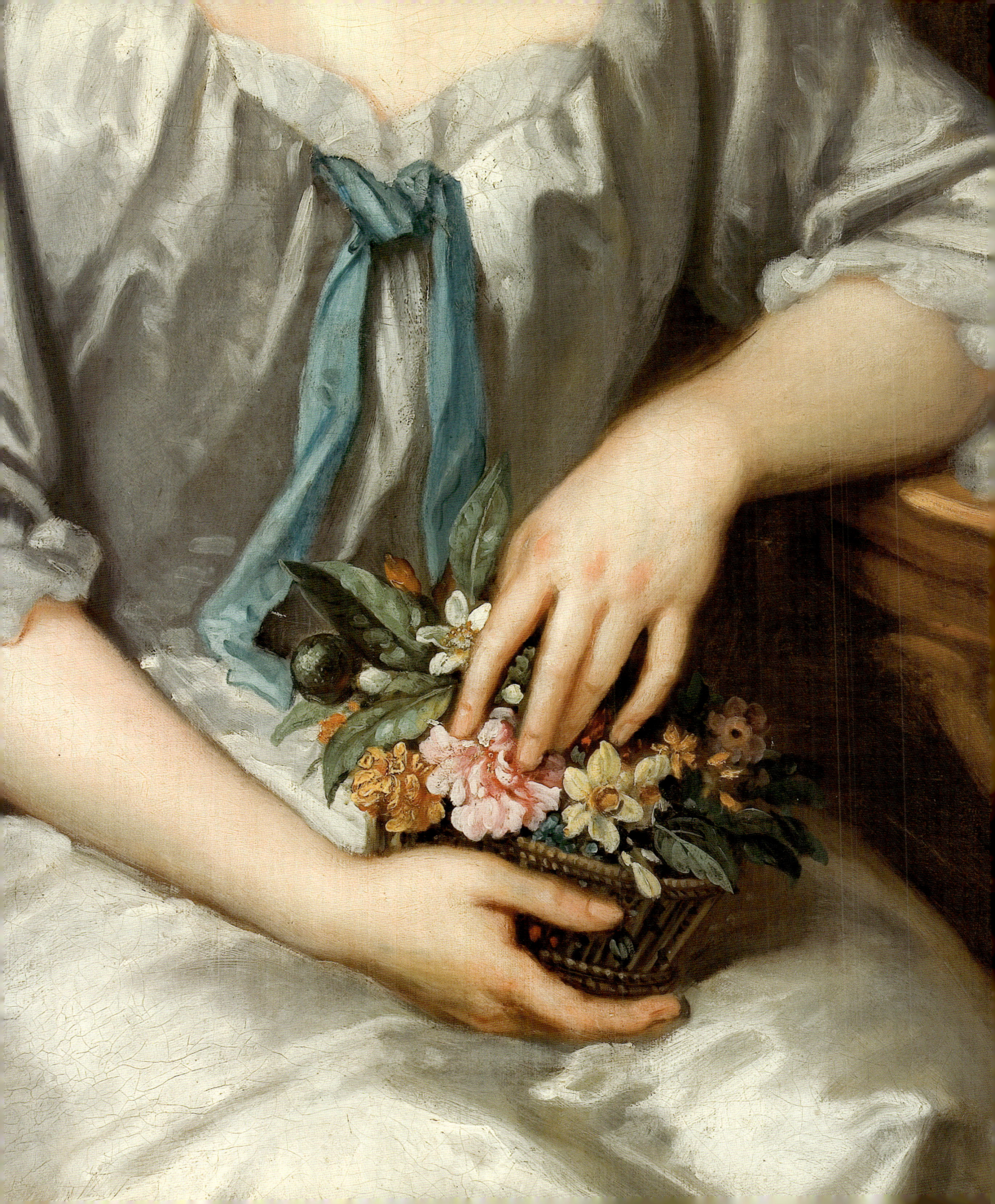

# Joseph Highmore 1693–1780

Joseph Highmore was amongst the finest British portrait painters in the thirty-three-year reign (1727–60) of King George II and also an occasional painter of historical and literary themes. He was an almost exact contemporary of William Hogarth whose narrative works had some influence on him. Highmore's portraits are lively and individual and are mainly of the middle classes. They range from full-lengths and conversation pieces to portraits on a small scale.

Born in London in 1693, Joseph Highmore was the nephew of the now forgotten Thomas Highmore (1660–1720), Sergeant Painter to William III, Queen Anne and George I. He abandoned law studies in 1713 for painting, at Godfrey Kneller's Academy, and continued to study there for about ten years, during which time it was taken over by James Thornhill, in 1716. He met Hogarth at St Martin's Lane Academy in 1720 and his portraits share some of Hogarth's sense of character. In 1732 Highmore travelled abroad, first to Düsseldorf to see Old Master paintings and then to Antwerp principally to study the greatest works by Rubens, his favourite artist. In 1734 he visited Paris where he responded directly to the French Rococo movement.

Highmore became a friend of the novelist Samuel Richardson and painted a series of illustrations to the writer's *Adventures of Pamela*. They were reproduced as engravings published in 1745 and became very famous. The influence of both Hogarth and French Rococo art can be seen in that narrative series. The twelve *Pamela* paintings are now equally divided between three museums: Tate, London, the Fitzwilliam Museum, Cambridge, and the National Gallery of Victoria, Melbourne, the last of which holds the largest public collection of paintings by Highmore. Highmore was also a writer on art whose publications included studies of Rubens.

In 1716 Highmore married Susanna Hiller, born in 1690 and thus three years his senior. After her death in 1750, aged sixty, the artist stayed a widower for the remaining thirty years of his life. Under his father's guidance Highmore's son Anthony became a semi-professional painter of portraits and topographical landscapes but gave up art when his father retired. The daughter Susanna married the Reverend John Duncombe fairly late in life, in 1761. Highmore retired from London and from painting in 1762 to live in Canterbury with his newly married daughter. By that time Joshua Reynolds was established as the leading portrait painter in London. Highmore died in Canterbury in 1780.

Highmore's great-great-grandson Frederick Morgan Payler emigrated from England to Australia in the second half of the nineteenth century and brought with him many of the family's portraits. The Gallery's portrait group was one of them.

## The artist's wife Susanna, son Anthony and daughter Susanna, c.1728
oil on canvas, 126.0 x 101.7 cm
Gift of the Art Gallery of South Australia Foundation 1994

This three-quarter-length portrait of the artist's wife and their only two children is a companion to the artist's self-portrait of the same size and probable date now held by the National Gallery of Victoria.[1] Painted near the beginning of Highmore's career, the date of the pair can be determined by the likely age of the children. The son Anthony, who was born in 1718, appears to be about ten years old and the daughter Susanna, who was born in 1725, could be no older than three years.[2] This gives a date of 1728, when his wife was thirty-eight and the artist was thirty-five and beginning to have some success.

The group shows similar poses and compositional structure to those used by Kneller. Highmore's drawing and modelling are not as strong or as solid as his teacher's but the faces are more individual. There is only a hint of the formulaic 'Kneller mask' although Mrs Highmore's pose is nearly identical to that of the Gallery's Kneller, *The Duchess of Bolton*, a painting that Highmore could have known, and many others like it. Highmore's fine rendering of flesh is much closer to Lely's and Van Dyck's than Kneller's. Nor has he neutralised the textures of the fabrics as Kneller and his studio tended to do; the surfaces of the drapery are more like Lely's, particularly Lely's earlier works of the 1650s and 1660s. The satin of his wife's white dress, his son's red

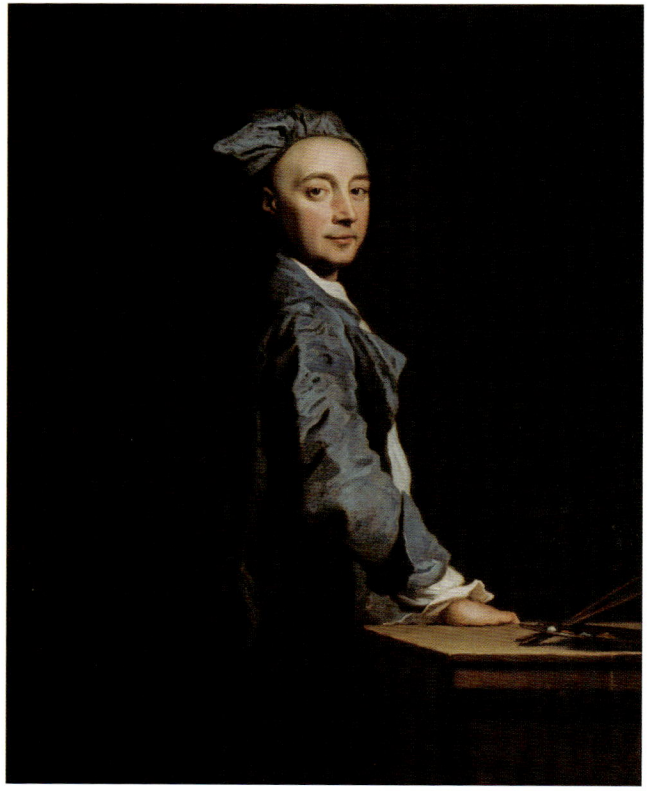

Joseph Highmore, *Self Portrait*, c.1728. Felton Bequest 1947, National Gallery of Victoria, Melbourne

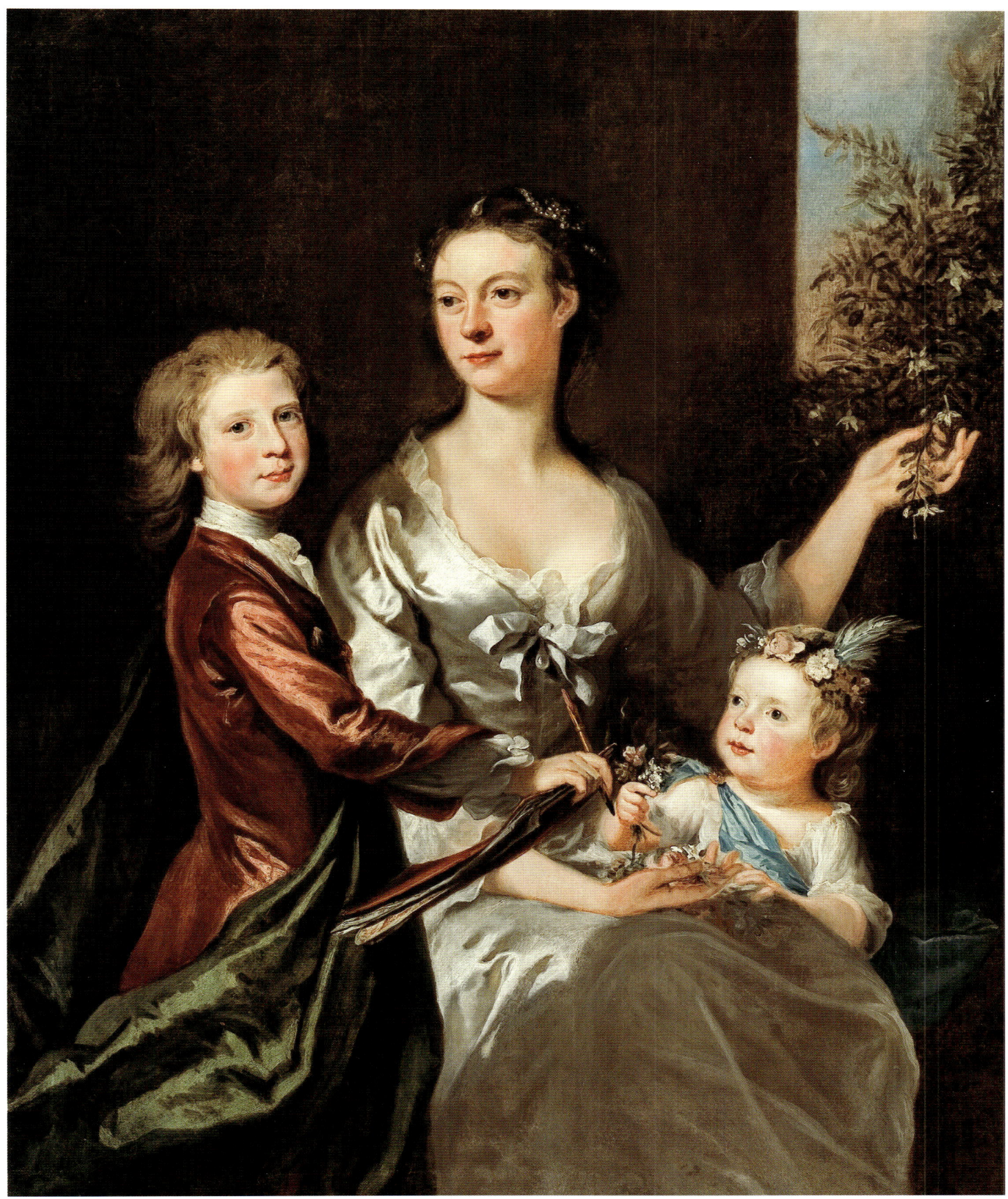

velvet coat and his daughter's cotton muslin are clearly and sensitively differentiated.

Highmore has made his wife graceful by extending her neck, arms and fingers. With her right hand she loosely gathers roses and other flowers into her lap while her left hand reaches to pick a spray of fragrant white jasmine. Fragrant flowers were commonly included in female portraits since the time of Van Dyck. Roses in particular alluded to Venus the goddess of love and beauty and therefore to the sitter's beauty and the artist's feelings for her. Flowers are a general allusion to youth and spring, but the plucking of a bloom hints at the fragility of beauty and life; a plucked bloom soon withers. A drop of water from the delicate blossoms echoes the drop-pearl above his wife's forehead and another hanging from the bow on her dress, at her heart; this alludes to her purity and virtue. Young Anthony is shown with a double-ended holder of red and black chalk and a folio of drawings. He is old enough to show a keen interest in drawing, no doubt encouraged by his father. The little daughter Susanna is in classical Roman fancy dress as Flora, the goddess of flowers, a garland of roses in her hair; she holds up a posy in one hand while fondling the flowers on her mother's lap with the other. The son is a budding professional artist; the daughter will bloom into womanhood.

The developing canons of British portraiture of the first half of the eighteenth century are interesting – the two-canvas family, with a separate father – but what engages us here is the artist's tender feeling towards his family. Although the three do not appear to be responding particularly to each other, Highmore's own relationship with each is touchingly revealed. He conveys the lively and cheerful warmth of his attractive wife, the close affection and approval he feels for his son and the delight he takes in his baby daughter. This is no routine commission; the artist, standing beside his palette and brushes, gazes out from the companion self-portrait with familial pride and love.

**Provenance:** Passed to the artist's son Anthony Highmore (1718–1799); thence to Anthony's fourth child John Field Highmore (1749–1794); thence to John's daughter Maria (1783–1814) who married on 12 May 1806 the Reverend William Payler, Rector of Patricksbourne and Bridge, Kent; thence to their daughter Charlotte Clara (b. 1809), who married the Reverend F. Morgan of Biddelsden Park, Buckinghamshire, who took the name of Payler in addition to his own; thence to their son Frederick Morgan Payler, an immigrant to Victoria; thence to Frederick's son the Venerable Frederick Trafford Morgan Payler (1872–1954), Archdeacon of Ballarat, Victoria; by whom sold in 1947 to Sir Keith and Lady Murdoch, Melbourne; sold (as *Family portrait*) to Michael Blanche and Lauraine Diggins, Melbourne; by whom lent to the Art Gallery of South Australia, Adelaide, from 1986 and sold to the Gallery in August 1994.

**Exhibitions:** *A Celebration: Recent acquisitions of heritage and contemporary art*, AGSA, Adelaide 1996. *Island to Empire: 300 Years of British Art 1550–1850*, AGSA, Adelaide 2005.

**Literature:** Alison Shepherd Lewis, *Joseph Highmore 1692–1780*, Ph.D. thesis, Harvard University, Cambridge, Massachusetts, 1975, no. 90, as *The Highmore Family*, pp. 435–36 (illus. fig. 59). Warren Mild, *Joseph Highmore of Holborn Row*, Ardmore, Pennsylvania, 1990, pp. 101–104, 229. *AGSA Foundation Fifteenth Annual Report 1994–1995*, Adelaide: AGSA (illus. front cover). Ron Radford et al., *Treasures*, Adelaide: AGSA, 1998, pp. 44-45. "Recent Acquisitions at the Art Gallery of South Australia", *The Burlington Magazine*, April 2003, London, p. 328.

**Condition:** Good; conserved in 1995 by Artlab Australia, Adelaide.

**Frame:** Probably original.

# William Hogarth 1697–1764

William Hogarth, a painter and engraver of satirical genre, and painter of conversation pieces and single portraits, was the most significant and original British artist of the first half of the eighteenth century. His "Modern Moral subjects" make him the first peculiarly British artist; his work looks forward into the nineteenth century rather than back onto the seventeenth. Before Hogarth, foreign artists from Holbein through to Van Dyck, Lely and Kneller had dominated British art for 200 years. He emerged as an independent artist not long after Kneller's death in 1723 and – a passionate nationalist – was determined to promote the idea of a British school of painting. He resented and opposed the patronage of foreign artists working in Britain, particularly the French. Nevertheless his elaborate conversation and narrative pictures are inspired by the French Rococo style and are the high point of what we can call the British Rococo.

Born in London in 1697, Hogarth was apprenticed in 1713 to an engraver Ellis Gambel and in 1720 studied art at the small St Martin's Lane Academy founded by John Vanderbank. During the 1720s he engraved and published a number of prints, chiefly satirical. His illustrations to Samuel Butler's *Hudibras* in the mid 1720s anticipated the moralistic narratives he invented and popularised. These were stories told in six to eight paintings. They exposed the follies and vices of his time in startling and cynical realism. Hogarth subsequently made engravings or had engravings made after the paintings. The most celebrated series are *A Harlot's Progress* 1731, *A Rake's Progress* c.1734, *Marriage à la Mode* c.1743, and *The Four Stages of Cruelty* 1751.

In 1729 he eloped with Jane Thornhill, daughter of the mural painter James Thornhill, which led to an estrangement between the artists, later reconciled. Hogarth admired and identified with his father-in-law's attempts to establish a British school of painting and after some success was able to support Thornhill's daughter comfortably.

During the late 1730s, in rivalry with the French painter Jean-Baptiste van Loo who had established himself as a portraitist in London in 1737, Hogarth turned to portraiture. His half-lengths, like this *William FitzHerbert*, often employed the feigned oval. His portraits are fresh and direct in treatment and characteristically responsive to the sitter's personality traits. He was the finest British portrait painter of his era and his best work depicts sitters from his own middle-class background.

In 1753 Hogarth published his approach to art and to the principles of the Rococo in his treatise *The Analysis of Beauty*. In 1757 he was appointed Sergeant Painter to the King, a post previously held by his father-in-law. He died in London in 1764.

## William FitzHerbert, early 1740s
oil on canvas, 62.3 x 75.0 cm
F. G. Halloran Bequest Fund 1994

William FitzHerbert of Tissington, Derbyshire, was from a landowning family and became a figure of considerable political influence. He entered parliament in 1761 as the member for Bramber, and later represented Derby. He was born in 1712, son of William and Rachel FitzHerbert of Tissington Hall; Rachel FitzHerbert was daughter and heiress of Thomas Bagshaw of Bakewell, Derbyshire. The son was educated in Derby and at Emmanuel College, Cambridge, before he joined the Inner Temple and was called to the Bar in 1739. His London residence was in Queen Street West, Cavendish Square.

FitzHerbert was a figure in London literary and theatrical circles, friends with David Garrick, Oliver Goldsmith, Samuel Foote and Arthur Murphy. Murphy recorded a dinner on 21 April 1759, the day his play *The Orphan of China* opened, when Hogarth, FitzHerbert, Foote and others gathered in great conviviality.[1] Later the same year FitzHerbert became Gentleman Usher, the daily waiter to the King, a post he held until 1763. He was also Commissioner of Trade and Plantations from 1765 to 1772 and Vice-President of the Society for the Encouragement of Arts, Manufactures and Commerce from 1761 to 1765.[2] FitzHerbert was also a good friend of Samuel Johnson, the greatest social commentator of the age. Johnson wrote: "I never knew a man who was so generally acceptable. He made everybody quite easy, overpowered nobody by the superiority of his talents, made no man think worse of himself by being his rival, seemed always to listen, did not oppose what you said. Everybody liked him".[3]

The bon viveur, renowned for his lavish entertainment of many friends, married Mary, eldest daughter of Littleton Poyntz Meynell of Bradley, Derbyshire, on 23 June 1744. His wife was an important influence on him. In her *Anecdotes* Mrs Piozzi quotes Johnson:

> That woman loved her husband as we hope and desire to be loved by our guardian angel. FitzHerbert was a gay, good humoured fellow, generous of his money and of his meat; desirous of nothing but cheerful society among people distinguished in some way or in any way, I think; for Rousseau and St Augustine would have been equally welcome to his table and to his house. The lady, however, was of another way of thinking; her first care was to preserve her husband's soul from corruption; her second to keep his estate entire for their children; and I owed my own good reception in the family to the idea she had entertained, that I was fit company for her husband, whom I loved extremely.[4]

When his wife died the loss of her influence doubtlessly

# William Hogarth

contributed to FitzHerbert's suicide over financial problems, the day after New Year 1772. He hanged himself with a bridle in his own stable. The death was recorded in *The Gentleman's Magazine*: "2 Jan Wm. FitzHerbert Esq. Member for Derby, suddenly. He was one of the Lords of Trade, an active magistrate and a gentleman universally esteemed."

Hogarth has captured FitzHerbert's distinctly benign character, his kind eyes and cheerful mouth. Although he was very much part of Hogarth's artistic circle and undoubtedly a friend, Hogarth has not flattered the sitter's rather plump appearance or lack of sharp intelligence. There is nothing artful in the matter-of-fact placement of the figure and the painting is a restrained arrangement of browns and greys applied with a full brush. The brown coat is trimmed with a band of grey-and-silver damask and silver-covered buttons. His grey French bag wig is tied by a black bow. Most British half-length portraits of the standard 30 by 25 inches do not include hands, but part of FitzHerbert's right hand and shirt flounce can be seen placed in his jacket. Hogarth's frequent use of the feigned oval is a hangover from the long British tradition of encasing and framing miniatures. The smart costume of the sitter and the style of painting date the picture to the early 1740s and it may indeed be a marriage portrait of 1744, when FitzHerbert was thirty-two.

Hogarth was not a prolific portrait painter and nearly all examples are now in public collections, this being one of only two of his paintings held in Australasian public collections.

**Inscription:** A nineteenth-century note on the reverse records that before relining the painting was signed on the back of the canvas "Hogarth pinx.ᵗ".

**Provenance:** The family of William FitzHerbert; collection of Henry Farrer Esq., FSA, 1863, his executor's sale, Christie's, London, 1 June 1866, lot 62; collection of Mr Earl Newton, Brookfield, Ohio from the 1950s; Historical Portraits Ltd, London.

**Exhibitions:** Historical Portraits Ltd, London, 1992. *A Celebration: Recent acquisitions of heritage and contemporary art*, AGSA, Adelaide, 1996. *Island to Empire: 300 Years of British Art 1550–1850*, AGSA, Adelaide, 2005.

**Literature:** Ronald Paulson, *Hogarth: His life, art and times*, New Haven and London: Yale University Press, published for the Paul Mellon Centre for Studies in British Art, 1971, vol. 2, p. 303. *Gainsborough's House Review*, 1992/93, unpaginated, (illus. Historical Portraits Ltd advertisement). Sale catalogue Historical Portraits Ltd, London: 1992, p. 4 (illus.).

**Condition:** Good; last conserved in 1992 in London.

**Frame:** Not original.

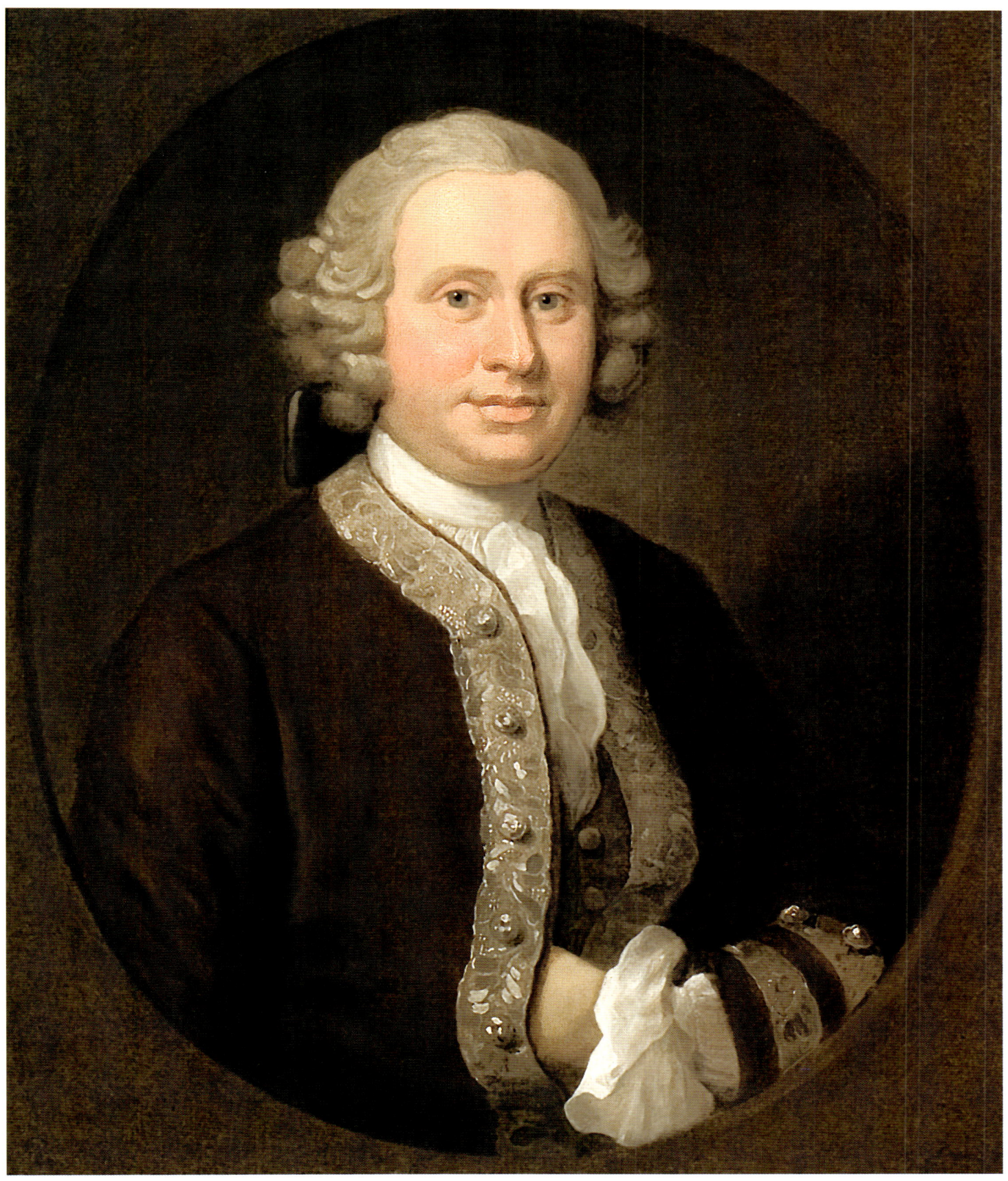

# Arthur Devis 1712–1787

Arthur Devis specialised in small informal portraits in domestic or landscape settings, less often single figures than groups disposed in easy familiarity. This genre, known then and now as the conversation piece, flourished in English art from the 1730s to the 1780s and derives from French Rococo painting. Antoine Watteau's follower Philip Mercier, who came to England around 1716, helped introduce it. Conversation pieces also show indebtedness to Dutch seventeenth-century pictures of everyday life, widely collected in Britain during the mid eighteenth century.

Devis's conversation pieces were popular with the landed middle classes in the 1740s and 1750s, particularly those from around his native Preston in Lancashire and the nearby counties of Chester and Derbyshire. Rather than a show of action, his figures display gentility, elegant deportment and status. They are rendered with fine almost-miniaturist detail. The art historian Joseph Burke aptly summed up Devis's somewhat awkward but charming pictures as "essentially a doll's-house world… His interiors have the rectilinear neatness and dovetailing precision of the model cabinet-maker's masterwork; his landscapes could be cut out for a toy theatre; and his silhouette figures positively invite the scissors".[1]

Born in Preston in 1712, Arthur Devis was the son of Anthony Devis who gained high local-political office there, and thereby influenced local commissions for his son. By 1728 Arthur Devis had left Preston and in the following year he was working in London for the Flemish topographical and sporting painter Peter Tillemans. From Tillemans he appears to have developed an interest in landscape painting and the use of thin translucent paint. Before 1742 he was established as a painter of conversation pieces with a studio in fashionable Great Queen Street, Lincoln's Inn Fields. After about 1748 Devis preferred to place his sitters out of doors whereas his earlier preference had been to arrange them in sparse domestic interiors.

Devis exhibited at the Free Society between 1761 and 1775 and in 1780, and became its president in 1768. By then his popularity was waning, but he was unwilling to accommodate his style to the reaction against Rococo art. Towards the end of his life he supplemented his income by repairing and cleaning paintings. After a studio auction in 1783 he retired to Brighton where he died in obscurity in 1787.

Arthur Devis's art was largely forgotten until a revival of interest in early-Georgian culture took place between the World Wars of the twentieth century. He had a few students, including his sons Thomas Anthony Devis (1757–1810) and Arthur William Devis (1762–1822), and possibly his half-brother Anthony Devis (1729–1816) who may have provided landscape backgrounds for Arthur's pictures.

## Portrait of a lady with a dog, c.1755

oil on canvas, 61.2 x 41.3 cm

Gift of Dorothy Spry 2002

This portrait is of an unidentified lady. Painted when Devis was at the height of his popularity and setting his single figures and groups out of doors, it has the greater sense of modelling and chiaroscuro found in his works from the mid 1750s. The sitter engages us with her direct gaze from behind a stone balustrade that divides the unusual composition in half, and upon which she rests her forearms over a draped kerchief. Divided from her on the viewer's side of the balustrade is a white miniature French poodle, a breed that began to be a popular lapdog in England in the mid eighteenth century. Behind her is the dark foliage of a tree and behind that a river landscape and the hint of a town view in the distance. In the left background a three-storeyed house with a stone pediment over its doorway is reflected in a middle-distance stream seen through the balustrade.

If this distinctive house, of Queen Anne's period, could be identified it might lead to the identity of the sitter. However, Devis sometimes invented the background of his outdoor portraits just as earlier he had usually invented grander or more correctly-furnished interiors for his sitters than their own. Moreover, the sitter of this portrait would not have owned the blue dress in which she is posed; it was one of his studio props and appears in a number of portraits of the mid 1750s and early 1760s. The dress is most notable in the double portrait of a Lancashire couple, *Edward Parker and his wife, Barbara, on the Terrace at Browsholme Hall, near Clitheroe*, 1757,[2] where Mrs Parker leans on an iron balustrade and holds by a ribbon the same hat seen on the stone balustrade in our portrait. The blue dress is worn again by Alicia Clarke of Ross-on-Wye, Herefordshire, in a double portrait with her sister Jane, of similar date to the Lancashire commission, and in a later and more populated group portrait of the Rookes-Leeds family of Bradford in Yorkshire,[3] and it recurs on further sitters in different colours than blue. The costume, a sumptuous blue sack and petticoat trimmed with flounce and furbelows, would have been used to dress a doll-like artist's lay-figure as a substitute for the absent sitter. Reliance on lay-figures varied considerably. The articulated joints, unlike a human model's, could hold a difficult pose indefinitely while an elaborate allegorical figure composition was in progress, and lay-figures, usually life-size, continued in use for such purposes into the twentieth century. However, Devis seems to have exploited the

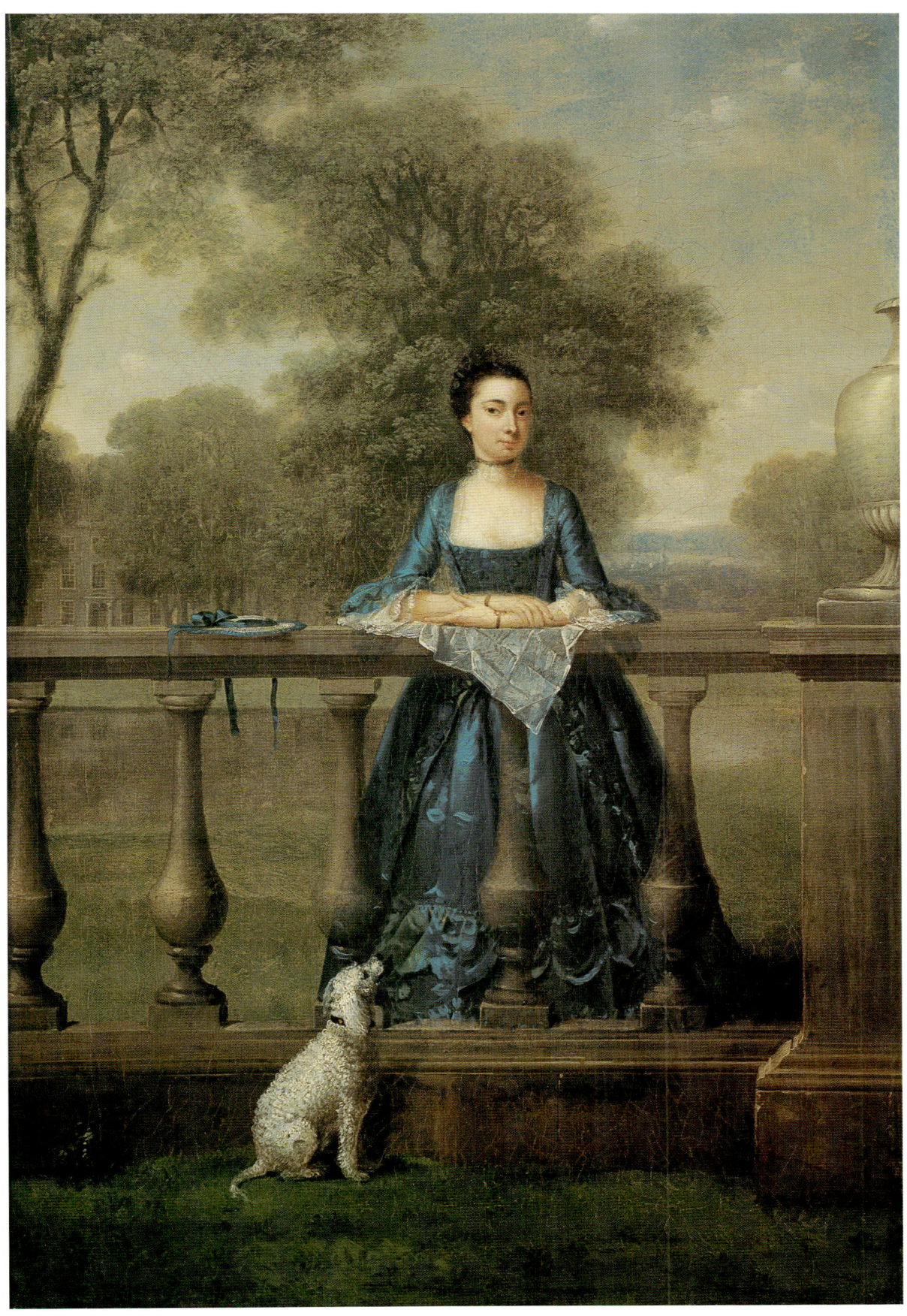

angular articulation and doll-like characteristics as an essential feature of his portraits of aspirational provincials; certainly the awkward look is characteristic of his art. Based on other doll costumes that have survived from Devis's studio, the lay-figure dress would have been about 30 inches (76 cm) high.[4]

Most of Devis's clients were from the country and would have sat for him briefly on a trip to London. During the sitting he would have painted only the faces – and in this instance perhaps the lapdog – and the remainder of the portrait, including the costume, would be completed in their absence.

Because husband-and-wife pictures of the same size were usually commissioned together one can assume the possible existence of a male pair for our portrait. Devis did a number of portraits in the same small size as the Gallery's in the mid-to-late 1740s but the only other known in this distinctive size (24 by 16½ inches) and painted in his subsequent style is the late-1750s *Sir Robert Rich, of Ross Hall, Suffolk, and Waverley Abbey, Surrey*.[5] As well as belonging to a similar period it shows the sitter leaning on a tree with a similar river landscape behind. The Gallery's portrait could possibly be its pair and therefore of Lady Rich. If so, her appearance in Suffolk or Surrey in the blue dress would be well distanced, as Devis customarily intended, from its other wearers in Lancashire, Yorkshire and Herefordshire.

**Provenance:** Sotheby's, London; bt 16 December 1988 by Robert Compton Jones, London; bt by Miss Dorothy Spry, Hunters Hill, Sydney, 14 March 1989.

**Exhibition:** *Island to Empire: 300 Years of British Art 1550-1850*, AGSA, Adelaide, 2005.

**Literature:** Stephen V. Sartin, *Polite Society by Arthur Devis 1712-1787: Portraits of the English country gentleman and his family*, Preston, Lancashire: Harris Museum & Art Gallery, 1983. "Recent Acquisitions at the Art Gallery of South Australia", *Burlington Magazine*, London, April 2003, p. 328.

**Condition:** Good; last conserved in London about 1988.

**Frame:** Not original.

# Tilly Kettle 1734/35–1786

Tilly Kettle was an accomplished London portrait painter, a follower of Joshua Reynolds. He became the first British artist of consequence among the many to work in India.

Born in Exeter, Devonshire, in 1734 or 1735, Kettle probably received early artistic tuition from his father who was a sign-painter. He undertook formal studies in London at the St Martin's Lane Academy where he was known to have painted versions of Reynolds's original portraits on loan to the Academy from Reynolds's studio assistant Giuseppe Marchi (1735–1808). Although from the age of twenty-one he regularly exhibited portraits at the Free Society of Arts, Kettle's earliest extant works date from a slightly later period, the beginning of the 1760s. These paintings are derivative of Reynolds's style and also show the influence of Allan Ramsay and possibly the more popular style of Francis Cotes.

Rejected, probably unfairly, for membership of the Royal Academy in 1769, Kettle travelled to India, where he remained for seven years at Madras. There he prospered, producing numerous portraits of the local princes and nabobs and other Indian subjects, occasionally shipping home paintings for exhibition in London. In 1776 he returned to England, a wealthy man soon to marry and build a house in Old Bond Street. By 1782 he was facing bankruptcy; his London career had been a financial failure and he retreated to Dublin. In 1786, attempting to regain his fortunes and his Indian reputation, he set out on an overland journey to India but fell sick and died near Aleppo in the Syrian desert, a premature end to his career.

## Woman with a muff, early 1760s
oil on canvas, 77.0 x 63.6 cm
South Australian Government Grant 1969

The pose and composition for this sensitive yet confronting portrait is possibly taken from Joshua Reynolds's *Ann Day*, 1760, in the Carnegie Museum of Art, Pittsburgh. Allan Ramsay was probably the first British artist to portray half-length portraits of women with their hands concealed in the fashionable French accessory of the muff. In 1754 Ramsay painted two such portraits, possibly inspired by French portraiture, for example, François-Hubert Drouais's *Duchess of Hamilton and Argyll,* and he used this distinctive half-length frontal pose[1] with and without muffs on numerous occasions until the beginning of the 1760s. Reynolds and likewise Kettle were possibly inspired by these Ramsay precedents.

Reynolds's *Ann Day* and Kettle's unknown middle-aged woman differ from Ramsay's muff portraits in that both show the sitter wearing a flat conical cloth hat known as a 'Woffington' and apparently made popular by the actress Peg Woffington. Reynolds's and Kettle's sitters both face the viewer front-on and similarly wear embroidered-satin and lace-trimmed coats and warm their hands inside a blue monkey-fur muff.[2] Soon after its completion in 1760 Reynolds's portrait was engraved by the leading mezzotint engraver James McArdell,[3] and a print from the edition is in the Art Gallery of South Australia's collection. Whether Kettle saw the original portrait by Reynolds or merely the engraving is not known. However, Kettle has made subtle but effective variations to the composition, pose and costume: the hat is broader and the muff is much larger, nearly a third of the picture's height, thus making the form more triangular and the composition more striking than in the portrait by Reynolds.

Kettle, like Ramsay, was more interested than Reynolds in capturing the differing textures of a sitter's garments and skin; Reynolds concentrated more on form and impasto effects than illusionistic surface. As can be seen here, Kettle's surface renderings and direct realism are close to Ramsay and so is his uncompromising portrayal of this sitter's plain features. On the other hand, the pitch of the emotional tone is more like Reynolds: the portrayal is sympathetic and we are conscious not only of this Englishwoman's commanding strength but also her sensitivity and sincerity, expressed partly through the delicate and subdued cool colour.

This undated portrait would probably have been painted in the first half of the 1760s, at the height of Kettle's fully matured style, and certainly well prior to his departure in 1769 for India. In the early to middle 1760s he was touring the English Midlands where the portrait may have been executed. Kettle, and by implication his clients, obviously liked this pose and he painted a number of sitters similarly; one such is *Portrait of Anne Howard-Vyse* in the Auckland Art Gallery.

The art historian Ellis Waterhouse wrote that "Kettle's portraits can be readily recognized by his tendency to render the human skull as of the shape of a football".[4] This sitter's firmly modelled head makes the comment seem particularly apt, if a little harsh.

# Tilly Kettle

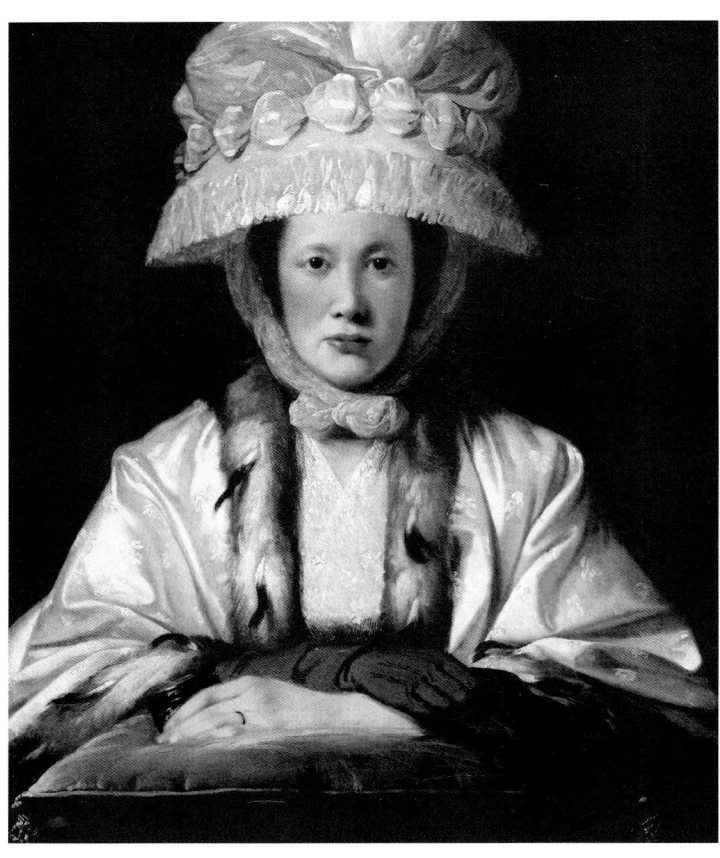

Tilly Kettle, *Portrait of Anne Howard-Vyse*, 1780. Mackelvie Trust Collection, Auckland Art Gallery, Toi o Tamaki, Auckland

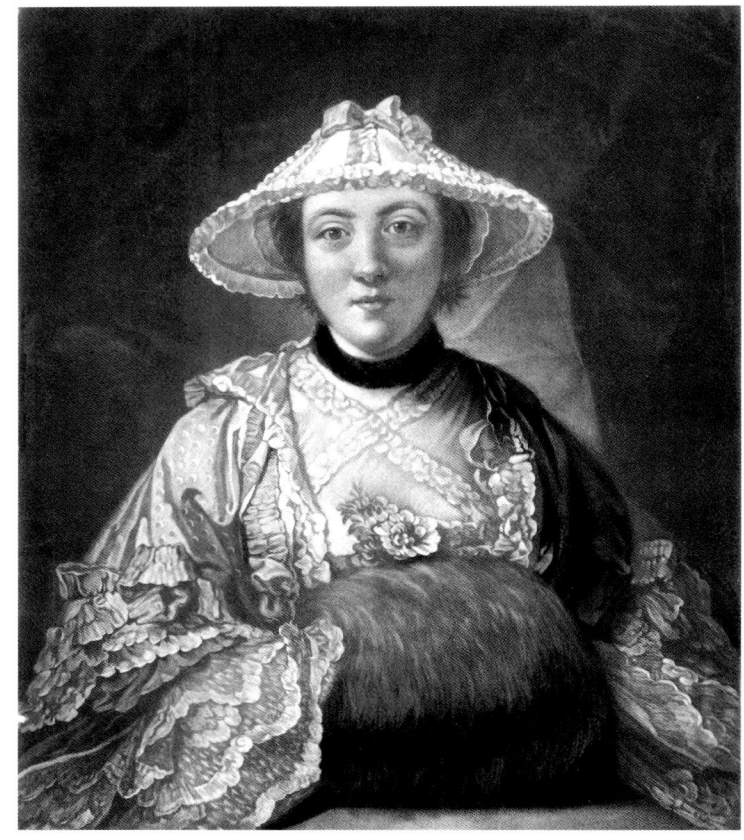

James MacArdell, 1729?–1765, after Joshua Reynolds, *Anne (Day), Lady Fenoulhet*, mezzotint on paper. South Australian Government Grant 1970, Art Gallery of South Australia, Adelaide

**Provenance:** Agnew's, London.

**Exhibition:** *Island to Empire: 300 Years of British Art 1550–1850*, AGSA, Adelaide, 2005.

**Literature:** John Baily, "A Portrait by Tilly Kettle", *AGSA Bulletin*, vol. 32, no. 2, October 1970. *Picture Book*, Adelaide: AGSA, 1972, p. 21 (illus.). Ron Radford in David Thomas et al., *Art Gallery of South Australia 1881–1981*, Adelaide: AGSA, 1981, p. 60. Peter Tomory and Robert Gaston, *European Paintings before 1800 in Australian and New Zealand Public Collections*, Sydney, 1989, p. 31, no. 71 (illus.). Jeremy Black, *History of England*, London, 1993, p. 102 (illus.).

**Condition:** Excellent; last conserved probably in London before acquisition.

**Frame:** Probably original.

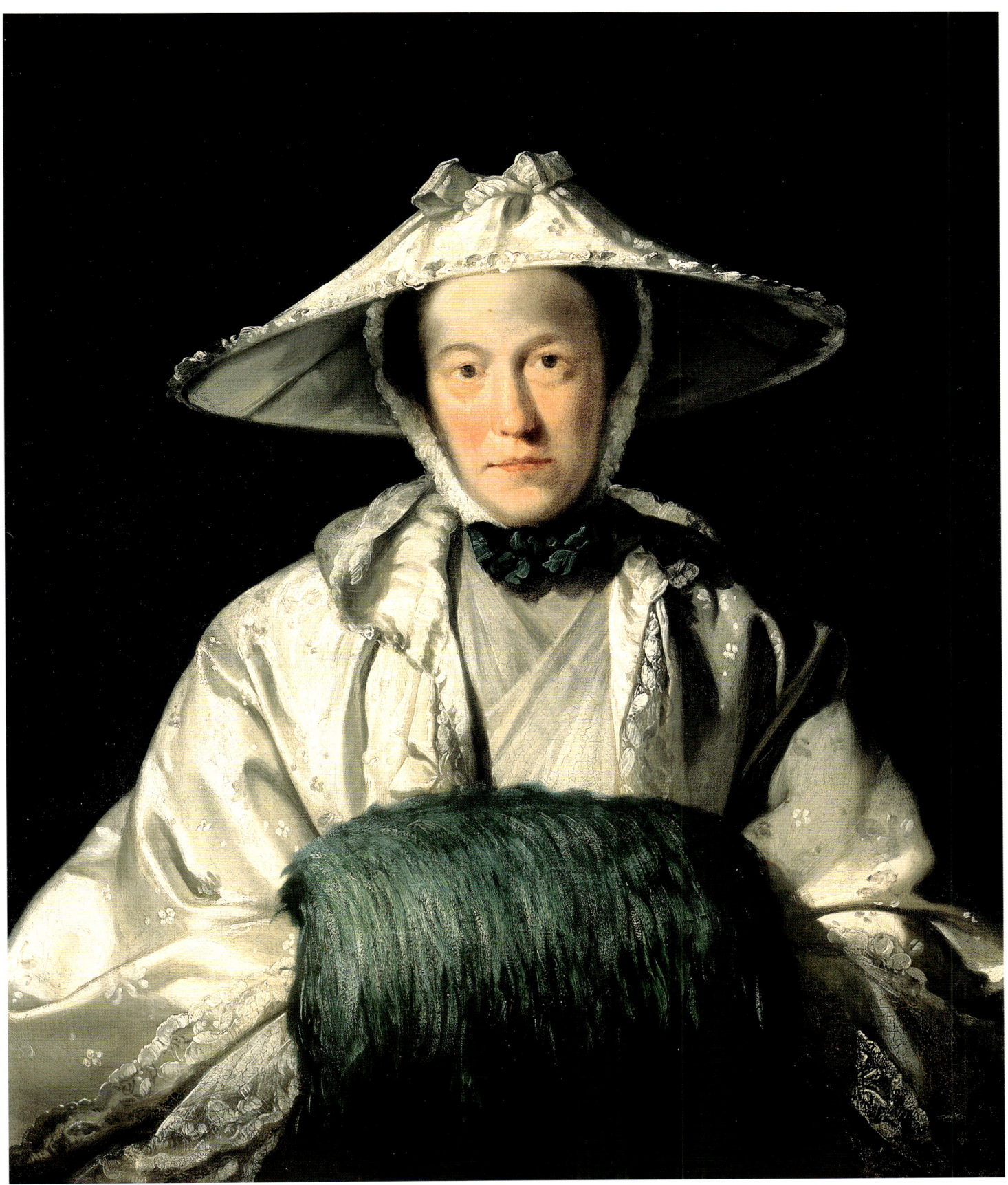

# Francis Swaine c.1720–1782

Francis Swaine was one of Britain's leading marine painters of the 1750s and 1760s. The marine specialisation, in which London had led Europe since the 1680s, became increasingly important since British mercantile and imperial expansion was very considerable at this period. After the 1763 peace that ended the Seven Years War, British naval power was even more crucial for the expanded colonial empire gained from France in India, the Caribbean and North America.

Born around 1720, Francis Swaine worked as a messenger for His Majesty's Navy in 1735 and by 1741 was probably painting as an assistant in the studio of the leading marine painter of the day, Peter Monamy (1681–1749), a friend of Hogarth's. In 1749 Swaine married Mary, Monamy's second surviving daughter, and it is probable that he inherited part of her father's studio works and possessions. Furthermore, Swaine inherited much of Monamy's style and his light and colourful palette. Whereas Swaine never exhibited at the Royal Academy, which was formed in 1768, he did exhibit regularly until his death at its predecessor rivals, the Free Society of Artists from 1761 to 1782 and the Society of Arts from 1762 to 1782. In 1764 his *A seapiece: a sunset view* gained second prize, of fifteen guineas, in the Society of Arts' first competition for "Best Original Sea piece on canvas". In the following year he received a prize of twenty guineas for the remarkable painting now owned by the Art Gallery of South Australia.

Various distinct categories of marine painting were introduced to England from the Netherlands by Willem van de Velde the Elder (1611–93) and his more influential son Willem van de Velde the Younger (1636–1707) who in 1674 became official marine painters to Charles II, the elder for painting 'seafights'. Besides seafights there were calms, beach scenes, storms and 'parade' pictures, the last designed to show a variety of types of vessel and usually enlivened by some fictive ceremonial action, such as the arrival of a dignitary. Swaine's teacher, Peter Monamy, had worked in the Van de Velde studio at Greenwich. A prolific output from Swaine included his speciality of finely-painted small pairs on copper, contrasting morning and dusk or calm and storm.

Swaine lived in London at Strutton Ground, Westminster, before moving to an address near Avery Farm, Chelsea, where he died in 1783. His son Monamy Swaine (*fl.* 1769–74) was also a marine painter, the third generation in the family but he also painted still-lives and genre pictures.

The National Maritime Museum, Greenwich, holds fourteen of Swaine's marine paintings.

## The Landing of the Sailor Prince at Spithead, 1765

oil on canvas, 106.6 x 167.5 cm

Gift of James & Ann Douglas in memory of Sholto & Alison Douglas 2001

Francis Swaine's best work seems to have been done in the 1760s, when he executed this impressive painting, one of his finest and largest surviving canvases. It belongs not only to the category of a marine 'calm', it is also a grand, royal 'parade'. It appears to be the painting, thought to be lost, that in 1765 gained an award from the Society of Arts for it bears the inscription "This picture gain'd a premium of 20 guineas / 1765". The donors' family, the Douglases had owned it in Scotland since the eighteenth century and in about 1900 it was inherited by the South Australian branch of the family. *The Landing of the Sailor Prince at Spithead* is the traditional title of the painting handed down through the Douglas family. However, there is no painting of this specific title exhibited.

The painting features ten naval vessels from various angles. Spithead, in modern times still a place for ceremonial coronation reviews of the Royal Navy, is at the entrance to Portsmouth, for centuries the principal base and dockyard for the navy. In this painting the prominent flagship – the ship that carries a fleet's commanding admiral – flies a Hanoverian Royal Standard that was current in 1765, and the kings of Great Britain and Ireland were then also Electors of Hanover. This main flagship is a direct copy of Van de Velde the Younger's *Royal Sovereign*, a 1703 painting that was widely copied by subsequent artists including Swaine's teacher and father-in-law Peter Monamy (see illus. p. 124). Indeed, given the profound influence of the Van de Velde studio in establishing a fashion for these paintings in Britain, it is no surprise to find that both Monamy in an important 1726 work, and Swaine here in 1765, appropriated an iconic image that would resonate with prize-awarding judges. However, like Monamy previously, Swaine updated the royal standard and ensign to current examples, evidently an acceptable practice in what may have been perceived from the start as an historical picture.[1]

George III was known as a Sailor Prince, but the best known of several so-called Sailor Princes over the centuries was his younger son who later became King William IV, and this painting was executed in William's birth year. The central rowing boat bears the Royal Standard on the prow meaning royalty was on board, and the figure in profile (in a yellow and white vest) sitting in the stern is possibly therefore meant to be the Sailor Prince of the picture-title. Even though the picture was painted later, more likely the figure represents George III when he was the Prince of Wales, before he ascended the throne in 1760, aged twenty-two.[2] On the other hand, parade seapieces of this kind were sometimes of imaginary ceremonies, pretexts for a shiplover's proliferation of vessels and riggings.

Unusually for a maritime painting of this early date it retains its original fine Rococo-style frame.

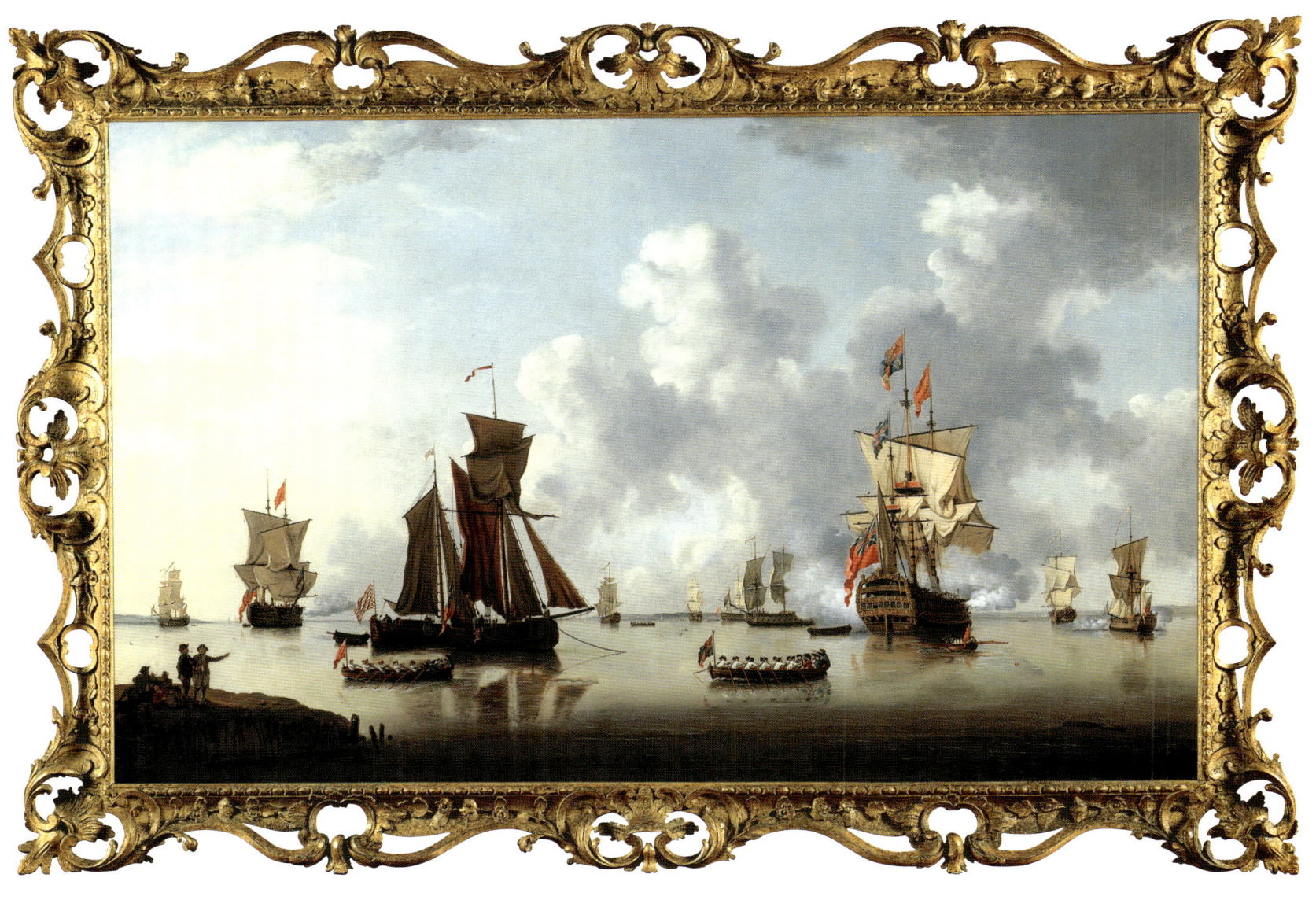

| | |
|---|---|
| **Inscription:** | Signed l.r., oil: "F Swaine Pinxit" (F and S in monogram). Inscribed and dated l.l., oil: "This picture / gain'd a premium of 20 guineas / 1765". |
| **Provenance:** | By family descent in the Douglas family, Kelso, Roxburghshire; by c.1790s with Andrew Douglas, Ednam House, Kelso; c.1805 to James Alexander Douglas, Woodside, Kelso; c.1901 with William Selby Douglas, Adelaide; early 1930s to Francis John Douglas, Victor Harbor, South Australia; 1962 to Sholto John Douglas; 1984 to James Douglas of Stonyfell, Adelaide, by whom given to the Art Gallery of South Australia in 2001. |
| **Exhibitions:** | Society of Arts, London, 1765. *Island to Empire: 300 Years of British Art 1550–1850*, AGSA, Adelaide, 2005. |
| **Literature:** | "Recent Acquisitions at the Art Gallery of South Australia", *Burlington Magazine*, April 2003, p. 330. |
| **Condition:** | Excellent; last conserved in 2001 by Artlab Australia, Adelaide. |
| **Frame:** | Original. |

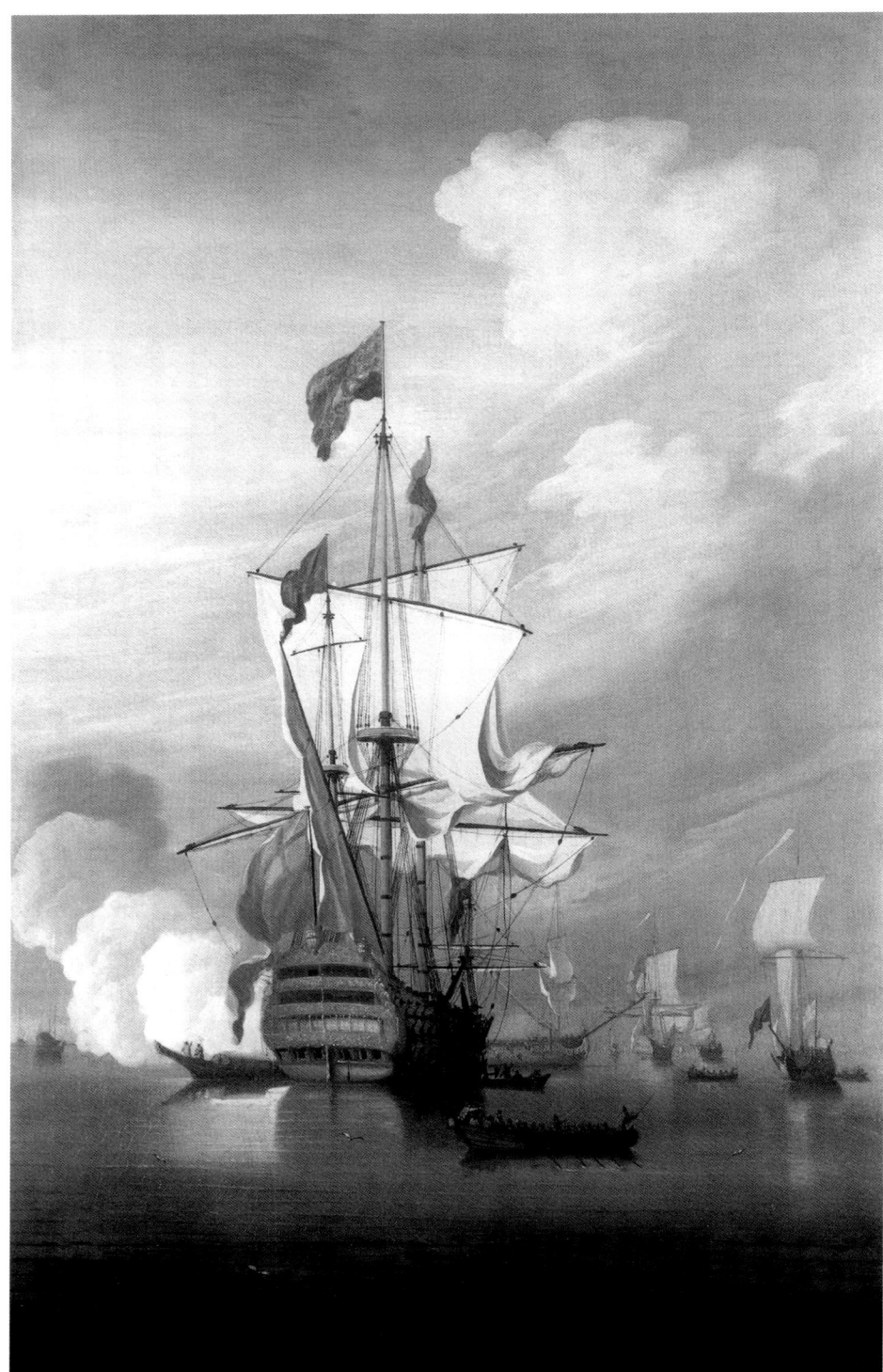

Peter Monamy, *The first-rate ship* Royal Sovereign, *stern quarter view, in a calm*, 1726. Private collection

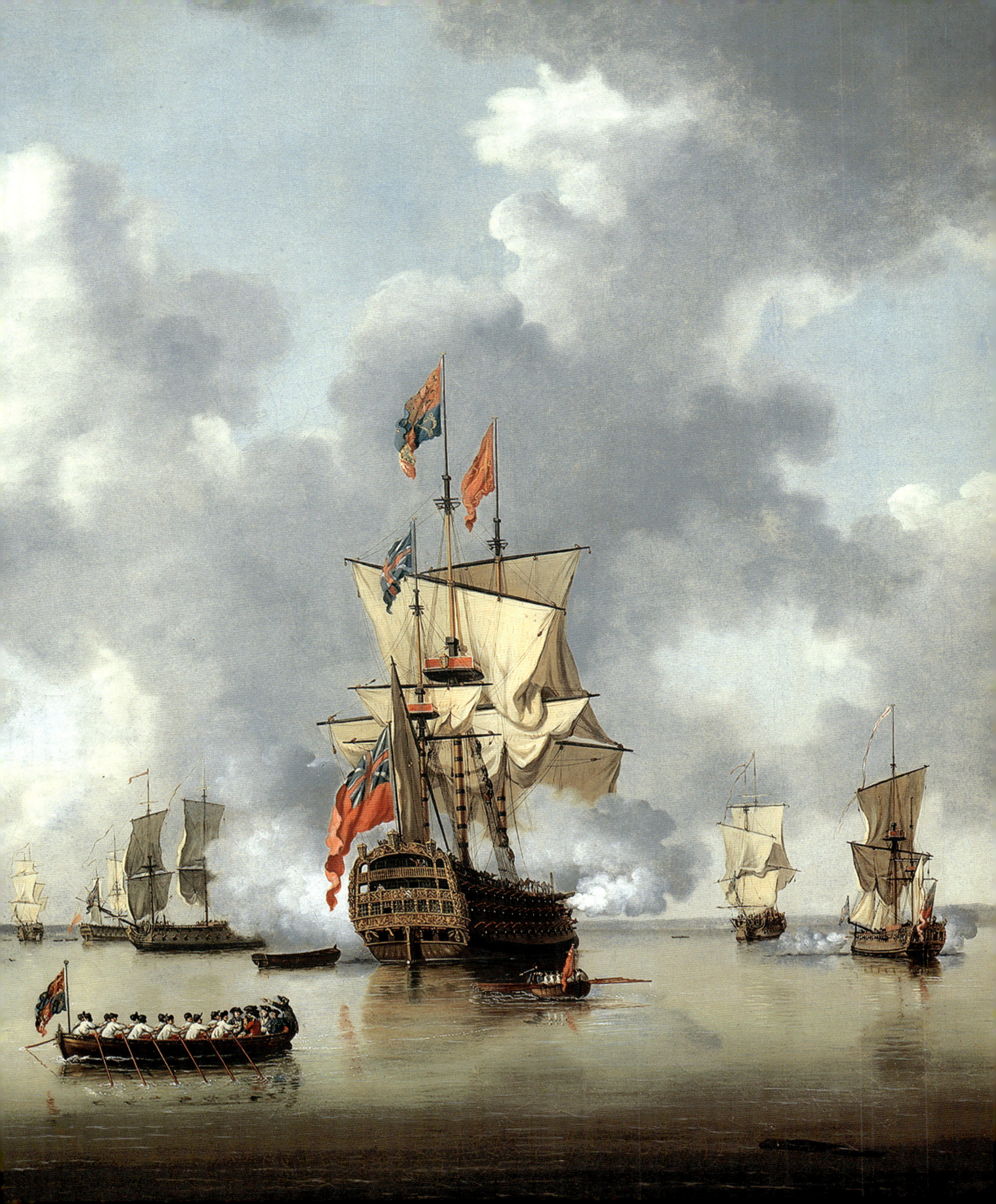

# Allan Ramsay 1713–1784

The Scottish-born Allan Ramsay was one of the leading British portrait painters of the eighteenth century and, with William Hogarth, certainly the finest of the 1740s and 1750s. In 1761 he was appointed a Painter in Ordinary to King George III and in 1767 became His Majesty's Principal Painter in Ordinary, the highest honour available to an artist in Britain. He was also an important figure in the Scottish Enlightenment, a classical scholar and master of many languages. He was the most erudite artist of the age and his *Dialogue on Taste*, 1755, deserves an honoured place among eighteenth-century discourses. Ramsay's sensitive and graceful realism also made his finest portraits equal to any done at the time in Europe.

Born in Edinburgh in 1713, he was the son of an eminent Scottish poet of the same name. In 1732–33 Ramsay studied painting in London under the little-known Swedish painter Hans Hysing (1678–1753) before returning to Edinburgh where for four years he set up a portrait practice. From 1736 to 1738 he studied in Italy. In Rome he worked with Francesco Imperiali (1668–1740) under whose guidance he was able to refine and polish his technique, and in Naples with the aged Francesco Solimena (1657–1747), the last significant exponent of the Italian Baroque style and then the most famous painter in Europe. From them he gained a feeling for the overall composition of a portrait, not just the head or the figure. It was probably Solimena who instilled in him his sense of firm modelling by dramatic contrasts of light and shadow, cool flesh tones and a taste for the graceful gesture.

Back in London in 1738 he was further influenced by the direct realism of Hogarth and for nearly a quarter of a century was unrivalled as a portrait painter, particularly in portraits of women on whom he bestowed great charm and sentiment. Despite success he felt the need to study again in Rome and between 1754 and 1757 he enrolled there at the French Academy. On return Ramsay consolidated his reputation for full-length portraits with statue-based Italianate poses and high finish, though his colour and elaborate accessories are reminiscent of the stylish French portraitists of the time.

Among the full-length portraits that found favour when he returned was one of the Prince of Wales. When the Prince succeeded to the throne in 1760 as King George III he commissioned Ramsay to paint the official coronation portraits of the new monarch and his young consort Queen Charlotte. By the mid 1760s Joshua Reynolds began to overtake Ramsay. In 1773, due to an accident that damaged his right arm, he gave up painting altogether and at the time of his death in 1784 was almost forgotten as a major artist. The importance of Ramsay's art has been fully reassessed only in recent years, particularly through the research of Alastair Smart whose 1992 monograph paralleled the exhibition he prepared for the National Portrait Galleries in Edinburgh and London.

## Allan Ramsay and studio

## King George III in coronation robes, c.1765?

oil on canvas, 236.2 x 158.7 cm
South Australian Government Grant 1924

George III, King of Great Britain and Ireland, and Elector of Hanover, was born in London in 1738 and, in succession to his grandfather George II, came to the throne in 1760 aged twenty-two. His long reign of sixty years extended from 1760 to 1820 during which time the British Empire lost control of its American colonies in 1776 but in 1770 claimed the eastern half of the continent that became known as Australia; the British settled New South Wales in 1788 as a distant gaol and strategic Pacific Ocean port. It was the second longest reign, after Queen Victoria's, of any British monarch's but towards the end of his life George III became mentally ill and was officially confined in 1811, after which his son the Prince of Wales, later George IV, was appointed Prince Regent. It is not generally appreciated that George III was a generous and influential patron of the visual arts and in 1768 was the first "Patron Protectionist and Supporter" of the new Royal Academy. Not since Charles I's death in 1649 had Britain had a monarch who took an active interest in art, particularly the decorative arts which flourished in his reign. It is therefore appropriate for the Art Gallery of South Australia that George III's portrait should preside grandly over our British eighteenth-century display of paintings and decorative arts.

This full-length portrait is one of many replicas, painted largely or wholly by Ramsay's studio assistants, of *King George III in coronation robes*. What is possibly the 1761 original is in the possession of Her Majesty Queen Elizabeth II and now hangs, with its companion portrait of Queen Charlotte, in the grand dining room at Buckingham Palace. In 1757 Ramsay had already painted a full-length of the king as Prince of Wales for his tutor and mentor the Earl of Bute; in 1758 the Prince in turn commissioned from Ramsay a full-length *3rd Earl of Bute*. Of the coronation portrait Ramsay wrote in 1766: "I painted, from the life, a whole length picture of him for Hanover, a profile for the coinage, and another whole length, which, after the Coronation, I, by his Majesties orders, dressed in Coronation robes. Soon after her Majesty's arrival, she likewise did me the honour to sit to me; and these two pictures in Coronation robes are the originals from which all the copies ordered by the Lord Chamberlain are painted."[1]

The commanding pose of the young king is based to some extent on the poses of Greco-Roman statues like the celebrated Apollo Belvedere in the Vatican. Reynolds's *Commodore Keppel* in Apollo pose has become famous but five years earlier, in 1748, Ramsay had painted *The Macleod*

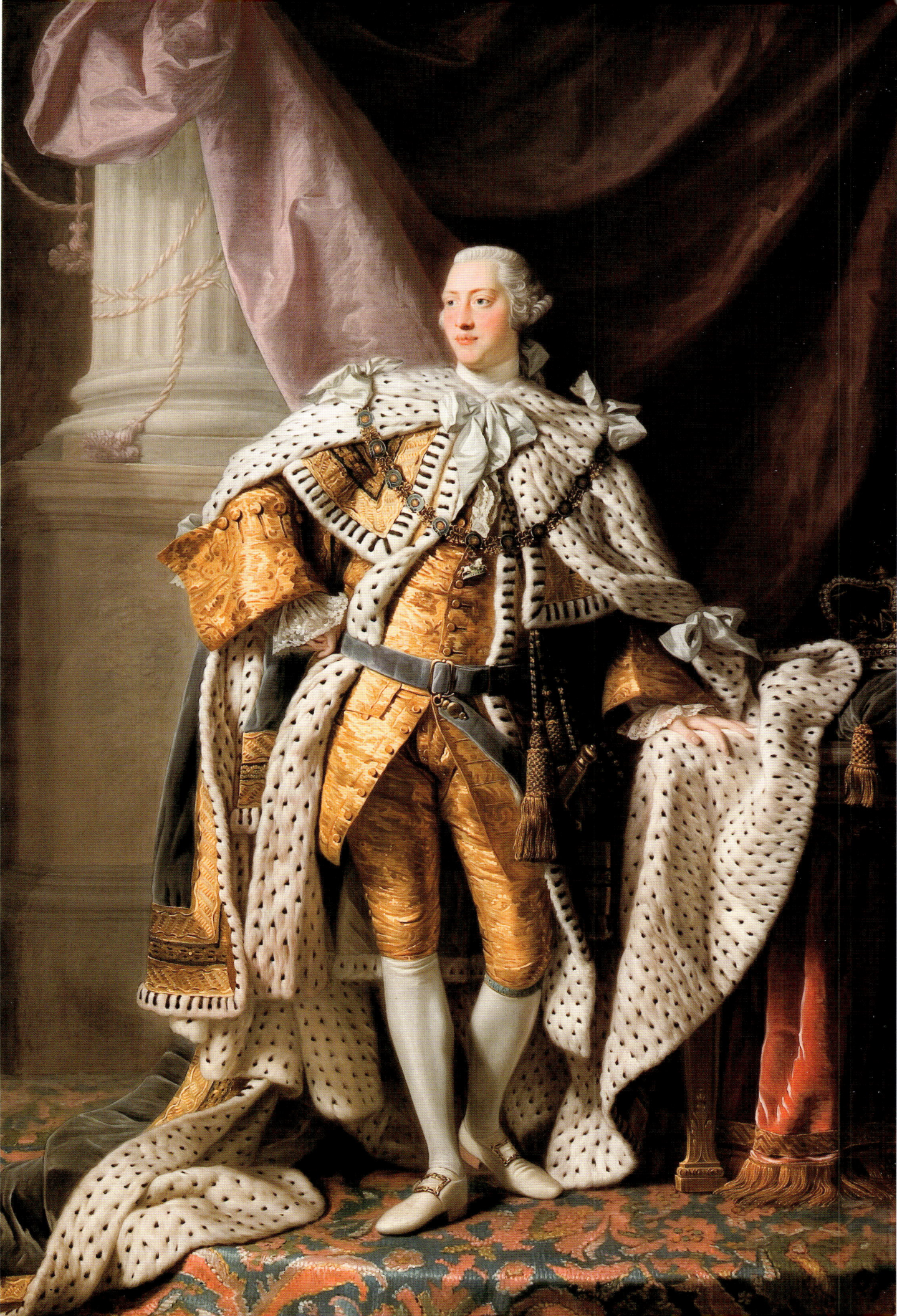

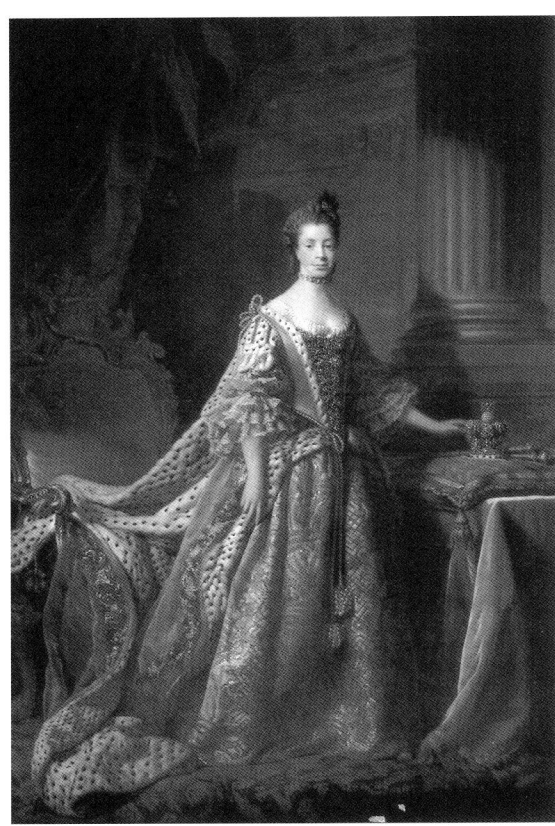

Allan Ramsay and studio, *Queen Charlotte in coronation robes*, c.1766. Purchased by the Commonwealth Art Advisory Board, National Gallery of Australia, Canberra

*of Macleod* as an Apollo Belvedere in red tartan trews. The art historian Ellis Waterhouse affirms, "…the marriage of the Italian grand style to British portraiture was primarily the achievement of Ramsay".[2]

The statuesque grandeur of a king in gleaming golden damask is made more magnificent by the wearing of the elaborate panoply of state, an ermine mantle and insignia of the Order of the Garter; the royal hand rests on a table beside the British crown, which sits upon a tasselled cushion. (The crown jewels were sent to Ramsay's studio in Soho Square where the artist insisted on 24-hour guards.) The sumptuous costume-piece is set on richly patterned carpet and backed theatrically with a large classical pillar and a pale rose-coloured curtain. In 1762 the writer and politician Horace Walpole admired the newly completed portrait and astutely commented: "The gold stuff and ermine are highly finished; rather too much, for the head does not come out so much as it ought."[3] The ostentatious decorative detail, high finish and pastel colours give it a French Rococo appearance, but with a much greater sense of formal grandeur. Sir Oliver Millar, Keeper of the Queen's Pictures, considered it the most distinguished state portrait of a monarch since the time of Van Dyck.

The coronation pair was completed in 1762 and Ramsay, with the help of assistants, was henceforth officially responsible for the vast number of copies in constant demand as royal gifts to members of his family and other sovereigns or to embassies and consulates and to colonial governors' residences throughout the British Empire.[4] Versions of Ramsay's portraits presented to American colonial governors were deliberately destroyed in the War of Independence.

At the end of 1762 Ramsay wrote, "I have resolved to give the last painting of all of them with my own hand",[5] and for several years he insisted on painting the head himself. David Martin (1737–1798), who had long been Ramsay's principal assistant, helped produce most of the copies until about 1769 after which Philip Reinagle (1749–1833) took over. Reinagle remained in Ramsay's service until the artist's death in 1784 and after Ramsay's accident in 1773 the artist had no hand in them. Reinagle is said to have painted as many as ninety pairs of the State portraits of the King and Queen. Altogether it appears that one-hundred-and-fifty pairs, plus twenty-six of the king alone and nine of the queen alone, can be listed.[6] They made Ramsay a very wealthy man; by the late 1760s he charged £84 each, his standard price for a full-length portrait.

Although the Gallery's example is a high-quality studio replica, some of the modelling of the flesh is a little mechanical compared with the early version in the royal collection. Ours could be a fairly early example executed by David Martin in the 1760s.[7] However, it is notoriously difficult to date the many replicas unless certain of the provenance.[8]

Bought by the Art Gallery of South Australia as early as 1924, this grand-manner portrait was only the second Old Master British portrait to enter the collection, well before the Gallery began to acquire British and Continental Old Master pictures more systematically.

**Provenance:** Offered by Charles Newman, London, through Sir William Sowden.

**Exhibition:** *Island to Empire: 300 Years of British Art 1550–1850*, AGSA, Adelaide, 2005.

**Literature:** *NGSA Catalogue of Paintings, Pastels and Sculpture*, 1940, no. 561, p. 113. *NGSA Catalogue of Oil and Water-colour Paintings and Pastels with Biographical Notes*, 1960, p. 207. David Thomas et al., *Art Gallery of South Australia 1881–1981*, Adelaide, AGSA, 1981, p. 58. Peter Tomory and Robert Gaston, *European Paintings before 1800 in Australian and New Zealand Public Collections*, Sydney, 1989, p. 40, no. 104 (illus.). Alastair Smart, *Allan Ramsay: Painter, essayist and man of the Enlightenment*, New Haven and London, 1992, p. 217. Alastair Smart, *Allan Ramsay: A complete catalogue of his paintings*, Yale University Press, 1999, published for the Paul Mellon Centre for Studies in British Art, p. 113. Jane Roberts (ed.), *George III & Queen Charlotte: Patronage, collecting and court taste*, London, 2004, pp. 24–26.

**Condition:** Excellent; conserved in 2004 by Artlab Australia, Adelaide.

**Frame:** Not original.

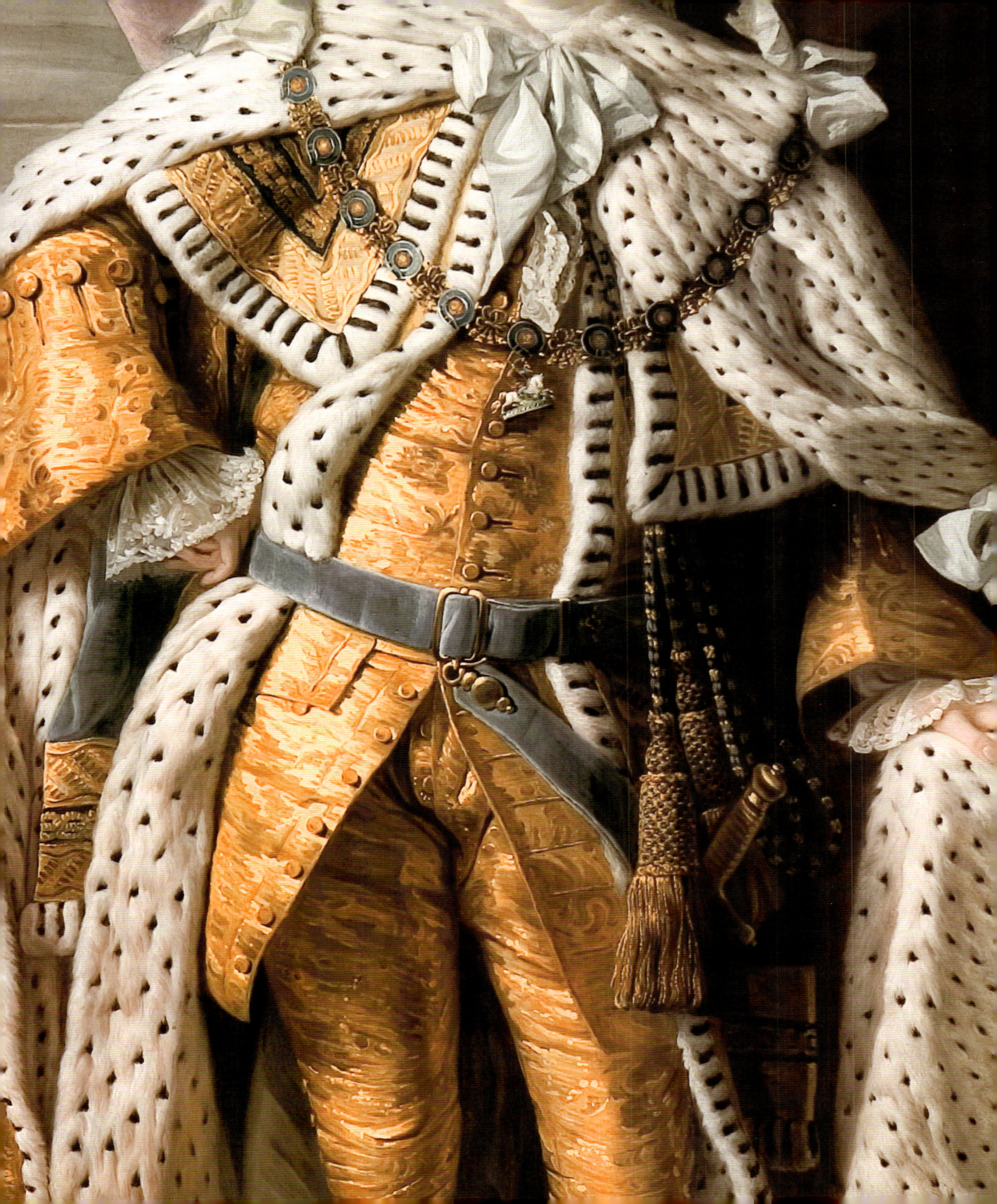

# Joshua Reynolds 1723–1792

Sir Joshua Reynolds became the most famous and influential artist of eighteenth-century Britain and with Gainsborough, Turner and Constable he remains one of the best-known of all British artists. His career spanned most of the second half of the eighteenth century, sometimes known as the golden age of British art. British art came of age. The many fine locally-born artists and craftsmen of international standard included the painters Allan Ramsay, Thomas Gainsborough, Francis Cotes, Richard Wilson, Joseph Wright of Derby, Thomas Lawrence, the furniture designers Thomas Chippendale and Thomas Sheraton, the silversmith Paul de Lamerie, the pottery manufacturer Josiah Wedgwood and of course the painter Joshua Reynolds himself. It was also the birth and early training period of the great nineteenth-century landscape artists J. M. W. Turner and John Constable. Reynolds's Grand Style of portraiture and history-painting dominated exhibitions at the Royal Academy that he had helped establish. In 1768 it was obvious he should be its first president, a post he held until his death in 1792. He received his knighthood in 1769 not only in acknowledgement of his gifts as a painter but also for raising the prestige and status of artists in British society.

Besides the example of his fine and various portraits Reynolds was influential also through his published "Discourses", fifteen lectures originally delivered between 1769 and 1790 to students and members of the Royal Academy. They were chiefly, although by no means exclusively, directed to the student of history painting, which Reynolds regarded as the highest branch of art.

Reynolds was born near Plymouth in 1723, the son of a clergyman. In 1740, at the age of seventeen, he commenced a two-and-a-half-year apprenticeship with Thomas Hudson (1701–1779), a leading portrait painter in London. In 1743 Reynolds set up an independent portrait practice in his native Devonshire and then later in London, producing routine portraits in the style of Hudson. Then in 1749 he set out for Italy where he spent two years in Rome, and a few weeks in Venice. In 1753 he settled again in London having learned much from past Italian masters, particularly the grand style of portraiture with learned allusions to classical antiquity; he generally married classical grandeur to the elegant local approach of Van Dyck, but sometimes switched to the more intimate and inward style of Rembrandt. By the mid 1750s he was running a highly successful and prolific studio that received well over a hundred commissions a year. By the mid 1760s he rivalled the older and more established royal portrait painter Allan Ramsay.

Reynolds was also a great art collector. He assembled the finest and largest collection of Old Master paintings and drawings owned by any artist in eighteenth-century Europe. The Art Gallery of South Australia owns a major drawing by Tintoretto that once belonged to Reynolds.

## Dr John Armstrong, 1767
oil on canvas, 76.5 x 63.8 cm
Morgan Thomas Bequest Fund 1934

Painted in mid-career, the year before he helped establish the Royal Academy, this is one of Reynolds's more intimate portraits. The sitter was a friend of many years: John Armstrong, M.D. (1709–1779), a noted physician, poet and essayist, especially remembered today as an author. He was born at Castleton, Roxburghshire, Scotland, in 1709 where his father, like Reynolds's at Plympton in Devon, was a parish clergyman. He studied medicine at Edinburgh University and took his degree in 1732. In 1746 he was appointed to the Hospital for Lame, Maimed and Sick Soldiers in London and in 1760 he was appointed physician to the British army in Germany. After the Peace of Paris he retired in 1763 on half pay; in 1769 he became director of the first London dispensary set up for children of the poor, situated in Red Lion Square. With his friend the artist Henry Fuseli he made a tour of France and Italy in 1771 and published his travel notes. Armstrong began to write poetry at an early age. His most successful effort and the one that established his fame was "The Art of Preserving Health", a didactic poem in four parts first published in 1744. It has become an English-language classic reprinted countless times, a masterpiece of blank verse and a work of austere imagination and weighty diction.[1]

In 1773 in his *Medical Essays* Dr Armstrong wrote about the reasons for his limited success as a medical practitioner. He confessed "he could neither tell a heap of lies in his own praise wherever he went; nor intrigue with nurses; nor associate, much less assimilate, with the various knots of pert insipid, lively stupid, well-bred impertinent, good-humoured malicious, obliging deceitful, waspy drivelling gossips; nor enter into juntos with people who were not to his liking". A contemporary colleague, a Dr Cuming of Dorchester, wrote: "[he] was a man of learning and genius, of considerable abilities in his profession, of great benevolence and goodness of heart, fond of associating with men of parts and genius, but indolent and inactive, and therefore totally unqualified to employ the means that usually led to medical employment, or to elbow his way through a crowd of competitors."[2]

Allan Ramsay, a fellow Scot, had painted Dr Armstrong's portrait in 1753. By 1767, when he painted this portrait of Armstrong, Reynolds had eclipsed Ramsay as the leading

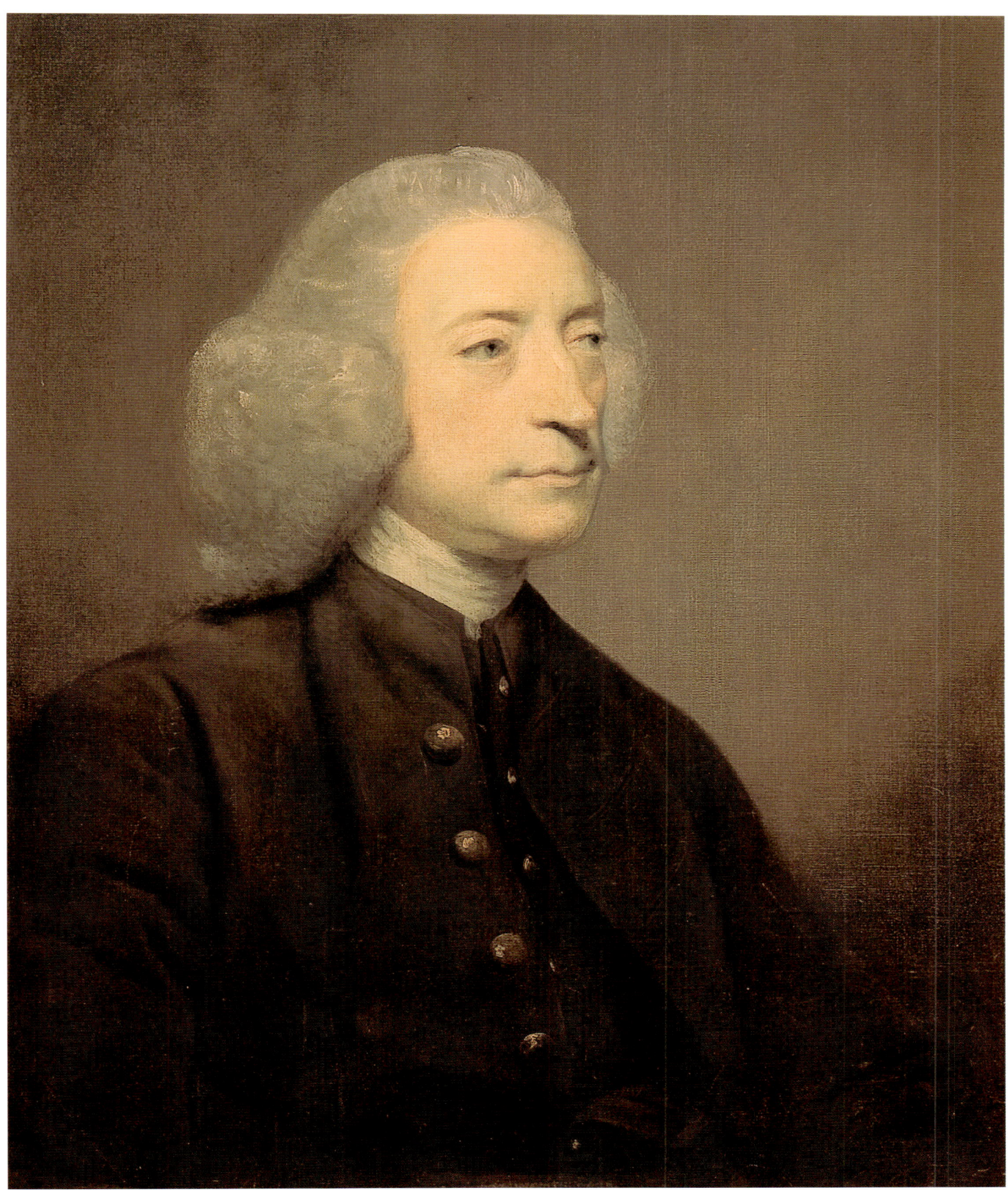

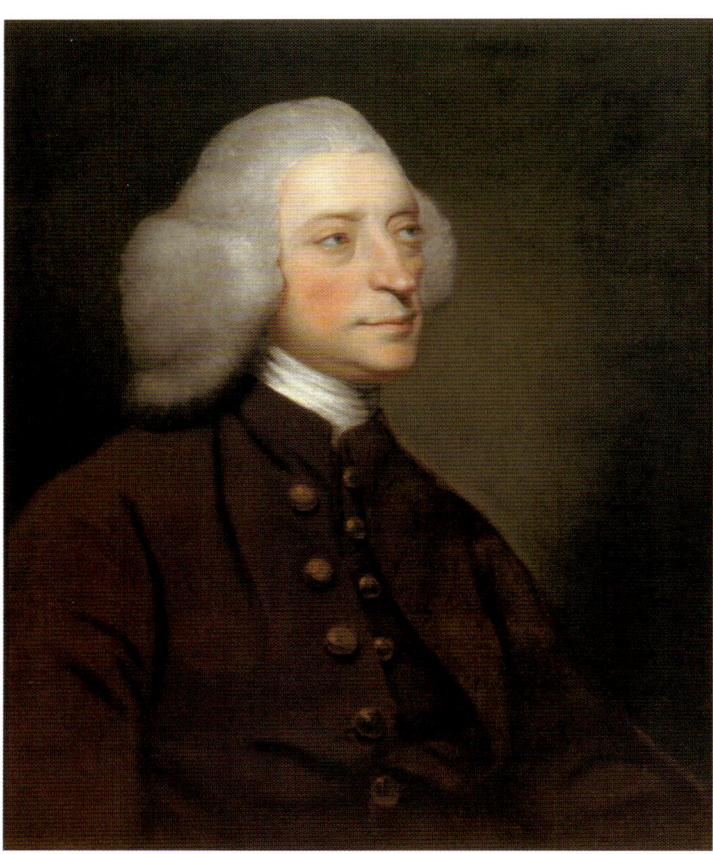

*Portrait of Dr John Armstrong*, c.1767. Gift of C. A. Ficke 1915, Figge Art Museum, Davenport, Iowa

artist of the time. Reynolds enjoyed associating with men of letters such as John Armstrong who in turn was "fond of associating with men of parts and genius" like Reynolds.

The portrait of the 58-year-old doctor – in a grey full-bottomed wig, white stock and dark brown coat and vest with brass buttons – displays the artist's ability to abandon the grand portrait style for an uncomplicated composition using a simple but refined restricted palette. Though in a cooler hue, like the paintings of Velázquez, it has some of the insight and subtle close tones and textures of Rembrandt. This is appropriate for Armstrong's private, shrewd and sometimes melancholic character; he is portrayed with an air of intelligent and sombre contemplation. Dr Armstrong was painted when Reynolds's admiration for Rembrandt was at its height and when the artist-collector already owned seventeen paintings he believed to be by Rembrandt.

The apparent simplicity of the composition is deceptive. It is not merely a straightforward head and shoulders of the kind that Thomas Hudson might have painted. Instead every part of the composition, not just the face, has been carefully considered and subtly worked up with warm and cool tones into a gently modulated and textured whole. It is the epitome of English reserve, restraint and good taste. The restrained palette, however, may be partly due to the fading of flesh-colour which was often the result of unsuccessful experiments in Reynolds's quest to emulate what he thought were the Old Masters' technical secrets concerning pigments and other materials.[3] A number of his portraits faded within his own lifetime, much to the distress of patrons.

Reynolds completed this highly-worked small portrait commission after nine one-hour sittings in 1767 and on 8 December was paid 36 pounds and 15 shillings[4], then his standard fee for this 30 by 24 inch size. A version of similar size, presumably painted by Reynolds's studio at about the same time, is in the Figge Art Museum, Davenport, Iowa. A third version is possibly a copy.[5] A 1777 mezzotint by Edward Fisher is inscribed "John Armstrong, MD. The suffrage of the wise, the praise that's worth competition is attained by sense alone and dignity of mind". At least four other engravings of the image followed, attesting to the sitter's importance.[6]

The portrait is one of the Gallery's early British Old Master purchases, bought in 1934. It was secured in London on the recommendation of the highly respected South Australian landscape painter Hans Heysen who was on a visit to Europe.

**Provenance:** John Armstrong, thence by descent; possibly Caleb Whitefoord, his sale at Christie's, London, 4 May 1810, lot 99, bt Solomon; Christie's, London, 26 April, 1830, lot 74 (owner John Green), bt Watts; taken to America for sale, W. Hayward, Boston, Massachusetts, 3 June 1840, lot 74; Christie's, 7 May 1841, lot 34; Sotheby's, London, 6 May 1926, lot 5; 8 May 1931, lot 86; bt from Tomas Harris Ltd, London, on the recommendation of Hans Heysen, 1934.

**Exhibitions:** Hayward Collection exhibition, Boston, 1840. *Island to Empire: 300 Years of British Art 1550–1850*, AGSA, Adelaide, 2005.

**Literature:** A. Graves and W. V. Cronin, *A History of the Works of Sir Joshua Reynolds*, London, 1899–1901, vol. 1, p. 30. *NGSA Catalogue of Paintings, Pastels and Sculpture*, Adelaide: AGSA, 1940, no. 842, pp. 160, 225. E. K. Waterhouse, *Reynolds*, London, 1941, p. 58. *NGSA Catalogue of Oil and Water-colour Paintings and Pastels*, fifth edition, Adelaide: NGSA, 1946, pp. 165–66. *NGSA Catalogue of Oil and Water-colour Paintings and Pastels with Biographical Notes*, Adelaide: NGSA, 1960, p. 211. *NGSA Picture Book of Selected Oil and Watercolour Paintings and Sculpture*, Adelaide: NGSA, 1960, p. 20. E. K. Waterhouse, "Reynolds's Sitter Book for 1755", *Walpole Society*, xli, 1966–68, p. 141. *Picture Book*, Adelaide: AGSA, 1972, p. 18 (illus.). David Thomas et al., *Art Gallery of South Australia 1881–1981*, Adelaide: AGSA, 1981, p. 64. Yarnall and Gerdts, iv, 1986, p. 2931. Peter Tomory and Robert Gaston, *European Paintings before 1800 in Australian and New Zealand Public Collections*, Sydney, 1989, p. 42, no. 109. David Mannings, *Sir Joshua Reynolds: A complete catalogue of his paintings*, New Haven and London, 2000, no. 73, pp. 65, 386 (illus.).

**Condition:** Fair; flesh tones probably faded, last conserved in 1998 by Artlab Australia, Adelaide.

**Frame:** Original.

# Joshua Reynolds

## Robert Henley, Second Earl of Northington, 1787
oil on canvas, 45.0 x 42.2 cm
A. R. Ragless Bequest Fund 1948

Robert Henley, second Earl of Northington (1747–1786) is notable for holding the post of Lord Lieutenant of Ireland with some distinction and popularity, albeit for a short period, from 30 April 1783 to his retirement in February 1784. He advocated annual parliaments and promoted Irish industry.

He was the only surviving son of Robert Henley, first Earl of Northington and a Lord Chancellor of England. The son was an elected member of parliament for Hampshire from 1768 until he succeeded to the earldom in 1772 and thus entered the House of Lords. In 1771 he was made a Knight of the Thistle. He died aged thirty-nine in Paris on 5 July 1786, returning from a trip to Italy. He never married, the title lapsed and his estates devolved upon his two sisters as co-heirs. Sir Nathaniel Wraxall in his *Memoirs* describes the second earl as "…unwieldy, vacillating, and destitute of grace, [which] seemed to disqualify him for any active exertions of body, nor were his faculties brilliant, but I have always heard that he gave great satisfaction, and was as much beloved as his infirmities permitted".[1]

From Joshua Reynolds's appointment books we know that Northington sat for him in December 1782 and January 1784. (Reynolds's appointment book for 1783 is missing.) It is probable that the 1782 sittings resulted in the half-length portrait now in the Musée Cognaq-Jay, Paris. The 1784 sittings, which were after Northington's 1783 appointment as Lord Lieutenant of Ireland, resulted in a grander seated three-quarter-length portrait in his peer's robes, holding an open paper in his right hand, and wearing the collar of the Order of St Patrick which George III had instituted in 1783 and for which the sitter was the second Grand Master. A final payment to Reynolds was made in April 1785 and the portrait may not have been finished until then; it was exhibited at the Royal Academy that year. From a review in the *General Advertiser*, 28 April 1785, we read: "His [Reynolds's] next best portrait is that of Lord Northington, in the robes of the Lord-Lieutenant of Ireland, which is likewise a fine likeness, and well executed. There is, however, somewhat of a stiffness in the drapery, and too great a compliment to the noble Lord's rotundity, which, by the measurement of the portrait, is one-sixth less than his lordship's weight and measure", and from the *Morning Herald*: "No. 122. Portrait of a Nobleman, a half-length of Lord Northington in his robes of Lord-Lieutenant of Ireland. The likeness is strong."[2] The portrait is now held by the National Gallery of Ireland, Dublin.

A studio replica the same size as Reynolds's three-quarter-length figure was later commissioned by one of Northington's co-heirs, his eldest sister Lady Bridget Tollemache, and paid for in February 1787, which was the year following his early death. The present-day peer Lord Henley, who is also a Lord Northington by a later creation in the peerage of the United Kingdom, owns that replica and also a similar but half-length portrait by Reynolds; both are held at Scaleby Castle, Cumbria.

In January 1788 Reynolds was paid "£25/5s" for a further posthumous copy, of the head only.[3] This is almost certainly the Gallery's portrait head of Lord Northington, in which part of the collar of the Order of St Patrick can be seen, with part of the red chair and curtains behind. It displays Reynolds's typical brushwork, particularly in the painting of the ermine fur robe, which is Titianesque. No doubt this version would have had some studio assistance, being a replica painted at the very end of the artist's long career. The 1788 payment means that one could conclude with some certainty that it was painted in 1787.

Although Lord Northington had no children (or because he had no children) he seems to have been concerned about posterity. He commissioned several other portraits in his relatively short life besides those by Reynolds. The earliest is by Reynolds's teacher, Thomas Hudson. Two – one of 1777, another 1781 – are by George Romney.[4]

Provenance: Miss Hickey; Agnew's, 1946; purchased on the advice of Harold Wright.
Exhibition: *Island to Empire: 300 Years of British Art 1550–1850*, AGSA, Adelaide, 2005.
Literature: A. Graves and W. V. Cronin, *A History of the Works of Sir Joshua Reynolds*, London, 1899–1901, vol. 2, p. 696. *NGSA Catalogue of Oil and Water-colour Paintings and Pastels with Biographical Notes*, Adelaide: NGSA, 1960, p. 211. Peter Tomory and Robert Gaston, *European Paintings before 1800 in Australian and New Zealand Public Collectionse*, Sydney, 1989, p. 42, no. 112. David Mannings, *Sir Joshua Reynolds: A complete catalogue of his paintings*, New Haven and London, 2000, p. 250, no. 875a.
Condition: Good; last conserved in 1997 by Artlab Australia, Adelaide.
Frame: Original.

# Joshua Reynolds

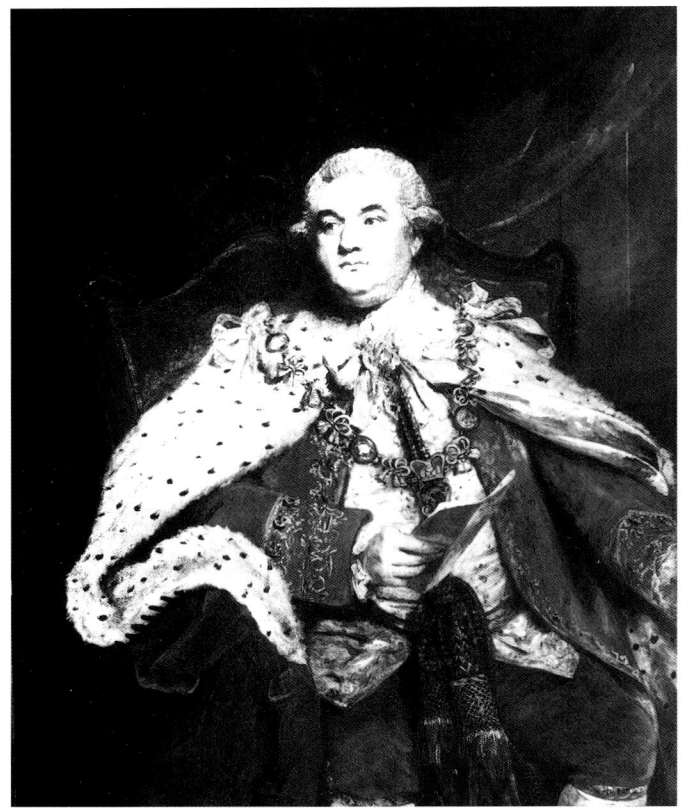

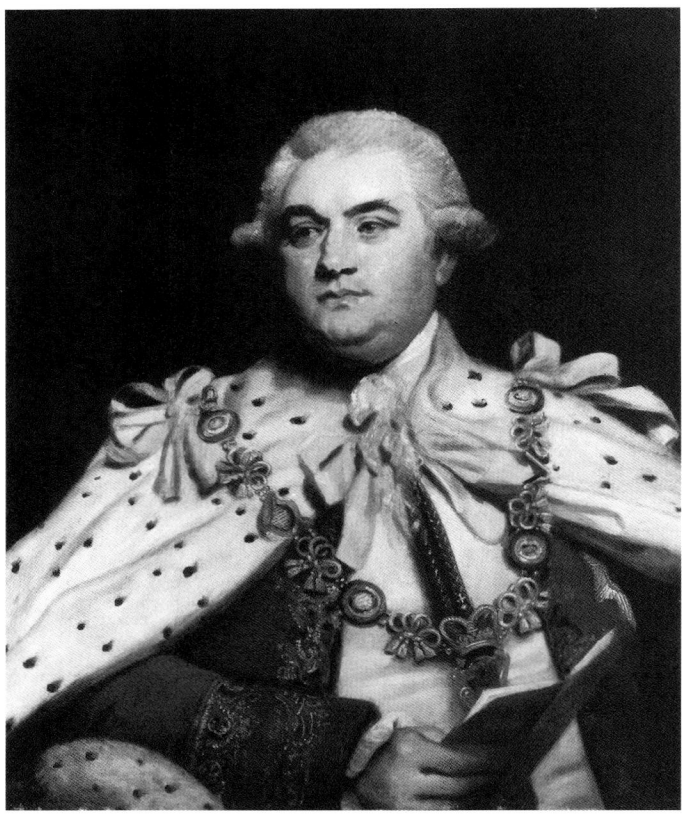

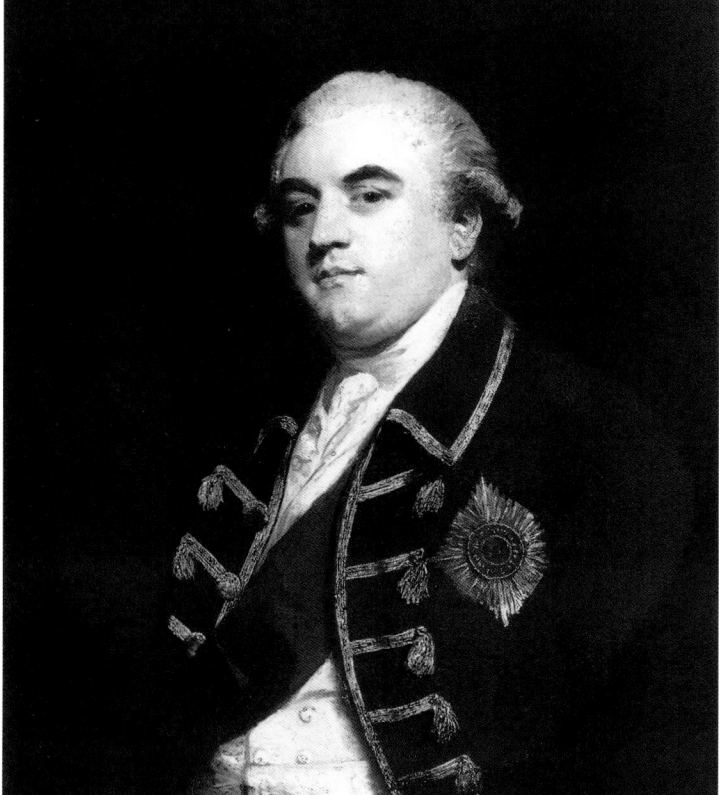

top right: Joshua Reynolds, *Robert Henley, Second Earl of Northington*, 1784. Photograph courtesy of the National Gallery of Ireland, Dublin

top left: Joshua Reynolds, *Robert Henley, Second Earl of Northington*, c.1787. Lord Henley, Carlisle

bottom: Joshua Reynolds, *Robert Henley, Second Earl of Northington*, c.1782. © P.M.V.P./ Joffre, Musée Cognaq-Jay, Paris

opposite: Joshua Reynolds, *Robert Henley, Second Earl of Northington*, 1787, oil on canvas, 45.0 x 42.2 cm.
A. R. Ragless Bequest Fund 1948

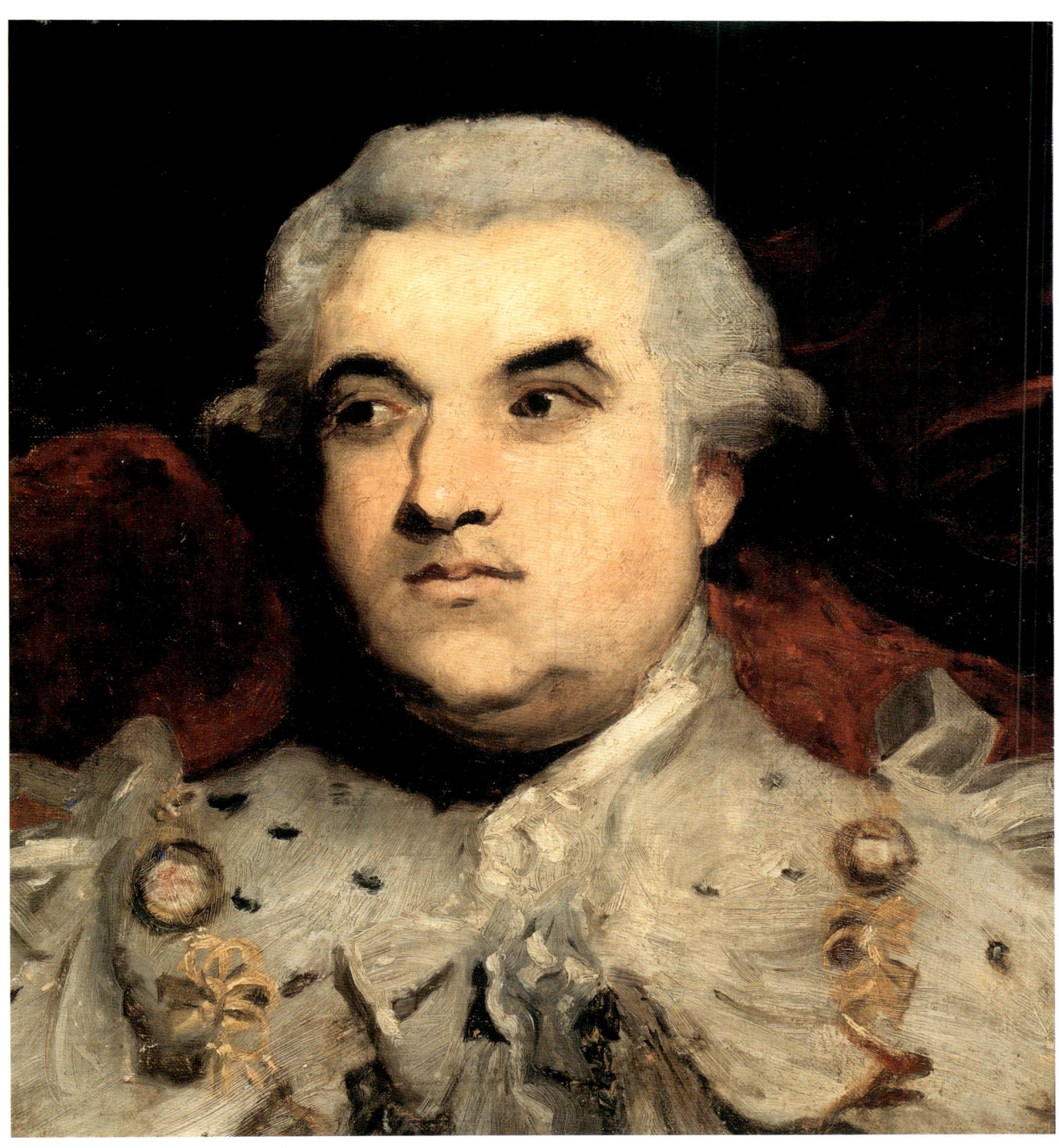

# Francis Cotes 1726–1770

Francis Cotes was a fashionable portrait painter whose practice in London in the 1760s was surpassed only by those of Allan Ramsay and Joshua Reynolds yet had been almost forgotten until relatively recently. He is known for the milk-and-roses complexions of his youthful, healthy and wealthy sitters in elaborate clothes. In the early 1760s he moved into a handsome and commodious studio in Cavendish Square where he executed pastel portraits of the royal family and then in 1767 a double full-length portrait of George III's younger sisters Princess Louisa and Princess Caroline (Royal collection). After the success of the royal portraits he received many commissions from notable people.

Cotes was born in London in 1726. He began his career in the late 1740s as a pastel artist, emerging from the English Rococo milieu and influenced by the Continental pastel tradition exemplified by Rosalba Carriera (1675–1757), who was much favoured by British tourists to Venice, and also by the French Jean-Étienne Liotard (1702–89), who was in England in the 1750s. Cotes first studied and mastered pastel drawing under George Knapton (1698–1778) and he continued to work chiefly in pastel for portraits throughout the 1750s. Although he continued to execute pastel portraits in the 1760s, he then mainly painted large oils but retained some of the colouring and decorative drawing quality of pastel. As an oil painter he used the basic portrait types being popularised in the 1750s by Ramsay and Reynolds, but his style also owes something to Johann Zoffany (1733–1810).

Cotes resisted, however, the trend led by Reynolds from the 1760s to classicise figures and costumes, and include classical props and allusions. He remained a late Rococo portrait painter who relied on realistic rendering of decorative costumes to give his paintings verve.

He was a founding member of the Society of Artists and active in the establishment of the Royal Academy, of which he was a foundation member and at which he exhibited before his early death in 1770 aged forty-four. Cotes's relatively short career and limited output may be the reason his name long fell almost into oblivion. He is now again considered to be, along with Ramsay, Reynolds and Gainsborough, one of the finest British portrait painters of his time.

## Elizabeth, Lady Jones, 1769
oil on canvas, 127.0 x 101.6 cm
A. M. Ragless Bequest Fund 1961

This striking portrait of Lady Jones was painted in 1769 at the height of Cotes's fashionable success, a year before his death. She was the eldest daughter and co-heiress of William Jones of Ramsbury Manor, Wiltshire, and in 1767 married William Langham who assumed the name Jones and who was created a baronet in 1774. He died in 1791. The companion Cotes portrait of her husband Sir William Jones Bt is the same size as hers and shows him wearing a green coat leaning on a fence in a landscape setting with his left leg up and a walking stick in his left hand and a hat in his right hand. It is held in a private collection in Britain.[1]

Lady Jones is portrayed three-quarter-length with a typically English landscape backdrop rather in the style of George Knapton and early Thomas Gainsborough. The oak tree on the left spreads above her and provides an autumn canopy for the portrait while dark clouds gather in the sky. She wears a white silk-and-lace gown with pink satin bows and neck ruff and a white lace bonnet featuring a small central floral-like bow also in pink satin. Her dress is remarkably similar to the white-and-pink dress worn by Princess Caroline in Cotes's grand double portrait of the royal sisters painted in 1767. Lady Jones's stylish, self-conscious pose is one of arrested movement, a mannerism for which the artist became known, rather like the qualities of fashionable portrait photographers in a later age. She faces us directly, a voluminous silk train held over her right arm while her left arm is extended as if pointing to her substantial property beyond. Despite Cotes's lack of interest in classical allusions the draped outstretched arm and fingers ultimately derive from classical statues like the Apollo Belvedere whose stance filtered through over a hundred years of British portraiture from Van Dyck and Lely to Reynolds. The gesture towards property resembles that in statues of Roman emperors. Yet this portrait is anything but classical. She is a robust, well-dressed Englishwoman with a glowing and healthy moon face. Her elaborate costume with frills, lace and bows echoes the pinks and whites of her complexion. Light powdery colours and decorative drawing of the costume echo the pastel technique and colours from which Cotes's art evolved. Paintings like this are a last flutter of the English Rococo. Cotes's virtuosity with luxurious costume and pleasant landscape make it easy to understand his fashionable success.

The painting and its pair followed a number of earlier portrait commissions carried out by Cotes for Lady Jones's family. Elizabeth's father was apparently the first to engage the artist when he commissioned his own portrait in 1764. This was followed by ten other commissions from the Joneses and their in-laws the Burdetts. Cotes was evidently a family favourite by 1769 when he painted the Gallery's portrait of Lady Jones and its companion of husband Sir William. The

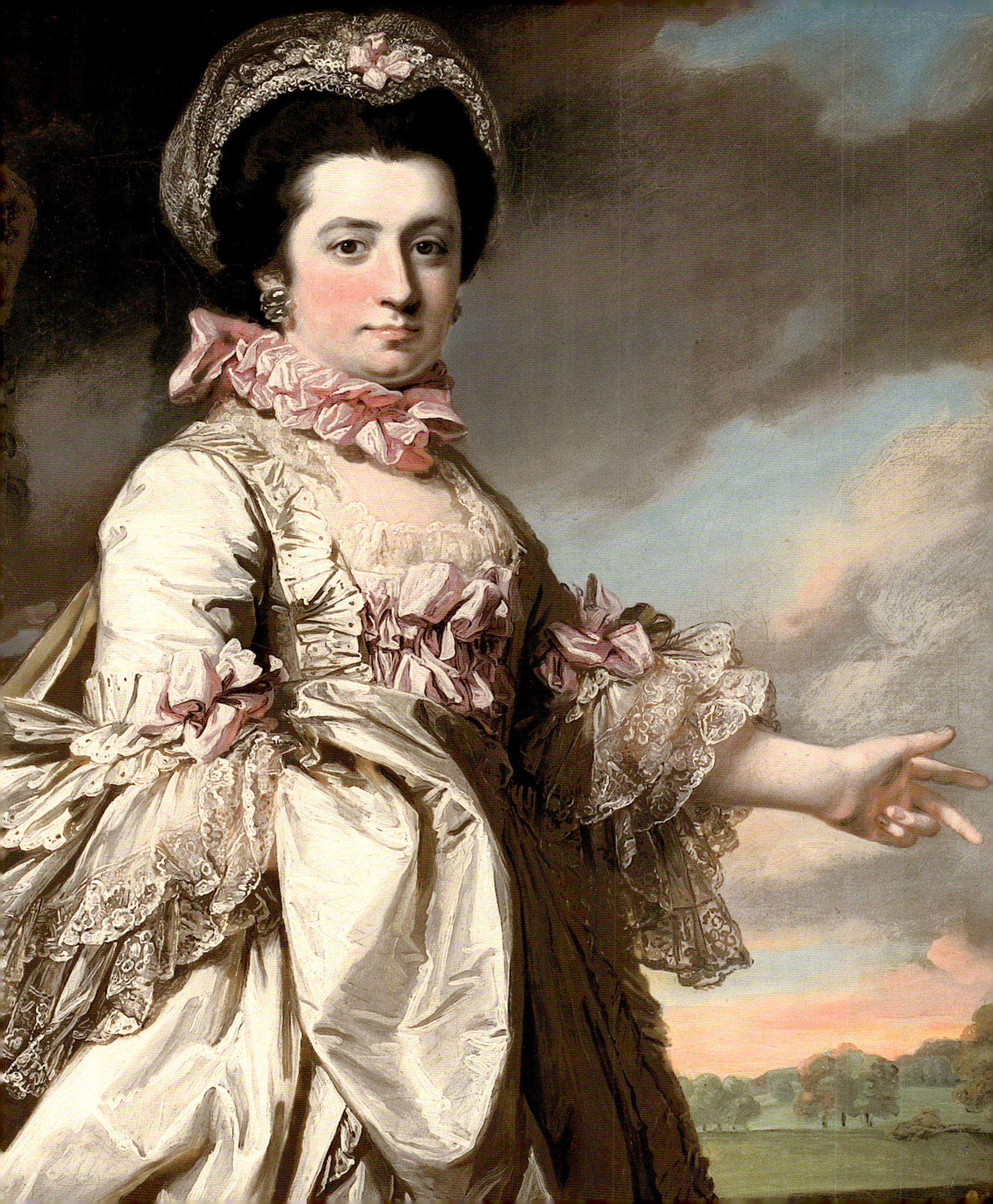

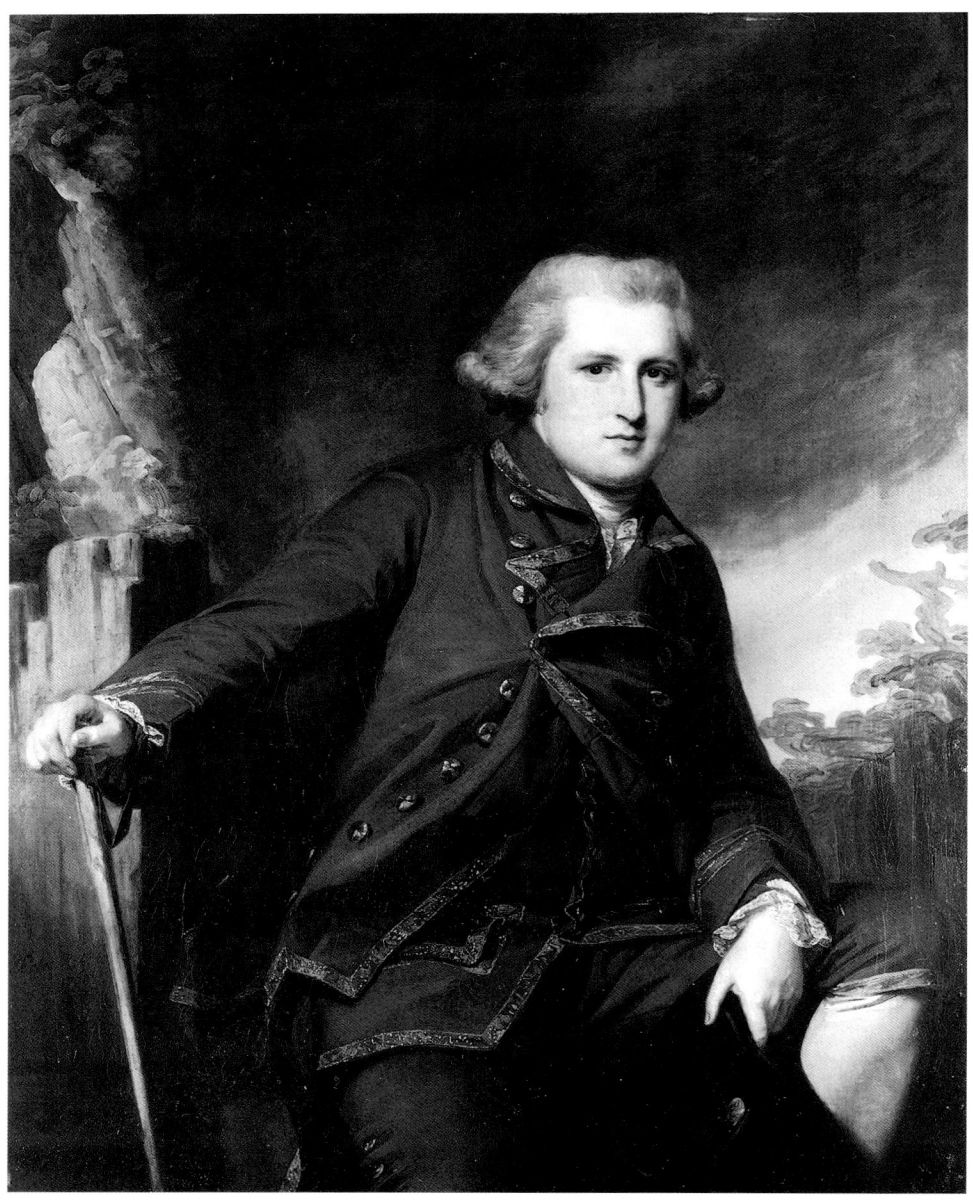

Francis Cotes, *Sir William Jones*, c.1769. Wimpole Hall, The Bambridge Collection, The National Trust.
Photograph: Photographic Survey, Courtauld Institute of Art

Joneses and Burdetts were in fact his best customers. Sir William and Lady Jones died without issue and all eleven portraits by Cotes came together in the Burdett family when they eventually inherited the Joneses' Ramsbury Manor. The portraits all remained there until the estate of Sir Francis Burdett, 7th baronet, was dispersed in Sotheby's sale on 2 December 1953. Our painting was bought by the American collector Walter P. Chrysler junior but it was returned to the London art market six years later.

Since Cotes was not prolific and his life was short it is perhaps not surprising that this is the only painting by him in Australasia.

**Inscription:** Signed and dated c. l., brown paint: "FCotes R.A. / 1769" (the initials "FC" in monogram).

**Provenance:** By family descent from the sitter to Sir Francis Burdett, 7th Bt, Ramsbury Manor, Ramsbury, Wiltshire; his sale Sotheby's, London, 2 December 1953, lot 54, bt by Spiller; Walter P. Chrysler Jnr, Provincetown, Massachusetts, his sale Sotheby's, London, 15 July 1959, lot 87; bt by the Art Gallery from Leger Galleries, London, on the advice of H. D. Molesworth, 1961.

**Exhibition:** *Island to Empire: 300 Years of British Art 1550–1850*, AGSA, Adelaide, 2005.

**Literature:** *Connoisseur*, May 1966 (American edition), (illus.). David Thomas et al., *Art Gallery of South Australia 1881–1981*, Adelaide: AGSA, 1981, p. 58. Peter Tomory and Robert Gaston, *European Paintings before 1800 in Australian and New Zealand Public Collections*, Sydney, 1989, p. 15, no. 13 (illus.).

**Condition:** Excellent; last conserved in 1998 by Artlab Australia, Adelaide.

**Frame:** Not original.

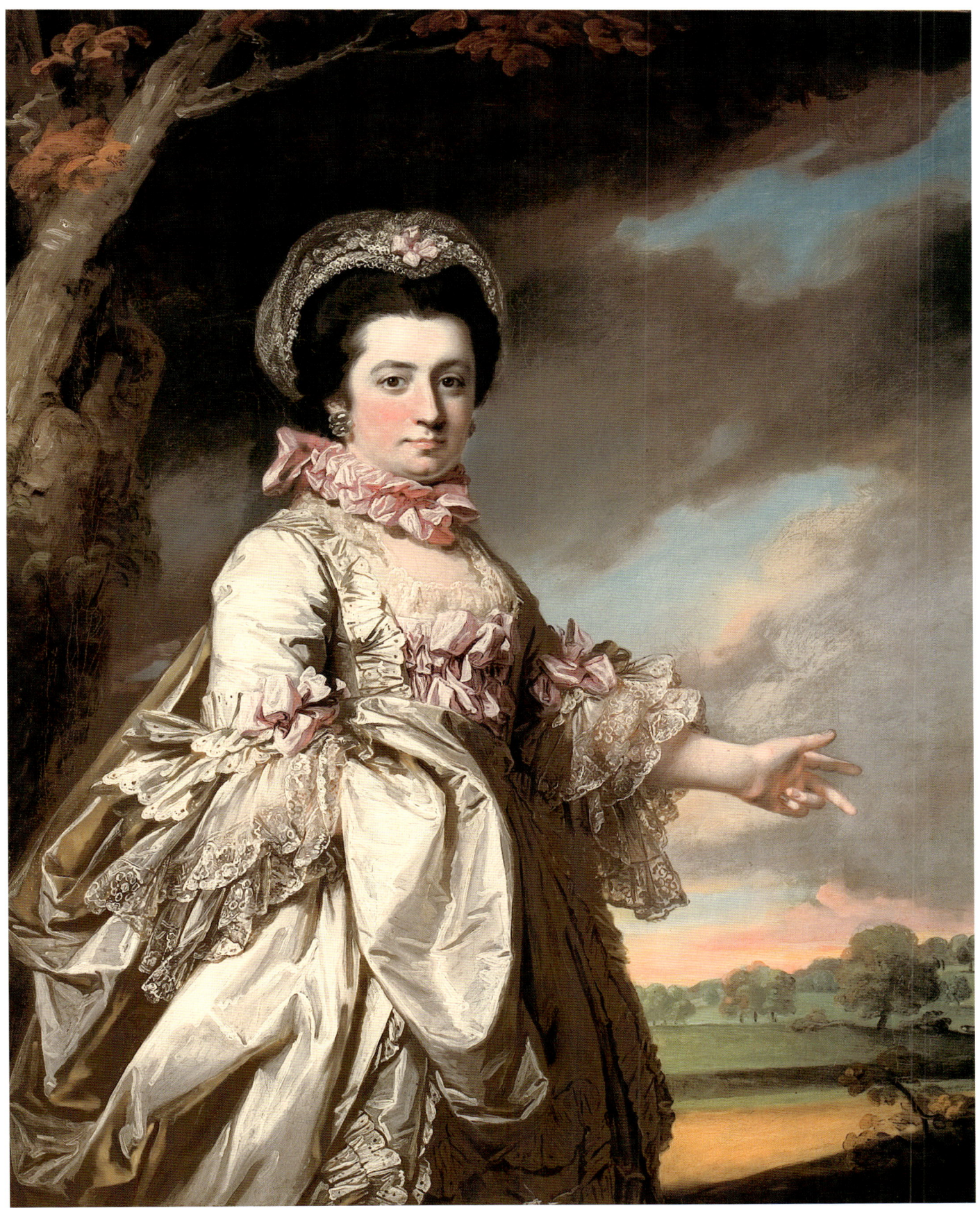

# Richard Wilson 1713–1782

Richard Wilson was the first major British artist to concentrate on landscape painting. Born in 1713 in Penegoes, North Wales, he had a lifelong love of the Welsh countryside but began his career as a portrait painter, which was usual for any British artist at the time. From 1729 there was a six-year apprenticeship in London under a little-known portraitist, Thomas Wright. From 1750 to 1757 he travelled through Italy, studying longest in Rome. In 1750 in Venice and in Rome in 1751 the landscape painters Francesco Zuccarelli (1702–1788) and Joseph Vernet (1714–1789) both encouraged Wilson to shift to landscapes, which he had done only occasionally in Britain. He was inspired by the art-haunted countryside of the Roman Campagna and the landscape paintings of the seventeenth-century Roman masters Gaspard Dughet (1615–1675), Nicolas Poussin (1594–1665) and above all Claude Lorrain (1600–1682). Using their formulas for composition, Wilson evolved an effective style of his own, broader in handling, more related to the actual scene and often cooler in colour than Italian landscape paintings.

In Rome Wilson found several British patrons for his landscapes. Back in England he continued to paint Roman landscape compositions and began to interpret British landscape, especially Welsh scenery, using the balanced composition and unified light beloved by the seventeenth-century Roman masters. This Italianisation helped raise the status of landscape painting in a nation obsessed with portraiture, but it also helped the British appreciate the beauty of their own country. By the 1760s and early 1770s Wilson had created a market for large oils of British landscape subjects, his classically balanced compositions fit to hang alongside the seventeenth-century masters already numerous in British collections. However, by the second half of the 1770s his market had waned.

Wilson was a foundation member of the Royal Academy in 1768 but in 1776 only his appointment, with a small salary, as the Academy's Librarian saved him from destitution. He retired to Wales about a year before his death, which occurred in 1782 exactly one hundred years after the death of his Roman exemplar Claude Lorrain.

## Cicero with his friend Atticus and brother Quintus, at his villa at Arpinum, c.1771–75
oil on canvas, 121.8 x 174.5 cm
Morgan Thomas Bequest Fund 1948

Wilson's Roman landscapes painted in Britain are either imaginary or derived from his topographical sketches made in Rome between 1750 and 1757, but *Cicero with his friend Atticus and brother Quintus, at his villa at Arpinum* is an exception and has a different, more complex origin. The left half of this Italian subject appears to be based on a sketch of Welsh scenery. That drawing and another in chalk, more summary and broadly suggesting the space and composition of the right-hand side of the painting, are now held in the Ashmolean Museum, Oxford. Nonetheless the overall balanced appearance is in conformity with conventional seventeenth-century Roman styles. The general colouring, the billowing clouds and spraying torrents suggest Gaspard Dughet; the basic concept, composition and space are distinctively Claudean. The source of the composition seems to be Claude Lorrain's *St George and the Dragon*, 1643, in the Wadsworth Atheneum, Hartford, Connecticut.

So this Italian scene was painted in London using Welsh landscape sketches interpreted through a composition by Claude Lorrain. It was executed towards the end of Wilson's career and takes its classical subject matter from the Roman consul Cicero's treatise *De Legibus* (*Of the Laws*). When Wilson exhibited the first of the four known versions of the work in 1770 he appended the exact reference to Cicero after the title in the Royal Academy exhibition catalogue.

The patrician Cicero, the celebrated orator and writer, is shown conversing with his brother and his friend at his birthplace Arpinum in a mountainous district between Rome and Naples. Cicero is the central figure, in the white toga. Atticus has just referred to Cicero's poem "Marius" and gestures towards the great oak at the right-hand edge of the composition. The painting refers to the following passage in *De Legibus*:

> Atticus: I recognise this as the very grove, and this oak, too, as the oak of Arpinum, the description of which I have often read in your poem on Marius. If that oak still exists, this must certainly be it; and, indeed, it appears extremely old.
>
> Quintus: Yes, my Atticus, it does exist, and always will exist, for it is a nursling of genius. No such long-lived stock can be planted by the care of an agriculturist as may be sown by the verse of a poet.
>
> Atticus: Do you feel inclined, since we have had walking enough for the present, and since you must now take up a fresh part of the subject for discussion, to vary our situation; and if you do, let us pass over to the island which is surrounded by the Fibrenus – for such, I believe, is the name of the other river – and sit down, while we prosecute the remainder of our discourse?
>
> Cicero: I like your proposal: for that is the very spot which I generally select when I want a place for undisturbed meditation, or uninterrupted reading or writing.
>
> Atticus: In truth, now I am come to this delicious retreat, I cannot see too much of it. Would you believe, that the pleasure I find here makes me almost despise magnificent villas, marble pavements, and sculptured palaces: Who would not smile at the artificial canals which our great folk call their Niles and Euripi,

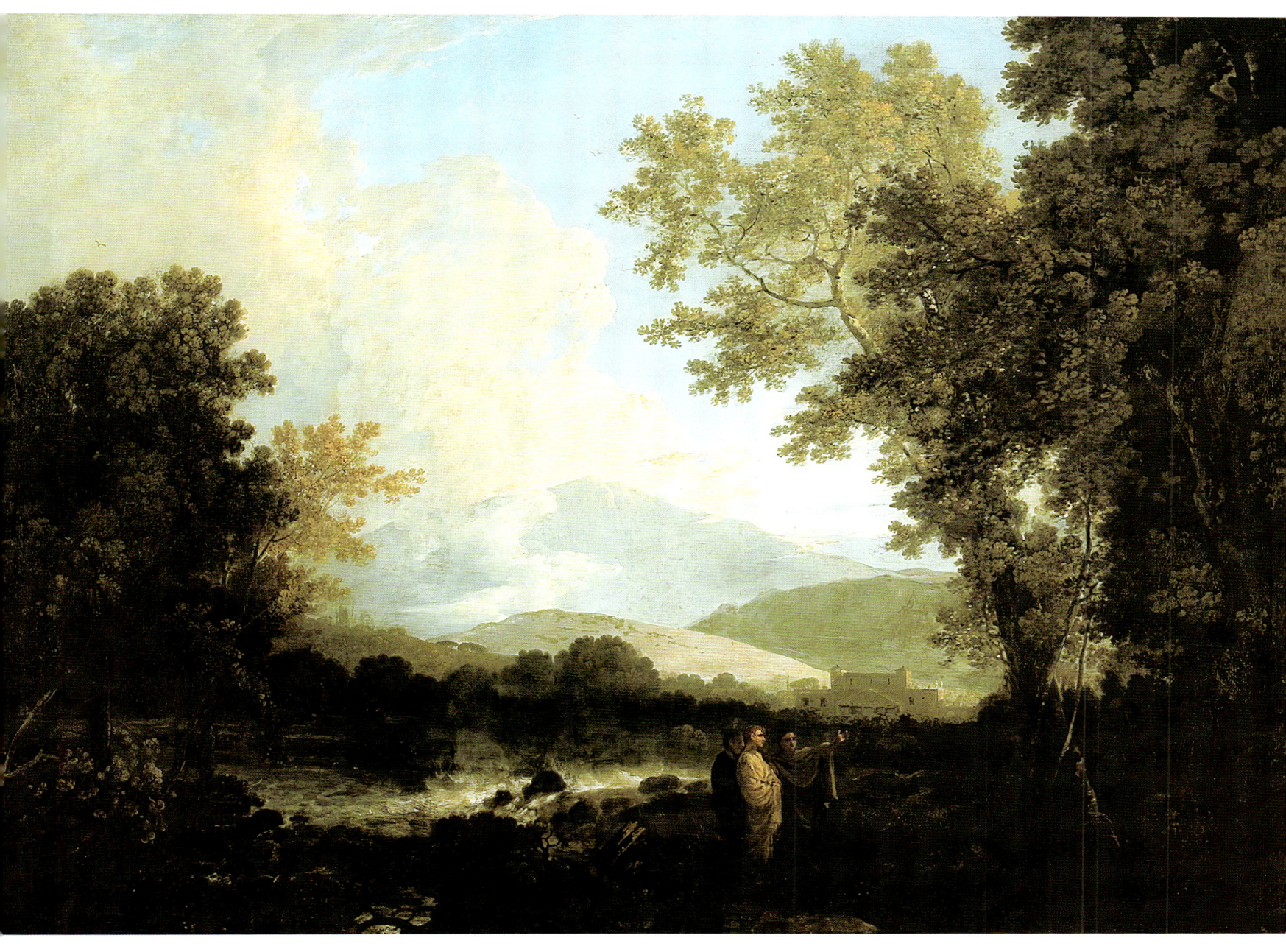

after he had seen these beautiful streams? Therefore, as you just now, in our conversation on Justice and Law, referred all things to Nature, so you seek to preserve her domination even in those things which are constructed to recreate and amuse the mind. I therefore used to wonder before, as I expected nothing better in this neighbourhood than hills and rocks (and, indeed, I had been led to form these ideas by your own speeches and verses) – I used to wonder, I say, that you were so exceedingly delighted with this place. But my present wonder, on the contrary, is, how, when you retire from Rome, you condescend to rusticate in any other spot.

Cicero responds by saying that Arpinum holds a special meaning for him as his birthplace, and as the home of his ancestors. Then Atticus continues, in words particularly applicable to Wilson's composition:

> But here we are arrived in your favourite island. How beautiful it appears! How bravely it stems the waves of the Fibrenus, whose divided waters lave its verdant sides, and soon rejoin their rapid currents! The river just embraces space enough for a moderate walk, and having discharged this office, and secured us an arena for disputation, it immediately precipitates itself into the Liris; and then; like those who ally themselves to patrician families, it loses its more obscure name, and gives the waters of the Liris a greater degree of coolness.[1]

At his peaceful and isolated villa, Cicero and his friends analysed the fundamental principles of justice and law, inspired to truth by the beautiful scenery around them. The idea of cultivated patricians inspired to virtue and wisdom in republican Rome – *De Legibus* dates from about 52 B.C. – by the simple life on their secluded country estates, far away from the distractions and corruptions of commerce, showy opulence and noisy crowds of the city, appealed to the landed gentry of eighteenth-century Britain. Sir Watkin Williams-Wynn, a baronet, the largest landowner in Wales and one of the wealthiest men in Britain, commissioned this second and much larger version of the painting probably after seeing the first in the Royal Academy exhibition of 1770. He doubtless intended to display it at his country seat Wynnstay in North Wales thus suggesting symbolic parallels with his own wise rule. It is not among the paintings recorded in his London town house; there Sir Watkin displayed Welsh views by Wilson.[2]

The Cicero subject had not previously occurred in work by Wilson or any other artist.[3] David Solkin has argued persuasively that the original Royal Academy version was partly provoked by current political events in Britain.[4] It was the time when John Wilkes, although democratically voted into Parliament several times, had been consistently denied his seat by a patrician Government. This had caused a storm between the rising middle class who demanded a more democratic government and the landed gentry who held power. In painting this picture, Wilson, a distant relative of Sir Watkin Williams-Wynn, has supported the status quo of the gentry who were, after all, his patrons and would understand the significance of Cicero's passage favouring the wisdom of traditional aristocratic rule. However, besides the pertinent classical theme and its local topical relevance at the time of "Wilkes and Liberty", it is possible that the Welsh appearance of Wilson's Italian landscape had inspired the classically-educated former grand tourist to commission this much larger version.

The first version of the painting, which is in a British private collection (see opposite), was almost certainly bought from the 1770 Royal Academy exhibition by another extensive landowner, Sir John Smith, of Devon; it was presumably the basis of the "Cicero" engraving that a publisher dedicated to Sir John in 1778.[5] (Before his emigration John Glover bought Sir John Smith's version and exhibited it in 1821 and 1822 alongside his own British landscapes.) Sir Watkin's larger commission was possibly completed in the year following its exhibition at the Royal Academy and almost certainly before 1775. Wilson followed it by at least two more smaller versions of the subject, thus making it the most popular of the artist's late historical landscapes.[6]

| | |
|---|---|
| Provenance: | Painted for Sir Watkin Williams-Wynn Bt; the Wynn family by descent until sold Sotheby's, London, 5 February 1947, lot 48, as *A Welsh Landscape*; with Leggatt, London; with Agnew's whence bought for the Art Gallery of South Australia on the recommendation of Harold Wright 1948. |
| Exhibitions: | British Institution, London, 1814, no. 161. Suffolk Street, London, 1833, no. 145. British Institution, London, 1848, no. 173. *Art Treasures*, Manchester, 1857, no. 36. *Hidden Treasures: South Australia's European Old Master paintings, Restorations and Re-attributions and South Australia's European Old Master drawings*, AGSA, Adelaide, 1989. *The Morgan Thomas Bequest Centenary Exhibition*, AGSA, Adelaide, 2003. *John Glover and the Colonial Picturesque*, Tasmanian Museum & Art Gallery, Hobart; AGSA, Adelaide; National Gallery of Australia, Canberra and National Gallery of Victoria, Melbourne, 2003–04. *Island to Empire: 300 Years of British Art 1550–1850*, AGSA, Adelaide, 2005. |
| Literature: | W. G. Constable, *Richard Wilson*, London, 1953, pp. 168–69, pl. 27b. David H. Solkin, *Richard Wilson: The Landscape of Reaction*, London: Tate Gallery, 1982, pp. 131–33, 235–36. Ron Radford, *Hidden Treasures*, Adelaide: AGSA, 1989, pp. 39, 74 (illus.). Peter Tomory and Robert Gaston, *European Paintings before 1800 in Australian and New Zealand Public Collections*, Sydney, 1989, p. 51, no. 138 (illus.). Ron Radford et al., *Selected Works*, Adelaide: AGSA, 1991, p. 19 (illus.). Kathleen Nicholson, *Turner's Classical Landscapes: Myth and Meaning*, New Jersey, 1990, p. 14 (illus.). David Hansen, *John Glover*, Hobart/Sydney: Tasmanian Museum & Art Gallery and Art Exhibitions Australia, 2003, pp. 39, 74 (illus.). |
| Condition: | Good/fair; some of the dark paint has sunk. Last conserved in 1987 by Artlab Australia, Adelaide. |
| Frame: | Not original, but a 1980s enlargement of an eighteenth-century frame contemporary with the painting. |

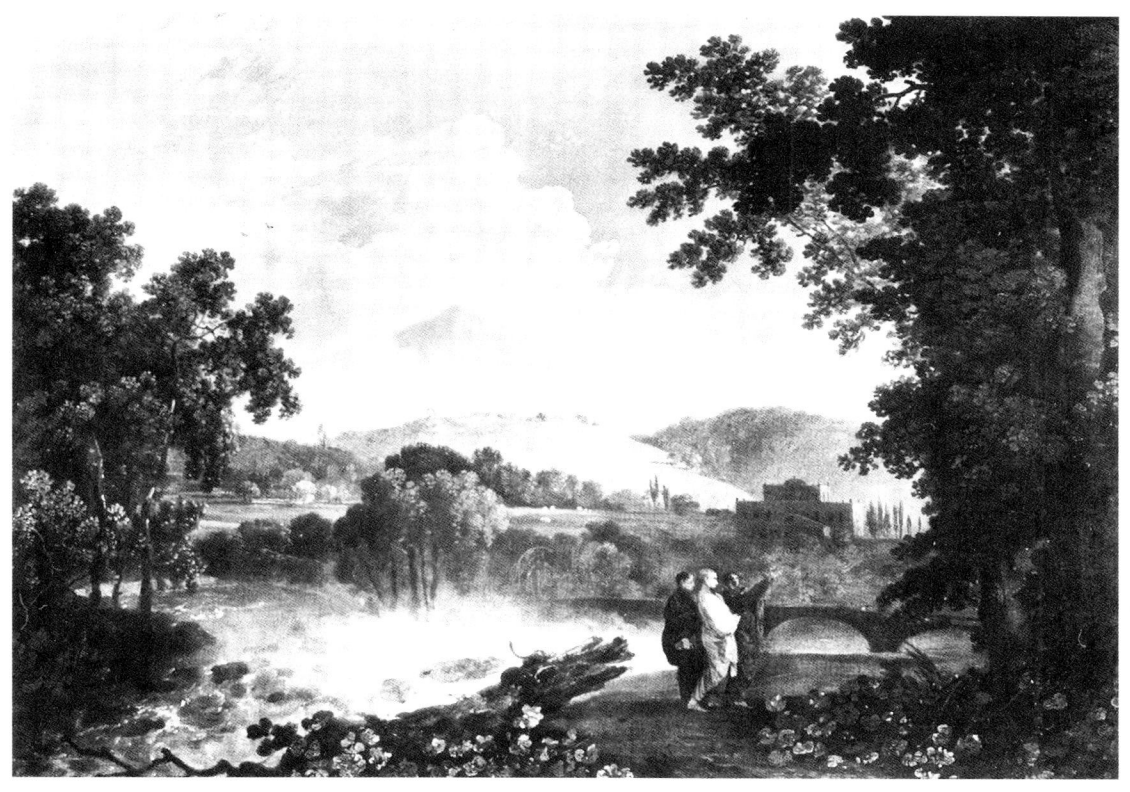

Richard Wilson, *Cicero and his two friends, Atticus and Quintus, at his Villa at Arpinum*, c.1769–70. Private collection

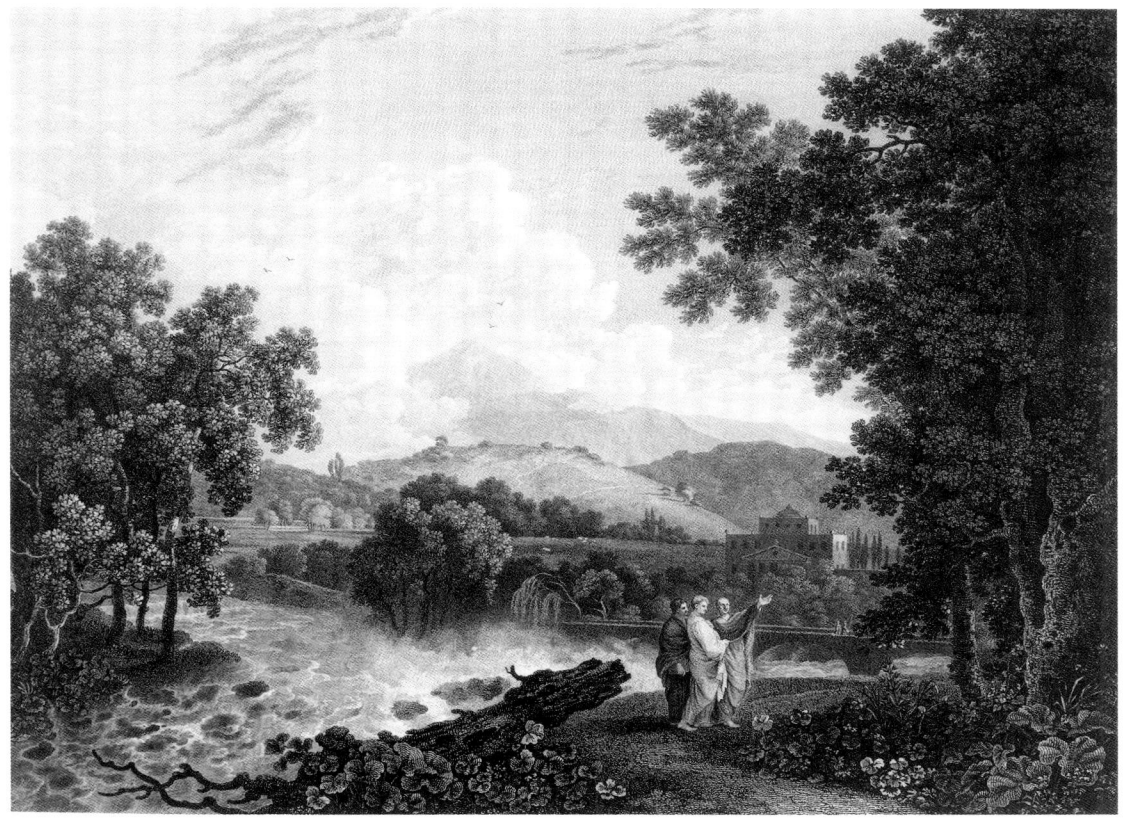

William Woollett after Richard Wilson, *Cicero at his villa*, 1778. © Copyright The Trustees of The British Museum, London

# Richard Wilson

## Dinas Bran from Llangollen, c.1772–75
oil on canvas, 82.5 x 104.1 cm
Gift of Gladys Penfold Hyland in memory of her husband Frank 1964

This North Wales landscape shows the village of Llangollen and surrounding mountains illuminated in morning light. The prospect, from the banks of the River Dee, framed by trees, leads the eye towards the village and then up the western slope of a mountain crowned by Castell Dinas Bran or, roughly anglicised from the Welsh, Crow Castle. The fourteenth-century bridge over the Dee and the tower of the village church of St Gollen can be seen in the middle distance; in the foreground four fishermen haul their nets across the river. Wilson's much larger first version of this scene was commissioned by Sir Watkin Williams-Wynn whose vast estate was nearby. Sir Watkin also commissioned the Gallery's large version of *Cicero with his friend Atticus and brother Quintus, at his villa at Arpinum* (p. 141).

Wilson has endowed the natural landscape with the pictorial devices of seventeenth-century Roman landscape painting – the classical balance, breadth, space and light conceived by Claude Lorrain – thus giving the view grandeur and thereby greater acceptability to his contemporary British market. The colour and mood also reflect the Roman landscapes of Gaspard Dughet. In the second half of the eighteenth century Richard Wilson assisted the new notion that ancient British castles could conjure up for the British a romantic nostalgia similar to that evoked by the ruins of the Roman Campagna: the lofty ruins of Castell Dinas Bran were as worthy a subject and as romantic as the Castel Sant' Angelo in Rome or the ruins of the Roman Forum; the bridge over the River Dee at Llangollen could be as worthy of depiction as the Ponte Sant' Angelo over the River Tiber, which in this painting it indeed resembles. Furthermore, the composition is remarkably similar to Claude's *Jacob, Laban and his daughters* at Petworth House, West Sussex.

Castell Dinas Bran, featured here and in the companion *View near Wynnstay* also commissioned from Wilson by Sir Watkin Williams-Wynn, had a special relevance for the patron. Sir Watkin owned much of the land overlooked by the ancient citadel. Importantly, the castle was known as one of the few large ruins surviving from before the English conquest of Wales and Sir Watkin took pride in tracing his lineage far back to Rhodri Mawr, a ninth-century Welsh king. Looking over the young lordling's estates, the dominant Dinas Bran (its altitude exaggerated in the composition) could be seen as a symbol of his family's traditional rule and benign authority over the land and its inhabitants.[1]

The first version and its companion were completed by 1771, intended for Sir Watkin's London town house no doubt as a reminder in the capital of his dominion over Denbighshire. The pair, both two-and-a-half-metres wide, and another two Welsh landscapes by Wilson hung in the neoclassical house designed and built for the grandee by Robert Adam in 1771–74, and still extant at 20 St James's Square.

This smaller, simpler version, probably painted within a year or two of the original, retains the fishermen drawing in a net but omits three foreground figures at work on a fallen tree and a washerwoman's riverside tub. There are at least another two versions: one in a British private collection, and the other in the Ferens Art Gallery, Hull. Two drawings are closer to our painting than to the first version. One of them is in the National Museum of Wales and once belonged to Paul Sandby, who in 1770 travelled and sketched in Wales with Sir Watkin Williams-Wynn.[2] The other is now at the Yale Center for British Art.

It is a pleasing coincidence that the Gallery should now own both the Sir Watkin Williams-Wynn version of *Cicero* and this version of his *Dinas Bran*. Sir Watkin's *Dinas Bran* and its companion *View near Wynnstay* are still together, at the Yale Center for British Art, New Haven; the *Dinas Bran* was shown in Adelaide in 1998 in the exhibition *This Other Eden: British Paintings from the Paul Mellon Collection at Yale*.[3]

**Provenance:** Captain E. N. F. Loyd; sold Christie's, London, 30 April 1937, lot 138, as *Welsh River Scene*, bt Hyam; to Frank and Gladys Penfold Hyland, Sydney.

**Exhibitions:** *Art Treasures*, Manchester, 1857, no. 38 as *Vale of Llangollen*, lent by Edward Lloyd. *Island to Empire: 300 Years of British Art 1550–1850*, AGSA, Adelaide, 2005.

**Literature:** W. G. Constable, *Richard Wilson*, London, 1953, pp. 175–76. David Solkin, 1982, pp. 130–33, 238. *Picture Book*, Adelaide: AGSA, 1972, p. 22 (illus.). Ron Radford et al., *Treasures*, Adelaide: AGSA, 1998, p. 48 (illus.).

**Condition:** Very good; last conserved in 1990 by Artlab Australia, Adelaide.

**Frame:** Original.

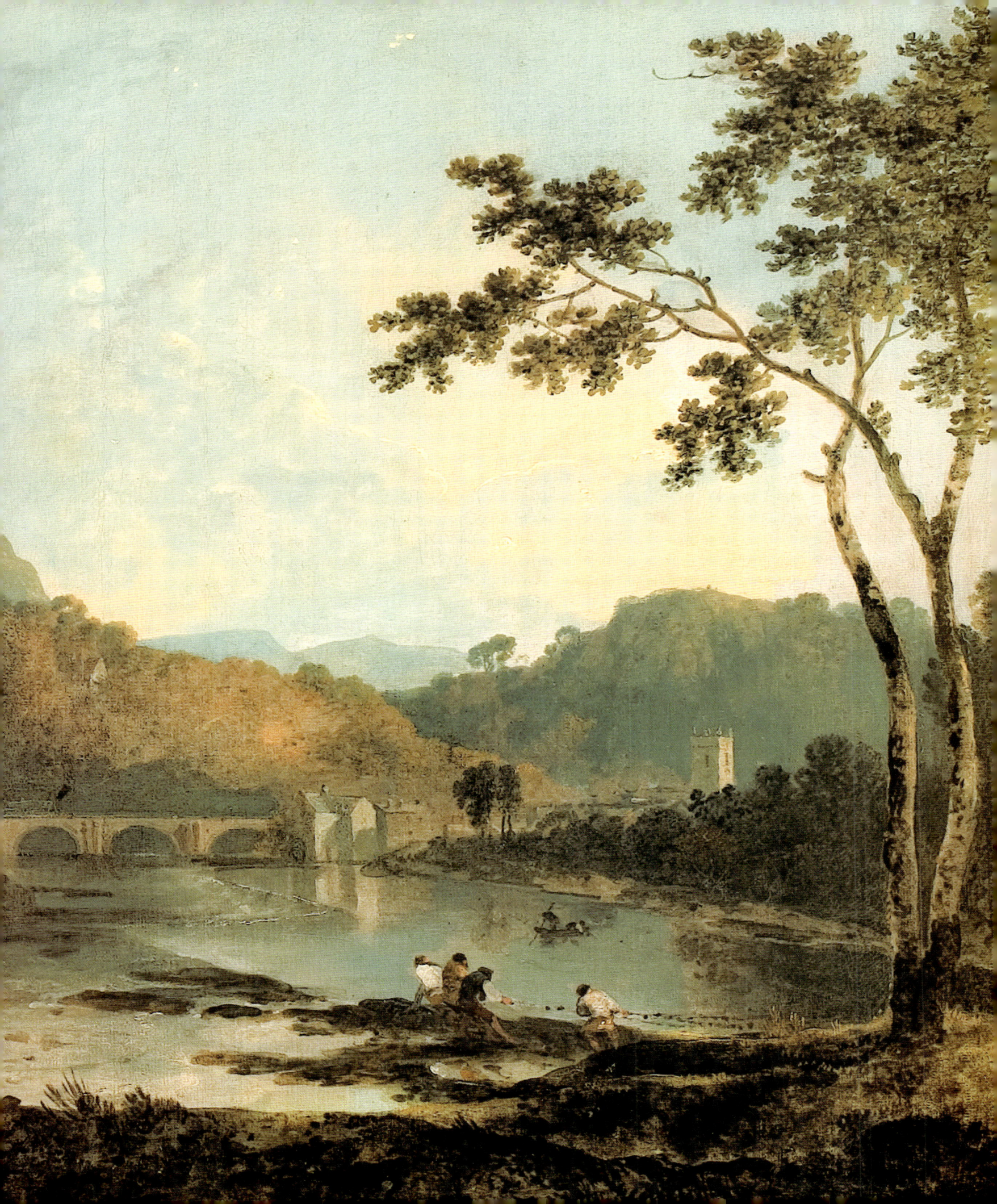

# Richard Wilson

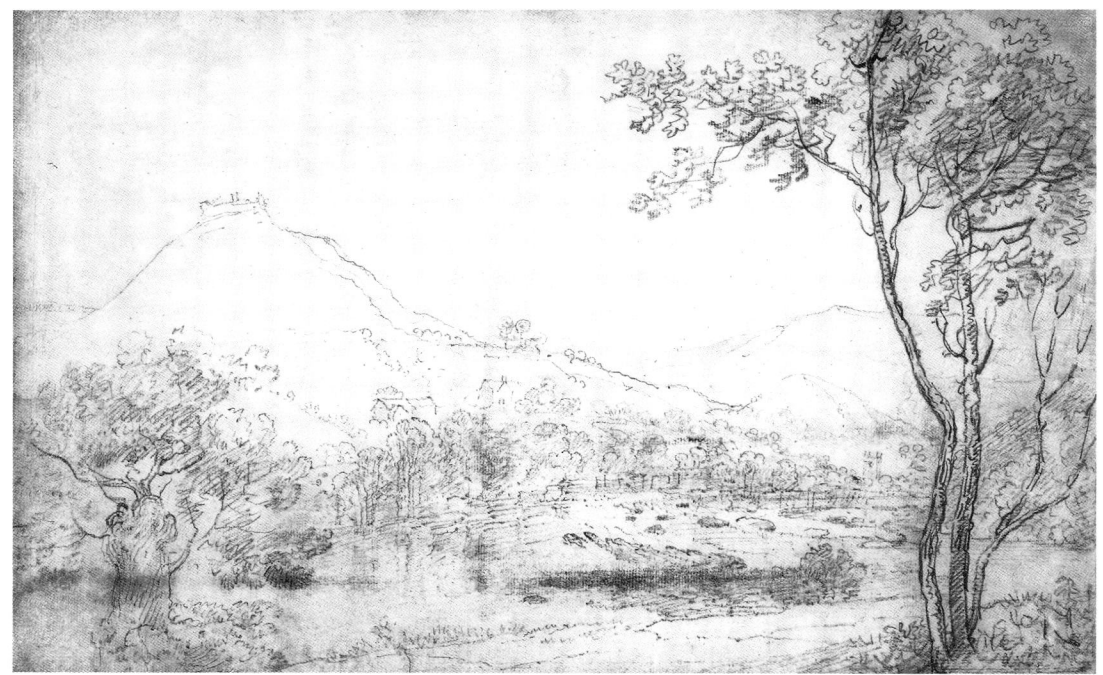

Richard Wilson, *Dinas Bran Castle, near Llangollen*, c.1770. Paul Mellon Collection, Yale Center for British Art, New Haven

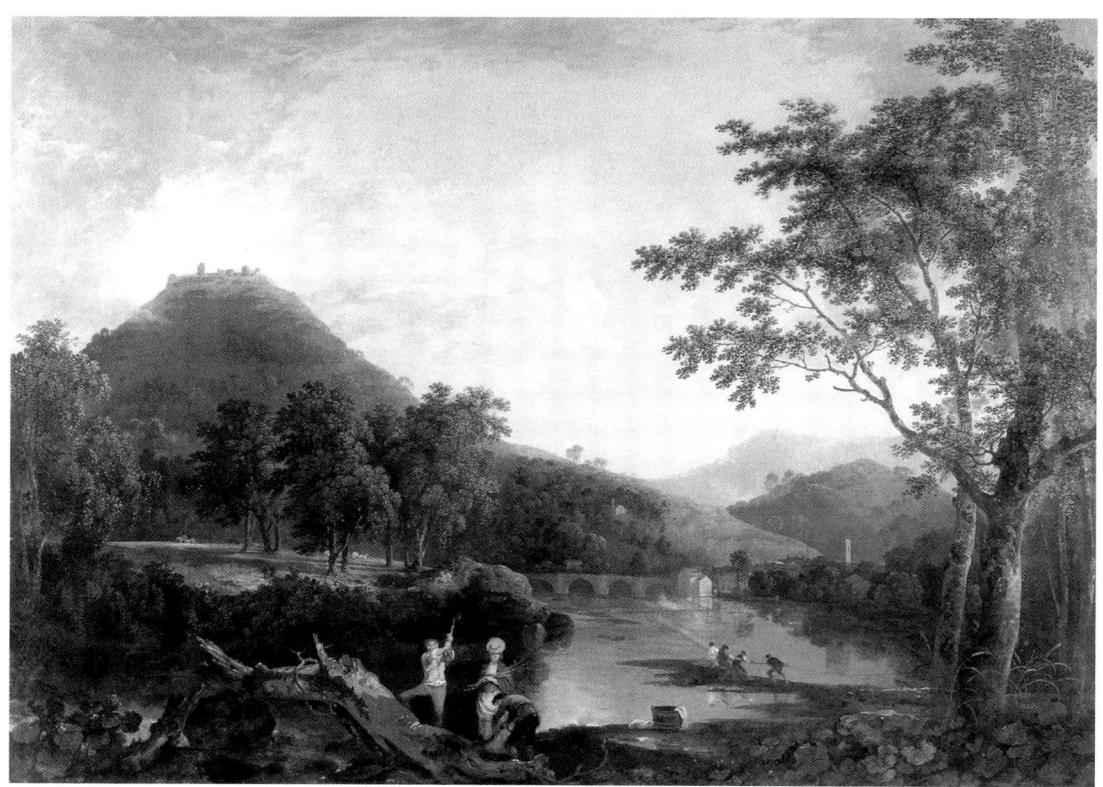

Richard Wilson, *Dinas Bran from Llangollen*, 1770–71. Gift of Paul Mellon 1976, Yale Center for British Art, New Haven

opposite: Richard Wilson, *Dinas Bran from Llangollen*, c.1772–75, oil on canvas, 82.5 x 104.1 cm.
Gift of Gladys Penfold Hyland in memory of her husband Frank 1964

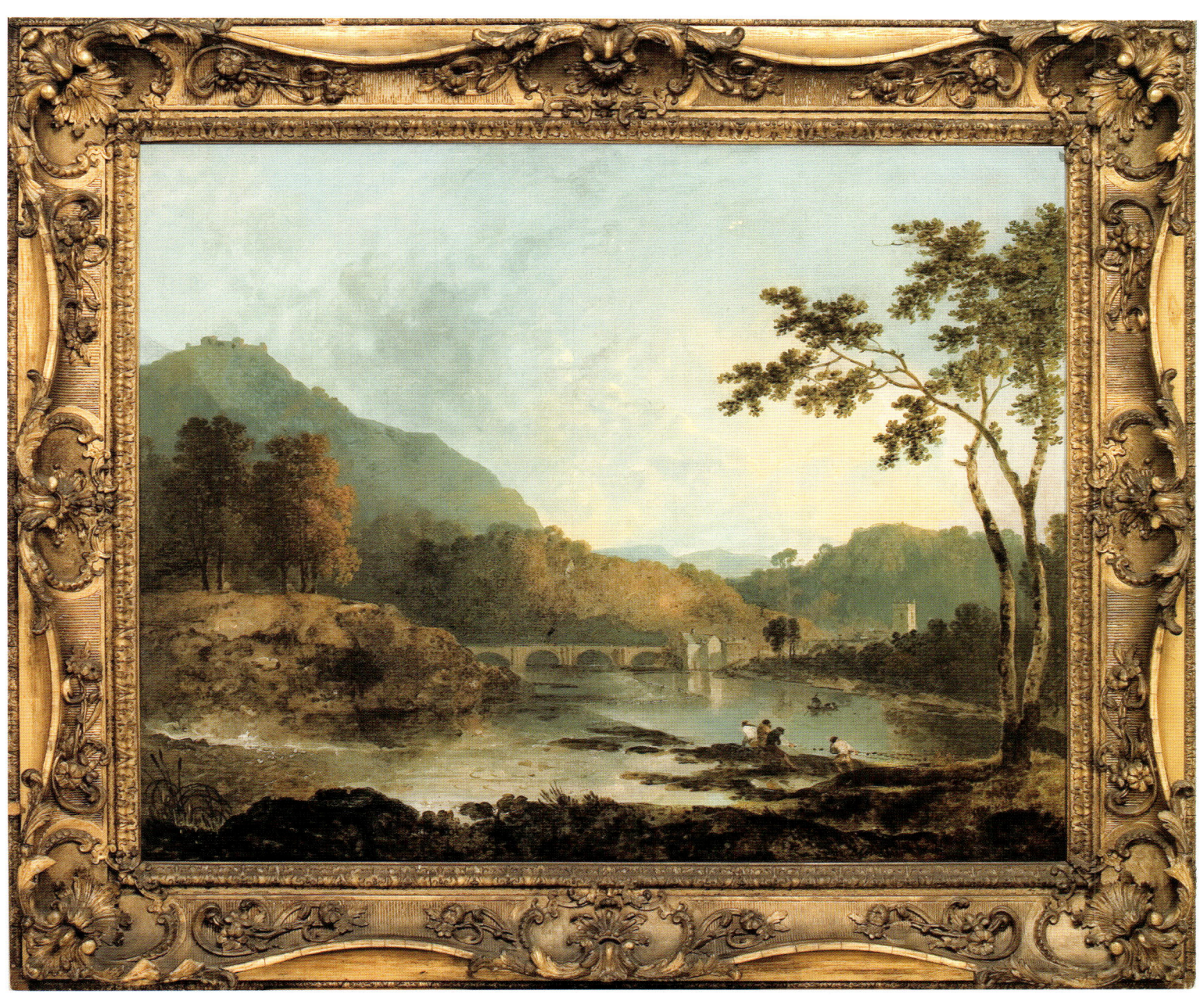

# Jacob More 1740–1793

Jacob More, a Scot, was the first major painter of Scottish landscape but he spent all of his later career in Rome. There he became, very briefly, the most esteemed European landscape artist of his time.

Born in Edinburgh in 1740, More was apprenticed to a goldsmith in 1757 then in 1764 changed his trade to become an apprentice for two years to the minor landscape painter and decorator Robert Norie until that artist's death in 1766. More then transferred his apprenticeship to Alexander Runciman, another Scottish landscape painter and decorator. In 1767 More's stage-set scenery for the New Theatre in Edinburgh was so well received that he determined to be a full-time landscape painter. By 1770 he was producing landscapes of the Scottish countryside in the style of the French artist Joseph Vernet (1714–1789), whose work he admired and who had some influence on him for the rest of his life. The Scottish storms and waterfalls brought him much acclaim when they were exhibited in Edinburgh and London.

In 1771 More left Edinburgh to live permanently in Rome and by the 1780s was famous, being known as 'More of Rome'. He became not only the leading landscape painter in Rome but also, for a short time, one of the most successful landscape painters in Europe. For much of his first decade in Rome he produced small watercolours and larger gouaches of the city but in the 1780s a steady demand for his oils included commissions for paintings of enormous size. The contemporary landscapes of Richard Wilson and Joseph Vernet, the seventeenth-century Roman masters Gaspard Dughet and above all Claude Lorrain were major influences on his art. Significantly, among the numerous Old Master paintings he owned in Rome were landscapes by Gaspard and Claude.

More produced many striking compositions of the Eternal City and died there in 1793. He left an unusually valuable estate of £7000.

Immediately after his death the romantic period of landscape painting took hold and highly crafted and tightly painted classical landscapes fell from popularity. For two hundred years Jacob More was almost forgotten.

## A distant view of Rome across the Tiber, c.1774
oil on canvas, 78.0 x 106.5 cm
A. M. & A. R. Ragless Bequest Funds 1979

This view is in More's earlier Roman style and probably dates from the mid 1770s. It may have been one of the four paintings sent to London for the 1775 exhibition of the Incorporated Society of Artists, the first works sent since his arrival in Rome in 1771[1] and the largest group he would ever send back for exhibition. It is possibly the painting exhibited as *A Landscape; a Sunset with a distant View of Rome*, a title that certainly fits the Gallery's painting. Jacob More, like Claude Lorrain, sometimes painted companion landscapes of sunrise and sunset and another of the four sent back in 1775 had a title that could be paired with this tranquil sunset landscape. *A Landscape; a calm, with a Bridge, on the Road to Tivoli*, no. 176 in the exhibition, may have been a companion morning scene to no. 177, which was the sunset with a distant view of Rome.[2]

The city is seen here from the north-east on the ancient Via Flaminia, the main highway from the north, probably near the Ponte Milvio over two miles outside the Porta del Popolo, the main entrance gate to Rome. In the distance are the dome of St Peter's, the Vatican, the Castel Sant' Angelo, the Ponte Sant' Angelo, the walls of Rome, and the Roman hills, villas and farmhouses. In the middle foreground is the River Tiber on which are two moored sailing boats, an empty rowing boat and a man rowing. In the immediate darkened foreground on the left three men are in animated discussion beside a fallen Roman column; below them a seated man watches. The small buildings and trees on the opposite riverbank are beautifully reflected in the glassy water. It is an accurate view of Rome depicted with classical balance and serenity.

The pink early-evening sunset glow and the large trees on the left deliberately echo landscape devices used by Claude Lorrain a century earlier. However, More's work has less nostalgia and romantic depth than Claude's and instead shows a lighter palette and tighter paint application closer in style to the smoother surfaces of Vernet. Like much of his work, it is topographically accurate whereas Claude painted only a handful of topographical views of Rome. Nonetheless, More, like Claude, also painted many pastiches or caprices depicting Roman ruins. Both the landscape caprices and the more topographical views such as the Gallery's may have been admired less by local Roman audiences than by the growing number of visitors on the Grand Tour in the last decades of the eighteenth century. For visitors More provided a kind of high-class tourist art; many of his landscapes were especially commissioned to send back to Britain. His paintings tapped into a market for the classical past and tourist Rome, and also made nostalgic reference to the landscapes of his highly esteemed and ardently collected predecessor Claude Lorrain.

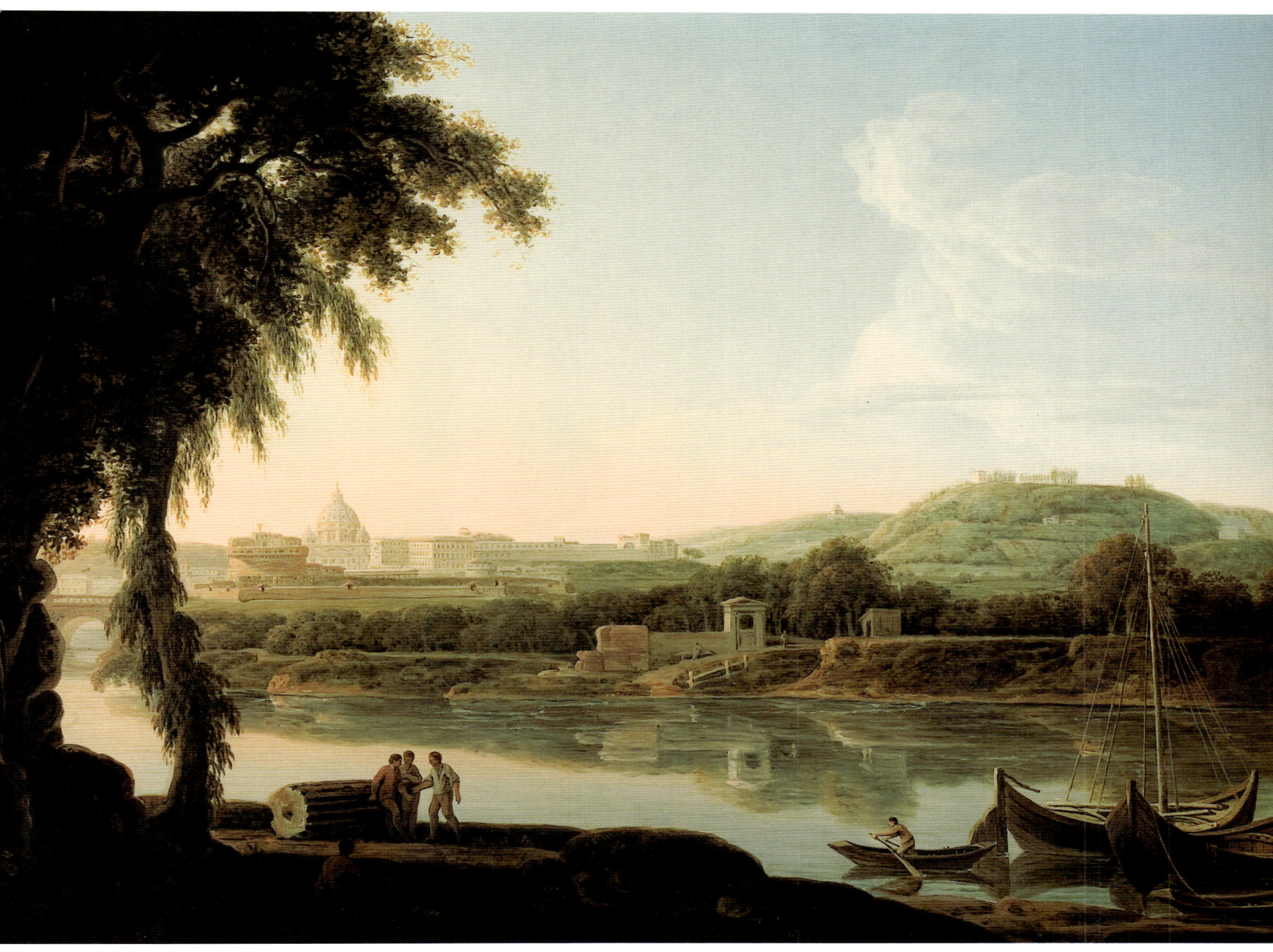

**Provenance:** Lady Mary Duncan, Dunbar near Edinburgh; Leger Galleries, London, by 1978.

**Exhibitions:** Incorporated Society of Artists, London, 1775, no. 177. *Island to Empire: 300 Years of British Art 1550–1850*, AGSA, Adelaide, 2005.

**Literature:** James Holloway, *Jacob More 1740–1793* (Scottish Masters Series), Edinburgh: National Galleries of Scotland, 1987, pp. 8, 22 (illus. no. 5). Peter Tomory and Robert Gaston, *European Paintings before 1800 in Australian and New Zealand Public Collections*, Sydney, 1989, p. 35, no. 83 (illus.). Patricia R. Andrew, "Jacob More: Biography and a checklist of works", *The Walpole Society 1989/90*, vol. 55, London, 1993, pp. 120–21, 163, 195 (illus. fig. 88).

**Condition:** Excellent; last conserved in London c.1978 prior to acquisition for South Australia.

**Frame:** Possibly original.

# Thomas Gainsborough 1727–1788

Thomas Gainsborough was arguably the greatest English artist of the second half of the eighteenth century, a golden age for British art, and one of the greatest European painters of the time. He made his living from portraits but claimed his first love was landscape and rustic genre painting. His paintings and drawings are romantic, attuned to the eye rather than the intellect. His feeling for rhythm, colour and texture combines with an extraordinary ability to evoke mood. The informality of Gainsborough's portraits was in direct contrast with the classical ideal that Reynolds presented in his history paintings and grand-manner portraits.

Gainsborough was born in 1727 at Sudbury, Suffolk. He trained as a painter in London from about 1740, influenced by the French painter-engraver Hubert Gravelot (1699–1773). Gravelot introduced him to the St Martin's Lane Academy which, under Hogarth's regime, was the centre of Rococo in English painting. Gainsborough at this time was influenced by the portrait painter Francis Hayman. In addition he began to paint landscapes, learning much from the seventeenth-century Dutch artists, especially Jacob van Ruisdael and possibly Salomon van Ruysdael and Meindert Hobbema, whose works were entering British collections in large numbers by the mid eighteenth century.

Gainsborough set up his own London studio in 1745. In 1748 he returned to Suffolk where he first worked back in Sudbury and from 1752 in Ipswich. He moved to Bath in 1759. There he had great success as a portrait painter and his style became much freer and more dashing, reflecting his profound appreciation and understanding of Van Dyck's English portraits. In Bath he was exceptionally successful at attracting commissions from the many visitors to the city and became Britain's finest regional portrait artist of all time; in 1768 he was a foundation member of London's Royal Academy. In 1774 he left Bath for London and became Reynolds's rival in portraiture. After a gap of three years he began to exhibit again at the Royal Academy in 1777 but picked a quarrel with the administration and stopped exhibiting there after 1782. Instead he exhibited at his house in Pall Mall and developed the 'family picture', a life-size genre painting designed to compete with the Old Masters. He died in London in 1788.

## Madam Lebrun, 1780

oil on canvas, 127.0 x 102.6 cm

Gift of Gladys Penfold Hyland in memory of her husband Frank 1964

Madam Franzisca Lebrun was a famous soprano and composer and the wife of Ludwig August Lebrun, an oboist, composer and member of the Mannheim Orchestra. They were married in 1778 and belonged to a very select group of chamber musicians commanding high salaries wherever they performed in Europe.

She was born Franzisca Danzi in Mannheim in 1756. She was the daughter of cellist Innocenz Danzi and elder sister of composer Franz Danzi. She made her debut in Antonio Sacchini's *La Contadina in corte* in 1772 and soon gained a leading position at the Mannheim Court Opera. In 1777 she created the role of the countess in Ignaz Holzbauer's *Günther von Schwarzburg*, which was written for her. In the same year she was granted leave of absence by Carl Theodor, the Prince Elector of the Palatinate and went to London to sing the lead in an opera season staying for a year. It was said that Franzisca Lebrun's vocal abilities were superior to those of any other woman then on the London stage, and there she published two sets of six sonatas for the keyboard and violin. In August 1778 she sang at the opening of La Scala, Milan in Antonio Salieri's *Europa riconosciuta*. Throughout her career she was constantly on tour including Paris, Vienna, Prague, Naples, Berlin and Munich. She died in Berlin in 1791 only five months after her husband. They had two daughters, Sophie who became a pianist and composer and Rosine who became an opera singer and then an actress.[1]

In November 1779 Madam Lebrun was in London for two opera seasons at the Kings Theatre and this is when she sat for Gainsborough at his studio in Schomberg House, Pall Mall, probably at the beginning of 1780. Gainsborough exhibited the portrait at the Royal Academy that year, along with six landscapes and a number of other portraits including one of the musician Johann Christian Fischer (Royal Collection, Windsor). The same chair from Gainsborough's studio appears in the Lebrun and Fischer portraits, and a number of others of this late period, including the famous portrait of Sarah Siddons, 1785, in the National Gallery, London, though in the Fischer portrait it has green upholstery not red.[2] Fischer, like Ludwig Lebrun, was a composer and oboist, and was Gainsborough's son-in-law. It was probably through Fischer that Madam Lebrun met the artist. Gainsborough was passionately fond of music and himself an amateur musician. Whereas Reynolds, Ramsay and Romney preferred the company of scholars and writers, Gainsborough enjoyed the company of musicians and other performers, and painted their portraits. Gainsborough's portraits of the two performers, the singer Franzisca Lebrun and the actress Sarah Siddons make an interesting comparison. Apart from using the same chair, these famous women of the stage share the same pose and the portraits are the same size. Painted five years earlier, the loosely painted portrait of the singer is like a rehearsal for the more formally posed, highly finished and colourful portrait

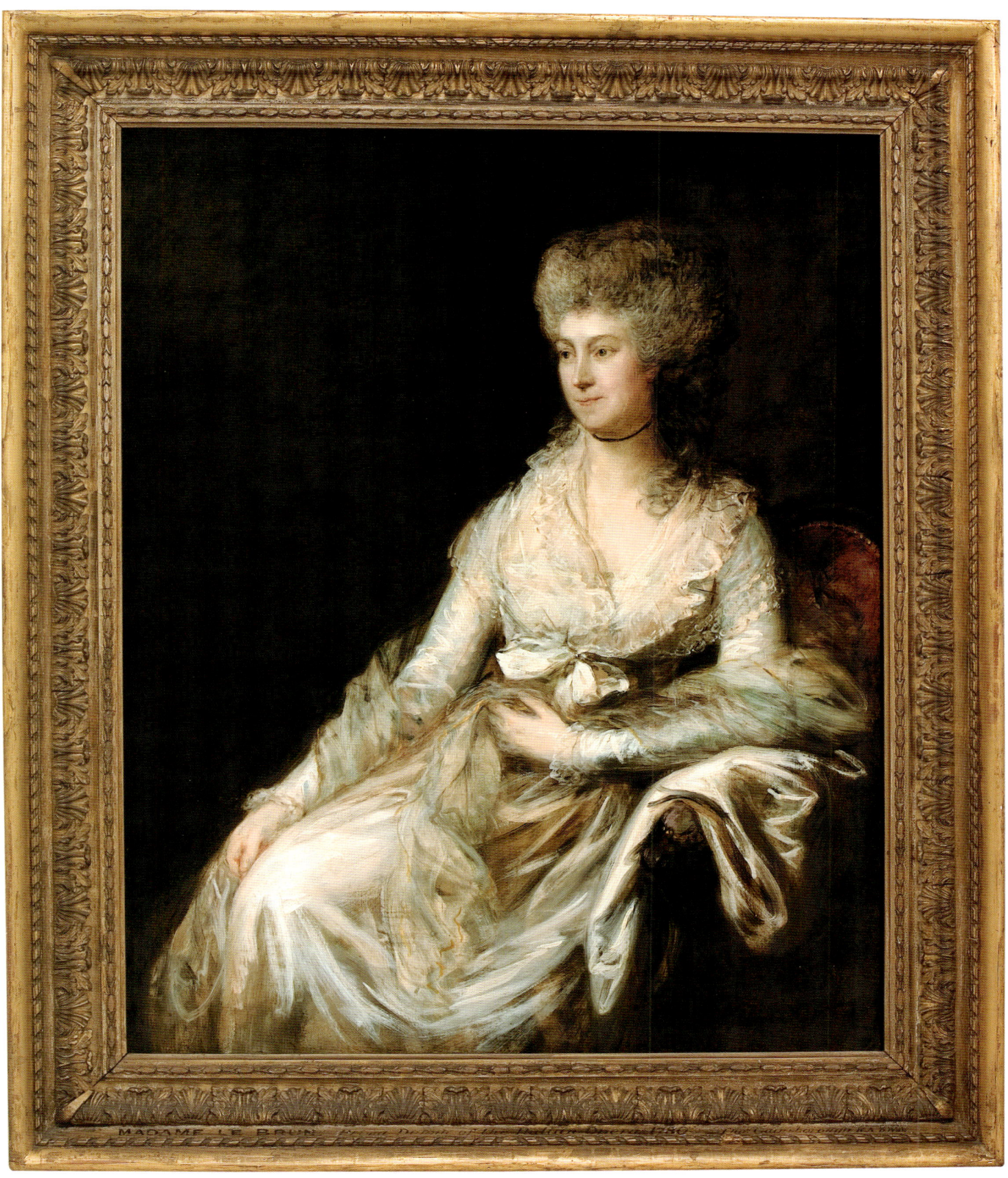

# Thomas Gainsborough

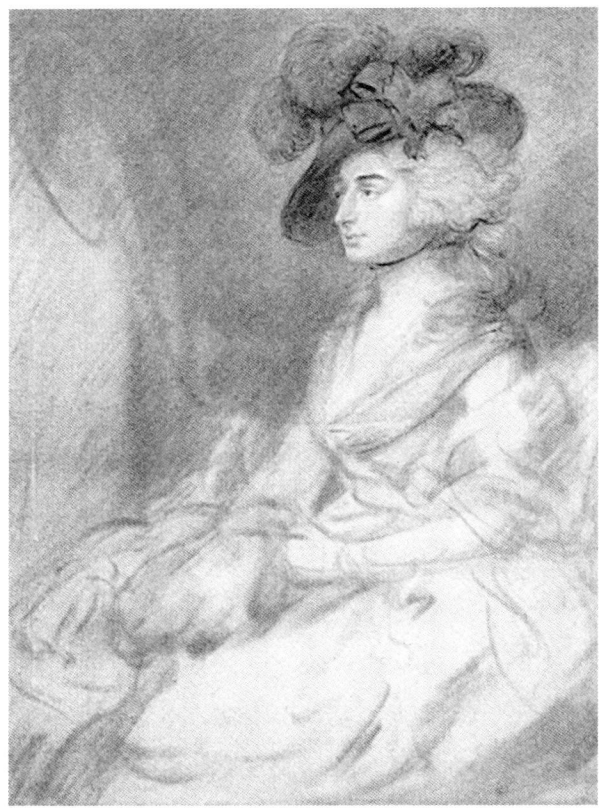

Thomas Gainsborough, *Study for the portrait of Mrs Siddons*, 1785? Cleveland Museum of Art, Cleveland, Ohio

of the actress. The hurried Lebrun portrait was probably not commissioned by the sitter and the Siddons portrait was certainly not, but conceived especially for Gainsborough's special studio showing of 1785/86. It is particularly useful to compare our sketch-like monochromatic portrait of Madam Lebrun with the freely drawn chalk drawing for *Mrs Siddons*, now held at the Cleveland Museum of Art, Cleveland, Ohio (see above).[3]

The Gallery's effervescent study of a young singer is one of the late portraits in which Gainsborough's energetic brushwork has become broad and increasingly bold. Indeed, while still capturing the sitter's likeness, character and mood, it is one of his most daringly abbreviated paintcraft performances. In 1788 after Gainsborough's death Reynolds nobly devoted his Fourteenth Discourse, for students and members of the Royal Academy, to his rival, with appreciation of "…all those odd scratches and marks which, on close examination, are so observable in Gainsborough's pictures, and which even to experienced painters appear rather the effect of accident than design. This chaos, this uncouth and shapeless appearance by a kind of magic, at a certain distance assumes form, and all the parts seem to drop into their proper places". Reynolds could have been describing the technique of this portrait of Madam Lebrun.

The spontaneity of the flickering touch resembles French Impressionist portraits of a hundred years later but the painting is more monochromatic and has the directness and tonality that we normally associate with drawing. It is like a drawing in paint, very like his own black-and-white figure studies in chalk. Gainsborough was not always interested in accurate representation – though he was excellent at facial likeness – and he has extended the slope of the sitter's shoulders and the length and proportion of her arms and legs. He was more concerned with the rhythms of the composition as a whole and the animation of the surface than with anatomical precision. The nervous brushwork gives a sense of momentary transition or arrested movement: has the sitter only just settled down and started to arrange her dress and silk stole or is she preparing to get up and take her leave? In this sympathetic portrait, most of which he would have enthusiastically dashed off in one or two sittings of not much more than an hour, Gainsborough captured the restless mood of a touring performer who must soon rush to another engagement. Her head only momentarily still, her mouth slightly pursed, she shows the alertness of a singer awaiting her cue.

Provenance: W. Stirling Crawfurd 1878; his widow the Duchess of Montrose; her sale Christie's, London, 14 July 1894; resold Christie's, London, 4 May 1895; Leopold Hirsch by 1900; his sale Christie's, London, 11 May 1934; Francis Howard, London; from whence purchased by Frank and Gladys Penfold Hyland, Sydney, c.1935.

Exhibitions: Royal Academy, London, 1780, no. 162. Royal Academy, London, 1878, no. 100. The Grosvenor Gallery, *Exhibition of the Works of Thomas Gainsborough, R.A. with historical notes*, London, 1885, no. 63. *Exposition Universelle*, British Pavilion, Paris, 1900, no. 51. *Island to Empire: 300 Years of British Art 1550–1850*, AGSA, Adelaide, 2005.

Literature: G. W. Fulcher, *Life of Thomas Gainsborough R.A.*, London, 1856, p. 184. G. W. Fulcher, *Life of Thomas Gainsborough R.A.*, 2nd edition, London, 1856, p. 188. Sir W. Armstrong, *Gainsborough and his Place in English Art*, London, 1898, p. 198. Sir W. Armstrong, *Gainsborough and his Place in English Art*, London, 1904, p. 272. William T. Whitley, *Thomas Gainsborough*, London, 1915, p. 167. Ellis Waterhouse, *Preliminary Check List of Portraits by Thomas Gainsborough*, Walpole Society, vol. 33, 1948–50, Oxford, 1953, p. 67. Ellis Waterhouse, *Gainsborough*, London, 1958, p. 78, no. 433. *NGSA Bulletin*, vol. 26, no. 2, October 1964. *Picture Book*, Adelaide: AGSA, 1972, p. 19 (illus.). Peter Tomory and Robert Gaston, *European Paintings before 1800 in Australia and New Zealand*, Sydney, 1989, pp. 22–23, no. 40 (illus.). Ron Radford et al., *Selected Works*, Adelaide: AGSA, 1991, p. 8. Julie Anne Sadie & Rhian Samuel, *The New Grove Dictionary of Woman Composers*, London, 1994, pp. 271–72 (illus.). Ron Radford et al., *Treasures*, Adelaide: AGSA, 1998, p. 48 (illus.). Alfried Wieczorek, Hansjörg Probst and Wieland Koenig, *Lebenslust und Frömmigkeit: Kurfürst Carl Theodor (1724–1799) zwischen Barock und Aufklärung*, Regensburg: Verlag Friedrich Pustet, 1999, band 2, p. 345 (illus.). Stanley Sadie (ed.), *The New Grove Dictionary of Music and Musicians*, 2nd ed., vol. 14, London, 2001, pp. 436–37 (illus.).

Condition: Good to fair; some of the whites have sunk. Probably not conserved since the early twentieth century when the former owners acquired the portrait in London.

Frame: Original.

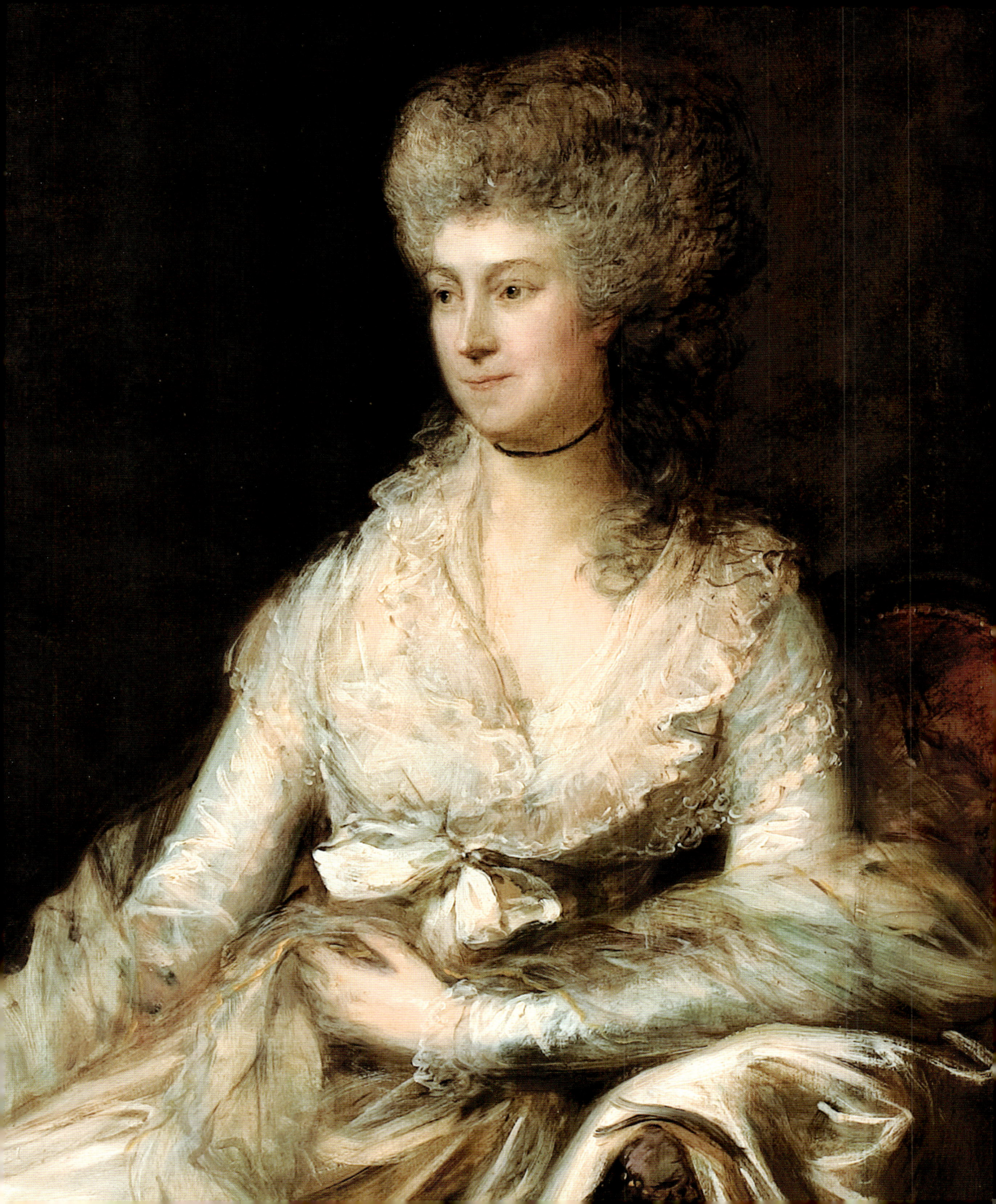

# Thomas Gainsborough

## Wooded upland landscape with shepherd and sheep and track winding around a knoll, mid 1780s

black and white chalks, ink wash on paper, 28.0 x 37.0 cm
Gift of the Friends of the Art Gallery of South Australia 1978

Gainsborough was one of Britain's finest draughtsmen and one of the most prolific. Over a thousand of his drawings are documented but he must have produced many more. Ten years after the artist's death William Jackson wrote of them in his *Character of Gainsborough*, published in 1798: "No man ever possessed methods so various in producing effect, and all excellent… The subject which is scarce enough for a picture is sufficient for a drawing, and the hasty loose handling which in painting is poor is rich in transparent wash of bistre and Indian ink".[1] Gainsborough was a brilliant and original technician who tirelessly experimented in various drawing media.

Most of the landscape drawings made during Gainsborough's 1750s Suffolk period are in pencil. Those drawings, like his landscape paintings, show the influence of Dutch seventeenth-century art. Landscape drawings of the early 1760s were mostly done in watercolour, often with added body colour; later in the same decade brown or grey wash drawings were the most common. It was not until the mid 1770s that Gainsborough used black and white chalks for the majority of his drawings, a practice he continued for the rest of his life, while continuing to experiment in other media and applications. For these broadly-executed late landscape drawings he used coarse paper. This Gallery drawing largely in black chalk is a characteristic example of this final London period and can be stylistically dated to the mid 1780s.

It is a fine example of a drawing most probably executed indoors in the evenings, which is when he usually worked on paper, after-hours from oil on canvas. The studio-composed drawings were often produced with the help of models. W. H. Pyne described how Gainsborough made "…thoughts for landscape scenery on a little, old-fashioned folding oak table, which stood under his kitchen dresser…this table, held sacred for the purpose, he would order to be brought to his parlour, and thereon compose his designs. He would place cork or coal for his foregrounds, make middle grounds of sand and clay, bushes of mosses and lichens, woods of broccoli".[2] To the drawings of these artificially composed landscapes he introduced shepherds, sheep or cattle.

In the case of the Gallery's drawing the staffage of the shepherd and a few sheep is suggested by the barest outlines and the main subject is the robustly executed trees on a gravelly knoll. In Gainsborough's own words, the purpose of the human and domestic-animal figures was to "fill a place (I won't say stop a gap) or create a little business for the Eye to be drawn from the trees in order to return to them with more glee".[3] The figures also give scale to the trees and other vegetation.

It is a peaceful rural scene pervaded by a mood of gentle melancholy. In the shade of an embankment a shepherd rests surrounded by his small flock of sheep. There is a certain Arcadian artificiality and perhaps the influence of Gaspard Dughet and a suggestion of the Roman Campagna. The balanced composition of trees and embankments and tracks is typical of the Arcadian settings Gainsborough began to create in the 1770s and continued for the remainder of his life.

Rhythmic flow is emphasised by the two paths that wind along both sides of the central knoll. This and the effects of light on the foliage and terrain are unifying elements in the composition, the entire surface of which is animated by the artist's vigorous nervous energy and his technical verve. The broad masses of the clumps of trees and the landform are broadly suggested rather than descriptively modelled. Gainsborough's late landscape drawings stand very much apart from the detailed topographical drawings of his British contemporaries and in this highly generalised landscape he was more concerned to evoke a peaceful absorption in the earth than to depict a specific place in the country.

The technique, composition and date of our drawing are close to a mid 1780s work, *Wooded landscape with figures, cattle, bridge over stream and church tower* in the Witt Collection, Courtauld Institute, London. In both drawings Gainsborough has used grey wash rather than the more usual stumped chalk to give added depth and plasticity to his black chalk and wash highlighted with white chalk. However, the work that relates closest in composition, size and technique to ours is *Wooded upland landscape with sheep*, also mid 1780s (Private collection). This and the Gallery's drawing were not only executed about the same time, they both feature similar landscape elements, though the *Wooded upland landscape with sheep* is darker and more deeply melancholic than the Gallery's *Wooded upland landscape with shepherd and sheep*.[4]

The Gallery's two Gainsborough drawings are its most significant eighteenth-century British drawings.

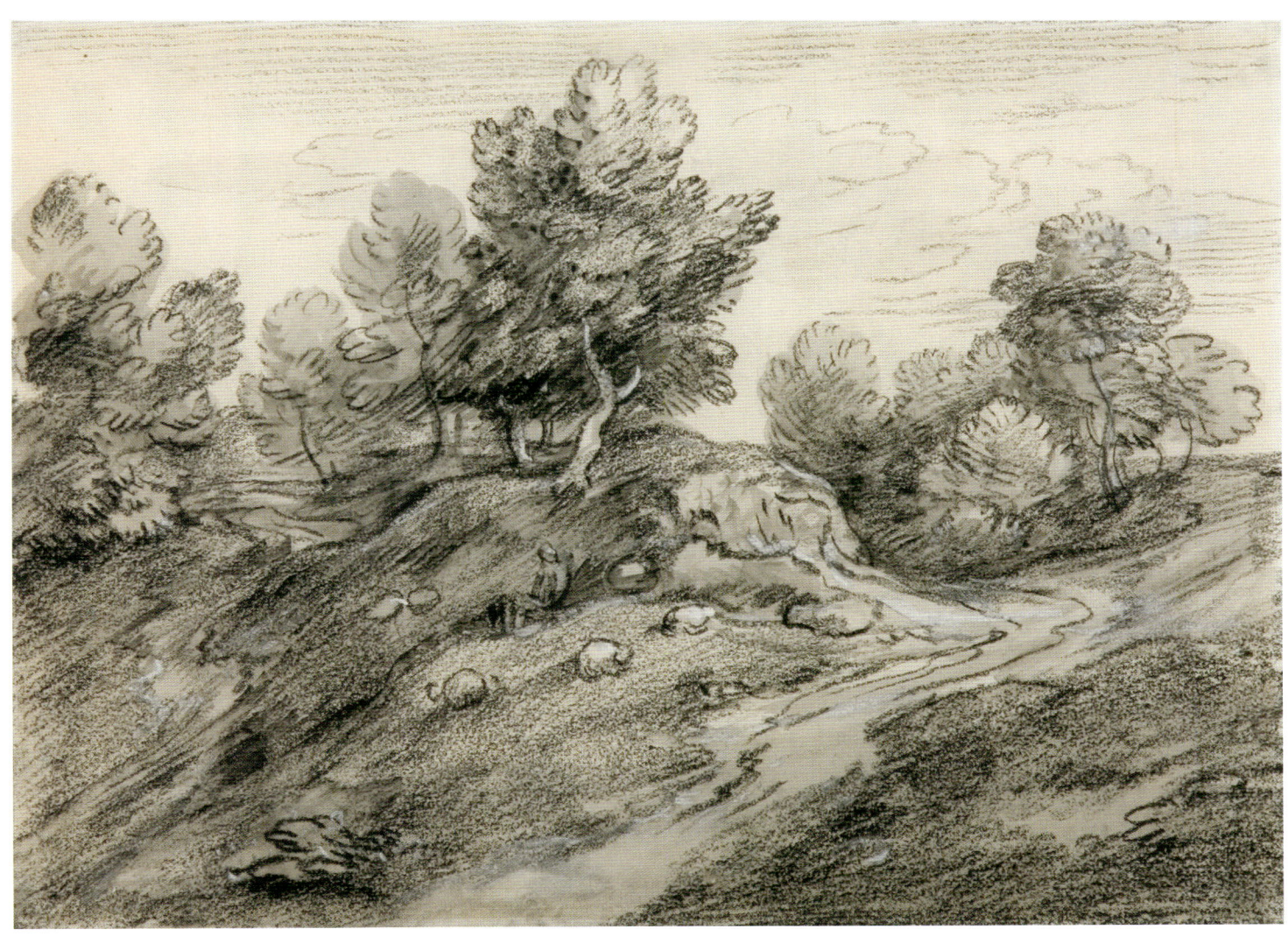

**Provenance:** Given by the artist to William Pierce, Cadogan Square, London; Henry Whitehead, London, thence by descent; sold by Miss Frances Whitehead, Sotheby's Whitehead Sale, 30 November 1978, lot 140; bt by the Art Gallery of South Australia on the advice of Dr Ursula Hoff and Alison Carroll, 1978.

**Exhibitions:** *Hidden Treasures: South Australia's European Old Master paintings, Restorations and Re-attributions, and South Australia's European Old Master drawings*, AGSA, Adelaide, 1989. *Island to Empire: 300 Years of British Art 1550–1850*, AGSA, Adelaide, 2005.

**Literature:** John Hayes, *The Drawings of Thomas Gainsborough*, London, 1970. *Important Eighteenth and Nineteenth Century English Drawings and Watercolours*, Sotheby's, 30 November 1978, lot 140 (illus.). John Hayes, *Gainsborough drawings: A supplement to the catalogue raisonné in Master Drawings*, vol. 21, no. 4, 1983, no. 956. Ron Radford et al., *Hidden Treasures*, Adelaide: AGSA, 1989.

**Condition:** Excellent.

# Thomas Gainsborough

## Wooded landscape with a building and pool, mid to late 1770s
black, red and white chalks on blue paper, 25.9 x 31.6 cm
Gift of William Bowmore AO OBE through the Art Gallery of South Australia Foundation 2004

Gainsborough remained a compulsive draughtsman throughout his career and his landscape drawings are among his best. They were a spontaneous self-expression created, for the most part, for the sheer love of drawing. This was in contrast with the Italian tradition of using drawings as preparatory studies for paintings.

The *Wooded landscape with a building and pool* is typical of Gainsborough's drawing style as it developed in the mid 1770s. He worked with rapid strokes to create the effect of a windswept landscape. The chalk medium is skilfully yet broadly and quickly applied. Short horizontal strokes indicate generalised areas of mass while looped feathery strokes define the tree foliage in more detail. The naturalistic landscape is not from a particular place but is constructed. It nonetheless evokes a sense of immediacy.

The overall composition is defined by a rhythmic arrangement of space and line. A bank on the left leads the eye down to a central mound with six trees growing from it (possibly meant to indicate birch trees), and the composition rotates around the clump. A track meanders towards and disappears into bushes on the left; through a clearing on the right can be seen a generic building of ambiguous architectural form, the broad tower probably meant to suggest a medieval church. In the foreground is a swampy pond or stream with reeds.

Although such subjects are common in Gainsborough's drawing œuvre and the style is characteristic, it was not contrived within conventions. Gainsborough, who became increasingly interested in chiaroscuro and effects of light, used alternating planes of light and dark masterfully to create a sense of spatial depth. White chalk is applied to suggest reflected light on the pool or stream, to highlight the roundness of the tree trunks and to offset glimpses of sky against the form of the forest. Black chalk is densely and confidently applied to create areas of stark contrast that throw the composition into relief.

Gainsborough's use of ready-coloured blue paper and chalk can be traced to Vittore Carpaccio, who in the early sixteenth century first used blue Venetian paper and chalk. The use of three chalks – black, red and white – reflects the French drawing tradition. (There are only touches of brown-red chalk on this drawing, to help make it less stark.) Drawing *aux trois crayons* had been popularised in the seventeenth century and most notably favoured by Antoine Watteau, to whose art Gainsborough began to make formal allusions in the 1760s.

This energetic, spiky drawing hints at the Dutch seventeenth-century landscape tradition whereas the Gallery's other Gainsborough drawing, a *Wooded upland landscape with shepherd and sheep and track winding around a knoll* of the mid 1780s, is more Italianate. Throughout his career the artist alternated between different landscape styles.

**Inscription:** Stamped on original mount, l. l., ink: "*T. Gainsborough*".

**Provenance:** Christie's, London, 19 November 1968; Agnew's, London; Christopher Lever, Windsor; William Bowmore, Australia.

**Exhibitions:** *The Fine Art of Giving: 90 Masterpieces from the William Bowmore Collection*, AGSA, Adelaide, 1999–2000, no. 38. *Island to Empire: 300 Years of British Art 1550–1850*, AGSA, Adelaide, 2005.

**Literature:** John Hayes, *The Drawings of Thomas Gainsborough*, London, 1970, p. 208, no. 430. John Hayes, *Thomas Gainsborough*, London: Tate Gallery, 1980. John Hayes & Lindsay Stainton, *Gainsborough Drawings*, Washington: International Exhibitions Foundation, 1983. Ron Radford, *The Fine Art of Giving*, Adelaide: AGSA, 1999, p. 74.

I am grateful for the help of Jane Messenger and Julie Robinson for their assistance with this entry.

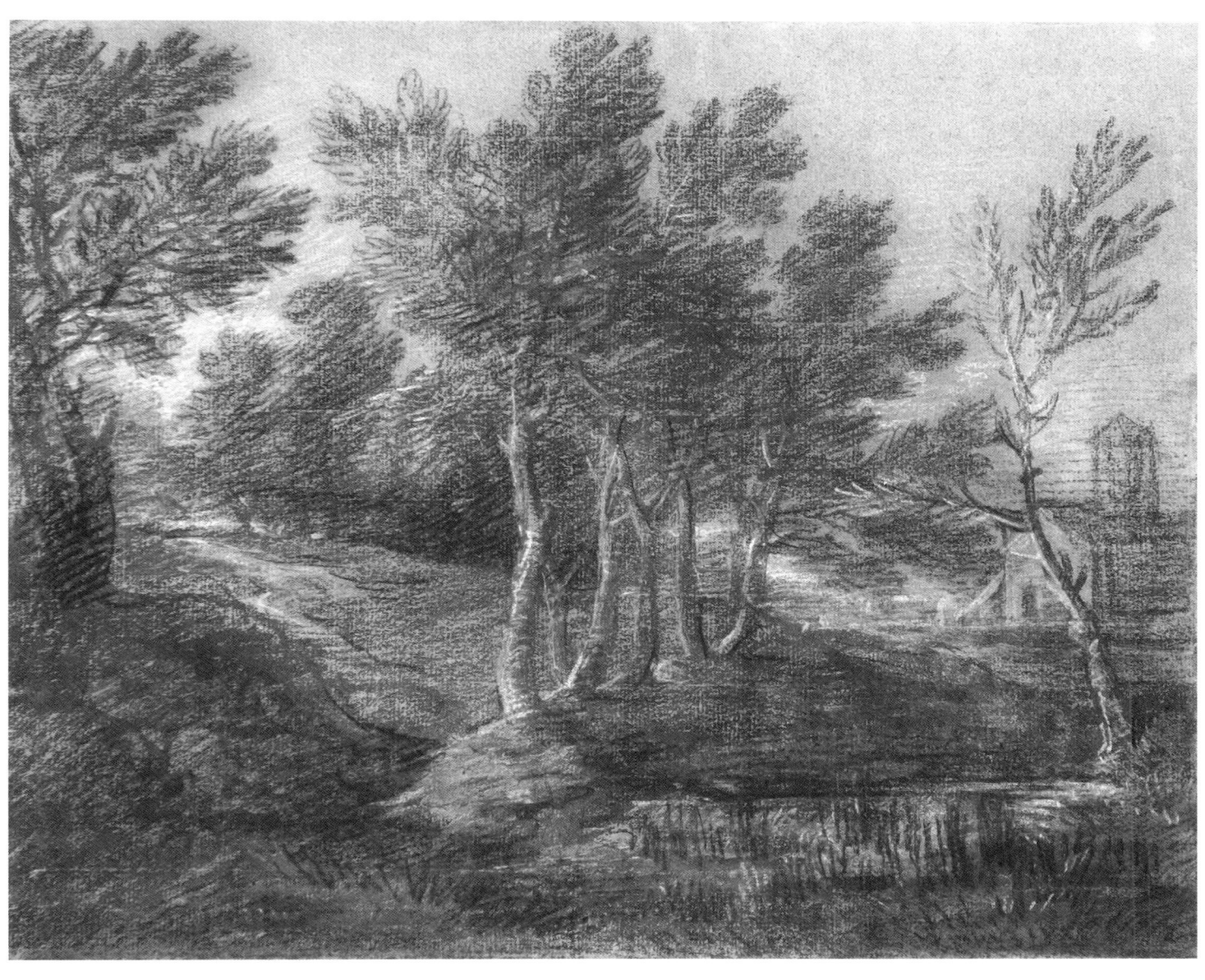

# Dominic Serres 1722–1793

Dominic Serres was probably the most successful of the many marine painters who flourished in Britain in the late eighteenth century. Among the foundation members of the Royal Academy in 1768 he was the only marine painter; in 1780 he was appointed Marine Painter to King George III.

Born in 1722 at Auch in Gascony, south-western France, he became a sailor. Working his way through the ranks he eventually became a master of a trading vessel. It was while he was trading to the West Indies in about 1758 that his ship was involved in an action with a British frigate and he was captured and brought to England. Following his release he became a student of marine painting, greatly influenced by the British marine painter Charles Brooking (1723–1759), whose student he may have been. His work also reveals awareness of paintings by Willem van de Velde the Younger (1633–1707) whose work was the ultimate model for all subsequent British maritime painting. Some of Serres's more ambitious works also show pretensions to the style of the major eighteenth-century French marine and landscape painter Joseph Vernet (1714–1789). Many of Serres's paintings record specific naval engagements with directness and clarity. His well-crafted scenes of ships in harbours or against coastlines display a very accurate knowledge of nautical rigging and coastal topography, no doubt informed by his youthful first-hand experience as a sailor.

In 1765 he became a member of the Society of Artists and in 1768 a foundation member of the Royal Academy. He was the teacher of his son John Thomas Serres (1759–1825), also a marine painter. Dominic Serres died in 1793.

## Foudroyant and Pégase entering Portsmouth Harbour, 1782, 1782

oil on canvas, 76.8 x 112.3 cm
Gift of Mrs David Evans and Mr Geoffrey O'Halloran Giles
in memory of their parents Mr and Mrs Hew O'Halloran Giles 1987

Portsmouth was, and is, the principal base of the Royal Navy and therefore a place that helped make Britain the greatest maritime power of the eighteenth century. In 1787, only five years after the defeated French ship seen in this painting was brought in to Portsmouth, a British fleet set out from the same harbour to establish a colony in New South Wales. In 1987 the gift to the Art Gallery of South Australia, from a South Australian family, of this Portsmouth Harbour painting marked the bicentenary of the First Fleet and the beginning of the nation now known as Australia.

Painted two years after he was made Marine Painter to George III, *Foudroyant and Pégase entering Portsmouth Harbour, 1782* records an event that took place in May 1782[1] following a British naval victory. It depicts a naval procession, a victorious entry into Portsmouth Harbour of the British *Foudroyant*, seen left, followed by the defeated French *Pégase*, seen to the right. The French were the greatest threat to British naval and imperial supremacy and the *Pégase*, with its 74 guns, had just been captured by the 80-gun *Foudroyant*, under Captain John Jervis, in the Bay of Biscay on 21 April 1782.[2]

In the painting we can see the defeated ship's white figurehead of the mythological winged horse Pegasus. On its masts we see the flying of the British Union Jack above a white flag, a sign of capture. The *Foudroyant*, which was the largest two-deck vessel in the British navy, is seen disappearing behind the square tower, with its naval flag flying. (The *Foudroyant* had been captured from the French in 1758 and recommissioned for Britain about the time that Serres himself was captured by the British.[3]) The captured *Pégase* shows rigging damaged in the battle. Over 600 of her crew were imprisoned, eighty having been killed and forty wounded.

The Portsmouth Dockyard records show that on 1 June 1782 the *Pégase* was put in No. 2 North Basin Dock for conversion into a receiving ship, so the triumphant procession probably took place on 30 May.[4] The victorious Captain Jervis stands while being rowed to shore in his barge, seen just to the right of the *Pégase*.

The painting is a good visual record of differing vessels in use at the time. The small vessels include a pinnace conveying junior officers with oarsmen seen to the left of the *Pégase* and to its left a hoy in full sail, as is also a cutter which can be seen in the far right of the composition. At the side of the *Pégase* is a small local fishing boat with its gaff-rigging. In the immediate foreground is a wherry, or water taxi, and another can be seen immediately behind *Foudroyant*.[5]

There is a welcoming crowd on the distant beach in front of the fortified sea wall. In the immediate foreground is a fisherman and his wife and to the left red-coated marines and ordinary seamen in blue coats take great interest in the spectacle.

Landmarks of the harbour and town of Portsmouth can also be clearly seen. The conspicuous structure that frames the view in the left foreground is the protective entrance tower

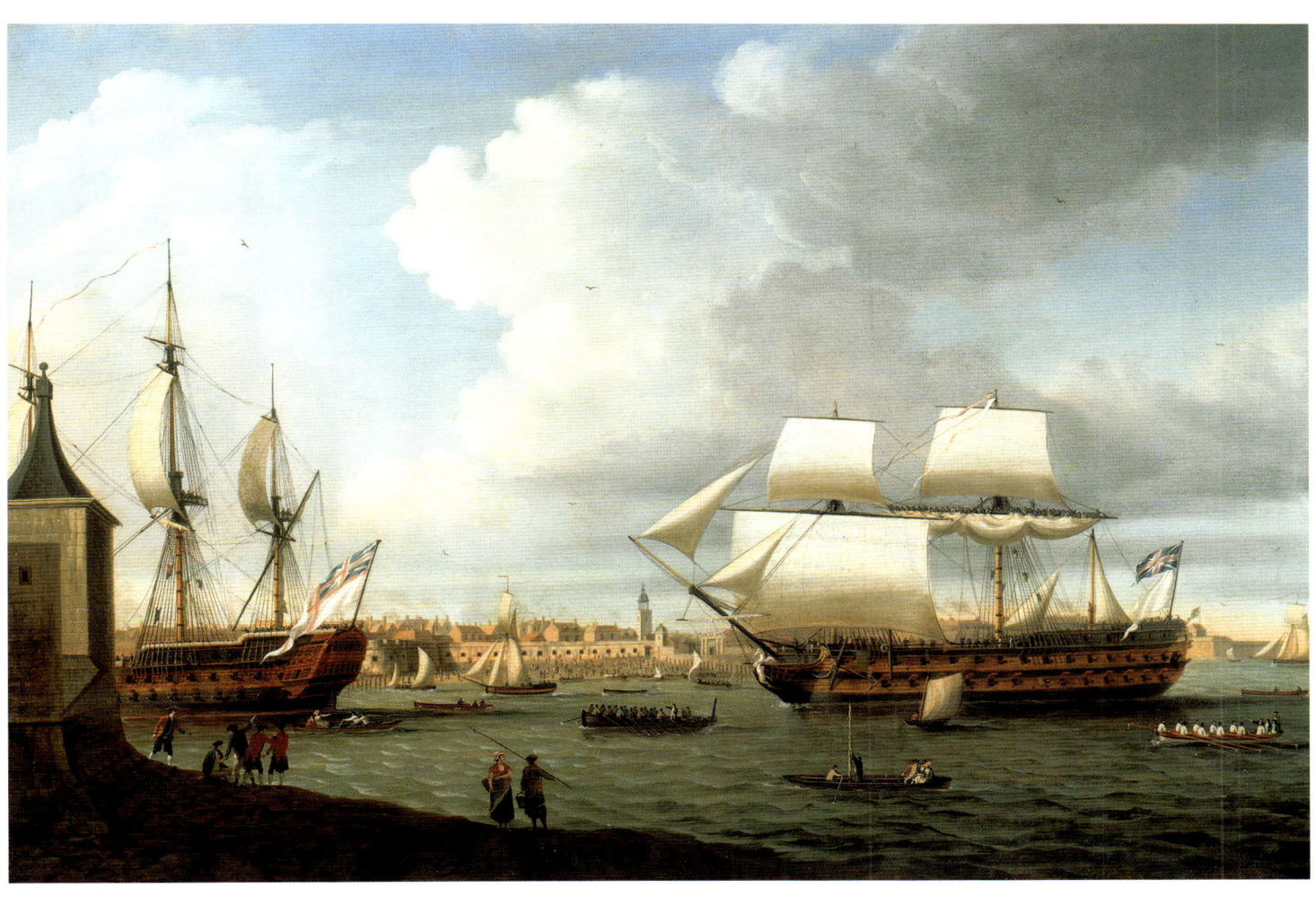

on the end of Fort Blockhouse. Visible in the distance to the right of the *Foudroyant* is the guardian fortress, the fifteenth-century Round Tower of Portsmouth and the defensive wall of the Eighteen-Gun Battery still extant today and built in the 1680s by King James II. At the centre of the painting is the tower of St Thomas's Cathedral, directly below the front sail of the *Pégase*. To the right of the cathedral tower is the town's classical gateway, King James's Gate, built in 1687. The fortifications seen to the extreme right of the painting were known as the Spur Redoubt.[6]

The painting was possibly commissioned by the much-esteemed Captain Jervis, who was knighted for this victory and later became Lord Vincent. However, the artist must have had strong personal feelings about the subject. In his days as a French sailor Serres had been captured by the British and brought to Portsmouth about the time the victorious *Foudroyant* itself was originally captured by the British. The scene would have seemed to him both familiar and poignant. Nevertheless he has depicted it serenely and with detachment, rather than as a scene of triumphalism and humiliation. Calm dignity and topographical accuracy are the chief characteristics of Serres's work.

Cleaning and restoration of the painting in 1988 revealed the signature and date. The attribution was thereby confirmed and the date enabled identification of the precise subject.

Although this is one of only two pre-nineteenth-century British oil paintings of a marine subject, and both are of the Portsmouth base, the Gallery holds a substantial and varied collection of English marine watercolours of this period and later. One is by Dominic Serres himself and another by his son John Thomas Serres.

| | |
|---|---|
| Inscription: | Signed and dated l.l. corner, oil: "Serres. 1782". |
| Provenance: | Oliver Symon collection, London; bt probably in 1962 by Hew O'Halloran Giles; thence to Geoffrey O'Halloran Giles and Diane Evans, 1986. |
| Exhibitions: | *Hidden Treasures: South Australia's European Old Master paintings, Restorations and Re-attributions and South Australia's European Old Master drawings*, AGSA, Adelaide, 1989. *Island to Empire: 300 Years of British Art 1550–1850*, AGSA, Adelaide, 2005. |
| Literature: | *NGSA Picture Book of Selected Oil and Water-colour Paintings and Sculpture*, Adelaide: NGSA, 1960, p. 224. Ron Radford, *Hidden Treasures*, Adelaide: AGSA, 1989, pp. 5–6 (illus.). Jeremy Black, *History of England*, London, 1993 (illus. frontispiece). |
| Condition: | Fair; conserved in 1988 and 2004 by Artlab Australia, Adelaide. |
| Frame: | Not original, but nonetheless late-eighteenth-century British. |

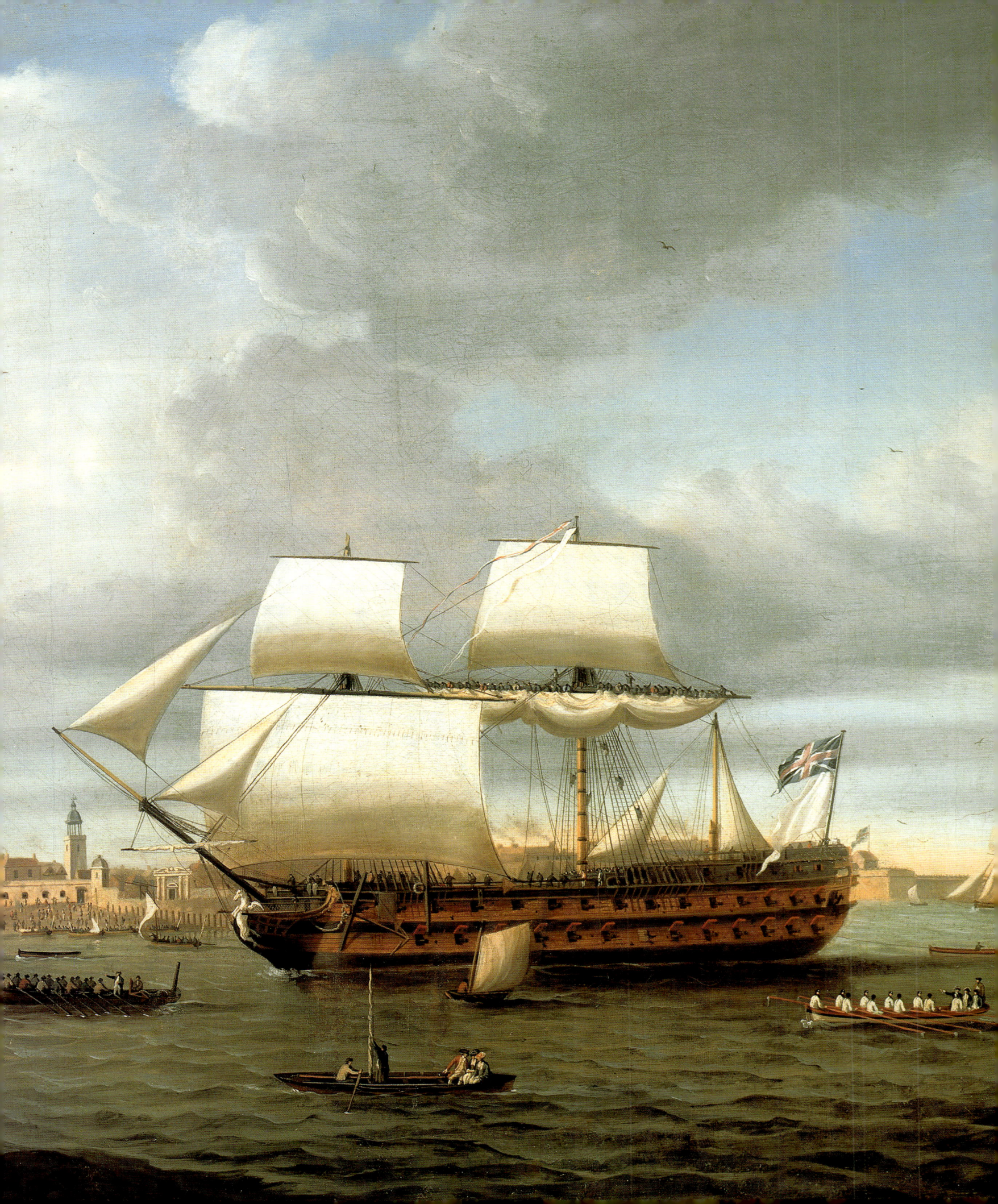

# Paul Sandby 1731–1809

Paul Sandby is regarded as the father of the peculiarly British tradition of landscape painting in watercolour. From the 1760s he played a key role in promotion of the medium, which by the time of his death in 1809 was flourishing as never before. In 1775 when he published *XII Views in Aquatinta from drawings taken on the spot in South-Wales* he conspicuously introduced to England the aquatint printmaking technique that was the most sympathetic way to reproduce and therefore popularise watercolour painting. In 1770 he spent six weeks at Wynnstay with the North Wales art patron Sir Watkins Williams-Wynn and he was the first landscape artist frequently to paint the rugged and mountainous scenery of Scotland and Wales. This repertory helped establish the conventions of the Picturesque movement in British art and contributed to the rise of Romantic landscape painting.

Born in Nottingham in 1731, Sandby began his career as a topographical draughtsman for the Board of Ordnance. From 1747 to 1751 he was employed on a military survey of Scotland. He reasserted his military connection later when, from 1768 to 1796, he was Chief Drawing Master at the Royal Military Academy, Woolwich. In 1768 he was a foundation member of the Royal Academy and his brother Thomas was its first Professor of Architecture. Almost from the outset Sandby's interest in pictorial landscape had far outstripped the dry recording expected of a military draughtsman. During the years from 1775 to 1786 he issued many prints made from his drawings of country houses and other places of interest.

Sandby regularly exhibited his watercolours and gouaches at the Royal Academy and his prominent presence there further aided the acceptance of watercolour as a serious medium for high art.

## Approaching Rochester and the Medway, 1786
watercolour on paper, 36.5 x 54.5 cm (sheet)
Morgan Thomas Bequest Fund 1956

Rochester is in Kent about thirty miles out of London where the road to Canterbury and Dover crosses the estuary of the River Medway. The distinctive Norman keep of Rochester Castle and the cathedral tower, both visible in this view,[1] indicate that the small city was once a significant river port. Two airy groups of foreground trees frame the ancient buildings in a rather Claudean pictorial fashion; on the right we see a bend on the navigable Medway.

However, Sandby holds our interest not by the topographically accurate distant view of Rochester or even the handsome compositional trees, but by his animation of the foreground road. A pedestrian woman traveller approaches briskly, preceded by her scampering dog. Behind her another traveller waters his horse at a pond. A gentleman on horseback receives information – about something over to the right – with a gesture from a local man. Some way along the road we can see another very small figure, a heavily burdened woman. Contented sheep and cattle, the livelihood of the district, occupy a patch of open ground looking into the view on the right. Rustic wooden cottages and sheds nestle under the great trees, and across the foreground lie rough logs, partly sawn, that once belonged to such trees. (Sandby often painted the woodyard and sawmill in Windsor Great Park, and other subjects of felling trees and carting timber.) The local man's gesture might be an offer to the passing rider of timber, or livestock, or work on carriage wheels in the shed at the centre of the picture. Human and natural processes add charm and warm geniality to the scene, and raise it far above topography.

The realistic informality, the flat landscape and the big sky show the unmistakable influence of seventeenth-century Dutch landscape painting. The subject of travellers and a barn-like roadside building beneath trees reminds us of landscapes by Salomon van Ruysdael, for example the Art Gallery of South Australia's *Halt at the coach-house* (1644). To a certain extent Sandby's restricted palette also recalls that master, whose works, with those of other Dutch landscape painters, were collected in great numbers in Britain by the mid eighteenth century. Like the Dutch, Sandby has captured the atmospheric effects of clear afternoon light. As in much of his art from the 1780s onwards, Sandby in this 1786 watercolour shows a much freer, more fluid manner than earlier in his career.

Rochester, fairly close to Woolwich and London, was a popular subject for Sandby in his later years. This watercolour precedes several others of Rochester. In 1794 he exhibited at the Royal Academy *A view of Rochester Castle* and *A view from Rochester Castle* (with Hazlitt, Gooden & Fox, London, in 1990). A large 1802 watercolour is held in a private collection in London, and two smaller and similar views, less finished and dating from the 1790s, are held by the Victoria & Albert Museum, London, and the Whitworth Art Gallery, Manchester.

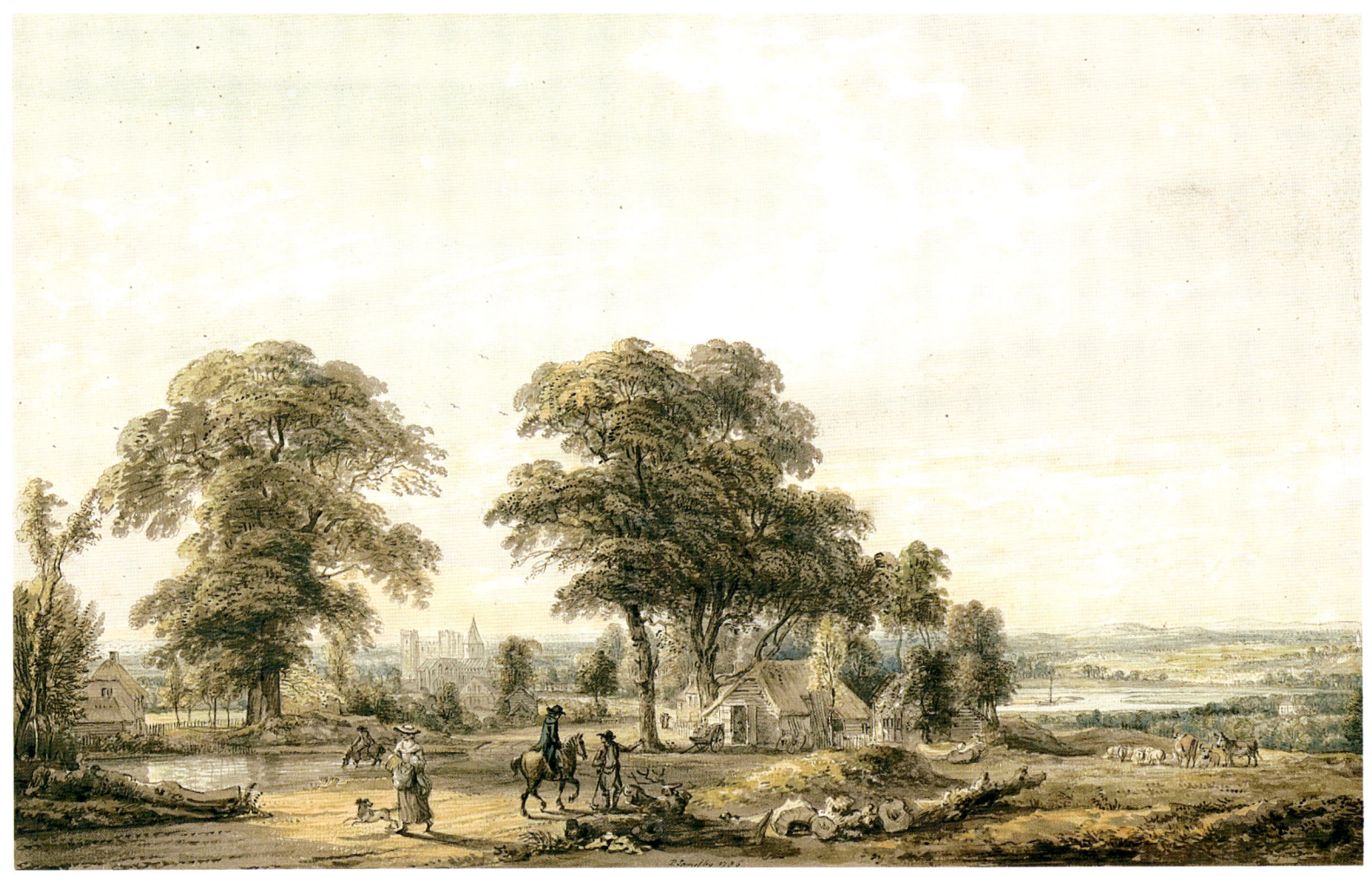

**Inscription:** Signed and dated l.c. pen & ink: "P Sandby 1786".

**Provenance:** Bought from the Fine Art Society, London, on the advice of H. D. Molesworth, 1956.

**Exhibitions:** *Paul Sandby Drawings*, 1981–82, City of Hamilton Art Gallery, Victoria; AGSA, Adelaide; National Gallery of Victoria, Melbourne and Art Gallery of New South Wales, Sydney. *Island to Empire: 300 Years of British Art 1550–1850*, AGSA, Adelaide 2005.

**Literature:** *NGSA Bulletin*, Adelaide: NGSA, vol. 17, no. 4, April 1956. Julian Faigan, *Paul Sandby Drawings*, Sydney: Australian Gallery Directors' Council, 1981, pl. 65.

**Condition:** Good; evidence of some fading.

# George Romney 1734–1802

George Romney for a short while after the death of Gainsborough in 1788 and from the last years of the ailing Reynolds (who died in 1792) was without rival as Britain's leading portrait painter. In the mid 1790s Thomas Lawrence assumed that mantle but, before he did so, Romney's later spontaneous and painterly portraits had provided a model for portraiture in the subsequent Regency period.

Romney usually presented his sitters as alert and open-faced but rarely attempted to disclose any depth of character. The technique of his mature works from the late 1770s was broad, confident and fluid. He seldom overworked the surface, as Reynolds tended to do. Consequently Romney usually finished his portraits twice as quickly, and unlike Reynolds's most remain in good condition.

Romney's reputation, high in his own time and again in the late nineteenth and early twentieth century, suffered in the second half of the twentieth century. His portraits can seem superficial, especially some rather sexist female portraits like those of the celebrity Emma Hart, later Lady Hamilton. Yet it was precisely this unquestioning attitude that made him such a successful society portrait painter. The 2002 retrospective exhibition at the National Portrait Gallery, London, attempted with some success to revive interest in his work. The exhibition and its accompanying book commemorated the bicentenary of the artist's death.[1]

Born in 1734 near Dalton-in-Furness in Lancashire (now Cumbria), Romney was largely self-taught but was apprenticed from 1755 to 1757 to an itinerant portrait painter named Christopher Steele (1733–1767), after which he established his own practice in Kendal and Lancaster. He moved to London in 1762 and visited Paris in 1764. His few surviving portraits from the 1760s are crisply drawn and very smoothly painted. The exhibition in 1768 of his masterful and complex *The Leigh family* (National Gallery of Victoria, Melbourne) marks the beginning of his successful career. From 1773 to 1775 he was in Italy and was especially impressed by the works of Titian in Venice and Raphael in Rome. When he returned to London – with a much more painterly technique, using coarser canvas and thicker paint like the Venetians – he took over Francis Cotes's impressive studio in Cavendish Square and no doubt some of the patrons of the artist who had died young in 1770. Romney certainly flattered the same strata of society as Cotes and within a year of his return became London's most fashionable portraitist. As his practice grew and his style became broader he painted directly onto the canvas without preparatory drawings. This sometimes led to sloppiness in technique and to portraits that fell into a formula.

Romney hated the drudgery of portrait sittings even more than did Reynolds and Gainsborough, and preferred intellectual company such as that of the sculptor and illustrator John Flaxman, the poet William Hayley and the visionary artist and poet William Blake. His chief ambition was to succeed as a history painter and he made thousands of pen drawings of literary and mythological compositions, rather in the style of Henry Fuseli, for paintings that were never executed. Romney refused to join or exhibit at the competitive Royal Academy. In 1798 he retired back to Kendal where he died four years later.

## Charlotte, Mrs Thomas Raikes, 1787

oil on canvas, 125.1 x 99.7 cm

Gift of Gladys Penfold Hyland in memory of her husband Frank 1964

This portrait was painted during Romney's most fashionable moment in the late 1780s and it is one of the most engaging of his late works. Charlotte Raikes, née Finch, was believed to be the natural daughter of the Honourable Henry Finch, younger son of Daniel, second Earl of Winchelsea and Nottingham.[2] She married Thomas Raikes (1741–1813) in London at St George's, Bloomsbury, on 8 December 1774. Raikes was a banker and a successful merchant with Russia and was for many years a Director and in 1797 the Governor of the Bank of England. At the time of this portrait the Raikeses lived at 10 New Broad Street in London and Freeland House, Kent, but later took a house in Upper Grosvenor Street. Raikes was a man of substance, a personal friend of the Prime Minister William Pitt the Younger and the reformist parliamentarian William Wilberforce. He died in 1814; Charlotte died in 1822.

The attractive Mrs Raikes sits on a red upholstered chair and poses playing at her spinet. She wears a powdered grey wig and a white linen gown cut in the style of a fashionable riding habit. The lawn frills of her chemise are draped over her shoulders and bosom. Romney had a good eye for placing the figure on the picture-surface to give it the greatest possible importance. This portrait is no exception and the placement is most inventive, a clearly-defined light figure against a dark background. The window above the spinet opens to a suggestion of deep, romantic landscape space.[3] The cool greens and moody indigo sky complement and contrast with the warm reds of the chair and the sitter's lips and with the crisp white of her dress. It is a highly satisfying orchestration of colour. The entire surface of this dashing composition is evenly painted with fluid, confident and summary brushwork.

The portrait is cheerful, and the sitter's gaiety is intended to be infectious. She turns to the viewer as if inviting accompaniment in her song. The painting makes few demands of us; the artist does not lead us to enquire about the inner character or thoughts of Charlotte Raikes. Romney wants us only to enjoy her enchanting appearance and light-hearted mood.

Long before Romney painted her, Charlotte had been

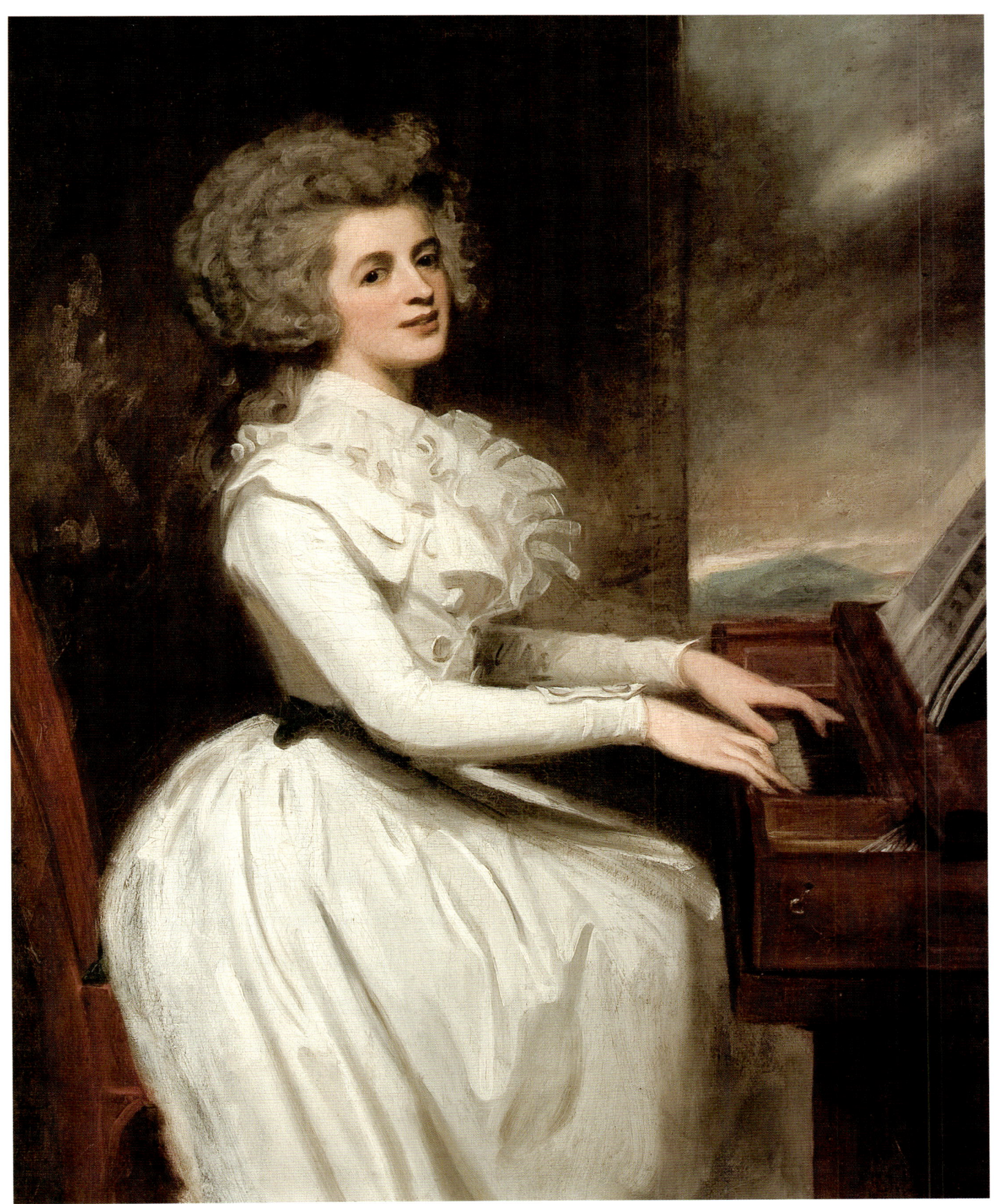

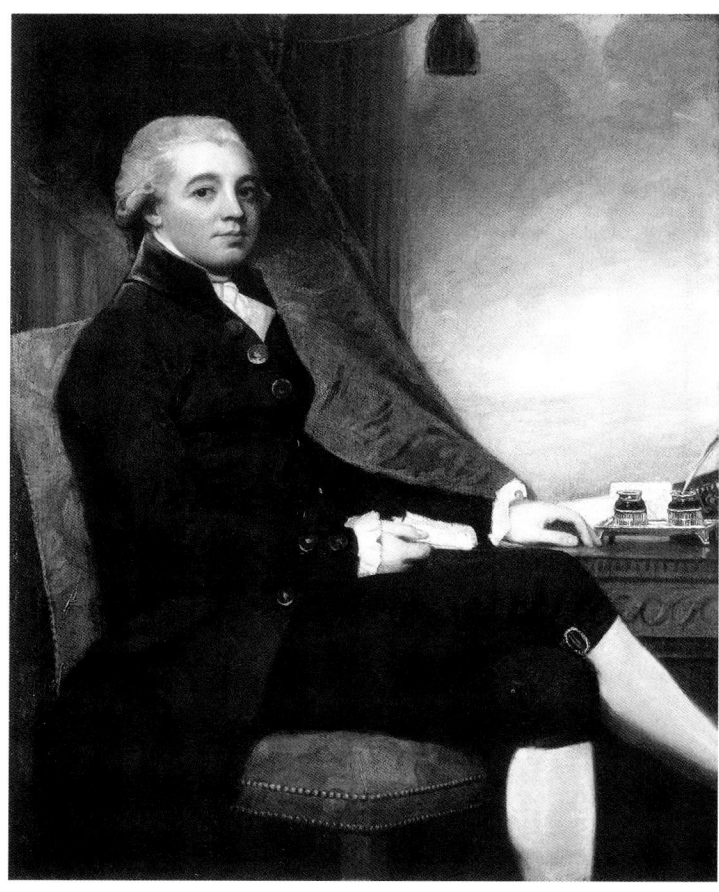

George Romney, *Thomas Raikes*, c.1786. Bank of England, London

portrayed in pastels by John Russell (1745–1806), the leading specialist in London for 'crayons'. Both Charlotte and Thomas Raikes were painted by Romney a number of times between 1785 and 1792.[4] In January 1786 Romney was paid for a portrait of Charlotte accompanied by one of their several children.[5] The Gallery's lively portrait of Charlotte playing the spinet resulted from four sittings mentioned in Romney's appointment diaries from December 1786 to May 1787.[6] In our portrait Romney painted her with much more dash and verve than in his earlier portrait of her in the role of mother. Having painted her before, Romney has not had to labour on her likeness. It is one of the most direct and confident of all his larger late portrait commissions. Nonetheless it could be said that her presentation is rather as a decorative possession – that the portrait is perhaps unwittingly about possession and status. Mrs Raikes does not play and sing for us, but for the husband who commissioned the portrait. It is a private performance. She and her accomplishments, and the expensive spinet, are status symbols, and the landscape possibly suggests her husband's possession of vast landholdings.

Romney also painted three portraits of her husband between the mid 1780s and the beginning of the 1790s. Romney had earlier painted portraits of Thomas Raikes's brothers Robert and Charles[7], so the Raikes family must be considered the artist's major patron of the 1780s.

This charming portrait was reproduced in early-twentieth-century publications around the time of the centenary of Romney's death, when the artist's work was most admired. It was therefore a well-known and respected work when it was purchased and brought to Australia by Frank and Gladys Penfold Hyland of Sydney, probably in the 1930s.

**Provenance:** Thomas Raikes; before 1888 T. Horatio Fitzroy Esq.; by 1902 Leopold Hirsch Esq., London; 1930s Frank and Gladys Penfold Hyland, Sydney.

**Exhibitions:** Old Masters exhibition, Burlington House, London, 1888, no. 35. *Island to Empire: 300 Years of British Art 1550–1850*, AGSA, Adelaide, 2005.

**Literature:** Herbert Maxwell, *George Romney*, London, 1902 (illus. facing p. 136). Humphry Ward and W. Roberts, *Romney*, 1904, vol. 1, p. 119 (illus. p. 104) and vol. 2, pp. 128–29. *NGSA Bulletin*, October 1964, vol. 26, no. 2 (illus.). Ron Radford in *Art Gallery of South Australia 1881–1981*, Adelaide: AGSA, p. 60. Peter Tomory and Robert Gaston, *European Paintings before 1800 in Australian and New Zealand Public Collections: Summary Catalogue*, Sydney, 1989, p. 44, no. 117 (illus.). Jeremy Black, *History of England*, London, 1993, p. 98 (illus.).

**Condition:** Excellent; probably last conserved in the 1960s.

**Frame:** Possibly original.

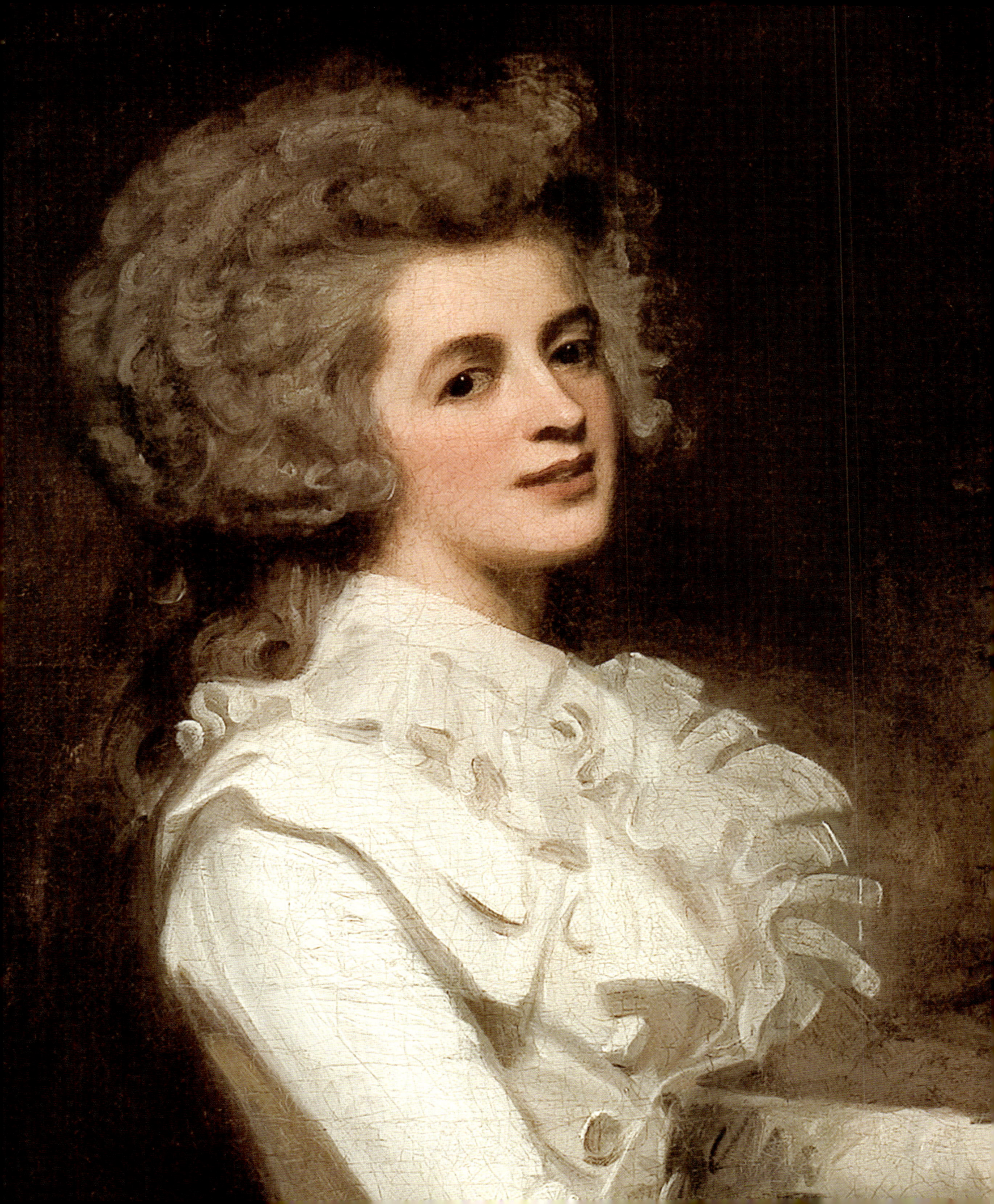

# George Romney

## Colonel Robert Abercrombie, 1788
oil on canvas, 76.5 x 63.0 cm
Gift of Phillips & Henderson, Adelaide 1982

This handsome half-length portrait of Colonel Robert Abercrombie, a Scot, was painted by Romney in 1788, the year after he painted the Gallery's portrait of *Charlotte, Mrs Thomas Raikes*, another work from the height of the artist's career.

Robert Abercrombie (later Sir Robert) was born in 1740 at Tullibody, Clackmannan, his father's seat in Scotland, and died in 1827. He entered the army at a young age, served in North America and returned in 1763 having risen to the rank of captain. Ten years later when trouble was brewing in the American colonies he again volunteered, was made a lieutenant-colonel and served with great distinction in the subsequent war. In 1781 he was promoted to colonel and made an aide-de-camp to young Prince Frederick, Duke of York.

In 1787 Robert Abercrombie became Colonel of the 75th Regiment and early in 1788 accompanied it to India. This portrait was painted just before he left for India and was doubtless commissioned because of the imminent departure. Romney's diary for 1788 records that "Colonel Abercrombie" gave the artist five sittings between 27 February and 8 March and that the portrait was paid for on 18 March, price 25 guineas.[1]

The sitter was wrongly identified in the past as Robert's even more distinguished brother Ralph Abercrombie (1734–1801), who was at one time also a colonel. However, Ralph Abercrombie was promoted to major-general in 1787, was away fighting in the war with France and therefore could not be the "Colonel Abercrombie" who is recorded in Romney's diary. Furthermore our portrait is of a younger man than Ralph. Robert Abercrombie would have been forty-eight years old in early 1788 and his older brother would have been fifty-five.[2] The London address to which this portrait was sent from Romney's studio on 30 April 1788 was 20 St James Street, St James's.[3]

The benevolent, open gaze of Robert Abercrombie, like other Romney portraits, is no doubt flattering to the middle-aged colonel but his pleasant countenance and character are well-recorded in letters. Sir John Shore, Governor-General of India when Abercrombie was stationed there, described his nature as "mild, conciliatory, and unassuming…a more reasonable, upright and zealous man never served the company…his greatest fault is his good nature".[4]

Like the portrait of Mrs Raikes, Colonel Abercrombie's is executed with effortless dexterity and confidence, the paint applied directly with no under-drawing and little need for over-working. Romney has placed the sitter elegantly onto the canvas. The warm dark background and the warm flesh tones of the face are complemented by the attractive cool green of the coat, highlighted with gold buttons, a partly visible lemon-coloured waistcoat and, at his throat, a white stock. The formal powdered wig is not for military occasions and the apparel is not a military uniform but a type of livery, almost certainly of Prince Frederick Duke of York's household; the gold braided buttons display a crown above a capital "F" for Frederick.

**Provenance:** Lord Cochrane of Cults; Agnew's, London, by whom sold to Mr T. D. Kelly, Adelaide, 20 July 1967; Theodore Bruce auction, Adelaide, 16 March 1982, lot 428.
**Exhibition:** *Island to Empire: 300 Years of British Art 1550–1850*, AGSA, Adelaide, 2005.
**Literature:** Humphry Ward and W. Roberts, *Romney*, London, 1904, vol. 1, pp. 1, 114.
**Condition:** Excellent; probably last conserved in London in the late 1960s.
**Frame:** Probably original.

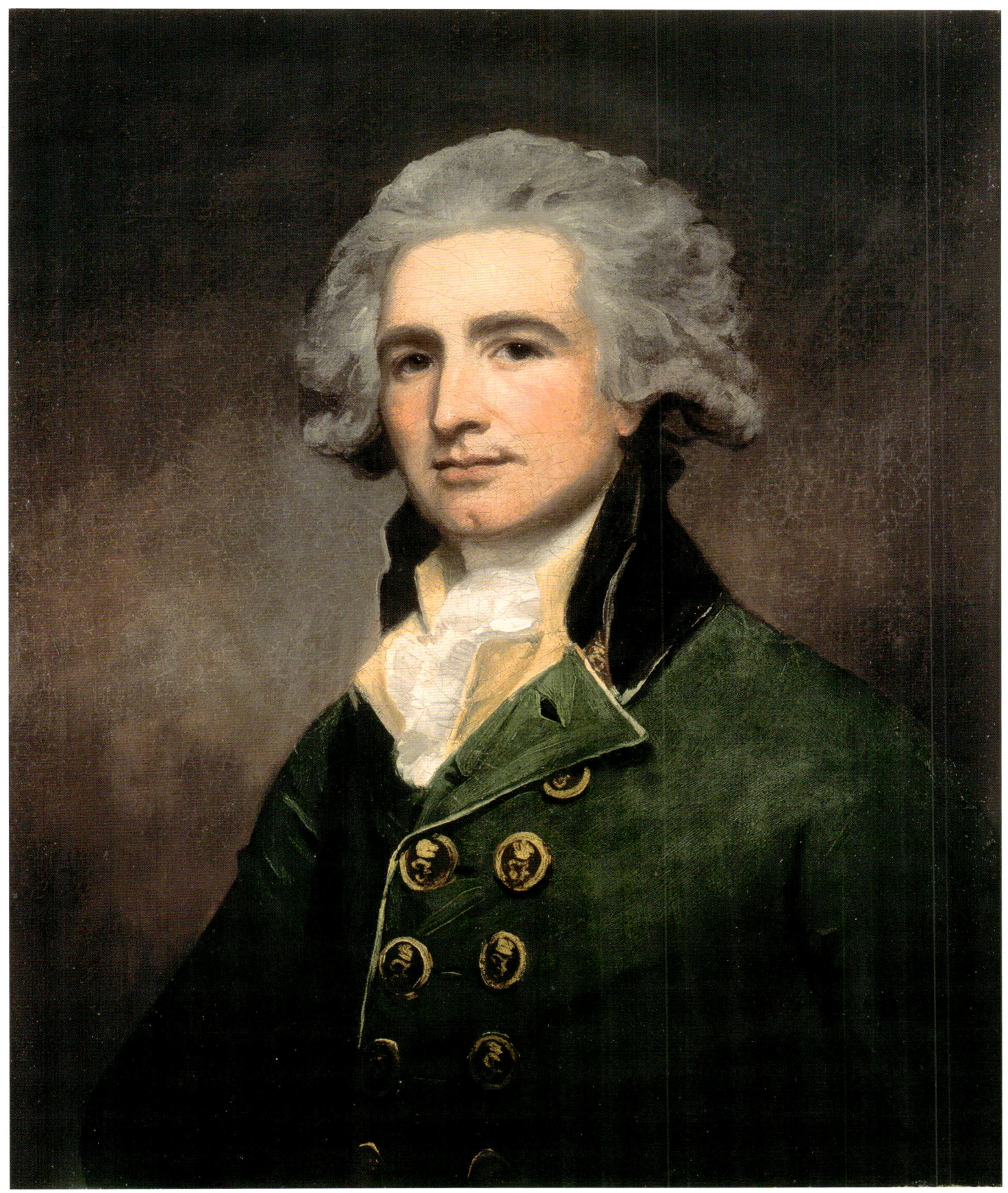

# Francis Wheatley 1747–1801

Francis Wheatley is known chiefly for prints that depicted aspects of everyday life in his own time and place. He was also a painter of history, of landscapes, and of portraits.

Born at Covent Garden, London, in 1747, he studied at William Shipley's School at the Society of Arts but was mainly self-taught. In 1762 he made a trip to the Low Countries where Dutch genre scenes and landscapes had an impact on his subsequent art. He visited Paris in 1777 and at the Salon probably saw paintings by François Boucher (1703–1770) and Jean-Baptiste Greuze (1725–1805). Sentimental moral subjects by the latter and peasant scenes by Gainsborough were to remain influential throughout his career.

Well established in London as a painter of portraits and conversation pieces, Wheatley fled his creditors to work in Dublin from 1779 to 1783. In 1786 he received commissions for two differing portraits of Arthur Phillip, appointed first Governor of New South Wales in October that year with instructions to establish a colony on the continent soon to be known as Australia, which he did at the beginning of 1788. Wheatley's standing portrait of Captain Phillip on an imaginary New South Wales shore is now in the National Portrait Gallery, London, and an oval bust-length portrait is in the Mitchell Library, Sydney.

In the late 1780s Wheatley began to participate in the schemes of printseller and publisher Alderman John Boydell and concentrated on elevated British subject pictures and popular genre for engraving. Wheatley's most famous works of this kind are *The Cries of London*. The fourteen small paintings showing the street-calls of itinerant London traders were exhibited at the Royal Academy (of which he had just become a full member) between 1792 and 1795 and shortly afterwards made into what became best-selling prints.

## The blind pedlar, 1794
watercolour on paper, 34.7 x 48.0 cm
South Australian Government Grant 1956

This watercolour was executed in 1794 when Wheatley was producing *The Cries of London* and enjoying the height of his fame. It is a rustic counterpart to that series of commercial enterprise in city streets, another approving image of the virtuous working poor.

A youthful pedlar sits on a bench between two standing kitchen maids at the back courtyard of a picturesque farmhouse. On his lap is a basket which includes cheap wares: a candlestick, a metal salt shaker, and a ribbon that he holds out for the two young women. His faithful dog has settled at his heels. The maids, not particularly interested in his wares, appear nonetheless to be over-attentive and protective towards the blind but handsome youth. We are invited to share their interest and sympathy.

Sentimental genre pictures of this kind, lightly-charged with sex, were Wheatley's forte. An immediately appealing subject, simple composition and clear execution were created for easy translation into prints. However, no print was made of this composition, though he might have wished for the extra income. He painted it in the year, 1794, that he was declared bankrupt, not for lack of professional success but because of his extravagant living.

Wheatley repeated the subject a number of times in the 1790s. There are two major oil paintings, *The pedlar*, 1791, and *The pedlar at the cottage door* (both in British private collections). A watercolour, *A travelling potter with his wares outside a cottage*, 1798, is at the Yale Center for British Art. Pedlars combined two of Wheatley's best-known themes of the 1790s, the street traders of his *Cries of London* and his peasants, especially women and children, outside a cottage door. The latter were derived directly from Gainsborough's famous *The cottage door*, c.1780, at the Huntington Library & Art Collections, San Marino, California.

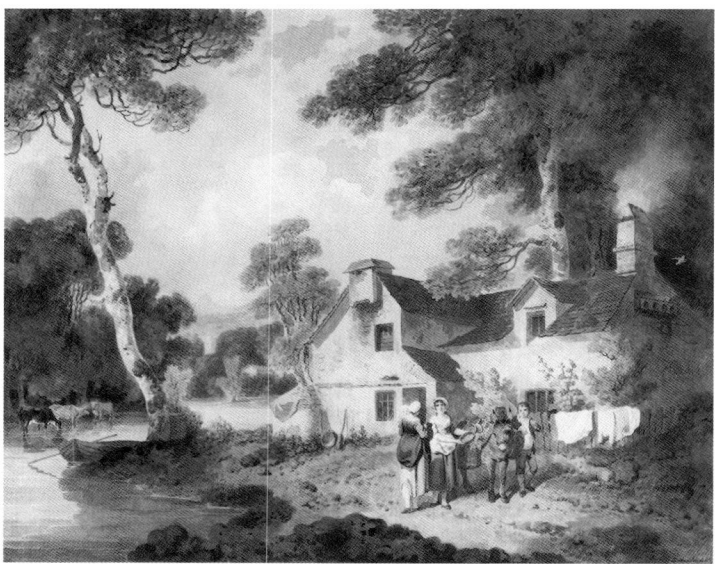

Francis Wheatley, *A travelling potter with his wares outside a cottage*, 1798. Yale Center for British Art, Paul Mellon Collection, New Haven

**Provenance:** Purchased from Appleby Bros, London, on the advice of H. D. Molesworth, 1956.

**Exhibitions:** *Exhibition of English Watercolours*, Mildura Art Gallery, Victoria, 1960. *Island to Empire: 300 Years of British Art 1550–1850*, AGSA, Adelaide, 2005.

**Condition:** Fair; evidence of fading.

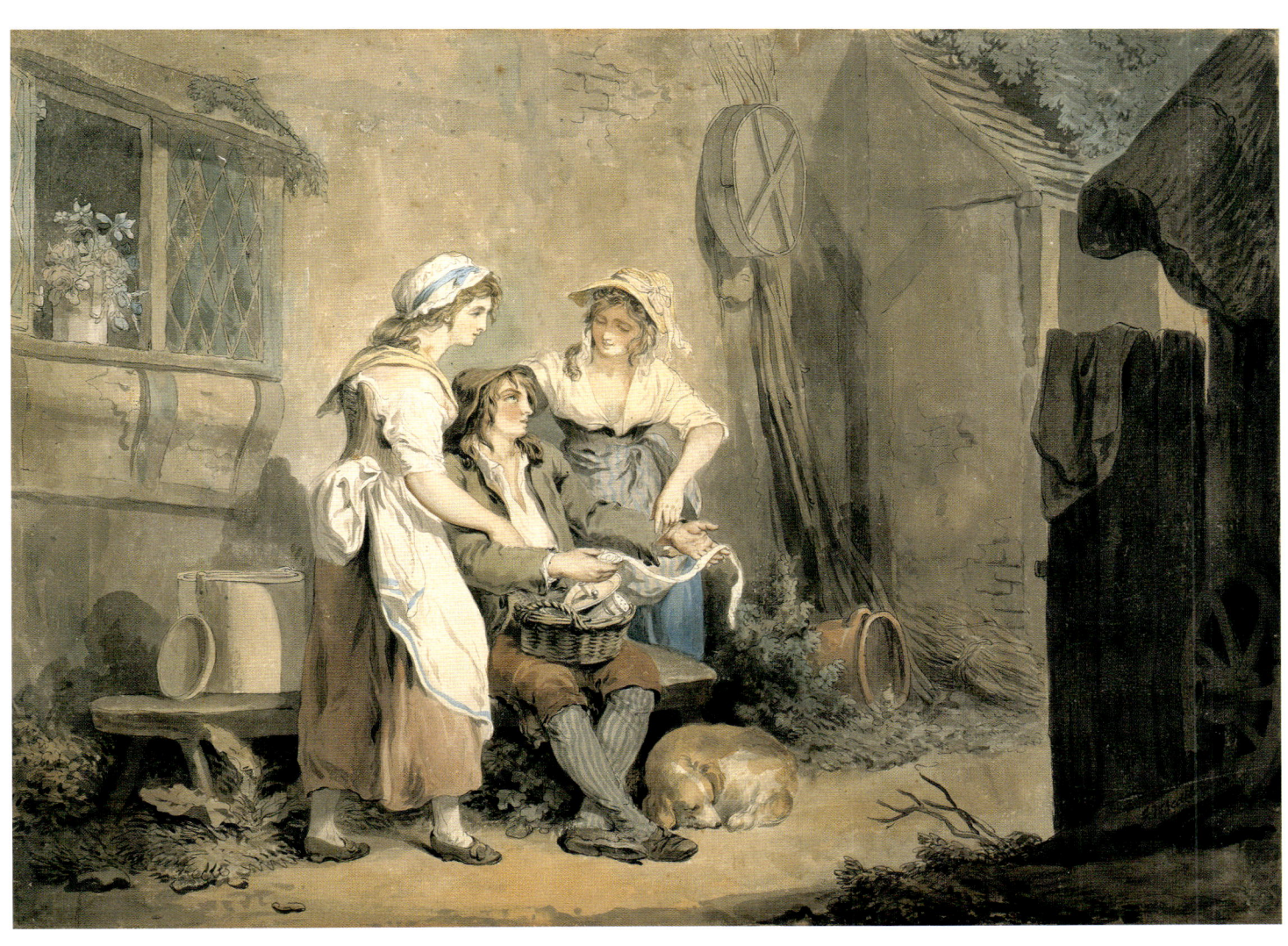

# Richard Westall 1765–1836

Richard Westall (like Francis Wheatley) is remembered mainly for his introduction of figure subjects and historical themes into British watercolour painting in the late eighteenth century, a time when it was dominated by landscape. His watercolours had a depth and richness of colour comparable to painting in oil, and he occasionally painted in oil. With only partial justification, his works are sometimes dismissed for being too pretty and sentimental.

He was the older half-brother and first teacher of William Westall, the first professional artist to paint Australian landscapes. William was the official topographer on the voyage of the *Investigator* when Matthew Flinders, from 1801 to 1803, circumnavigated the continent and for the first time charted the full extent of the Australian coastline.

Richard Westall was born in 1765 at Hertford. In 1779 he was apprenticed to a heraldic engraver in London but took evening art-lessons and in 1785 was admitted to the Royal Academy Schools. By the later 1780s he was exhibiting regularly at the Royal Academy and became a full member of the Academy in 1794.

He produced many anecdotal and classical figure compositions, and occasional light-hearted rustic subjects, often intended for popular engravings. Many of the sentimental subjects, particularly his earliest works, display a tendency towards Rococo decoration and frivolity but by the mid 1790s his subjects and style took on a firmer Neoclassicism.

## The birds' nest, 1794
watercolour, gouache on paper, 44.0 x 35.8 cm
South Australian Government Grant 1955

When Westall painted *The birds' nest* in 1794 his style was firming towards Neoclassical precision. In an Italianate garden a young mother with two pretty daughters indulges her young son in the discovery of a thrush's nest with hatchlings. Rococo playfulness has given way to a pre-Victorian sweetness and sentimentality. On the large Neoclassical vase behind the group is a low relief depicting a biblical subject, *The Presentation in the Temple*, in which the infant Jesus is presented to the Elders by Mary and Joseph to be consecrated to the Lord. Just as the infant Christ is being initiated so is the innocent son undergoing instruction in the wonders of God's creations. As symbolic doves of purification hover over the Virgin in the relief, the mother thrush flies above the figures in the garden.

It is possible that Richard Westall used his young half-brother William, then thirteen years old, as the basis for the dark-haired boy. The mother could be based on Richard's young stepmother (William's mother) and the sisters embracing in the background could be modelled on Richard's sisters (William's half-sisters) Mary and Ann.[1]

The composition and the white-costumed figures are fashionably classical in style; the figures and the nest form a regular triangle with the marble vase at its apex. The mother and younger daughter are intent on the nest while the older daughter observes the mother bird just flown to the upper edge of the watercolour. This daughter will soon fly from the family nest. The arrangement of the three women suggests the Three Graces of Greek mythology, goddess personifications of charm, grace and beauty. Their Neoclassical dress conforms with the garden and its great vase beneath what appears to be an overhanging Roman pine. The overall colouring is rich and especially enlivened by the prominent crimson of the boy's velvet suit. Tall stands of colourful hollyhocks grow at the base of the vase and the foreground is decorated with straying morning-glory vine and honeysuckle.

Westall was a close friend of the young portrait painter Thomas Lawrence and was living with him at Lawrence's parents' house at the time this picture was executed. Lawrence's influence is clearly seen here and it is interesting to compare Westall's small watercolour *The birds' nest* with Lawrence's large portrait *Lady Elizabeth Manners* (Cleveland Museum of Art). They were painted the same year and in both we see sweetness and elegance in a classical garden setting. Both were exhibited with success at the Royal Academy in 1794.[2] Westall received not only popular success with this stylish anecdotal work but also the admiration of his artist peers. *The birds' nest* and his twelve other exhibits ensured his early election to full membership of the Royal Academy that year, simultaneously with his younger friend Thomas Lawrence, soon to be the darling of Regency society as their chief portrait painter.

The scene is clearly composed and defined for easy translation into a print for popular enjoyment. Its purpose was fulfilled four years later, in 1798, when Charles Knight made an engraving.

Throughout the 1790s Westall produced similar compositions

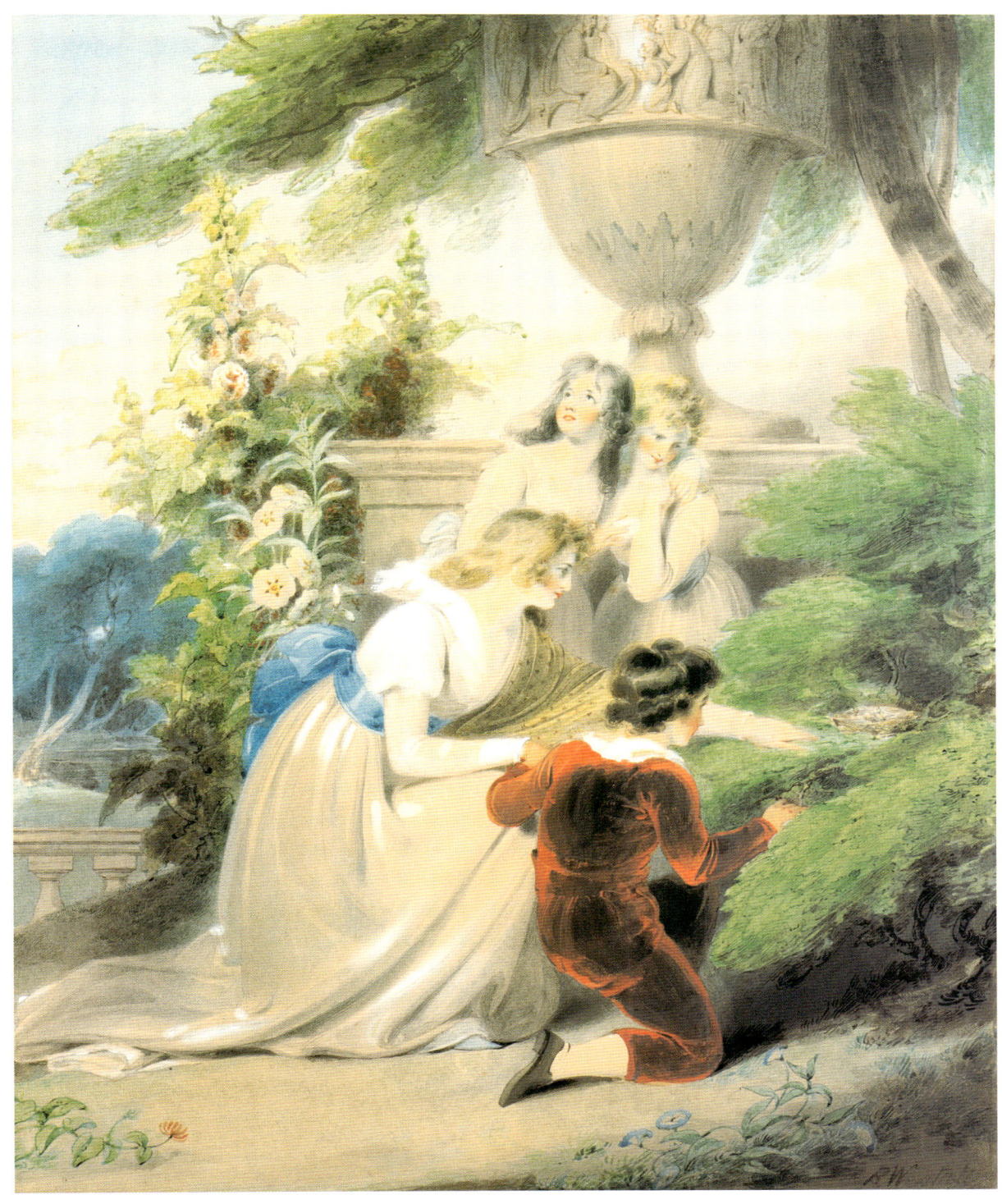

173

of charming children or young adults in ornate gardens, with titles like *The sensitive plant* and *Innocent mischief*, and these too were engraved as popular prints. They embodied popular perceptions of desirable pastimes for the leisured upper classes, and were created largely for a hardworking and prosperous middle class. The market for such pictures was not confined to Britain; at the beginning of the nineteenth century Westall's paintings and prints, like those by other of his English contemporaries, had a wide Continental audience, particularly in middle-class Germany.

It is instructive further to compare Westall's *The birds' nest* with the Gallery's *The blind pedlar* by Francis Wheatley (p. 171) which is also of 1794. The contrast between a well-groomed family in a formal front garden and kitchen maids and pedlar at a back door is obvious. Yet these scenes of class contrast were both intended to appeal to the same middle-class buyers and offer romantic notions of the idle rich and the happy poor. Westall himself sometimes painted sentimental scenes of rural low-life with titles such as *The reaper's child asleep*, 1793, but unlike Wheatley's and, especially, George Morland's rusticities Westall's low-life characters are remarkably unconvincing. They seem to be playing at being peasants. Westall was more at home with upper-class gentility, as in *The birds' nest*.

**Inscription:** Signed l.r. brush & wash: 'R. Westall'. Dated '1794'.

**Provenance:** Purchased from Agnew's, London, on the advice of H. D. Molesworth, 1955.

**Exhibitions:** Royal Academy, 1794, no. 413, possibly as *Spring. Exhibition of English Watercolours*, Mildura Art Gallery, Victoria, 1960. *Regency: British Art & Design 1800-1830*, AGSA, Adelaide, 1998, no. 128. *Island to Empire: 300 Years of British Art 1550-1850*, AGSA, Adelaide, 2005.

**Literature:** Ron Radford in Christopher Menz, *Regency*, Adelaide: AGSA, 1998, pp. 74-75. Ron Radford, "William Westall and the Landscape Tradition" in Sarah Thomas, *The Encounter, 1802*, Adelaide: AGSA, 2002, p. 106 (illus.).

**Condition:** Excellent.

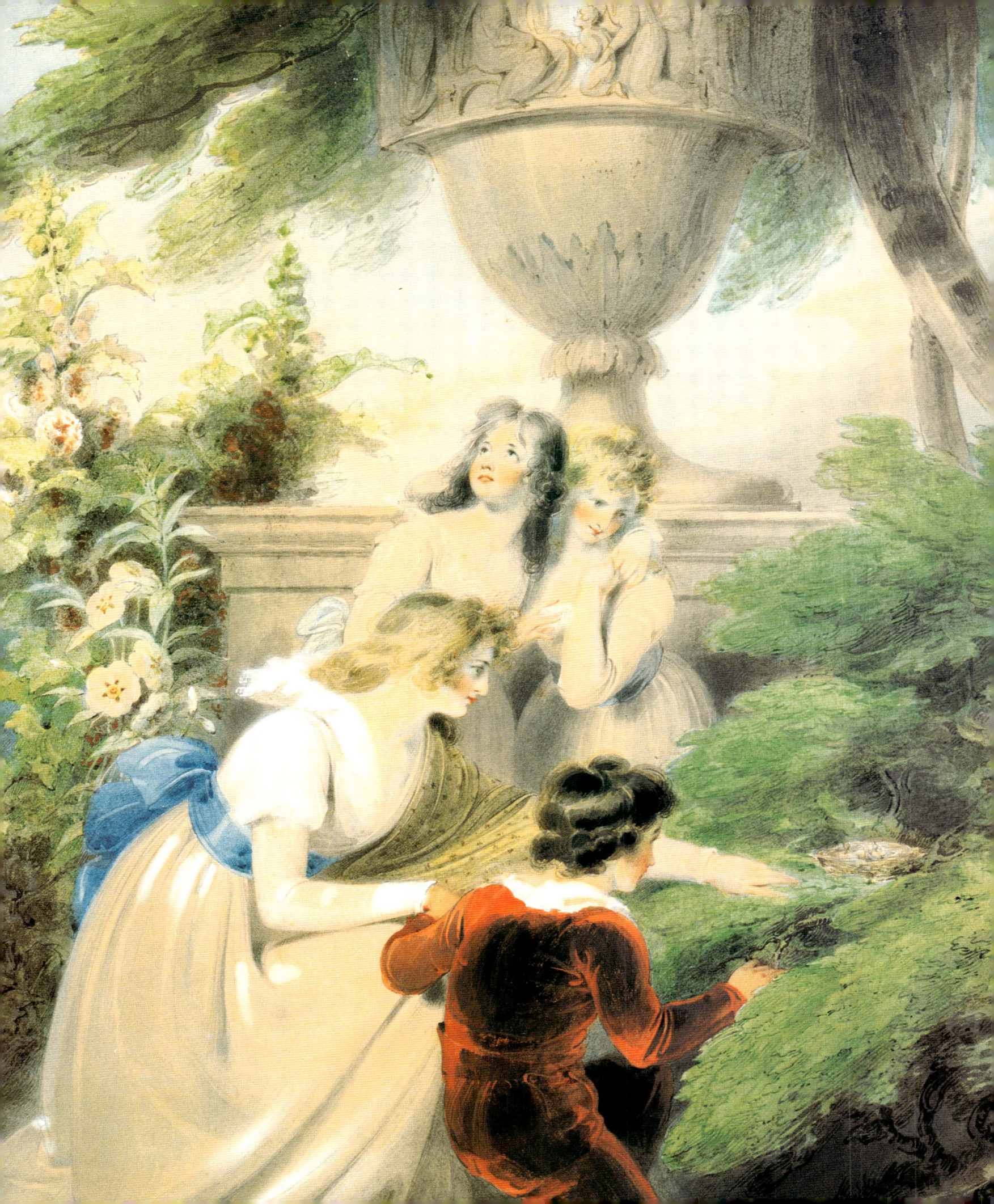

# George Morland 1763–1804

George Morland is famous for his picturesque depictions of tumbledown farmyards, country inns, endearing runt animals, harmless gypsies, happy peasants and romantic smugglers and fishermen. His popularity coincided with a craze for the rustic picturesque at the end of the eighteenth century and his own colourful personality and eccentric dress helped make him a celebrity.

Born in London in 1763, Morland was taught at a very early age by his artist father. Henry Morland began exhibiting the precocious son's work when the boy was fourteen. When the restrictive apprenticeship to his father expired in 1784 George began to follow the sentimental genre scenes of Francis Wheatley who was then enjoying success in London. Morland's earliest dated painting, St Valentine's Day, 1786–7 (Victoria & Albert Museum, London), was part of The Progress of Love, a popular series executed in collaboration with Wheatley. By 1790 Morland had established a reputation as an independent painter of moral and domestic scenes that were particularly attractive to the printsellers' wider market for engravings. Characteristic of his work up till then was Laetitia, a harlot's progress, a Hogarth-like series of six pictures that serialised a young woman's slide from innocence to vice. He married the older sister of the animal-painter James Ward, whose work he influenced.

About 1790 Morland began his unusually successful paintings of rustic low-life, probably in response to the commercial appeal of a new sensibility, the cult for a nostalgic simple-life picturesque. His compositions were made into engravings by many artists, one being Benjamin Duterrau (1767–1851) who became a significant Australian early-colonial history and portrait artist after his emigration late in life to Hobart. Prints of Morland's work were popular not only in Britain but also on the Continent, especially in Germany and France.

Morland was a pioneer in the marketing of his own work. Instead of finding a buyer, or waiting for commissions, or fighting for exhibition space at the Royal Academy or other exhibiting institutions, Morland simply sold most of his production to a middleman, a dealer who found a buyer or arranged for the work to be engraved. Morland then was free to paint the subjects of his choice, when he pleased and the size he wished. A hitherto rare arrangement in Britain, the practice required very popular, immediately appealing work that a dealer could readily sell – which is exactly what Morland produced. The system had its own potential to corrupt. Between about 1790 and 1794 Morland created the best of his rustic genre pictures, full of vitality and spontaneity, with inventive compositions, but later it became too easy for him. Together with the devastating effects of his growing drunkenness, this caused his paintings from the mid 1790s onwards to become repetitive and in some cases downright sloppy.

Alcohol was the main cause of his death in 1804 at the age of forty-one. Three years later no fewer than four books appeared on his life and art. Other books followed through the nineteenth century. Virtually nothing substantial has been published on Morland since 1907, which is indicative of the critical regard in which he was held then and now.

## Outside the Bull's Head, mid 1790s
oil on canvas, 49.2 x 64.8 cm
Gift of Gladys Penfold Hyland in memory of her husband Frank 1964

The Gallery's picture of drinkers and talkers outside a small thatched inn, a subject close to drunkard Morland's heart, is one of several repetitions of an earlier painting. The subject and setting were easily appealing: the inn and its side fence are properly rustic and shaded by a large and romantically gnarled oak; Morland's own shaggy dog of indeterminate breed, often included in his compositions, is seen here faithfully waiting and enlivens the pleasurably rough foreground of long grass and stones. It is a scene that makes little demand on the viewer and derives from Wheatley's cottage-door subjects and less directly from Gainsborough's earlier and more complex rural images of peasants at their cottage doors. Such rustic scenes ultimately derive from seventeenth-century Dutch paintings, extensively collected in Britain in the eighteenth century. By the time Morland painted this canvas the genre was well-tried but had only just gained huge popularity in Britain. Morland boosted the genre as well as reaping its rewards.

In 1790 the first version of Outside the Bull's Head was one of Morland's first essays in rural daily life. Its success can be measured in part by the number of versions. The crisply-painted first version, signed and dated, measured 27 by 35 inches.[1] The Gallery's version is smaller, 19 by 25 inches. A little-known artist, D. Brown, made a good copy of the original work in 1792 and inscribed his name and date above the door of the inn.[2] In France, A. Masson made a popular but undated engraving of this composition. Throughout the 1790s Morland continued to paint differing scenes of drinkers outside country inns, places where he himself was spending more and more time.

The closest in size and composition to our Outside the Bull's Head is one called The Fish Inn (private collection). The National Gallery of Scotland, Edinburgh, holds a similar but more elaborate painting entitled The public house door, 1792. The Tate, London, owns a small 1792 composition of two drinkers outside a tavern.

The Gallery's version is not dated but on stylistic grounds appears to be executed about the mid 1790s. Although it has solid form the paint application is generalised and lacks the vitality of slightly earlier canvases. However, it is not one of the later works in which quality markedly deteriorated.

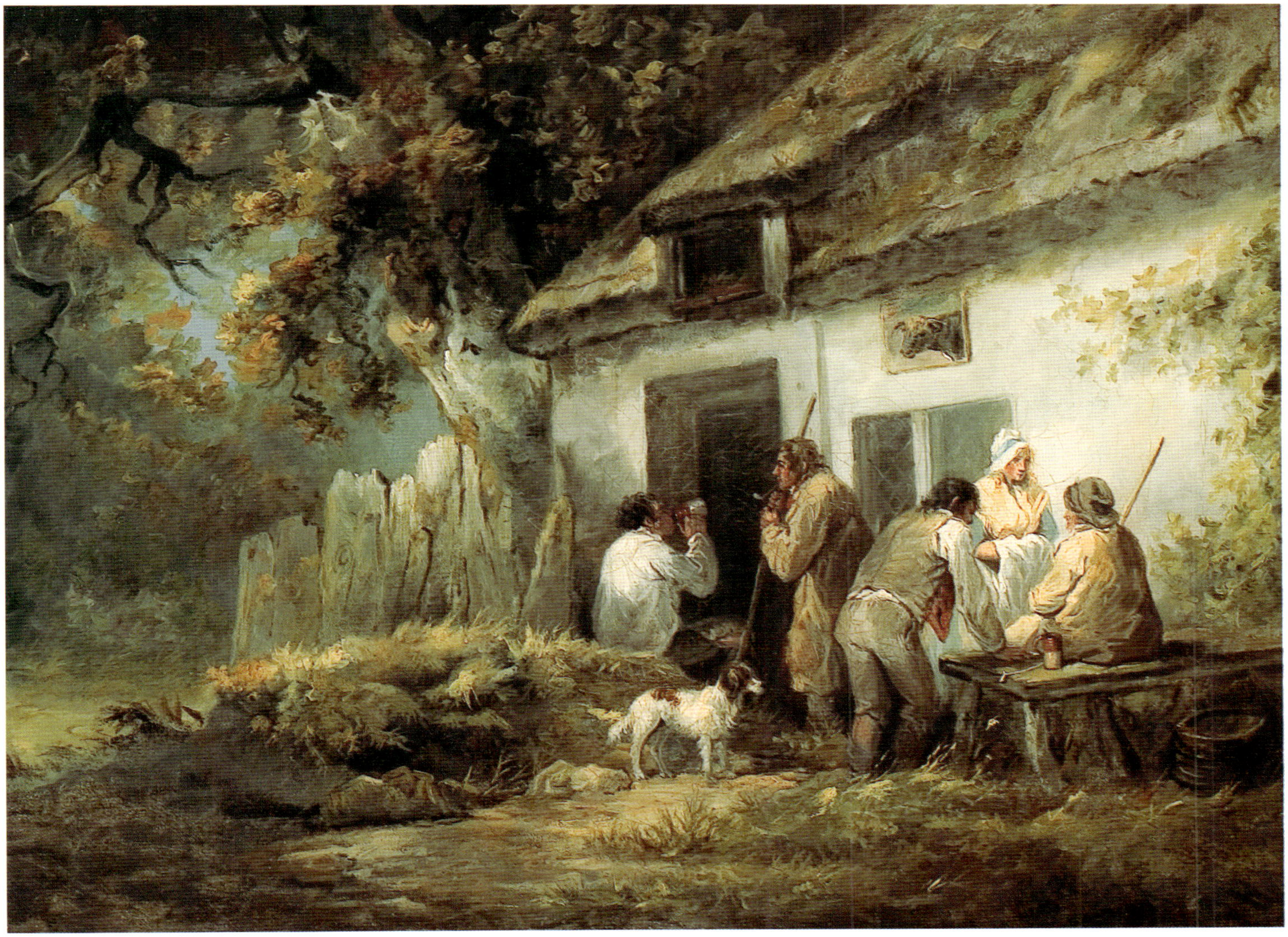

| | |
|---|---|
| **Provenance:** | Purchased in London probably in the 1930s by Frank & Gladys Penfold Hyland, Sydney. |
| **Exhibition:** | *Island to Empire: 300 Years of British Art 1550–1850*, AGSA, Adelaide, 2005. |
| **Literature:** | *NGSA Bulletin*, Adelaide: NGSA, vol. 26, no. 2, October 1964, unpaginated. Peter Tomory and Robert Gaston, *European Paintings before 1800 in Australian and New Zealand Public Collections*, Sydney, 1989, p. 36, no. 87 (illus.). |
| **Condition:** | Good; conserved 1993–94 by Artlab Australia, Adelaide. |
| **Frame:** | Probably not original, but late nineteenth century. |

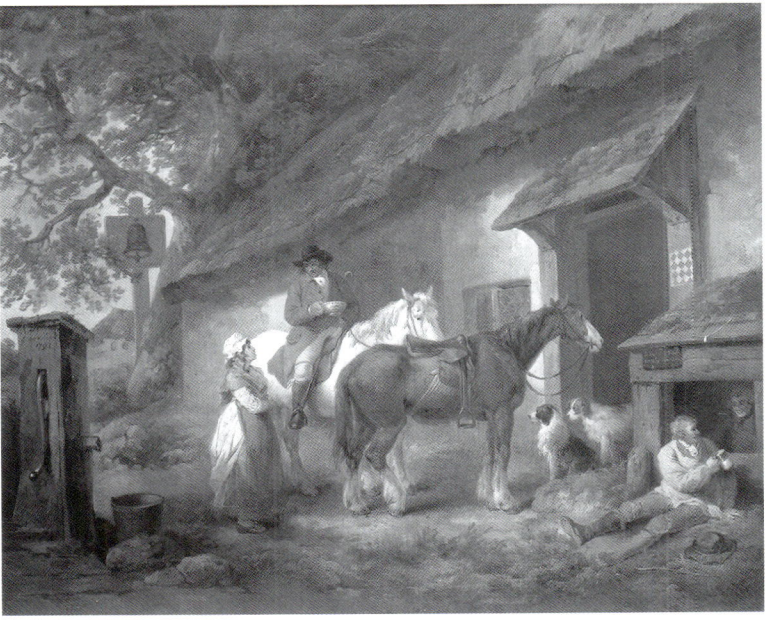

George Morland, *The public house door*, 1792. The National Gallery of Scotland, Edinburgh

# Martin Archer Shee 1769–1850

Martin Archer Shee followed the grand manner of English portraiture exemplified by the work of Joshua Reynolds. The style prevailed throughout the second half of the eighteenth century and remained in vogue almost until the middle of the nineteenth century. Although largely forgotten now, Shee was famous in his day. His extraordinarily long career as a portrait painter began in the 1780s, he became President of the Royal Academy in 1830, and retained the position until his own death in 1850. He was the last survivor of the 'Golden Age' of British portrait painting.

Shee was born in 1769 into an Irish Catholic family in Dublin, where he received his first training as an artist at West's Academy. In 1783 the death of his father forced Shee to turn to portraiture to support himself. His first portraits in pastel display the influence of the Irish portrait painter Hugh Douglas-Hamilton but he turned to oil painting. Encouraged by the American portrait painter Gilbert Stuart to move to London – although in Dublin Stuart himself was a fugitive from London competition – Shee arrived there in 1788 at the age of eighteen, hoping for good training and professional success. The following year, encouraged by Joshua Reynolds, he began to study at the Royal Academy Schools. He was soon introduced to patrons by his nabob cousin George Shee and began to receive commissions, many from Irish Catholics who continued to support him throughout his life.

The year 1798 marked a significant turning point in what was to be a long and successful career. Shee exhibited a very large portrait of his Irish kinsman George O'Shea at the Royal Academy, was paid the handsome sum of £108 for it, and received much praise.[1] This was the portrait now in the Art Gallery of South Australia. It was crucial in assisting his prompt election to the Royal Academy as an Associate. In 1799 he acquired George Romney's fine house and studio in Cavendish Square. (Romney, who had retired to the country, had in turn acquired the studio from Francis Cotes's estate, and it is interesting that Shee was asked to complete two of Romney's unfinished portraits.) His success was now assured and at the beginning of 1800 he was elected a full Academician. Commissions for similar large-scale portraits of military and naval sitters came his way from the end of the 1790s, including two full-length portraits, 1800 and 1801, of the Duke of Clarence. Shee painted the Duke again after he became William IV, and also painted his consort Queen Adelaide in whose honour the capital city of South Australia is named. The artist seems ill at ease with his female sitters, however, and may be better remembered for his charming and sensitive portraits of children.

Although Shee's early work strongly reflected the grand style of Reynolds, by the beginning of the nineteenth century it showed the influence of Hoppner and later of Lawrence. On Lawrence's sudden death in 1830 Shee was an obvious choice to be the next president of the Royal Academy, due as much to his long professional standing and his tactful temperament as to his artistic skills. He was knighted that year and continued to exhibit at the Royal Academy until 1845. In 1838 the Royal Academy commissioned from its president a portrait of the young Queen Victoria, the year after her ascendancy to the throne. Sir Martin Archer Shee died in London in 1850.

## Major O'Shea of the Loyal Cork Legion, 1798

oil on canvas, 233.7 x 157.5 cm

Gift of Alexander Melrose 1930

This huge double portrait of a soldier and a horse, exhibited at the Royal Academy in 1798 with the title *Major O'Shea of the Loyal Cork Legion*, was the artist's first significant popular success in the most important exhibition in London, and perhaps a calculated populist manoeuvre. The slightly exotic Irish major dominates with his authoritative statuesque stance, sabre in hand, dressed in a bright red and white military outfit, and standing in front of an imposing horse who wears a saddle of hair or shaggy fleece. In the background is a glimpse of a castle fortress in a barren landscape, romantically lit by a dark and cloudy sky, hinting at the drama of battle. Although not as inspiring as the best grand-manner portraits by Reynolds and Gainsborough, this work is nonetheless immediately striking and it is easy to see why it impressed Shee's contemporaries and resulted in further commissions. He was very much at home with military gentlemen and in the following year he exhibited at the Royal Academy another equestrian portrait, *Major Vickers of the 2nd Life Guards with black servant*, which helped his election to full membership of the Academy. With two early equestrian successes Shee amusingly remarked, "I *rode* into the Academy".[2] Indeed, the spectator-conscious horse in our painting engages us with its direct stare more than does Major O'Shea himself.

The painting came into the South Australian collection in 1930 as a gift from the Gallery's generous benefactor and Board Member, Alexander Melrose. He had purchased it in London the year before at Christie's with the title *Major George O'Shea of the Loyal Cork Legion*[3] but was already corrupted on arrival in Adelaide to the shorter title of *Major-General O'Shea*. The significance of the painting in the artist's career is rehearsed in the biography written by his son Martin Shee and published in 1860. However, one can find little information about the supposed sitter and only a little more about the Loyal Cork Legion in which he is supposed to have been a major. George Shea was born in Cork about 1754. There were units of volunteer yeomanry styled The Cork Legion (Infantry) and The Cork Legion (Cavalry)

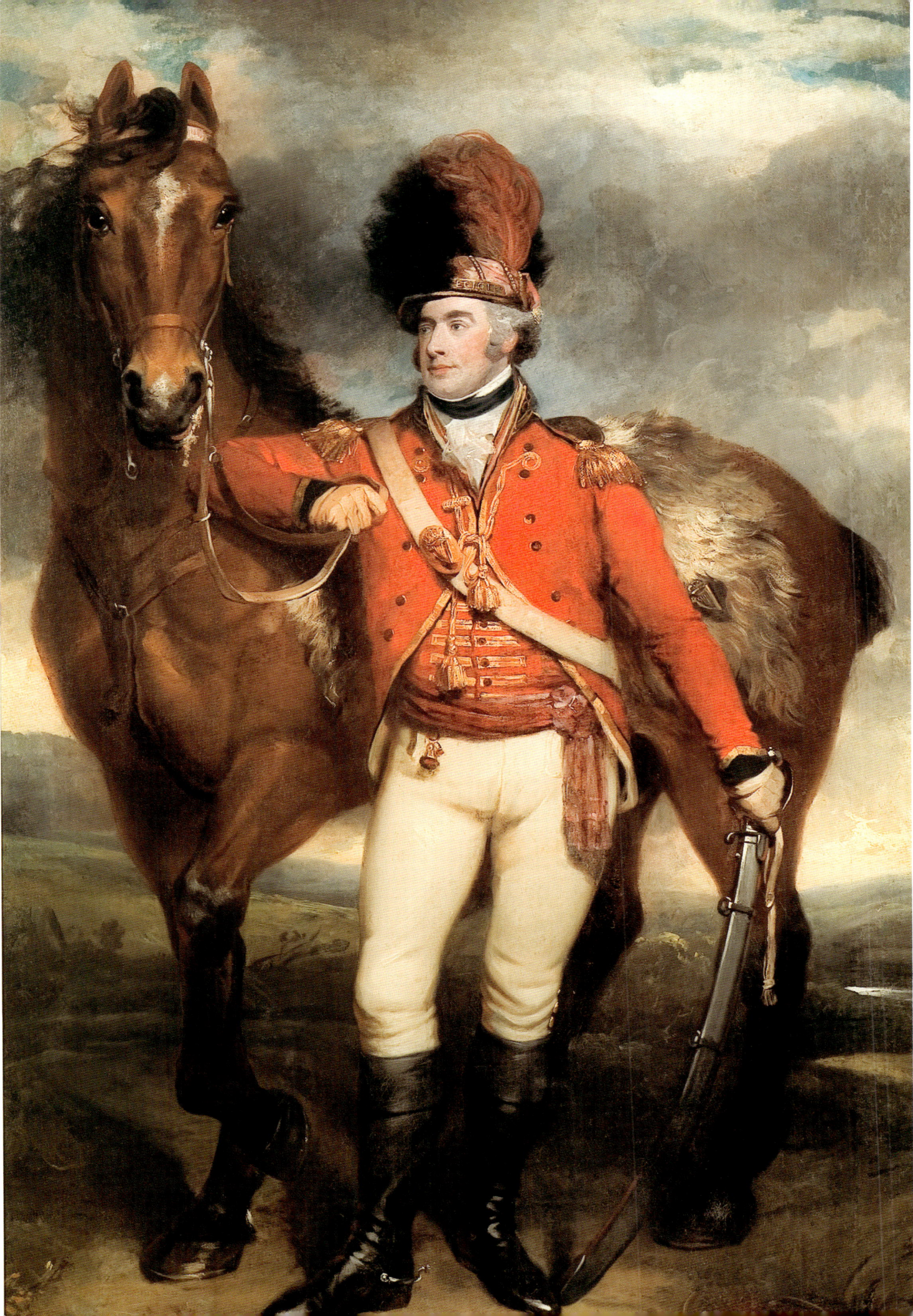

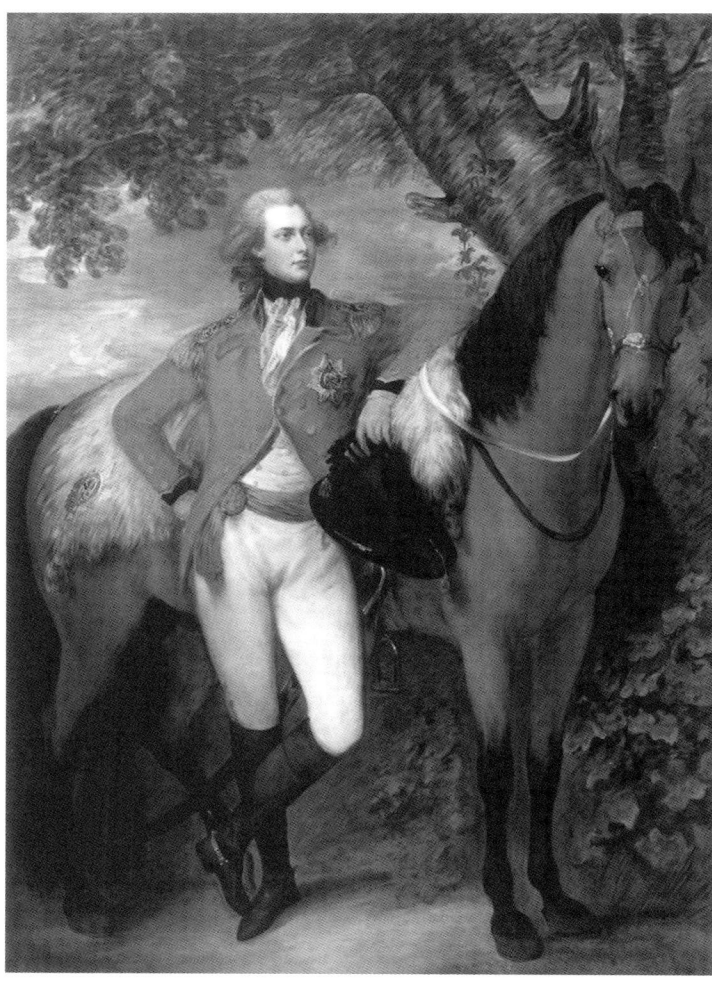

Thomas Gainsborough, *George, Prince of Wales*, c.1782. Waddesdon Manor, The National Trust

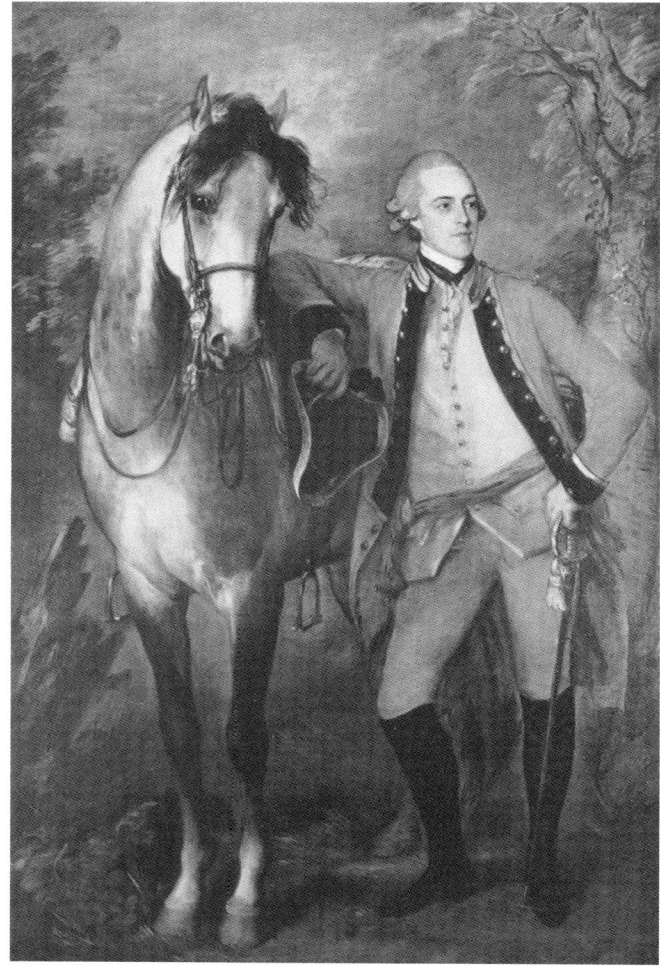

Thomas Gainsborough, *Edward, 2nd Viscount Ligonier*, 1771. Huntington Library & Art Collections, San Marino, California

which were established in 1796–97. The prefix 'Loyal' seems to have become attached to the infantry unit, which by 1805 was styled The Loyal Cork Legion Riflemen whereas our man with his horse would be attached to the cavalry.[4] The only evidence of the 'Major' is in a 1797 volume entitled *District Corps Ireland*. Listed under Cork Legion, Fourth Company, the second-lieutenant's name has been crossed out and the name "George Shea" written in.[5] The year 1798, the date of our portrait, was the time of the Irish Insurrection. O'Shea may possibly have been promoted by then from lieutenant to major because of his involvement, and that may have been the reason for commissioning in the same year a celebratory portrait from his kinsman Martin Archer Shee. Nevertheless it seems likely that this grand military portrait was a collusion between sitter and artist, a promotional gambit for them both, and an exaggeration of George O'Shea's military credentials.

The portrait owes a stylistic and compositional debt to Reynolds who had died six years earlier and whose lectures Shee would have attended at the Royal Academy Schools. The composition and basic idea of a red-coated officer in plumed hat standing in front of his horse follows a tradition set by Reynolds's striking 1756 portrait of Captain Robert Orme and his horse (National Gallery, London), a composition Reynolds reused a number of times. It was a popular model for artists well into the nineteenth century.

However, in spite of the similarity to Reynolds's equestrian subjects and technique, Shee's more immediate inspiration, at least for the composition, may have come from Reynolds's rival Gainsborough. Young Shee may even have heard Reynolds's Fourteenth Discourse, a stirring memorial lecture on Gainsborough given to the students and members of the Royal Academy in December 1788.[6] Gainsborough's 1771 equestrian portrait of Shee's countryman Edward, second Viscount Ligonier (Huntington Library & Art Collections, San Marino, California), painted at the time of the sitter's succession to the Irish viscountcy, is very close to Shee's composition of the Irish major. Gainsborough's red-uniformed viscount leans on his horse with his right arm while his left clutches a sabre as in Shee's painting. An even closer model for our painting could be Gainsborough's later portrait of *George, Prince of Wales*, c.1782 (National Trust, Waddesdon Manor, Buckinghamshire). In that composition, although the standing figure and the horse are in a reverse pose to Shee's composition, most of the elements are otherwise the same (see p. 180). Even if Shee did not actually see the royal portrait he could have been aware of it from a famous and well-circulated engraving published in 1783 by John Raphael Smith. The reversed image in the engraving is remarkably similar to the Gallery's portrait by Shee. In the second half of the eighteenth century a strong tradition of full-scale uniformed male portraits standing with their horses provided a wealth of imagery for Shee to draw upon when painting this and later commissions.

Shee painted his showy Major O'Shea at the very end of the eighteenth century, and would produce other portraits in a similar manner for almost another half-century. At the end of a golden age of eighteenth-century British portraiture, the painting also ends the chronology of the Gallery's sizeable collection of interesting eighteenth-century British portraits by nearly all the major British portrait artists.

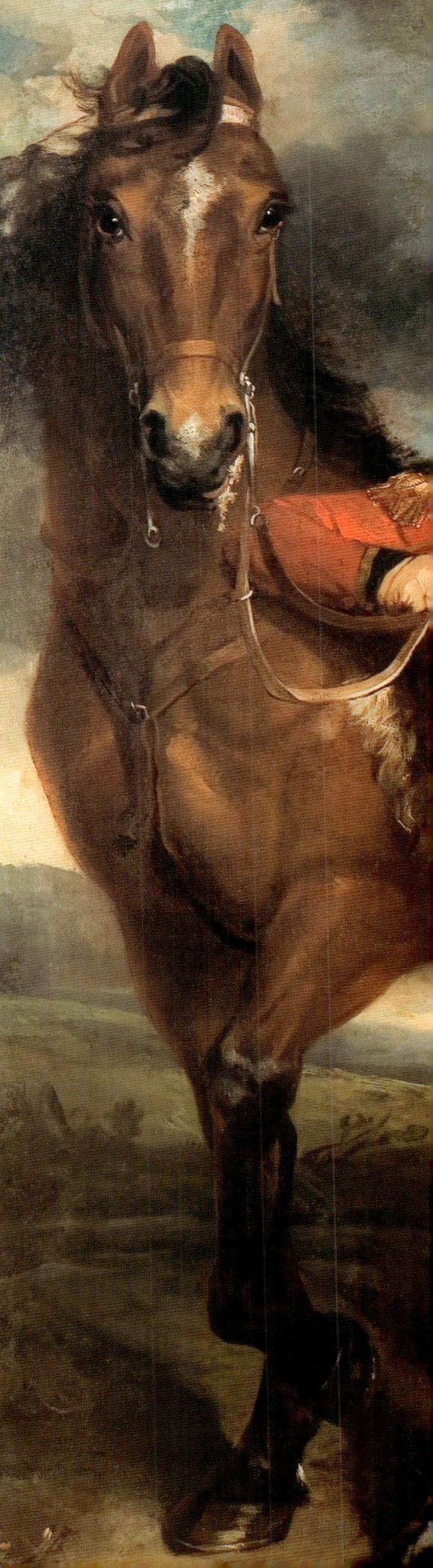

**Provenance:** Christie's, London, 19 July 1929, lot 79; Alexander Melrose, Adelaide, 1930.

**Exhibitions:** Royal Academy, 1798, no. 239. *Regency: British Art & Design 1800–1830*, AGSA, Adelaide, 1998, no. 121. *Island to Empire: 300 Years of British Art 1550–1850*, AGSA, Adelaide, 2005.

**Literature:** Martin Shee, *Life of Sir Martin Archer Shee*, London, 1860, vol. 1, p. 213. *NGSA Catalogue of Paintings, Pastels and Sculpture*, 1940, no. 756, p. 144. *NGSA Bulletin*, vol. 7, no. 1, 1945. *NGSA Catalogue of Oil and Water-colour Paintings and Pastels*, fifth edition, 1946, p. 179. *NGSA Catalogue of Oil and Water-colour Paintings and Pastels with Biographical Notes*, 1960, p. 226. Peter Tomory and Robert Gaston, *European Paintings before 1800 in Australian and New Zealand Public Collections*, Sydney, 1989, p. 45, no. 122. Ron Radford in Christopher Menz, *Regency*, Adelaide: AGSA, 1998, pp. 70, 71.

**Condition:** Fair/poor; much original paint loss; last conserved in 1993–94 by Artlab Australia, Adelaide.

**Frame:** Original.

# Michael Angelo Rooker 1746–1801

Michael Angelo Rooker was a topographical watercolour painter especially known for his ruined castles and abbeys but who also produced scenes of rural cottages, streets, city buildings and country seats. His crumbling ruins are devoid of romantic grandeur or sublimity and instead are bathed in clear sunlight to illuminate a mass of meticulous detail. The painstaking renderings of architecture are usually enlivened by human and domestic-animal activity.

Born Michael Rooker in London in 1746, he followed his artist (and actor) father Edward and became an engraver. Father and son both worked as engravers for Paul Sandby, who was also Michael Rooker's watercolour teacher. It was Sandby who gave the nickname "Michael Angelo" that Rooker adopted. He abandoned engraving in 1779 to work as a scene-painter at the Haymarket Theatre and to pursue his primary interest in landscape watercolours. He occasionally painted in oil.

He was a Foundation Associate of the Royal Academy when it was established in 1769 and thenceforth until his death regularly showed his topographical works at its exhibitions. Unlike most of his contemporaries Rooker never went abroad. In 1788 he began a series of summer walking tours making sketches in various parts of England and Wales. The drawings produced on those tours remained in his possession at the time of his death in London in 1801.

### A view of a ruined castle, c.1798
watercolour on paper, 26.4 x 36.4 cm
Elder Bequest Fund 1960

This is a fine and characteristic example of Rooker's work, one of his meticulous renderings of an overgrown castle in ruins. The crumbling material fabric of the ancient building is painted with virtuoso technique, the individual stones and the plants growing from them depicted visibly in bright daylight. We can admire the medieval pile but we are not meant to be transported by the drama of its romantic history as Peter De Wint later aimed to do in the Gallery's *Kenilworth Castle* (p. 247). The castle is not illuminated by striking evening light to feed our imagination as in the Gallery's later *Alnwick Castle* by J. M. W. Turner (p. 211). This image is Picturesque not Romantic, and the scene is presented prosaically with apparent topographical, architectural and archeological accuracy. It is domesticated by the use of foreground sheep and cattle, a shepherd, and smoke coming from what is possibly a kiln chimney; the smoke seems too vigorous for a mere cottage fire. Light fluffy clouds sail behind the towering pile against a pale blue sky, not the lurid sunset sky characteristically provided by Turner for his *Newport Castle*, c.1796 (Tate, London)[1], a subject similar to Rooker's and close in date. Furthermore, Rooker's castle pile is hardly more prominent in the composition than the foreground repoussoir trees that create space and add satisfying compositional balance.

However, unlike most of Rooker's work, this is not an accurate recording of a known castle, only an approximation of one. His accurate portrayals of ancient architecture were appreciated in his day but here the castle appears to be a compositional pastiche, though executed with the conviction of topographic plausibility.

This composition is partially derived from Rooker's on-the-spot watercolour sketch, *Castle at Newport on Usk, South Wales*, now in the collection of the National Gallery of Scotland, Edinburgh. The Gallery's watercolour, although larger, more highly finished and carefully composed than Edinburgh's, is probably not specific enough to be Rooker's Newport subject exhibited at the Royal Academy in 1797. The small size of the Edinburgh sketch, its lack of compositional devices or elaborate foreground staffage exclude it, too, as one of the pair of watercolours exhibited together that year as catalogue no. 417 under the titles of *Llandilo Caermarthenshire* and *Newport on Usk, Monmouthshire*. Those two watercolours would have been larger exhibition pieces, more composed and finished than Edinburgh's sketch.

The Gallery's watercolour takes from Edinburgh's Newport sketch only the basic idea of a ruined towered castle on a river, but retains the distant buildings across the river as well as the roof and chimney of the building in the right foreground of the composition. If we compare the Edinburgh sketch of the towers with the castle tower pile in the Gallery's watercolour, we see that the artist has taken only some of the structure's features and invented the rest, making the ruin more dynamically interesting and architecturally picturesque. He has placed a small hillock and valley between the castle and the viewer. He added mature trees to the right and surrounded the castle with luxuriant vegetation rather than the stark protuberance of the actual architectural site. Unlike today's surviving Newport Castle towers, which sit on the muddy banks of the River Usk, Rooker's castle is situated high above and further from the river. Furthermore, the closest tower here is much taller than the one adjacent, giving the building a more Gothic elongation than in actuality. Yet

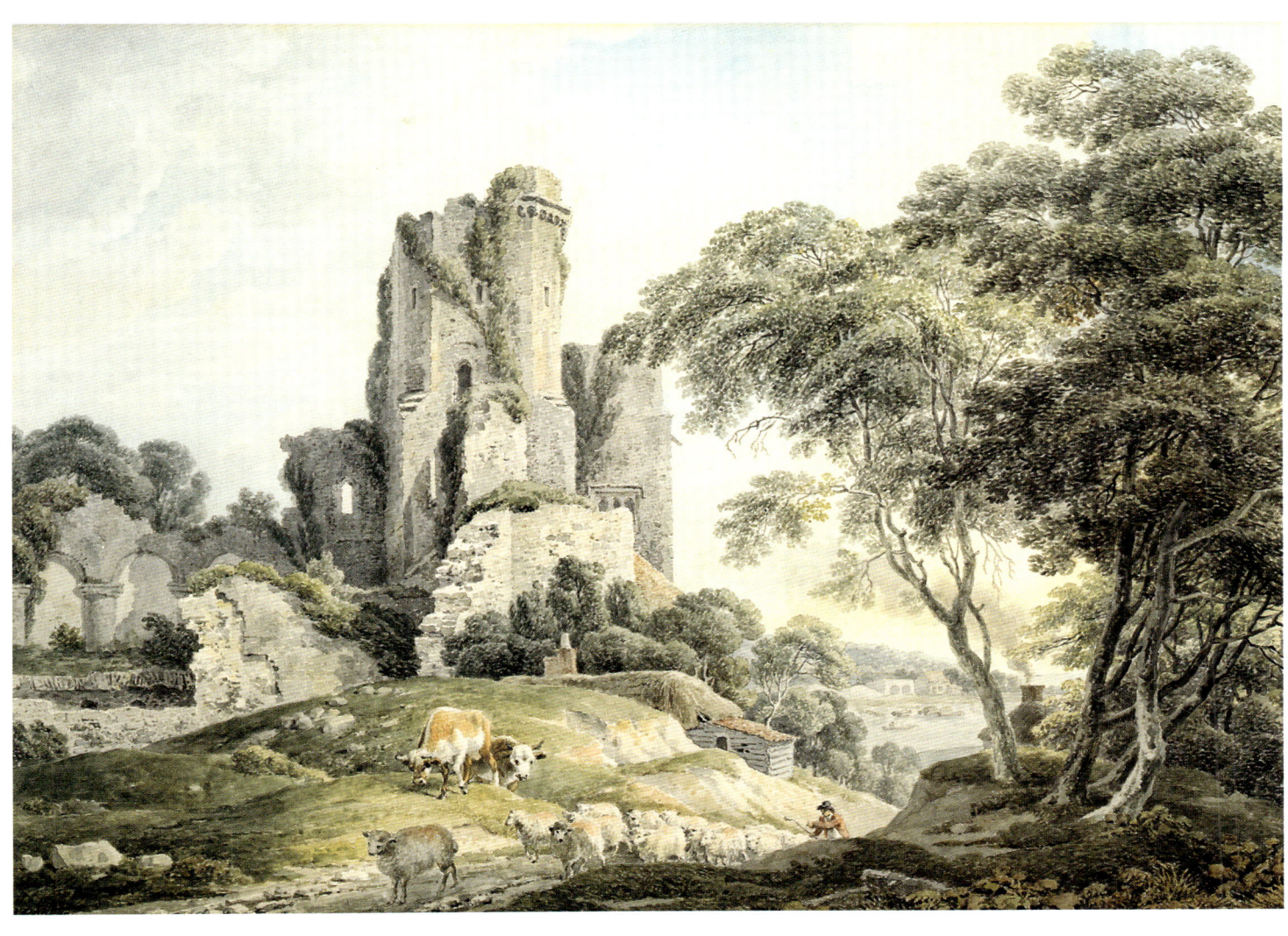

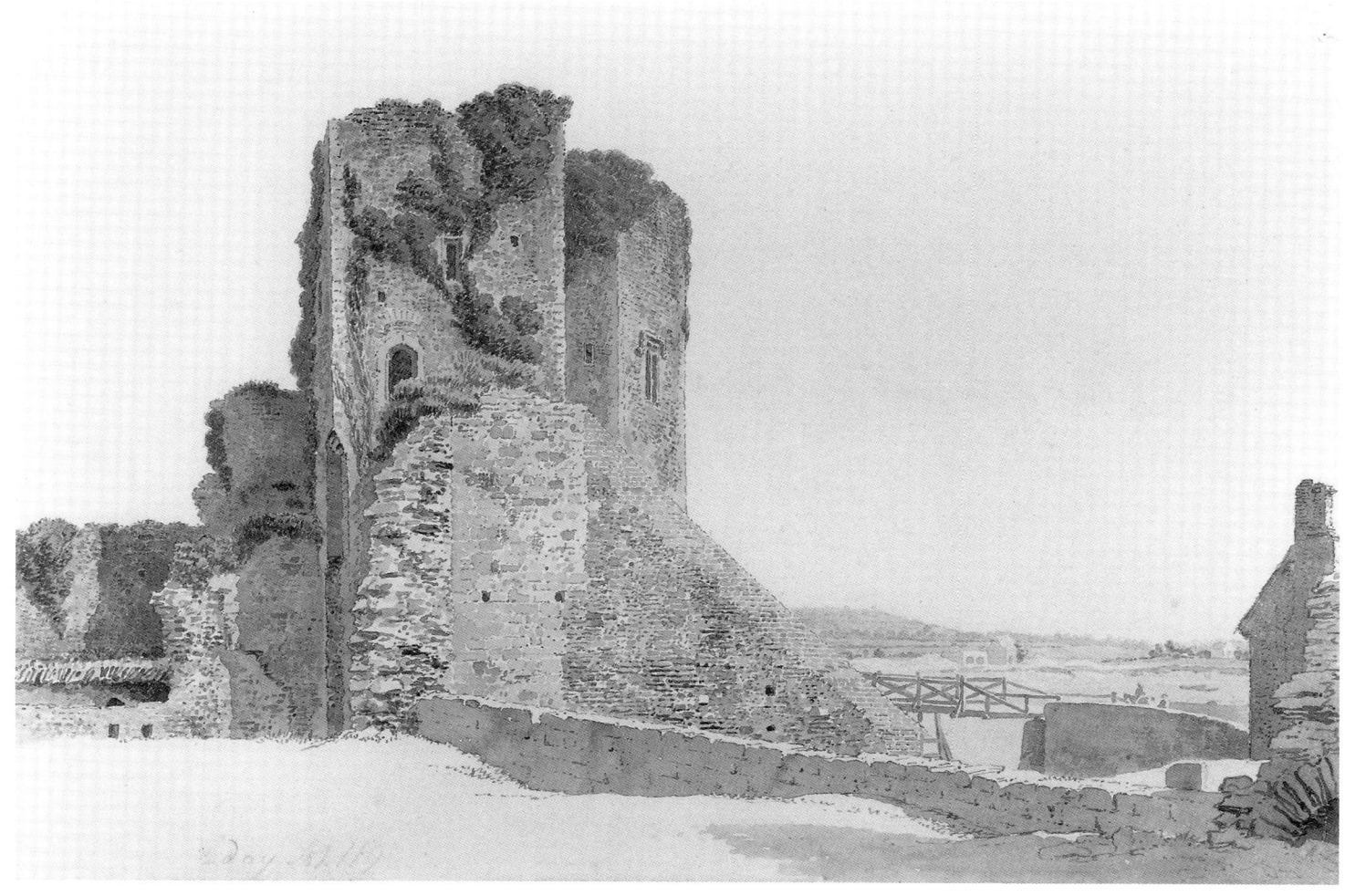

Michael Angelo Rooker, *Castle at Newport on Usk, South Wales*. National Gallery of Scotland, Edinburgh

the castle scene is otherwise not Gothicised but mild and domesticated and also modernised. A shepherd follows his flock of sheep towards us along the foreground road, observed from above by two curious cows. The scene is humanised further by a boatman on the distant river and what is possibly industrial smoke billowing from the chimney of the half-hidden kiln-like building on the right.

We can perhaps assume that Edinburgh's small sketch of Newport Castle was Rooker's starting-point both for the Gallery's painting and the presumed highly-finished watercolour painting of Newport exhibited at the Royal Academy in 1797. We can consequently conclude that the Gallery's was done as least as early as 1797 and possibly shortly afterwards. The Gallery's watercolour could therefore be one of the two with the non-geographically-specific titles of *A landscape* (catalogue nos 829 and 845) that Rooker exhibited at the Royal Academy in 1799. Among all his works hung at the Royal Academy from its inception these are two out of only six that do not mention specific places in the title.[2] Since Rooker died in February 1801 the Gallery's watercolour could be among his last paintings, executed in his most assured manner.

**Provenance:** J. Leger & Son, London, on the advice of H. D. Molesworth, 1960.

**Exhibitions:** *Regency: British Art & Design 1800–1830*, AGSA, Adelaide, 1998, no. 118.
*Island to Empire: 300 Years of British Art 1550–1850*, AGSA, Adelaide, 2005.

**Literature:** Ron Radford in Christopher Menz, *Regency*, Adelaide: AGSA, 1998, pp. 69–70 (illus.).

**Condition:** Good.

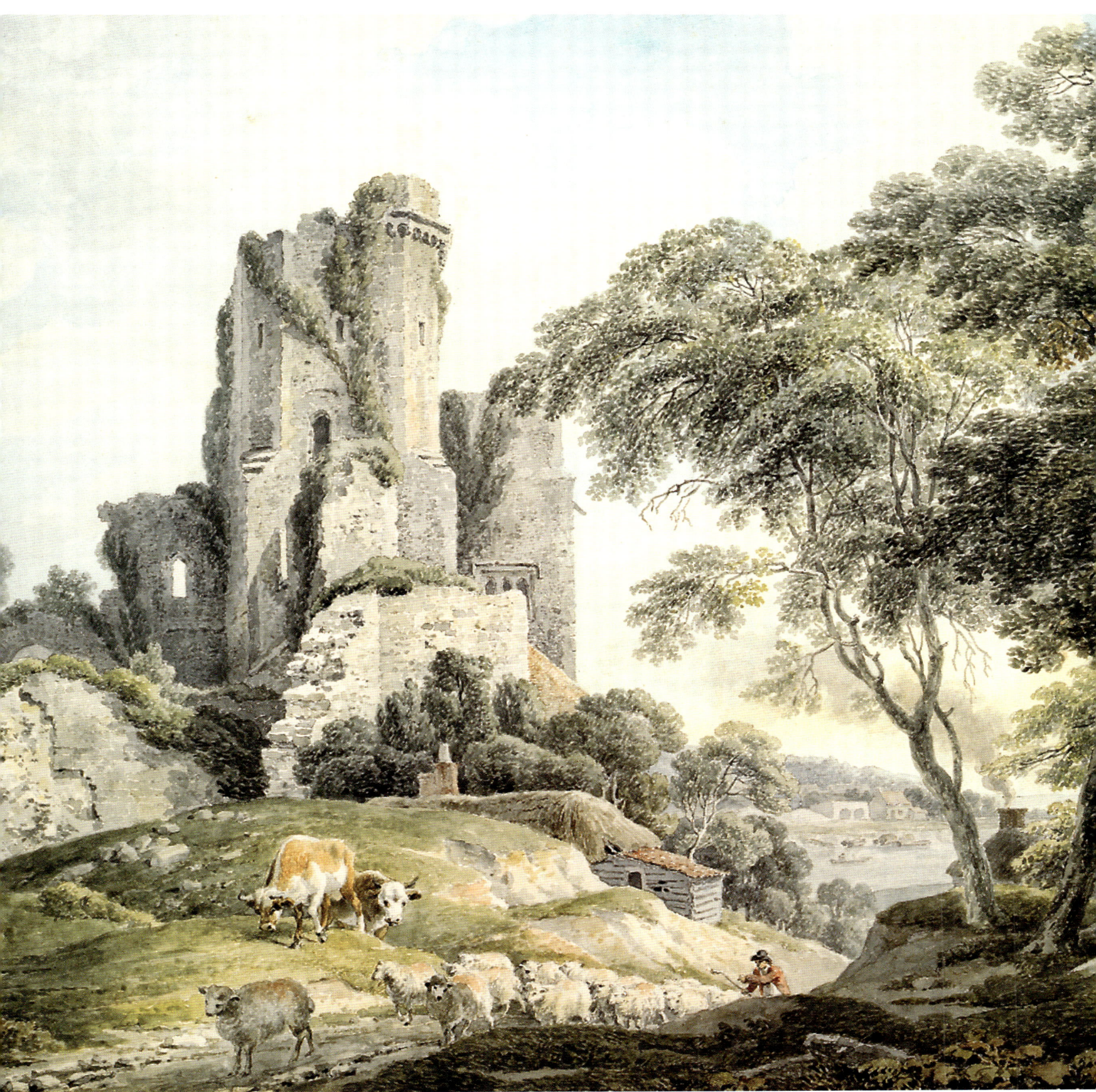

# Thomas Rowlandson 1756–1827

Thomas Rowlandson was the most talented and successfully prolific of the comic British draughtsmen of his time. He was an acute social commentator on the foibles of late-eighteenth- and early-nineteenth-century British life. No class, no profession, no human activity escaped his satire. He followed and greatly contributed to a distinctly British tradition of humorous and biting social commentary that has flourished in art since William Hogarth in the early eighteenth century, and has strong parallels in British literary wit. The immediate appeal of his humour has often disguised the fact that, at his best, he was one of the greatest British draughtsmen.

Born in London in 1756 and showing an early inclination to draw, Thomas Rowlandson was admitted in 1772 to the Royal Academy Schools where he later won a silver medal for drawing. In 1774 he visited Paris and the next year he exhibited for the first time at the Royal Academy. Paintings and drawings by the history painter John Hamilton Mortimer exerted the strongest influence on the development of his style and he eventually collected no less than fifty-two of that artist's works, many of them satirical. Hogarth was also a significant influence on Rowlandson's style and humour, particularly his satirical engravings. From the very beginning of his long and prolific career Rowlandson displayed a talent for extracting humour from any situation. He died in London in 1827.

### The Brilliants, c.1801
pen & ink, watercolour, pencil on paper, 30.0 x 44.5 cm
A. R. Ragless Bequest Fund 1960

Rowlandson's mid-career watercolour drawing *The Brilliants* depicts the London men's club of that name. Its membership largely comprised actors and journalists who usually met after the theatre in a room at the Swan Inn, Chandos Street, Covent Garden. There they drank and cavorted into the early hours. The club was formed at the end of the eighteenth century and was succeeded by a slightly more respectable and larger offshoot called The Eccentrics which survived well into the nineteenth century. It is likely that Rowlandson himself was a member of The Brilliants. He mixed with actors and Jack Bannister, one of the greatest actors of the time, was an intimate life-long friend of Rowlandson's. The high-spirited companions were known to enjoy over-drinking together into early morning.

In this highly animated drawing Rowlandson has brutally satirised the club, reducing its activities solely to competitive drunkenness. Around the table the rollicking members are vigorously toasting and imbibing. They are all in different but advanced stages of intoxication. Some are already vomiting while bottles are still being opened and glasses charged. A young man on the left has fallen backwards on his chair to the floor. Another standing on the left appears to be simultaneously vomiting and urinating into a jug on a chair. He is balanced on the right of the composition by a man standing among empty bottles while opening another held between his legs. A standing, shouting figure at the rear centre has unwittingly sent hats flying from above the fireplace with his waving arms. Such excessive drunkenness was the norm in Rowlandson's day and has remained almost acceptable behaviour among young bachelors as a sign of rebellious blood and male camaraderie.

Another version[1] of this composition, in a private collection, predates the Gallery's. That 1798 version has the same basic composition of inebriated men slouching in dining chairs around a table in a well-furnished room. The detail, positioning and caricaturing of the figures vary as Rowlandson's spontaneous style could never repeat a picture exactly. Among the major differences in the earlier version are an empty fallen chair in the left foreground and many more empty bottles in the right foreground. The earlier version also omits the saucy touch of the two women lurking behind the screen, one holding and probably delivering a sealed invitation or message. The room in the first version also has an elaborately decorated plaster ceiling and a chandelier. The plain ceiling, simpler neoclassical cornice, fire surround and striped curtains in the Gallery's watercolour might suggest a slightly later, Regency-style interior. On the right wall hangs what looks like a Dutch or British seascape, a fashionable item to collect in late-eighteenth- or early-nineteenth-century Britain.

An engraving was made from the 1798 version of *The Brilliants* and published on 15 January 1801 by Rudolph Ackermann. Our version was probably an opportunistic repetition produced after the engraving was published. The main difference in the engraved version is the inclusion on the wall, left of the mirror, of a sheet of paper on which the rules of the Brilliants Club are written:

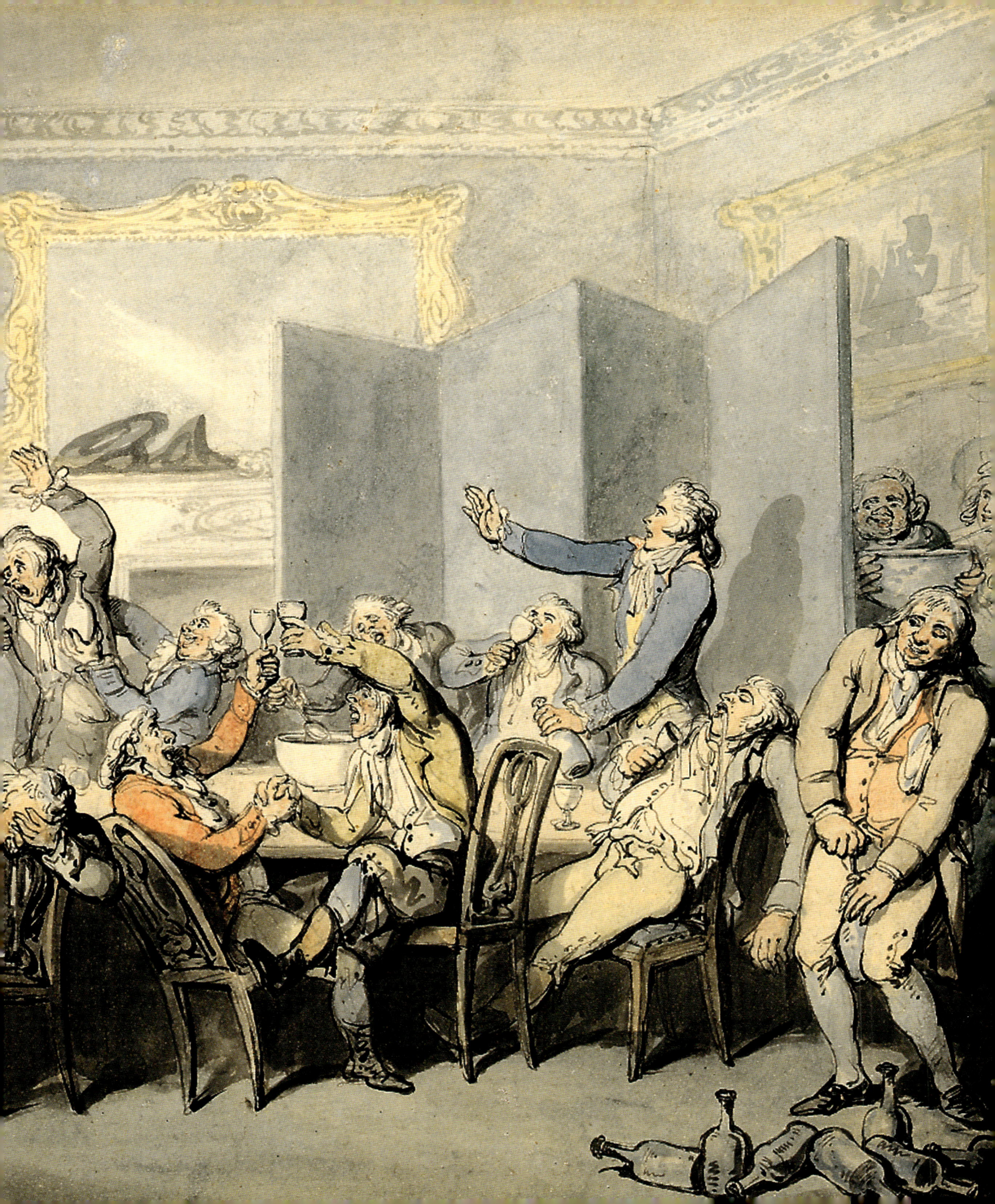

# Thomas Rowlandson

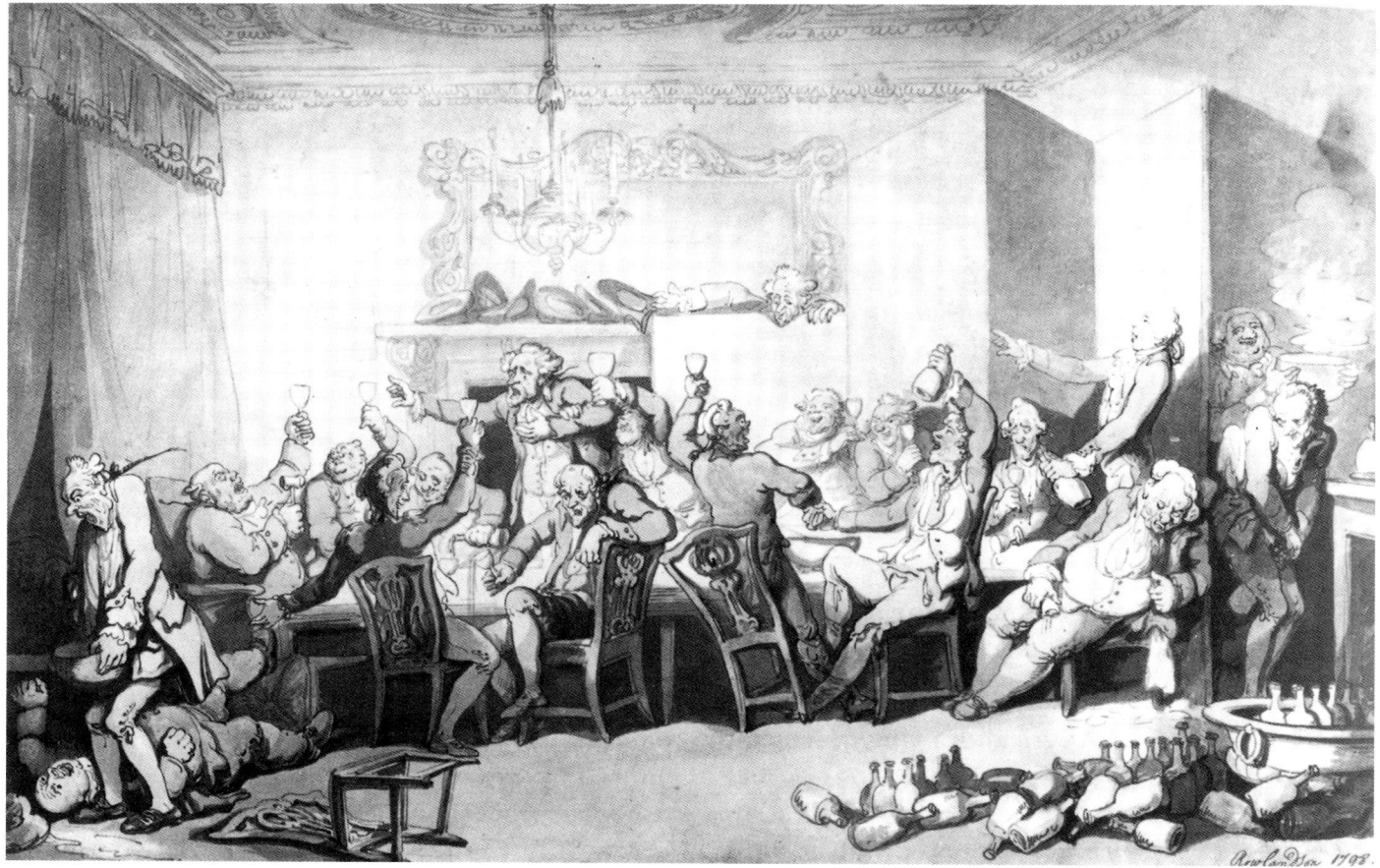

R. Ackermann, after Rowlandson, *The Brilliants*, 1801, (published by R. Ackermann)

1st  That each member shall fill a half-pint bumper to the first toast.
2nd  That after twenty-four bumper toasts are gone round every member may fill as he pleases.
3rd  That any member refusing to comply with the above regulations to be fined; compelled to swallow a bumper of salt and water.

It is possible that the white bowl seen here on the table held the warm salty water. Rowlandson had no qualms in presenting, indeed revelling in, the obscene spectacle, made all the more outrageously provocative by appearing as a parody of Leonardo's famous *The Last Supper*, a composition then well known from engravings.

A more immediate precedent to the composition of both versions of *The Brilliants* is Rowlandson's own *The Hunt Supper*, c.1790 (Victoria & Albert Museum) which shows an even more boisterous drunken group around a table in a room similar to those which appear earlier in the century in Hogarth's work. Hogarth's painting *A Midnight Modern Conversation*, 1730–31 (Yale Center for British Art) or its 1732–33 engraving must be a source for both Rowlandson's compositions of riotous debauchery at men's clubs.

The Gallery owns two other drawings and many prints by Rowlandson.

**Inscription:** Signed l.r. pen & ink: "T. Rowlandson".
**Provenance:** Charles A. Cohen Esq.; purchased 1960 from Leger Galleries, London, on the advice of H. D. Molesworth, 1960.
**Exhibitions:** *Master Prints and Drawings AGSA*, Adelaide, 1978, no. 16. *Regency: British Art & Design 1800–1830*, AGSA, Adelaide, 1998, no. 119. *Island to Empire: 300 Years of British Art 1550–1850*, AGSA, Adelaide, 2005.
**Literature:** Joseph Grego, *Rowlandson the Caricaturist*, London, 1880, vol. 2, pp. 24–26. *NGSA Bulletin*, vol. 21, no. 3, 1960. Alison Carroll, *Master Prints and Drawings AGSA*, Adelaide: AGSA, 1978, p. 12 (illus.). John Hayes, *The Art of Thomas Rowlandson*, Alexandria, Virginia: Art Services International for Baltimore Museum of Art, Maryland, 1990, no. 46. Ron Radford in Christopher Menz, *Regency*, Adelaide: AGSA, 1998, pp. 32, 70.
**Condition:** Good.

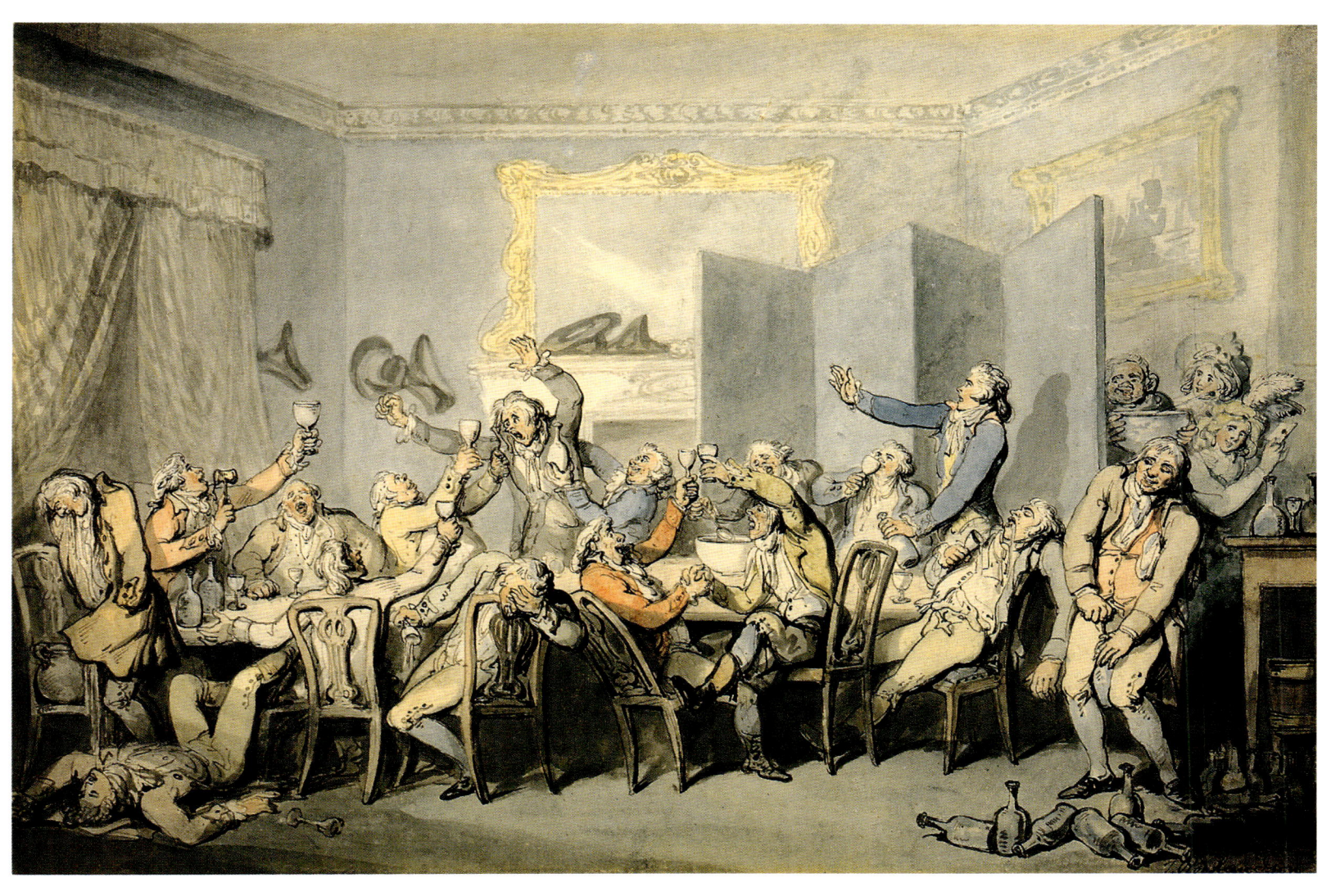

# William Blake 1757–1827

A passionate, visionary philosopher and poet as well as a watercolour artist and engraver, William Blake was the strangest artistic personality ever to flourish in Britain. In the 1790s his work had shifted fully to Romanticism but although he was highly antagonistic to the conventions represented by Joshua Reynolds, President of the Royal Academy, he shared Reynolds's deep admiration for classical antiquity and the art of Michelangelo. However, Medieval Gothic art was another strong and most unusual influence.

Born in 1757, Blake was the son of a London hosier who placed him, aged ten, in the best preparatory school for young artists and then apprenticed him at fourteen to James Basire (1730–1802), engraver to the Society of Antiquaries. An engraver's focus on line characterises Blake's work throughout his career. Basire started him drawing Gothic tombs in Westminster Abbey. After the 1772–79 apprenticeship Blake joined the Royal Academy Schools in 1779–80, and exhibited regularly at the Royal Academy from 1780 to 1808. He was on friendly terms with Henry Fuseli and Thomas Stothard, as well as John Flaxman, who introduced him into a dilettante literary circle which in 1783 printed his *Poetical Sketches* of 1769–78. From 1784 to 1787 Blake joined in partnership with James Parker as an engraver and printseller. By 1788 he had developed a new technique of "illuminated printing" to illustrate his own writings.

In 1818 Blake met the young artist John Linnell who commissioned illustrations for *The Book of Job* (1821–26) and Dante's *Divine Comedy* (1824–27), but the latter were unfinished at Blake's death. Blake was admired in his last years by a group of young artists who called themselves 'The Ancients'; they included Linnell, Samuel Palmer, George Richmond, Edward Calvert and Frederick Tatham, his executor and first biographer.

Ignored in his lifetime save by a few artists and a handful of patrons, Blake came to be regarded as the greatest of English poet-painters. His art was the expression of a personal form of prophetic Christianity, part visionary, part philosophical. It reflects current artistic and literary fashions, but more important are the elements derived from wide reading and an exceptional visual memory. His very precise rendition of things imagined made for a most distinctive style and extremely original inventions.

## St Paul before Felix and Drusilla, c.1803
watercolour on paper, 37.5 x 35.5 cm
Gift of William Bowmore AO OBE through the Art Gallery of South Australia Foundation 1995

A number of episodes in the *Acts of the Apostles* were intended to affirm the authority of the earliest Christian saints. The text for this biblical illustration describes St Paul taken before Felix, governor of Caesarea, the principal seaport city of Roman Palestine. Paul confronts and evangelises the proconsul and his wife:

> And after certain days, when Felix came with his wife Drusilla, which was a Jewess, he sent for Paul, and heard him concerning the faith in Christ. And as he reasoned of righteousness, temperance, and judgment to come, Felix trembled, and answered, Go thy way for this time; when I have a convenient season I will call for thee. (Acts 24: 24–25)

In a starkly neoclassical-cum-neogothic style, Blake forcefully conveys the New Testament story.

St Paul, in chains, is accompanied by a gaoler with keys and Roman soldiers, the most prominent of whom is encased in a kind of medieval chain-mail armour; they mostly take care not to attend to the apostle's words or notice their governor's agitation. Paul is even taller than his muscular guards, an elongated columnar figure in a golden robe. His uplifted arm, with a vertical index finger reaching the edge of the picture, points to the Lord like an antenna gathering psychic energy for transmission across empty but thunderous space to the startled governor and his consort. Paul exudes immense power.

Felix and Drusilla are seated on a high plinth and their robes fuse over their laps as if to suggest a single, solid base for a statuary group, disturbed only by the human touch of a footstool for the smaller wife. The solidity comes alive as four raised hands tremble together above the falling drapery and two faces lean forward in a mixture of anxiety and understanding. Blake may have been familiar with a passage in Josephus, the first-century Jewish historian, who made it clear that Felix obtained the hand of Drusilla, a daughter of Agrippina I, by dishonourable means.

The confrontation, with its warning of a Last Judgement, is conveyed simply and unambiguously, as if by actors in a passion play on a narrow stage with minimal sets and props. The watercolour paper has darkened but it was always largely a tonal composition and like much of Blake's work could have transformed easily into a black-and-white print.

*St Paul before Felix and Drusilla* is one of the many religious works commissioned by Blake's most important patron Thomas Butts (1757–1845). They probably first met as early as 1793 but most of the commissions flowed from 1799 to 1816. Butts was a clerk in the Muster-master's office, dealing with enlistment of soldiers, but was well off. Nearly all Blake's surviving biblical illustrations – 137 Old Testament subjects and thirty-eight New Testament in various media – come from the Butts collection. Butts also commissioned

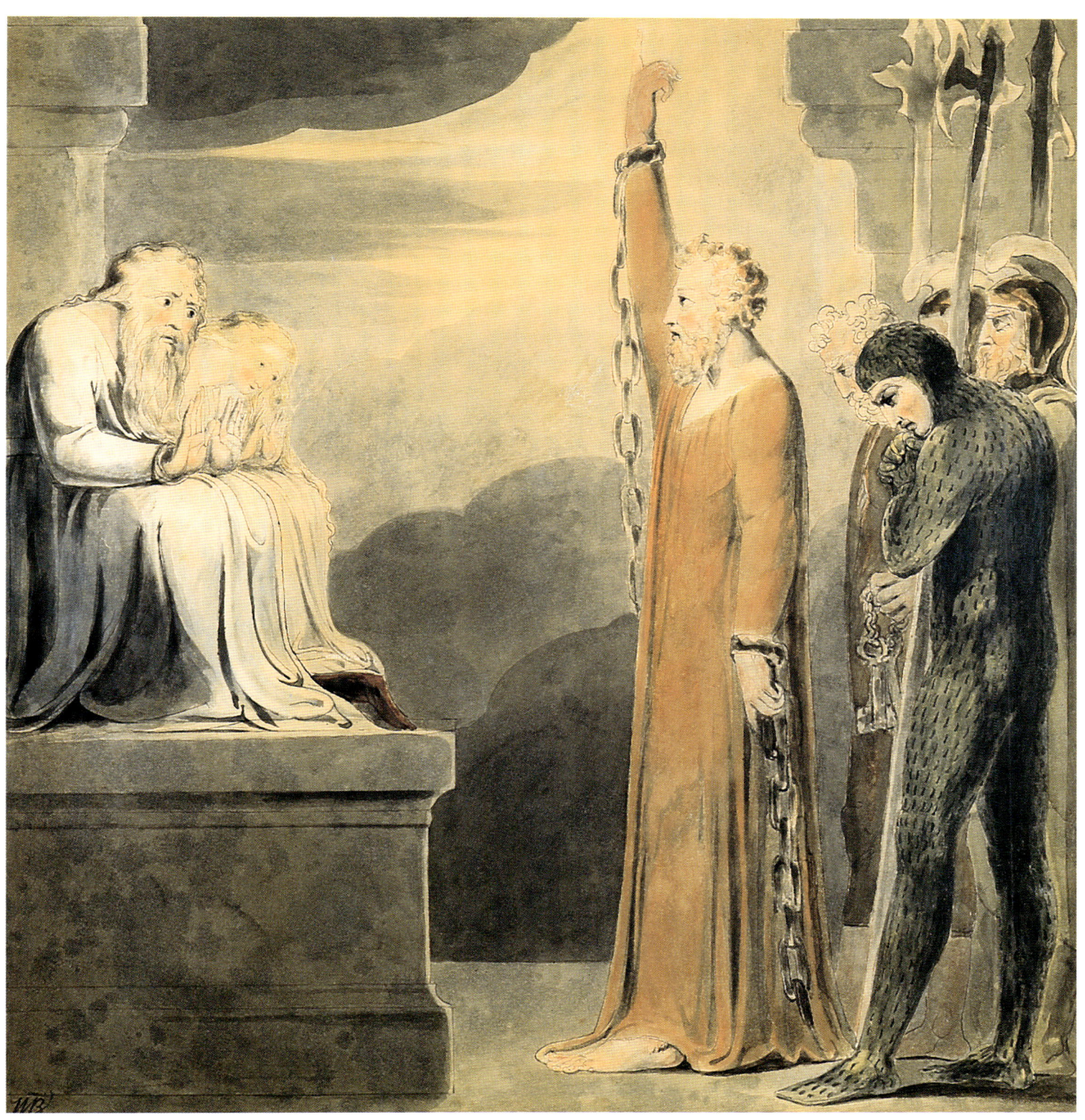

a portrait miniature of himself, his wife and son (British Museum, London).[1] In 1799 and 1800 Butts's commissions were usually executed in tempera, but Blake then began to make biblical watercolours and eventually produced over eighty for his patron.[2]

All of these watercolours, although slightly different in size, are part of a unified series, most of which he painted from 1800 to 1806. The five that illustrate St Paul were almost certainly executed between 1801 and 1803. In a letter of July 1803 to Butts from Blake, who was still at Felpham, listing seven drawings "on the Stocks" for Butts, no. 6 was "St Paul Preaching" which is probably our watercolour.[3]

A number of works in the series had pencil inscriptions on the original mounts, in copperplate handwriting, with titles above the illustration and a text below. The inscription on the Gallery's mount is one of the very few to survive, though cropped at the bottom. These pencil inscriptions were believed to be by Blake's wife, but Butts or his family are other possibilities. They were certainly there before 1852 which is when the series began to be dispersed by Butts's son.[4]

Blake stood in the long tradition of English nonconformist Protestantism, and was attracted to strong biblical subjects, like this, in which St Paul provides an example of evangelical zeal, courageous personal faith, and high moral values in the face of religious persecution. In the early nineteenth century, nonconformists like Blake could still identify with these themes in the face of an established Church of England armed with the weapons of power and privilege.

**Inscription:** Signed l.l., pen and ink: "WB". Inscribed centrally on upper mount, pencil, in copperplate handwriting: "Felix and Drusilla." Inscribed similarly on mount l.l.: "Acts ch: 24$^{th}$: v. 25$^{th}$:" / beginning l.r. "And as he reasoned of righteousness, temperance, and Judgement to come, / Felix trembled, & said, Go thy way for this time, when I have a / …" [inscription on mount is cut off here].

**Provenance:** Thomas Butts; Thomas Butts junior, sold at Foster's, 29 June 1853, lot 130; J. C. Strange; Harvey, offered, catalogue c.1865; Robson and Co., sold 1904 to W. Graham Robertson; sold at Christie's, London, 22 July 1949, lot 44, purchased Waller Wheeler; bt by C. A. Stonehill; bt by Mrs Hannah D. Rabinowitz; bt c.1971 by C. A. Stonehill; Lucien Goldsmidt, New York; Scott C. Elliot, New York; bt 1974 by Roland, Browse & Delbanco; bt 1975 by William Bowmore, Newcastle, New South Wales.

**Exhibitions:** *Paintings, Drawings and Sculpture Collected by Yale Alumni*, Yale University Art Gallery, New Haven, Connecticut, May 1960, no. 174. *A Celebration: Recent acquisitions of heritage and contemporary art*, AGSA, Adelaide, 1996. *Regency: British Art & Design 1800-1830*, AGSA, Adelaide, 1998, no. 94. *The Fine Art of Giving, 90 Masterpieces from the William Bowmore Collection*, AGSA, Adelaide, 1999, no. 13. *Island to Empire: 300 Years of British Art 1550-1850*, AGSA, 2005.

**Literature:** William Michael Rossetti, *Annotated Catalogue of Blake's Pictures and Drawings*, vol. 2, 1863. Kerrison Preston, *The Blake Collection of W. Graham Robertson, Described by the Collector*, 1952, pp. 160-61, no. 62. Geoffrey Keynes, *William Blake's Illustrations to the Bible*, 1957, p. 46, no. 156 (illus.). Kathleen Raine, *William Blake*, London, 1970, p. 105. Geoffrey Keynes, *Blake Studies*, 1971, p. 156. Martin Butlin, *The Paintings and Drawings of William Blake*, New Haven, 1981, p. 365, pl. 607. *Blake: An Illustrated Quarterly*, vol. 30, no. 4, spring 1997, Rochester, New York: Department of English, University of Rochester, p. 112 (illus.). Ron Radford in Christopher Menz, *Regency*, Adelaide: AGSA, 1998, pp. 56, 57 (illus.). Ron Radford et al., *Treasures*, Adelaide: AGSA, 1998, p. 55 (illus.). Angus Trumble in Radford, *The Fine Art of Giving*, Adelaide: AGSA, 1999, pp. 56, 73 (illus.).

**Condition:** Good/fair; the paper has darkened.

**Frame:** Not original, but retains original inscribed inlay mount.

# Robert Hills 1769–1844

Robert Hills's carefully detailed watercolours of farm animals in rural scenery introduced the traditional stippled technique of English portrait miniatures into landscape painting. With this painstaking method he recorded British light, landscape and livestock. His livestock studies, which concentrated on sheep and deer, are part of the broad tradition of animal painting in Britain and more particularly they respond to a new interest in specific livestock breeds at the beginning of the nineteenth century. Hills was also one of the early promoters of the fashion for watercolours and was involved with the formation of watercolour societies.

Born in Islington, London, in 1769, Hills received lessons from John Alexander Gresse (1741–1794). He began his artistic career as a painter on glass which may help to explain his adoption of the stippled technique of miniature painting, often executed on porcelain or ivory and sometimes on glass. Hills entered the Royal Academy Schools in 1788, first exhibited at the Academy in 1791 and continued to exhibit there until 1824. Between 1798 and 1815 he issued a series of etchings of different types of farm animals which gained him a considerable reputation in this field. With James Ward (1809–1859), John Claude Nattes (c.1765–1822), William H. Pyne (1769–1843) and Samuel Shelley (1756–1808) he was one of the five central members of the Sketching Club which began in 1800. From this club the influential Society of Painters in Water-Colours, of which Hills became the first secretary, was formed in 1804 to promote and exhibit British watercolour paintings, and he continued to exhibit there – some six hundred paintings – between 1805 and 1844.

Robert Hills and James Ward accompanied one another on animal-painting trips around Britain at the beginning of the nineteenth century. Hills was also often asked to contribute animals in the watercolour landscapes of other artists, namely George Barret junior (1767–1842) and G. F. Robson (1788–1833). The farm animals in the Gallery's watercolour by Robson, *View of the City of Wells*, c.1810s, could have been painted by Hills.

In 1815 he visited the Low Countries, including the site of the Battle of Waterloo. In 1831 he went to Jersey and the other Channel Islands and returned there with Robson two years later.

On his field trips Hills executed detailed sketches on the spot, sometimes in pencil, often in watercolour. Many of these sketches survive and are usually accompanied by notes and annotations in a form of shorthand, a method James Ward also used. Back in his studio, Hills would combine these sketches and notes of details of nature and animals into highly finished compositions using his stippled technique. Although some of these works appear over-laboured, others are fresh and sparkling with natural sunlight, which he captured more accurately than most of his fellow watercolourists.

## Soay sheep in a landscape, c.1805
watercolour on paper, 32.4 x 43.8 cm
Mortlock Bequest Fund 1957

This fairly large watercolour landscape with horned sheep of the rare and ancient Soay breed[1] is a characteristically fine example of Hills's art. The small flock of nine sheep are resting in a patch of gentle light and late afternoon warmth. They are gathered in a little dip on a hill slope overhung by what look like oak or beech trees, of which the artist often made on-the-spot studies. The well-fed Soay sheep take on a sculptured roundness. Hills's careful stippling reproduces the different textures of nature: the fleecy sheep, the grassy slopes, the flaky tree trunks, the gravelly foreground and the leafy branches silhouetted against a tremulous sky. The stippling, which is difficult to capture in the reduced scale of reproductions, gives the work an effect of shimmering richness.

The painting was probably a commission to record this rare breed of sheep. Formerly confined to the remote island of Soay in the St Kilda group beyond the Outer Hebrides – the westernmost outlier of Scotland – they are thought to be the oldest and most primitive breed of sheep herded into Europe from Asia in the early Neolithic period. They are hardy and swift and have apparently remained unchanged for over six millennia. Both the ewes and rams have distinctive curved horns and are small. Their faces are dark and the wool is coarse but short, and in colour ranges from fawn to brown. The wool is shed naturally each year and is collected and used for hand-spinning and knitting yarns. The setting for these lighter-coloured and neater than usual Soay sheep is obviously not the rocky islands of St Kilda but a gentle rolling mainland. The flock would have been a novelty possession of a progressive landowner, and worthy of a commissioned picture. The countryside could be south of London in west Kent or Surrey, where Hills found many of his landscapes.

Like many of his watercolours it is undated, and it is very difficult to date Hills's work. On stylistic grounds and to some extent on the time when he was known to record many diverse breeds of sheep, it may be dated between 1800 and 1810, possibly about 1805. He made a series of fine etchings of sheep, issued with a frontispiece in 1809 although the

# Robert Hills

individual etchings range from 1798 to 1808. Hills's stippled style is often broader at the very beginning of the nineteenth century but by about 1820 the stipples are much more refined, becoming almost invisible. The Gallery's picture seems to be about halfway along the stylistic evolution.

This work from the beginning of the nineteenth century pre-dates by at least forty years the detailed realism of the Pre-Raphaelites and early Victorian super-realists. Hills's animal paintings are serious, however, and avoid the mid-nineteenth-century tendency of animal watercolourists to sentimentalise their creatures.

Robert Hills's farm animal watercolours would have appealed to landholders and farmers at a time when there was a great interest in improved husbandry, scientific breeding, and accurate knowledge of British livestock. His friend James Ward also took advantage of the market for such subjects. Hills was able to make his animals especially appealing by placing them in beautiful and typically English landscapes. For this reason his work also attracted city buyers.

The subject of this watercolour would have held favour with the staff and Board of the Art Gallery of South Australia when it was purchased in the 1950s. Australia's economy then depended heavily on sheep, as wool was by far its largest export, and still remains a major Australian export today. In the 1950s a much-repeated phrase was coined by the then Prime Minister, Sir Robert Menzies: "Australia rides on the sheep's back".

**Provenance:** Purchased 1957 for the Art Gallery of South Australia from Appleby Bros, London, on the advice of H. D. Molesworth, 1957.

**Exhibitions:** *Regency: British Art & Design 1800–1830*, AGSA, Adelaide, 1998, no. 110.
*Island to Empire: 300 Years of British Art 1550–1850*, AGSA, Adelaide, 2005.

**Literature:** Ron Radford in Christopher Menz, *Regency*, Adelaide: AGSA, 1998, pp. 65, 66 (illus.).

**Condition:** Excellent.

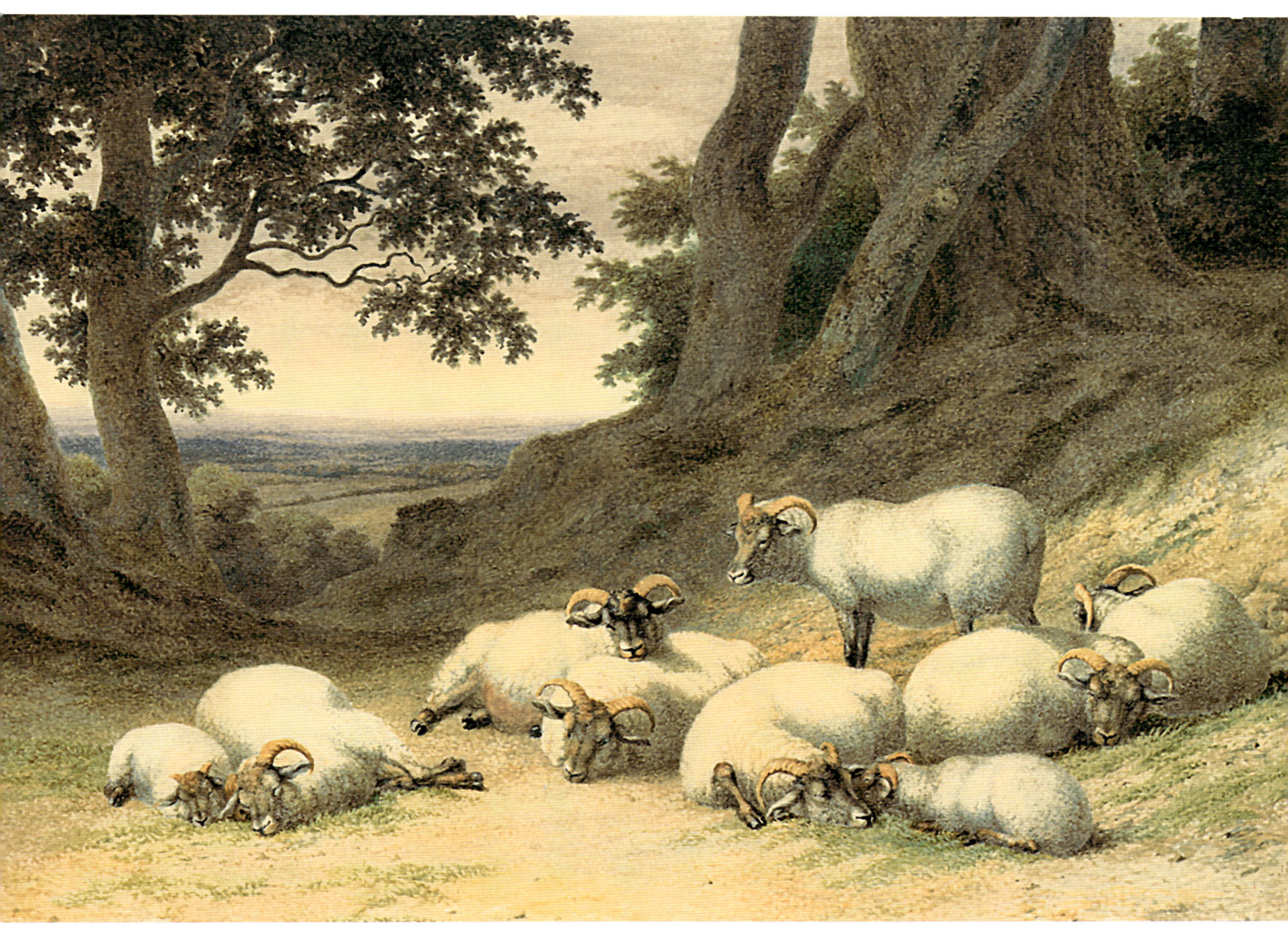

# Thomas Lawrence 1769–1830

The golden age of British grand-manner portrait painting included the great artists Ramsay, Reynolds, Gainsborough and Romney and culminated at the very end of the eighteenth century with a painter of great dash and of equal talent, Thomas Lawrence. He continued into the first third of the nineteenth century the swagger portrait tradition that had emanated from Van Dyck in the first third of the seventeenth century. Lawrence's portraits range from the regal and the imperial to the informal and the intimate. They often flatter, are usually very stylish in both subject and virtuoso technique, and are invariably Romantic in mood. Only twenty-three when he succeeded Reynolds in 1792 as Painter in Ordinary to King George III, Lawrence became the first British-born painter to enjoy an international reputation, partly because he was later commissioned to paint all the leaders of the allied victory over Napoleon. His fluid style remained an aspiration for British – and Australian colonial – portraiture until the mid nineteenth century.

Thomas Lawrence was born in Bristol in 1769, grew up in a coaching inn at Devizes on the road to fashionable Bath and became a child prodigy. His talents were exploited by his father who took him first to Bath, where he executed portraits mainly in pastel, and then at the age of eighteen to London. During his first year there, in 1787, he studied briefly at the Royal Academy Schools. Queen Charlotte granted sittings when he was twenty. The striking royal portrait and a very impressive full-length of the actress Miss Farren appeared at the Royal Academy in 1790, created a sensation, and launched him into fame. His style changed little thereafter. In 1794, just before his twenty-fifth birthday, he became the youngest full member of the Royal Academy.

After the first defeat of Napoleon in 1814, it was officially proposed that Lawrence travel to the Congress of Vienna to complete a set of portraits of the successful military leaders and heads of state. The Prince Regent (later George IV) sat for Lawrence and the following year knighted him in preparation for the Continental portrait campaign. Sir Thomas eventually set out in 1818, first for the conference at Aix-la-Chapelle, then to Vienna and later to Rome where he spent most of 1819, staying in Paris on his return journey. Some, including Prince Metternich and the Duke of Wellington, had already been painted in London but now he received sittings from all the architects of the new order, including the emperors of Austria and Russia, the king of Prussia and Pope Pius VII. To hang the series George IV created the Waterloo Chamber at Windsor Castle, one of the great nineteenth-century interiors, destroyed by the castle fire in 1992, but recreated shortly after; the paintings were unharmed.

When the second President of the Royal Academy, Benjamin West, died in 1820 Sir Thomas Lawrence was his natural successor as president. Lawrence was also a compulsive art collector, particularly of Old Master drawings. He died in 1830.

## Caroline Matilda Sotheron, c.1808

oil on canvas, 126.7 x 101.1 cm

Gift of William Bowmore AO OBE through the Art Gallery of South Australia Foundation 1998

According to family tradition over one hundred years, the subject of this portrait was Lucy Sarah Sotheron,[1] born in 1810 or 1811 and the only child of Admiral Frank Sotheron (1765–1839) of Kirklinton, Nottinghamshire, and Darrington Hall, Yorkshire, and his first wife, Caroline Matilda Barker (1787–1812). Lucy married in 1830 and the portrait was therefore thought to be a very late work by Lawrence, possibly painted just before his death in the same year as the supposed sitter's marriage.

However, recent research has revealed that this is Lucy's mother. A family miniature by John Wright (1745–1820) is based directly on this portrait by Lawrence, and an inscription on a now lost folding case for the miniature identified the sitter as Caroline Sotheron.[2] Caroline died aged twenty-five on 29 May 1812, only three years or so after her 1808 marriage to Frank Sotheron, and left behind the one-year-old Lucy. The miniature that John Wright based on Lawrence's portrait was commissioned immediately following Caroline's death. Stylistically, moreover, the painting is of a far earlier date than the late 1820s and is close to Lawrence's c.1806 portrait of *Miss Clements* in a very similar pose, costume and background.[3]

Lawrence also painted a standing portrait of Caroline's husband Frank Sotheron[4] in full naval uniform and clasping a sword. (In 1819 he eventually rose to become a Vice-Admiral.) The portrait of Frank Sotheron is the exact same size and of a similar period to this portrait of Caroline Matilda Sotheron. Therefore it can be concluded that they were probably commissioned in 1808 as a marriage pair, when she was twenty-one.

Mrs Sotheron sits outdoors dressed in white muslin, high-waisted, loose, and consciously neoclassical in its fashionable allusion to body-revealing marble drapery. A fringed salmon-pink shawl is not only a precaution against outdoor chill, it also protects the white dress from being soiled by the stone seat at the base of a classical column. She holds an outdoor straw bonnet dangling from a ribbon in an inconspicuous corner of the composition. The glimpse of an extensive

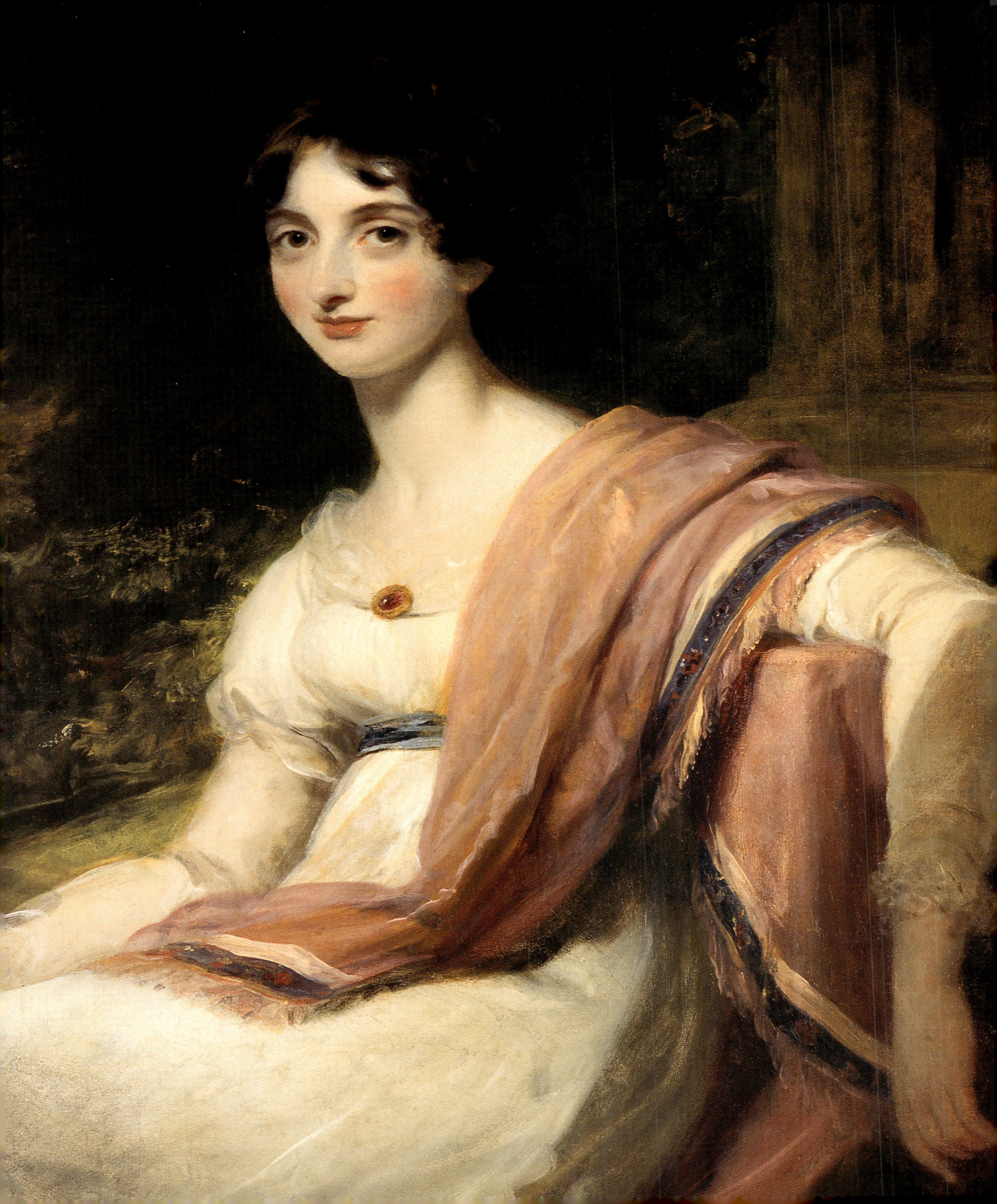

romantic landscape beyond generalised foliage may hint at her husband's landholdings. The substantial column, a frequent device in grand portraits from Van Dyck onwards, reinforces the lady's status as a person of substance. Economic implications of property and marriage often impinged on portrait commissions of young women – as they do at the same moment in the novels of Jane Austen.

Lawrence was known to flatter his younger sitters. In this portrait he has elongated the neck and limbs in the interest of languid Mannerist elegance for an image of leisure and ease. Characteristic of Lawrence, and some other Regency portrait painters, is the way he has also enlarged the eyes and made the mouth smaller, thus sweetening her appearance. The contrast between high finish at the centre (the face, the jewel at her breast, the fringe on the shawl) with the sketchy quality at the edges of the composition (the landscape, the thinly painted arms, hands and bonnet) are a peculiarity of many of Lawrence's portraits at the time.

The composition of a woman in white relief against a dark background displays a Neoclassical simplicity more typical of contemporary French portraits than British, and it alludes to seated female portraits in marble from classical antiquity. Lawrence may have been aware here of his French contemporaries as well as classical sculpture.

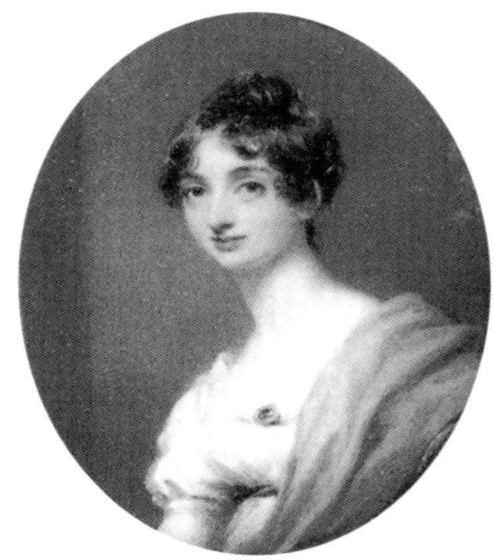

John Wright, after Thomas Lawrence, *Caroline Matilda Barker, Mrs Frank Sotheron*, 1812. The Clarke Collection, On long-term loan to the Scottish National Portrait Gallery, Edinburgh

**Provenance:** Duveen sale, Plaza Hotel, New York, 29 April 1915, lot 12; with Duveen again, 1923; with Scott & Fowles, New York, 1950; Frederick Vanderbilt, by whom bequeathed to his niece, Margaret Louise Van Alen Brugière, and sold from her estate, Christie's, 28 November 1969, lot 194; bt by Agnew's; 1970 or 1971 to the William Bowmore Collection, New South Wales, until 1998.

**Exhibitions:** *Regency: British Art & Design 1800–1830*, AGSA, Adelaide, 1998, no. 112. *The Fine Art of Giving, 90 Masterpieces from the William Bowmore Collection*, AGSA, Adelaide, 1999, no. 17. *Island to Empire: 300 Years of British Art 1550–1850*, AGSA, Adelaide, 2005.

**Literature:** Kenneth Garlick, *Sir Thomas Lawrence: A complete catalogue of the oil paintings*, New York, 1989, no. 733, p. 267. Angus Trumble in Menz, *Regency*, Adelaide: AGSA, 1998, no. 112, pp. 65, 67. Dr Stephen Lloyd, *Portrait Miniatures from the Clarke Collection*, Edinburgh: Scottish National Portrait Gallery, 2001, no. 65, pp. 88–89. Angus Trumble in Ron Radford, *The Fine Art of Giving*, Adelaide: AGSA, 1999, pp. 46–47. Ron Radford, "Recent Acquisitions at the Art Gallery of South Australia", *The Burlington Magazine*, April 2003, p. 329.

**Condition:** Good; conserved in 1998 by Artlab Australia, Adelaide.

**Frame:** Original.

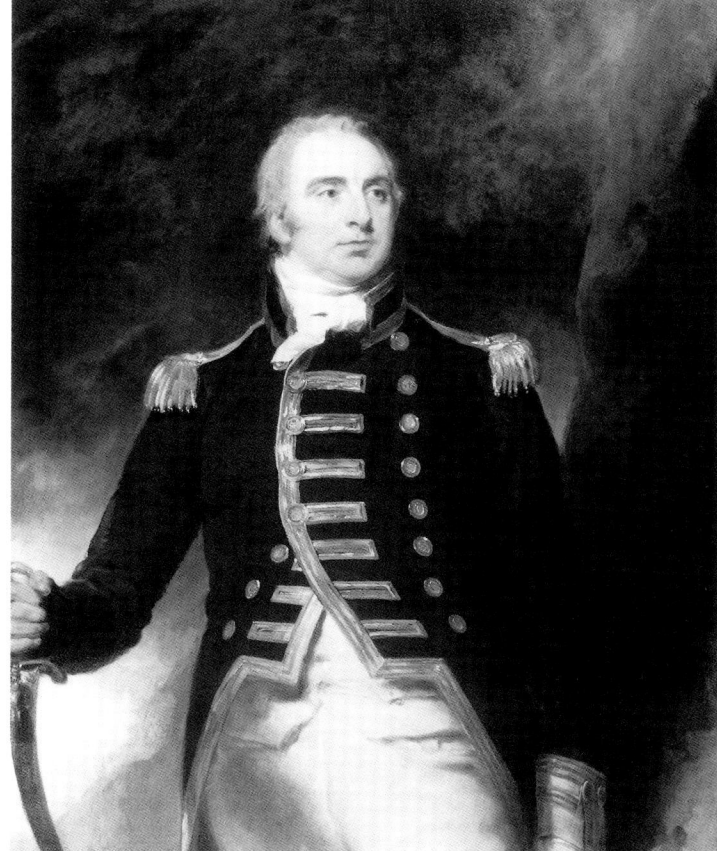

Thomas Lawrence, *Admiral Frank Sotheron*, c.1808. George Eastman Collection, Memorial Art Gallery of the University of Rochester, Rochester, New York

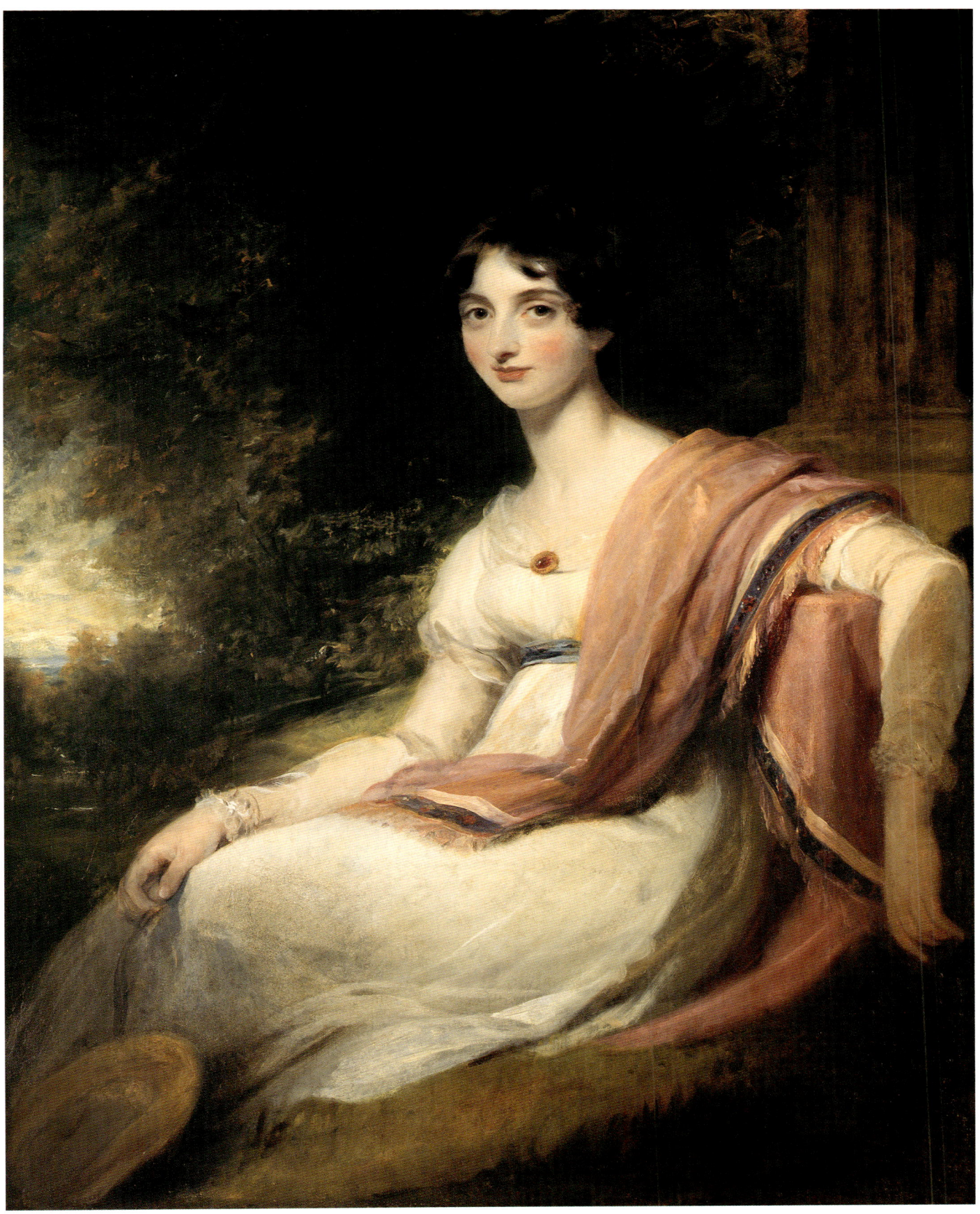

# Thomas Lawrence

## The son of Countess Meerveldt, 1819
pencil, black, red & blue chalks, grey wash on paper, 46.8 x 33.5 cm
V. B. F. Young Bequest Fund 1993

It was during his five-month official stay in Vienna from early December 1818 to 3 May 1819 that Lawrence executed this engaging portrait. In Vienna, apart from his portraits of leaders destined for the Waterloo Chamber at Windsor Castle, he undertook several other commissions and executed twelve private portrait drawings that he listed in a letter sent to Joseph Farington from Rome. The list included drawings of Princess Razoumowski, Count and Countess Esterhazy and Lady Selina Meade as well as, to quote directly from it, "Comtesse Murveldt's son".[1]

The small three-quarter-length portrait of the pretty child engages us with his big eyes as he clutches a flag, perhaps a liberation victory pennant. He is about twelve years old and fashionably dressed in the style for upper-class boys. A finely-written inscription, barely perceptible along the sitter's right arm, strengthens the modelling of the form and cleverly becomes the shadow of the arm.

The rhyming-verse inscription reads: "*T. L. – of my Name the Initials I write, for I tire to behold it again, But the name that can ne'er be too long in my sight, Nor too fix'd in my Heart is <u>Vienne</u>!*"[2] It may imply Lawrence's fondness not only for Vienna but perhaps also for the boy's mother. As mentioned, after leaving Vienna he recorded the drawing as "Comtesse Murveldt's son" but it is very probable that Murveldt was his spelling of Meerveldt and that the boy's mother was Theresa, Countess Meerveldt. Though she had married General Count Max Meerveldt some time after 1815 her first husband was Count Phillip Josef Kinsky and Kinsky is likely to be the father of our young sitter; hence Lawrence referred not to the son of Count Meerveldt but to the son of the Countess.[3] The inscription also implies that the drawing was executed at the end of the artist's stay in Vienna, probably in April 1819 as he left Vienna on 3 May, and by then had tired of signing his name to so many commissions. Also implied is nostalgia for Vienna after a presumably pleasant few months there.

The drawing is executed with a sharp lead pencil outline highlighted by black, red and blue chalks and strengthened by thin grey wash. This was a standard Neoclassical portrait-drawing technique in the early nineteenth century. Lawrence helped make it popular in Britain and it was used later by a number of early-colonial Australian portrait artists, among them Thomas Bock (1790–1855) but the technique is especially visible in more mannered late Regency drawings by Thomas Griffiths Wainewright (1794–1847).

Both were convict artists transported to Tasmania and are well represented in the Gallery's collection. Lawrence's portrait drawing, with its refinement and its delicate yet tight classical precision, shows the artist as a consummate draughtsman. It displays strength and skill often lacking in British draughtsmanship; for instance Reynolds's drawings by comparison are weak. Like Reynolds, though, Lawrence was an avid collector of Old Master drawings and owned the greatest such collection ever assembled in Britain.

The Gallery also holds a student drawing by Lawrence, a male classical nude subject that probably dates from the late 1780s when he was still influenced by Reynolds's Discourses and classical subjects. It belonged to Lawrence's sister and was brought to Adelaide by a direct descendant.

**Inscription:** Signed l. r., pencil: "T. L.". Not dated. Inscribed l. r. [along arm of sitter], pencil: "T. L. - of my Name the Initials I write, for I tire to behold it again, But the name that can ne'er be too long in my sight, Nor too fix'd in my Heart is <u>Vienne</u>!".

**Provenance:** Harnach Palace, Freyung, Vienna; bought for the Art Gallery of South Australia from Sotheby's, London, 19 November 1992, lot 46.

**Exhibitions:** *Regency: British Art & Design 1800–1830*, AGSA, Adelaide, 1998, no. 143. *Island to Empire: 300 Years of British Art 1550–1850*, AGSA, Adelaide 2005.

**Literature:** D. E. Williams, *The Life and Correspondence of Sir Thomas Lawrence*, vol. II, London, 1831, p. 146. Allan Cunningham, *Life of Sir David Wilkie*, London, 1843, vol. 2, p. 365. Kenneth Garlick, *A Catalogue of the Paintings, Drawings and Pastels of Sir Thomas Lawrence* in Walpole Society, vol. XXXIX, London, 1964, p. 238. Walter Armstrong, *Lawrence*, New York, 1969 (reprint of 1913 edition), p. 186. Sotheby's, *Eighteenth and Nineteenth Century British Paintings and Drawings*, 19 November 1992, lot 46. Ron Radford in Christopher Menz, *Regency*, Adelaide: AGSA, 1998, p. 79.

**Condition:** Good; evidence of some fading.

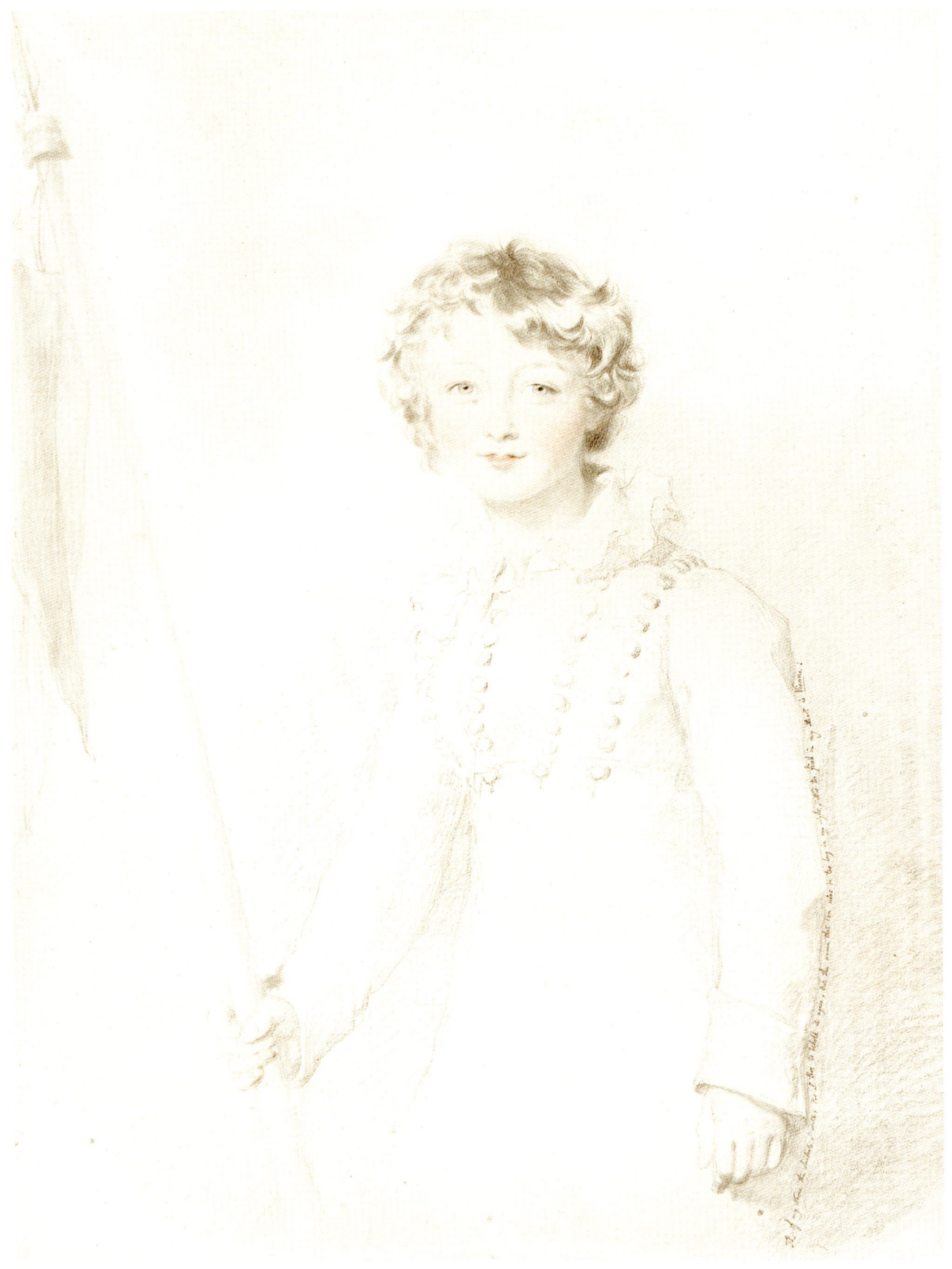

# Henry Raeburn 1756–1823

Henry Raeburn is the best known artist who worked in Scotland. Though it was unusual for a major British painter to sustain a flourishing career outside London his life as a very successful portrait painter was spent in Edinburgh, undoubtedly helped by romantic interest in Scotland generated by the novels of Walter Scott. (In 1810 Raeburn exhibited in London a *Portrait of W. Scott, Esq., author of The Lay of the Last Minstrel, Marmion, etc.*) The characterisation of his sitters was unusually frank and his highly distinctive tonal style of painting was similarly bold and direct: without any preliminary drawing he used a square brush to lay one tone beside another with no gradation in the modelling. He frequently used tone as colour and made increasing use of dramatic effects of contrasting light and dark.

Born in 1756 at Stockbridge near Edinburgh, he was the son of a prosperous mill owner, Robert Raeburn, and Ann Elder. At the age of sixteen he was apprenticed to the Edinburgh goldsmith James Gilliband. He was encouraged to draw by David Deuchar, a seal-engraver and etcher, and by David Martin, Allan Ramsay's former assistant and the first artist to make a comfortable living from portraiture in Scotland. In Edinburgh Alexander Runciman (1736–1785) could have been an influence for he did not follow Ramsay's practice of careful preliminary drawings but instead cultivated spontaneity so as to record the impact of a sitter's presence. Nonetheless, Raeburn was largely self-taught which possibly accounts for his unusual style.

In 1784 Raeburn spent two months in Reynolds's London studio on his way south to study abroad for three years. He was in Italy, but there has been speculation about a visit as well to Spain because of what is thought to be the influence of Velázquez. Raeburn returned and settled in New Town, Edinburgh in 1788 to practice as a portrait painter and achieved instant success. After his early mentor David Martin died in 1797 Raeburn was recognised as the leading portrait painter in Scotland. He exhibited at the Royal Academy in London only rarely before 1810 but after that did so regularly, with critical acclaim. He became an associate of the Royal Academy in 1812, and in 1815 he became a full Academician.

Raeburn was knighted during George IV's State Visit to Edinburgh in 1822. He died in 1823 shortly after being appointed the King's Limner for Scotland. His influence on subsequent Scottish portrait painters was strong, most notably on John Watson Gordon.

## Archibald Trotter of Bush, 1810
oil on canvas, 76.4 x 63.3 cm
Gift of William Bowmore AO OBE through the Art Gallery of South Australia Foundation 1998

The sitter of this attractive, spare portrait is the young Scottish gentleman Archibald Trotter (1789–1868) of Dryden, Castlelaw and Bush, all in Midlothian just south of Edinburgh. He worked for the East India Company.

In 1911 James Greig published a list of Raeburn's works that included "Trotter, Archibald, of Bush, Midlothian" and also a "Trotter, Mrs., of Bush",[1] present whereabouts unknown, and apparently not of the wife Archibald married in 1813 for she was Laura Maria, the second daughter of Thomas Chase of the Madras Civil Service. In Algernon Graves' *A Century of Loan Exhibitions 1813–1912* our portrait and a portrait of *Mrs Ann Trotter of Bush*, who was Archibald's mother, is mentioned as exhibited in the Raeburn exhibition of 1876.[2] "Mrs Ann Trotter" is a usage that implies a widow, and if the lost portrait was indeed from a companion commission it was for a mother and son, a much less common occurrence than a husband-and-wife commission.[3] Our portrait (and his widowed mother's) was probably triggered by the heir's coming of age in 1810.

The composition of this elegant Regency portrait is simple and straightforward. There is a Scottish no-nonsense directness – no columns, drapery, elaborate chairs or other artifices or pretensions. The handsome 21-year-old man is at ease in the standard half-length format and his fresh features, lemon waistcoat and white stock emerge from a dark Rembrandtesque space. Raeburn's characteristic shadowy background, the dark high-collared coat and subduing of the shine of the brass buttons, prevent any drift of attention away from the face. The paint application, as in all Raeburn's portraits, is executed broadly, fluidly and tonally. There appears to be no under-drawing or reworking. The features are dexterously and confidently blocked in with simple stepped gradations of mainly warm tones, a distinguishing feature of Raeburn's portraiture.

Provenance: Archibald Trotter (1789–1868), Bush, Midlothian; his son Lt-Col. Robert Archibald Trotter (1814–1894), Bush, Midlothian; Lt-Col. Trotter's nephew and heir Alexander Edmund Coutts Trotter (1846–1913); A. E. C. Trotter's kinsman and heir Richard Durant Trotter who sold the Bush and Dryden properties, Midlothian, in 1946; Thomas Agnew & Sons, London, after 1952; Agnew's again 1972; William Bowmore AO OBE, New South Wales, from 1973.

Exhibitions: Raeburn Exhibition, Edinburgh, 1876, no. 278. *Regency: British Art & Design 1800–1830*, AGSA, Adelaide, 1998, no. 116. *The Fine Art of Giving: 90 Masterpieces from the William Bowmore Collection*, AGSA, Adelaide, 1999, no. 14.

Literature: Dr John Brown, Raeburn exhibition catalogue, Edinburgh, 1876. James Greig, *Sir Henry Raeburn, R.A.*, London, 1911, p. 61, as *Archibald Trotter, of Bush*. Angus Trumble in Christopher Menz, *Regency*, Adelaide: AGSA, 1998, p. 69. Ron Radford, *The Fine Art of Giving*, Adelaide: AGSA, 1999, p. 22–23 no. 14 (illus.).

Condition: Excellent; last conserved possibly in London before 1972.

Frame: Original.

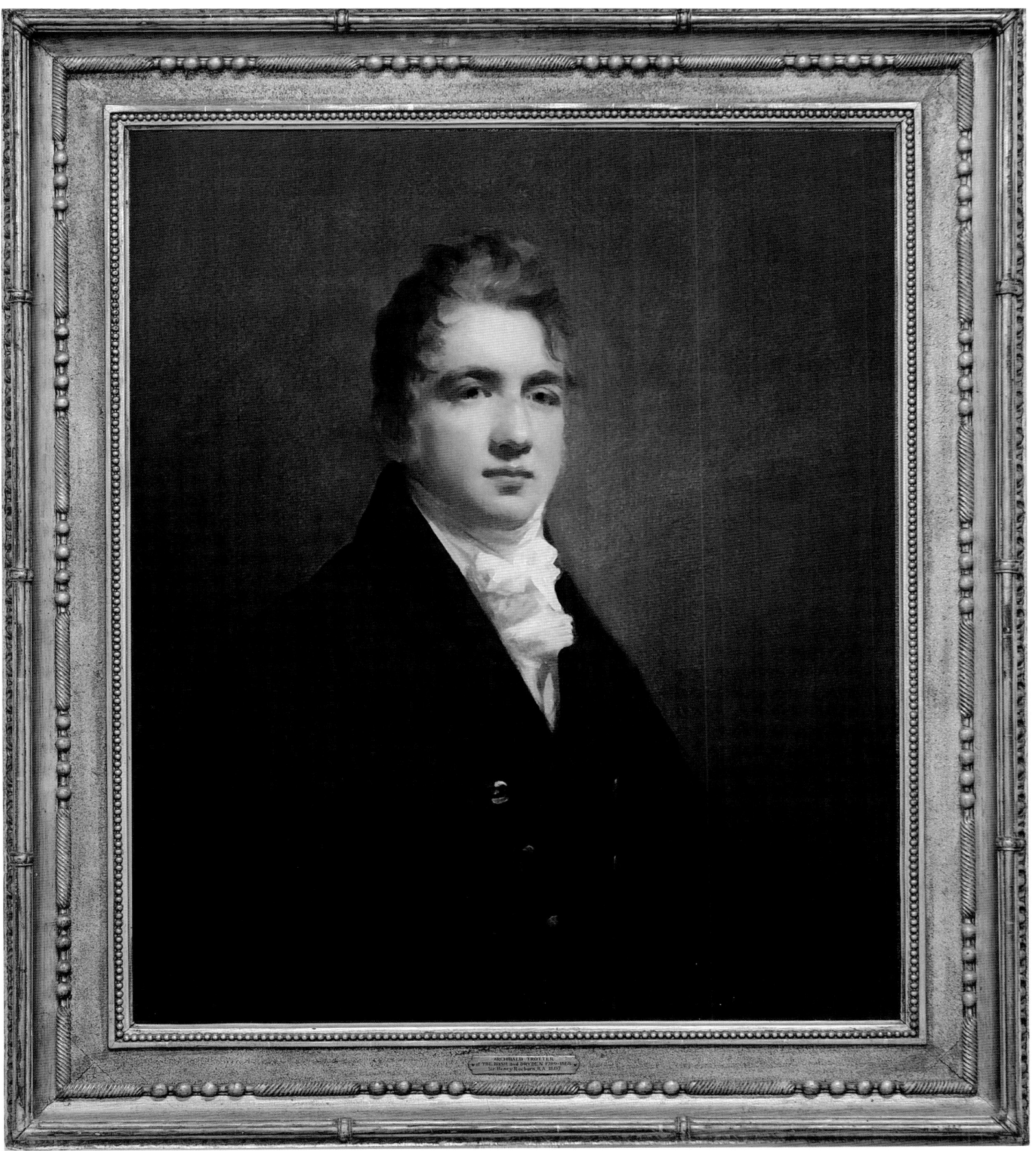

# John Sell Cotman 1782–1842

John Sell Cotman was one of the most original artists of those who made watercolour an important movement within English landscape painting; his style combined naturalism with a distinctive sense of flat pattern that appealed to the modernist taste of later centuries. He and the older John Crome (1768–1821), who was chiefly an oil painter, led the early-nineteenth-century Norwich School of landscape art that flourished from 1803 to 1833 at their native city in Norfolk. The Norwich School was the first and most artistically significant regional centre of art-making, exhibiting and teaching to develop in England.

Born in Norwich in 1782, Cotman moved to London in 1798 where he became acquainted with Dr Thomas Monro, the great enthusiast and patron of watercolours. He became a member of the Sketching Club set up by the watercolourist Thomas Girtin and he first exhibited at the Royal Academy in 1800. In 1803–05 he spent his summers in Yorkshire. In 1806 Cotman returned to Norwich where he worked as a drawing master, shifting to nearby Yarmouth from 1812 to 1823 to teach drawing for the Dawson Turner family. Dawson Turner was the motivating force behind Cotman's summer tours to Normandy, in 1817, 1818 and 1820, which resulted in splendid series of "Architectural Antiquities" in both watercolour and etching.

Cotman was elected an associate member of the Old Water-Colour Society in 1825. He left Norwich in 1833 and became Professor of Drawing at King's College, London. In 1841 he made his last sketching tour of Norfolk, and died the next year. The Art Gallery of South Australia owns six of his many etchings. He painted only a handful of oils.

## The old pigeon house, Downham Market, c.1810
oil on canvas, 32.5 x 39.7 cm
Gift of William Bowmore AO OBE through the Art Gallery of South Australia Foundation 1999

This is one of Cotman's rare landscapes in oil. Like his other oils, which he began to execute after his return from London to Norwich in 1806, it is carried out in thin paint a little like watercolour. Formerly known as *The orchard house*, the subject recurs in a rare softground etching, a presumably unique example of which is in the Norwich Castle Museum (see opposite),[1] and the etching is signed and inscribed by the artist with the title *The old pigeon house, Downham Market*. Whereas the background in the oil shows a line of trees with water in the distance, the background of the etching shows a windmill to the right of the building.

The painting was executed about 1810 during the artist's most creative first period of working in Norwich. It is similar in composition and technique to his oil *Ferry house at Bristol*, 1808–10 (National Galleries of Scotland), and like that work it may have been preceded by an earlier watercolour now lost.

The pigeon house was near the small town of Downham Market, which is on the River Ouse in Norfolk about twenty kilometres inland from King's Lynn. It is at the edge of the Fens which are marshland that was drained over the years for agriculture. The simple building is windowless and of unusual form. W. F. Dickes described it in 1905 as "a tall, oblong erection of Cob [a mixture of compressed clay, gravel and straw], such as is used in clay countries, framed in timber and thatched, standing on a brick platform, to which access is gained by steps from the gravel walk in the foreground. Willow trees are grouped near the building".[2] The dilapidated structure was probably originally an orchard house for storing fruit. The door we see above improvised wooden steps might have been intended originally for access to loaded wagons at the brick platform or, during high water in the Fens, for a barge; the building might have had a similar purpose, in the wetter seasons before extensive drainage, to that depicted in the much larger warehouse in *Ferry house at Bristol*. By the time of the painting and etching the orchard house was abandoned and given over to pigeons. Behind it is a roadway, indicated by the post-and-rail fence and the row of old willows that frame the composition. The willows are not present in the more topographical etching and evidently were inserted into the painting for pictorial effect. The tall cob-and-thatch object is a curiosity well suited to Cotman's artistic purpose, with its rustic simplicity, its timber-framed rectangularities of form, and its flat planes of warm colour. Solidity and a sense of light are established by the sunlit face of the building and the darker shadows on the side and at the steps.

In this tiny painting the picturesque rural subject has been translated into a monumental and stately composition of light and colour. Cotman's painting pre-dates by a decade or more the pre-Impressionist light-filled Italian oil sketches that Camille Corot completed out of doors in Italy, and also pre-dates Charles Eastlake's sunny Italian sketches like the Gallery's *Cypress trees at the Villa d'Este*, 1817 (p. 225).

Cotman's painting once belonged to the Pre-Raphaelite sculptor Thomas Woolner who came briefly to Australia in the gold rush of the early 1850s. Woolner's Australian portrait relief sculptures, and other British works, are well represented in the Gallery's collection.

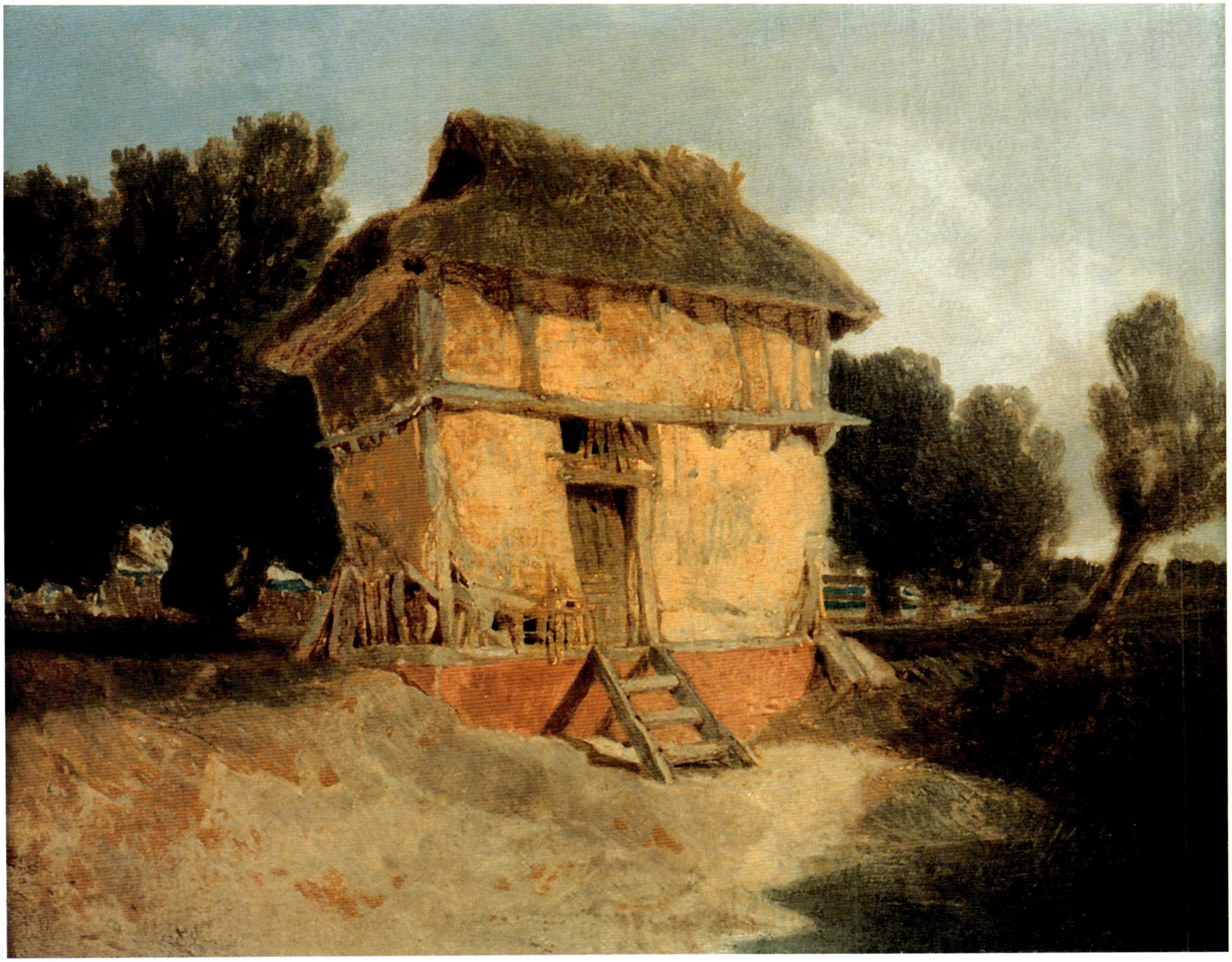

**Provenance:** Thomas Woolner, London (by 1888); The Hon. Mrs Wood; Miss M. Deakin by 1958; Thomas Agnew & Sons, London; Agnew's, 1970; William Bowmore Collection, New South Wales, from 1970.

**Exhibitions:** Grosvenor Gallery, London, 1888, no. 272. *Oil Paintings by J. Crome and J. S. Cotman*, Agnew's, London, 1958, no. 60. *Paintings and Drawings from Agnew's, London*, David Jones Art Gallery, Sydney, 1970, no. 20. *Regency: British Art & Design 1800–1830*, AGSA, Adelaide, 1998, no. 99. *The Fine Art of Giving: 90 Masterpieces from the William Bowmore Collection*, AGSA, Adelaide, 1999–2000, no. 15. *Island to Empire: 300 Years of British Art 1550–1850*, AGSA, Adelaide, 2005.

**Literature:** W. F. Dickes, *The Norwich School of Painting*, London, 1905, p. 305. Thomas Agnew & Sons, *Paintings and Drawings from Agnew's, London*, Sydney: David Jones Art Gallery, 1970, no. 20. Angus Trumble in Christopher Menz, *Regency*, Adelaide: AGSA, 1998, p. 59. Angus Trumble in Ron Radford, *The Fine Art of Giving*, Adelaide: AGSA, 1999, pp. 22, 58–59.

**Condition:** Good; last conserved in 2004 by Artlab Australia, Adelaide.

**Frame:** Possibly original, cut down from an eighteenth-century frame.

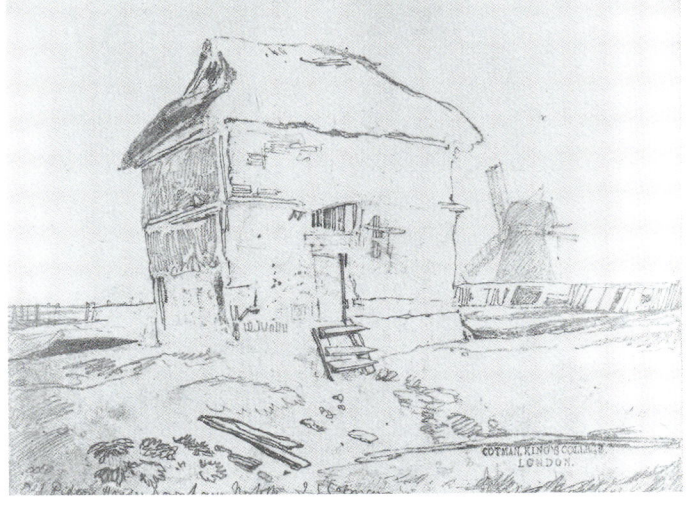

John Sell Cotman, *The Old Pigeon House, Downham*, softground etching. Norwich Castle Museum and Art Gallery, Norwich

# J. M. W. Turner 1775–1851

J. M. W. Turner is Britain's greatest artist, the finest landscape painter of the European Romantic movement, and the most creative and prolific exponent of watercolour painting in Western art. His radiant golden landscapes are today amongst the best known and best loved of all British works of art. Turner's extraordinary energy, tireless inquisitiveness and unflagging inspiration enabled him to create hundreds of oil paintings and many thousands of watercolours, and to show an almost infinite inventiveness, especially in his miraculous effects of light. He should be regarded as Claude Lorrain's greatest follower and towards the end of his life he pushed Claude's glowing golden-lit landscapes to a vaporous, almost abstract, culmination. Nevertheless, other significant artists of the past also inspired him: Gaspard Dughet, Nicolas Poussin, and seventeenth-century Dutch masters, including Rembrandt, Aelbert Cuyp and the seascape artists. Turner borrowed openly and freely from the subjects and inventions of these masters but always transformed them through his own personal vision.

Born in 1775 at Covent Garden, London, Turner was initially trained as an architectural draughtsman under Thomas Malton (1748–1804). He joined the Royal Academy Schools in 1789, aged fourteen, and in the mid 1790s achieved an early reputation as a painter of topographical and antiquarian watercolours. About 1794 he met the collector and mentor of watercolour painters, Dr Thomas Monro, who employed him and Thomas Girtin to copy and colour watercolour drawings by Edward Dayes, Thomas Hearne and J. R. Cozens.

Throughout his career Turner travelled extensively in Britain to Wales, Yorkshire, Scotland and the Lake District to seek romantic scenery for his own watercolours and oils. He first visited the Continent in 1802, admired works by the great Italian and Dutch masters at the Louvre, and travelled to Switzerland. He first toured Italy in 1819, and made many more productive trips to the Continent in later years.

Unlike his contemporary and rival John Constable, Turner's rise to fame was meteoric. He was only twenty-four in 1799 when elected an Associate of the Royal Academy and three years later he was a full Academician. Turner continued to exhibit regularly and prominently at the Academy, often dazzling and bewildering his fellow artists, until his death in 1851.

## Scarborough town and castle: morning: boys catching crabs, c.1810
watercolour on paper, 68.5 x 101.5 cm
On long-term loan to the Art Gallery of South Australia since 1987

This masterpiece of watercolour painting from the beginning of Turner's middle period depicts South Bay at the English seaport of Scarborough, with the town and the remains of the medieval castle in the background. Scarborough is on the Yorkshire coast in the north of England and faces east into the morning sun. It was the site of a Roman signal station, the remains of which are visible on the cliffs. The castle on the headland was built in the twelfth and thirteenth centuries. The town has traditionally been known for its herring fishing but in the late seventeenth century it also became a spa resort and from the eighteenth century onwards people flocked there to take dips in the North Sea.

The scene shows Scarborough bathed in the soft light of morning. The tide is out, the waves are gently purling in and the early mist has almost cleared. Nature is tranquil but the small city is busy and hard-working. In the foreground five young boys are catching crabs, probably to sell. On the left two women lay out washing to dry on the cliff rocks and on the remains of an old wooden seawall; it is a big professional wash, perhaps from a ship's voyage, not their domestic laundry. On the right a man is fishing at the water's edge and men unload cargo from a beached fishing vessel into a horse-drawn cart. Stationary shipping with sails furled can be seen docked by the town where buildings descend to the shore. The only sign of recreation – or health cure – is in the centre at middle distance where a horse-drawn bathing machine, a hut on wheels, is entering the sea. (Scarborough claims that bathing machines were a local invention.)

Pictorially the scene is reminiscent of Dutch seventeenth-century riverport paintings that show working life at the start of a peaceful day. The naturalism of this beach watercolour is far removed from Turner's oil paintings of classical coasts and seaports inspired by Claude Lorrain. Nevertheless, the diffused golden glow ultimately derives from Claude's coastal scenes albeit modified by the influence of Aelbert Cuyp, the Dutch master of rural life who also bathed his naturalistic scenes in Claudean light. Turner greatly admired the art of Cuyp but here he is closer to the seventeenth-century Dutch seascape artists such as Jan van de Cappelle (1626–1679) and Willem van de Velde the Younger who later worked in Britain or the coastal scenes of Jacob van Ruisdael. Turner often quotes his favourite Old Masters, but makes them his own. This composition is carefully, even classically, balanced in a predictable way yet Turner captures, as no other artist has, a natural sense of receding distance and glowing atmospheric light.

The scene of daily life is less prosaically naturalistic than similar works by his Dutch forerunners. In *Scarborough town and castle: morning: boys catching crabs* Turner is less interested in the descriptive and anecdotal than in a broader

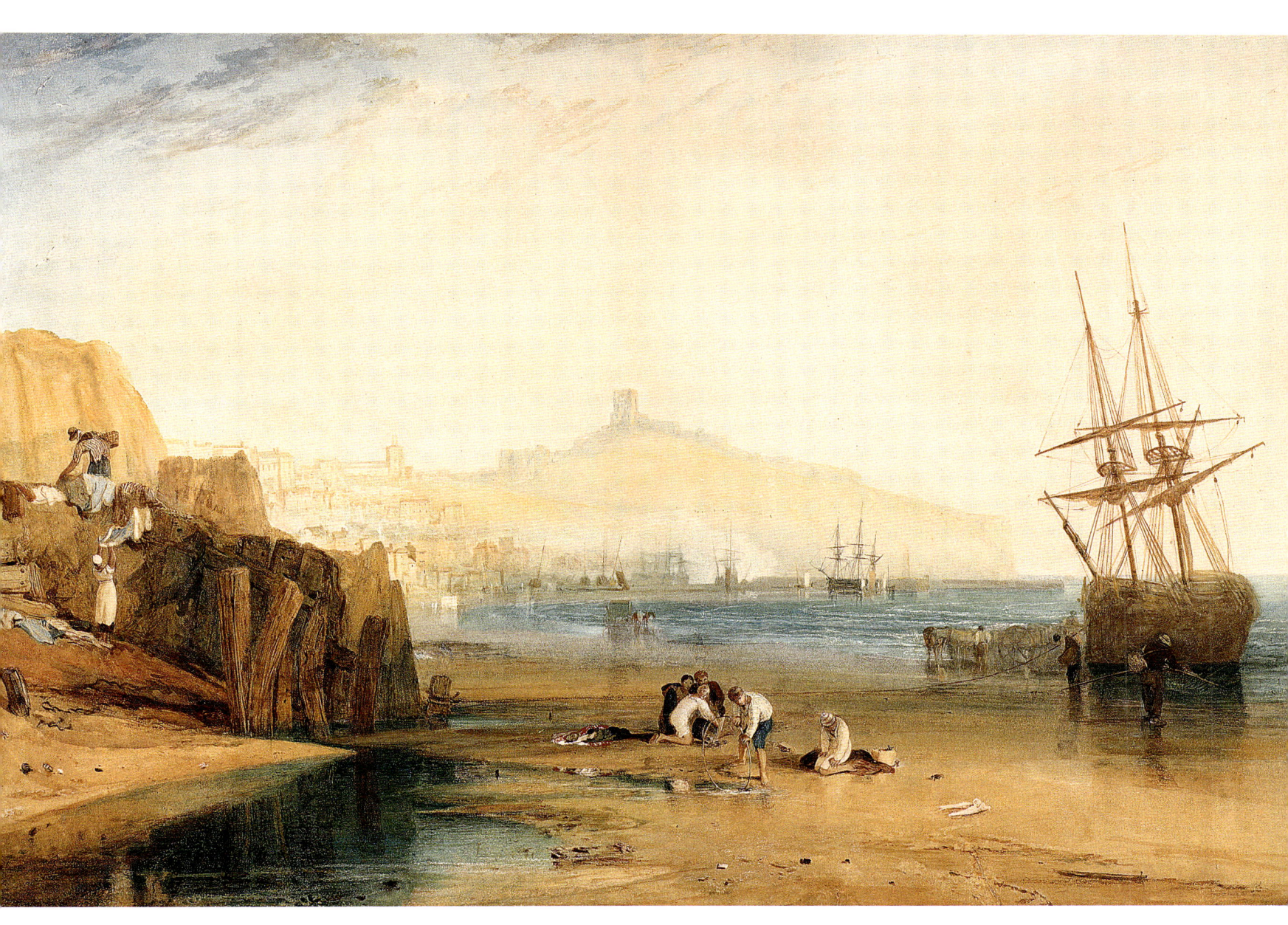

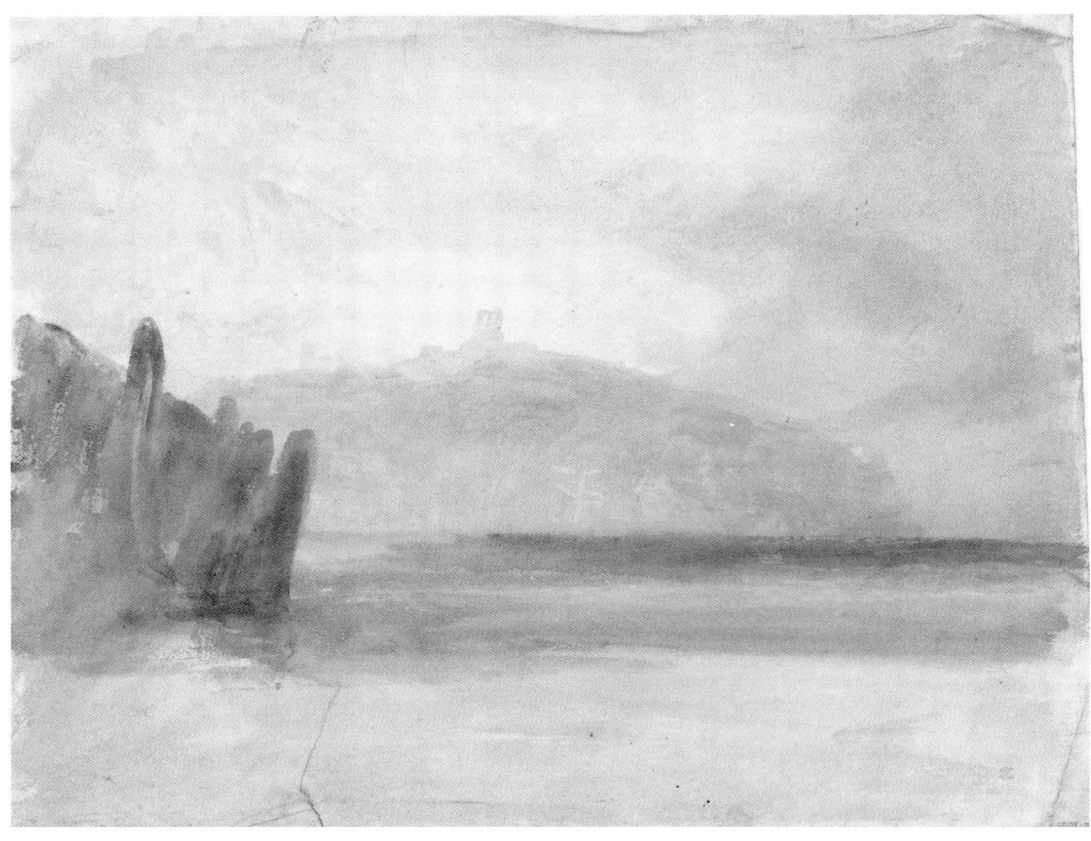

J. M. W. Turner, *Scarborough*. © Tate, London 2004

cycle of continuity, a sense of place, the full richness of the everyday in a good productive society of men, women and children. At the very centre of the composition, high in the distance, is the ruin of the town's medieval castle near fourth-century Roman remains. The castle looms above the town but a hilltop church also watches over the place. The town faces the shore, the source of its fishery income and its attractions as a resort. And the beach is populated by Scarborough's working men and women with their young male offspring, their hope for the future, conspicuously grouped in the immediate centre of the scene. The past links with the present, an ancient Roman seaport is now also a modern spa town. These continuities show humankind working with and making a living from nature. Unified by radiant light the scene transcends naturalism and becomes an ideal of social harmony and cyclical history.

This beach scene followed a number of major oil paintings of flat beaches and rivers, among them *Sun rising through vapour; fishermen cleaning and selling fish*, c.1807 (National Gallery, London), *Trout fishing in the Dee*, c.1809 (Taft Museum, Cincinatti), and *Fish market on the Sands, Hastings*, c.1810 (Nelson-Atkins Museum, Kansas City). With their Netherlandish foreground flatness, they are immediate forerunners and relate in subject matter and composition to *Scarborough town and castle: morning: boys catching crabs*.

Evidently pleased with his subject, Turner used it several times. This is the largest and most finished version and unlike the bulk of his watercolours, which are small sketches, it was conceived as a large and elaborate exhibition picture – not a watercolour drawing or sketch but a watercolour painting. It was exhibited at the Royal Academy in 1811.[1] A large "colour beginning" the same size as this finished watercolour, of the same view but with a more detailed treatment of the posts and pool to the left, is held by the Tate, London, which also has a smaller version. The Wallace Collection, London, holds another smaller version, without the boats, dated 1809. In about 1825 Turner used a similar view of the town, though from a nearer viewpoint, to make a watercolour, also in the Tate, for *The Ports of England* series that was engraved and published in 1826.[2]

This watercolour made for a major exhibition was originally owned by one of Turner's most enthusiastic early patrons, Walter Fawkes of Farnley Hall near Leeds in Yorkshire. It is probable that Fawkes commissioned this display piece

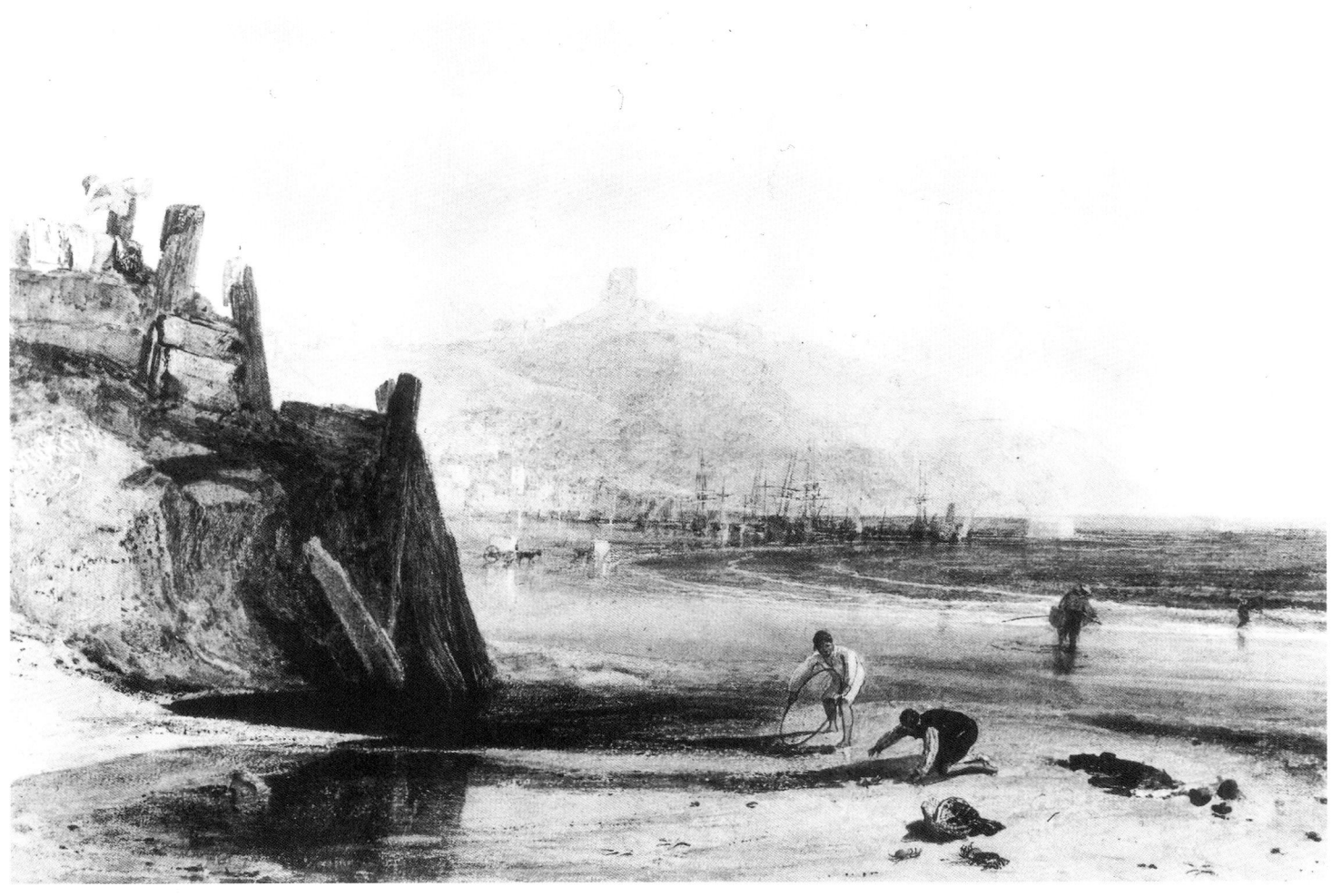

J. M. W. Turner, *Scarborough Castle: Boys crab fishing*, 1809. By kind permission of the Trustees of The Wallace Collection, London

after seeing one of the smaller earlier versions or sketches of the subject. Turner stayed with the Fawkes family in 1810 during a visit to Yorkshire that included Scarborough, and the picture was probably commissioned then. (He had first visited Yorkshire in 1797.) Turner revisited Farnley Hall almost every subsequent year until 1824. Fawkes collected two hundred of Turner's watercolours and seven oils and in 1819 opened his London house in Grosvenor Place so that visitors might see his vast collection of watercolours by Turner and other artists. A newspaper provides a first-hand account: "The intermediate apartments were filled with finished drawings by leading names and sketches by Turner, of Yorkshire scenery…".[3] No doubt this watercolour view of Scarborough shore was prominent among them. It has been included in most of the significant exhibitions of Turner's work since.

**Provenance:** c.1811, Walter Ramsden Fawkes of Farnley Hall, Yorkshire; Estate of Walter Fawkes, Christie's, London, 2 July 1937; Sir Frederic Hamilton; 1956, Lady Hamilton; 1968, Mrs William Crabtree, UK; On long-term loan to the Art Gallery of South Australia since 1987 from a private collection, South Australia.

**Exhibitions:** Royal Academy, 1811, no. 392. Leeds, 1839, no. 17. *Agnew's 150th Anniversary Exhibition,* 1967, no. 43. *Turner 1775–1851*, Royal Academy, London, 1974–75, no. 77. Royal Academy, 1975, no. 113. *J. M. W. Turner at the Grand Palais,* The British Council, Paris, 1983–84, no. 118. *Turner,* National Gallery of Australia, Canberra and National Gallery of Victoria, Melbourne, 1996, no. 43. *Regency: British Art & Design 1800–1830*, AGSA, Adelaide, 1998, no. 88. *Turner: The great watercolours,* Royal Academy, 2001. *Island to Empire: 300 Years of British Art 1550–1850*, AGSA, Adelaide, 2005.

**Literature:** Andrew Wilton, *Turner 1775–1851*, London: Tate and Royal Academy, 1974, p. 63. Michael Lloyd, *Turner*, Canberra: National Gallery of Australia, 1996, p. 109 (illus.). Ron Radford et al., *Treasures*, Adelaide: AGSA, 1998, p. 54 (illus.). Ron Radford in Christopher Menz, *Regency*, Adelaide: AGSA, 1998, pp. 7, 71–72. Eric Shanes, *Turner: The great watercolours*, London: Royal Academy, 2001, p. 129, no. 44.

**Condition:** Good.

**Frame:** Probably original.

# J. M. W. Turner

## Alnwick Castle, c.1829
watercolour on paper, 28.2 x 42.2 cm
South Australian Government Grant 1958

In direct contrast to *Scarborough*'s bayside activities bathed in golden morning light (p. 207), Turner's deserted view of *Alnwick Castle* is a haunting riverside nocturne. Illuminated only by the cold light of the moon, a highly romantic Gothic citadel guards the river in which it is reflected. *Scarborough* is open, light and golden; *Alnwick Castle* is mysterious, dark and indigo.

Alnwick Castle still stands on the river Aln in the small town of Alnwick, Northumberland, in the north of England about thirty miles beyond Newcastle and about the same distance south of the Scottish border. It was a border fortress. The castle was built in its present form in the twelfth century by the powerful de Vescy family and since the fourteenth century has been the seat of the Percy family, first as the Earls and later as the Dukes of Northumberland. It was one of the first Norman citadels to depart from the simpler square keep surrounded by a walled enclosure. Although much altered today, it preserves the basic twelfth-century design of a circular keep composed of a series of towers surrounding a courtyard with two outer courts.

In 1750 when Canaletto painted the castle it was in a near-ruinous state.[1] Soon afterwards, in the 1760s, it was restored for the first Duke of Northumberland by the architect Robert Adam and it is their version of the castle that Turner painted, along with the Lion Bridge designed in 1773 by Robert's brother John Adam. Turner's contemporary, the watercolourist Samuel Prout, on a visit to Alnwick Castle in 1814 noted in his diary, "…the Duke's architect for the tower-house conduit, etc. manifests a wretched want of judgement and feeling for harmony. On the battlements of the towers are figures of warriors, they have an extraordinary effect, perhaps not improving the grandeur of the noble pile".[2] The giant stone warriors are seen here against the sky; they were originally Medieval but mostly replaced by Robert Adam.[3]

This watercolour was executed probably in 1829 but the young Turner had first visited Alnwick in 1797, and it was then that he made the drawing in his *The north of England sketchbook* (Tate Britain, London) from which he developed the watercolour more than thirty years later. He exhibited *Alnwick Castle* in July 1829 at the Egyptian Hall, Piccadilly, with about forty other watercolours that would shortly be engraved for his *England and Wales* series. Many of these, including *Alnwick Castle*, were acquired by Thomas Griffith who later became Turner's agent. The next year, 1830, the watercolour was engraved by J. T. Willmore and published in the *England and Wales* series. The firm lines and clear silhouettes were clearly intended from the start for translation into an engraved print. In 1835, exhibited at the Royal Manchester Institution, *Alnwick Castle* was titled *Moonlight*.[4]

The effect of light transforms a straightforward pictorial description of a fortress and bridge into a romantic Gothic fantasy. Moonlit towers, battlements and arched bridge could

J. M. W. Turner, *Alnwick Castle and Bridge from the North-West*, [from *North of England Sketch Book*], 1797. © Tate, London 2004

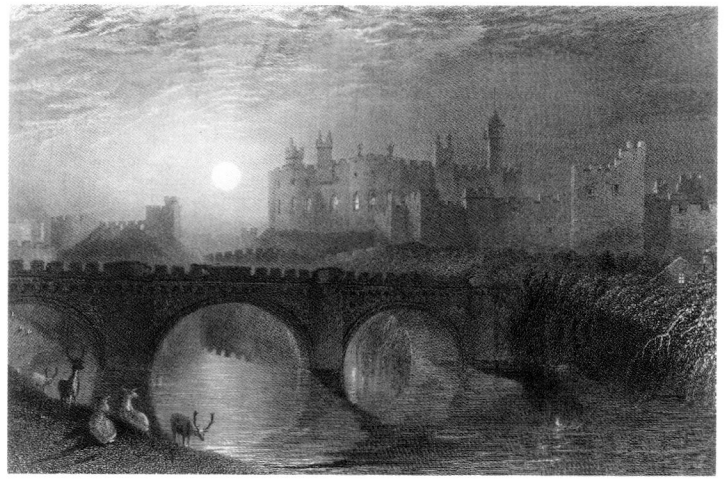

J. T. Willmore after J. M. W. Turner, *Alnwick Castle*, [from *England and Wales* series,] 1830. © Copyright The Trustees of The British Museum, London

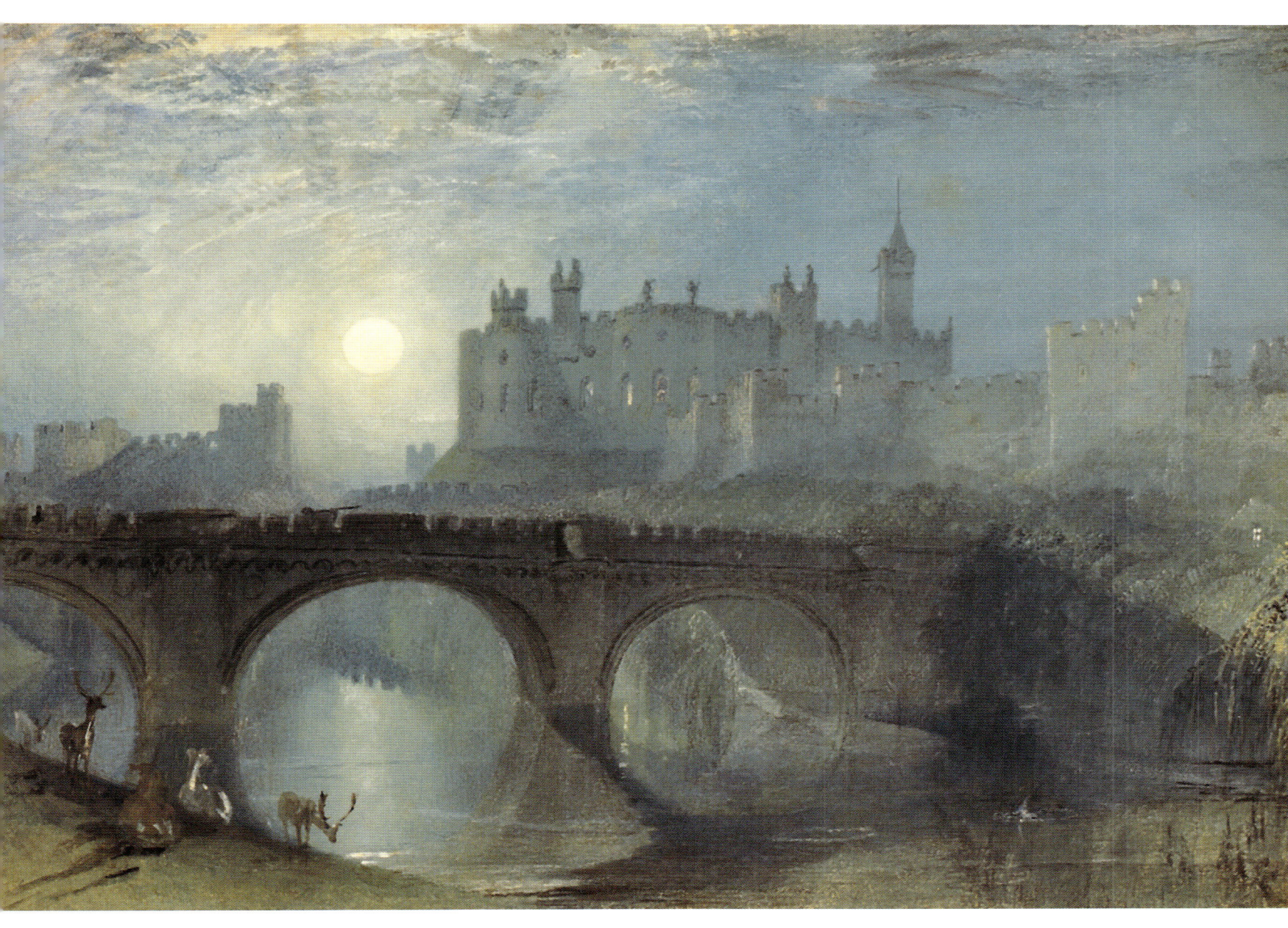

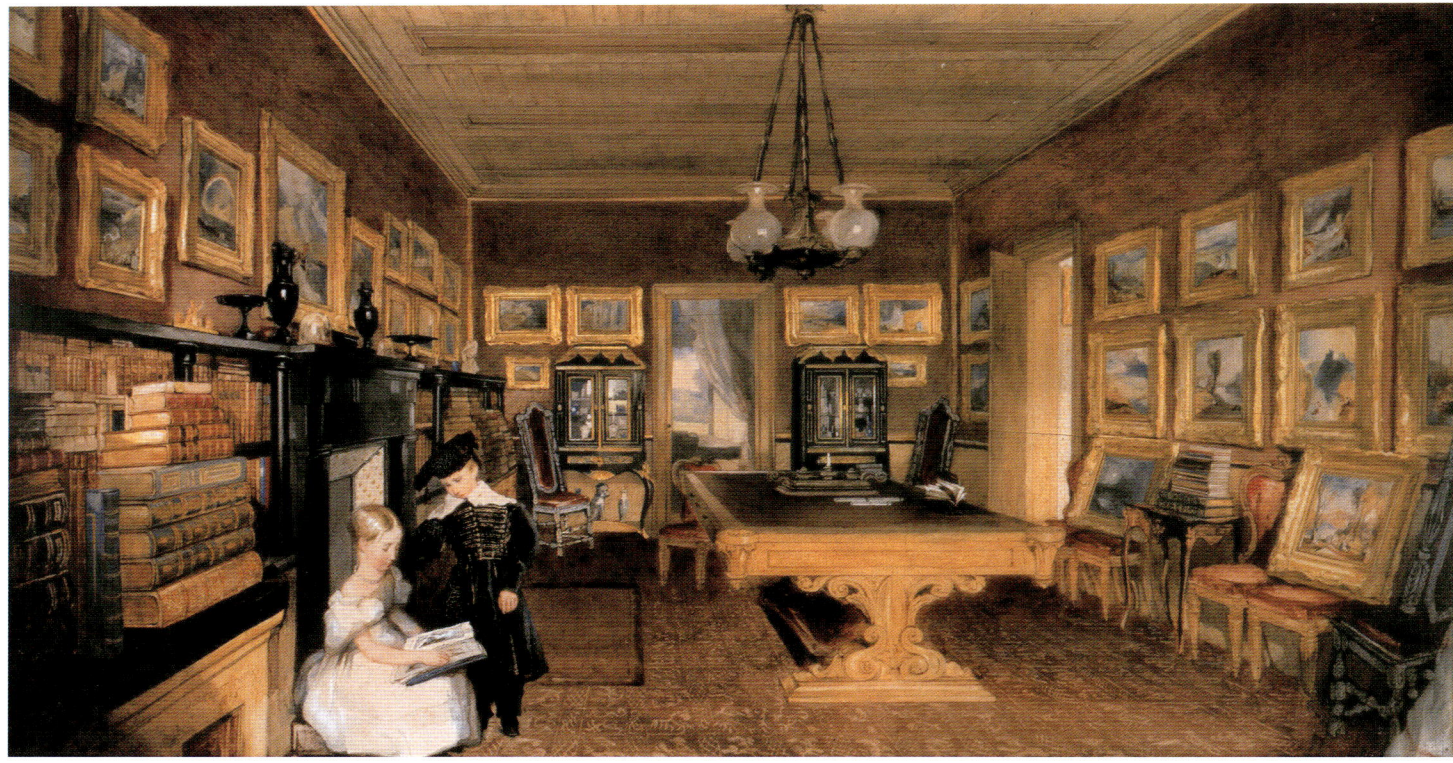

John Scarlett Davis, *The Library at Tottenham, the seat of B. G. Windus, Esq.*, 1835. © Copyright The Trustees of The British Museum, London

be a moody backdrop for a stage set. Silhouettes of the deers' antlers echo the Gothic pinnacles. Painted when Romanticism and its taste for the Gothic was replacing the centuries-long European obsession with the Classical, *Alnwick Castle* is probably the most striking, theatrical and Romantic of Turner's many castle views.

Turner would have been well aware of Claude Lorrain's famous poetic painting, traditionally known as *The enchanted castle* (National Gallery, London)[5] in which a castle at the water's edge is silhouetted against an evening sky. The darkest and most mysterious of all Claude's paintings (and darkened by the crime of time), it was the one that most appealed to Gothic taste in the nineteenth century and was immortalised in 1818 by the Romantic poet John Keats. Turner's love of Claude, and his knowledge of the nocturnes of his own immediate predecessor, Joseph Wright of Derby, may be his starting points here, but his fascination with the drama of light takes his *Alnwick Castle* beyond his predecessors' views and expresses the intensity of his own poetic vision.

Some time before 1835 Thomas Griffith sold *Alnwick Castle* to one of the greatest patrons of Turner's watercolours, B. G. Windus, who owned more than two hundred of his works. The British Museum has an 1835 watercolour by John Scarlett Davis that shows Windus's library crowded with Turner's watercolours. Leaning on a chair before the right-hand doorway our *Alnwick Castle* is recognisable (see above).

**Provenance:** Thomas Griffith, c.1829; B. G. Windus before 1835; F. N. Fordham Esq.; Brian G. Hamilton; Mr P. Stamp, bought for the Art Gallery of South Australia from Appleby Bros, London, on the advice of H. D. Molesworth, 1958.

**Exhibitions:** Egyptian Hall, London, 1829. Royal Manchester Institution, 1835. Fine Art Society, London 1946. Appleby Bros, London 1958. *Turner*, National Gallery of Australia, Canberra and National Gallery of Victoria, Melbourne, 1996, no. 63. *Regency: British Art & Design 1800–1830*, AGSA, Adelaide, 1998, no. 124. *Turner: The great watercolours*, Royal Academy, London, 2001, no. 92. *William Turner: Licht und Farbe*, Folkwang Museum, Essen and Kunsthaus Museum, Zurich, 2001, no. 155. *Island to Empire: 300 Years of British Art 1550–1850*, AGSA, Adelaide, 2005.

**Literature:** David Hill, *Turner in the North*, New Haven and London: Yale University Press, p. 71 (illus.). Walter Armstrong, *Turner*, p. 39. Michael Lloyd, *Turner*, Canberra: National Gallery of Australia, 1996, p. 77 (illus.). Ron Radford in Christopher Menz, *Regency*, Adelaide: AGSA, 1998, no. 124, pp. 71–72. Eric Shanes, *Turner: The great watercolours*, London: Royal Academy, 2001, p. 208, no. 92 (illus.). Andrew Wilton, *William Turner: Licht und Farbe: eine Ausstellung in Zusammenarbeit mit Tate*, Cologne, 2001, p. 348, no. 155, p. 218 (illus.).

**Condition:** Excellent.

# John Flaxman 1755–1826

John Flaxman was Britain's first and most celebrated Neoclassical sculptor. In the 1790s engravings published after his illustrations to Homer, Æschylus, Hesiod and Dante made him a crucial figure in the spread of Neoclassicism throughout Europe and for a while more famous on the Continent than any other British artist. The outline engravings were of seminal interest to painters as diverse as William Blake, Ingres, Goya, the German Nazarenes and later the English Pre-Raphaelites, Walter Crane and Aubrey Beardsley. His monuments in marble were a major contribution to British sculpture and a significant influence on Victorian tomb sculpture. He was a designer for Wedgwood and also provided designs for the royal goldsmiths Rundell, Bridge & Rundell.

Born in York in 1755, Flaxman was the son of a maker of plaster casts. The family moved to London shortly after his birth. In 1769 he became one of the first students at the newly established Royal Academy Schools and won a silver medal. The next year he began to exhibit at the Royal Academy's annual exhibitions. Flaxman was strongly influenced by classical Greek and Roman sculpture and by the pictorial decoration on ancient Greek vases. Later he also admired the simplicity and directness of late-Medieval and early-Renaissance painting and sculpture – particularly the sculpture of Lorenzo Ghiberti (1370–1455). In 1775 he began designing ceramics for Wedgwood's 'Etruria' factory and most notably modelled, in wax, Neoclassical reliefs for reproduction on the newly perfected 'Jasper' ware. In 1787 he travelled to Italy with Josiah Wedgwood's assistance and remained in Rome until 1794. In Rome his commissions for illustrations and sculptures came largely from English patrons.

Flaxman was elected an associate of the Royal Academy in 1797, a full member in 1800, and in 1810 he became the first Professor of Sculpture at the Academy. He joined the Swedenborg Society in 1810 and was a committee member in 1815 and 1817; the strong religious beliefs of Swedenborg greatly affected Flaxman's life. He died in London in 1826.

John Flaxman, 1755–1826, designer
Paul Storr, 1771–1844, silversmith

## Dessert stand, 1812/13

silver gilt, glass, 62.0 x 38.0 x 38.0 cm
Mr & Mrs J. H. Borthwick and family fund assisted by the Art Gallery of South Australia Foundation 1993

This dessert stand is also a significant piece of Regency sculpture. John Flaxman designed the classical figures and base for Rundell, Bridge & Rundell (1724/25–1843), a firm which received a royal warrant in 1797 and was appointed Crown Jewellers in 1820. The impressive object demonstrates the adoption of full Neoclassical style, particularly the robust Greek Revival, in Regency Britain. It also exemplifies the taste for opulent, expensive and massive tableware. Primarily for decoration, such centrepieces were placed along the axis of a banqueting table where they would hold decorative pyramids of fruit or occasionally arrangements of flowers.

The standing females are caryatids, based on the figures that support a porch of the Erechtheum temple on the Acropolis at Athens. Caryatids reappeared during the Renaissance and again after the emergence of Neoclassicism during the eighteenth century, but were particularly favoured within the movement's more scholarly Greek Revival at the beginning of the nineteenth century. Copies of the Erechtheum caryatid porch at St Pancras's Church, 1819–22, designed by W. & H. W. Inwood, are the most notable example in Regency architecture, and very conspicuous on Euston Road in London.

This style of dessert stand, with three caryatids supporting a bowl as if it were a ceremonial offering, was popular enough for Rundell's to supply over a dozen between 1809 and 1816. They were produced in various sizes, with slight variations, and the Gallery's example, hallmarked for the date 1812–13, is one of the larger and more impressive. These glamorous silver gilt objects were equally at home on the dining table or side table, where they were arranged decoratively, demonstrating their owners' wealth, taste and status. Smaller versions are in the Waterloo Chamber of the Wellington Museum, Apsley House, London and the Banqueting Room of the Royal Pavilion, Brighton. (The celebrated views by John Nash of the interiors of the Royal Pavilion show how grandly the silverware was displayed during the Regency period in the Banqueting Room. The table is usually set for the dessert course, based on the Nash view. The gilded silverware decorates the dining and side tables and was originally from the Londonderry and Ormonde collections, two famous Regency services. Much of this silver was supplied by Paul Storr.)

The silversmith Paul Storr (1771–1844) managed Rundell's silver plate workshops from 1807 and by 1811 was a partner in the firm. Another partner, the sculptor William Theed II (1764–1817), was the chief modeller when Flaxman's design was first executed in silver.[1] The fine craftsmanship in carrying out Flaxman's idea makes the dessert stand one of the high points of the decorative arts in the Neoclassical style of the Regency period. Storr was Britain's leading goldsmith

# John Flaxman

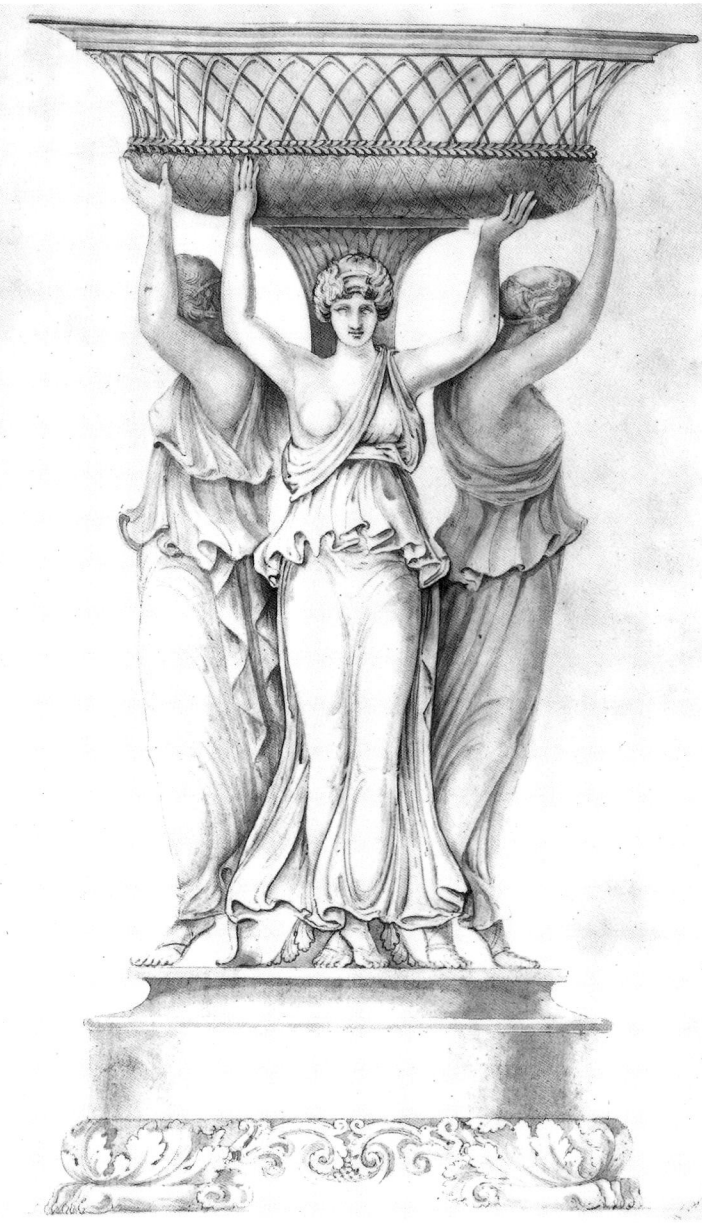

John Flaxman, *Design for a dessert stand*. V. & A. Images/Victoria & Albert Museum, London

and silversmith at the time. He was apprenticed to Andrew Fogelberg in 1785 and completed his apprenticeship in 1792 when he joined William Frisbee (represented in the Gallery's collection by a pair of dessert-dish covers). In 1793 Storr entered his own hallmark and was working independently in London and had established his leading position. He supplied Rundell's with silver from at least as early as 1799, and continued to use his own registered hallmark during the twelve years he worked within the firm, which he left in 1819 to establish his own business.

The design concept of the dessert stand was attributed until recently to the sculptor Thomas Stothard (1755–1834), who from 1809 to 1815 also designed silver for Rundell's and later designed decorations for the Grand Staircase and the Throne Room at Buckingham Palace. However, a design drawing held by the Print Room at the Victoria & Albert Museum is securely attributed to Flaxman[2] and is described as follows:

> Design for a fruit stand, the bottom section of which is adapted from a design for a silver-gilt candelabrum, one of a pair designed by John Flaxman for George IV when Prince of Wales, in the Royal Collection at Windsor Castle. These bear the maker's mark of Paul Storr and are dated 1809–10…. The three female figures in this design, which support a dish with basket-work sides, were also used for the central section of a silver-gilt dessert stand made for…[the] Prince Regent…[by] Paul Storr, dated 1817.[3]

The drawing indicates a deep bowl and a circular base. The Gallery's shallower bowl and higher tripod base supported by shells and festooned with flowers and leaves gives our variation more classical authenticity.

This sculptural stand ranks as the most impressive piece of Regency metalwork in an Australian public collection.

Inscription: Impressed marks on: lower platform "[lion passant]", "R", "[king's head]"; base of each acanthus leaf "[lion passant]", "[king's head]", "P.S"; upper platform "[lion passant]", "R", "[king"s head]"; back of drapery near lower hem of each caryatid "[king's head]", "[lion passant]", "P.S".

Provenance: Lady Astor, Hever Castle, Kent, c.1991; Asprey (Bond Street) Ltd, London.

Exhibitions: *Regency: British Art & Design 1800–1830*, AGSA, Adelaide, 1998, no. 88. *Island to Empire: 300 Years of British Art 1550–1850*, AGSA, Adelaide, 2005.

Literature: Christopher Menz, *Regency*, Adelaide: AGSA, 1998, pp. 21, 55. Ron Radford et al., *Treasures*, Adelaide: AGSA, 1998, p. 52.

Condition: Excellent. It apparently once had the coat of arms of the original owner on the base immediately under the caryatid figures but this was removed when it went on the market.

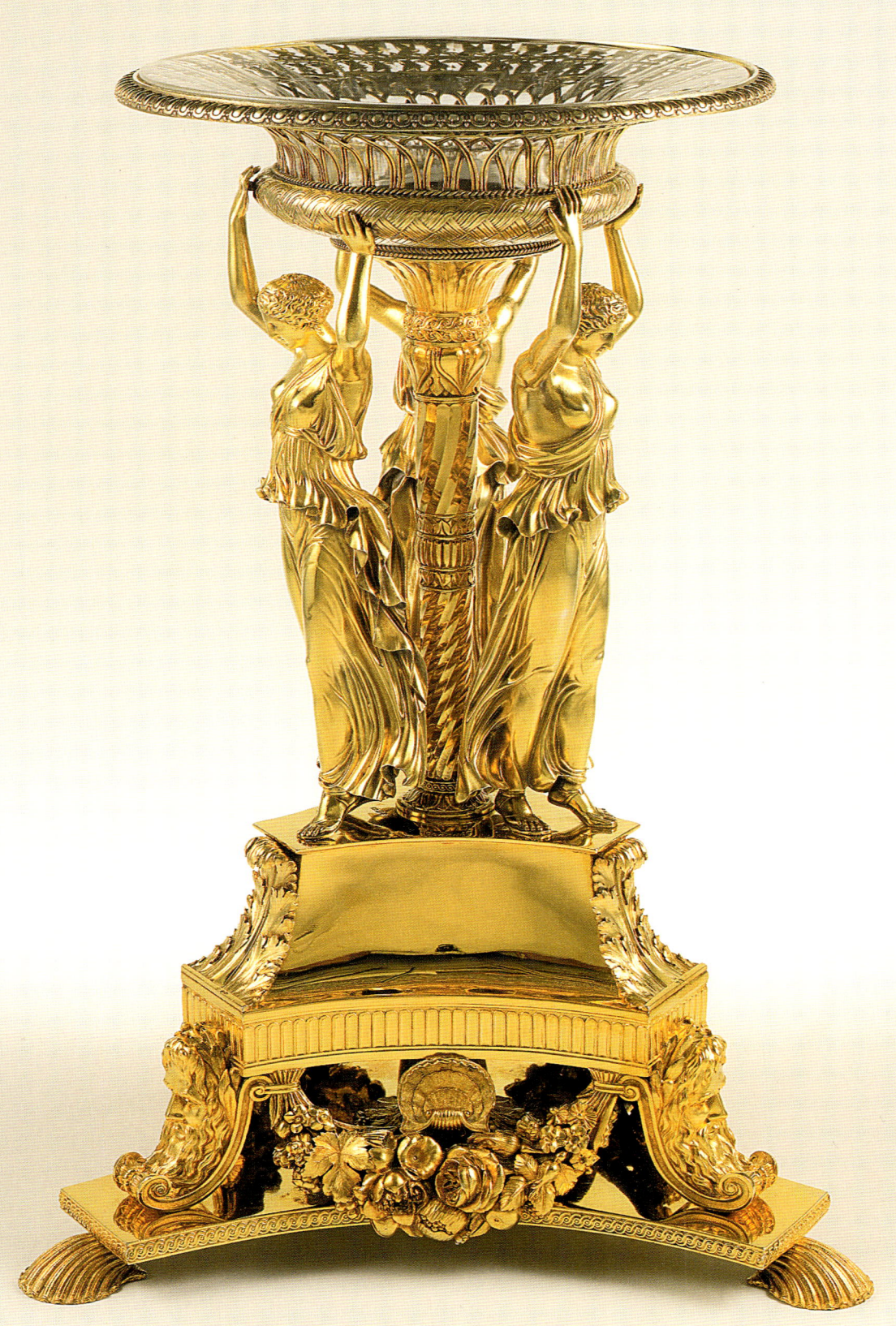

# John Flaxman

## Arcana Cœlestia: Novitiate spirits surrounded by a heavenly sphere, late 1790s?
pen & ink, ink wash, pencil on paper, 13.2 x 20.2 cm
South Australian Government Grant 1980

This drawing is one of Flaxman's eleven identified illustrations for *Arcana Cœlestia*, sometimes called *Heavenly Secrets*, a major work by the Swedish mystical philosopher and theosophist, Emanuel Swedenborg (1688–1772). Swedenborg's writings strongly influenced Flaxman's intense religious beliefs. The artist's drawings were apparently not intended for a specific publishing project but were personal ruminations over an extended period of time.

As early as 1784 Flaxman joined the newly established Theosophical Society which was founded to promote, translate and publicise Swedenborg's books, among them the twelve-volume *Arcana Cœlestia*, first published in 1747–56. In London in 1810 Flaxman was one of the founders of another association, The Society for Printing and Publishing the Writings of the Hon. Emanuel Swedenborg, and it has been suggested that his Swedenborg drawings were executed then.[1] The drawing *Arcana Cœlestia 464, Enoch Raised to Heaven* (Princeton Museum collection) is dated 1792 and is a finished presentation drawing unlike all the other *Arcana* illustrations, and was created while Flaxman was in Rome. It is likely that the remainder were done over the ensuing decades when he was again living in London.[2]

*Arcana Cœlestia* is an exegesis of the first two books of the Old Testament, Genesis and Exodus, with cross-references to almost every other part of the Bible. In his introduction Swedenborg makes the remarkable statement: "I have been allowed constantly and without interruption for several years now to share the experiences of spirits and angels, to listen to them speaking and to speak to them myself. I have been allowed therefore to hear and see astounding things in the next life." Flaxman's artistic imagination was inspired by such statements. What Swedenborg saw in the spiritual world is particularly relevant to this drawing.

It illustrates a specific incident in paragraph 542 of *Arcana Cœlestia* when Swedenborg describes how novitiate spirits are allowed temporarily to glimpse and experience heaven. Three bodily spirits are seen in the drawing. The supine foreground figure is overwhelmed by intense joy, covering his eyes with his arm to signal that he is unable to endure any more of the emotion. A second overwhelmed figure lies prostrate behind him. The background figure kneels in prayer but turns his head up towards the vision of circling angels above. The rendering of the earthly figures is almost cubically simplified, using a firm classical line in pen and ink, strengthened by grey wash. In the celestial sphere the hovering angels are hinted at by only suggestions of line.

Martha Gyllenhaal has pointed out that the celestial circle of angels and the praying figure ultimately derive from imagery in the *Story of Adam and Eve* reliefs designed around 1437 by Lorenzo Ghiberti for his doors of the Baptistry in Florence.[3] Flaxman greatly admired Ghiberti's sculpture. Gyllenhaal has also identified another Flaxman drawing, in the British Museum, which relates to the same paragraph of *Arcana Cœlestia* and illustrates the experience of the novitiate spirits. This, too, is a pen-and-ink drawing but without wash.[4]

| | |
|---|---|
| Inscription: | Inscribed l.r., pencil: "542 A : C". |
| Provenance: | Christopher Powney and Heim Gallery, London; Stanhope Shelton, Monks Eleigh, Suffolk. |
| Exhibitions: | *John Flaxman*, Heim Gallery, London, 1976, no. 37. *Prints and Drawings Acquisitions 1980-81*, AGSA, Adelaide, 1982. *Regency: British Art & Design 1800-1830*, AGSA, Adelaide, 1998, no. 135. *Island to Empire: 300 Years of British Art 1550-1850*, AGSA, Adelaide, 2005. |
| Literature: | Christopher Powney, *John Flaxman*, London: Heim Gallery, 1976, no. 37 (illus.). David Irwin, "John Flaxman's Drawings", *Burlington Magazine*, May 1976, p. 333 (illus. pp. 335-36). Martha Gyllenhaal, "John Flaxman's Illustrations to Emanuel Swedenborg's Coelestia", *Studia Swedenborgiana*, vol. 9, no. 4, 1996, plate VII, pp. 17-19. Ron Radford in Christopher Menz, *Regency*, Adelaide: AGSA, 1998, p 76. |
| Condition: | Good. |

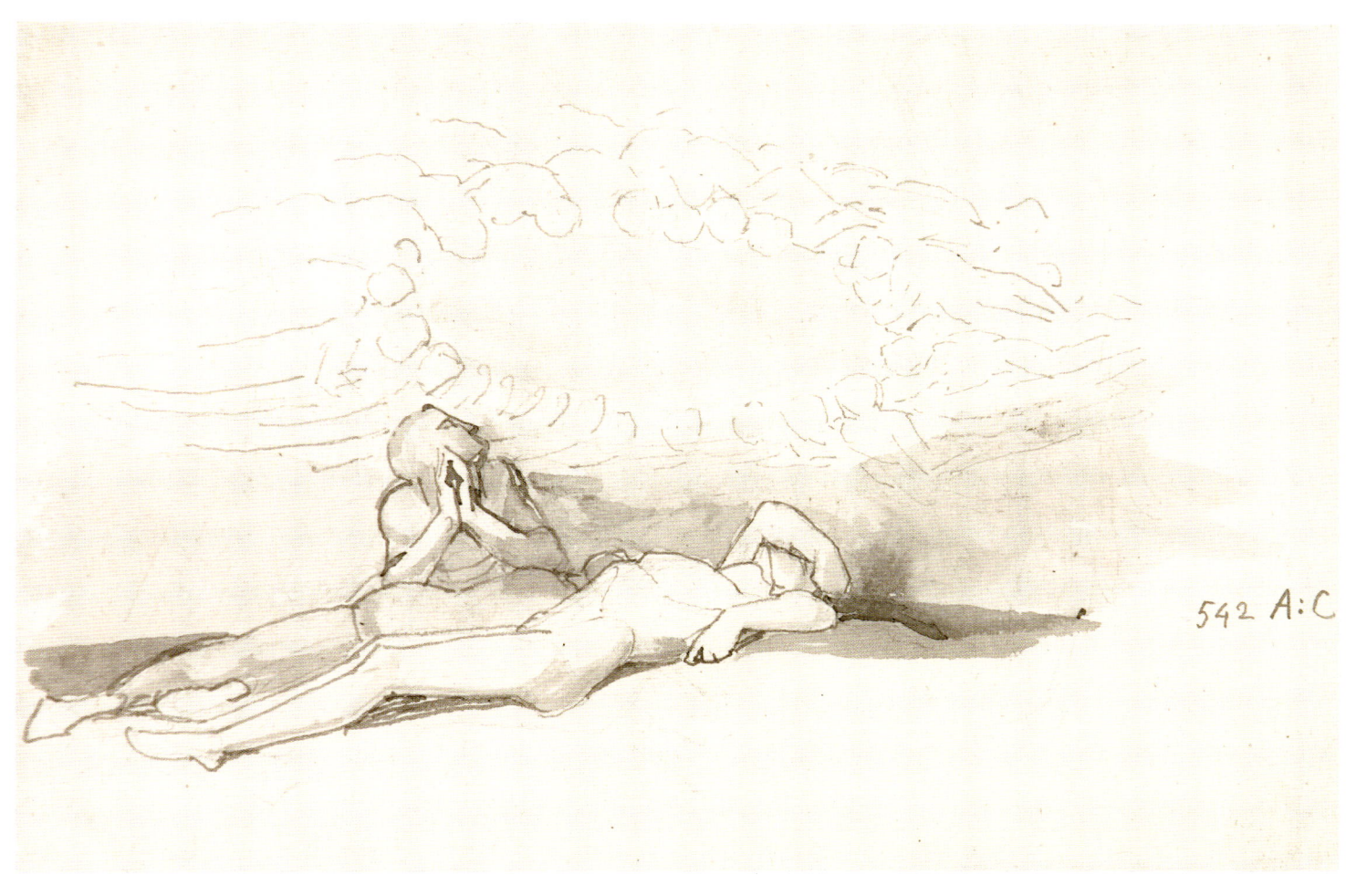

# Ferdinand Bauer 1760–1826

Ferdinand Bauer is regarded as the greatest natural-history artist of all time. He worked prolifically in his birthplace Austria and in Britain but a momentous trip to Australia inspired perhaps his finest works. A member of the scientific party on Matthew Flinders's circumnavigation voyage of Australia, Bauer chose to remain in Sydney for a period after Flinders's departure in 1803. He was the most important artist to come to Australia before John Glover's arrival in Tasmania thirty years after Bauer's first landfall in Western Australia. Bauer was in Australia and Australian waters for less than four years – December 1801 to June/July 1805 – and was enormously productive. His contribution was probably more important for Australian culture than that of two other itinerant nineteenth-century artists who stayed for equally short but significant periods: Augustus Earle for four years in the 1820s and Charles Conder for six years in the 1880s.

However, granted his importance to Australian colonial art, here we are chiefly concerned with Ferdinand Bauer's two substantial periods of work in Britain. The first was from 1787 to 1801; towards the end of the second, which was from 1805 to 1814, he produced his only surviving oil painting, the Gallery's still-life of *Passionflowers*.

Ferdinand Lukas Bauer was born in 1760 at Feldsberg, Austria (now Valtice, Czech Republic). He was a son of Lukas Bauer, a court painter for Prince Josef Wenzel von Liechtenstein; his mother, Theresia, after her husband's premature death, taught Ferdinand and his brothers to emulate their father's painting methods. Ferdinand's eldest brother Josef eventually succeeded their father as court painter of still-lives for the Liechtensteins at their summer residence at Feldsberg whereas Franz (1758–1840), two years older than Ferdinand, became another botanical artist, eventually working under the name Francis Bauer in England.

Franz and Ferdinand trained at Feldsberg with the botanist Dr Norbert Boccius who taught them an exacting scientific technique using a colour code to record plants promptly from life, before finishing the picture later in the studio. The brothers' skills were further refined in Vienna by working for Nikolaus Joseph von Jacquin, director of the botanic gardens and professor of botany at the university.

In 1784 John Sibthorp (1758–96), professor of botany at Oxford, was in Vienna on his way to study afresh the plants of the eastern Mediterranean, and employed Ferdinand as his painter on scientific fieldwork in Italy, Greece and Asia Minor. It was Bauer's first taste of life as a travelling natural-history artist. Back in Oxford, by the end of the project he had made nearly a thousand large watercolours. His second expedition began in 1801 on HMS *Investigator* under Captain Matthew Flinders, undertaking a hydrographic survey of the New Holland coasts for the Admiralty (the name Australia was not yet in use) but also, on Sir Joseph Banks's advice, carrying a party of naturalists. Banks, president of the Royal Society and leader of the scientific establishment in Britain, had already been employing Ferdinand and Francis Bauer, and recommended that Ferdinand be appointed natural-history artist to the expedition. The scientific leader on the voyage was the botanist Robert Brown (1773–1858). He collected previously unclassified specimens whose exact colouration Bauer recorded with a chart of up to one thousand shades. In 1805 Bauer returned to London with a wealth of preparatory material: 1500 drawings of plants and 230 drawings of mammals, reptiles and fish. The drawings had been rapidly executed in pencil, and many of them would be later transformed into finished watercolours, some of which in turn were engraved for publication in Flinders's *A Voyage to Terra Australis* (1814) and in Bauer's *Illustrationes floræ Novaæ Hollandiæ*, which appeared in parts from 1813.

Bauer left London for Vienna in 1814 and continued painting both wild and cultivated plants. His career ended when he became seriously ill in 1825 and he died unmarried in Vienna early in the following year.

## Passionflowers, 1812
oil on wood panel, 34.3 x 25.0 cm
Mary Overton Gift Fund 2000

*Passionflowers* is one of only four paintings in oil known to have been painted by Bauer, all exhibited in London at the Royal Academy in 1813.[1] The other three, present whereabouts unknown, were *Group of Flowers*, *Group of Flowers from New Holland*, and *Group of Flowers from Cape of Good Hope*. The vast body of his work was in watercolour or pencil on paper.

Exuding a striking exoticism, both the botanical species and the butterfly included in this pyramidal floral arrangement originate from Brazil. Bauer never visited South America but he would have had no trouble seeing specimens in the Royal Botanic Gardens at Kew or Vienna at Schönbrunn. The passionflower, of which there are three species depicted in this painting, seems to have fascinated Bauer throughout his career. The first painting dedicated to the subject was completed when he was still a student in Feldsberg, and the last was painted the year before he died. This 1812 still-life is his only portrayal in oils. The British watercolour boom was subsiding and watercolours were not encouraged by the Royal Academy. It is likely that Bauer executed *Passionflowers* and his other three oil paintings hoping to be taken seriously as an exhibition artist by this British institution of the highest artistic prestige. His father and oldest brother had painted still-lives in oil of flowers and game for their princely patrons,

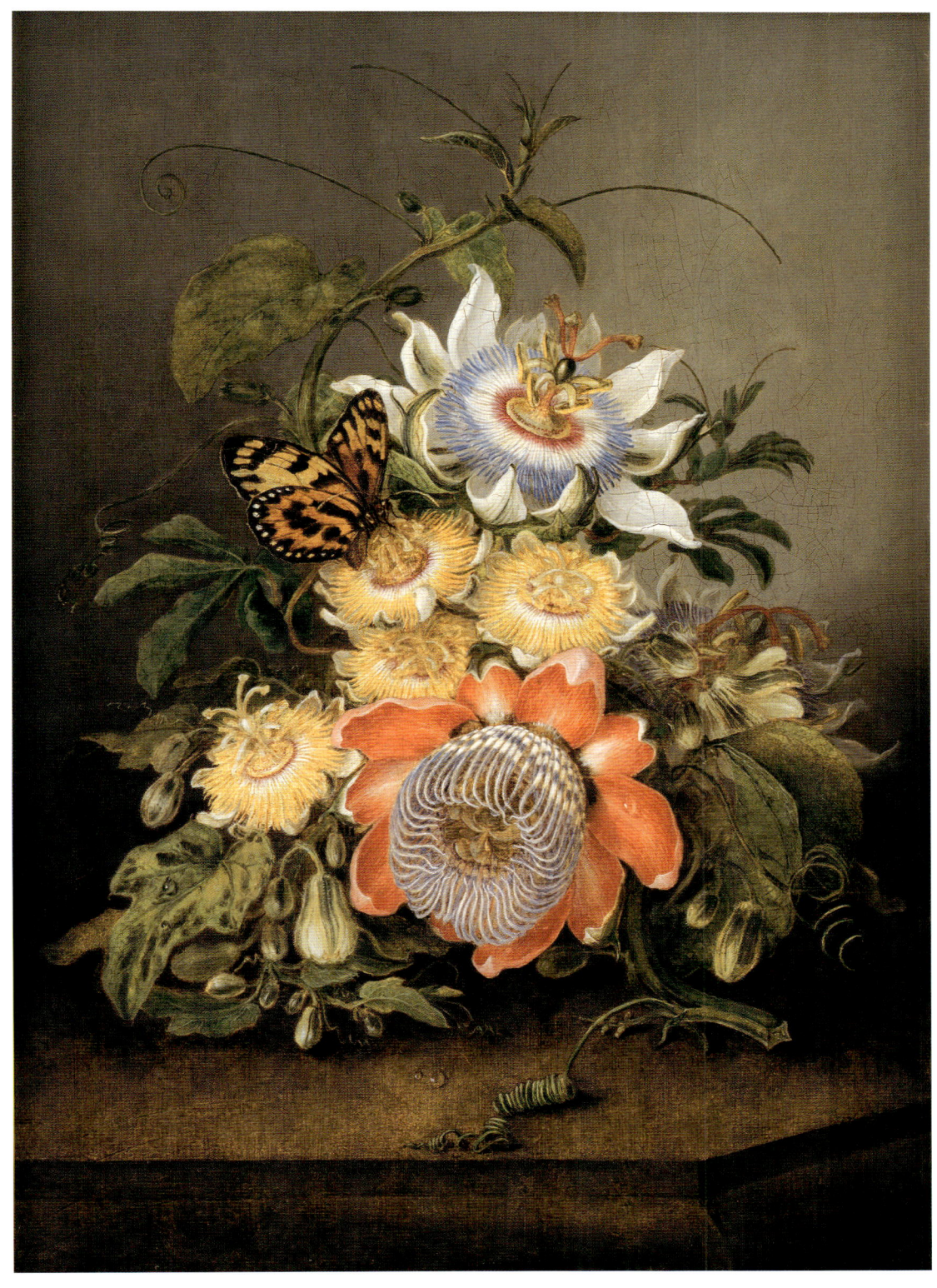

the Liechtensteins.

The three different passionflowers are posed as a rather unlikely combined spray – only one stem readily visible – on what appears to be a sideboard. Diminutive droplets of water on the furniture top, and on a leaf and a petal, suggest the sprays have been freshly picked. With stems exposed and out of water they will soon die, as will the short-lived butterfly. These allusions to the transience of life take the painting into the realm of seventeenth-century Dutch still-life painting, which indeed Bauer's realist style plainly emulates.

The passionflower received its symbolic name from Christian missionaries in its native South America early in the seventeenth century. They saw the cruciform of the stamen and the delicate parts of the flower as icons of Christ's passion.[2] However, the complex and beautiful flower structure may have been what particularly attracted Bauer, as it extended and showcased his great technical virtuosity.

Nevertheless, detailed as this tiny oil is, it lacks the refinement and subtlety of Bauer's watercolours, and it appears that he never again attempted to paint in oil. He left London permanently the year after he exhibited his four oils at the Royal Academy.

This is the only authenticated painting by Ferdinand Bauer held in an Australian public collection. It is unfortunate that none of his watercolours can be seen in Australia.

**Inscription:** Signed l.l., oil: "Fer.d Bauer". Inscribed and dated verso c., pen & ink: "Fer.d Bauer / 16 May 1812"

**Provenance:** From the mid twentieth century William Leonard Hughes, Llanelli, Carmarthenshire, South Wales; thence to his grand-daughter Janet Wareing, Lancashire, 1997; Hordern House, Sydney, 1999.

**Exhibitions:** Royal Academy, 1813, no. 731. *The Encounter, 1802: Art of the Flinders and Baudin Voyages*, AGSA, 2002. *Island to Empire: 300 Years of British Art 1550–1850*, AGSA, Adelaide, 2005.

**Literature:** Sarah Thomas, *The Encounter, 1802*, Adelaide: AGSA, 2002, pp. 98–99 (illus.).

**Condition:** Excellent; last conserved in 1999 in Sydney.

**Frame:** Not original.

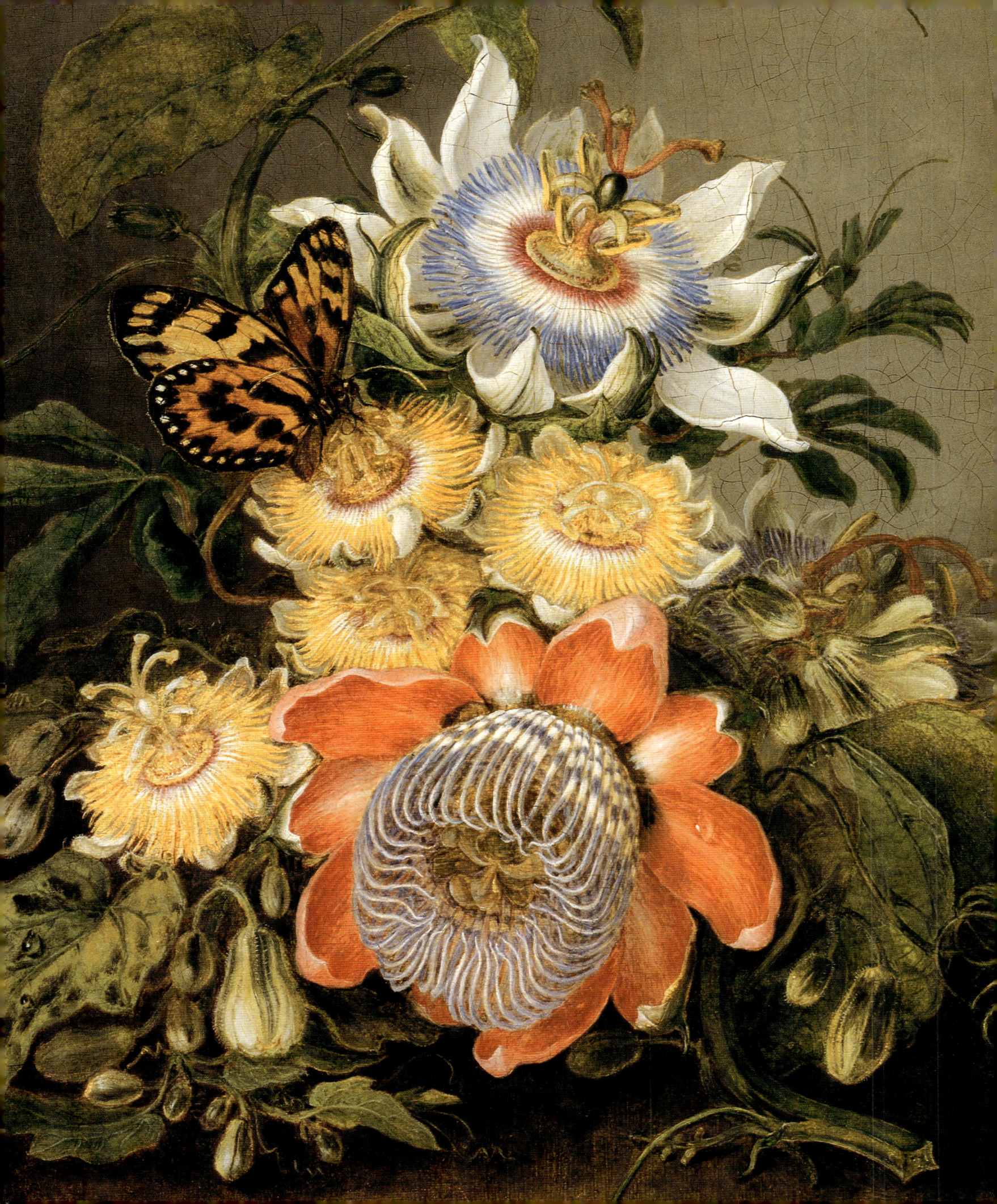

# Francis Chantrey 1781–1841

Francis Chantrey was the most successful and prolific British sculptor of portrait busts in the first third of the nineteenth century, and probably the finest. He was also a sculptor of monuments and tomb sculptures. His busts, nearly all of eminent men, are based on the classical Roman portrait format but show artistic inventiveness, dignity and a sensitivity to the sitter's character. His contemporary, the English genre painter C. R. Leslie, was justified in describing him as "the Reynolds of Portrait sculpture".

Chantrey was born in 1781 in the village of Norton near Sheffield and was the son of a small tenant farmer and carpenter. In 1797 he was apprenticed in Sheffield to Robert Ramsay, a decorative carver, a dealer in plaster models and prints and also an art restorer. However, Chantrey cancelled his apprenticeship in 1802 and set up as a portrait artist in crayons and miniatures and at the end of that year went to London. He studied at the Royal Academy Schools and in 1805 began to receive commissions for sculptured busts. It is claimed that only after seeing and being inspired by the Parthenon Marbles – brought to London by Lord Elgin and visible to artists from 1806 at his house in Park Lane and later bought for the British Museum – did Chantrey develop his astonishing talent for carving marble to resemble living flesh. In about 1809 he married his cousin Mary Ann Wale, whose dowry of over £1000 helped him set up a comfortable house and well-equipped studio in Pimlico.

In 1811 Chantrey received his first major success at the Royal Academy exhibitions with a bust of the radical politician Horne Tooke, and won a competition to execute his first larger sculpture in marble, a statue of King George III for the City of London. (It was destroyed in a 1940 air raid that bombed the Guildhall.) He was proud of the royal statue and in 1815 he took his mentor Antonio Canova, whom he had met in Rome earlier that year, to see it when Europe's most famous sculptor was visiting London. From the time he finished the 1811 City of London commission Chantrey's career was secure. He had a large sculpture workshop in which assistants helped him make hundreds of marble busts. He produced no less than seventeen standard busts of George IV and thus fashioned a memorable public image of that king. As well as George III and George IV he was also commissioned to make busts of King William IV and the young Queen Victoria; hers was his last work.

Chantrey exhibited at the Royal Academy from 1804, was elected an associate in 1815 and a full member in 1818, was knighted in 1835 and died in 1841 leaving a fortune of £150,000 to his wife for life and, after her death, to the Royal Academy. The Chantrey Bequest was for "the encouragement of British Fine Art in Painting and Sculpture".

## King George III, 1813
marble, 72.0 x 58.0 x 24.0 cm
Morgan Thomas Bequest Fund 1951

This bust of George III is dated 1813. Some time between December 1809 and mid 1810 Chantrey had obtained at least two sittings with the ailing monarch who was then over seventy years old.[1] His sitter was already suffering from the mental derangement that led to confinement and the declaration of a Regency in February 1811. It is not certain who commissioned the sittings, perhaps intended for a portrait to celebrate the Golden Jubilee in 1810 of the King's fifty-year rule, perhaps preparatory to the commission that the City of London placed in 1811 for its full-size statue of the King. It is also not known who commissioned the Gallery's bust though it might have been the first Earl of Brownlow, at whose Belton House the bust seems to have been recorded, in a descendant's ownership, in the mid twentieth century.[2] In 1813, the year of its completion, the Royal College of Surgeons commissioned a similar bust, completed in 1814, which it still holds.

In spite of his habitual use of the devices of a Roman classical sculptural base and classical robes (which hang over the royal chain of office and the royal insignia of the Order of the Garter), the Gallery's bust is nonetheless a decidedly unclassical portrait. The King is wearing a wig that was fashionable in the late eighteenth century, and his features are not as idealised as those of ancient Roman emperors. Instead he is a jowly-faced, weak-chinned, round-shouldered old man. The open mouth and intense stare can be read as an expression of bewilderment, indeed appearing almost disturbed. This George III lacks the assertively patrician qualities we see in Chantrey's later busts of George IV and William IV. In spite of the inclusion of the chain of highest office, Chantrey has produced not a symbol of kingship but a realist portrait of a vulnerable human. Of course, realism is a striking characteristic of ancient Roman portrait heads of the Republican period and one can perhaps read the portrayal as an affirmation of parliamentary constitutional monarchy. This sympathetic yet undignified bust of the old King in classical drapery on a classical base should be compared with the Gallery's painting, by Allan Ramsay (p. 127), of him in the classical pose of a commanding monarch but dressed in modern coronation robes, a young man full of youthful promise.

A work from the very beginning of Chantrey's successful career, the sculpture shares with the one-year-later version a more highly-polished marble finish as well as a more painstaking realism of style than is found in his later productions. Chantrey probably would have charged £125, the same price he received for the version commissioned by the Royal College of Surgeons.[3]

The Chantrey studio's mass production of busts of George IV and William IV are admittedly fine but this 1813 portrait of George III is more sensitive. It and the Royal College of Surgeons' 1814 version are Chantrey's only known busts of the king who was hidden away by 1813 and died in 1820.

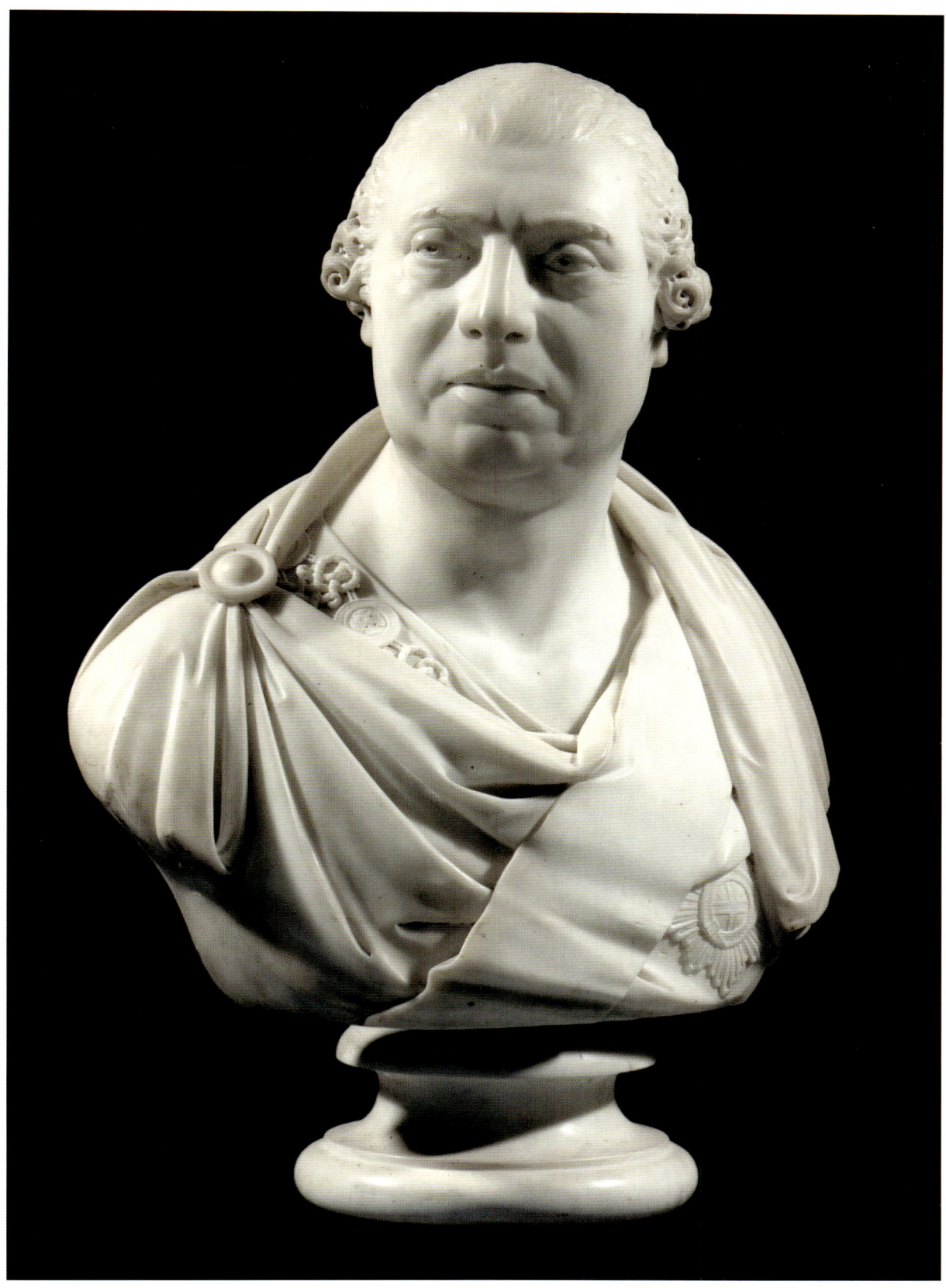

| | |
|---|---|
| **Inscription**: | Incised on back column: "CHANTREY / Sculptor / 1813". |
| **Provenance**: | Belton House, Lincolnshire; bought for the Art Gallery from Gerald Kerin, London, on the advice of H. D. Molesworth 1951. |
| **Exhibitions**: | *Regency: British Art & Design 1800–1830*, AGSA, Adelaide, 1998, no. 153. *Island to Empire: 300 Years of British Art 1550–1850*, AGSA, Adelaide, 2005. |
| **Literature**: | Ron Radford in Christopher Menz, *Regency,* Adelaide: AGSA, 1998, pp. 34, 81. |
| **Condition**: | Excellent. |

# Charles Eastlake 1793–1865

Charles Eastlake's achievements as a painter have been dramatically overshadowed by his mid-nineteenth-century fame as a connoisseur, scholar and art-politician. His career culminated in election as President of the Royal Academy and a knighthood in 1850 and, finally, his appointment in 1855 as the first professional Director of the National Gallery in London. His lasting contributions are the inspired purchases for the National Gallery of late-Medieval and early-Renaissance Italian and Flemish masters, acquired against the prevailing taste of the period. His contemporaries generally considered the works too primitive. Although these great acquisitions were relatively inexpensive Eastlake had a certain amount of opposition. Therefore in 1864, when he was invited to make the first purchases for Australia's first art museum, the National Gallery of Victoria, he did not venture to suggest affordable pre-Renaissance masterpieces for Melbourne. He instead purchased largely contemporary British paintings, some with historical British themes – all of which he must have considered culturally instructive for the infant colony.

His lofty official position in the mid-Victorian art world of the British Empire has obscured his own classical figure compositions and landscapes. And those works have been responsible in turn for the obscurity of his oil-studies executed in the open air, of which the Gallery's is one of the most delightful examples.

Charles Lock Eastlake was born in 1793 in Plymouth, which was also the birthplace of Joshua Reynolds, who had died the year before Eastlake's birth. Reynolds's commanding art-world position and his academic principles are what Eastlake was eventually to emulate. At grammar school in Plymouth, Eastlake was one of the first pupils of the young watercolour artist Samuel Prout, uncle and teacher of the Australian colonial artist John Skinner Prout (1805–1876). He studied in London as the first pupil of the history painter Benjamin Robert Haydon who also originally hailed from Plymouth. Under Haydon he gained a strong academic training in technique and subject matter which was significant for his subsequent development.

In 1814 and 1815 Eastlake was in Paris to study the vast gathering of art treasures in the Louvre, many of which Napoleon had plundered from all over Europe. Then in 1816 he travelled to Rome and remained based in Italy for the next fourteen years. He also visited Greece. In Rome he came in contact with the German brotherhood of religious painters known as the Nazarenes, whose meticulously finished paintings closely followed the simplicity of style and the religious sincerity of the Italian masters before Raphael. It was the Nazarenes who helped consolidate Eastlake's own art and taste. They, and German art historians working in Italy, introduced him to Italian fourteenth- and fifteenth-century painting, masterpieces of which he was later to buy for the National Gallery. He died in Pisa in 1865.

## Cypress trees at the Villa d'Este, 1817
oil on card, 26.0 x 24.2 cm
d'Auvergne Boxall Bequest Fund and South Australian Government Grant 1990

Painted on the spot in 1817, this tiny and charming view of the ancient cypress trees at the bottom of the famous gardens of the Villa d'Este dates from Eastlake's first visit to Tivoli. The painting is among the finest of the thirty small oil sketches he executed during the visit but the place so enchanted him that he was inspired to return many times.

Only a couple of hours from Rome, the picturesque hills of Tivoli, with their sublime cascades, had been a refuge from hectic city life, and a summer retreat, since classical antiquity. From the Renaissance its beautiful natural scenery and its cliff-top ruins, in particular the circular Temple of the Sybil, made Tivoli a place to which most artists, particularly landscape painters, undertook a pilgrimage. The great seventeenth-century landscape painter Claude Lorrain made many sketching trips to Tivoli and his near-contemporary, the landscape artist Gaspard Dughet, even had a house there.

The gardens of the sixteenth-century Villa d'Este[1] are a spectacular and steeply sloping series of terraces holding one hundred ponds and fifty fountains. The formal arrangement is emphasised by neat box and tall laurel hedges. The garden is studded with a profusion of statues, grottoes, gargoyles and other grotesque decorations that help to make it a masterpiece of Italian Mannerist landscape architecture. Although today the garden is fully restored to its original magnificence, by the end of the eighteenth century it had fallen into disrepair, becoming a romantic wasted garden that appealed greatly to artists of that time.

Artists were particularly attracted to the ancient cypresses, especially the paired rows conspicuously and centrally planted at the bottom of the garden around what is known as the Rotunda of Cypress. They are what Eastlake records in this painting. These large and dramatically twisted trees, believed to have been planted in the later part of the sixteenth century, feature in pictures by many artists[2]. The row on the left survives into the early twenty-first century, partly propped up by scaffolding. Claimed to be the oldest cypresses in Italy, they still delight amateur and professional photographers.

Eastlake painted his subject from the lower central steps of the near-vertical gardens, with the Villa d'Este high behind him. A front entrance, now rarely used, can be seen between the trees, beyond which are the rooftops of the village and the hills of Tivoli. Like Fragonard before him, Eastlake has

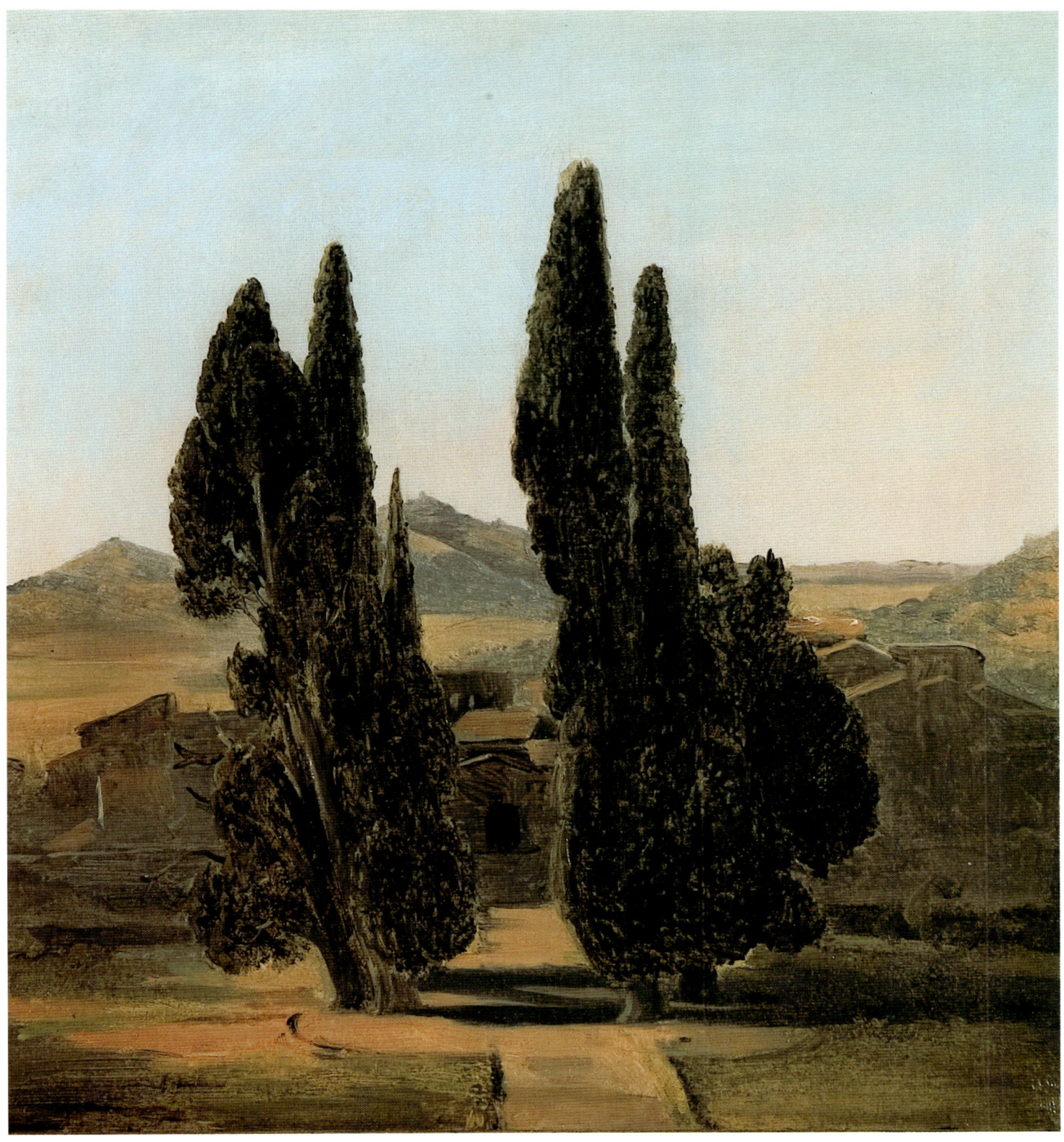

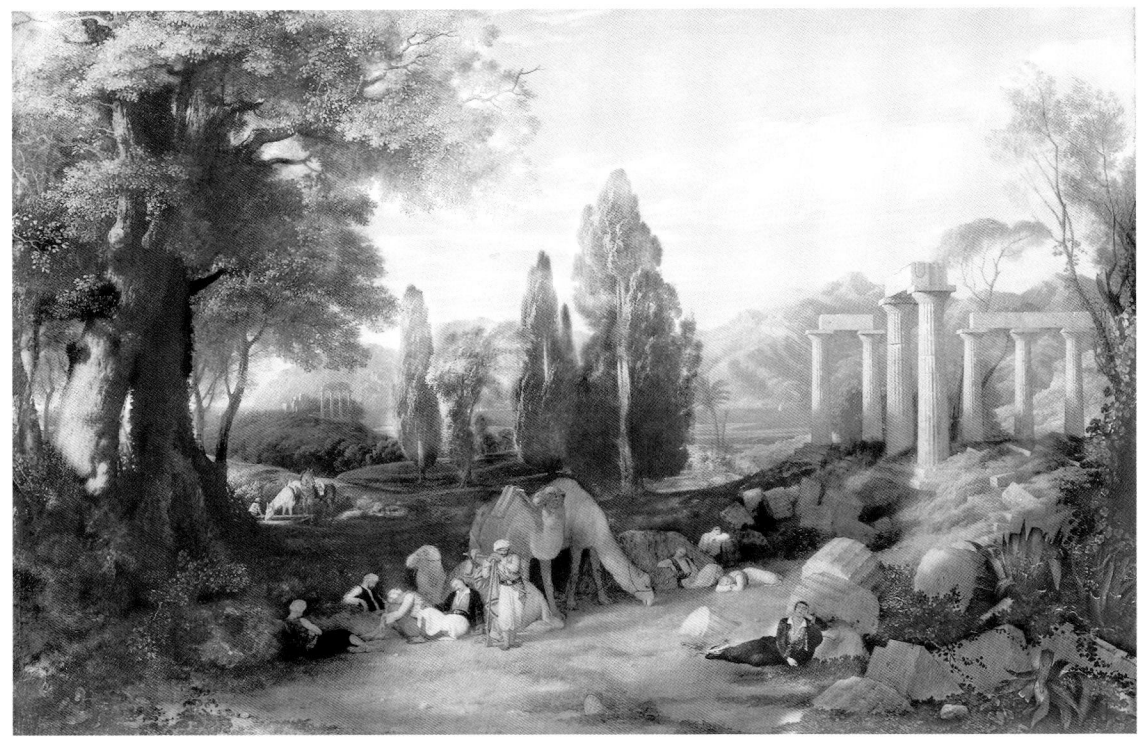

Charles Eastlake, *Lord Byron's 'Dream'*, 1827. © Tate, London 2004

placed the aisle of trees in the centre of the composition, their vertical sculptured shapes the main focus in what is almost a symmetrical parody of a balanced classical landscape. By the end of the eighteenth century vertical cypresses were romantically associated with ancient ruins and had become the trees of European graveyards. They were and still are seen by romantics as living monuments to the passing of time. Appreciation of their pointing verticality coincided with the Gothic Revival in the early nineteenth century. But Eastlake has not explored the romantic potential of the cypresses in this painting; he was to leave that to a later composition. Here he was more concerned to register the clarity of their form against clear Italian sky in the brilliant southern European sunlight that has long fascinated northern European artists.

This is a rare and tantalisingly early British example of an artist actually finishing an oil landscape out of doors in front of the subject, a spontaneous notation of the light and the colour of a particular place at a particular moment. More than forty years later it was the process which the French Impressionists would make the raison d'être of their art. By 1817 Constable was also exploring the possibilities of the oil sketch; Richard Parkes Bonington, the other English master of spontaneous outdoor painting, would do so a little later, in the 1820s, as would the French precursor of Impressionism, Camille Corot.

Perhaps Eastlake in this direct study was responding to his early training as an outdoor watercolourist under Samuel Prout. It is more likely, however, that he was following an academic procedure common since the eighteenth century of on-the-spot oil sketches to be used as reference material for compositions worked-up to greater complexity in the studio. He recalled these Villa d'Este cypresses in his large studio painting *Lord Byron's Dream*, 1827 (Tate, London) (see above) where cypresses are placed centrally in the background with Greek ruins. However, Adelaide's exquisite oil sketch has a freshness and clarity not found in Eastlake's overworked studio pieces.

Provenance: Painted for Jeremiah Harman, Higham House, Woodford, Essex; W. Fuller Maitland (1813–1876), Stansted Hall, Essex, thence by descent; Agnew's, London.

Exhibitions: *Images of Victorian Life*, Agnew's, London, 1990, no. 4. *A Celebration: Recent acquisitions of heritage and contemporary art*, AGSA, Adelaide, 1996. *Regency: British Art & Design 1800–1830*, AGSA, Adelaide, 1998, no. 101. *Island to Empire: 300 Years of British Art 1550–1850*, AGSA, Adelaide, 2005.

Literature: *Images of Victorian Life*, London: Agnew's, 1990, no. 4. Ron Radford in Christopher Menz, *Regency*, Adelaide: AGSA, 1998, p. 60 (illus.).

Condition: Excellent; conserved in London prior to acquisition.

Frame: Not original.

# Samuel Howitt 1756–1822

Born in 1756 of an old Nottinghamshire Quaker family, Howitt was at first a country gentleman living at Chigwell, Epping Forest, Essex, where he was devoted to field sports. He took up painting only when financial difficulties forced him to do so, after which he moved to London and attended a Dr Goodenough's academy at Ealing. On marriage to Thomas Rowlandson's sister his work of the 1780s and 1790s took on a less animated version of his brother-in-law's style, not only in characterisation but also in the technique of pen-and-ink outline with watercolour. Howitt's subjects recorded the outdoor activities that he himself enjoyed, namely hunting and horse-racing. The Gallery has a lively watercolour drawing from this period, a horsey adventure subject entitled *The Smugglers alarmed by Excise Men*. He produced a few popular rustic scenes and from 1785 exhibited intermittently at the Royal Academy.

At the beginning of the nineteenth century Howitt's interests shifted towards natural history. He illustrated a number of sporting and zoological works including *Miscellaneous Etchings of Animals*, 50 plates (1803), *British Field Sports*, 20 plates (1807), Captain T. Williamson's *Oriental Field Sports*, 41 plates (1807), *A New Work of Animals principally designed from the Fables of Æsop*, 56 plates (1811), *Groups of Animals*, 24 plates (1811) and *The British Sportsman*, 70 plates (1812).

Howitt occasionally painted in oil and was a fine etcher. He died in Somers Town, London, in 1822.

## Kangaroos (Didelphis Gigantia), c.1818
watercolour on paper, 24.7 x 18.4 cm
South Australian Government Grant 1955

This illustrative study of two kangaroos was executed about 1818, near the end of Samuel Howitt's career. It is among the earliest recordings made from life in Europe of these Australian marsupials. Kangaroos had been visually recorded since James Cook's voyage traced the east coast of Australia in 1770 and from the first years after British colonisation in 1788. However, most early images produced in Europe of this then novel creature were based on George Stubbs's painting of c.1773, itself based on a stuffed specimen skin that had been brought back to England in 1770 by Joseph Banks who had accompanied Cook on the South Sea voyage. Stubbs's image was engraved, engraved copies were made of those engravings, and they were likewise copied. So by about 1820 many images of the best known of Australian native animals were scarcely recognisable as kangaroos at all. They often looked like giant rats and sometimes were hardly distinguishable from possums. Thus Howitt's depiction from life could have been somewhat surprising to people who had not seen a kangaroo in the flesh.[1]

Howitt's watercolour drawing appears to have been done from live zoo specimens and relates to his other kangaroo illustrations which occur, together with sketches of other Australian animals (some mistakenly identified), in a sketchbook now held at the Yale Center for British Art.[2] His inscription on one of the Yale kangaroo studies, sketchbook page 56, is "*Life summary specimens*" and on ours it is "*From life many times*". The Gallery's drawing is very similar to the one on page 56 of the Yale sketchbook. The Yale study reverses both kangaroos and adds another kangaroo lying between them. Apart from the reclining central kangaroo in the sketchbook version, they are almost mirror images.

In the Gallery's version Howitt has washed in a suggestion of an Australian coastal habitat but otherwise it is so close to the one in the sketchbook that it was probably once part of that book. The size of the Gallery's watercolour sheet is exactly that of the sketchbook pages, of which page 57 is missing; pages 54 to 56 are of kangaroos. Howitt's hand-written index to the sketchbook has ditto marks indexing page 57 under those identifying the kangaroos on pages 54, 55 and 56 and he has written "T Lying O. NSW", possibly an abbreviation of "Two [kangaroos] lying, of New South Wales". Thus the Gallery's drawing could well be the missing page 57 of the Yale sketchbook. The artist himself may have removed the page, perhaps as a gift. If it is from the Yale sketchbook then it would be of the same date which must be after 1817, the latest watermark date in the Whatman's paper of the book.

Although Howitt's images of the kangaroos are meant to be scientific specimens – hence his inscription *Didelphis Gigantia* on the Gallery's watercolour – and therefore are more accurate than the distorted engravings based on other engravings, they are nonetheless somewhat stylised. He has made the heads of the pair of kangaroos and their joey in the pouch sentimentally appealing, even rather toy-like. With exaggerated size of eyes and ears they take on an endearing doe-like appearance. He was in fact very fond of deer which he regularly illustrated, presenting them in an overly gentle

# Samuel Howitt

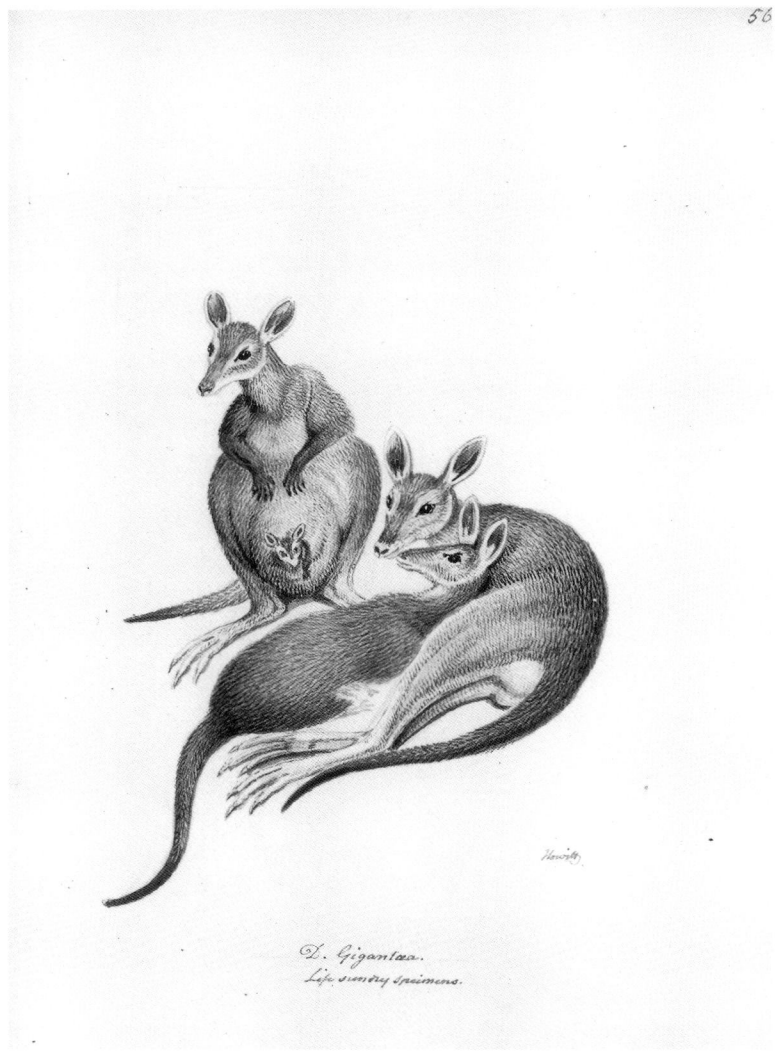

Samuel Howitt, *Sketchbook of Samuel Howitt, p. 56: D. Gigantea. Life sundry specimens*. Paul Mellon Collection, Yale Center for British Art, New Haven

manner. Howitt, like his brother-in-law Rowlandson, was prone to characterisation and even his published natural-history studies are sentimentalised; the foxes in his *Fables of Æsop*, for instance, are crafty. Howitt has not only exaggerated the kangaroos' heads, their bodies also take on the appearance of soft toys. His natural-history illustrations often transgressed empiric scientific recording.

From an Australian point of view, this watercolour drawing (and its sketchbook companions) is not only of interest as an early recording made in Britain of the animal which has long been Australia's national symbol. Its date coincides with the invocation of the kangaroo, by the first colonial poet Barron Field, as "Thou Spirit of Australia".[3] It is also an example of the specialist British practice from which much of Australia's non-Aboriginal artistic tradition originated. Natural-history painting, recording the curiosities of what was to European eyes a strange land, was the dominant motivation of Australian art for the first twenty years of European settlement.

Inscription: Signed l.l., pen & brown ink: "Howitt". Inscribed pencil: bot. c., "Didelphis Gigantea."; l.r. "from Life many times".

Provenance: Purchased from P. & D. Colnaghi, London, on the advice of H. D. Molesworth, 1955.

Exhibitions: *Regency: British Art & Design 1800–1830*, AGSA, Adelaide, 1998, no. 111. *Island to Empire: 300 Years of British Art 1550–1850*, AGSA, Adelaide, 2005.

Literature: *NGSA Catalogue of Oil and Water-colour Paintings and Pastels with Biographical Notes*, Adelaide: NGSA, 1960, p. 127. Ron Radford in Christopher Menz, *Regency*, Adelaide: AGSA, 1998, p. 66 (illus.).

Condition: Excellent.

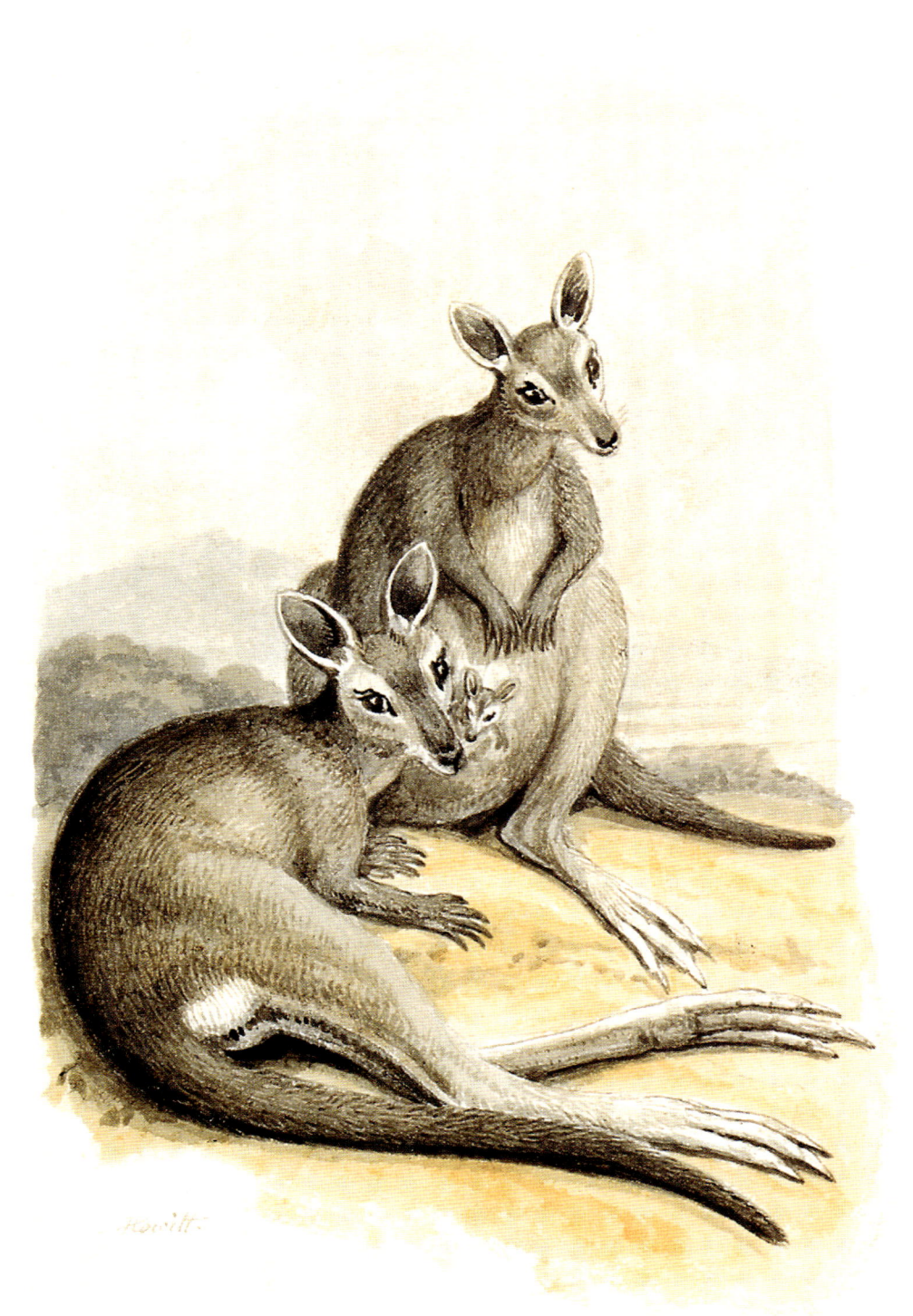

*Didelphis Gigantea*

# John Glover 1767–1849

John Glover is now most admired, both in Australia and Britain, for his oil paintings of Tasmanian landscapes. Executed after his arrival in Hobart from London in 1831, aged sixty-four, they are the climax of his long career and they make him Australia's most significant early-colonial artist. However, his career as a watercolour and oil painter in England is also significant. His ease with classical landscape composition earned him the title of an "English Claude". (He owned two landscapes by Claude Lorrain which he sometimes exhibited with his own for favourable comparison, and he owned a version of the Gallery's *Cicero with his friend Atticus and brother Quintus, at his villa at Arpinum*, 1771 (p. 141), by Richard Wilson who in his day had been another "English Claude".) But Glover, as well as following Claude and other seventeenth-century Italian masters, had another manner for farming and animal subjects, based on Dutch realism.

Born at Houghton-on-the-Hill, Leicestershire, in 1767, he was the son of a farmer; his parentage and childhood surroundings may help explain his continuing love of pastoral landscape. While working as a young drawing master at nearby Appleby he made trips from the Midlands to London and took lessons from William Payne (c.1760–c.1830) and John "Warwick" Smith (1749–1831).

Glover's professional career as a painter began in Lichfield, Staffordshire, the local cathedral city to which he moved with his young family in 1794 and had close contact with an unusually lively provincial intelligentsia. There he continued to teach, but he sent paintings to London and first exhibited at the Royal Academy in 1795. He painted for a while in oils but for the first two decades of the nineteenth century he preferred watercolour, a medium he helped popularise and which reaped him a fortune. He was a founding member of the Society of Painters in Watercolours and following the success of its first exhibition in 1805 he moved to London. A leader in his professional specialisation, he was President of the Society for two terms, founded its successor Society of Painters in Oil and Water-Colours in 1812, and in 1823 was partly responsible for establishing the Society of British Artists with which he annually exhibited many oil paintings.

Summer sketching tours from Lichfield to picturesque sites in Wales and the Lake District had begun in the early 1790s; Yorkshire, Durham and Scotland came later. For a few years from around 1817 Glover owned a farm on Ullswater, Cumberland (now Cumbria). In 1814 Glover made a journey abroad to Germany, Switzerland and France and in 1818 travelled mainly in Italy. He later executed many Italian and some Swiss views based on the sketchbook studies made on these two foreign tours. The boom in watercolour painting had subsided and he began to paint regularly in oils again but had less critical success than with watercolour; in 1818 he failed in a submission for membership of the Royal Academy. From 1820 he presented his own solo exhibitions as well as showing with the various associations. In 1830 he decided to follow his three emigrant sons and their families to Tasmania, then known as Van Diemen's Land.

On his arrival in Hobart in 1831 and then from 1832 on his farm at Mills' Plains near Evandale in northern Tasmania, Glover continued to paint Italian and British landscapes in oils, partly to satisfy a local demand for nostalgia. But he also painted colonial homestead portraits and agricultural progress, mountainous landscapes, and landscapes that included the Aborigines thought to be heading towards extinction. His light-filled naturalism made these the first oil paintings to capture distinctively Australian light, vegetation and landform. Glover died in 1849 in Tasmania at the farm he had named Patterdale after the village near his former Lake District retreat.

The Art Gallery of South Australia holds an exceptionally fine and comprehensive collection of Glover's British and Australian oil paintings, watercolours and drawings.

## Cattle. The last Gleam of the Setting Sun, 1816
oil on canvas, 163.0 x 246.0 cm
Given to honour the achievements of Ron Radford as Curator and Director,
Art Gallery of South Australia (1980–2004)
M. J. M. Carter Collection 2005

This very large canvas occupied by the decided realism of seemingly life-size cows and botanically-specific weeds contrasts with Glover's smaller and earlier more generalised watercolours. It was one of his most ambitious oil paintings, deliberately intended to impress in a public display, though at two-and-a-half metres wide it was still a metre less expansive than another cattlepiece by him of similar date held by the Bowes Museum, Barnard Castle, Durham. The Bowes Museum cattlepiece, probably a commission from an Agricultural Revolutionist, is dominated by a portrait of a Durham bull who is posed to display his improved breed and fine condition. From the time of Glover's youth there had been a demand for such portraits, reflecting the modernised British beef breeding that Robert Bakewell had pioneered in the Glover country of north-west Leicestershire. Our Adelaide cattlepiece is more a matter of art, though these animals are specific enough to be identified as Shorthorns but the front cow could be a Jersey. Both breeds are productive milking cows, but in the early nineteenth century the Jersey was also prized by grand landowners chiefly as decorative parkland cattle.[1]

Glover's model for this composition was not the greatest eighteenth-century painter of animals, George Stubbs, or even his own contemporary James Ward who had earlier made his reputation with large paintings of livestock. The prime influences on Glover were seventeenth-century Dutch, not eighteenth-century British: Paulus Potter, notorious for his painting of a life-sized bull, and Aelbert Cuyp who painted cattle in landscapes bathed in golden light.

In 1817 at the Society of Painters in Oil and Watercolours Glover exhibited lifelike portraits of bulls, goats, cows and asses.[2] A much repeated anecdote is that a cattleman who called at the exhibition with a bulldog had difficulty restraining his dog from attacking a bull in one of Glover's large canvases.[3] *Cattle. The last Gleam of the Setting Sun* was exhibited in 1816 and specifically referred to in a letter by Thomas Uwins: "Glover's great big cows have entirely failed, not withstanding the frog [*sic*, no frog is depicted], the snail, and the dandelion. There happening to be a great many cows on the side of the room on which these are hung, some wicked wit said, it resembled a Smithfield cattle show, and this opinion has been repeated rather too often for the interest of the Exhibition".[4]

This cattlepiece may emulate the scale of a few of Potter's canvases but its style is much closer to Cuyp's landscapes, especially paintings like *Cows with seated herdsman* (Frick Collection, New York) or *Cattle near Dordrecht* (National Gallery, London). The latter composition also features a reclining young herdsman with his dog. Glover used this motif in another work, a watercolour of Durham. In 1830 a copy that Glover had made after Cuyp was included in his pre-emigration disposal sale.

The golden light that pervades *Cattle. The last Gleam of the Setting Sun* is derived from Cuyp, but Glover was also directly influenced by the suffused light in landscapes by Claude Lorrain. The background of framing trees and distant castle ruin remains more a Claudean ideal than Leicestershire realism though there is also a farm cottage in the distance to the far left. The young herdsman lies on his back in sympathy with his sunset cows but nonetheless manages to play with his dog. It is a serene painting of bovine tranquility in the presence of a human carer. In the left foreground the beautifully painted dock leaves, dandelions and a snail, a still-life in itself, is a conventional device used by Cuyp and other Dutch landscape painters, notably Jan Wijnants; in 1797 Glover had made an etching of dock leaves, perhaps intended as a teaching aid to sell to pupils. In the right foreground is the suggestion of a pond or stream with a bank and reeds.

This painting is more complex than his commissioned portraits of single animals, which were sometimes scoffed at by critics and fellow-artists. It is designed for a market that included progressive landowners but Glover also raises the tone with his learned allusions to the Dutch and Italian Old Masters. There is, as well, an infusion of personal nostalgia for his parents' farm. The distant landscape evokes the Roman paintings of Claude Lorrain but it could also evoke a view of his birthplace Houghton-on-the Hill, looking down towards the valley of Ingarsby which he would have seen daily in his Leicestershire childhood.

| | |
|---|---|
| **Provenance:** | John Barkes, Sydney and London, 1983; M. J. M. Carter, Adelaide. |
| **Exhibitions:** | Society of Painters in Oil and Watercolours 1816, no. 65. *The M. J. M. Carter Collection: A Private View of Australian Colonial Art*, AGSA, Adelaide, 1993. *Regency: British Art & Design 1800-1830*, AGSA, Adelaide, 1998, no. 104. *John Glover and the Colonial Picturesque*, Tasmanian Museum & Art Gallery, Hobart; AGSA, Adelaide; National Gallery of Australia, Canberra and National Gallery of Victoria, Melbourne, 2003-04, no. 36. *Island to Empire: 300 Years of British Art 1550-1850*, AGSA, Adelaide, 2005. |
| **Literature:** | Basil Long, "John Glover", *Walkers Quarterly*, no. 15, April 1924, p. 29. Ron Radford, *19th-Century Australian Art: M. J. M. Carter Collection*, Adelaide, AGSA, 1993, pp. 23-24. Ron Radford in Christopher Menz, *Regency*, Adelaide, AGSA, 1998, p. 61. David Hansen, *John Glover and the Colonial Picturesque*, Hobart/Sydney: Tasmanian Museum & Art Gallery and Art Exhibitions Australia, 2003, pp. 65 (illus. pp. 166-67). |
| **Condition:** | Excellent; conserved in London prior to the Gallery's acquisition. |
| **Frame:** | Not original. |

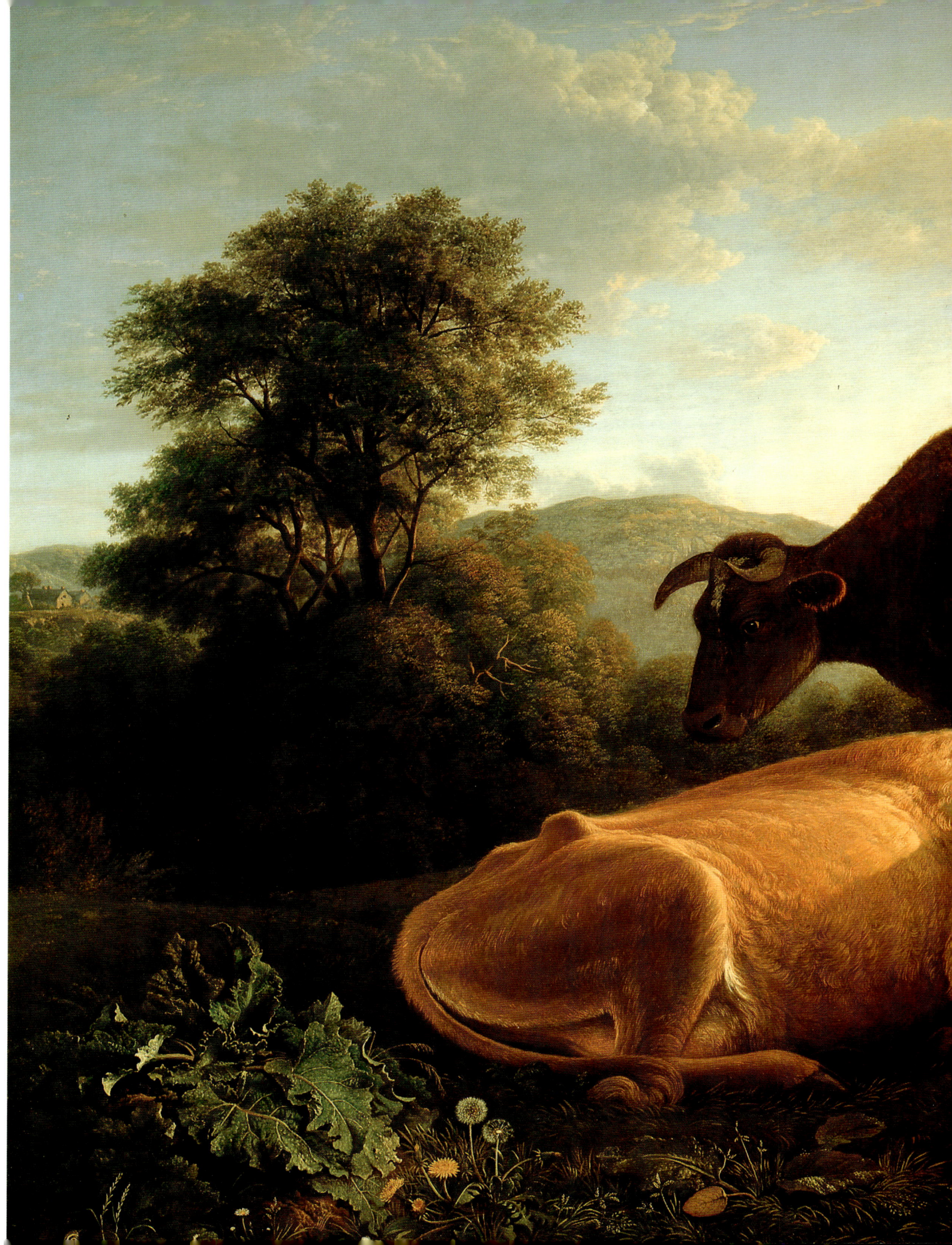

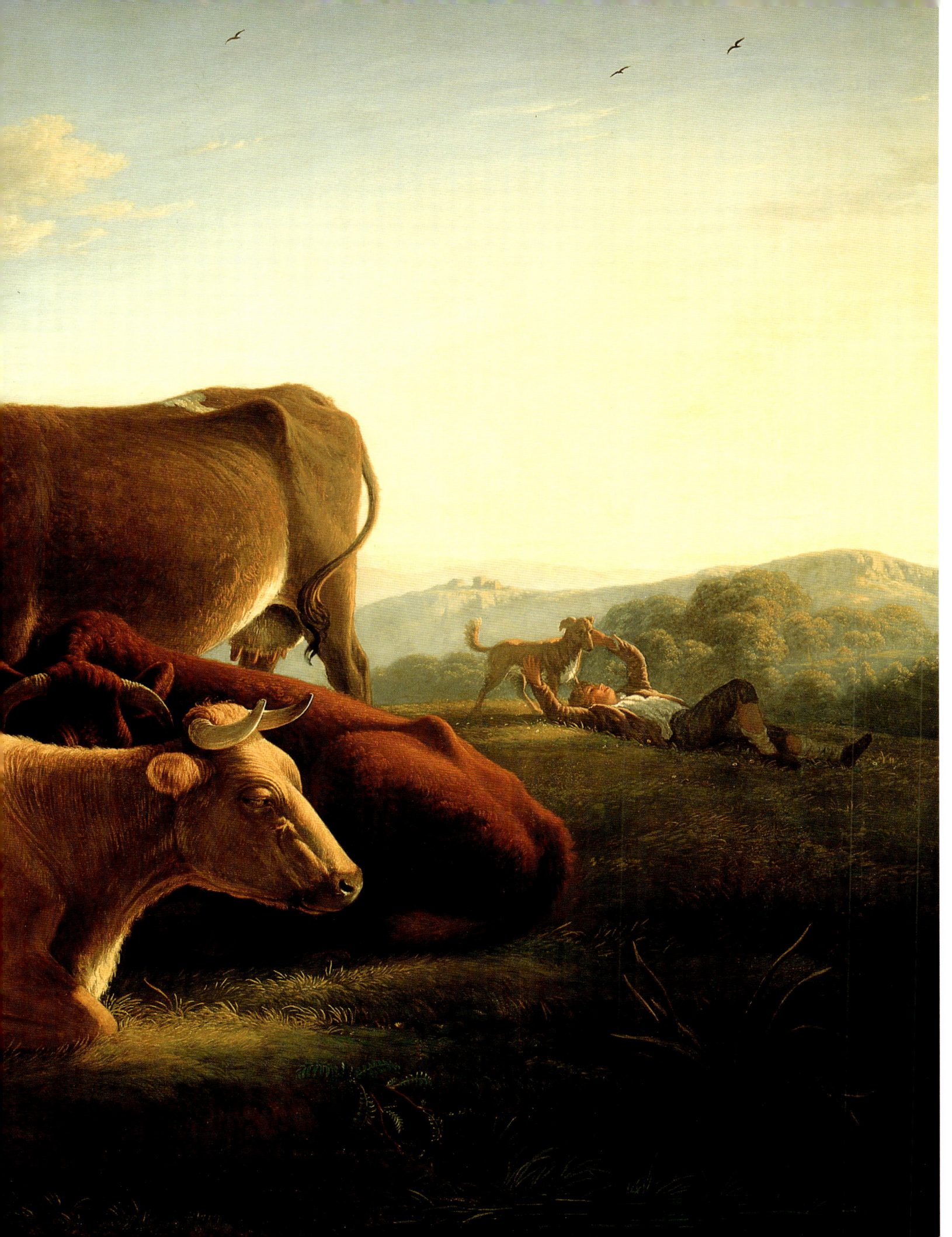

# John Glover

## Twilight, Ullswater, mid 1820s
watercolour on paper, 27.5 x 41.5 cm
J. C. Earl Bequest Fund 1986

Glover first visited the picturesque lakes of Cumberland and Westmorland in 1793 and his debut painting at the Royal Academy in 1795 was a *View of Ryddol, Cumberland*. The Lake District since the 1770s had been a favourite destination for British tourists, who there found scenery to match the canonical landscape styles of Salvator Rosa, Gaspard Dughet and Claude Lorrain. With fellow-artists Robert Hills and William Green, Glover made a thorough tour of the Lake District in 1803 and after further visits in 1807, 1808, 1809 and 1815 he bought Blawick Farm near the village of Patterdale around 1817; it was sold in 1820 but by 1824 Glover's sketchbooks reveal a total of at least nine tours to Cumbria. A third of his pictures in the annual exhibitions from 1805 at the Society of Painters in Water-Colours were of the Lake District, more than those by any of his contemporaries.

This delightful watercolour has survived in unusually fresh condition whereas most of the earlier watercolours that made Glover rich and famous are now faded ruins. It depicts the southern end of Ullswater from above Glover's Blawick Farm; the village of Patterdale is out of sight to the left. The craggy mountain is Helvellyn, Glenridding Dodd is lower on the shore at the centre, and Sheffield Pike is further right. The glassy lake surface is screened by a foreground of trees that rhyme pictorially with the background mountains. The trees are rendered with his characteristic split-brush method that saved time while depicting textured foliage. A small flock of sheep shelters between these trees and the foreground outcrops of rock.

The tranquil scene is bathed in twilight, the time of day favoured by Claude Lorrain but although Claude was conventionally associated with Coniston Water, Gaspard Dughet with Windermere and Salvator Rosa with Derwent Water, Glover thought of the Lake District – and Ullswater in particular – chiefly in terms of Gaspard Dughet. Of a similar view in oil, David Hansen says: "Glover found the whole combination in his beloved Ullswater, and in this work there is a particular synthesis of Claude and Gaspard Dughet (Gaspard Poussin). There is Claude's 'delicate sunshine over the cultivated vales, the scattered cots, the groves, the lake' in the foreground and middle distance, while 'the grand pencil of Poussin [crowns] the whole with the majesty of the impending mountains'". The quotations come from a tourist guide published in 1753.[1]

However, this is not at all like Glover's earlier Claudean pastiches in watercolour. It is a scene of miraculous realism and has a clarity of vision absent from the more generalised and popular watercolours that he produced in the first one-and-a-half decades of the nineteenth century. In this regard it is also closer to the approach of seventeenth-century Dutch realism. Its precise naturalism and clarity point towards his subsequent and final decade of splendidly realistic Australian landscapes.

There exist at least two oil paintings of the subject, perhaps three. One large landscape entitled *Ullswater* (private collection London)[2] shows the lake and mountains from a viewpoint similar to the Gallery's watercolour, but although it includes sheep it has a very different foreground with a Claude-like tree and a ruin on the right. The Art Gallery of New South Wales, Sydney, holds *Ullswater, early Morning*, c.1824 (formerly known as *Ullswater from Patterdale*), which shows the lake and mountains from a slightly different angle but has the same meticulous depiction of the Lake District mountains. The foreground in the Art Gallery of New South Wales's picture is a studio pastiche, a Claudean device with an uneasy relationship to the highly realistic background, and its foreground features cows not sheep.

Glover exhibited an oil painting titled *Ullswater from Patterdale* at the Royal Academy in 1825 (no. 282) which is possibly the slightly larger, better resolved composition in the private collection. There also exists in a private collection another watercolour of the subject.[3] All four or five similar views would probably have been done about the same time, probably in the mid to late 1820s. By 1820 he had sold Blawick Farm and these works made in his London studio are a final tribute to the beloved Lake District that he had recorded over a period of thirty years.

**Provenance:** Bought from Nevill Keating Pictures, London, 1986.
**Exhibitions:** *Regency: British Art & Design 1800–1830*, AGSA, Adelaide, 1998, no. 107.
*Island to Empire: 300 Years of British Art 1550–1850*, AGSA, Adelaide, 2005.
**Literature:** Ron Radford in Christopher Menz, *Regency*, Adelaide: AGSA, 1998, pp. 33, 64. David Hansen, *John Glover and the Colonial Picturesque*, Hobart/Sydney: Tasmanian Museum & Art Gallery and Art Exhibitions Australia, 2003, pp. 172, 180.
**Condition:** Excellent.

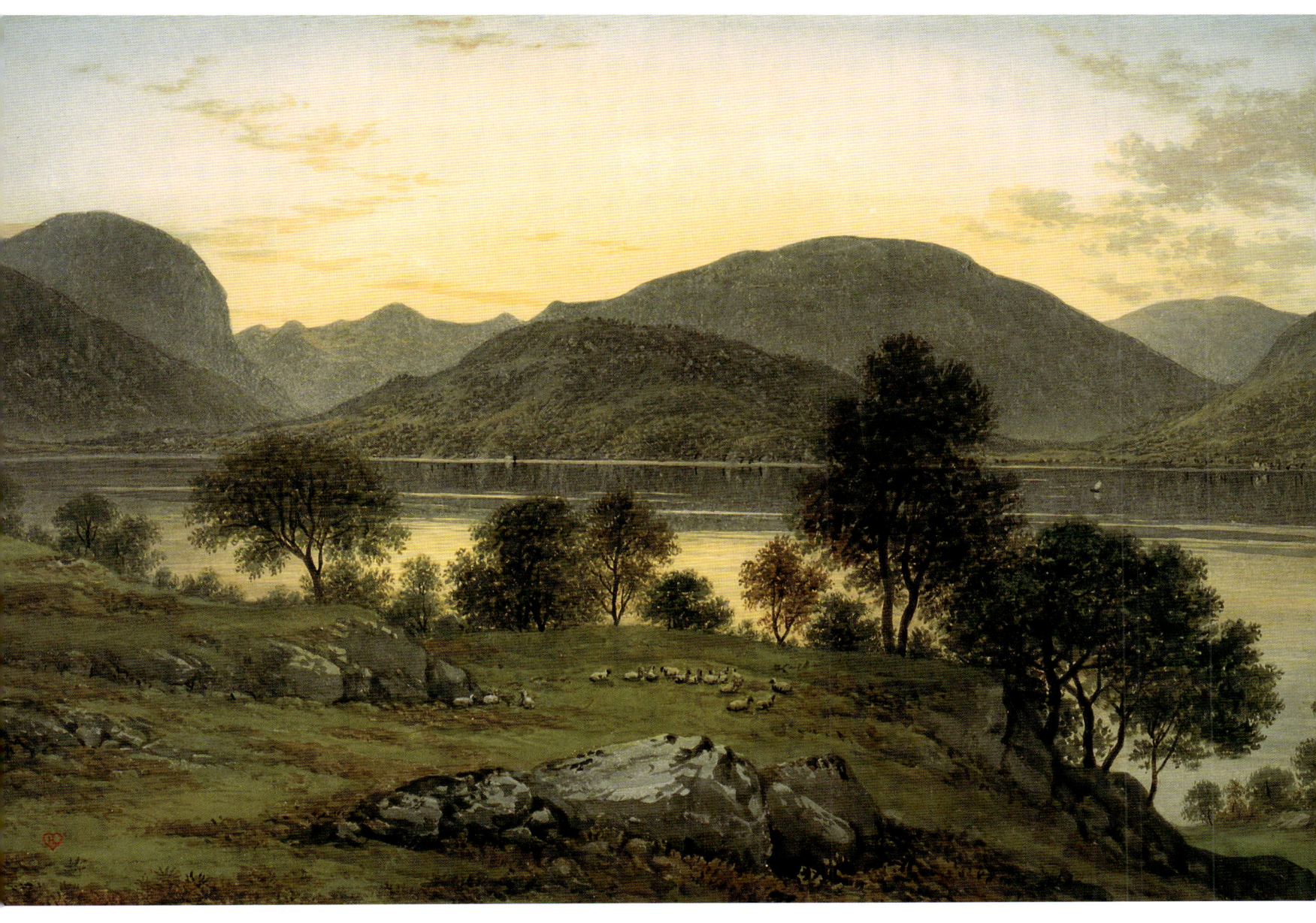

# John Glover

## North End, Hampstead Heath, c.1826
watercolour on paper, 22.5 x 38.5 cm
Gift of M. J. M. Carter through the Art Gallery of South Australia Foundation 2004

This domesticated semi-rural landscape subject was already in the 1820s a suburb of London. Hampstead Heath, north-west of the city, is an elevated, undulating and gravelly region that was originally covered with gorse and heather and used for rough grazing. The village of Hampstead became a fashionable mineral-springs spa at the beginning of the eighteenth century and in the early nineteenth century the North End of the Heath abounded with laundresses who used the gorse and heather to dry and bleach linen. Artists visited from the 1780s onwards. Glover exhibited a *Hampstead Heath* in 1811 and made sketches there again in 1816 (sketchbook 5).[1]

By the time he painted *North End, Hampstead Heath* in the mid 1820s the village was a sought-after rustic suburb. John Constable rented a cottage there from July 1819 and painted many of his now famous oil sketches of the Heath. The land had escaped the forces of industrialisation and the area was fiercely fought over to preserve its archaic pastoral quaintness.

Glover has taken pleasure in depicting this unlikely rural atmosphere, only a short coach ride or a long walking distance from what was then the largest city in the world and the centre of a worldwide empire. It is Frognal Farm on the northern outskirts of Hampstead. The village dwellings and farm buildings back onto a common where cattle come for water; at the centre we also see low farm buildings and a horse cart and a rustic thatched shed. The pond and the remarkably uneven foreground are probably the result of the gravel mining that continued throughout the nineteenth century in many areas of the Heath. The soil supports scant pasture but there are regular clumps of heath. Towards the left are three seated women and sheltered under the trees are two men. They are not farmers, rural workers or laundresses, but well-dressed leisure-seekers from London enjoying the rusticity. The dense clump of trees screens their moment of country experience from the farmyard and the village and the vast sprawl of London, which can be seen encroaching in the hazy distance.

It is probable that Glover sketched this view in the company of his fellow watercolour artist John Varley (1778–1842), who often stayed at John Linnell's house on visits to Hampstead Heath. The Victoria & Albert Museum holds a watercolour by Varley, dated 1826 and titled *Frognal, Hampstead*, which depicts the exact same view.[2] As Glover also knew John Linnell they both possibly stayed with him on this excursion. Glover did a preliminary on-the-spot drawing for this work, held by the Dixson Galleries at the State Library of New South Wales, Sydney,[3] and the watercolour was probably completed in his studio. For Londoners it would have been an appealing and saleable subject.

This landscape is quite unlike Glover's earlier stereotype English or Italian scenes seen through the golden gaze of Claude Lorrain. It is one of his later works of well-observed realism, partly influenced by the conventions of seventeenth-century Dutch art, like the landscapes of Jacob van Ruisdael and Meindert Hobbema. Although the landscape lacks the standard classical framing device of large formulaic foreground trees, the gravelly undulating foreground and the light-green and sandy colours do have some of the qualities found in the Arcadian foregrounds of Gaspard Dughet, another seventeenth-century master whose Italian paintings Glover admired and of which he had made copies.

Glover was painting fewer watercolours in the 1820s as the watercolour market was saturated and the fashion had subsided after a depression that followed the Napoleonic Wars. Those he did paint adhered to a general British trend towards greater realism, seen in the landscapes of John Linnell (1792–1882), William Mulready (1786–1863) and John and Cornelius Varley. Glover was probably also influenced by the realism of Constable, who was scathing of Glover's work. Like its contemporary *Twilight, Ullswater*, this small watercolour of unpretentious, cosy naturalism comes close to the confident realism later evident in his finest Tasmanian oils, many of which he sent back in 1835 and 1836 for exhibition in London.

**Provenance:** Spink, London before 1986; sold from Rex Irwin Art Dealer, Sydney, 1986, to M. J. M. Carter, Adelaide.

**Exhibitions:** Society of British Artists, London, 1827, no. 703. Rex Irwin Gallery, Sydney, 1986. *The M. J. M. Carter Collection: A Private View of Australian Colonial Art*, AGSA, Adelaide, 1993. *Regency: British Art & Design 1800–1830*, AGSA, Adelaide, 1998, no. 106. *John Glover and the Colonial Picturesque*, Tasmanian Museum & Art Gallery, Hobart; AGSA, Adelaide; National Gallery of Australia, Canberra and National Gallery of Victoria, Melbourne, 2003–04, no. 51. *Island to Empire: 300 Years of British Art 1550–1850*, AGSA, Adelaide, 2005.

**Literature:** Ron Radford, *19th-Century Australian Art*, Adelaide: AGSA, 1993. Ron Radford in Christopher Menz, *Regency*, Adelaide: AGSA, 1998, p. 64. David Hansen, *John Glover and the Colonial Picturesque*, Hobart/Sydney: Tasmanian Museum & Art Gallery and Art Exhibitions Australia, 2003, pp. 184–85.

**Condition:** Good; evidence of some fading.

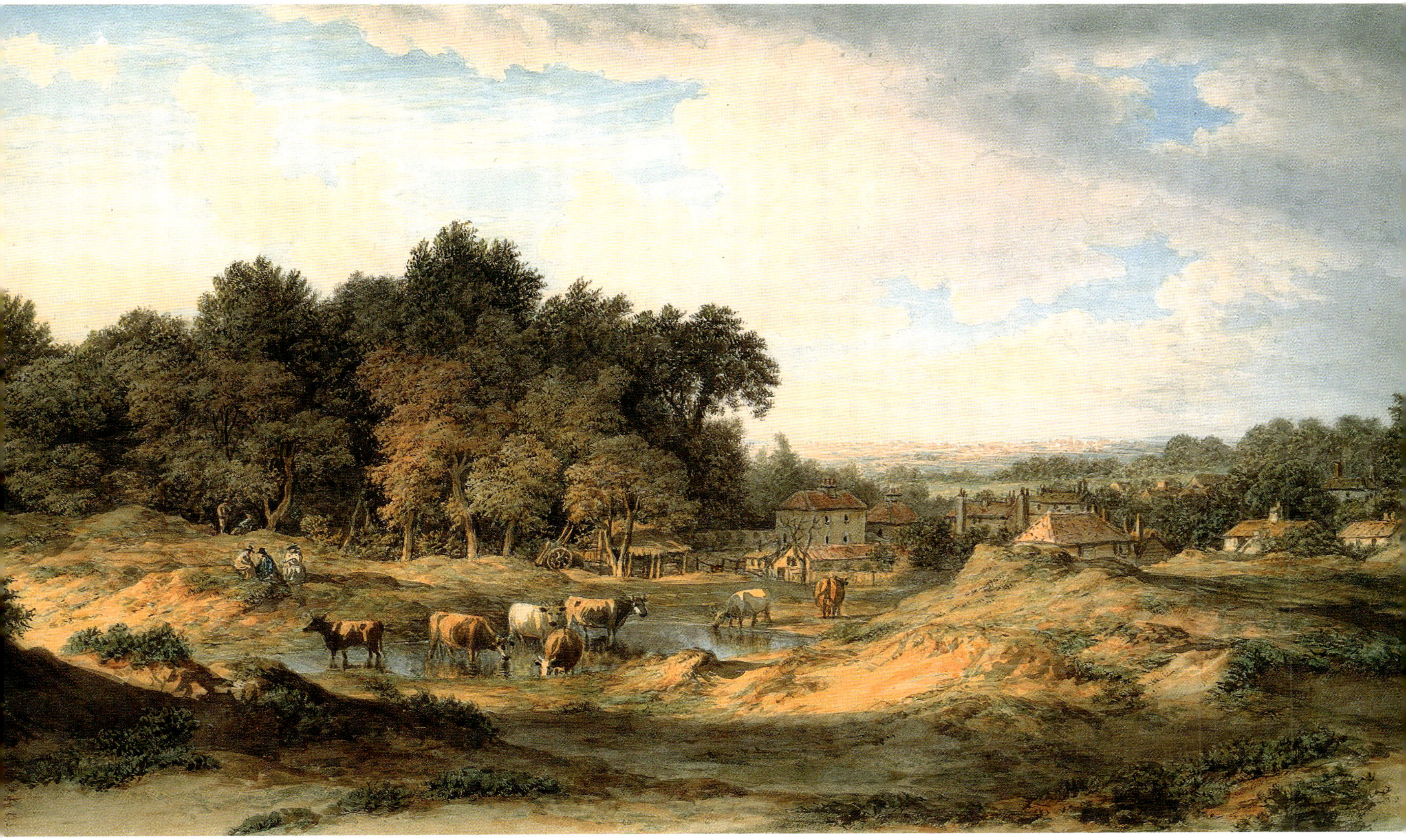

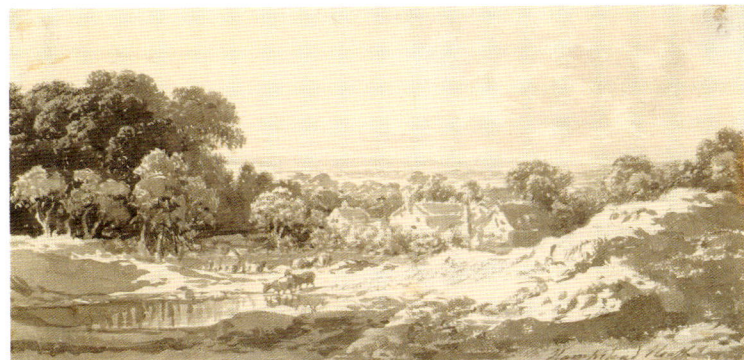

John Glover, [*North End, Hampstead Heath*], c.1825. Dixson Galleries, State Library of New South Wales, Sydney

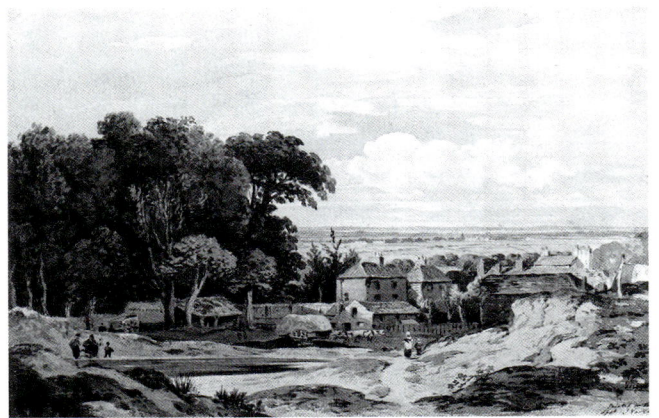

John Varley, *Frognal, Hampstead*, 1826. V. & A. Images/Victoria & Albert Museum, London

# James Ward 1769–1859

James Ward has long been best known for spirited animal pictures, though in recent decades attention has been given to his few large romantic landscapes in which animals assume a diminished role. In the early nineteenth century Ward's art was central to the distinctly British tradition of animal painting. The tradition began with Thomas Barlow, was much extended in the eighteenth century by George Stubbs and continued in the nineteenth century with artists like James Ward, Thomas Sidney Cooper, Edwin Landseer, J. F. Herring and Herring's sons. Robert Hills, Samuel Howitt, John Glover and others also played a part in the continuing history of animal painting. The long tradition of British portraiture extended to an animal department, embracing pets, champion horses and prize livestock.

Born in London in 1769, Ward was a precocious draughtsman and was apprenticed in 1781–82 to the famous engraver John Raphael Smith, thereby following the professional lead of James's brother William who had become a very accomplished engraver. James broke his apprenticeship to work for William and by the end of the 1780s was extremely competent. In the 1790s he began to paint and engrave his own compositions of popular genre subjects in the manner of Francis Wheatley and George Morland; he made engravings of Morland's paintings and became his brother-in-law. James Ward's proficiency led to his appointment in 1794 as Painter and Engraver in Mezzotint to Prince Frederick, Duke of York.

At the end of the 1790s he began to exhibit oil paintings at the Royal Academy. These included horses owned by royalty and many large paintings of cows, the latter earning him a reputation as an "English Paulus Potter", after the seventeenth-century Dutch artist known to have painted cattle life-size. The Board of Agriculture and the leading print-seller John Boydell jointly commissioned Ward to paint two hundred portraits of representative breeds of cattle, sheep and pigs of Great Britain for which he was to be paid £3000. The series was not completed as Boydell went bankrupt but thereafter Ward was to be known almost exclusively as an animal painter and was hailed as the greatest such artist of his day.

Partly as a reaction against his narrow reputation, in 1803 Ward painted the first of his showpiece monumental landscapes, the dramatic *Bulls fighting with a view of St Donatt's Castle in the background*, and in 1804 *The Boa Serpent*. Both were executed with quasi-Baroque vigour and showed the influence of Rubens whose landscapes Ward greatly admired. In 1811 he began an even more ambitious essay in the romantic sublime, the vast *Gordale Scar* which was his largest canvas and secured his election to full membership of the Royal Academy. The *Bulls fighting*, now in the Victoria & Albert Museum, and *Gordale Scar*, in the Tate, London, have both in the 1980s been the subjects of small but special publications and it is for these striking works that he has again become known. This would have pleased him.

James Ward died at the age of ninety in 1859, poor and almost forgotten. An early biographer stated: "He was in truth a survivor of the past, a straggler from the age of Reynolds and Gainsborough, and the newer art movement which was heralded by the advent of Millais, Leighton, and Watts, had in it no place for him".[1]

## Portrait of Dash, a Favourite Spaniel, the Property of Lady Frances Vane-Tempest, 1819

oil on canvas, 88.9 x 104.1 cm
South Australian Government Grant 1959

Lady Frances Vane-Tempest commissioned this portrait of the handsome, well-groomed Dash on 17 March 1819. Ward charged the substantial sum of £94/10/-. The frame, which is almost certainly the one that still surrounds the painting, was another 12 guineas.[2] Work of this kind earned James Ward his reputation and income for most of his long career.

Frances Anne Vane-Tempest was born on 7 February 1800, the only child of Sir Henry Vane-Tempest and Anne, Countess of Antrim. An heiress to very large estates in Durham and the north of Ireland, Lady Frances married, as his second wife, Charles William Stewart, third Marquess of Londonderry (1778–1854) on 3 April 1819. On their marriage he took the surname of Vane, and on 28 March 1823 he was additionally created Earl Vane and Viscount Seaham. She died in 1865.

The commission was ordered only two weeks before her marriage, so when the picture was exhibited as *Portrait of Dash, a Favourite Spaniel, the Property of Lady Frances Vane-Tempest* she was the Marchioness of Londonderry. If she was to leave her beloved dog behind she at least would have his image preserved for her fond memory, and in association with the name she bore in his day. Possibly, however, the painting or the dog was a wedding present for her husband-to-be. In any case the painting would have hung in the Regency couple's palatial new mansion Wynyard Park at Wolviston, County Durham, now County Cleveland.

Dash was painted at the height of Ward's career and like most of the artist's animal portraits it is not merely a straightforward descriptive record of the animal. It is a portrait in the grand manner. The noble creature faces us while displaying the full side of his luxuriant tan-and-white coat. He fixes us with an engaging stare. Unlike other

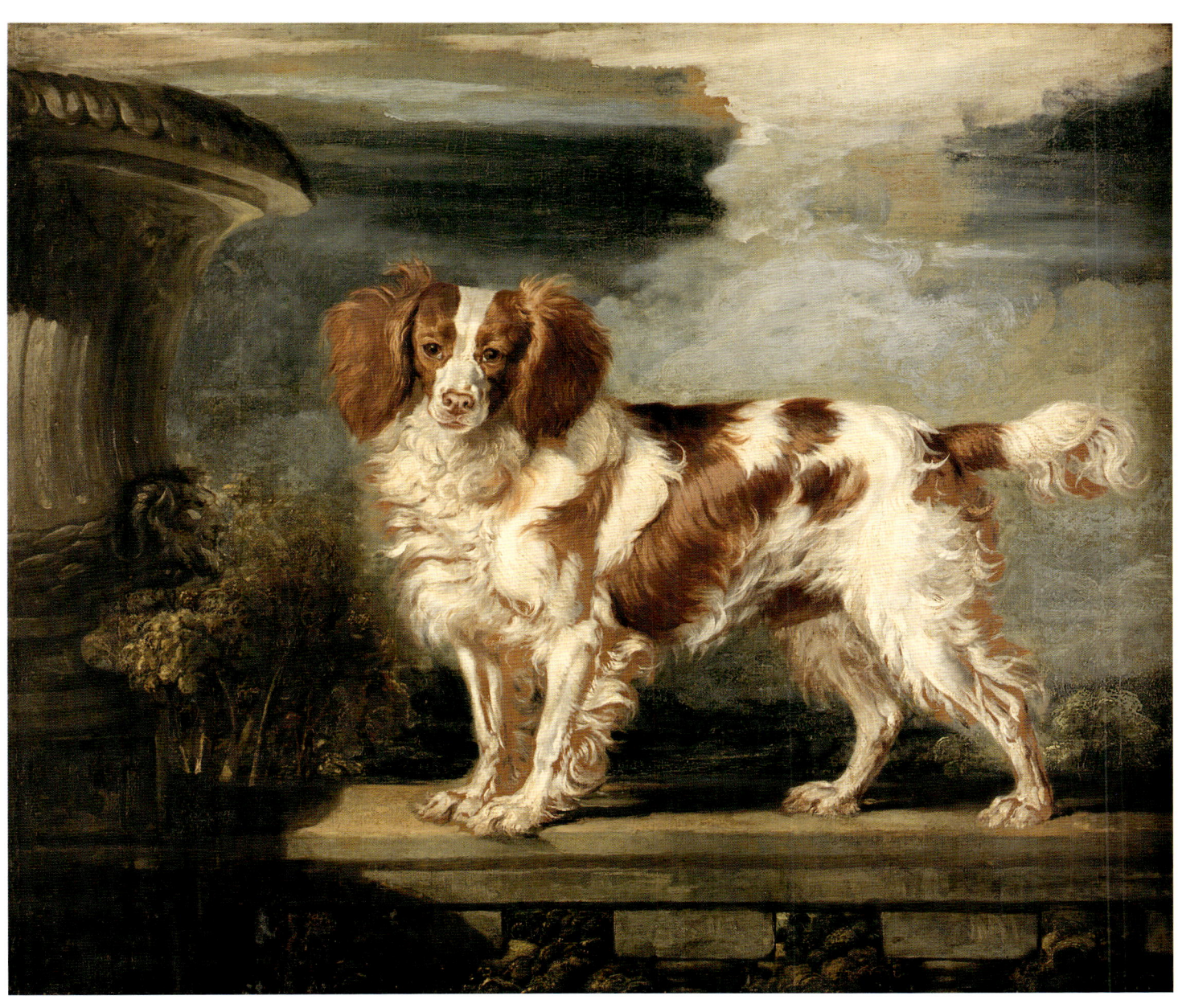

portraits of favourite pets, shown in either cosy domestic interiors or pretty gardens, he stands high on a classical stone balustrade as if overlooking landed property like a statue on a pedestal. His status overshadows the large classical urn on the left. He is portrayed in the manner expounded by Joshua Reynolds and, indeed, the deft and vigorous broad brushwork suggests the Old Masters, particularly Titian who often incorporated similar but smaller dogs in his compositions. The indication of dark romantic landscape and threatening sky also reminds us of moody seventeenth-century landscapes by Salvator Rosa, another Italian master Ward much admired. The picture was intended to hang in a great house and would have had to hold its own in the company of grand ancestral portraits and Old Master paintings.

It is a work that demonstrates the increasing seriousness in Britain of animal painting, especially portraits of pets. It is interesting to note that in the Gallery's *Portrait of a lady with a dog*, c.1755 (p. 117), painted by Arthur Devis over sixty years earlier, the poodle is small and on the ground below a balustrade on which its owner leans beside a classical urn. In Ward's painting the owner has disappeared and now it is the dog we see elevated onto the balustrade beside the urn.

This spaniel portrait was exhibited at the Royal Academy the year it was painted. It obviously impressed as it led to similar commissions. The Earl of Powis's two pictures of his King Charles spaniel Rover, one of which is now in the Tate, appeared at the Royal Academy in 1821 and were even larger than Lady Frances's Dash. Other spaniel portraits followed; one painted in 1836 was of Ward's own dog.

**Provenance:** Knight, Fox, Rutledge, 1958; Thomas Agnew & Sons, London, purchased on the advice of H. D. Molesworth, 1959.

**Exhibitions:** Royal Academy, London, 1819, no. 324. *Regency: British Art & Design 1800–1830*, AGSA, Adelaide, 1998, no. 125. *Island to Empire: 300 Years of British Art 1550–1850*, AGSA, Adelaide, 2005.

**Literature:** David Thomas et al., *Art Gallery of South Australia 1881–1981*, Adelaide: AGSA, 1981, p. 60. Ron Radford in Christopher Menz, *Regency*, Adelaide: AGSA, 1998, pp. 72–73.

**Condition:** Excellent; last conserved in 1999 by Artlab Australia, Adelaide.

**Frame:** Original.

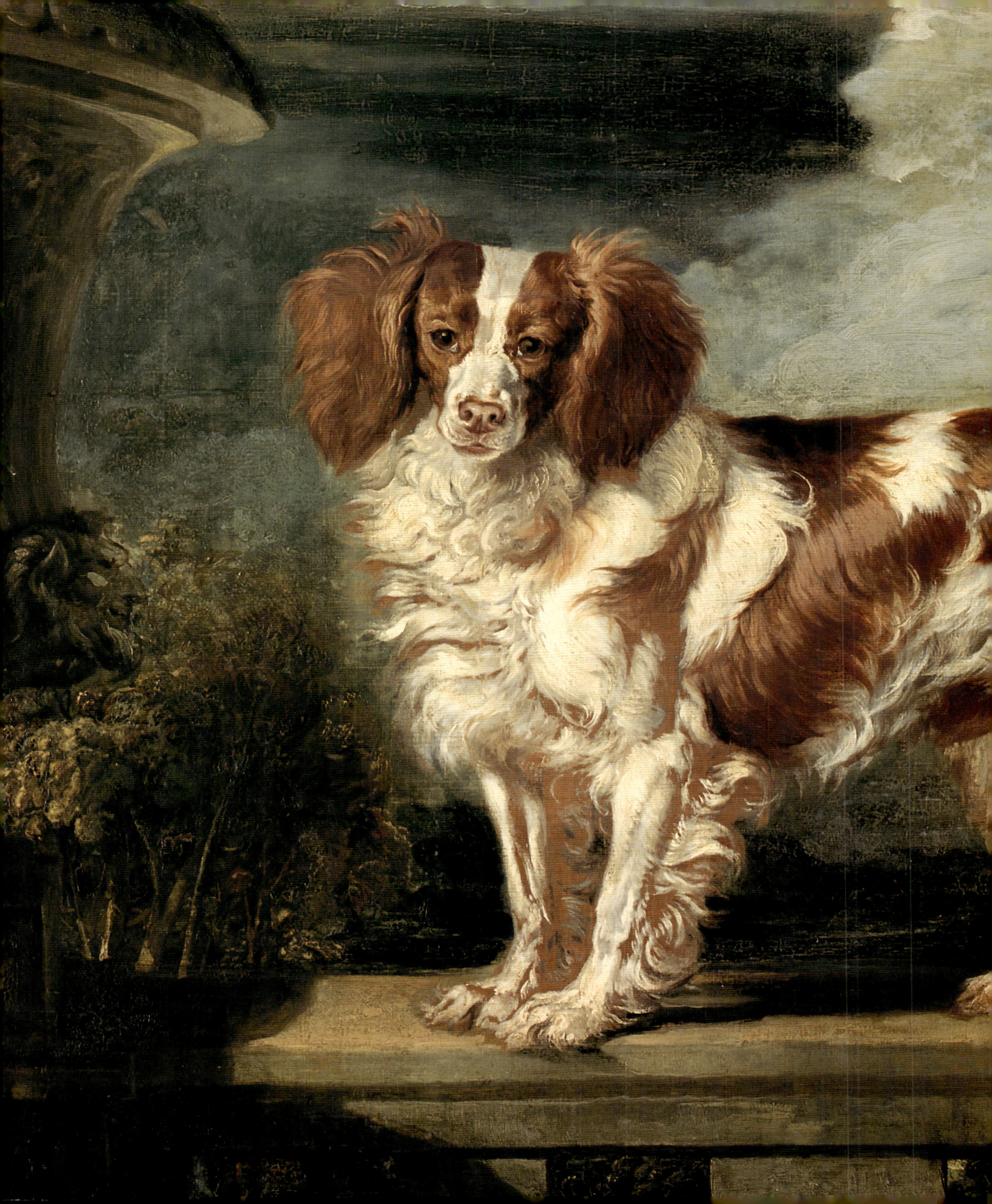

# J. J. Halls 1776–1834

John James Halls was a talented and moderately successful portrait and history painter in Regency London, but he is now almost forgotten.

Born in Colchester, Essex, in 1776, Halls was living in London by 1791 when as a youth he first exhibited a landscape at the Royal Academy. He later entered the Royal Academy Schools in 1798 and was on friendly terms with Henry Fuseli with whom he travelled to Paris in 1802. He moved in the same circle as some of the most distinguished early-nineteenth-century British painters including Hoppner, Lawrence, Blake, Turner and Wilkie. In 1813 he gained a premium of 200 guineas at the British Institution for his *Raising of Jairus's Daughter*.

Although Halls aspired to full-scale history painting he resorted, like most British artists at the time, to establishing himself as a portrait painter and from about 1813 onwards he only exhibited portraits at the Royal Academy. His career in portraiture flourished in the 1810s and the first half of the 1820s. Of the 108 paintings he exhibited at the Royal Academy between 1798 and 1827, almost ninety percent were portraits, mostly of the landed gentry, or professional and commercial families and politicians. The pinnacle of his career was a commission to paint Princess Mary, Duchess of Gloucester, the fourth daughter of George III and Queen Charlotte, a picture that he exhibited in 1817 at the Royal Academy. He gave up exhibiting in 1827 and died in London in 1834.

## Thomas Wilson, c.1823
oil on canvas, 76.8 x 64.4 cm
J. C. Earl Bequest Fund assisted by Shirley and Honor Cameron Wilson 1997

Thomas Wilson was a prosperous lawyer and also an art connoisseur and collector. In 1838 he emigrated from London to the infant British colony of South Australia, where he made an invaluable contribution to its civic and cultural life.

Born in 1787 and trained in law in London, Wilson's education included time on the Continent where he studied foreign languages. He became a successful solicitor. His maternal grandfather Thomas Major (1714–1799) was an accomplished engraver and close friend of the sculptor Joseph Nollekens (1737–1823), and a colleague of a number of artists associated with the formation of the Royal Academy in 1768. Wilson grew up with much knowledge of art and the significant personalities of the British art world.

As his legal practice prospered he began to assemble, and systematically document, an art collection that focused on European Old Master prints: early Italian, German, Flemish, British and Dutch etchings and engravings, especially Rembrandt's. He published a scholarly catalogue of his own print collection and a catalogue raisonné of Rembrandt's etchings, one of the first in English. Wilson also collected watercolours and drawings by British artists, and brought with him to Adelaide nearly 100 brush drawings by John Glover. That artist had emigrated in 1831 and was already in Tasmania but these were the first works by Glover to come to the Australian mainland; nineteen of them are now in the collection of the Art Gallery of South Australia and are listed in this present catalogue.

In Dulwich, a suburb south of London, Wilson built Dulwich Place, a large and fashionable Regency house with remarkable grounds, and in Wales he bought a large country estate, Abbey Cwm Hir, north of Llandrindod Wells in Radnorshire (now Powys). After a disastrous land speculation he had to sell his properties, including the print collection, part of which went to the British Museum. This prompted his emigration in 1838.

Wilson quickly established a busy legal practice in Adelaide, became a prominent participant in the colony's vigorous social, political and intellectual life, and in 1842 was elected the second Mayor of Adelaide. In March 1843 he delivered the first public lecture on art to be held in Adelaide and in June of the same year the first lecture on literature.[1] In 1854, appropriately for a city soon to be renowned for its outstanding women artists, he gave the first lecture in Australia on European women artists, and had it published.[2] He helped arrange the colony's first general art exhibition in 1847, was a founder of the (Royal) South Australian Society of Arts in 1857, the year of the Society's first exhibition, and advocated the necessity of a public art collection in Adelaide. He died in 1863, eighteen years before the establishment of the then-named National Gallery of South Australia.

J. J. Halls's dignified portrait of Thomas Wilson shows the sitter aged thirty-six and at the height of his legal career in London. Halls was most likely a friend of the sitter. Wilson wears a conservative black coat with brass buttons over a crisp white waistcoat, kerchief and upturned collar, the usual dress of a professional city man. He sits upright and alert in a stout office chair upholstered in red leather and holds a loosely-rolled legal document. His formal appearance must have varied little in his adult life, since nearly twenty years later he was similarly described:

> No man seems to possess more of the attributes of ubiquity than Mr Wilson. Visit whatever part of Adelaide you may, during the hours of business, there you are sure to meet with him – despite the burning heat of an Australian summer's sun – dressed in

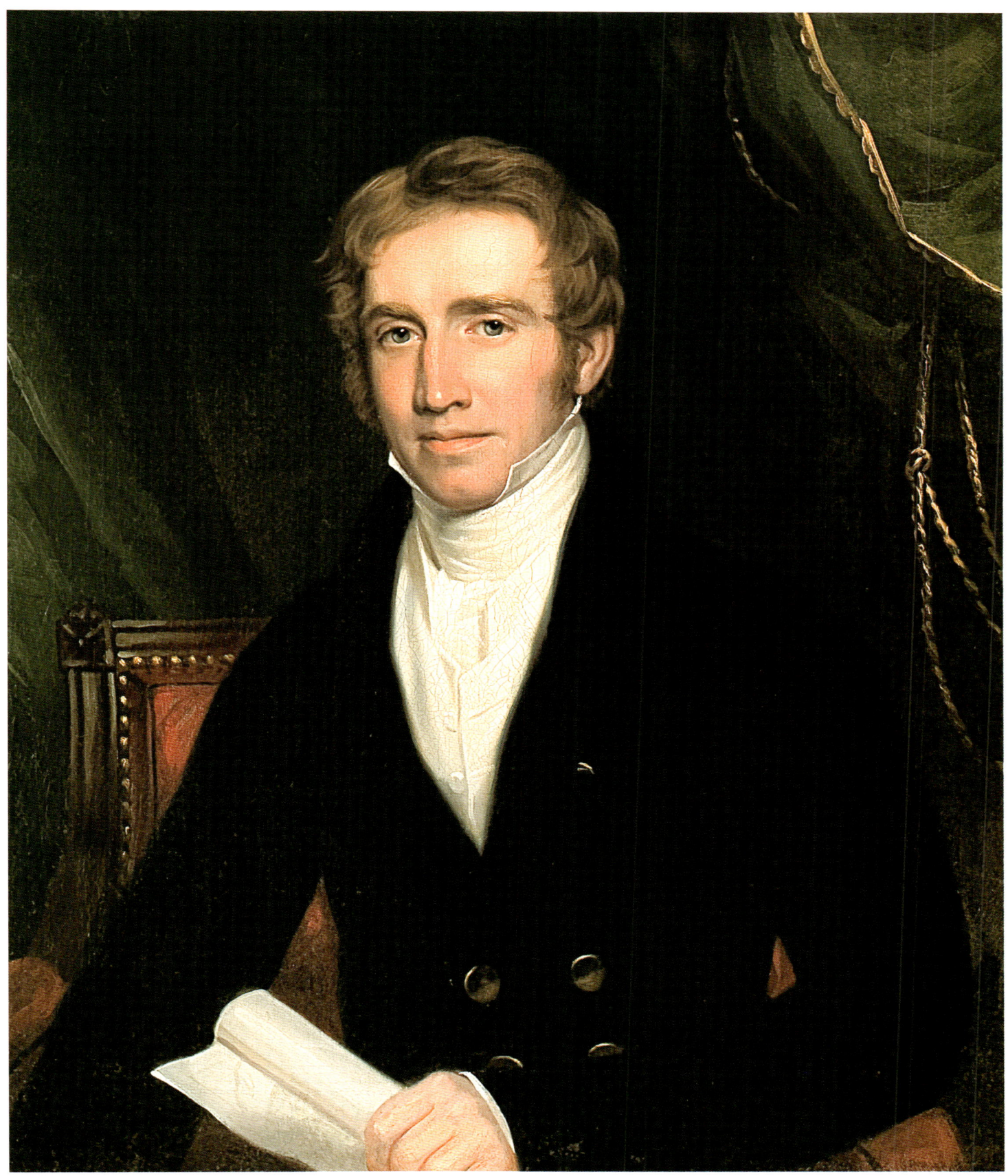

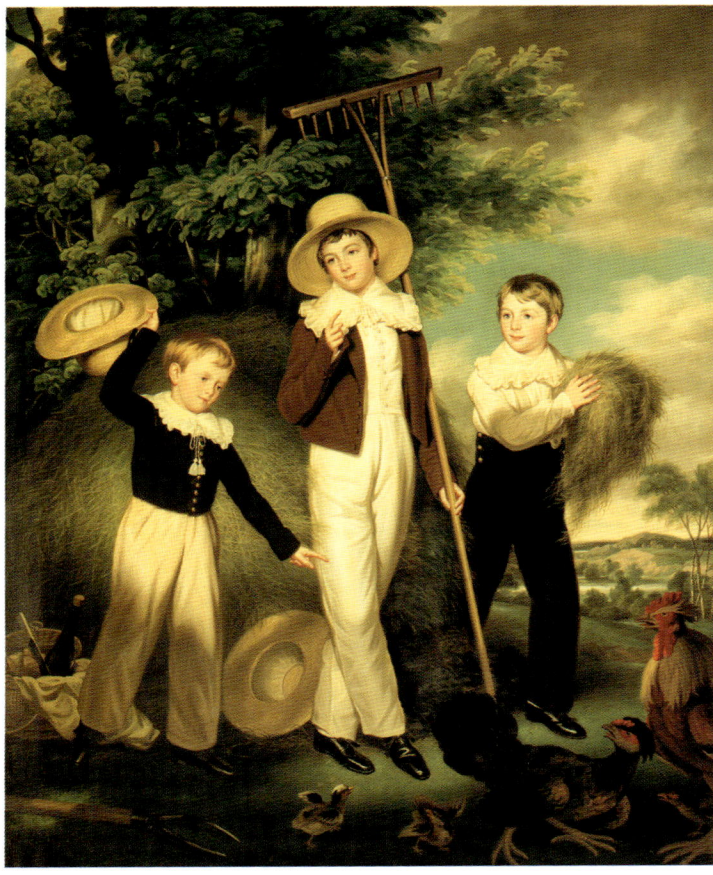

J. J. Halls, *The young haymakers*, 1827. Private collection

a suit of black – and most commonly with a bundle of papers hanging loosely in his hand.³

Wilson's handsome face is enlivened by the hint of a smile and bright intelligent eyes and framed by a fashionably windswept Regency coiffure. Dark-green gathered drapes with gold braid fill the right-hand corner of the composition. The modelling of his features has a firm Neoclassical crispness that distinguishes Halls's portraits from the more painterly quality of contemporaries such as Raeburn, Hoppner and Lawrence. This attractive half-length portrait was exhibited at the Royal Academy in 1823, discreetly titled *T. Wilson, Esq*.

Almost four years later Wilson commissioned Halls to paint a full-length group portrait of his three young sons, two of whom were also to play an important part in South Australia's history. The large and charming outdoor scene, the artist's last exhibited work, appeared at the Royal Academy in 1827 as *The young haymakers: portraits of the sons of Thomas Wilson, Esq*.; the landscape setting perhaps is a reference to the Wilsons' Welsh landholding.⁴ From 1992 to 2002 the picture was on loan from the Wilson family in Adelaide to the Art Gallery of South Australia and shown prominently adjacent to Halls's portrait of Wilson in the Gallery's exhibition *Regency: British Art & Design 1800–1830* of 1998.

**Provenance:** Thomas Wilson, London c.1823, thence by family descent in Britain to Lt Col. Eric Wilson, V.C., Dorset, from whom bought in 1997 by the Art Gallery of South Australia.

**Exhibitions:** Royal Academy, 1823, as *T. Wilson, Esq.*, no. 80. *Regency: British Art & Design 1800–1830*, AGSA, 1998, no. 108. *Island to Empire: 300 Years of British Art 1550–1850*, AGSA, Adelaide, 2005.

**Literature:** Algernon Graves, *Royal Academy Exhibitors, 1769–1904*, London: Royal Academy, 1905–06, vol. 3, p. 361. S. C. Wilson and K. T. Borrow, *The Bridge over the Ocean: Thomas Wilson (1787–1863), Art Collector and Mayor of Adelaide*, Adelaide, 1973, p. 45 (illus. fig. 13) (then thought to be lost). Angus Trumble in Christopher Menz, *Regency*, Adelaide: AGSA, 1998, p. 64.

**Condition:** Excellent; last conserved in 1997 by Artlab Australia, Adelaide.

**Frame:** Possibly original, more likely to be the slip for a more elaborate Regency-style frame.

# Peter De Wint 1784–1849

John Clare (1793–1864), poet of the natural world and a contemporary of De Wint, wrote in his *Essay on Landscape*: "The only artist that produces real English scenery in which British landscapes are seen and felt upon paper with all their poetry and exillerating [sic] expression of beauty about them is De Wint."[1]

A disciple of Thomas Girtin's watercolour style, De Wint is widely known for his expansive vistas of flat landscape executed with a confident breadth of handling, usually on coarsely textured paper. His peaceful rural scenes seem oblivious to, or perhaps consciously avoid, the social upheavals of his time brought about by the Industrial Revolution. During his prolific period in the 1820s and 1830s there were great riots by rural labourers. The disruption of the countryside by rapidly expanding cities, rural enclosures and mechanical farming methods that took away the traditional livelihood of tens-of-thousands of country people are not even hinted at in his open, often sunny, always optimistic and productive landscapes. As Thackeray wrote: "[One] might have called for a pot of port at seeing one of De Wint's haymakings… everything basked lazily for him, and one wondered whether he remained torpid in winter."[2] De Wint's works are nostalgic romantic landscapes of reaction.

He was born of Dutch extraction at Stone, near Hanley, Staffordshire, in 1784. In 1802 he was apprenticed in London to the pastel portraitist and notable mezzotint engraver, John Raphael Smith, the publisher for whom Turner and Girtin coloured prints as youths. After serving only four years of his apprenticeship, De Wint and his fellow apprentice and future brother-in-law William Hilton (1786–1839) set up lodgings in Golden Square, Soho. The Hilton connection would take him to Lincolnshire for many landscape subjects throughout his life. Their neighbour in London was the watercolourist and distinguished teacher John Varley. De Wint had painted mainly in oil before this but now took watercolour instruction from Varley who introduced him to the circle of Dr Thomas Monro. Monro was the most influential patron of English watercolours and De Wint would have become acquainted with Monro's vast collection, particularly the works by Girtin. Girtin, who had died young in 1802, is the essential transitional figure in English watercolour painting from the topographical eighteenth-century style to the Romantic landscapes of the first half of the nineteenth century, and was De Wint's closest forerunner.

In spite of his profitable success as a watercolour painter, De Wint, like other artists of his time, had to supplement his income by making illustrations for engraved publications. It is interesting to note here that in 1820 he was asked to make detailed watercolours from sixty-two sketches of Sicily by Major William Light, as a basis for engravings in W. B. Cooke's *Sicilian Scenery*, published in 1823.[3] In 1837 Light, by then a colonel, would be the founder and planner of the British colonial city of Adelaide, South Australia.

De Wint's watercolour style had matured by about 1811, the year he became a full member of the Society of Painters in Water-Colours. Over the next forty years of his career he made few stylistic changes but he did alternate between quick sketches and more detailed, elaborate works. This, combined with the fact that De Wint never signed or dated his watercolours, makes it very difficult to follow any chronological development or sequence in his work.

## Kenilworth Castle, c.1827
watercolour on paper, 50.7 x 69.2 cm
South Australian Government Grant 1955

Although De Wint painted the subject of *Kenilworth Castle* many times the Gallery's version can be dated with some confidence to 1827. It was almost certainly the work exhibited that year with the Society of Painters in Water-Colours. Ours is a large exhibition watercolour and therefore coincides with the painting of this title exhibited at the high price of thirty-five guineas, twenty guineas being an average price for De Wint's work around that time. The Gallery's is the largest and most highly worked of the known versions of Kenilworth Castle.

Kenilworth Castle, in the English midland county of Warwickshire, has romantic historical associations from early Norman to Elizabethan times, which is when it became the seat of the Queen's favourite, Robert Dudley, Earl of Leicester, who entertained her lavishly there. It was immortalised in Walter Scott's popular novel *Kenilworth*, first published in 1821, only a few years before De Wint painted this watercolour.[4] A visitors' guide to the castle published in the 1820s says, "…as we tread the ground so much famed in history as Kenilworth, the mind is naturally affected with a pleasing pensive melancholy".[5]

This is the mood that De Wint evokes. It is not one of the fresh wash drawings that John Clare so lovingly described as "…those rough sketches taken in the fields…of open air and sunshine" and instead has some of the qualities Clare disliked in the picturesque watercolours by other artists: "mountains lifting up the very plains with their extravagant attitudes… ruins with their worn and mossy claptrap for effect."[6] De Wint produced simple watercolour sketches of Dutch-like flat landscapes, often taken around Lincoln with grain-harvesting and haymaking, as well as conventionally imposing views that included such institutional subjects as cathedrals, country houses and castles. The latter compositions were the ones enlarged and highly finished in his studio.

# Peter De Wint

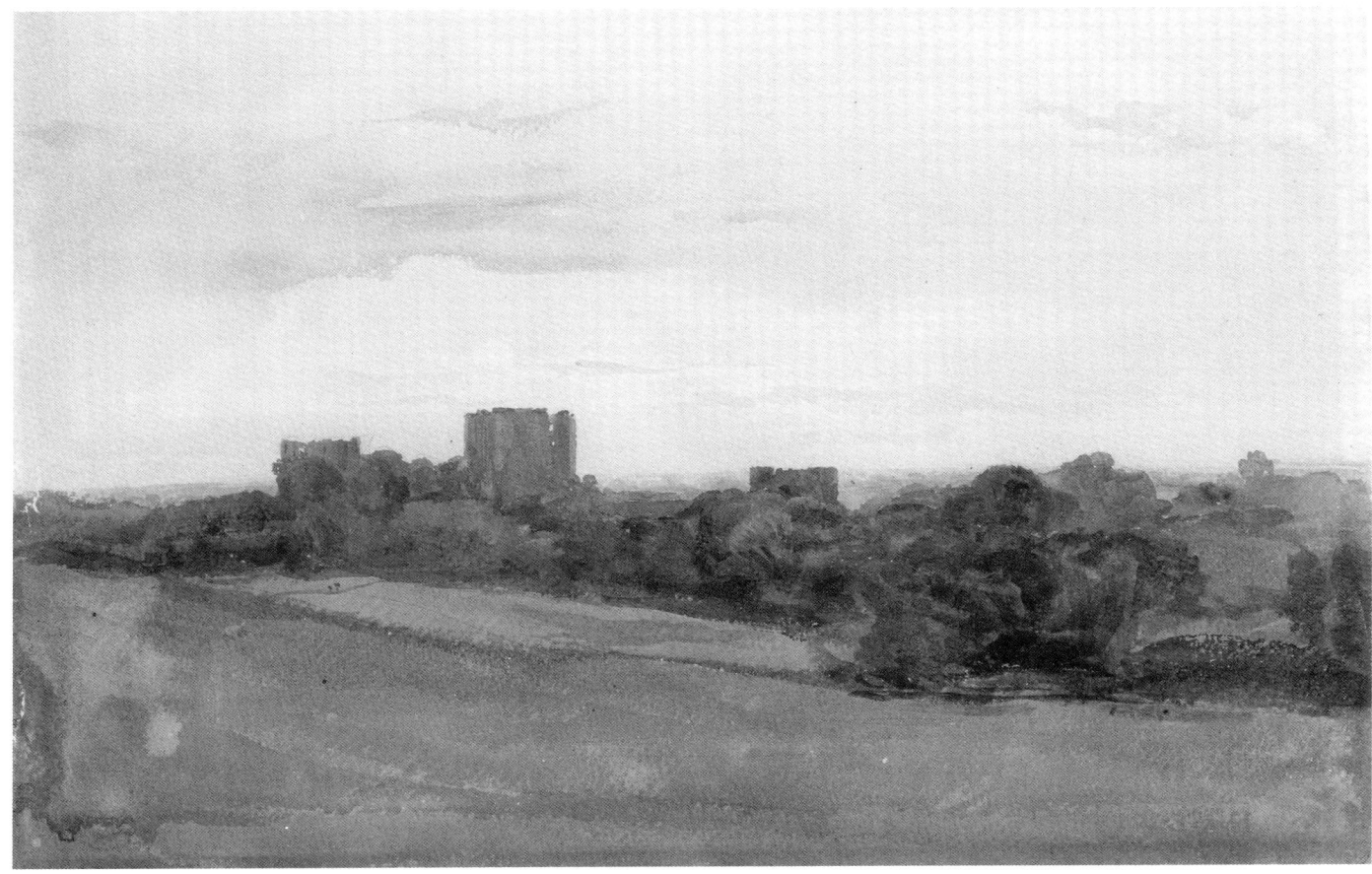

Peter De Wint, *Kenilworth Castle*. © Tate, London 2004

If by the 1820s Kenilworth Castle was one of the artist's traditional institutional subjects, De Wint's balanced composition and careful rendering is also 'institutionalised'. It follows the spirit and grand style of none other than the great Claude Lorrain[7] who painted in Rome two hundred years earlier. The middle-distant Medieval ruins, like Claude's Roman ruins, are silhouetted against a sky radiating with the warm glow of a setting sun. This magical Claudean light is reflected up from foreground water and it backlights the classically balanced framing foliage. By capturing the golden light De Wint transforms the subject from mere topography into a landscape of poetry, evoking the passage of time. In doing so he is stylistically linked to his great contemporary J. M. W. Turner, as is amply demonstrated in the Gallery's romantic *Alnwick Castle*, c.1829 (p. 211), a similar subject to Kenilworth Castle and of similar date, and also in Turner's earlier *Scarborough*, c.1810 (p. 207), a landscape infused with Claudean light. Like the oil paintings and finished watercolours by Turner (and Claude long before) De Wint's *Kenilworth Castle* was a careful working-up of the composition in his studio, developed from on-the-spot watercolour sketches.[7]

This romantic castle was a favourite artist's subject, painted by many of De Wint's contemporaries. They included Turner, Michael Angelo Rooker, David Cox and James Ward.

**Provenance:** Earl of Cavan (possibly Frederick Rudolf Lambart, the 10th Earl of Cavan, 1865–1946) by 1906; J. Leslie Wright (1862–1954); bought for the Art Gallery of South Australia through the Fine Art Society, London, on the advice of H. D. Molesworth, 1955.

**Exhibitions:** *Society of Painters in Water-Colours*, London, 1827. *Royal Academy Winter Exhibition*, 1906. *Regency: British Art & Design 1800–1830*, AGSA, Adelaide, 1998, no. 100. *Island to Empire: 300 Years of British Art 1550–1850*, AGSA, Adelaide 2005.

**Literature:** "A Group of English Water-colours", *NGSA Bulletin*, vol. 17, no. 2, October 1955, [pp. 2, 6]. *Picture Book*, Adelaide: AGSA, 1960, p. 21. Ron Radford in Christopher Menz, *Regency*, Adelaide: AGSA, 1998, p. 60.

**Condition:** Excellent.

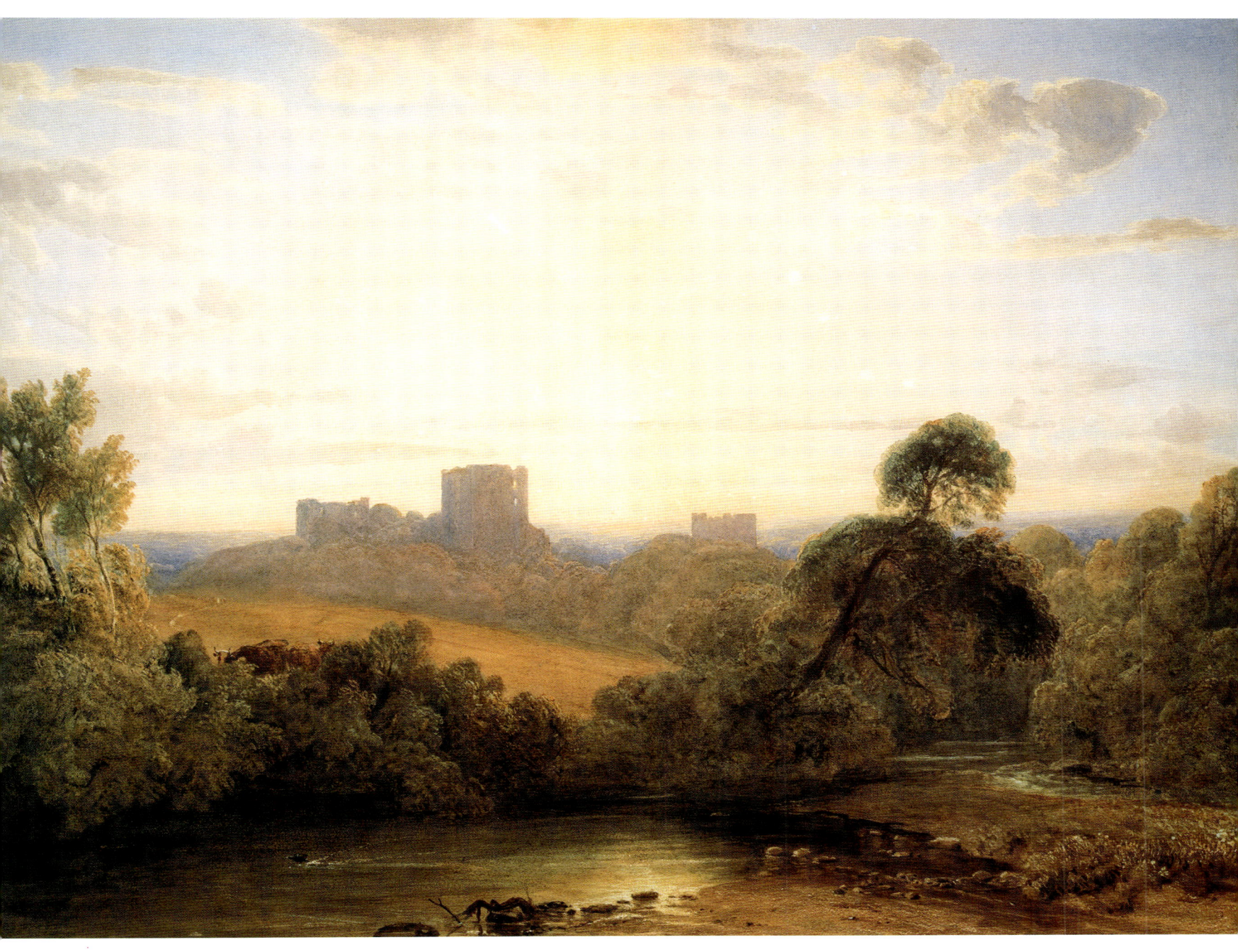

# T. Sidney Cooper 1803–1902

Thomas Sidney Cooper was renowned throughout the Victorian era as a painter of large cows in natural landscape settings. He was also a very fine pre-Victorian animal painter as the Gallery's 1834 painting testifies. Cattle made a fortune for him over a long nineteenth-century career that ended in 1902, aged ninety-nine, just after the end of Victoria's reign.

Born in 1803 in Canterbury, in a house on High Street, Cooper was a largely self-taught child prodigy. He undertook a haphazard apprenticeship as a decorator of wagons and coaches and theatrical scenery after the Archbishop of Canterbury first noticed him drawing the tower of Christ Church Cathedral on a slate. He gained early recognition for livestock portraiture but abandoned such work once he had developed a more academic and sophisticated style of animal painting. Summoned to London by an uncle, he took the opportunity to draw sculptures in the British Museum and pictures at the Angerstein Collection that was bought in 1824 to be part of the future National Gallery. In 1824 he attended the Royal Academy Schools but could not afford to continue when his uncle withdrew an allowance; he returned to Canterbury.

In 1827 Cooper left England for extended study in Brussels. There he met the painter Eugène Verboeckhoven (1799–1881) who taught him how to imitate the masters of seventeenth-century Dutch landscape and animal painting, in particular the great painters Aelbert Cuyp and Paulus Potter. Returning to London in 1831 (just after another sometime painter of cows, John Glover, had left permanently for Tasmania), Cooper established his reputation with pictures of cows in the "Dutch style", but which incorporated the recent British movement towards realistic landscape. He soon was nicknamed "Cow" Cooper to distinguish him from an Abraham "Horse" Cooper. He added cows and other domestic animals to the paintings of fellow artists Thomas Creswick and F. R. Lee.

Cooper exhibited with considerable success at the British Institution and the Society of British Artists. From 1833 he also exhibited regularly at the Royal Academy – indeed 266 pictures were exhibited there over seventy years without any annual break – and he became an Associate of the Academy in 1845. In 1848 Queen Victoria summoned him to Osborne to paint a portrait of her favourite Jersey cow 'Buffie'. There he suffered an exchange with the Prince Consort about the conventionally artistic dock leaves introduced into the foreground but perceived as weeds by the prince, who joked: "Well, they are beautifully painted, and doubtless assist the composition, but they do not give evidence of good farming." For the queen he painted one other animal portrait, of Princess Alice's pet lamb 'Milly'.[1]

In 1850 Cooper left London and built a large house at Harbledown on the outskirts of Canterbury. He died a wealthy man in 1902, and remained a local hero in Canterbury, but having risen so high in the nineteenth century his reputation fell dramatically in the twentieth. Today in an urban technological age he is again justifiably given recognition for his highly technical skill in painting farm animals in atmospheric rural landscapes.

## Fording a brook, suburbs of Canterbury, 1834
oil on canvas, 96.2 x 133.7 cm
Gift of Dorothy Spry 2000

This is a masterpiece from Cooper's early period and finer than his better-known Victorian work. He had begun to exhibit his oils only one year before he painted *Fording a brook, suburbs of Canterbury*.

Like many of his other works, the subject is a dairy herd at milking time: the cattle are fording a shallow stream in the charge of a dog (at the centre) and a boy on a donkey bringing up the rear. The boy on the donkey engages with a gypsy man and woman who are camping by roadside trees on the left. The centre foreground is given to a confrontation between the herd's bull with the border collie who controls the droving when the boy loiters. Despite the inclusion of the bull, the dairy herd is presumably on its way to early evening milking. The glow of late afternoon sky illuminates the ancient city of Canterbury seen on the horizon. Cooper's earliest memories included his attempts to sketch Canterbury Cathedral and here, centrally framed by stark gnarled oaks, we have a distant but clear depiction of the cathedral. The rural boy understood the daily rituals of milking time just as well as the regular pilgrimages to Canterbury Cathedral.

The flat, wet landscape with cattle owes much to seventeenth-century Dutch landscape art, but also relates to a British tradition of painting farm animals for landowners. The subject of cattle in golden light is a particular tribute to Cuyp. The landscape itself with the brown feathery foliage of old oaks against a big cloudy sky recalls early work by Salomon van Ruysdael and the tonal landscape painters who worked in Haarlem in the first half of the seventeenth century. However, this post-Regency canvas has a greater sense of specificity and naturalism, painted in the wake of more realist British landscapes led by Turner and Constable. It also reflects a boom in farm-animal paintings that accompanied the supremacy of British agriculture in the early nineteenth century.

Cooper described this subject as "an elaborate composition – cattle going through water to a road fringed with gnarled oaks, with an evening effect". In 1833–34 he may have produced an earlier version, sold for £15 to an art dealer named Crib, who carried it away "under his arm".[2] Cooper recorded that this crucial sale was the beginning of his

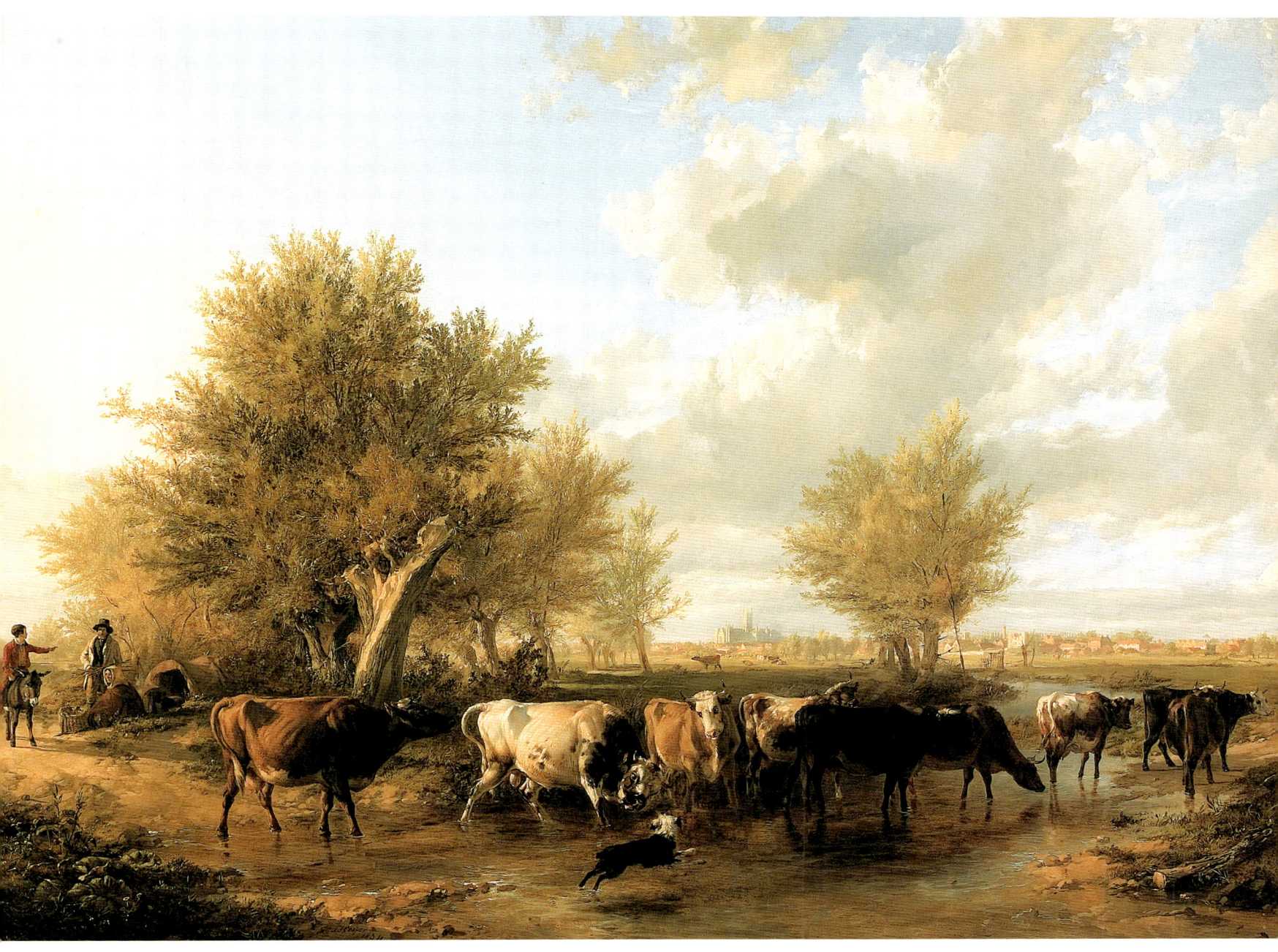

successful career. The Gallery's large painting – which could not be carried so easily under an arm – was almost certainly the version exhibited in London under the title *Fording a brook, Canterbury*, at the British Institution, in 1835.[3] The addition of "*Suburbs of Canterbury*" to the title comes from an inscription on a stretcher at the back of the canvas.

The Gallery also owns a more typical Victorian watercolour of a cow and three sheep by Cooper, dated 1883 and therefore painted when he was at the height of his fame and popularity. The watercolour was bought in London in 1899 as part of the first group of contemporary art purchases made by the curator H. P. Gill with the Gallery's generous Elder Bequest Fund. Other paintings by Cooper that entered Australian public collections from the late nineteenth century onwards likewise gave less prominence to cattle than to sheep.

| | |
|---|---|
| Inscription: | Signed and dated l.l., black paint: "T. S. Cooper/ 1834". Inscribed reverse stretcher bot. r., black ink (inverted): "[illeg.]…ing a Brook / [illeg.]… 13 Portland Terrace/ Regent's Park/ suburbs of Canterbury". |
| Provenance: | William Ernest Duncombe, third Baron then first Earl of Feversham (1829–1915); thence to his grandson the second Earl (1879–1916); thence to his son the third Earl (1906–1963); Christie's, London, 9 June 1967, lot 4444, *Cattle crossing stream*, bt P. Polak of Polak, St James's, whence sold to Mr H. Bell-Wilson; bt from Mr Bell-Wilson by Robert Jones Fine Art Ltd, London, whence sold 1989 to Miss Dorothy Spry, Hunters Hill, Sydney. |
| Exhibitions: | Probably British Institution, London, 1835, no. 384, *Fording a brook, Canterbury*. *Island to Empire: 300 Years of British Art 1550–1850*, AGSA, Adelaide, 2005. |
| Literature: | T. Sidney Cooper, *My Life*, London: Richard Bentley & Son, 1891, pp. 139–40. Stephen Sartin, *Thomas Sidney Cooper, C.V.O., R.A., 1802–1902*, Leigh-on-Sea, Essex, 1976, pp. 21–23, and no. E16, p. 53. Brian Stewart, *Thomas Sidney Cooper of Canterbury*, Rainham, Kent, 1983, p. 17 (illus.). Angus Trumble, "A youthful masterpiece by 'Cow' Cooper", *The Adelaide Review*, March 2000, p. 33 (illus.). |
| Condition: | Excellent; last conserved in 2000 by Artlab Australia, Adelaide. |
| Frame: | Original. |

# John Linnell 1792–1882

John Linnell's long and ultimately very successful career extended through most of the nineteenth century. He is mainly known as a landscape painter and his landscapes provide a stylistic link between three phases of British nineteenth-century landscape: the direct realism of his rivals John Constable and William Mulready, the precise detail of the Pre-Raphaelites in the mid nineteenth century, and the more generalised popular realism of late-Victorian landscape painting. He was also a highly accomplished portrait painter. His financial success is a measure of British taste and middle-class patronage throughout the nineteenth century. Before the 1820s most of his works for sale were highly naturalistic landscapes in watercolour but as the watercolour market subsided he devoted himself, from the 1820s to the 1840s, to portrait commissions in oil. By the 1850s popular taste had changed to landscapes in oil and Linnell then took to landscape painting for the rest of his life and became by far the wealthiest landscape painter in nineteenth-century Britain. This is not to say that Linnell pandered to popular taste. He remained faithful to his own almost religious doctrine of truth to nature.

Linnell was born in London in 1792. In 1804, aged twelve, he became a pupil of the influential watercolourist John Varley at whose studio he met two other young artists, William Henry Hunt and William Mulready, and was profoundly influenced by their devotion to realism. In 1805 he also enrolled at the Royal Academy Schools, under Henry Fuseli, where he learned not only to draw the figure but also to appreciate classical art, particularly that of the Italian Renaissance masters. Linnell later made small saleable copies of Renaissance paintings. Varley introduced Linnell to Dr Thomas Monro's evenings where he met many of the British watercolourists and was exposed to Monro's huge collection of their work.

From opposing disciplines – on one hand the guidance of nature encouraged by Varley and Mulready, and on the other the classical teachings of the Royal Academy – Linnell learned that the skill of an artist lay in ability to select only what is necessary from what is observed.

In 1818 Linnell met and became friendly with the visionary poet and painter William Blake. Both artists were intensely religious and found kinship in their mutual belief that all aspects of nature, its forms, moods and effects, take on a metaphorical significance beyond casual appearance. It was Linnell who commissioned the much older artist to produce his Job engravings and Dante plates. And it was Linnell who introduced Samuel Palmer to Blake, who had a profound impact on the young painter; later, in 1837, Linnell's daughter Hannah married Samuel Palmer.

## Mr Clare and Mrs Clare, 1834
oil on oak panels, 25.2 x 20.2 cm and 25.4 x 20.1 cm
Public Donations Fund 1983

This pair was painted by Linnell in 1834 midway through his profitable thirty-year career as a portrait painter. From about 1820 to about 1847 portraits were his main specialisation but after that Linnell referred such commissions to George Richmond. The Gallery's small pair is similar in technique and format to Linnell's other work at the time, among them his portraits of fellow artists William Mulready, William Collins, Thomas Phillips and Augustus Callcott. Those interesting portraits, like the Gallery's pair, show Linnell's technique of applying and building up translucent coloured glazes of oil and copal to achieve depth and colour in the shadows. The method of using oil varnish rather as if it were watercolour came to Linnell (and Mulready) from John Glover.

The heads and shoulders of the husband and wife are simply but elegantly placed in the vertical format. The likenesses are direct and penetrating without any ostentation or flourish. They contrast with the more fashionable and flashy portraits, often of aristocratic sitters, by Sir Thomas Lawrence, the President of the Royal Academy, who had died only four years previously. Linnell was known for down-to-earth portraits of middle-class sitters who included professionals, businessmen and tradesmen as well as fellow artists.

We can assume that these are good likenesses of the elderly couple but we do not know who the Clares were. They could have been related to John Clare the nature poet (1793–1864, certified insane and confined in 1837) who associated with artists including Linnell and De Wint. The portraits are signed and dated but came from a Tasmanian collection without further identification. However, they are identifiable as a Mr and Mrs Clare recorded in the artist's "Portrait Sketch-book" held by the British Museum. This book and another devoted to his landscapes do not contain preparatory sketches but were put together by Linnell late in life and filled with record sketches, a form of Liber Veritatis like that made by Claude Lorrain to document his landscapes. Linnell created the authentication system for his son James, in 1879, from his journals, his cash account book and from memory.

The page that documents and names the Gallery's 1834 portraits contains thumbnail sketches of three-quarter-length busts of the same sitters but they are recorded as on canvas and larger, 17 by 14 inches (43.0 x 35.5 cm) (see p. 252).

# John Linnell

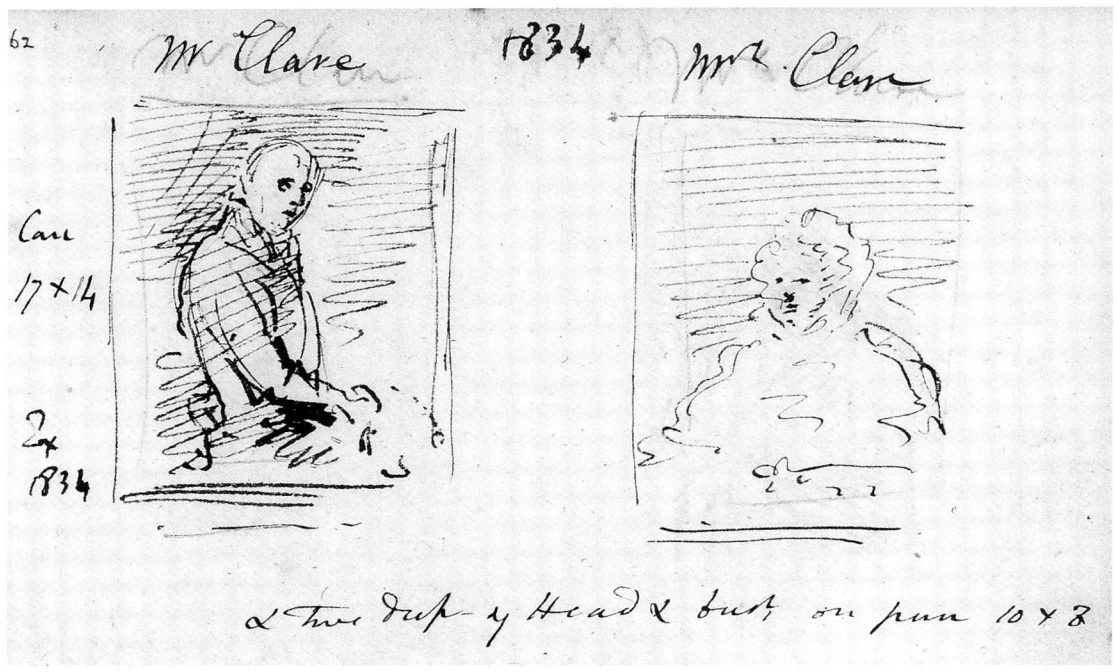

John Linnell, *Study for the paintings "Mr Clare" and "Mrs Clare"*, 1834. © Copyright The Trustees of The British Museum, London

Under those sketches Linnell noted: "+ two Dup[licates] of head and bust on pan[el] 10 x 8", doubtless referring to our smaller half-lengths which are indeed on wood panels 10 by 8 inches (25.4 x 20.3 cm). It was not at all unusual for commissions to include additional versions of a portrait, one kept by the client while others went to various members of the family, perhaps on the occasion of a marriage, or departure for the colonies. The latter might have been the case with this pair of portraits, believed to have come to Tasmania in the nineteenth century. Linnell in 1825 had already painted a pair of emigration portraits, one of Ralph Darling and the other of his wife and children, just before Darling left Britain to be Governor of New South Wales (National Library of Australia). Many settlers with the surname Clare came to Tasmania in the early and later nineteenth century.[1]

These paintings have an interesting similarity in style to the intimate portraits by Thomas Bock and his pupil Robert Dowling, portrait painters in colonial Tasmania who were Linnell's contemporaries. The Gallery holds similarly-scaled portraits by the Tasmanian artists.

**Inscriptions:** Both signed and dated l.r.: oil: "J. Linnell.f. /1834".
**Provenance:** Private collection Tasmania by 1982; to Masterpiece Fine Art Gallery, Hobart, whence bought 1983 for Art Gallery of South Australia.
**Exhibitions:** *Regency: British Art & Design 1800-1830*, AGSA, Adelaide, 1998, no. 113. *Island to Empire: 300 Years of British Art 1550-1850*, AGSA, Adelaide 2005.
**Literature:** Ron Radford in Christopher Menz, *Regency*, Adelaide: AGSA, 1998, p. 67.
**Condition:** Very good; conserved in 1997 by Artlab Australia, Adelaide.
**Frame:** Original.

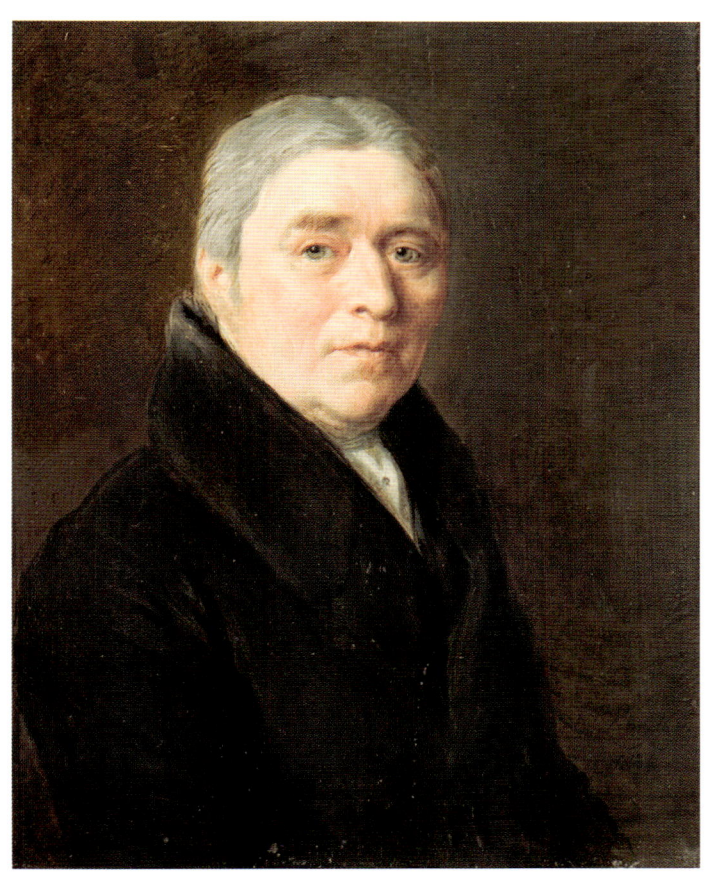
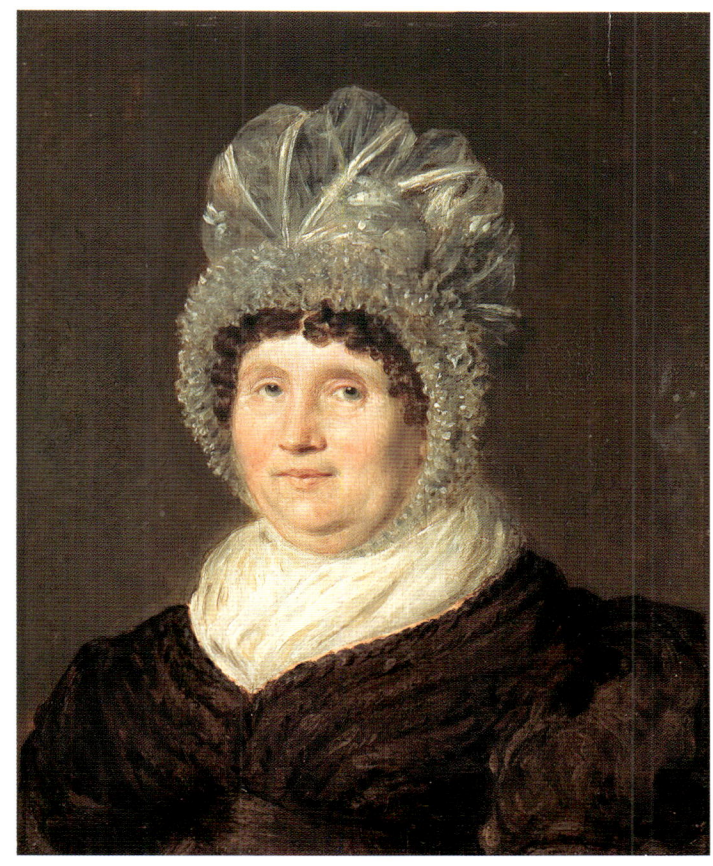

# John Gibson 1790–1866

John Gibson worked most of his life in Rome where he became one of the leading exponents of European Neoclassicism in the nineteenth century. He was admired nearly as highly as the two major Neoclassical sculptors, Antonio Canova (1757–1822) and Bertel Thorvaldsen (1770–1844). His patrons were American, Italian and German as well as British, and academies throughout Europe eventually honoured him.

Born in 1790, he was the son of a Welsh market gardener who had settled in Liverpool in 1799. He trained under the sculptor F. A. Legé (1779–1837) and from 1810 exhibited drawings and models at the Liverpool Academy. In 1817, to pursue his studies of the Antique, he went to London, met the Neoclassical sculptor John Flaxman who encouraged him go to Rome, and departed for Italy later the same year. In Rome, Gibson studied under Canova and under his guidance produced his first original sculptures. Gibson later received instruction from Thorvaldsen, and these two acknowledged masters of Neoclassical sculpture were his most important formative influences. In 1819 Gibson received his first commission and he soon became a favourite of English collectors in Rome, the leading figure in a colony of British sculptors working there. Among the others were Lawrence Macdonald (1799–1878), Joseph Gott (1786–1860) and Richard James (fl.1850–1900). He also helped the next generation of sculptors in Rome, among them Henry Timbrell (1806–1849), William Calder Marshall (1813–1894) and Mary Thornycroft (1814–1895).

Gibson declined many offers of work in London, though he exhibited at the Royal Academy from 1816 to 1864 and was elected an associate member in 1833 and a full member in 1838. Gibson revisited England in 1844–47 and 1850 to execute statues of Queen Victoria, one of them for the House of Lords, and to supervise the installation of major commissions in his home city of Liverpool. Many of his commissions came from patrons in Liverpool, particularly from its wealthy industrialists and merchants. The shipping heir Henry Sandbach (1807–1895) and his wife Margaret commissioned a number of works between 1839 and 1865 and among many other patrons at Liverpool were the manufacturers Richard Alison and Robert Preston.

In 1864 he was granted the Legion of Honour by the French government and after his death was honoured by a marble statue at the Glyptothek in Munich, alongside those of Canova, Thorvaldsen and others. One of the wealthiest sculptors of his day, he left most of his fortune, some £32,000, to the Royal Academy, together with the statues and models from his studio.

## Portrait of a woman, c.1840

marble, 63.5 x 49.5 x 22.9 cm

Gift of Max Carter, Geoffrey Hackett-Jones, Delcie Norton and Lady Porter
through the Art Gallery of South Australia Foundation Collectors' Club 2002

We do not know who sat for this elegant post-Regency portrait though almost without exception Gibson's few portraits were of his personal friends. It is difficult to date the work with any certainty but considering the costume and hairstyle it is probably from the late 1830s. The sitter may have some connection with the Sandbach family who were his friends and patrons. Of his recorded female portrait busts, two are yet to be traced: a Mrs Mainwairing and Viscountess Clifton (possibly Mary, Viscountess Clifton of Lanhydrock, Bodmin, Cornwall). It is doubtful our bust is one of those sitters.

Gibson's sculptures are notable for technical excellence, subtlety of composition, clarity of form and delicate modelling. His portraits, and this one in particular, are virtuoso essays that balance the competing imperatives of obtaining a likeness and idealising in conformity with Neoclassical style. He sought to achieve ideal beauty through the study of the human form, perfected according to the standards of Greek, or Greco-Roman, sculpture. Gibson regarded "novelties in sculpture" as "signs of ignorance" and was a consistent opponent of the use of modern costume in portraiture: "The human figure concealed under a frock-coat and trousers is not a fit subject for sculpture". It is no surprise to find that our sitter's diaphanous, Regency-style apparel speaks of a fashion from earlier decades than Gibson's heyday, and probably earlier than the execution of the portrait.

The bust has Neoclassical elegance in profile, a stylised silhouette of a woman whose hairdo refers to ancient Roman classical hairstyles with a high-netted bun. From the front it has the softer realistic modelling of an early-Victorian woman. Gibson is important because his output charts the transition in sculpture from Regency to Victorian styles. His Neoclassicism was tempered by newly awakened forces of naturalism; the emotional and the pictorial in art undermined the dominance of the classical aesthetic. This portrait sculpture perfectly demonstrates the transition from Regency Neoclassicism to Victorian realism.[1]

Inscription: Inscribed verso, incised in marble: "I GIBSON FECIT / ROMÆ". Incised in marble left side: "I. GIBSON FECIT".
Provenance: David Lowe, Melbourne, 1974; Renée and Keith Free, Sydney.
Exhibition: *Island to Empire: 300 Years of British Art 1550–1850*, AGSA, Adelaide, 2005.
Condition: Good; the surface shows some weathering from outdoor exposure probably in the early to mid twentieth century. Cleaned in 2002 by Artlab Australia, Adelaide.

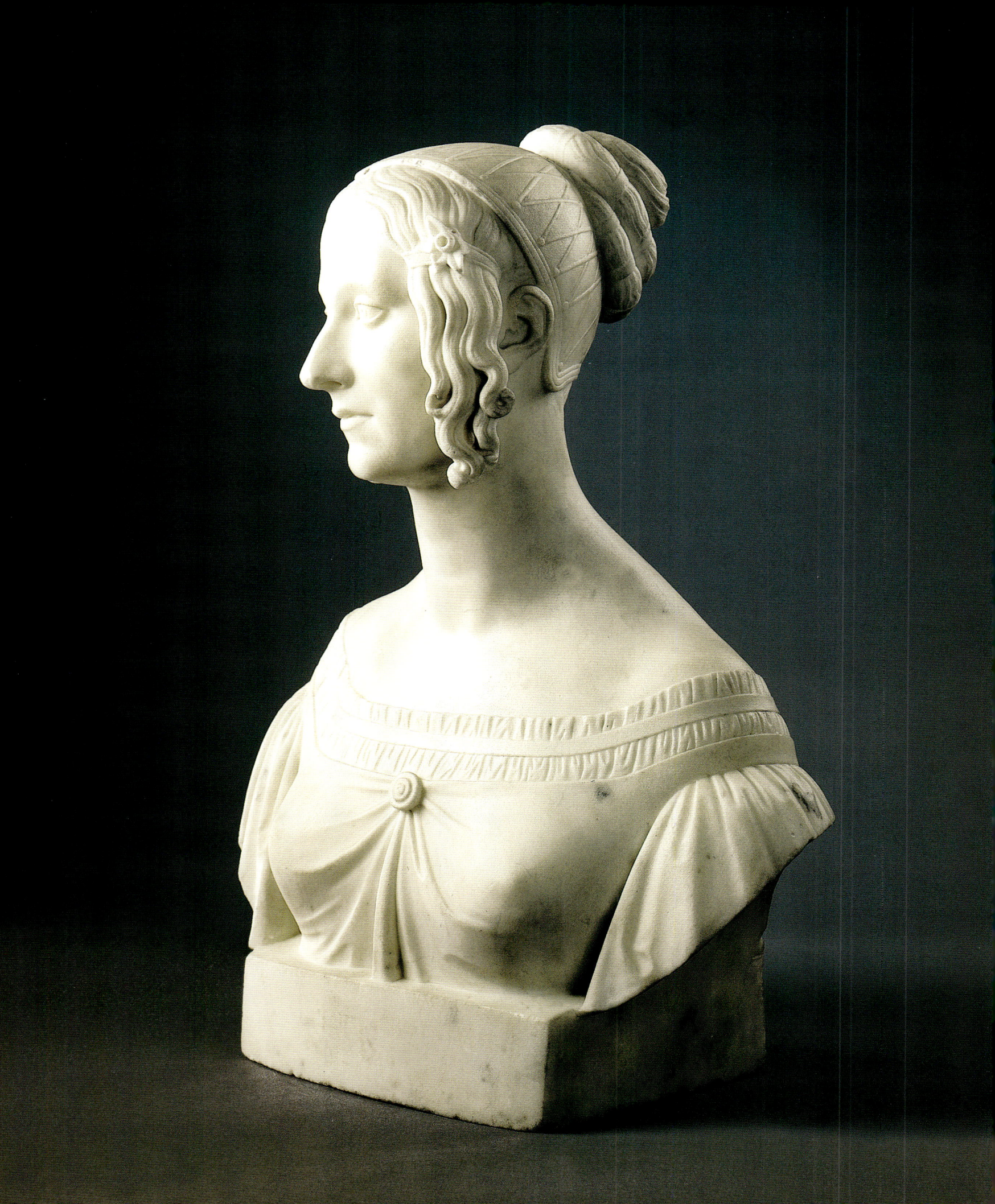

# J. F. Herring senior 1795–1865

J. F. Herring senior was the most celebrated racehorse painter in mid-nineteenth-century Britain but also painted other animals, and rural scenes. Among his racehorse portraits there were no fewer than thirty-three consecutive winners of the St Leger at Doncaster, twenty-one Derby winners and thirty-four winners of the Oaks at Epsom. His hunting, shooting and coaching subjects concentrated on horses but included their owners, trainers and jockeys. He painted dogs and goats as well and had an odd passion for portraying lop-eared rabbits. Of less specialist and more general interest are numerous farmyard and farming pictures which are a meticulous record of rural life. Over 500 of his paintings were engraved, and the prints became a popular and lucrative sideline. His paintings and prints were intended for display in inns, trainers' lodges and tack rooms, games rooms as well as gentlemen's studies, but only occasionally for the parlour. His prosperous career coincided with an early- to mid-nineteenth-century passion for equestrian and farm-animal portraits.

Born in Surrey in 1795 and brought up in London, John Frederick Herring was self-taught but had loved fast transport and therefore sketched horses from childhood. In 1814, aged nineteen, he became a stage-coachman based at Doncaster in Yorkshire. In his spare time he decorated coach panels and painted on inn signs with horses and other animals. About 1820 he became a full-time painter of animals and in 1830 shifted to another racing and racehorse-breeding town, Newmarket in Suffolk, where he hoped to gain more commissions for horse portraits. With his return to London in 1833 he entered the most interesting phase of his career; it brought a broadening of his hitherto rather tight technique, a wider range of subject matter and important new clients, particularly royalty. In the 1840s he began the farm pictures, such as the Gallery's *Autumn*, that are his best-loved works. In 1853 he shifted back to the country, this time to a farm in Kent near Tonbridge, where he died in 1865.

J. F. Herring's younger brother Benjamin (1806–1830) was a sporting painter but died young. Three sons also became animal and sporting painters: John Frederick junior (1825–1907), Charles (1828–1856) and Benjamin junior (1830–1871).

## Autumn, 1846
oil on canvas, 45.5 x 70.5 cm
Gift of Geoffrey B. Angas Parsons through the Art Gallery of South Australia Foundation 1984

*Autumn*, painted in 1846 at the height of Herring's career, is from a set of four-seasons farming subjects. The series was made popular by high-quality coloured prints executed by J. Harris and published in 1847 by Messrs Henry Graves & Co. The prints are inscribed "Animal Painter to HRH the Duchess of Kent", who was Queen Victoria's mother. The four paintings of the seasons belonged to Charles Cammell Esq. of Wadsley House, Sheffield, and he probably commissioned them. All feature horses and all but *Winter*, where the horses shelter inside a stable, depict beautiful farmland landscapes. The particular region is unidentified but it is possibly South Yorkshire around Sheffield where the patron Cammell lived, or the nearby Doncaster where Herring had lived for seventeen years.

The cycle of the four seasons has a long history in European art. It occurs in late-Medieval manuscripts and stained glass. The best-known early paintings are by Pieter Bruegel the Elder in the sixteenth century and Nicolas Poussin in the mid seventeenth century. It was not an uncommon theme in British art in the early nineteenth century. In Adelaide the colonial artist S. T. Gill painted series of the twelve months and the four seasons in the early 1840s soon after arrival in South Australia and only a few years before Herring painted his seasons in England.

*Autumn* is the most attractive of Herring's four seasons and is one of his finest paintings. It presents the warmth and satisfaction of harvest time. Half the composition is given to three handsome carthorses that have been unhitched to relax near their hay wagon, visible at the left edge of the composition. A grey ruminates, a well-bred bay and a brown gaze alertly at a departing horseman and another harvest wagon at work in the distance. Herring here displays his skill as a horse painter, relishes the beautiful sheen of their coats and tails and the particularities of their harness. Attention lavished on the horses does not detract from the sunny rural landscape on the right.

Judging from the shadows it is probably an early-afternoon break. The hay carter, wearing a smock, listens to the standing foreman in the red waistcoat and top hat. (The model for this foreman figure appears in other works by Herring, for instance *The broken pipe*, 1844.[1]) They have chosen to rest and water the horses at a pond or stream, visible in the foreground. The departing rider is probably the squire, accompanied on foot by the gamekeeper with rifle. With their two dogs they are keeping an eye out for game birds in the stubble of the already-harvested foreground field. The hay carter's little black sheepdog watches the game dogs with consuming interest, and is probably the same animal that is the central focus in Herring's *The broken pipe*. It could be Herring's own dog. In the distance a team loads sheaves of grain into a horse-drawn wagon, and grazing sheep spread over the far distant hill.

The conscious theme is benign co-operation between humankind and domesticated animals, working together

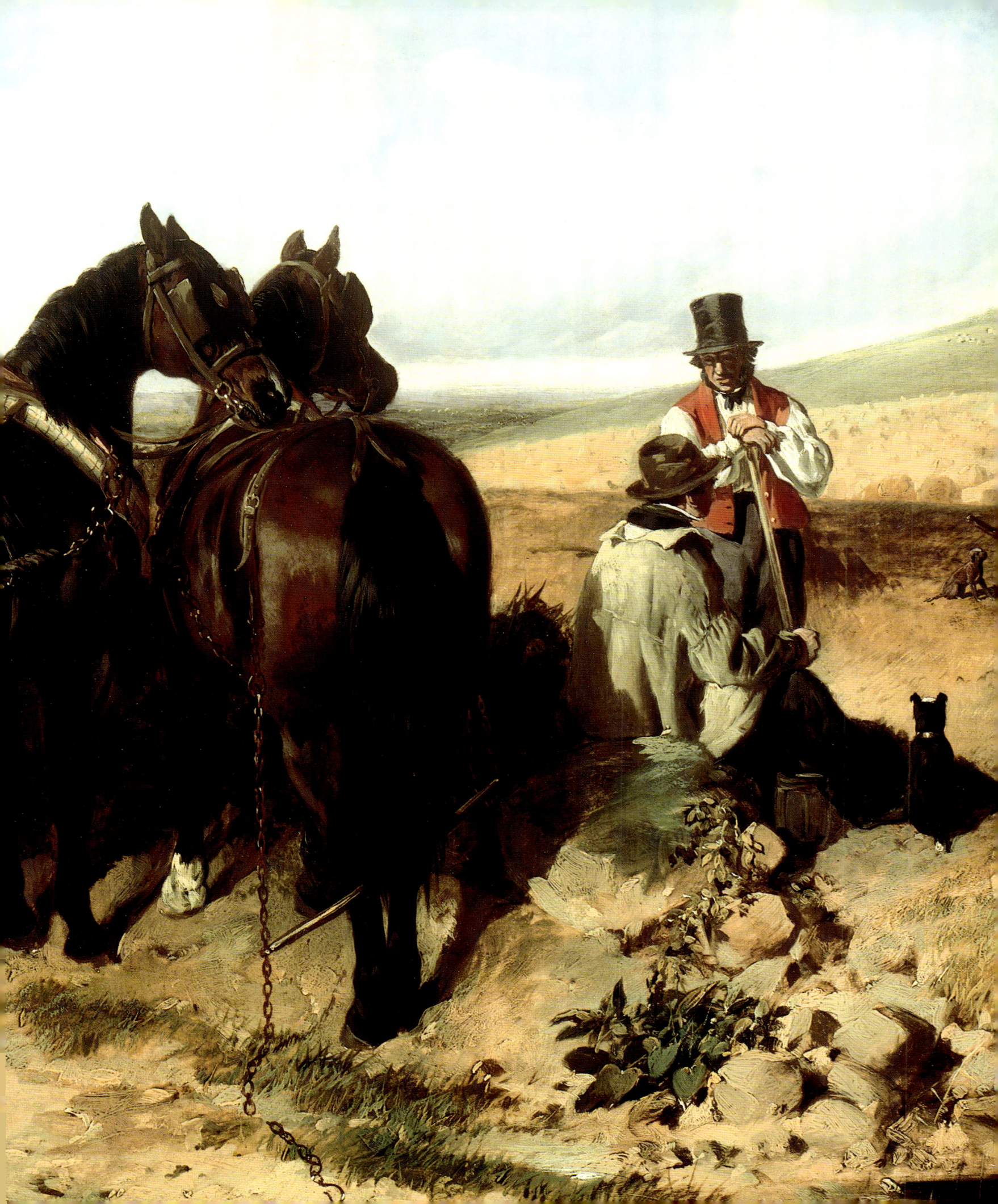

# J. F. Herring senior

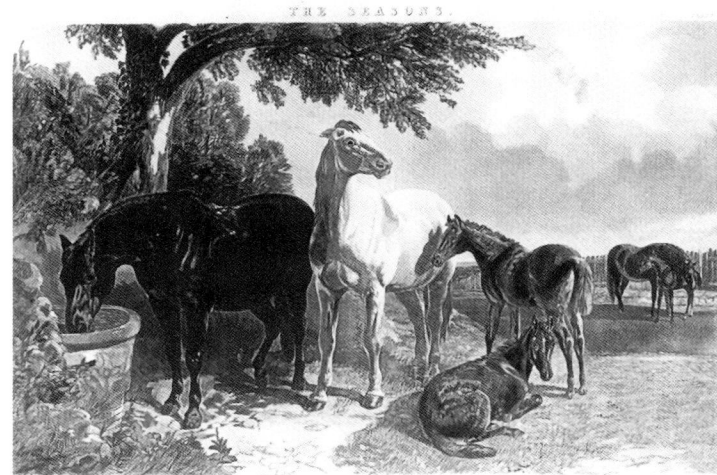
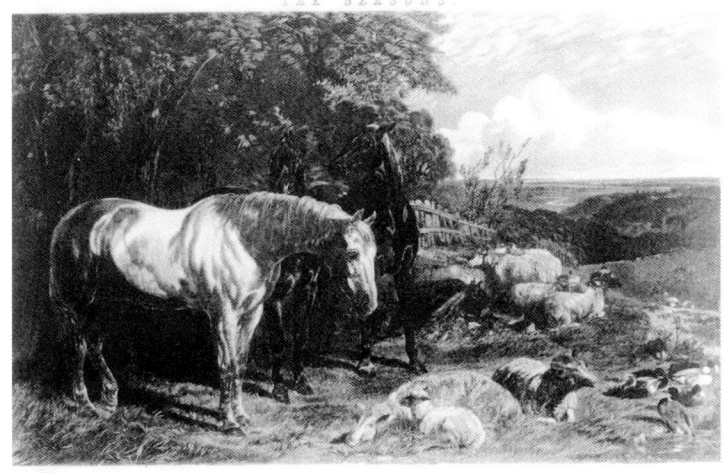
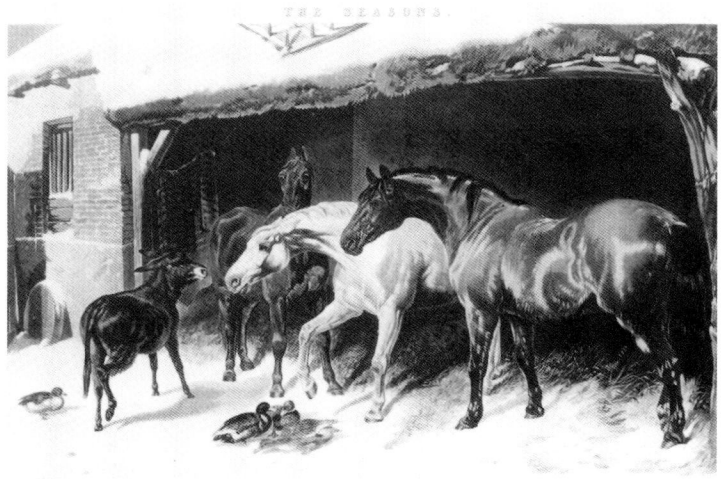
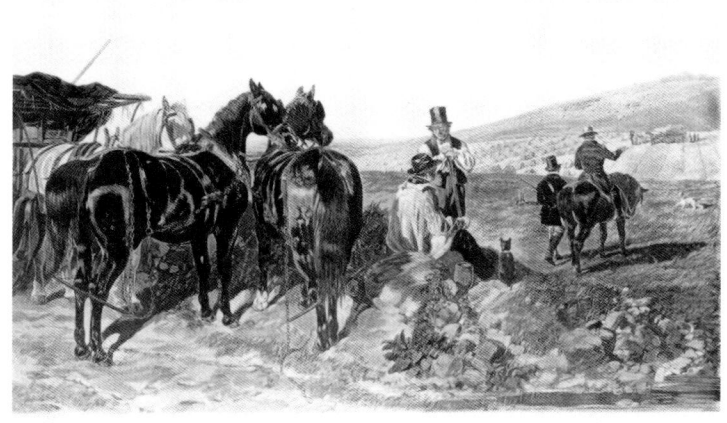

to reap the rewards of a bountiful land, in harmony with the seasons. The pleasant warmth of autumn sunshine accompanies the sense of pride and satisfaction in a year's production successfully achieved; it is a happy climax to the agricultural year. Part of the artistic success of *Autumn* is due to its pleasant colour harmony, its balance of warm browns, reds and gold contrasting with cool greens and blues. Much later, in 1859, Herring painted another major wheat-gathering subject, entitled *Harvest time*[2].

In all Herring's prolific output of more than 700 paintings over nearly half a century, his agricultural seasons, including this *Autumn*, were singled out after his death as the artist's most memorable. In 1865, along with twelve other works, they received special mention when the *Art Journal* published his obituary.[3]

top left: J. Harris, after J. F. Herring, *Spring*, from the series *The Seasons*, 1847, (published Henry Graves & Co. London)

top right: J. Harris, after J. F. Herring, *Summer*, from the series *The Seasons*, 1847, (published Henry Graves & Co. London)

bottom left: J. Harris, after J. F. Herring, *Winter*, from the series *The Seasons*, 1847, (published Henry Graves & Co. London)

bottom right: J. Harris, after J. F. Herring, *Autumn*, from the series *The Seasons*, 1847, (published Henry Graves & Co. London)

**Inscription:** Signed and dated l.r. corner, oil: "J.F.Herring.Sen<sup>r</sup>./1846".

**Provenance:** London art market 1953; purchased by the donor Geoffrey B. Angas Parsons, London, 1953.

**Exhibition:** *Island to Empire: 300 Years of British Art 1550–1850*, AGSA, Adelaide, 2005.

**Literature:** *Art Journal*, London, 1865, p. 328. Ron Radford et al., *Selected Works*, Adelaide: AGSA, 1991, p. 21 (illus.).

**Condition:** Excellent; last conserved in 1984 by Art Gallery of South Australia conservation laboratory.

**Frame:** Original.

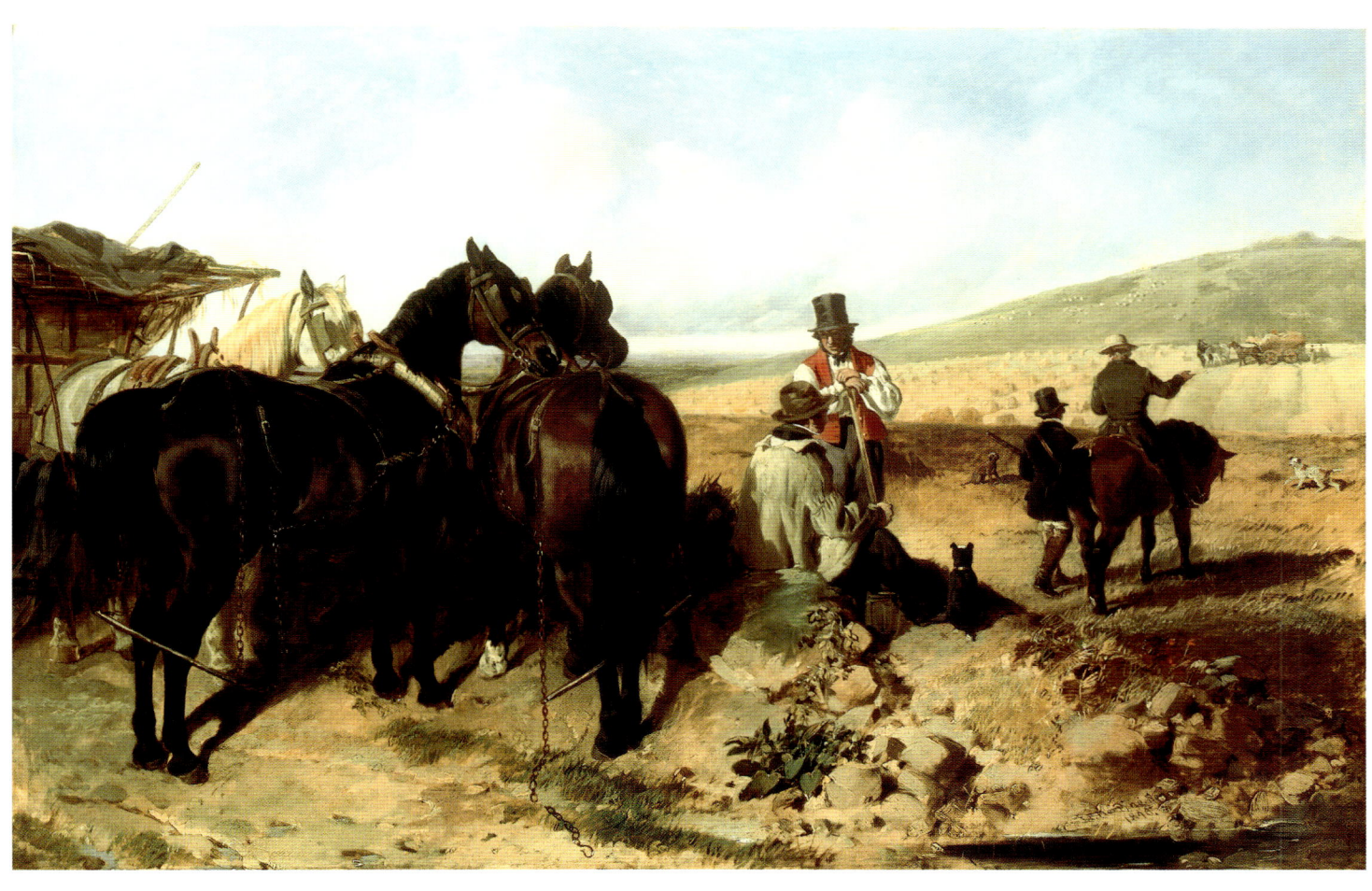

# Samuel Prout 1783–1852

Samuel Prout was one of the first English artists to specialise in watercolours of romantic scenery on the European Continent, but he began his career painting what had become routine picturesque views of British Medieval ruins and rustic cottages. After the Battle of Waterloo in 1815, followed by peace in Europe, it became safe and popular to travel again. From the early 1820s Prout popularised the scenery of the Grand Tour: Normandy, the Low Countries, the Rhine, Switzerland and Italy, particularly Venice. His work reached a wide public through the print trade and through various series of engravings and lithographs. His particular skill with architectural subjects won him the admiration of the critic John Ruskin who wrote that Prout had an "…appreciation and realisation of Continental character in his work – a locality and life which have never yet been reached by any other of our architectural draughtsmen…".[1] Prout's striking views are notable for meticulous architectural detail and rendering of masonry texture but they are also animated and made congenial by a focus on local inhabitants going about their everyday business. The figures were not merely staffage, but integral to the composition and the human-interest atmosphere. John Ruskin, writing in 1843 sets him on a pedestal: "He is the most dexterous of all our artists in a certain kind of composition. No one can place figures as he can, except Turner. …Prout's streets are the only streets that are accidentally crowded: his markets the only markets where one feels inclined to get out of the way."[2]

Born in 1783 in Plymouth, a port and naval base in Devon, Prout was first trained at the local grammar school by his headmaster Dr John Bidlake, an amateur artist who inspired both Samuel and his fellow-pupil and future artist Benjamin Robert Haydon towards romantic subject matter, including seapieces. Plymouth prided itself as the birthplace of the celebrated Sir Joshua Reynolds, first President of the Royal Academy. In London young Prout, with Haydon, met the history painter and subsequent President of the Royal Academy, Benjamin West, but more important to Prout's development was his meeting with the publisher John Britton (1771–1857). Britton employed him to illustrate antiquarian subjects and country houses that could be easily translated into steel-engravings for the *Beauties of England and Wales* (1801–15). At this early period of his career Prout painted views of churches, monuments, cottage scenes and prehistoric monuments in the style of the watercolourist Thomas Hearne.

He settled permanently in London in 1808 and worked for the publishers Thomas Palser & Rudolph Ackermann on an 1811–19 series that depicted the scenery of Devon and elsewhere in Britain. His Continental tours began in 1819, continued every year through the 1820s except 1828, and generated the majority of his most successful and memorable works. Watercolours by Prout in the Gallery's collection include views of Germany and France, as well as his native Devon. In 1829 George IV appointed him the royal Painter in Watercolour in Ordinary.

Samuel Prout was the uncle of the colonial watercolourist John Skinner Prout, also born in Plymouth, whom he taught. The nephew arrived in Sydney in 1840, worked there for four years and then in Hobart until his return to England in 1848; he was one of the liveliest landscape artists and teachers in the Australian colonies.

Samuel Prout's work, much admired when promoted by Ruskin in his lifetime and immediately after, was somewhat neglected in the twentieth century.

## Salving from the wreck, 1848
watercolour on paper, 67.2 x 97.5 cm
Elder Bequest Fund 1955

This shipwreck is not only one of the most spectacular subjects painted by Samuel Prout, it is also one of the largest of all his watercolours and probably the last of his many versions of the subject.[3] It was inspired by the wreck of the *Dutton* on the Plymouth coast on 26 January 1796. Ruskin records that Prout, then aged twelve, and the older Haydon sat awestruck watching the gnashing foam gradually break up the great East Indiaman. They both resolved to paint the scene, "…but Haydon, always incapable of acknowledging and remaining loyal to the majesty of what he had seen, lost himself in vulgar thunder and lightning. Prout struggled to some resemblance of the actual scene, and the effect upon his mind was never effaced".[4]

The massive hull dominates the shore on which the ship is grounded. It has not yet broken up, but one can imagine the groaning of the wooden hulk. The masts have snapped off and the sails drape the hull like a shroud. Under a threatening sky crewmen and others, dwarfed by the huge ship, struggle against waves and time to save the cargo. True to form, Prout has chosen not to over-dramatise the danger but simply to record the event. There is a feeling that in spite of the tragedy things are under control. On the right a young man seated on a pile of salvage calmly observes the teamwork, as if Prout has depicted himself, more than half a century earlier, committing the event to indelible memory for use in future paintings.

He first exhibited a version of this shipwreck subject in 1811 at the Associated Artists in Water-Colours. What was apparently another version was at the Royal Academy in 1817. At least a further nine were exhibited at the Society of Painters in Water-Colours between 1815 and 1834.[5] It is interesting that his 1820 version titled *Dismasted Indiaman* and his smaller *Shipwreck* (1821), of a similar subject, were bought by William Fawkes who also owned Turner's earlier coastal view *Scarborough town and castle: morning: boys catching crabs* (p. 207). Prout's 1821 version of the shipwreck, *A man-of-war ashore,* was bought by Thomas Griffith who later became

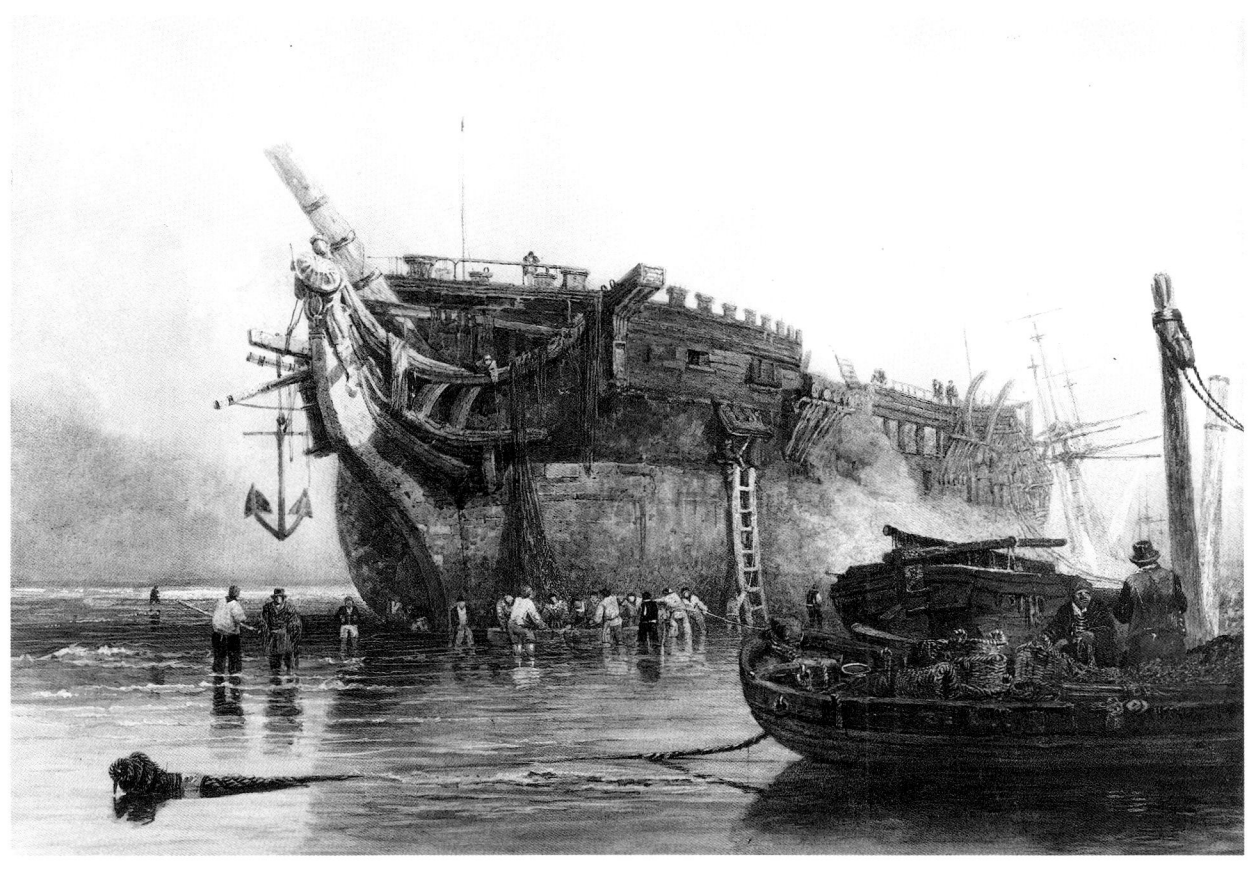

Samuel Prout, *An East Indiaman Ashore*. The Whitworth Art Gallery, The University of Manchester

Turner's agent and owned our c.1829 Turner watercolour *Alnwick Castle* (p. 211). Griffith's was the same large size as the Gallery's later version.⁶

A review in the *Magazine of the Fine Arts* says of the shipwreck exhibited in 1821 at the Old Water-Colour Society: "Mr Prout's broad large style is extremely well adapted to subjects containing large masses, such as shipping, old buildings, and distant groups, and his mode of execution seems most rapid and masterly." The reviewer, however, shared the doubts of later critics about "the use of a brown colour which is substituted for shades, preserving the chiaroscuro, and obtaining warmth where it ought not to exist". At the same time a reviewer in the *Somerset House Gazette* was impressed: "When we look at the gigantic style displayed in his pictorial representation of that ingenious work of man, a huge ship; when we behold its stupendous bulk, thus portrayed on thirty inches of paper…we are lost in the disparity of human intellect and see in this picture, as in the writings of Shakespeare…."⁷

There is no record of the Gallery's signed and dated 1848 version being exhibited in Prout's lifetime – he died only four years after its execution – so it is probable that such a large watercolour, more than three feet wide, may have been specially commissioned. On the other hand the artist may have painted and kept this monster watercolour for his own indulgence, reliving the vivid childhood memory of the shipwreck near Plymouth more than half a century later.

Apart from his shipwreck scenes Prout mainly exhibited Continental views. Therefore this *Salving from the wreck* not only climaxed the versions of his most repeated British subject but was also probably his very last sizeable British subject.

**Inscription:** Signed l.l., incised into paint layer: "S Prout". (S and P intertwined). Dated below signature, brown watercolour: "1848".

**Provenance:** Bought from the Fine Art Society, London, 1955, on the advice of H. D. Molesworth, 1955.

**Exhibition:** *Island to Empire: 300 Years of British Art 1550–1850*, AGSA, Adelaide, 2005.

**Literature:** "A Group of English Water-Colours", *NGSA Bulletin*, vol. 17, no. 2, October 1955, pp. 2, 4, 6. *NGSA: Catalogue: Oil and Water-Colour Paintings and Pastels with Biographical Notes*, Adelaide: AGSA, 1960, p. 203.

**Condition:** Excellent.

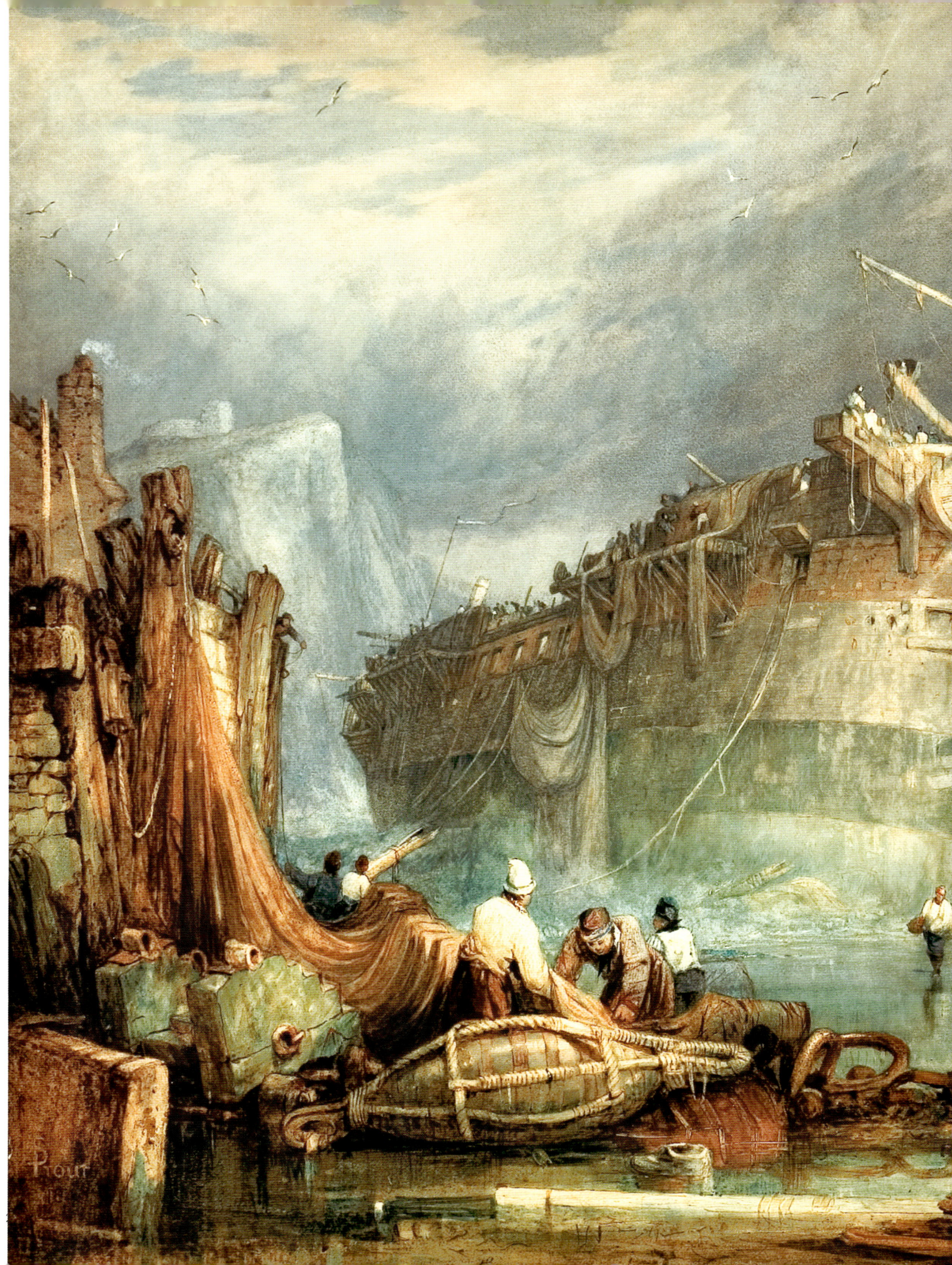

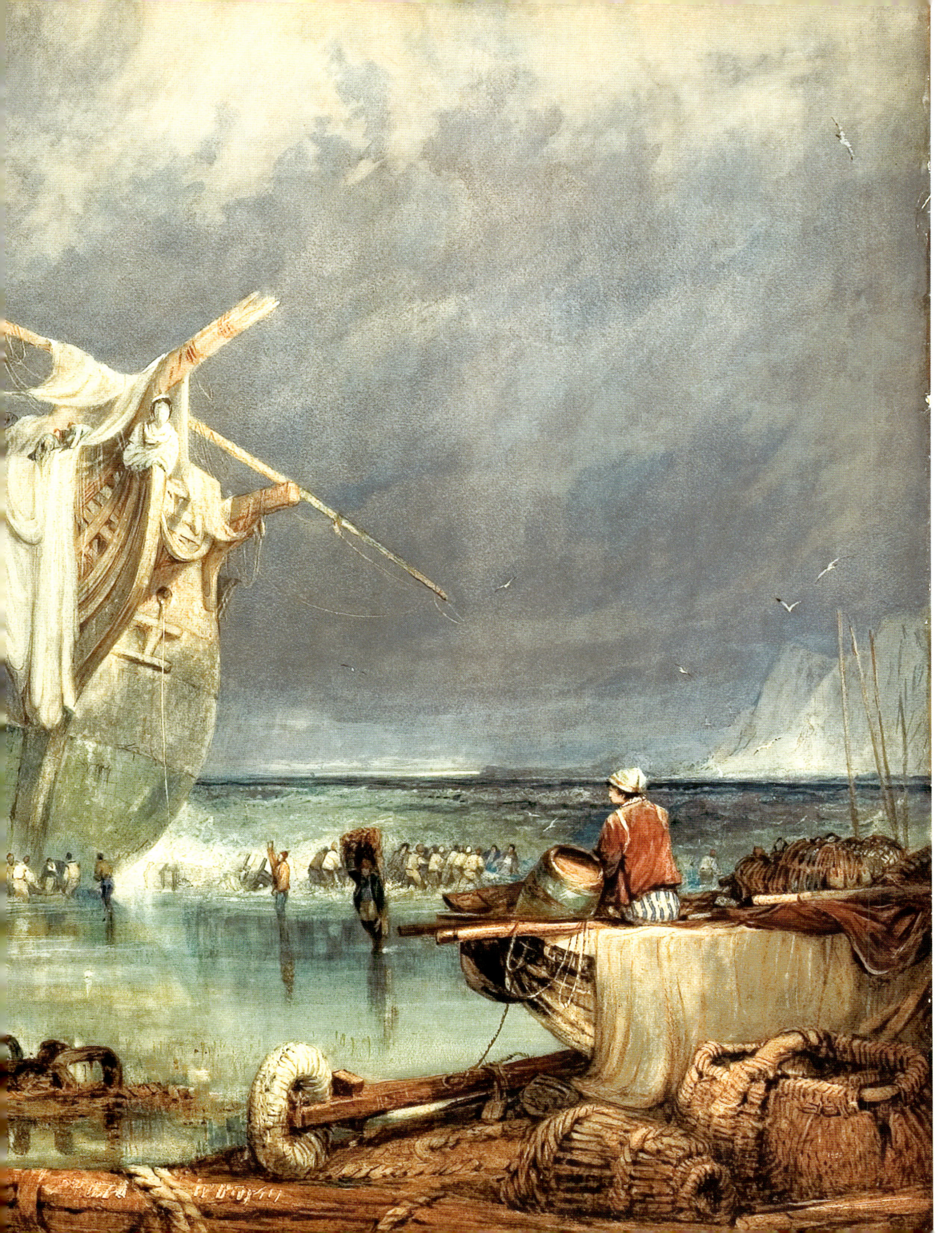

# Lionel Constable 1828–1887

Lionel Constable was the youngest son of John Constable who, with J. M. W. Turner, was the greatest and the best-known English landscape painter of all time. In 1982 a Lionel Constable exhibition at the Tate Gallery distinguished a small œuvre from the work of his famous father and identified him as an independent artist.

Born in 1828 at Hampstead, Lionel Bicknell Constable was the seventh and last child of John and Maria Constable. His mother died later the same year and his father died in 1837 when he was only nine. In 1847 he attended F. S. Cary's School of Design (Sass's Academy) in Bloomsbury where an older brother Alfred had studied earlier. He exhibited at the Royal Academy from 1849 to 1855. Lionel Constable was also an enthusiastic amateur photographer.

Although Lionel's small oil landscapes are similar to and rely heavily on those of his father, his work has characteristics of its own. He used a higher colour key, less contrast between light and dark and his paint is thinner; he generally had a lighter touch than his father. John Constable's brushwork is vigorous and robust with dramatic contrasts of light and dark. Lionel's work shows less concern with structure and form and greater concern with flattened picture planes and this may have been partly due to his interest in photography. His light-toned and painterly landscapes pre-date French Impressionism. Unlike his father he only painted very small works, nearly all of them oil sketches. He appears to have given up painting around 1855. However, until work by the other artist son, Alfred Constable, has been more securely differentiated, Lionel's output must remain speculative.

## attributed to Lionel Constable
### A summer sunset, c.1850
oil on paper on wood panel, 14.0 x 21.0 cm
Gift of Ethel Brookman Kirkpatrick 1959

## attributed to Lionel Constable
### Dawn, c.1850
oil on paper mounted on canvas, 17.4 x 24.7 cm
Gift of Ethel Brookman Kirkpatrick 1959

These small landscapes are typical of Lionel Constable's work but were formally attributed to him only in 1985.[1] Before that they were thought to be by his father John Constable and came into the Gallery's collection as such. The close tones and light touch of the thin paint are characteristic of Lionel's paintings. The low horizon and pinkish sky in *A summer sunset* and the light feathery strokes of the waves and clouds in *Dawn* are also typical qualities of his.

The paintings are of roughly similar size, around five by nine inches, and seem to be intended as a pair: sunset over the land and dawn over the water. The pink sky in the sunset landscape silhouettes the small trees against a very low horizon while in the dawn seapiece a similarly vast sky rises behind a tiny sailing ship on the horizon.

The paintings appear to have been completed in front of the motif. Since nearly all of Lionel Constable's known paintings were executed between 1849 and 1855 these too should be placed around 1850. They are not preparatory oil-sketch studies but, like all his other works, would have been intended as finished works for exhibition and sale. At the mid century this was still unusual in England. Oil paintings completed out of doors in front of the subject became a common practice only after the rise of French Impressionism in the 1860s.

**Provenance:** Benjamin Brookman, London, 1899; inherited by his daughter Florence Brookman in 1932; inherited by Florence Brookman's sister, Ethel Brookman Kirkpatrick, in 1940; given with other pictures into safe keeping at Victoria House, London, during the London blitz in 1941; after Mrs Kirkpatrick's death (1950) rediscovered at Victoria House in 1958 and, at her widower P. T. Kirkpatrick's request, in 1959 given in her name to the Art Gallery of South Australia.[2]

**Exhibition:** *Island to Empire: 300 Years of British Art 1550–1850*, AGSA, Adelaide 2005.

**Literature:** "The Brookman Kirkpatrick Pictures", *NGSA Bulletin*, vol. 21, no. 2, Adelaide: NGSA, October 1959, pp. 1–3. *NGSA Catalogue of Oil and Water-Colour Paintings and Pastels with Biographical Notes*, Adelaide: NGSA, 1960, p. 57. Ursula Hoff, *European Paintings before 1800 in the National Gallery of Victoria*, Melbourne: National Gallery of Victoria, 1995, pp. 60–61, 67.

**Condition:** Excellent; last conserved in 1992 at Artlab Australia, Adelaide.

**Frames:** Possibly not original.

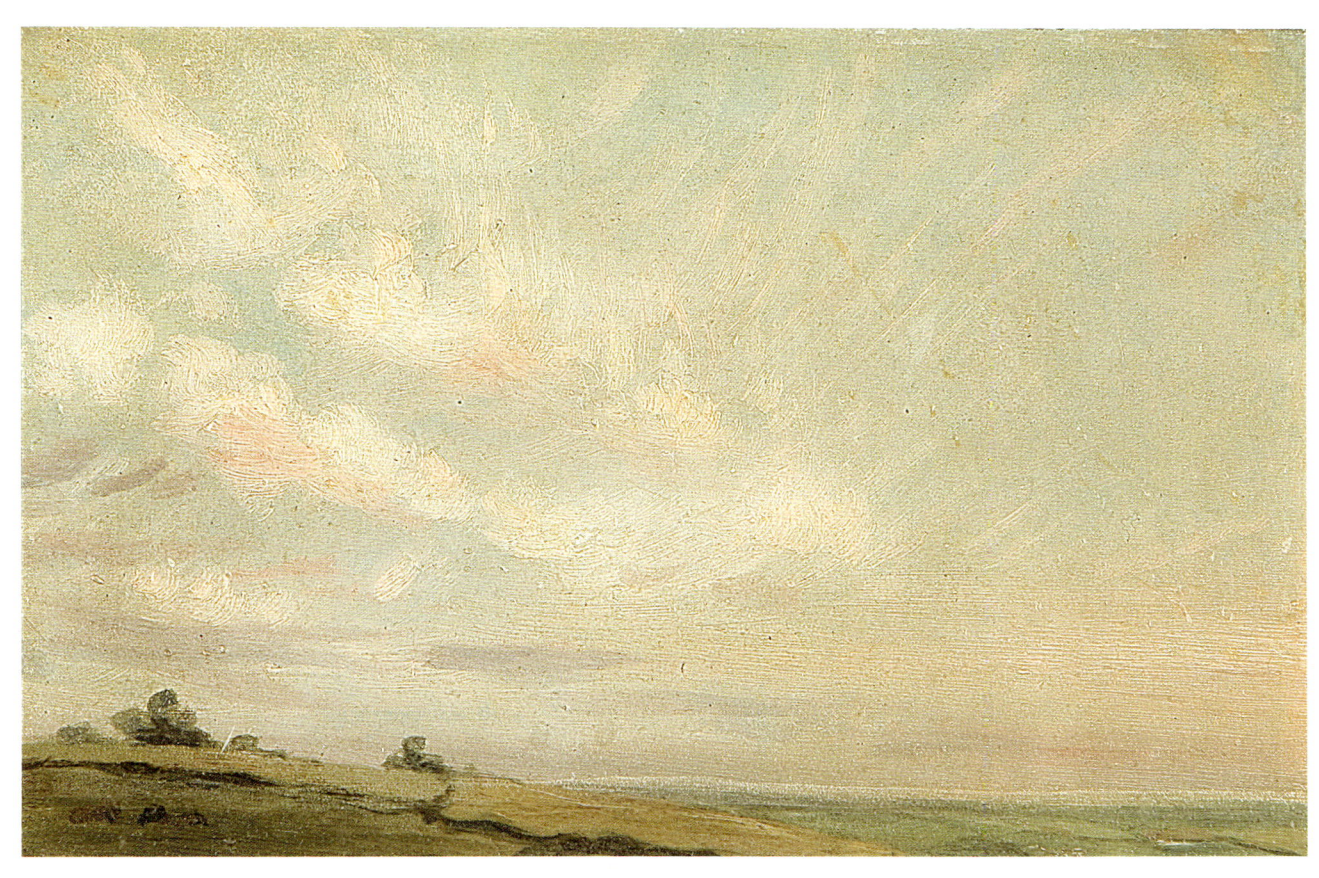
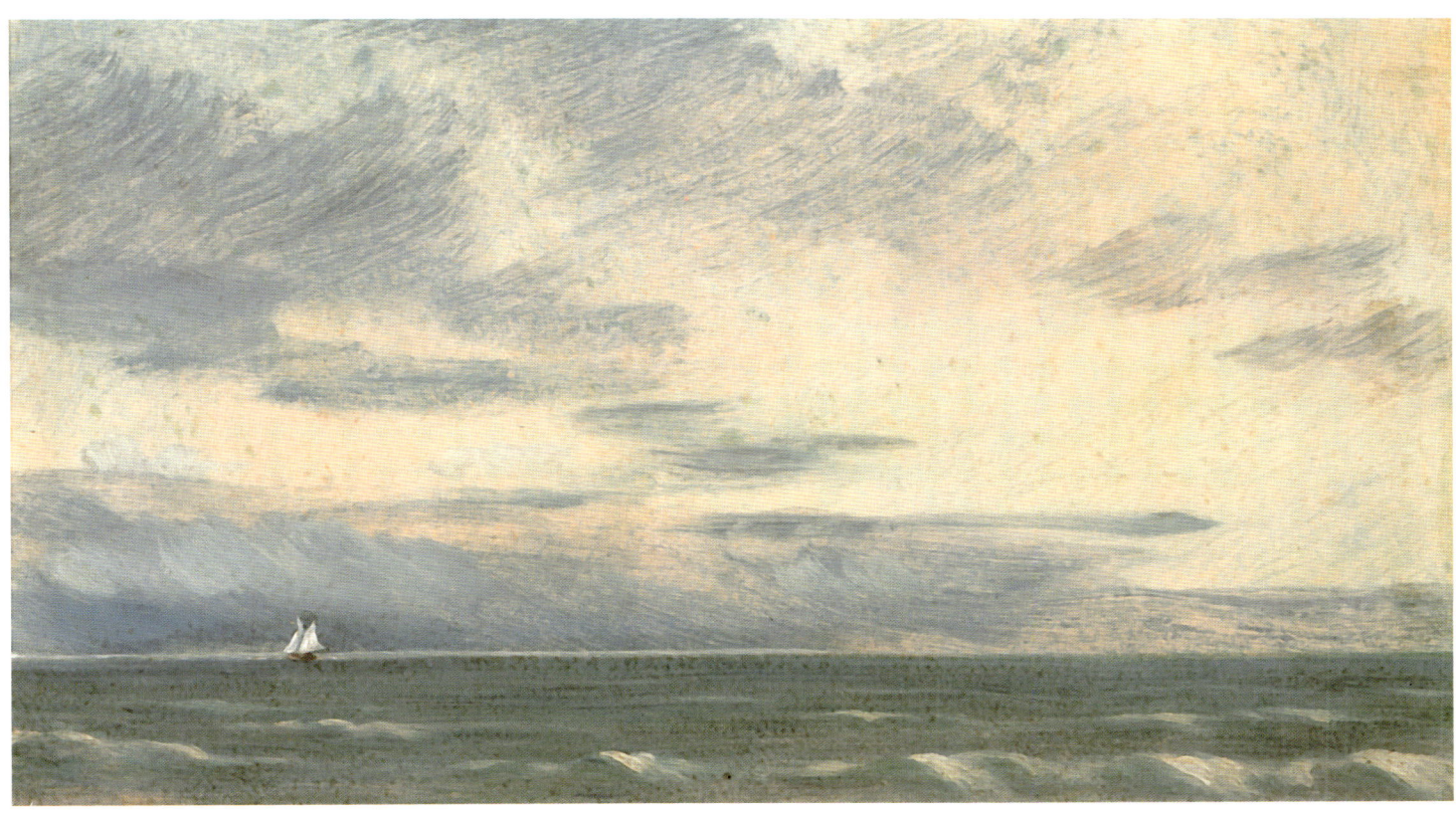

265

# Samuel Palmer 1805–1881

After Turner and Constable, Samuel Palmer's paintings and prints are among the major achievements of British landscape art in the first half of the nineteenth century. Palmer is especially admired today for the intensely visionary landscapes painted early in his career and inspired by William Blake and early German and Flemish engravings. He continued to paint inspired landscapes in watercolour but his later work was more conventional, showing greater concern both for naturalism and for the commonly acknowledged masters of landscape painting.

Palmer was born at Newington, London, in 1805 and developed a passion for poetry at an early age. He began his training in watercolour painting at thirteen under William Wate (working c.1815, died 1832). In 1822, while still in his teens, he met the landscape and portrait painter John Linnell who introduced him to the prints of Albrecht Dürer and Lucas van Leyden and, in 1824, to the ageing visionary William Blake himself. Palmer was deeply religious and he began to paint small, almost biblical dreams of a pastoral paradise. He became the leader of a group of young artists who called themselves 'The Ancients'. In the second half of the 1820s and early 1830s they met at the village of Shoreham in Kent, where Palmer had a house. They were all devoted to the work of William Blake, particularly his 1820 wood-engravings for the Pastorals of Virgil.

Palmer, even more than his fellow Ancients, deliberately turned his back on nineteenth-century progress. The more literal-minded John Linnell, who sometimes had an overbearing influence on Palmer's life and art, consistently pressed him to paint more directly from nature.

In 1837 Palmer married Linnell's daughter Hannah and the couple embarked on what was to become a very influential two-year stay in Italy where Palmer fell under the spell of the past Roman landscape painters Gaspard Dughet, Nicolas Poussin, Salvator Rosa and above all Claude Lorrain. The influence of those masters, and of Italian scenery, was to remain with him for the rest of his life, filtered through the Romanticism of his great contemporary, J. M. W. Turner.

Back in England Palmer lived in London. He was elected an associate of the Old Watercolour Society in 1842 and a full member in 1854. In 1849 he taught himself etching, became a member of the Etching Club in 1854 and published a series of very fine prints of which the Gallery has nine. From 1862 he lived at Redhill, Surrey, and died there in 1881.

## The rustic dinner, c.1853
watercolour, body colour on paper, 53.3 x 75.5 cm
South Australian Government Grant 1956

Samuel Palmer's painting is a mid-nineteenth-century view of English countryside, possibly the Surrey Downs looking over the Weald, but seen through the seventeenth-century landscape art of Claude Lorrain. The ten children, older girls in charge, are not likely to be resting from harvest labour for we can see adults hard at work with sheaves of corn a short distance away. It is more likely a picnic for young excursionists from a nearby town or village, come to a hilltop with shade and a fine view. The shade is probably from beeches but they could be compositionally mistaken for Roman pines and they form a classical repoussoir that frames the rolling English landscape and creates an effect of spacious distance. A tiny village with a church spire can just be seen in the distance to the left. The season is late summer, the land is golden, the sky clear and the harvest is ready to be gathered. Since the mid 1830s the artist had regularly used this tree-framed formula for distant, often hazy, landscapes and continued to rely on it for many watercolours up to the 1860s.[1]

Scenes of sweet young children in English landscapes dominated Palmer's work throughout the 1850s and early 1860s. For those compositions he drew upon a long Western tradition of peasant harvesting images, from the work of Pieter Bruegel the Elder and Nicolas Poussin to numerous eighteenth- and early-nineteenth-century British landscape artists such as George Lambert (1700–1765) and John Glover (1767–1849). Palmer was as obsessed with harvest subjects as his father-in-law John Linnell, for whom they signified a biblical typology. In 1828 Linnell wrote to Palmer: "Pray inform me…if the harvest is begun in your part yet for I should like to see something of that glorious type of the everlasting harvest of the spirits, the gathering of the saints – hoping that none of us will be found among the tares."[2]

In this watercolour the children who have settled into picturesque farming territory are a variation on Claude Lorrain's young shepherds and shepherdesses. Much mid-Victorian British art was devoted to a cult of children and their innocent world and the well-dressed and responsibly-behaved girls and boys appear to be playing rustics at a workers' dinner. This Arcadian scene of youth, joy and abundance was probably painted in 1853, the year in which the artist's second son was born and when first son Thomas More Palmer would have been twelve. The boy on the left-hand side looks to be around that age and could be the model.

The watercolour was bought by the Gallery from a Sydney dealer and collector with the title *Harvest picnic*. It is almost certainly the picture that Palmer exhibited at the Old Watercolour Society in 1853 as *The rustic dinner*.[3]

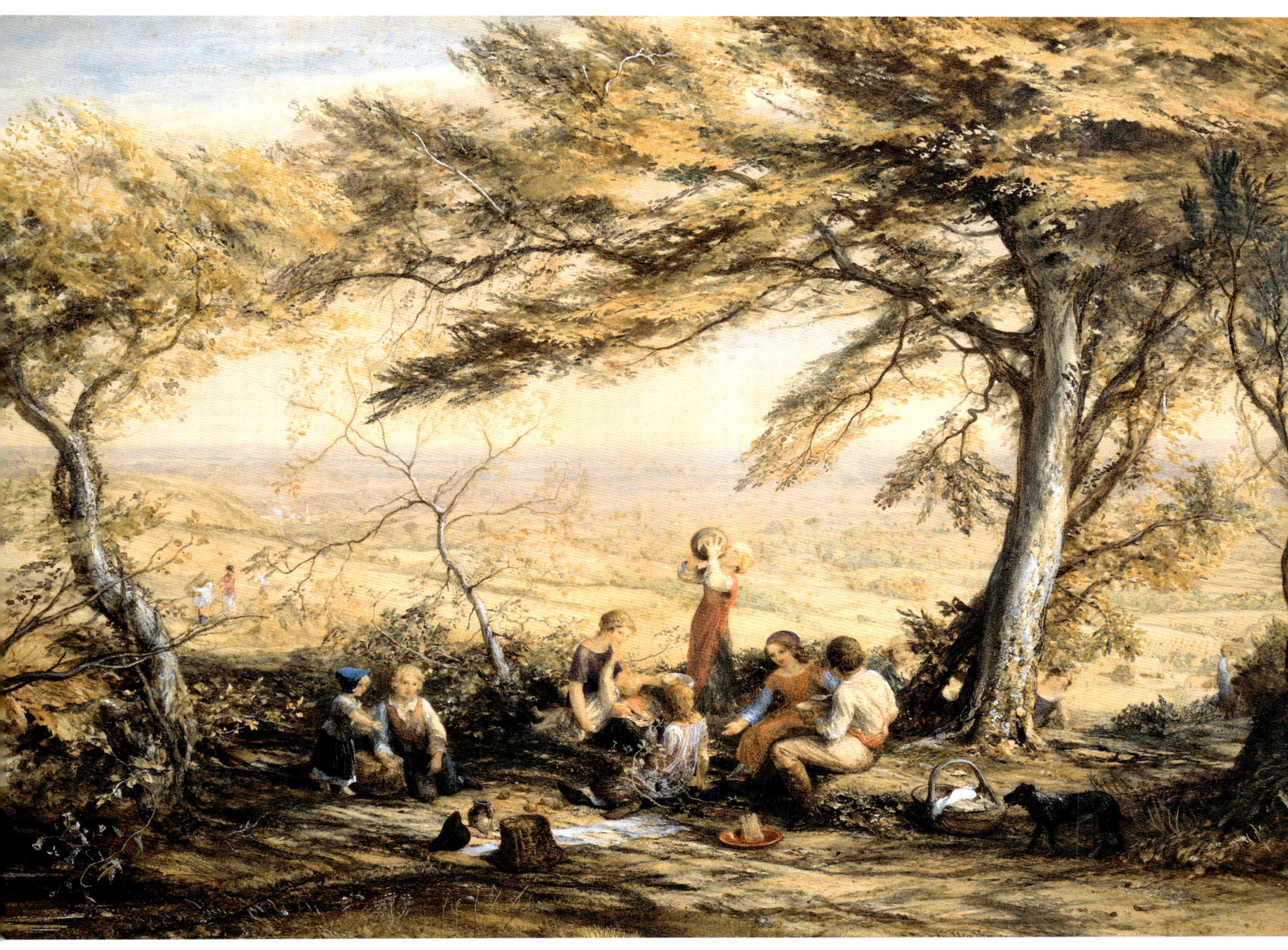

**Inscription:** Signed l.r. corner, grey watercolour: "S. Palmer".

**Provenance:** John Young, Sydney, possibly from late 1920s; bought by Art Gallery of South Australia from Young's widow, 1956.

**Exhibitions:** Probably *The rustic dinner*, Old Water-Colour Society, 1853, no. 18. *Island to Empire: 300 Years of British Art 1550–1850*, AGSA, Adelaide, 2005.

**Literature:** *NGSA Catalogue of Oil and Water-Colour Paintings and Pastels with Biographical Notes*, Adelaide: NGSA, 1960, pp. 189–90. *NGSA Picture Book of Selected Oil and Watercolour Paintings and Sculpture*, Adelaide: NGSA, 1960, p. 23. Raymond Lister (ed.), *The Letters of Samuel Palmer*, 2 vols, Oxford, 1974, p. 494[?]. Raymond Lister, *Catalogue Raisonné of the Works of Samuel Palmer*, Cambridge, 1988, p. 174, no. 515.

**Condition:** Fair; somewhat faded.

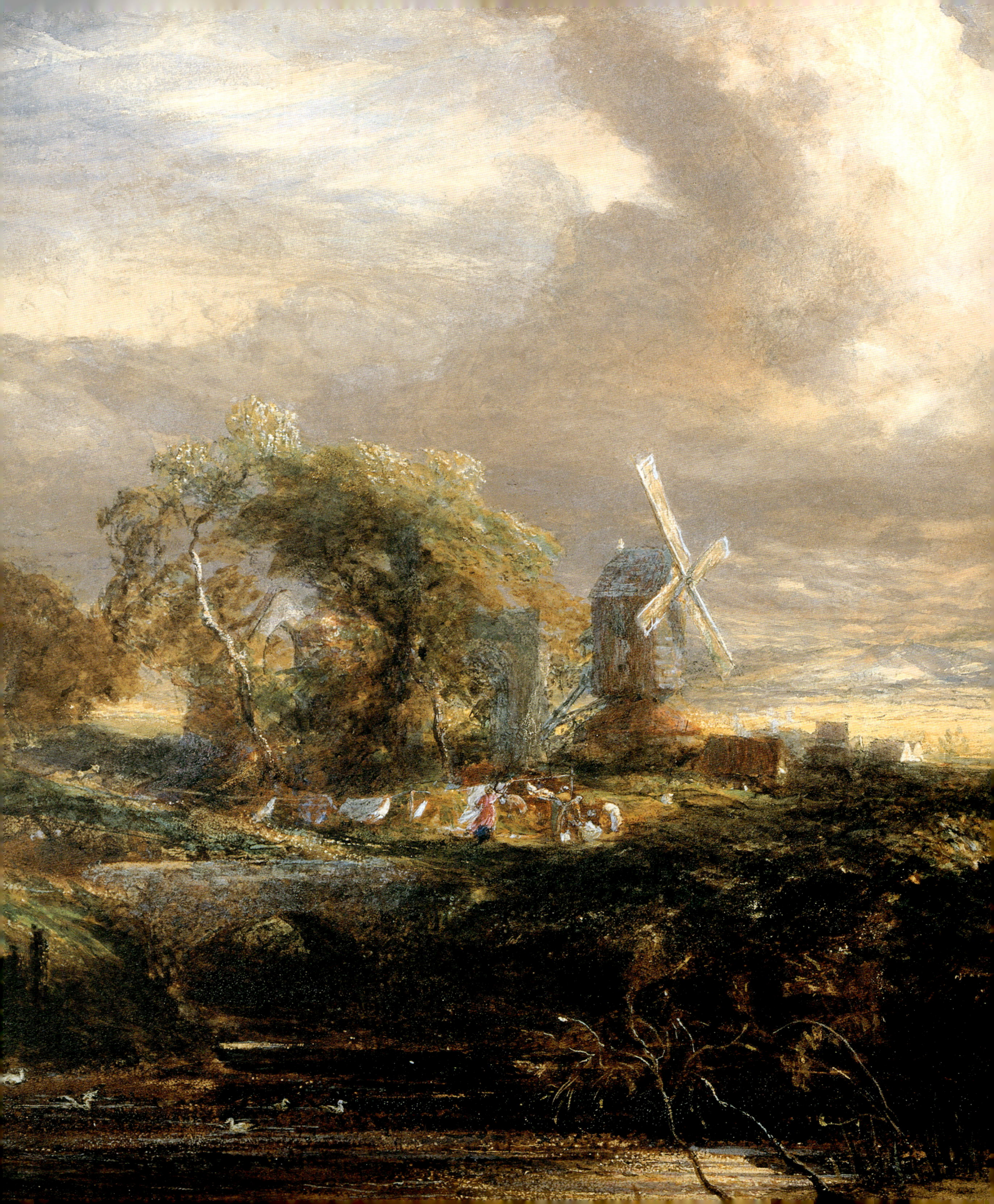

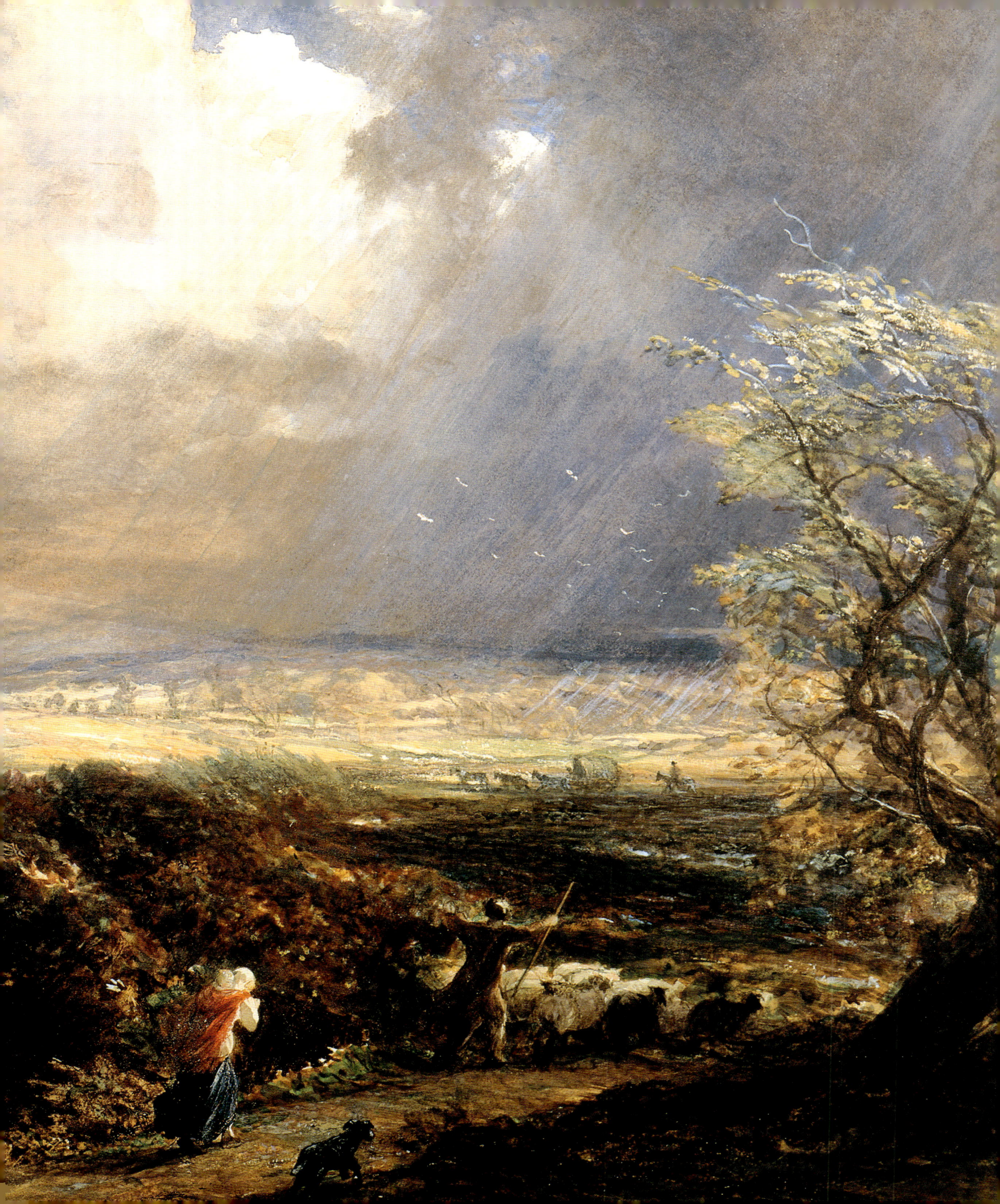

# Samuel Palmer

## Summer storm near Pulborough, Sussex, c.1851
watercolour, body colour on paper, 50.4 x 70.6 cm
A. R. Ragless Bequest Fund 1955

If the Gallery's sunny English picnic scene by Samuel Palmer was inspired by the Italian classical landscape tradition of the seventeenth century, this *Summer storm near Pulborough, Sussex*, draws heavily on the alternative Dutch tradition of more brooding realism in seventeenth-century landscape painting.

The rolling Sussex Downs is a rich mixed-farming area of southern England. The composition is based on a small watercolour sketch presumably made on the spot near Pulborough on the River Arun in West Sussex. A sheet exists with wash drawings of windmills done at this time.[1] The windmill could have been based on one at Margate, on the Kent coast, where there were several in the early 1850s.

This large studio version is more highly considered and more dramatically Romantic than the direct outdoor study. Black clouds have gathered, wind has risen and driving rain is already falling though there is a glimpse of distant sunshine. In the foreground a herdsman gestures to prevent his sheep stampeding off the road; his wife follows carrying a child on her back and beside her is an unhappy but faithful dog. To the left, near the windmill and a ruined church, women scurry to retrieve washing from a clothesline. At the edge of the darkness a horse-drawn covered wagon and a rider stoically proceed toward a farmhouse visible beyond the mill. Within the darkness bits of sunlight illuminate the travellers and the roadside stream and bridge. The streaming skirts of the foreground woman, the flapping washing, flitting birds, waving trees and mounting clouds emphasise the force of wind and rain. In this way Palmer builds tension and drama.

Working in Rome, Nicolas Poussin and his brother-in-law Gaspard Dughet had painted storm-threatened landscapes, but Palmer's low-lying composition with domineering clouds owes most to seventeenth-century Dutch art. Dutch realism was a growing influence in the development of British landscape in the first half of the nineteenth century, whereas the Italian influence waned. Turner, Glover and Palmer himself, all of them loyal to the Italian landscape tradition, also relied on the Dutch model for naturalistic depiction of weather. In its naturalism and weather effects, however, this painting also owes much to the realism of Constable.

Around 1851 *Summer storm near Pulborough, Sussex* and a similar landscape that Palmer painted shortly afterwards[2] were both dominated by the striking image of a windmill. Jacob van Ruisdael, Aelbert Cuyp and Rembrandt featured windmills in their Dutch landscapes, often to suggest the symbolism of stability, hope and the presence of God in the midst of turbulence and stress. The powerful windmill here plays a comparable role.

In 1848 Palmer had painted a similar-sized but more Italianate storm scene with the same basic composition. It was a subject from John Bunyan's *The Pilgrim's Progress* and it illustrated *Christian Descending into the Valley of Humiliation* (Ashmolean Museum, Oxford). The tower of the Palace Beautiful against a threatening sky plays the same compositional role as the windmill in the Gallery's painting of sheep descending into the valley of Pulborough and shares the same symbolism as the steadfast windmill in this later composition. At the time of the subject from Bunyan, Palmer and his wife were mourning the death of their three-year-old daughter Mary Elizabeth. And at the same date John Linnell painted two stormy landscapes, *Noah: The Eve of the Deluge* (Cleveland Museum of Art, Ohio) and *The Last Gleam* (private collection). Palmer's own illustration to *The Pilgrim's Progress* and Linnell's biblical Deluge are important forerunners that led to the composition of this brilliant atmospheric watercolour. *Summer storm near Pulborough, Sussex* is not only a study of weather. It is also a pilgrimage, with a flock, heading towards a possible deluge.

Palmer returned to his theme of windmill and storm twenty-eight years later. In 1879, near the end of his life, he painted *Hastings to Covert: A threatening rain storm*, which is now in the Victoria & Albert Museum, London.

**Provenance:** Rt Hon. Lord Joicey, DSO, Christie's, London, 13 May 1955, lot 24, bt by the Fine Art Society; bought for the Art Gallery of South Australia on the advice of H. D. Molesworth, 1955.

**Exhibitions:** *Exhibition of English Watercolours*, Mildura Art Gallery, Victoria, 1960. *Island to Empire: 300 Years of British Art 1550-1850*, AGSA, Adelaide, 2005.

**Literature:** *NGSA Bulletin*, Adelaide: NGSA, vol. 17, no. 2, October 1955. *NGSA Catalogue of Oil and Water-Colour Paintings and Pastels with Biographical Notes*, Adelaide: NGSA, 1960, pp. 189-90. Raymond Lister, *Catalogue Raisonné of the Works of Samuel Palmer*, Cambridge: 1988, pp. 170-71.

**Condition:** Excellent.

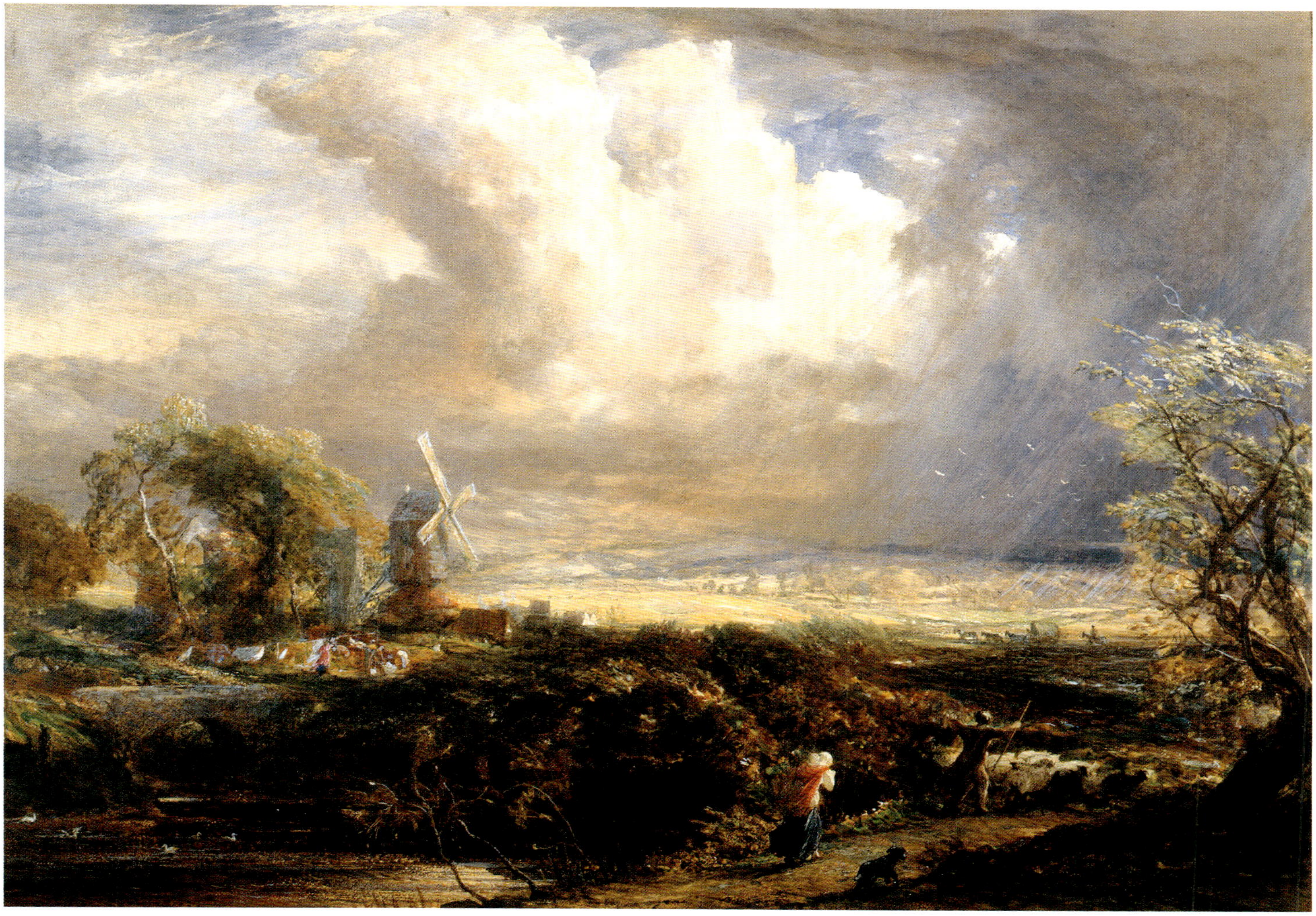

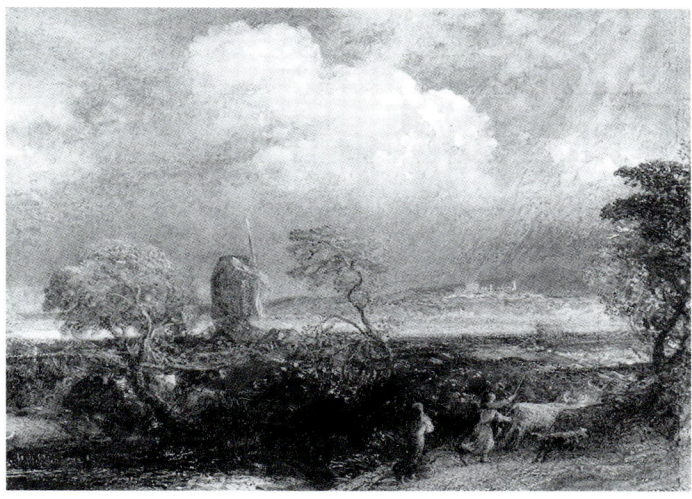

Samuel Palmer, *Hastings to Covert: A threatening rain storm*, 1879.
V. & A. Images/Victoria & Albert Museum, London

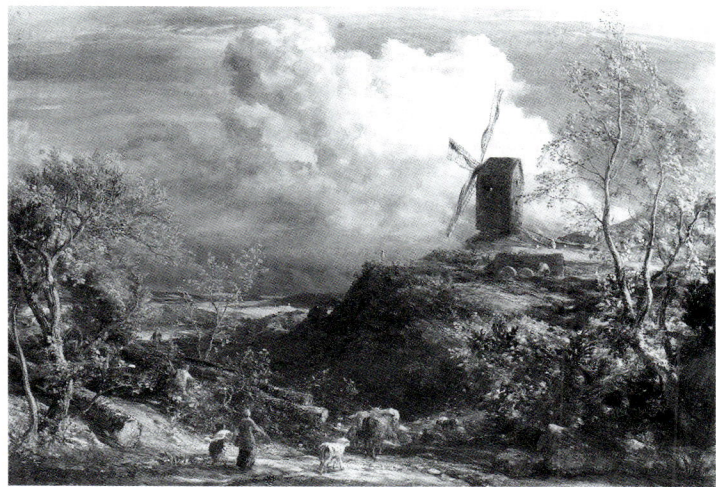

Samuel Palmer, *Landscape with windmill, figures and cattle*, c.1851.
V. & A. Images/Victoria & Albert Museum, London

# William Holman Hunt 1827–1910

Holman Hunt was one of the central figures of the Pre-Raphaelite Brotherhood, a group of seven young and ambitious artists who came together in 1848 with ideas about reforming British art. John Everett Millais and Dante Gabriel Rossetti were the other founders of the anti-academic Brotherhood. Believing that British art had become pretentious in style, sloppy in brushwork, dull in colour and trivial in content, they wished to return to the purity and seriousness of Christian art from before the time of the (to them) overrated Raphael and his Bolognese seventeenth-century followers, hence 'Pre-Raphaelite'. They perfected a style – based less on quattrocento precedents than on Van Eyck – with meticulous attention to detail, clear luminous colour and potent symbolism, particularly religious symbolism. Hunt was the driving force behind the movement, coined the name Pre-Raphaelite, and was the only member who remained faithful to the Brotherhood's ideals. Throughout a long career he painted with the commitment, passion and detailed precision of a medieval manuscript-illustrator. He was also the Pre-Raphaelites' most original colourist.

Born in London in 1827, he began his formal training in 1844 at the Royal Academy Schools (where he met Millais) and supported himself by making portraits and copies of paintings. In 1846 he exhibited at the Royal Academy for the first time, with some success. His early use of Keats's poetry for subject matter inspired his search for original iconography. Then in 1847 when he encountered writings by the art critic John Ruskin, who would soon champion the Pre-Raphaelites, Ruskin's *Modern Painters* gave Hunt a sense of mission. He was convinced there should be a total unity between intense realism and high symbolism and that every detail of a painting should be filled with meaning. These became the characteristics of early Pre-Raphaelite art generally and of Holman Hunt's art in particular.

In his twenties Hunt painted some of his best-known works: *The Hireling Shepherd*, 1851–52 (Manchester Art Gallery), *Valentine rescuing Sylvia from Proteus*, 1851 (Birmingham Museum & Art Gallery), *The Awakening Conscience*, 1851–52 (Tate, London), and the most famous of all his pictures *The Light of the World*, 1851–53 (Keble College, Oxford). Important late paintings include *The Shadow of Death*, 1870–73 (Manchester) and *The Lady of Shalott*, 1886–1905 (Wadsworth Atheneum, Hartford, Connecticut). In 1854–56 he was in Egypt and the Holy Land and chose a Dead Sea setting for *The Scapegoat* (Lady Lever Art Gallery, Port Sunlight, Merseyside). He was in Palestine again during 1869–72, 1875–78 and 1892 seeking the exact historical and archeological backgrounds for his religious pictures.

Holman Hunt exhibited at the Royal Academy from 1846 to 1874 and at the Old Watercolour Society from 1869 to 1903. In 1904 when he completed another version of *The Light of the World* with a life-size Christ (St Paul's Cathedral, London) it was the most popular and most-engraved image in the British Empire; it toured the Empire in 1905–06 to Canada, New Zealand, South Africa and Australia, including Adelaide, and attracted vast crowds. After his death in September 1910 such was Hunt's fame that crowds flocked to see his cremated remains interred in St Paul's Cathedral.

## Christ and the Two Marys, 1847 & 1897
oil on canvas over wood panel, 117.5 x 94 cm
d'Auvergne Boxall Bequest Fund 1964

*Christ and the Two Marys,* which Holman Hunt also referred to as "The Resurrection Meeting", is the artist's first attempt at the new Pre-Raphaelite manner and hence a most significant painting in mid-nineteenth-century British art. It was the first of his many religious paintings. Begun in 1847, the year before the Pre-Raphaelite Brotherhood was formed, the artist chose an important subject, but an unusual one. The Gospel according to St Matthew, chapter 28, tells how Mary Magdalene and Mary, mother of the apostles James and John, came to Jesus' sepulchre: "And behold, there was a great earthquake: for the angel of the Lord descended from heaven, and came and rolled back the stone from the door…and said unto the women…he is not here: for he is risen…and go quickly, and tell his disciples…and [they] did run…. And as they went to tell his disciples, behold, Jesus met them, saying, 'All hail'. And they came and held him by the feet, and worshipped him".

This first astonishing encounter with the risen Christ signifies the beginning of Christianity, and was therefore an appropriately lofty subject with which to begin a mission of artistic reform. Christ stands with arms raised to greet the two Marys with "All hail", but his posture also evokes the crucifixion and, in a further layer of meaning, offers benediction. The bands of his grave clothes are unravelling as if to release the spirit as well as the embalmed body of Jesus, and he generates a rainbow aura of power and optimism. Mary Magdalene is prostrate as if to repeat her earlier act of wiping his feet with her hair while the other Mary is on her knees, head bowed and hands held up in both prayer and trepidation. The lurid colours of the heavenly clouds, the distant mountains and the city of Jerusalem are properly startling for this depiction of a moment, soon after an earthquake at dawn on the first day of the week, when two women are greeted by a resurrecting Christ.

In order to achieve the luminous clarity characteristic of fifteenth-century devotional paintings Hunt experimented for the first time with painting colours thinly into a white semi-dry oil ground instead of the usual underpaint layer of brown-

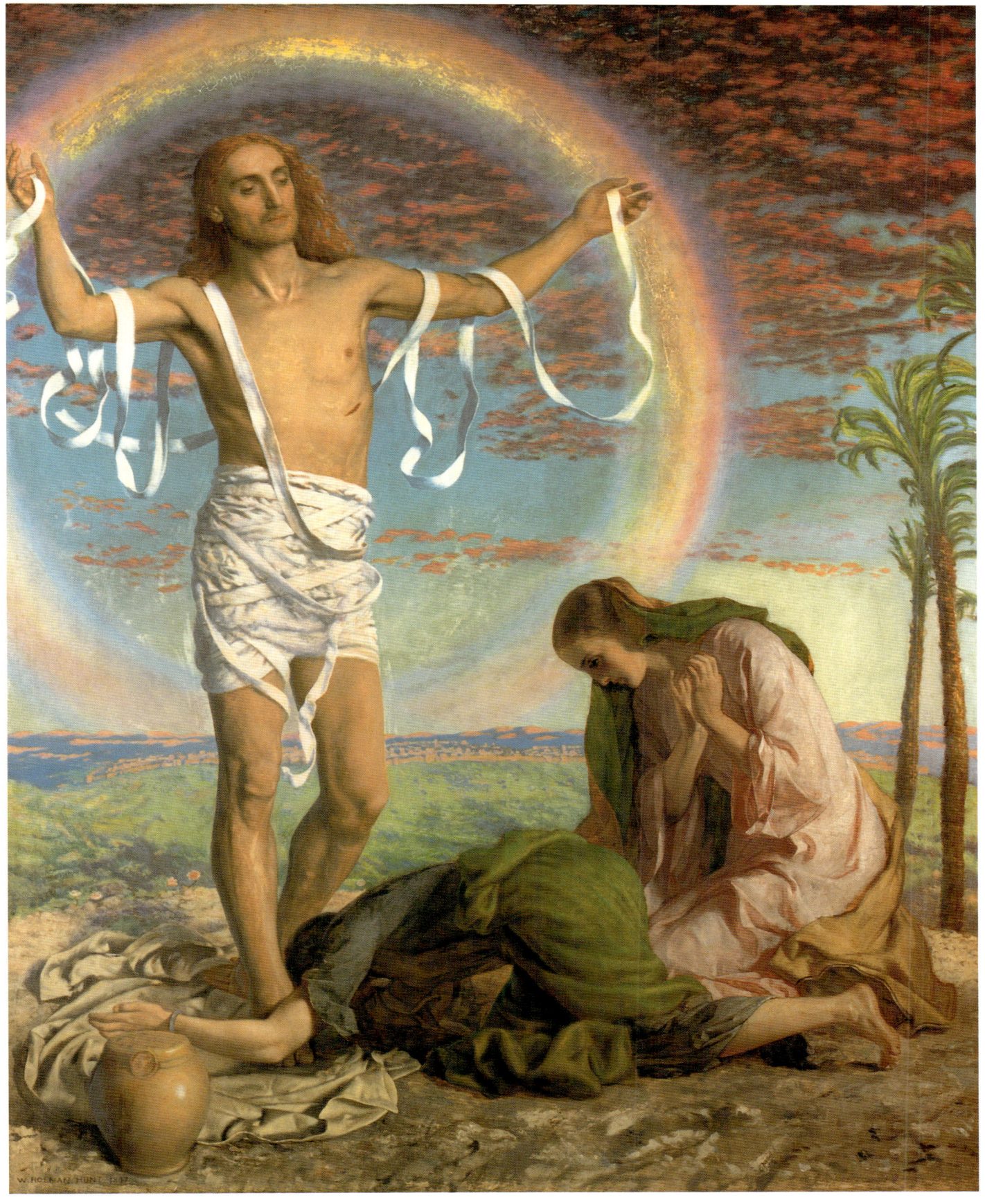

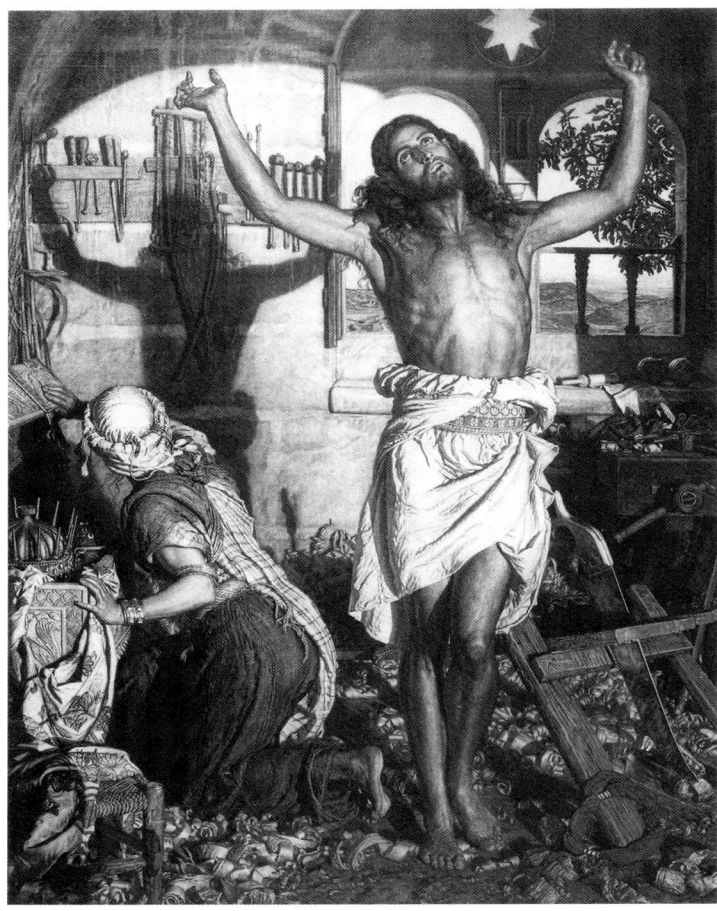

William Holman Hunt, *The shadow of death*, 1870–73. Manchester Art Gallery

grey "dead colouring". The procedure is discernible in his two Marys, particularly Mary Magdalene's blue-grey blouse. After this Millais and Rossetti immediately experimented with the luminous technique.

The number of extant preparatory drawings for *Christ and the Two Marys* attests to Hunt's careful construction of the picture and to the significance he accorded the painting. He was still a student at the Royal Academy life class and a life study exists for the figure of the suppliant Mary Magdalene as well as thumbnail drawings of different exploratory poses for the composition. These indicate that Christ was originally conceived with an extended left arm and a bowed head and looking into the face of a prostrate Magdalene.[1] Pentimenti on the picture reveal a more sharply upraised left arm and Christ's head further to the right. X-rays confirm this and also reveal that Christ was originally leaning on a staff. Hunt subsequently rejected that idea and instructed the supplier of his art materials to extend the canvas with a strip of about five centimetres along the bottom and a similar strip along the right-hand edge, which made the Christ figure less central but the women more so.[2] In addition, probably much later, in the 1890s, the left edge was extended by unwrapping the tacking margin which gave another two-and-a-half centimetres in which to manoeuvre a new pose for "the Saviour".[3] The figures of the two Marys remained mostly unchanged and the simplicity and clarity of their early-Renaissance style can be appreciated. The palm trees were studied from a specimen in Kew Gardens and from a branch given to Hunt by the curator there.[4]

The artist had great difficulty with the figure of Christ and apparently with the new technique. He aimed to avoid traditional imagery and instead to achieve immediate communication with ordinary "unaffected" people so that they might "see this Christ with something of the surprise that the Maries themselves felt on meeting Him as One who has come out of the grave".[5] He wanted to paint a real and credible Christ in a real and credible Palestinian landscape, that is to bring extreme feelings into the modern world. It was an ambitious work in both concept and technique, intended as a starting point from which to develop a new and intense style for religious painting. However, because of his technical, compositional and conceptual problems, together with the realisation that he could not finish the painting in time for the 1848 Royal Academy exhibition, Hunt became dispirited and abandoned the work.[6] He did not it take up again until half a century later.

An old inscription on a back label probably from the beginning of the twentieth century, reads:

> "Christ …the Two Maries" / by W Holman-Hunt / The Two Maries painted …[illeg.]… / WHH was 19 – Then put aside / face to the wall. / At the age of 70 WHH / painted the Christ (roughly sketched) / …[illeg.]… background / …[illeg.]… / Mountains of Mo…[illeg.]…"

At seventy it must have been a cathartic act returning to the painting after half a century of neglect. In 1897 Hunt was finishing off or tidying up his life's work and beginning to think about posterity and his central role in the Pre-Raphaelite movement; eight years later his autobiography appeared under the title *Pre-Raphaelitism and the Pre-Raphaelite Brotherhood*. Although the painting is conspicuously signed and dated "W. HOLMAN HUNT. 1847." this inscription was possibly added as late as 1897 or at the time of his 1906–07 retrospective exhibitions.

When Holman Hunt returned to the figure of Christ he made a variation on the pose in his *The Shadow of Death*, where the carpenter Jesus stretches with arms upheld as if

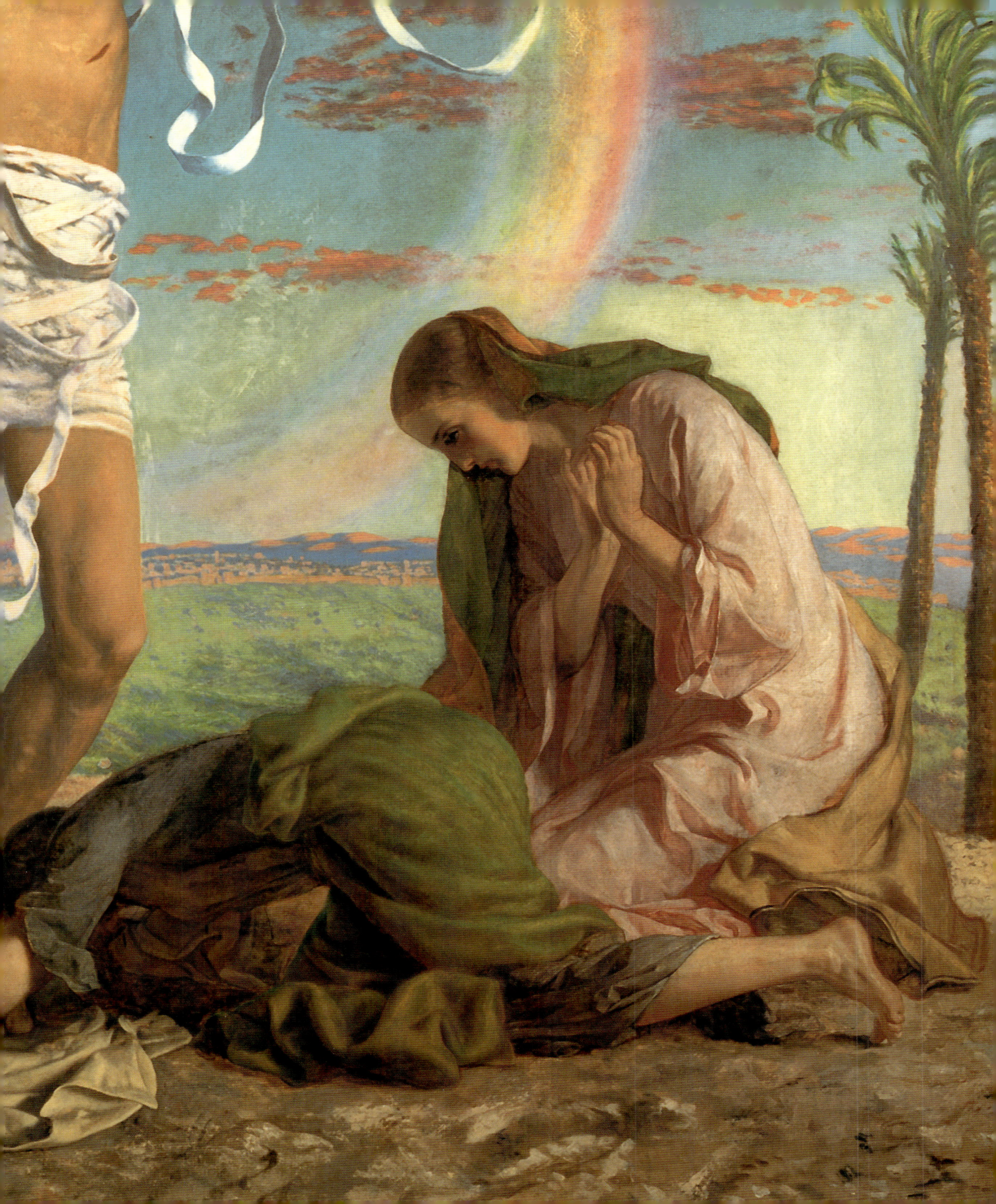

to prefigure his crucifixion. Hunt's model in 1897 was a very distinctive red-headed Italian named Luigi Delucca.[7] Delucca also posed for the last of the three versions of *The Light of the World* (1899–1904). In *Christ and the Two Marys* the torso was originally more side-on, and in the underpainting the nipple is perceptible. The torso does not have the high finish and detailed modelling of the Christ in *The Shadow of Death*. The foreground, the background mountains and the sky were mainly painted in the 1890s. Hunt had lived for years at a time in Jerusalem, and watercolours executed on the spot in Palestine were used for later works, among them the landscape background in this painting. Although the resurrection took place in Jerusalem and the city is summarily indicated, the note on the back label tells that the background is the Mountains of Moab, which are seventy kilometres away, along the far shore of the Dead Sea, and not visible from Jerusalem.

Because of failing eyesight Holman Hunt produced very little around the turn of the century. In 1905 in his autobiography he illustrated *Christ and the Two Marys* as an "unfinished" painting.[8] However, he allowed it to be seen, uncatalogued, in the final weeks of his retrospective exhibition at Manchester in 1906, and it was a formal inclusion in the follow-on exhibitions in Liverpool and Glasgow. Its presence in the book and the exhibitions confirms his high regard for this seminal work.

If *Christ and the Two Marys* can be regarded as the first Pre-Raphaelite painting it was also one of the last. After 1897, Hunt's new compositions were very few. Instead there were repeat subjects, and other unfinished paintings to complete; he was relying heavily on studio assistants. When he returned to *Christ and the Two Marys* it was a very old-fashioned picture, and he was the only surviving member of the original seven Pre-Raphaelites.

A key work, conceived and partly painted in 1847, the painting looked forward to a new direction in British art in the second half of the nineteenth century. It is therefore a highly appropriate conclusion for a book that outlines British art from 1550 to 1850.

**Inscription:** Signed and dated l.l.: "W. HOLMAN HUNT. 1847."

**Provenance:** By descent to the artist's grand-daughter Mrs Michael Burt, sold Christie's, London, 3 July 1964, bt Leger Galleries, London. Bought by the Art Gallery of South Australia on the advice of H. D. Molesworth, 1964.

**Exhibitions:** *The Collected Works of W. Holman Hunt*, Manchester City Art Gallery, 1906–07 (not in catalogue). *The Art of William Holman Hunt, O.M., D.C.L.*, Walker Art Gallery, Liverpool, 1907, no. 51. *Pictures and Drawings by William Holman Hunt, O.M., D.C.L.*, Glasgow, 1907, no. 11. *Liverpool Autumn Exhibition*, Walker Art Gallery, Liverpool, 1923, no. 994. *William Holman Hunt*, Walker Art Gallery, Liverpool and Victoria & Albert Museum, London, 1969, no. 8. *Art Treasures from Adelaide: From the Collection of the Art Gallery of South Australia*, Art Gallery of New South Wales, Sydney, 1977. *The Pre-Raphaelites*, Tate Gallery, London, 1984. *Morris & Company: Pre-Raphaelites and the Arts & Craft Movement in South Australia*, Art Gallery of South Australia, Adelaide, 1994. *Love & Death: Art in the Age of Queen Victoria*, Art Gallery of South Australia, Adelaide; Art Gallery of New South Wales, Sydney; Queensland Art Gallery, Brisbane and Toi o Tamaki Auckland Art Gallery, Auckland, 2001–02. *Island to Empire: 300 Years of British Art 1550–1850*, AGSA, Adelaide, 2005.

**Literature:** W. Holman Hunt, *Pre-Raphaelitism and the Pre-Raphaelite Brotherhood*, London, 1905, vol. 1, pp. 77–85. *The Collected Works of W. Holman Hunt*, Manchester City Art Gallery, 1906. *The Art of William Holman Hunt, O.M., D.C.L.*, Liverpool: Walker Art Gallery, 1907. *Pictures and Drawings by William Holman Hunt, O.M., D.C.L.*, Glasgow, 1907. *Liverpool Autumn Exhibition*, Liverpool: Walker Art Gallery, 1923. A. C. Gissing, *William Holman Hunt: A biography*, London, 1936, pp. 20, 23–24. Mary Bennett, *William Holman Hunt*, Liverpool: Walker Art Gallery/London: Arts Council of Great Britain, 1969, pp. 21–22, 64–65, pl. 5. Alan Bowness et al., *The Pre-Raphaelites*, London: Tate Gallery, 1984, pp. 32, 50–51, 221–23. Anne Clarke Amor, *William Holman Hunt: The True Pre-Raphaelite*, London, 1989, pp. 30, 270. Ron Radford et al., *Selected Works*, Adelaide: AGSA 1991, p. 22. Ron Radford in Christopher Menz, *Morris & Company: Pre-Raphaelites and the Arts & Craft Movement in South Australia*, Adelaide: AGSA, 1994, pp. 12, 80–81. Ron Radford et al., *Treasures*, Adelaide: AGSA, 1998, pp. 60–61. Angus Trumble, *Love & Death*, Adelaide: AGSA, p. 90, 91 (illus.).

**Condition:** Fair; evidence of crocodiling in sky, particularly on the rainbow. Last major conservation in 1993 by Artlab Australia, Adelaide.

**Frame:** Original, probably framed by the artist for his retrospective exhibition in 1906.

## Follower of Hans Holbein the Younger King Henry VIII

1. Under the supervision of David Crombie, Senior Paintings Conservator at National Museums Liverpool Conservation Division, the panel was examined at Artlab Australia under normal light and under the microscope, as well as with an Infra Red vidicon. A composition X-ray image of the picture has also been made. No treatment has been carried out since the painting was acquired around 1964.

   Metal leaf appears to have been used in several areas of the painting – gold leaf has been used underneath the tunic and sleeves; silver leaf has been used underneath the red gown and gold leaf mordant gilding used on the jewel highlights. The use of silver leaf under the red gown paint is the most obvious parallel to the techniques of The Walker's Henry VIII and has been noted on a number of other paintings of this date, including the Henry VIII portrait group. This is an indication that the painting follows mid-sixteenth-century painting practice. The combination of both gold leaf and silver leaf is unique. David Crombie was jointly responsible for the conservation of the Liverpool and other full-length versions of Henry VIII portraits, see note 2. Dendrochronology dating has not yet been able to be undertaken on the oak panel in Australia.

2. Until the mid 1980s this painting was attributed to Lucas Horenbout (see Paget 1970, pp. 8-18). Lucas Horenbout (c.1490/95-1544) is the supposed founding father of the important English tradition of miniature painting and was thought to have painted larger panel portraits. He arrived from Flanders in 1525 and immediately became a court painter to Henry VIII. In London he came under the influence of Hans Holbein the Younger; it was believed he in turn taught Holbein the art of the portrait miniature. More recent opinion is that Horenbout did not paint large portraits and this work therefore could not be by him.

3. Xanthe Brooke and David Crombie, *Henry VIII Revealed: Holbein's Portrait and its Legacy*, London, 2003.

4. The version of Henry VIII dated 1540 is still labelled at the Galleria Nazionale d'Arte Antica, Palazzo Barberini, Rome, as being by Hans Holbein the Younger himself. No Holbein scholar now accepts it as an autograph work; consensus gives it to a close follower.

## Cornelius Ketel Richard Goodricke of Ribston, Yorkshire

1. Roy Strong in *The English Icon: Elizabethan & Jacobean portraiture*, 1969, gives the famous 'Sieve portrait' of Elizabeth I to Cornelius Ketel (Pinacoteca Nazionale di Siena).

2. Karel van Mander, *Lives*, 1604.

3. Charles Alfred Goodricke, *History of the Goodricke Family*, London, 1885, p. 14.

4. Richard Goodricke matriculated from Cambridge in May 1576. *Alumni Cantabrigienses: A Biographical List of all known students, graduates and holders of office at the University of Cambridge, from the earliest times to 1900*, Part I, Cambridge, 1922.

5. J. W. Clay (ed.), *Dugdale's Visitation of Yorkshire, with additions*, London, 1899, pp. 53 and 54. Charles Alfred Goodricke (ed.), *History of The Goodricke Family*, London, 1885, pp. 14 and 15. Letter from Janet Grant, The College of Arms, London, 29 May 2004. I am also grateful for Mark Weiss for much of the biographical information on the sitter and the portrait itself.

6. Also known as Tycho's comet, after the Danish astronomer Tycho Brahe whose resulting studies helped confound Aristotle's ancient notions that the heavens were fixed and that the planets moved in crystal spheres.

7. No definite heraldic significance for either family can be found for the swan image but it could symbolise his wife's descent from so many kings. Swans were given royal status and had royal implications from the twelfth century onwards; any wild swan was the king's property. The swan could also be an allusion to Venus, the ancient Roman goddess of love; swans traditionally pull Venus' chariot.

8. Mark Weiss has pointed out that a portrait illustrated in Roy Strong's *The English Icon*, no. 122 (p. 175), attributed to George Gower and possibly of Sir Philip Sidney, is firmly dated to 1579 and was the earliest known portrait with such a large millstone ruff.

## George Gower Portrait of a lady

1. The three versions of the 'Armada portrait' are in the William Tyrwhitt-Drake collection, Bath, at Woburn Abbey, and the National Portrait Gallery, London, where the image has been cut down at the sides. There is another variant, privately held (London), with no ships in the background. Recent scholarly opinion is that all are by different hands, the version at Woburn Abbey more likely to be by Gower.

2. I am grateful to Avril Hart and Clare Brown of the Victoria & Albert Museum for their assistance with the costume description (letter to the author 16 September 1993).

3. Roy Strong, *The English Icon*, pp. 167-184. Sir Roy Strong, then Director, Victoria & Albert Museum, authenticated the attribution (letter to the author 13 September 1984).

## Isaac Oliver Man with fair hair and beard

1. Roy Strong, *The English Renaissance Miniature*, London, 1984, p. 76.
2. Sumner & Walker, 1999, pp. 46-47.
3. Letter dated 28 July 2004 from Katherine Coombs, Curator, Paintings, Victoria & Albert Museum, with support from Alan Derbyshire, Miniatures Conservation, Victoria & Albert Museum. Letter dated 22 August 2004 from Roy Strong to the author.

## Robert Peake the Elder Frances, Lady Reynell of West Ogwell, Devon

1. Weiss 2002, no. 10, ascribed to English School 1602. There exists a portrait of Sir Richard's wife Lucy painted by Marcus Gheeraerts and exhibited in 2001 at the Weiss Gallery, London, *A Noble Visage: early portraiture 1545-1660*, no. 10 (illus.).

2. Much of this information, including biographical information, comes from Mark Weiss, *Tudor and Stuart Portraits*, Sydney: Rex Irwin Art Dealer, 1997, pp. 1-2.

# Notes pp. 56–64

### Anthony van Dyck  A married couple

1. Susan J. Barnes, Nora de Poorter, Oliver Millar and Horst Vey, *Van Dyck: A Complete Catalogue of the Paintings*, Yale University Press, 2004, p. 109. In this entry it is stated, "Like a number of early portraits, this very thinly painted work is not in good condition…". However, it is painted both thinly and with areas of quite thick paint. More importantly, when cleaned and layers of discoloured varnish and overpaint were removed, it was found that the original paintwork was in remarkably good condition.
2. W. R. Valentiner, *Art in America*, August 1922, pp. 204, 209.
3. Susan J. Barnes et al., *Van Dyck: A Complete Catalogue of the Paintings*, p. 109.
4. Susan J. Barnes, letter to the author 14 November 1993.
5. Michael Jaffé, letter to the author 12 November 1993.
6. Christopher Brown and Hans Vlieghe, 1999.
7. The painting had been given in 1889 to the Detroit Institute of Arts by James E. Scripps as a portrait by Cornelis de Vos of Frans Snyders and Margaretha de Vos.
8. W. Adler, 1980.
9. Egbert Haverkamp-Begemann, letter to the author 12 November 1993.
10. Van Dyck did on-the-spot landscape drawings from nature either for relaxation or to use as a basis for landscape backgrounds to his portraits or figure compositions. The Art Gallery of South Australia holds a landscape drawing by Van Dyck probably executed in Britain in the mid 1630s.
11. Ron Radford, 1993.

### Anthony van Dyck  A wooded ridge

1. The attribution to Van Dyck and its placement in his English period was supported by Professor Michael Jaffé and Dr Horst Vey, see auction catalogue lot 170, and in an oral communication between Professor Jaffé and the author in May 1990. Martin Royalton-Kisch also confirmed the attribution to Van Dyck when he saw the drawing at the Art Gallery of South Australia in 1997.
2. Martin Royalton-Kisch, *The Light of Nature: Landscape drawings and watercolours by Van Dyck and his contemporaries*, London: British Museum, 1999, p. 22.

### Marcus Gheeraerts the Younger  Magdalen Poultney, later Lady Aston

1. Strong 1969, p. 303, no. 312.
2. Her death date of 9 March 1613 in her 34th year is clearly recorded on a monument to her in the north cross of Westminster Abbey. Other dates for the Fortescue and Poultney families have been researched by Peter O'Donoghue of the College of Arms, London.
3. I am grateful to Avril Hart and Clare Brown of the Victoria & Albert Museum for their assistance with the costume description (letter to author 16 September 1993).
4. Before conservation in 1997, close inspection of the paint surface revealed that the outline of Magdalen's features, hands and dress had been slightly strengthened by a dark outline at a later date, probably in the first half of the nineteenth century. Apparently, this practice was not uncommon: as portraits darkened with age, smoke and dirt, the sitter's features and general form were sometimes later emphasised for visibility in lamplight or dark rooms or long galleries. Also in the early nineteenth century with the revived Gothic taste there grew a renewed interest in formerly unfashionable Elizabethan and Jacobean portraits, and linear emphasis on sometimes over-cleaned images deliberately exaggerated their medieval look. In this painting the heavy metallic-like folds in the skirt and curtains were emphasised. Sir Arthur Aston (1798–1859) is believed to have had some of the family portraits cleaned, reframed and regilded probably in the 1840s. As Sir Arthur was minister plenipotentiary to the Court of Spain in the late 1830s and early 1840s it could be that he was also aware of and admired sixteenth-century Spanish portraits which have similar stiff formal qualities.

   The 1997 cleaning revealed the two moles on Magdalen's right cheek that had been painted over. With the Tate version (which has not been cleaned), neither microscopic examination nor infra-red has revealed any trace of the facial moles. It is possible that the overpainting in Adelaide's version and redelineation of the form was done when Sir Arthur Aston sent the paintings to Agnew's of Manchester for treatment in the 1840s. The original Agnew's label is still on the back of the stretcher (upper centre) of the Gallery's portrait and others that originally hung at Aston.

   The 1997 cleaning and conservation also revealed that the gold braid and fringe on the chair and curtains shows copious use of shell gold which is also the case in the Tate version.
5. The Tate has long identified and labelled the sitter of its painting of Lady Aston as Gertrude Sadler (*Tate Gallery 1978–80: Illustrated catalogue of acquisitions*), as does Roy Strong in *The English Icon* in which he also illustrates our Gallery's version. The confusion is due to the simultaneous existence of two Sir Thomas Astons, only distantly related. Gertrude Sadler married Sir Thomas Lucy Aston (after 1627 Lord Aston of Forfar) in about 1607 and therefore Gertrude Sadler would have been far too old to be the subject of the two portraits. The Gallery's portrait and the Tate's are of a young woman no more than twenty. Since Magdalen Poultney was born in 1600 and the costume can be dated to about 1620 the identification seems conclusive. The Aston family mourning portrait by Souch at Manchester (see mention of the painting later) also records Magdalen's likeness and is a further confirmation that the sitter is Magdalen Poultney. Furthermore, the Adelaide, London and Manchester portraits are recorded together in an 1862 inventory of Aston Hall (see note 6 below) and almost certainly were all sold at the Aston Lodge sale in 1927. (As was Melbourne's full-length Kneller of 1711, a portrait of a later Sir Thomas Aston – the grandson of our Sir Thomas.) On the other hand Julian Treuherz, in "New Light on John Souch of Chester" (*Burlington Magazine*, May 1997), discusses the Aston group mourning portrait and acknowledges that the Lady Aston on the deathbed was a "Pounteney" but suggests that the foreground figure could be a sister of the deceased woman. This would not make sense in the context of the intimate Aston family portrait in mourning.
6. Karen Hearn, Tate Curator of Sixteenth and Seventeenth Century

British Art, does not believe that the Tate's less elaborate version of Lady Aston is by Marcus Gheeraerts the Younger and therefore, by implication, neither is our version (which she has not seen). Both versions have an unusual blue cast to the whites of the eyes, use shell gold on the braid and fringes, and have other distinctive qualities which would indicate they are by the same artist or workshop. Both versions lack the pearly translucent flesh tones that documented and proven works by the artist possess, as Hearn adeptly demonstrated in her exhibition and publication *Marcus Gheeraerts II: Elizabethan artist in focus*, 2002. However, it is largely in the artist's works on panel, where he has used a slightly different technique, that the pearly flesh quality is overt, and has become increasingly so over time. Late works by Gheeraerts on canvas seem not so obviously to possess this quality. Certainly both versions of the Magdalen Poultney portrait have a more opaque coarseness in the handling of the flesh tones, which may indicate that they were mainly painted by the artist's studio. Little is known so far about the details of Gheeraerts's studio workshop practice. It is also possible that the works could have suffered in earlier conservation. Adelaide's version for instance had outlines of the forms strengthened, possibly in the early to mid nineteenth century. The Tate version has not been conserved. Both versions have similar poses, props, compositions and the sombre mood consistent with Gheeraerts's other full-length works of the period. Furthermore, the exact dating of the subject to 1620 or possibly 1621 by the very specific costume precludes authorship by other major Jacobean painters of full-length portraits such as William Larkin or Robert Peake as they were dead by 1619, and the modelling of the face is very unlike the other major Jacobean painter of full-length portraits Paul van Somer. And Karen Hearn does not believe the portraits are by the Cheshire artist John Souch who later painted the death portrait of Lady Aston. It is possible, however, that both portraits are by an artist yet to be identified.

7. On the other hand our portrait could have been painted to commemorate Magdalen's coming of age in 1621 and the Tate's version, though based on Adelaide's, commissioned later, on her marriage. The latter seems unlikely since her parents and grandparents were dead by the time of her marriage, unless in the highly unusual circumstance that her brother or one of her sisters wished for such a portrait. It is possible too, that the portraits were commissioned by the independently wealthy heiress herself and that she presented her grandmother with one of them. Magdalen Poultney and Thomas Aston were married in 1627; the first of their four children (all of whom died young) was born in 1630. Sir Thomas's grief is recorded in a Latin inscription on the painting by Souch, as is the fact that Aston's dead wife was aged thirty-five years, therefore confirming her birth date of 1600. Her marriage in 1627 would make Magdalen a considerably older bride than most of her time.

8. I am grateful to Karen Hearn for the suggestion of this possibility.

9. Aston Hall archives, schedule of family portraits, August 1862: "Twin Sisters…", nos 4 and 5. I am grateful to Howard D. Talbot, a descendant of Sir Thomas Aston, who drew my attention to this in an undated letter of early 1981.

10. The deathbed portrait group by Souch includes portrayals of Sir Thomas and their only surviving child Thomas, the Poultney heir who died two years later. The Latin inscription on the black-draped cradle reads in translation: "He who places his hope in flesh will become bones." This combines with the other melancholic inscription on the nautical cross that the father and son clasp: "By contrast with the earth, the seas and the stars are fixed and measurable." The painting is full of allusions to death and melancholy and it was in this mood that Sir Thomas could possibly have commissioned the painting-in of the broken windowpanes seen in Adelaide's portrait, to symbolise Magdalen's broken life (also see the following note 11).

11. For example, similar shattering of diamond-shaped windowpanes appears in an earlier melancholic portrait, of Henry Wriothesley, 3rd Earl of Southampton, painted in 1603 and attributed to Gheeraerts's brother-in-law John de Critz (collection the Duke of Buccleuch). That painting commemorates Southampton's imprisonment in the Tower of London for his part in the Essex rebellion for which he was condemned to death, the sentence later commuted to imprisonment for life. Presumably the shattered pane referred to his shattered life and the painful break with his family. As no one has yet produced a firm explanation for the cracked windowpanes in Jacobean portraits, and given the fact that glass was not easily replaceable, it is an equally plausible explanation that artists who included cracked windowpanes were simply recording actual cracked panes and demonstrating their illusionary skills.

12. "The Broken Heart", in John Hayward (ed.), *John Donne: A selection of his poetry*, Harmondsworth, Middlesex, 1986, p. 53.

13. Lady Aston's epitaph on a marble tablet in the chapel at Aston:

> Heere, reader, in this sad but glorious cell
> of Death, lyes shrinde a double miracle
> of women and of wife, and each soe best
> Shee may be Fames payre coppy to the rest.
> The virgin heere a blush soe chast might learne
> Till through the blood shee virtue did discerne;
> Heere might the Bryde upon her wedding day
> At once both knowse to love and to obey,
> Till shee grewe wife soe perfect and refynd
> To bee but body to her husbands mynd.
> The tender Mother heere might learne such love
> And care, as shames the pellican and dove,
> But Fame and Truth noe more, for should you fynd
> And bring each grace and beauty of her mynd
> Wonder and envy both would make this grave
> Theyr court, and blast that peace her ashes have.

# Notes pp. 68–84

### Cornelius Johnson  A lady, thought to be Catherine Fenn

1. Sotheby's, 11 July 1984.
2. First identified by the present author after a visit to Parham Park, West Sussex, in 1998.
3. Vicary Gibbs (ed.), *The Complete Peerage of England, Scotland, Ireland, Great Britain and the United Kingdom, extant, extinct or dormant*, London, 1910, p. 431. The *Col. of State Papers*, 1635. I am also grateful to Patricia Kennedy, Parham Park, for her assistance with biographical information on Catherine Fenn.
4. Ellen Chirestein, "Lady Elisabeth Pope: The Heraldic Body", in Lucy Gent and Nigel Llewellyn (eds), *Renaissance Bodies*, London, 1990, p. 40.
5. I am grateful to Avril Hart and Clare Brown of the Victoria & Albert Museum for their assistance with the costume description (letter to the author 16 September 1993).
6. Karen Hearn, *Marcus Gheeraerts II: Elizabethan artist in focus*, London: Tate, 2002, p. 46.

### Michiel van Miereveld  George Villiers, Duke of Buckingham

1. T. V. Wilks, "The Picture Collection of Robert Carr, Earl of Somerset Reconsidered", *Journal of the History of Collections*, vol. 1, 1989, p. 90. In a letter dated 11 February 1611 Miereveld stated he was willing to spend only three months in Britain but negotiations had foundered by February 1612 and he never came.
2. Oliver Millar, *The Age of Charles I: Painting in England 1620-1649*, London: Tate Gallery, 1972, p. 10. Millar states it was young Prince Charles not his older brother Prince Henry who first tried to induce Miereveld to Britain. Charles I, as well as possessing the portrait by Miereveld of Prince Maurice of Nassau, also owned a half-length portrait (1610) of Sir Edward Cecil. Cecil was most probably the first Englishman to commission a portrait by Miereveld.
3. His many official titles and positions especially irked members of the House of Commons who complained to the King in 1626 that too much power was entrusted to one man. In this formal complaint they listed the full concentration: "Duke, Marquis and Earl of Buckingham, Earl of Coventry, Viscount Villiers, Baron of Whaddon; Great Admiral of the kingdoms of England and Ireland…Master of the Horse of our sovereign lord the King; Lord Warden, Chancellor and Admiral of the Cinque Ports and of the members thereof; Constable of Dover Castle; Justice in Eyre of the forests and chases on this side the river Trent; Constable of the castle of Windsor; Gentleman of His Majesty's bedchamber; one of His Majesty's most honourable Privy Council in his realms both in England, Scotland and Ireland; and Knight of the most honourable order of the Garter". At the end of that year Chancellor of the University of Cambridge could have been added to the list.
4. Roger Lockyer, *Buckingham: The life and political career of George Villiers, First Duke of Buckingham 1592-1628*, London and New York, 1981, p. 461.
5. Charles Richard Cammell, *The Great Duke of Buckingham*, London, 1939, and Roger Lockyer, *op. cit.* Both these lengthy and heavily-researched books paint a much more favourable history of Buckingham.
6. Oliver Millar, *The Age of Charles I*, p. 18.
7. Lockyer, *op. cit.*, p. 409.
8. Lockyer, p. 307.
9. Millar, *op. cit.*, p. 18.
10. Millar, *op. cit.*, p. 2. Another was in the collection of Sir Gyles Isham, Bt, see *The Connoisseur*, 1936, pp. 128-29. Christie's auction 18 May 1994, lot 135. An engraving of this image of the Duke was executed in 1626 by Miereveld's son-in-law Willem J. Delff (1580-1638), and confirms the date and the attribution to Miereveld. Nevertheless the image has from time to time been ascribed erroneously to Daniel Mytens and Cornelius Johnson.
11. See Mark Weiss, *A Noble Visage: Early portraiture 1545-1660*, London: Weiss Gallery, 2001, no. 19. In all probability it was Miereveld's model that was used for the face and the lace collar in Mytens's several portraits of the Duke. An autograph version by Mytens, dated 1626, is in the collection of the Duke of Grafton, Euston Hall, Suffolk.

### Peter Lely  Portrait of a man, thought to be George Booth, Lord Delamere

1. Oliver Millar, *Sir Peter Lely*, London: National Portrait Gallery, 1978, p. 34, no. 2. The portrait was purchased in 1957 as Lord Delamere but at Christie's sale of 15 June 1928 it was catalogued as Sir George Howard. Other portraits of Sir George Howard cannot sustain any likeness to our sitter.

### attributed to Matthew Dixon  Portrait of a man

1. George Vertue, British Library Ms. Addl., f.53ᵛ (Vertue's folio 62ᵛ) and mentioned in Mary Edmond, "Nicholas Dixon, limner: and Matthew Dixon, painter died 1710", *Burlington Magazine*, no. 967, October 1983.
2. The five Ecton Hall portraits were sold at Sotheby's, 12 October 1955, lots 74-78. Photograph mounts of these works are held at the Witt Library. The portraits appear to have had similar conservation problems to the Gallery's painting.
3. Dr Malcolm Rogers, then of the National Portrait Gallery, London, first suggested this very plausible attribution in 1983.

### Mary Beale  Mary Wither of Andwell

1. Mark Weiss, 2002, no. 24, and letters to Mark Weiss from the College of Arms, London, 22 and 25 March 2002.
2. Letter to the author 10 October 2003 from Tabitha Barber, Curator Seventeenth and Early Eighteenth Century Art, Tate, London.
3. Tabitha Barber, *Mary Beale: Portrait of a seventeenth century painter, her family and her studio*, London: Geffrye Museum, 1999, pp. 14 and 67.

### Simon Verelst  Portrait of an Ambassador

1. The artist Jonathan Richardson told George Vertue that Verelst charged £110 for a half-length (George Vertue, *Anecdotes of Painting in England*, London, 1828, vol. III, p. 66), whereas the more highly esteemed court painter Peter Lely had charged only £40.
2. *NGSA Bulletin*, vol. 6, no. 2, October 1944.

3. *Loc. cit.*
4. Dr Malcolm Rogers, then Deputy Director, National Portrait Gallery, London, first suggested the highly plausible attribution to Simon Verelst in a letter to the author 15 December 1988. The author has checked the work against other portraits by Verelst and there would seem little doubt that he is the artist. An attribution to John Closterman had been proposed a few years earlier. In 1944 the Gallery noted that Godfrey Kneller and John Riley had also been suggested as possible artists (*NGSA Bulletin*).

### attributed to Nicolas de Largillierre  Portrait of a Frenchman

1. Alistair Laing, in a letter from Patrick Matthiesen to the author 6 December 1988, first suggested the plausible attribution to Largillierre. The author has been able to view earlier paintings by the artist to support the attribution. When the portrait was bequeathed to the Gallery in 1957 its artist was unknown and the subject was erroneously thought to be King Louis XIV of France.
2. *Jean-Baptiste Tavernier*, 1679 (Herzog Anton Ulrich-Museum, Brunswick); see *Largilliere and the Eighteenth Century Portrait*, Montreal Museum of Fine Arts, 1982, pp. 100–101.
3. Largillierre's oval portrait of *Charles Le Brun*, in the Mobilier National, Paris, and another version c.1685 (Bayerische Staatsgemäldesammlungen, Munich) is in a painted oval, as is the portrait of *François Adhemar de Monteil, Comte de Grignan, Governor of Provence* (Musée Calvet, Avignon). A Largillierre portrait of a man of almost identical size and format to the Gallery's oval portrait appeared at the Bischoffsheim sale, Christies, 7 May 1926 (see mount in Witt Library). There also exists a series of oval preparatory portraits of the Aldermen of the City of Paris painted in the mid 1690s (one in Musée d'Art et d'Histoire, Geneva, another in Museu Nacional de Arte Antiga, Lisbon, and a third in Muzeum Narodowe, Warsaw). All these early oval portraits by Largillierre relate in some way in style to the Gallery's portrait.

### Nicolas de Largilliere  Frances Wollascot, an Augustinian nun

1. George Vertue Notebooks, V, *The Walpole Society*, vol. 26, 1937/38, p. 105, (1741–52), p. 105; Inventory of Portraits at Coughton Court, ms., 1855, p. 10.
2. Sister Mary Benedict, St Augustine's Priory, Ealing, London, letter to the author 30 April 1992.
3. Pauline Johnstone, *High Fashion in the Church*, Leeds, 2002, p. 98.
4. Pauline Johnstone, Lewes, Sussex, letter to the Art Gallery of South Australia, 11 July 1991.
5. The title of the book is in capitals on three lines: "PENSÉE / CRÉ / TIENNE".
6. Bernard Tyssèdre, "Largillière's Portrait of Elizabeth Throckmorton", *Art News*, vol. 64, 9 January 1966, pp. 45–47. See Jean Baptiste Oudry, *Reflections sur la manière d'étudier la couleur en comparant les objects les uns avec les autres* (1749), Paris, 1844, pp. 44–45. These references are cited in *Largillierre and the Eighteenth Century Portrait*, Museum of Fine Arts, Montreal, 1982, pp. 246, 247, 274–276.

### Jean-Baptiste Monnoyer  Still-life with basket of flowers

1. I am indebted to Margaret Bowman's unpublished thesis on Monnoyer for the most up-to-date biographical information on the artist, particularly his dates in England.
2. The painting was bought in London in 1927 by Miss J. Turnbull of Melbourne.

### James Thornhill  Minerva and the Gods of Olympus: A design for the hall ceiling at Easton Neston

1. See inscriptions on reverse of sheet under Inscriptions.

### Godfrey Kneller  Lady Henrietta Crofts, Duchess of Bolton

1. The painting is signed and inscribed by the artist "G. Kneller. Baron$^{et}$ F" and therefore cannot be dated earlier than 1715. (The "F" is an abbreviation for the Latin "fecit" meaning "done by".)
2. Chaloner J. Smith, *British Mezzotint Portraits* (4 vols), 1878–83, no. 19.
3. It is not absolutely clear whether the Duchess of Bolton died on 27 February 1729 or 1730, but most sources say 1730.
4. The flowers, like the sitter herself, have been somewhat generalised, which is characteristic of Kneller. He was interested in flowers, but they are not painted with the same degree of botanical detail and subtlety employed by his friend and contemporary Monnoyer, whose portrait Kneller painted on Monnoyer's return to London before 1698. The Gallery has a fine and characteristic example of Monnoyer's flower painting (*Still-life with basket of flowers*, 1690s) which depicts flowers in a similar though much larger wicker-basket to that held by the Duchess of Bolton. Monnoyer is believed to have painted the flowers in earlier portraits by Kneller and others in Britain, and so also did his son Antoine who painted in Britain to 1747. Could Antoine Monnoyer have painted the flowers in this basket? Kneller might have been too elderly and busy to cope with them.
5. J. Douglas Stewart, 1983. It is possible that the Victoria & Albert Museum drawing, Stewart's no. 42 (plate 100b) and more probably the British Museum drawing no. 46 (plate 101c), are the drawings for the Duchess.

### Joseph Highmore  The artist's wife Susanna, son Anthony and daughter Susanna

1. The convention of the three-quarter-length informal family portrait in British art ultimately derives from Van Dyck. Highmore's group relies heavily on the then century-old formula filtered as it was through Van Dyck's followers Peter Lely and Godfrey Kneller, Highmore's teacher. It is interesting to note that Lely owned Van Dyck's *Family group* (Detroit Institute of Arts) and *Family of Endymion Porter* (private collection) and Van Dyck's influence can clearly be seen in Lely's *The Cotton family*, 1660 (Manchester Art Gallery). In a similar format Kneller painted *The Duke of Chandos and family* (National Gallery of Canada, Ottawa) in 1713, the year Highmore joined Kneller's Academy. If one were to cut off the fathers on the left in Lely's *The Cotton family* and in Kneller's

Chandos family what would remain in both paintings is a centrally placed mother with a standing son on her right and a daughter on her left. This is precisely the format of the Gallery's Highmore family group. Highmore's separate *Self-portrait* of the same size, now in Melbourne, is as if cut off from the left side of the picture, and intended to hang to the left of the family group. Vertical family portraits, one of the husband, the other of the wife and children (instead of one larger horizontal picture) were a format developed in British art in Highmore's time and continued in middle-class commissions until the mid nineteenth century.

The composition and pose of Highmore's companion *Self-portrait* also seems to be based on Lely and Van Dyck models. It resembles the pose and composition of Van Dyck's self-portraits, both painted and engraved, and also Lely's *Self-portrait* in the National Portrait Gallery, London.

2. The National Gallery of Victoria holds a later portrait, 1745–47, by Joseph Highmore of his son Anthony Highmore and another, 1745–50, of his daughter Susanna Highmore. Those two, the self-portrait and Adelaide's group portrait were four of seven works sold in Melbourne in 1947. They were brought to Australia, probably around 1865, by a great-grandson of Anthony Highmore, Frederick Morgan Payler who was the father of Frederick Trafford Morgan Payler, Archdeacon of Ballarat, Victoria, who sold the works in 1947. (Ursula Hoff, *European Painting and Sculpture before 1800*, Melbourne: National Gallery of Victoria, fourth edition, 1995, p. 151, where they are assigned much later dates than here.) I am also grateful for information supplied by Jane Clark (letter to the Art Gallery of South Australia, 2 July 1986). In the recent past Highmore's wife Susanna has been wrongly named Anna Maria in this portrait.

### William Hogarth  William FitzHerbert

1. Ronald Paulson, *Hogarth: His life, art and times*, New Haven and London: Yale University Press, published for the Paul Mellon Centre for Studies in British Art, 1971, vol. 2, p. 303.
2. W. S. Lewis (ed.), *Horace Walpole's Correspondence*, vol. 32, pp. 73–74. Walpole also mentions (vol. 38, pp. 263–264) that FitzHerbert was removed from the prestigious position of Gentleman Usher because he was an old acquaintance of the political dissident John Wilkes.
3. James Boswell, *The Life of Samuel Johnson LL.D.*, vol. 3, p. 134.
4. J. L. Smith-Dampier, *Who's Who in Boswell?*, 1935, p. 127. I am also indebted to Historical Portraits Ltd, London, and especially to Elizabeth Einberg, former Assistant Keeper, Tate, for drawing my attention to contemporary biographical information on the sitter and general information on the painting.

### Arthur Devis  Portrait of a lady with a dog

1. Joseph Burke, *English Art 1714–1800*, London: Oxford University Press, 1976, p. 303.
2. Stephen V. Sartin, *Polite Society by Arthur Devis 1712–1787: Portraits of the English country gentleman and his family*, Preston, Lancashire: Harris Museum & Art Gallery, 1983, no. 42. In 1983 it was with Leger Galleries, London.
3. *Op. cit.*, no. 45, *Alicia and Jane Clarke, of Walford Court, Ross-on Wye, Herefordshire*, c.1758, and no. 51, *Edward Rookes-Leeds and his family, of Royds Hall, Low Moor, Yorkshire*, c.1763–68. The same or similar dress can be seen also in other portraits by Devis.
4. *Op. cit.*, pp. 23–26, 67–68.
5. *Op. cit.*, no. 39, as of 1756–58; collection Museum of the King's Own Royal Regiment, City Museum, Lancaster.

### Tilly Kettle  Woman with a muff

1. An especially good later example is Ramsay's *Martha, Countess of Elgin*, c.1764 (collection Earl of Elgin and Kincardine).
2. Aileen Ribeiro notes a similar muff in Reynolds's portrait *Mary Pelham*, 1757, which also may be monkey skin. Letter to the author 3 May 1989.
3. John Baily, "A Portrait by Tilly Kettle", *AGSA Bulletin*, vol. 32, no. 2, October 1970.
4. Ellis Waterhouse, *Painting in Britain 1530–1790*, Harmondsworth, Middlesex: Penguin, 1969, p. 186.

### Francis Swaine  The Landing of the Sailor Prince at Spithead

1. Frank B. Cockett, *Peter Monamy 1681–1749 and his Circle*, Woodbridge, Suffolk, 2000, pp. 71, 73.
2. Frank B. Cockett correspondence with Adam Free, June 2002. Much of the information on the ships and maritime information was supplied by Frank B. Cockett; letter to the author dated 23 October 2004. I am also grateful for the assistance of Adam Free.

### Allan Ramsay  King George III in coronation robes

1. Jane Roberts (ed.), *George III & Queen Charlotte: Patronage, collecting and court taste*, London, 2004, p. 24.
2. Ellis Waterhouse, *Painting in Britain 1530 to 1790*, Harmondsworth, Middlesex: Penguin, 1953, p. 142.
3. Horace Walpole, *Anecdotes of Painting in England* (ed. F. W. Hilles and P. B. Daghlian), Yale University Press, 1937, vol. 5, p. 56.
4. A pair of Ramsay royal portraits hung until 2003 at Admiralty House, the Sydney residence of the Governor-General of Australia. They belong to the National Gallery of Australia, Canberra. The first governors of New South Wales received replicas of a different pair of royal portraits in coronation robes, seated not standing, the originals painted in 1779 by Reynolds, whose ledger notes that those for first governor Arthur Phillip were "small". (The pair of Reynolds replicas given to third governor Philip Gidley King, probably in 1791, were huge, 280 x 178 cm, and have been at the present Government House in Sydney since 1846, donated by King's widow.)
5. Alastair Smart, 1992, p. 217.
6. Jane Roberts, 2004, p. 24.
7. Correspondence from Jacob Simon, Curator, 18th Century Portraits, National Portrait Gallery, London.
8. I am indebted to Alastair Smart for much of the information about the versions of the George III portrait.

# Notes pp. 130–152

### Joshua Reynolds  Dr John Armstrong

1. Dr Armstrong's other notable literary works include: *Synopsis of the History and Cure of the Venereal Disease*, 1737; *The Economy of Love*, 1737; *Benevolence, an Epistle to Eumenes*, 1751; *Taste, an Epistle to a Young Critic*, 1753; *The Forced Marriage*, 1754; *An Epistle to John Wilkes*, 1760; *Day*, 1760; *A Short Ramble through France and Italy*, 1771.
2. *Dictionary of National Biography*, London, 1885, vol. 11, p. 94.
   I am grateful to John A. Armstrong, chairman of the Clan Armstrong Trust for supplying further biographical information on Dr John Armstrong.
3. At the back of Reynolds's first ledger is a technical note: "Dr Armstrong painted first in olio poi Vernic / iato / poi cera, solo poi cera e vernicio." This is a little ambiguous but it seems he painted first in oil and then waxed, possibly with coloured wax glazes, and then varnished. (Mannings p. 65)
4. Graves & Cronin, *loc. cit.*
5. The Davenport museum's version, which has been seen by the author, has higher-coloured flesh tones, sharper features and smoother, less textured overall surface, all of which would indicate that Reynolds had less of a hand in it. The Adelaide version is more typical of the artist's faded colours and highly worked surface. According to information on Witt Library mounts there is a third version which came up at a Christie's sale on 16 July 1937, again on 10 March 1939, and then in a Sotheby's sale on 26 July 1939; it had a provenance before 1899 from the Marquess of Bute. The Adelaide version was acquired in 1934 and the Davenport's in 1915.
   In 1899 Graves & Cronin recorded three versions: one belonging to Baroness Burdett-Coutts, a replica with the printseller Mr Dexter, and another belonging to the Marquess of Bute.
6. Craves & Cronin record five engravings as follows: E. Fisher, 12½ x 10 inches; T. Trotter, 1782, 4 x 2½ inches; Cook, 4⅝ x 2¾ inches; S. W. Reynolds, 5½ x 4⅜ inches; F. Engleheart, 1821, 3¾ x 3 inches.

### Joshua Reynolds  Robert Henley, Second Earl of Northington

1. Henry B. Wheatley, *The Historical and Posthumous Memoirs of Sir Nathaniel William Wraxall 1772–1784*, London: Bickers & Son, c.1884, p. 59.
2. Graves & Cronin, *loc. cit.*, vol. 2, p. 696.
3. *Ibid.*, and Mannings, *loc. cit.*, p. 250.
4. Humphrey Ward & W. Roberts, *Romney*, London, 1904, vol. 2, catalogue raisonné, p. 113; see also p. 72 after entry James Harris, Lord Malmesbury.

### Francis Cotes  Elizabeth, Lady Jones

1. In 1764 Francis Burdett, Elizabeth Jones's brother-in-law, commissioned three portraits of himself and one of his wife Mary Eleanor, Elizabeth's sister. Cotes painted Eleanor's sister-in-law Elizabeth Burdett in 1766 and twice again in 1767. In the latter year Sir Robert Burdett, father-in-law of Elizabeth Jones's sister Eleanor, commissioned a portrait of himself.

### Richard Wilson  Cicero with his friend Atticus and brother Quintus, at his villa at Arpinum

1. Cicero, *De Legibus*, book II, iii, translated C. W. Keynes, London, 1948, p. 377.
2. Wilson's *View near Wynnstay, the Seat of Sir Watkin Williams-Wynn, Bt* and its companion *Dinas Bran from Llangollen* (both Yale Center for British Art) hung at St James's Square. (The Art Gallery of South Australia has a version of Wilson's *Dinas Bran*.) See Solkin 1982, p. 238, who mentions Benjamin Booth recording these Welsh views hanging at Sir Watkins's St James's Square house.
3. In 1780 in Rome the Scottish artist Jacob More painted *Landscape: Cicero at his Villa* for Lord Bristol. More could have seen Wilson's original painting when it was exhibited at the Royal Academy in 1770, or the Gallery's version before he left for Rome in 1771, or he could have seen the Woollett engraving after Wilson of 1778.
4. David Solkin 1982, pp. 131–33, 235–36. I am greatly indebted to David Solkin for his ideas and research on the composition.
5. Engraving after Wilson's "Cicero" by William Woollett, published 1778.
6. W. G. Constable, *Richard Wilson*, London, 1953, pp. 168–69.

### Richard Wilson  Dinas Bran from Llangollen

1. David Solkin, 1982, pp. 130–33, 238. I am much indebted to David Solkin for his ideas and research on the first version.
2. W. G. Constable, 1953, pp. 175–76.
3. *This Other Eden: British Paintings from the Paul Mellon Collection at Yale*, New Haven, Connecticut/ Sydney: Yale Center for British Art/ Art Exhibitions Australia, 1998, no. 26

### Jacob More  A distant view of Rome across the Tiber

1. This early date is confirmed by Patricia R. Andrew, author of a doctoral thesis on Jacob More and of the substantial Walpole Society publication.
2. James Holloway 1987, p. 8. Patricia R. Andrew 1993, appendix A, p. 195. The whereabouts of no. 176 in the 1775 London exhibition is unknown. The painting was once attributed to Thomas Daniell (1749–1840) by Leger Galleries.

### Thomas Gainsborough  Madame Lebrun

1. Much of this biographical information on Franzisca Lebrun came from Julie Anne Sadie & Rhian Samuel, *The New Grove Dictionary of Woman Composers*, London, 1994, pp. 271–272, and Stanley Sadie (ed.), *The New Grove Dictionary of Music and Musicians*, 2nd ed., vol. 14, London, 2001, pp. 436–37.
2. Gainsborough's red studio chair seen in the portraits of Madam Lebrun and Mrs Siddons features earlier and most prominently in the portrait of his musician friend *Karl Friedrich Abel*, c.1777 (Huntington Library & Art Collections, San Marino, California).
3. Hugh Belsey has also pointed out a much closer comparison to the Madam Lebrun portrait is that of a later (probably nineteenth century) Gainsborough pastiche entitled *Miss Moleyns* now lost but known from an illustration in the Sedelmeyer Catalogue, Agnew's, 1913. It is very close in pose, dress and even the coat over the chair,

# Notes pp. 152–178

but has a different face, firmer modeling than in our painting. However, from the illustration it appears as a rather staid pastiche with none of Gainsborough's vitality and animation evident in the Lebrun portrait.

I am also indebted to Hugh Belsey for some other information on the painting especially the early literature about the painting. (Correspondence to author 12 November and 10 December 2004.)

### Thomas Gainsborough  Wooded upland landscape with shepherd and sheep and track winding around a knoll

1. William Jackson, *The Four Ages*, London, 1798, p. 157.
2. W. T. Whitley, *Gainsborough*, London, 1915, quoted p. 369.
3. Gainsborough to William Jackson, Bath, 23 August (no year), in Mary Woodall, *The Letters of Thomas Gainsborough*, London, 1963, no. 49, p. 99.

### Dominic Serres  Foudroyant and Pégase entering Portsmouth Harbour, 1782

1. Information supplied by Royal Naval Museum, H.M. Naval Base, Portsmouth, 6 December 1990.
2. W. Laird Clowes, *The Royal Navy: A history from the earliest times to the present*, London, 1899, pp. 80–83. For his victory Captain John Jervis was rewarded with a K.B. and permitted to bear on his coat-of-arms a winged horse. He was later in command of the British fleet at the Battle of St Vincent in 1797 and, as Lord Vincent, was a notable Lord of Admiralty. He was Nelson's mentor.
3. Francis Swaine painted the *Capture of the Foudroyant by H.M.S. Monmouth* (National Maritime, Museum, Greenwich) depicting the action which took place on 28 February 1758.
4. See note 1.
5. I am indebted to James Taylor and Brian Lavery from the National Maritime Museum, Greenwich, for much of this naval and nautical information. Letters to author 6 May and 9 June 1993. I am also indebted to Mrs D. L. Wood of Adelaide and to H.M. Naval Base, Portsmouth, for relevant naval history and other information.
6. I am grateful to Katy Ball, Assistant Local History Officer, Portsmouth City Council, for the information about the historical buildings of Portsmouth. Letter to the author 29 June 1994.

### Paul Sandby  Approaching Rochester and the Medway

1. The present author identified the subject in 1990. The former title was *Landscape with figures*, see Julian Faigan 1981.

### George Romney  Charlotte, Mrs Thomas Raikes

1. Alex Kidson, *George Romney 1734–1802*, London: National Portrait Gallery, 2002. The exhibition was shown at the Walker Art Gallery, Liverpool; National Portrait Gallery, London; Huntington Library & Art Collections, San Marino, California.
2. All the peerages describe Henry Finch as unmarried. He died in 1761.
3. Alex Kidson emphasises that the dramatic and panoramic scenery of Romney's Cumbrian childhood influenced his colour and appreciation of romantic landscape such as can be seen in the landscape background in this portrait. Kidson quotes Flaxman: "The rainbow, the purple distance or the silver lake taught him colouring…." Kidson also quotes Romney's son John in a similar fashion: "…varied often by storms and tempests, often by brilliant and glowing sunsets, often by that wild and skimming action of clouds, which forebodes storms, or by that gloominess of atmosphere, or dark accumulation of cloud in the horizon, which foretells rain…must have afforded him fine ideas of the sublime."
4. Humphry Ward & W. Roberts in *Romney*, vol. 2, London, 1904, pp. 128–29. The Romney appointment diary for 1785 is missing and therefore a full list of what he painted that year is not known. The Bank of England owns a similar sized portrait of Thomas Raikes by Romney that could be considered the companion to the Art Gallery of South Australia's portrait of his wife Charlotte, although Romney painted two other versions of the Thomas Raikes portrait.
5. Although Romney's accounts record that on 29 January 1787 he received payment for a portrait of "Mrs Raikes and Child", Ward & Roberts's 1904 catalogue of Romney's works doubted that it was ever executed. However, a Witt Library mount illustrates a portrait of a Mrs Raikes and Child that came up for sale in a Christie's auction in July 1913. The likeness is unmistakably that of Charlotte Raikes.
6. Ward & Roberts, vol. 1, p. 110. The sittings were on 20 December 1786, 28 February, 27 April and 17 May 1787.
7. *Op. cit.*, vol. 2, p. 128.

### George Romney  Colonel Robert Abercrombie

1. Humphry Ward & W. Roberts, *Romney*, 1904, vol. 2, p. 1. The sittings were 27 and 29 February, 4, 6 and 8 March 1788.
2. The sitter was correctly identified by the present author in 1983. Ward & Roberts wrongly identify him as Ralph Abercrombie.
3. Ward & Roberts, *loc. cit.*
4. *Dictionary of National Biography*, vol. 1, London, 1880, p. 47.

### Richard Westall  The birds' nest

1. Ron Radford in Sarah Thomas, *The Encounter, 1802*, p. 106.
2. It is possibly *Spring*, no. 413 at the Royal Academy exhibition, 1794.

### George Morland  Outside the Bull's Head

1. Singer sale, Christie's, 21 February 1930, bought by Ellis & Smith. Witt Library mount, Courtauld Institute, London.
2. Witt Library mount, Courtauld Institute.

### Martin Archer Shee  Major O'Shea of the Loyal Cork Legion

1. Martin Shee, *Life of Sir Martin Archer Shee*, London, 1860, vol. 1, p. 213. This tells that the sitter was a kinsman. In the eighteenth century Shee, Shea, O'Shee and O'Shea were often interchangeable; for instance brothers in the same family sometimes varied their surname from each other.
2. *Ibid.*
3. Christie's, 19 July 1929, lot 79. In Christie's record catalogue there is a hand-written notation, presumably made at the time of the

auction: "(may be James McMahon Coppinger)". (Correspondence from Margie Christian, Christie's, 11 April 1990)
4. Undated 1991 letter to the author from Kenneth Ferguson of The Military History Society of Ireland.
5. Information from Patrick Yarnold, Consulting Genealogist, Guildford, Surrey, 6 November 2004.
6. By then Shee had enrolled at the Royal Academy Schools on the advice of Reynolds but did not officially commence until the beginning of 1789.

### Michael Angelo Rooker  A view of a ruined castle

1. Newport Castle, Newport, Gwent, still stands on the banks of the Usk in South Wales. The surviving fourteenth- and fifteenth-century towers are the work of the Earls of Stafford, later Dukes of Buckingham, but theirs was not the earliest castle at the Newport site.
2. In the 1775 Royal Academy Rooker exhibited *Portrait of an old oak* (no. 249) and *A ruin* (no. 259). In 1786 he exhibited *Landscape and ruins* (no. 58) and *Landscape with ruins* (no. 112). All his other Royal Academy exhibits bear titles that name specific buildings or places.

### Thomas Rowlandson  The Brilliants

1. Formerly in the Bernard Landau collection, Sotheby's, 4 December 1957, lot 52.

### William Blake  St Paul before Felix and Drusilla

1. Butlin, 1981, pp. 316–17.
2. *Ibid.*
3. Kathleen Raine, *William Blake*, London, 1970, p. 105.
4. Butlin, *op. cit.*, pp. 335–36.

### Robert Hills  Soay sheep in a landscape

1. The watercolour was received in 1957 with the title *Landscape with sheep*, which obviously needed to be more specific. I am especially grateful to Graeme Gatley, Educational Manager Wool, at the Marleston College of TAFE, Adelaide, who first identified the sheep as being of the Soay breed and supplied information on them. (Letter to the author 7 April 1993.)

### Thomas Lawrence  Caroline Matilda Sotheron

1. Garlick, 1989, p. 267, no. 733, illus.
2. This identification was first suggested by the author on stylistic grounds in correspondence, 30 June 2003, with Kenneth Garlick, who confirmed the possibility. It was later substantiated by Robin Francis, Head of Archive & Library, National Portrait Gallery, London, after researching the Sotheron family papers deposited there by Garlick. The reference for the inscription on the lost gold case of the 1812 miniature is in George C. Williamson, *Catalogue of the Collection of Miniatures the Property of J. Pierpont Morgan*, London, 1906–08, pp. 99–100, no. 367. The 1812 miniature by John Wright after Lawrence is recorded in the exhibition catalogue by Dr Stephen Lloyd, *Portrait Miniatures from the Clarke Collection*, Edinburgh: Scottish National Portrait Gallery, 2001, no. 65, pp. 88–89 (the Clarke Collection is on permanent loan to the Scottish National Portrait Gallery).
3. Private collection United States; see Garlick, 1989, p. 169, no. 191 (illus.).
4. Garlick, 1989, p. 267, no. 732, illus., now in the George Eastman Collection, University of Rochester, New York.

### Thomas Lawrence  The son of Countess Meerveldt

1. Allan Cunningham, *Life of Sir David Wilkie*, London, 1843, vol. 2, p. 365.
2. Kenneth Garlick does not believe the inscription is by Lawrence himself as the writing is not particularly like his hand. However, it is difficult to imagine who else could have written such a personal inscription. (Letter from Kenneth Garlick to the author 19 August 2003.)
3. A 1793 portrait of the Countess by Élisabeth Vigée-Lebrun is in the collection of the Norton Simon Museum, Pasadena, California.

### Henry Raeburn  Archibald Trotter of Bush

1. James Greig, *Sir Henry Raeburn, RA*, London, 1911, p. 61.
2. Algernon Graves, *A Century of Loan Exhibitions 1813–1912*, London, 1914, vol. III, 'R to U', p. 975.
3. Archibald's father Robert Trotter died in 1807 three years before the mother and son commission.

### John Sell Cotman  The old pigeon house, Downham Market

1. Known from the late nineteenth century as *The Orchard House*, see W. F. Dickes, *The Norwich School of Painting*, London, 1905, p. 305.
2. Dickes, *loc. cit.*

### J. M. W. Turner  Scarborough town and castle: morning: boys catching crabs

1. Andrew Wilton, RA 1974.
2. A colour sketch for this later composition of Scarborough is also held by the Tate. The mezzotint for *The Ports of England* was engraved by T. Lupton. Turner also made a drawing of this later composition, dated 1825, and now held by the Fitzwilliam Museum, Cambridge. For the title vignette which may have been etched by Turner himself see Andrew Wilton, *Turner in the British Museum: Drawings and Watercolours*, London, 1974, p. 64.
3. Andrew Wilton, *The Life and Works of J. M. W. Turner*, London, 1979, pp. 117, 360.

### J. M. W. Turner  Alnwick Castle

1. The painting by Canaletto of the castle in ruins is still at Alnwick Castle.
2. Richard Lockett, *Samuel Prout 1783–1852*, London, 1985, p. 170.
3. The 4th Duke of Northumberland found Adam's work frivolous and demolished most of it a hundred years after it was built. The architect of this second restoration, which remains today, was Anthony Salvin. (I am grateful to Lady Richard Percy who supplied much of the information about the castle.)

4. Andrew Wilton, *The Life and Works of J. M. W. Turner*, London, 1979, p. 395.
5. The painting by Claude was held privately in Britain in Turner's day, publicly auctioned in 1795. Now owned by the National Gallery, London, its title has returned to Claude's original *Pysche in front of the Palace of Amor* and it has been fairly recently cleaned.

### John Flaxman  Dessert stand

1. Shirley Bury, "Flaxman as a designer of silverwork" in David Bindman (ed.), *John Flaxman, R.A.*, London: Royal Academy and Thames & Hudson, 1979, pp. 140–48.
2. Christopher Menz, then Curator of European & Australian Decorative Arts at the Art Gallery of South Australia, first provided the attribution to Flaxman. I am greatly indebted to him for most of the information on the object.
3. "Volume of Designs for Gold and Silver Plate for the Royal Goldsmiths Rundell, Bridge & Rundell …" (E.119-1964, p. 43), Print Room, Victoria & Albert Museum, London.

### John Flaxman  Arcana Cœlestia: Novitiate spirits surrounded by a heavenly sphere

1. David Irwin, *John Flaxman*, London, 1979, pp. 118, 227, notes 88–90. Powney, 1976.
2. Gyllenhaal, 1996, p. 8.
3. *Op. cit.*, pp. 18–19.
4. *Op. cit.*, p. 17.

### Ferdinand Bauer  Passionflowers

1. Apparently not exhibited by the Royal Academy as a group: *Passionflowers* was no. 731, *Group of Flowers* no. 596, *Group of Flowers from New Holland* no. 640, and *Group of Flowers from Cape of Good Hope* no. 714.
2. The multiple symbolism of the flower was first documented in the early seventeenth century by Emmanuel de Villegas, a member of the Augustinian order, and can be seen in each of the three species in *Passionflowers*. The tendrils represent the whips used to scourge Christ; the central flower column is the pillar of the scourging. The seventy-two radial filaments are generally seen as the Crown of Thorns, but sometimes seen as a halo; the three stigma and the five anthers are the nails and the wounds respectively, while the style represents the sponge used to moisten Christ's lips. The red stain visible in two of the species symbolises the blood of Christ, and the leaves can represent, according to their shape, either the spears or the grasping hands of the soldiers. The symbolism of this and other plants was one means of teaching the gospels.

### Francis Chantrey  King George III

1. Alex Potts, *Sir Francis Chantrey 1781–1841: Sculptor of the Great*, London: National Portrait Gallery, 1980, p. 13.
2. Rupert Gunnis, *Dictionary of British Sculptors 1660–1851*, London: Odhams, 1953, p. 94, gives a list of Chantrey's busts including two of George III. At 1814 Gunnis lists the Royal College of Surgeons' bust. At "1810?" he lists a George III at Belton House, Lincolnshire, which suggests he connected the 1809/10 sittings with the bust at Belton but did not know whether the object bore a date. Gunnis's preface is dated 1951 (in the second edition of his dictionary) so the bust might have been out of reach, moving around the art market or heading to Adelaide, just when he hoped to examine it. In 1815 John Cust of Belton House, Grantham, was created Earl Brownlow and Viscount Alford; he is a possible candidate for commissioning a sitting in 1810 and a bust that was completed in 1813. In 1984 the 7th Baron Brownlow gave Belton House to the National Trust.
3. Potts, *loc. cit.*

### Charles Eastlake  Cypress trees at the Villa d'Este

1. In 1550 Cardinal Ippolito II d'Este of the powerful patrician family from Ferrara (and later Modena) was appointed civil Governor of Tivoli and converted the Benedictine convent to his Villa d'Este. Cardinal Ippolito employed many mural painters to decorate the villa under Taddeo Zuccaro's principal scheme, but most attention and money was lavished on elaboration of the garden for which the Villa d'Este at Tivoli has become renowned.
2. After Claude Lorrain in the seventeenth century, the artists who recorded the gardens and the ancient cypresses of the Villa d'Este in the eighteenth century included the French painter Jean Honoré Fragonard (Albertina, Vienna) and the English artist Thomas Jones (private collection, United Kingdom). Artists of the first half of the nineteenth century who recorded the cypresses after Eastlake included Samuel Palmer in 1838 and 1839 (Pierpont Morgan Library, New York; Yale Center for British Art, New Haven, Connecticut; Ashmolean Museum, Oxford), Camille Corot in 1843 (Louvre, Paris) and many German romantic landscape painters who followed the German Nazarenes to Rome, including J. W. Schirmer in 1840 and Oscar Achenbach in 1850 (both in Kunstmuseum, Düsseldorf).

### Samuel Howitt  Kangaroos (Didelphis Gigantia)

1. By 1791 live kangaroos had been brought back to London and could be seen at a trunk-makers shop in the Haymarket. By the 1820s there was a herd of kangaroos in Windsor Great Park, see Tim Flannery, *Country*, Melbourne, 2004, p. 24.
2. Yale Center for British Art, Samuel Howitt Sketchbook, Registration no. B 1977.14.9395–9452.
3. From "The Kangaroo" in Barron Field, *First Fruits of Australian Poetry*, 1819.

### John Glover  Cattle. The last Gleam of the Setting Sun

1. Elspeth Moncrieff et al., *Farm Animal Portraits*, Woodbridge, Suffolk: Antique Collectors' Club, 1998, p. 199. Note also that a painting by Gourlay Steell, *Favourite Cattle at Windsor*, 1776, pl. 45, includes three breeds, Shorthorn, Hereford and Jersey, and that T. Sidney Cooper's *The Victoria Cow 'Buffie'*, 1848, colour pl. 104, p. 120, of Queen Victoria's favourite cow at Osborne, is a Jersey. On inspecting the latter painting, Prince Albert commented on the dock-leaves in the foreground and the artist responded:

"'The privilege of my branch of art…is to take advantage of objects of still-life, to assist the composition of a work, and for pictorial combination; and such accessories as dock leaves are considered allowable to avoid the monotony…of grass and earth.' 'Well', said the Prince jocosely, 'they are beautifully painted, and doubtless assist the composition, but they do not give evidence of good farming'."
2. Leigh Hunt, *Literary Pocket Book; or, Companion for the Lover of Nature and Art*, London, 1819-23, in which Glover's specialisations are advertised as "landscapes and animals".
3. Hansen, p. 166.
4. Letter from Thomas Uwins, 14 May 1816, in Sarah Uwins, *A Memoir of Thomas Uwins, RA: with letters to his brothers during 7 years spent in Italy and correspondence with the late Sir Thomas Lawrence, Sir Charles Eastlake, A. E. Chalon RA. and other distinguished persons* (1858), East Ardsley, Wakefield: EP Publishing, 1978, pp. 44-45.

### John Glover  Twilight, Ullswater

1. Hansen, p. 180. Quote from John Brown, *Description of the Vale of Keswick* (1753).
2. With Agnew's in 1964; 29 by 44 inches.
3. Sotheby's, June 1994, lot 69.

### John Glover  North End, Hampstead Heath

1. Hansen, p. 184.
2. I am indebted to David Hansen who drew my attention to this Varley watercolour. It is illustrated in Hansen, p. 184.
3. Dixson Galleries, State Library of New South Wales, Sydney, DGA30.

### James Ward  Portrait of Dash, a Favourite Spaniel, the Property of Lady Frances Vane-Tempest

1. C. Reginald Grundy, *James Ward, R. A.*, London, 1909, p. vii.
2. Ward's Account Book now at the Royal Academy, p. 62. I am grateful to Edward J. Nygren for drawing my attention to this information (letter to the author 22 April 1992).

### J. J. Halls  Thomas Wilson

1. Wilson & Borrow, 1973, pp. 155-66.
2. Thomas Wilson, "Eminent Female Artists", a lecture read at the North Adelaide Institute on 17 January 1854, Adelaide.
3. Wilson & Borrow, p. 150.
4. The family tradition is that the landscape background in the boys' portrait was meant to depict Thomas Wilson's Welsh land-holding of Abbey Cwm Hir.

### Peter De Wint  Kenilworth Castle

1. J. W. and A. Tibble, *The Prose of John Clare*, London, 1951, p. 212.
2. W. M. Thackeray, *Critical Papers in Art*, 1911 edition, p. 269.
3. *Sicilian Scenery*, engraved by J. Meddiman and others, printed by Rodwell and Martin, London, 1823.
4. A different view of the castle by De Wint was used to illustrate a reprint of Scott's *Kenilworth* (with other novels) in 1833. See note 8.
5. Francis Smith, *An Historical and Descriptive Guide to Leamington Spa with an account of Warwick and Kenilworth*, London, (first published in the 1820s and reprinted in 1831), in section headed "Town and Castle of Kenilworth", not paginated.
6. Tibbles, *op. cit.*, p. 212.
7. De Wint was observed alongside John Glover at the British Institution copying a painting by Claude, from Lord Egremont's collection, the finished results praised in the press. Although this painting after Claude is lost, a small pen-and-ink landscape drawing inscribed "after Claude" survives. (Hammond Smith, *Peter De Wint*, London, 1982, p. 69).
8. One of the sketches used as a basis for the Gallery's large composition may have been the smaller (almost half the size) and more spontaneous watercolour now in the Tate. Its middle-distant view of the castle and trees is closer to the Gallery's than the other known De Wint views of the castle which are held by Eton College, the Royal Collection at Windsor, and a private collection (with Spink in 1973). Catalogue entries for exhibitions in the 1840s suggest views of the castle other than those mentioned above. A De Wint sketchbook held by the Usher Gallery, Lincoln, which contains mainly floral subjects, also has a drawing of the castle.

### T. Sidney Cooper  Fording a brook, suburbs of Canterbury

1. Elspeth Moncrieff et al., *Farm Animal Portraits*, Woodbridge, Suffolk, 1996, pp. 118-21.
2. T. Sidney Cooper, *My Life*, 1891, pp. 139-40. Stephen Sartin, 1976, believes that the presumed smaller and larger versions may be one and the same painting but admits it difficult to prove. Our painting is dated 1834. The incident with Crib is recorded to have happened in 1833.
3. Angus Trumble, 2000.

### John Linnell  Mr Clare and Mrs Clare

1. There were at least eighteen families that bore the name Clare in Tasmania in the nineteenth century. It is worth noting that John Glover surely would have known the poet John Clare who was close to Glover's friend De Wint. However, the nearest certain Tasmanian connection is that Glover himself knew Linnell. Could these works have belonged to Glover or his family in Tasmania?

### John Gibson  Portrait of a woman

1. I acknowledge the assistance of Adam Free in researching this sculpture.

### J. F. Herring senior  Autumn

1. Oliver R. Beckett, *J. F. Herring and Sons*, London, 1981, pl. 33.
2. Beckett, *op. cit.*, pl. 43. Christie's, British Paintings sale, 15 July 1992, lot 94.
3. *Art Journal*, London, 1865, p. 328.

# Notes pp. 260–276

### Samuel Prout  Salving from the wreck

1. Quoted in Richard Lockett, *Samuel Palmer (1783–1852)*, London, 1985, p. 64
2. John Ruskin, *Modern Painters (1843)*, 1906 Edition, vol. I, Chapter VII, p. 121.
3. Another version of the same subject, *A man-of-war ashore*, was bought by Thomas Griffith for £25 from the Old Water-Colour Society exhibition of 1821. It measured 26½ by 38½ inches, the same size as *Salving from the wreck*. (Lockett, p. 65)
4. John Ruskin, *Modern Painters*, London, 1906, five volumes.
5. Richard Lockett, 1985, pp. 176–82.
6. See note 3.
7. Quoted from the *Somerset House Gazette* in Lockett, 1985, p. 65.

### Lionel Constable  A summer sunset and Dawn

1. The two paintings were attributed to Lionel Constable by Leslie Parris, Tate, London. Parris was co-curator and co-author, with Ian Fleming-Williams, of the 1982 Tate exhibition and catalogue, a pioneering work which for the first time attempted to distinguish Lionel Constable's work from that of his father and brothers. Following the receipt of photographs of the Gallery's pair, Parris confirmed the author's attribution to Lionel, or possibly Alfred, in a letter to the author dated 23 July 1985. Anne Lyles, Tate, reconfirmed the attribution to Lionel in a letter to the author dated 11 October 2004.
2. These paintings carry the same type of exhibition label as another from the Brookman collection now at the National Gallery of Victoria; see Ursula Hoff, 1995, pp. 60–61, 67. The label of Adelaide's *A summer sunset* reads: "Purchased by us from the collection of Hugh Constable, 1899", "us" being Benjamin Brookman, of Adelaide, who went to live in London in 1890. The date 1899 is still visible on the label of *Dawn*. The label on the back of Melbourne's painting is now largely destroyed. See *NGSA Bulletin*, October 1959, for the provenance.

### Samuel Palmer  The rustic dinner

1. Raymond Lister, 1988, p. 174.
2. John Linnell letter to Samuel Palmer, 7 August 1828, quoted in Raymond Lister (ed.), *The Letters of Samuel Palmer*, Oxford, 1974, vol. 1, p. 25.
3. Lister, 1988, p. 174, no. 18.

### Samuel Palmer  Summer storm near Pulborough, Sussex

1. Raymond Lister, 1988, pp. 170–71. The landscape sketch and the sheet of windmill studies are in private collections.
2. *Landscape with Windmill, Figures and Cattle*, c.1851, Victoria & Albert Museum. The composition is reversed.

### William Holman Hunt  Christ and the Two Marys

1. Judith Bronkhurst, "William Holman Hunt" in Alan Bowness et al., *The Pre-Raphaelites*, London: Tate Gallery, 1984, pp. 50–51. The preparatory drawings were then in the collection of Mrs Elizabeth Burt, the artist's grand-daughter.
2. The Conservator Christopher Payne of Artlab Australia, Adelaide has confirmed this after close inspection and X-ray of the painting. He also confirmed that the two Marys were painted earlier and found some evidence of painting into damp white paint, especially the blue-grey part of the prostrate Mary. Pale sky above the two Marys is also early. However, the jar, shroud, Mary Magdalene's hair and arm, and the tail of the ochre cloak of the other Mary were all painted later. The palms, although painted earlier, were also extensively reworked later, as was the upper sky. (Notes by Christopher Payne, 4 June 1993.)
3. Christopher Payne suggests that this was probably done in 1897 when the painting was also relined. (Conservation report 7 October 1993.)
4. W. Holman Hunt, *Pre-Raphaelitism and the Pre-Raphaelite Brotherhood*, London, 1905 (reprinted New York, 1967), vol. 1, pp. 78–79.
5. Holman Hunt, *Pre-Raphaelitism*, vol. 1, p. 85.
6. *Op. cit.*, p. 81. Holman Hunt began *The Eve of St Agnes* soon after *Christ and the Two Marys* since he thought it would sell better. He claimed he painted much of *The Eve of St Agnes* by lamplight, which indicates he needed to work in daylight for the more radical *Christ and the Two Marys*. *The Eve of St Agnes* was in the 1848 Royal Academy exhibition.
7. Oral information from Marcus Delucca, the red-headed great-grandson of the sitter, in whom a strong family resemblance is still evident. (Adelaide, 26 June 1987.)
8. Holman Hunt, *Pre-Raphaelitism*, vol. 1, p. 77. Illustrated with "(*Unfinished*)" after the caption title.

# Collecting British Art in Adelaide

The British colony of South Australia, with its capital named after King William's consort Queen Adelaide, was established in 1836, the last of the British colonies to be settled in Australia. It was founded as an ideal colony under Edward Gibbon Wakefield's theory of Systematic Colonisation; it always prided itself on being convict-free and thus more civilised than the other Australian colonies. Whereas Tasmania, Western Australia, Victoria and Queensland were colonised from the original convict settlement of New South Wales, the Province of South Australia was established directly from Britain. It is often said that Adelaide was the most English of the colonial capitals even though it was one of the cities Britain established furthest away from London.

It is not surprising then that when in 1881 the good fathers of South Australia decided it was time to set up their own 'National Gallery' in Adelaide (having earlier established on North Terrace a library, a museum and a university), most of the first acquisitions were of British art. The National Gallery of South Australia, as it was then called, was opened by Queen Victoria's young grandsons Princes Albert Victor and George Frederick (later King George V) only forty-five years after settlement. Even though one of the first gifts in 1881 was a late-eighteenth-century copy after Sir Joshua Reynolds, most of the acquisitions of paintings in the first decades were of contemporary British art. This was also the case with the other Australian public collections established before the end of the nineteenth century. Earlier works of art were acquired later. But whereas Melbourne's distinguished collection of European Old Master paintings – the largest in Australasia – was for the most part put together in the first half of the twentieth century, it was only from the mid twentieth century that Adelaide began acquiring a steady stream of early British and Continental European paintings. A mere handful of works pre-dating 1850 was acquired before then. (Sydney's much smaller early British collection also began to develop from the mid twentieth century.) Nearly forty percent of Adelaide's Old Master painting collection, like Melbourne's, is British and the rest Continental. In Melbourne and Adelaide, the only Australian cities to establish large art-historical collections in all media, the acquisition of British Old Masters was not necessarily differentiated from the acquisition of other European Old Masters. Most works were acquired in London, initially with the assistance of London-based advisers. Considering how sizeable and representative Adelaide's early British collection now is, it may come as a surprise to discover how recently it has come together, in a concentrated period and with more care than money. Although the Gallery has been building its collection over a period of thirteen decades, most of the pre-1850 British material was assembled in just four decades: the 1950s and 1960s and then – more than half of it – in the 1980s and 1990s.

Nonetheless, the first purchase of a British Old Master painting came in the nineteenth century. In 1896 the Gallery bought from a local collection what was mistakenly thought to be a portrait of James II by an unknown artist, now safely attributed to the seventeenth-century Dutch–British painter of flowers and portraits, Simon Verelst. It was nearly thirty years before the Gallery made another early British purchase, in 1924. That acquisition was another king, a version of Allan Ramsay's coronation portrait of George III, the British monarch who lost the American colonies but soon planted others in Australia. In 1930 the pastoralist, lawyer and benefactor Alexander Melrose added a Lely School portrait and Regency-period portraits by Martin Archer Shee and John Watson Gordon. Melrose died in 1945 leaving the Gallery, among other things, an early British watercolour by G. F. Robson and a European work by John Skinner Prout painted after he returned to Britain from Tasmania.

The South Australian landscape painter Hans Heysen, while on a trip to Europe in 1934, was asked by the Art Gallery Board to find early works for the collection. Among those he secured was an admirable and subtly painted bust by Joshua Reynolds of the artist's friend Dr John Armstrong. In 1946 Queen Mary (widow of George V who as a young prince had opened the Gallery in 1881) gave the Gallery some of Queen Adelaide's possessions for its decorative-arts collection. She had earlier given other works, but included in this gift there were Regency miniatures in oil on papier mâché of King William IV and Queen Adelaide by Samuel Raven after Mrs James Green (Miss Mary Byrne).

Only a few early oil paintings were acquired in the first half of the twentieth century but a handful of British drawings and watercolours trickled into the collection, mainly from bequests, like those of David Murray in 1908 and Miss Sarah Crabb in 1925. Of these, the bequest of a Thomas Lawrence drawing in 1931 by Miss E. Bloxam of Adelaide, a direct descendant of Lawrence's sister, is of special interest. Unlike the Gallery's strong late-Victorian and Edwardian collections, acquired when they were contemporary art, by the late 1940s the small group of pre-1850 British and other European works was still so thin and unrepresentative that it could not be seriously considered as a cohesive art-history collection.

Then in 1948, without precedent, eight interesting European Old Master paintings, including three British pictures, arrived in Adelaide from London. They had been secured there by Board member Sir Lloyd Dumas during a 1947 visit. He was acting on directions from the Art Gallery Board, chaired by Sir Edward Morgan, and on advice from Director Louis McCubbin, to find a London adviser to buy early European paintings. In early 1946, not long after the restrictions of the war, the Board had resolved to buy pictures in London dating from the sixteenth to the eighteenth centuries, but the Director of the National Gallery in London, Sir Philip Hendy, declined the Board's invitation to help advise because of his pressing workload. In London Sir Lloyd Dumas engaged the very competent authority Harold Wright, who since 1925 had advised the Gallery on prints, now to advise as well on the purchase of European paintings pre-dating 1800. The three British pictures among the eight secured[1] were the solemn and elegant Jacobean portrait attributed to Marcus Gheeraerts, *Magdalen Poultney, later Lady Aston* (c.1620), Richard Wilson's grand classical landscape, *Cicero with his friend Atticus and brother Quintus, at his villa at Arpinum* (1771), and another Joshua Reynolds painting, a small portrait of *Robert Henley, Second Earl of Northington* (c.1787). The welcome arrival of the eight paintings nearly doubled the Gallery's pre-1800 collection. The annual report for the year ending 30 June 1948 made much of these acquisitions, stating proudly: "These works represent very significant phases in European art and their addition to the collection enriches and widens its scope and is of inestimable value to the artist and the layman in studying the evolution of painting. Two galleries have been set aside for their display, where they are shown with examples of furniture of the 16th to 18th centuries, which provide the right setting and atmosphere."

It is clear that the Gallery at long last was committed to building an historically representative European collection, then the only such collection in Australia after Melbourne's. (Sydney, as mentioned, built a smaller collection later, and later still Brisbane acquired about a dozen early British works.) It was late to attempt to build a substantial collection and, though better endowed than Sydney, Adelaide was not as well resourced as Melbourne which had its very generous Felton Bequest. Nonetheless the Board and Director now had the resolve to proceed. Building a collection from such a distance, with no staff travel and limited money was a challenge. Furthermore, the Gallery did not have a Curator of Paintings and Sculptures until after the mid 1960s. Trusted advisers had to be found in London. Strange as it may seem today, the advisers were not paid, but enjoyed pursuing and buying works of art for a public institution of the British Empire and the authority it gave them with dealers in the relatively depressed post-war London art market. Presents of South Australian wine and other token gifts were all the advisers received. There was much goodwill.

In 1949 the Board engaged none other than Sir Kenneth Clark to be its adviser. The distinguished connoisseur and former director of London's National Gallery had visited Adelaide that year. He was asked to advise on European paintings of all periods and indeed he even advised on the purchase of Australian colonial works in Britain, which resulted in three Australian masterpieces by John Glover. In his few years as London adviser to the Gallery he recommended wisely in many areas, stating in his autobiography: "I had been asked to buy pictures for the Adelaide Gallery, as well as for that of Melbourne, and as the grant was quite small I was much more successful."[2] Although he acquired Continental Old Master paintings, as it happened his recommended British works were all post-1850.

In 1950 the Gallery also engaged H. D. Molesworth, the Keeper of Sculpture at the Victoria & Albert Museum, to advise on the purchase of sculptures. He acquired the earliest British works in the collection, a pair of fifteenth-century Nottingham alabaster reliefs and also Francis Chantrey's sensitive marble bust of George III, among numerous other early European sculptures. In 1955 after Kenneth Clark gave up advising for the Gallery, Molesworth, by then Keeper of Woodwork at the V. & A., was asked to buy pictures for the collection. In a revealing letter dated 25 February 1955 Gallery Director Robert Campbell, prompted by Molesworth, outlined what he perceived the Gallery's acquisition policy to be:

> The Board's policy is roughly to possess a small collection – possibly, I might almost say probably, of the works of minor masters, as the important men are undoubtedly beyond our reach – showing the general trends in European painting since the 14th century, this group of pictures to serve as a background for a much more comprehensive representation of 18th, 19th and 20th century painting, the bias in favour of British and Australian schools.
>
> I think the Gallery does now possess something like this background, very sketchy it's true, but I can't see how, without a very considerable outlay and a good deal of luck, it can be anything else. I enclose a list of our principal early pictures.
>
> As you are not very keen about the kind of contemporary English paintings that Kenneth Clark was buying for us, we will, as you suggest, look round for someone else in London who will purchase contemporary works for us.
>
> I like very much your idea of a group of early English watercolours and so does the Board. In fact, over two years ago I asked Sir Kenneth to look out for some, but he never did.[3]

As a result of Molesworth's efforts, from 1955 to the early 1960s a steady stream of excellent early British watercolours came into the collection. These included such major works as Turner's *Alnwick Castle* (c.1829), Samuel Palmer's *Summer storm near Pulborough, Sussex* (c.1851), Paul Sandby's *Approaching Rochester and the Medway* (1786), Michael Angelo Rooker's *A view of a ruined castle* (c.1798), Thomas Rowlandson's *The Brilliants* (c.1801), Peter De Wint's *Kenilworth Castle* (c.1827), Samuel Prout's *Salving from the wreck* (1848) and many other first-class British watercolours and also drawings from the late eighteenth century to the mid nineteenth century. At the same time pre-1800 British oil paintings were bought, often on Molesworth's advice. The only authenticated Peter Lely painting in Australia was bought in 1957; the only James Ward painting, an animal portrait of the spaniel *Dash*, in 1959; and the only portrait by the distinguished mid-eighteenth-century portrait painter Francis Cotes was bought in London in 1961 indirectly from the Chrysler Collection in America. Until 1966 Molesworth purchased well and imaginatively for the Gallery with almost embarrassingly small sums of money. He was always looking for "bargains" for Adelaide, especially major works by lesser-known artists. Perhaps he tried too hard as the Gallery Board, in spite of its low budget, would have preferred well-known artists and did not always appreciate his creative acquisitions by artists they did not know. He was reasonably patient with the Gallery and understood the difficulties posed by little money, long distance, slow communication and sometimes miscommunication. The Board could not afford to bring him out to Adelaide to see the collection as he would have wished, just as it also could not afford to send the Director to London. But Molesworth's frustration often came to the fore in correspondence. For one thing he never believed the Gallery's

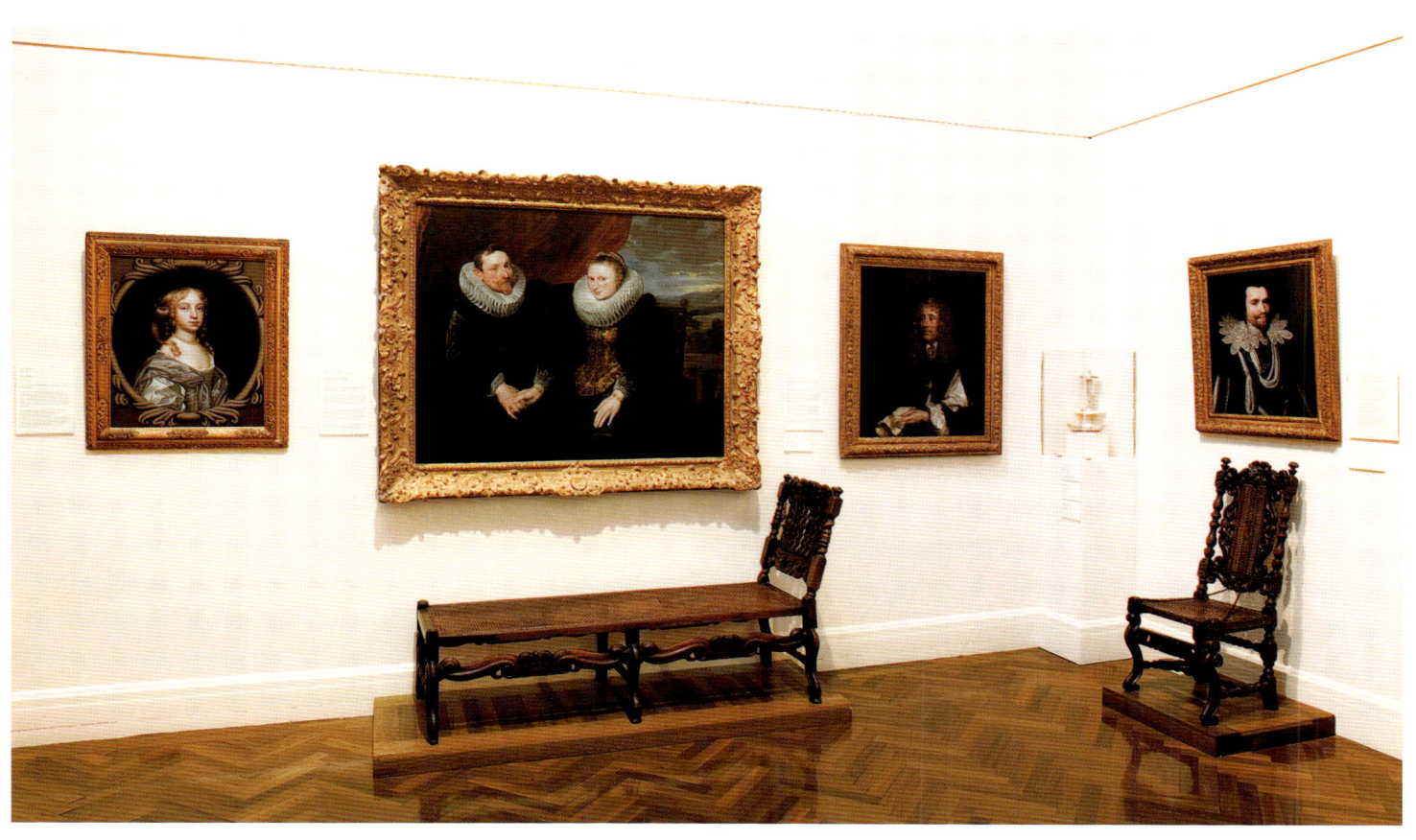

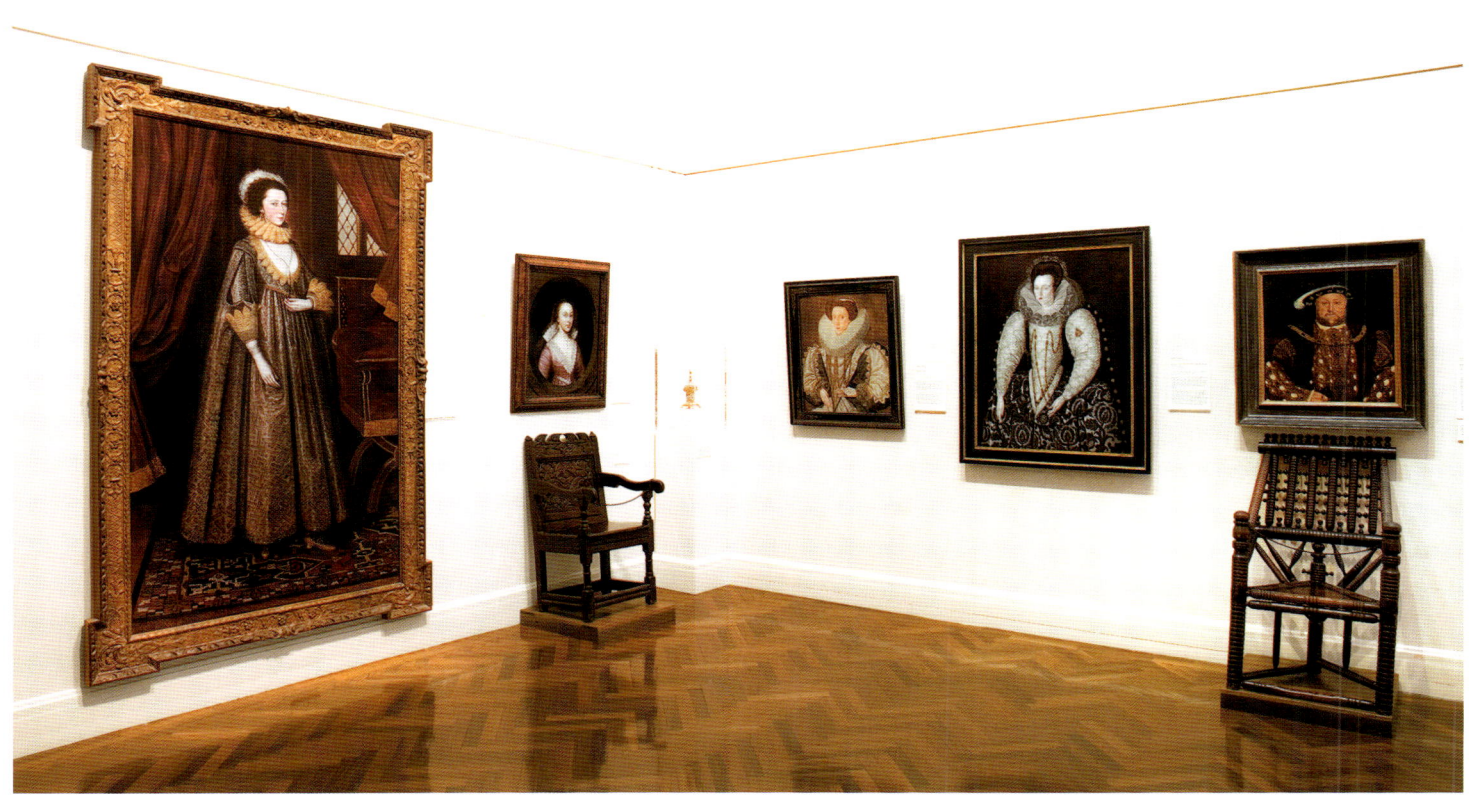

acquisition policy and its requests were specific enough. He wrote on 13 October 1959: "As I am sure you must appreciate, merely to ask for pictures is rather like a woman telegraphing to Paris for a frock without taking the trouble to state whether morning, afternoon, or evening, size, weight and shape or anything else." To use his own words, he often tried "to clarify your fairly hazy buying policy".[4]

Knowing that South Australia was a great wine-growing region and that the Board members understood their wines, of which he was a grateful recipient, in a letter of 22 August 1960 he drew an analogy between collecting and wine appreciation which is as amusing as it is patronising:

> …if you <u>don't</u> want the interesting, but lighter, wines <u>don't</u> order them. If you do, then <u>don't</u> expect that a miracle is going to happen and that an ordinary 3$^{eme}$ cru of even a decent year is suddenly going to taste like a 1$^{er}$ of the best vintage. Muller as a watercolourist or Clarkson Stanfield or any of the others could never be like Girtin or Turner but many people may enjoy their delicate flavour and learn much if only by comparison. …Perhaps you will tell me and decide whether to stock the cellar only with further bins from the great houses, or have the courage to take some lighter wines as well.[5]

The Board and Director never quite resolved this dilemma, but fine inexpensive works recommended by Molesworth continued to enter the collection. The Assistant Director Ron Appleyard, on an overseas Gulbenkian Foundation scholarship, met Molesworth in London in 1964 and wrote back to the Gallery on 22 August, warning Robert Campbell: "…beware the person who dares not share his views!"[6] Molesworth certainly had the most decisive influence on Adelaide's early European collection in the 1950s and 1960s. By early 1967, after he retired from the V. & A. and when the correspondence between him and the Gallery petered out, a new adviser, Christopher White, was engaged to consult on purchasing works on paper, but otherwise Molesworth's services as an adviser on early paintings were not replaced.

Independently of Molesworth's recommendations from London, the year 1964 was very significant for the Gallery and its international collections: it was the year of the great Penfold Hyland gift from Sydney. Gladys Penfold Hyland lived there with her Adelaide-born husband Frank, a member of the wine-making family. From the 1930s they had assembled Australia's most remarkable collection of early European paintings and decorative arts. (James Fairfax, a later Sydney donor to the Gallery's Old Master collection, claims it was his visits as a youth to their house to see their collection which inspired his own ambitious collecting.) Gladys Penfold Hyland was impressed by Adelaide's early collections which were always well displayed and maintained and which had similarities to their own. Long after her husband's death she therefore considered the Gallery an appropriate and worthy home for their collection, which had after all been put together with Adelaide money. In 1964 she presented it to the Gallery in memory of her late husband. The Art Gallery of South Australia was highly excited with its coup. There were seven Old Master paintings[7] and a very high-quality collection of English silver, furniture and porcelain from the sixteenth to the eighteenth centuries. It was the single largest and most valuable gift of foreign works the Gallery had yet received and was to remain so until William Bowmore's splendid gifts of paintings and sculptures throughout the 1990s. The Penfold Hyland gift included four British pictures – a fine landscape by Richard Wilson, *Dinas Bran from Llangollen* (c.1772–75), a well-known and well-documented George Romney portrait, *Charlotte, Mrs Thomas Raikes* (1787), a typical rustic inn scene by George Morland, *Outside the Bull's Head* (c.1792), and above all a splendid late sketch-like painting by Thomas Gainsborough, a portrait of the German soprano *Madam Lebrun* (1780).

The year 1964 was also significant for another major British acquisition. The Gallery bought what is probably its most important British oil painting of the first half of the nineteenth century, Holman Hunt's pioneering 'pre' Pre-Raphaelite painting *Christ and the Two Marys*, which the artist commenced in 1847 but finished fifty years later. It was one of Molesworth's last finds for the Gallery but members of the Board and staff were divided over whether or not it should be acquired, feeling uncomfortable that it had been painted by the artist over two such divided periods. One can also sense that the passionate religious imagery was rather too much for some of Adelaide's very Protestant Board members. Here this extraordinarily interesting painting, the artist's first of many memorable religious pictures, concludes the chronological catalogue of the Gallery's British works from 1550 to 1850 on a high note.

It is only at this point, in 1964, that at last the Gallery could claim a collection outlining British (and wider European) art of the past. Although the collection was still fairly small, many major eighteenth-century artists such as Reynolds, Gainsborough, Romney and Wilson were well represented and there was a very substantial collection of early-nineteenth-century watercolours. Even at this date Adelaide had a small but better representation of seventeenth-century British painting than Melbourne. Certainly the early British collection was much more representative than the holding of Continental art. British paintings already constituted about forty percent of the Old Master collection, a proportion mentioned earlier as maintained to the present day.

The Penfold Hyland boost seemed to further strengthen the Gallery's resolve to develop a representative collection of British and Continental European art. In 1965 it bought, without Molesworth's advice, the earliest British painting held in Australasia, a portrait of King Henry VIII, painted around 1540 by a follower of Holbein, and secured in London by Board member Sir Alexander Downer. Less than two years later, in 1967, the Gallery bought from a Melbourne private collection a portrait of another historically memorable Englishman, that of the controversial and influential *George Villiers, Duke of Buckingham* (c.1625), the most powerful man in Britain in his day and one of the most illustrious European art collectors of all time. The striking portrait is by the Dutch artist Michiel van Miereveld who painted many English sitters and probably had some influence on British portraiture; it was the Gallery's second portrait by the artist. The last British acquisition in the 1960s was the sensitive mid-eighteenth-century portrait of a woman by Tilly

Kettle secured by Director John Baily. Most of these major British paintings accumulated in the previous two decades were proudly and prominently illustrated in the Gallery's first colour picture book, compiled by John Baily and published in 1972. The book serves as a reminder of how the collection had been transformed by the beginning of the 1970s and what the Gallery then regarded as its major acquisitions.

A new Curator of European and Australian Paintings & Sculptures, Ian North,[8] was appointed in 1971 and over the next decade or so the Gallery focused on contemporary Australian, European and American art. It was a phase in which the collection was brought abreast of the times; it was felt that the so-called contemporary collection needed updating. This was also a time when prices for the art of the past were escalating and the Gallery considered its collections of early work to be representative enough for its small income, and that contemporary art was both more relevant and affordable. The policy was seen as markedly progressive within the Australian art museum context. It also accorded with the Director's determination to reduce the influence of the 'Old Adelaide Establishment' on the Gallery, and to make it more accessible and popular with artists and public. That stance in turn reflected the left-leaning political times, which saw Don Dunstan elected Premier of South Australia in 1970, and Gough Whitlam Prime Minister of Australia in 1972. The only early British painting acquired in the 1970s was a rare work by the eighteenth-century Scottish landscape artist who worked in Rome, Jacob More. It was the Director David Thomas who advocated its acquisition, albeit with the curator's full support. Earlier, in 1977, a new Curator of Prints & Drawings, Alison Carroll, pressed to resume the acquisition of Old Master drawings, which were still inexpensive. This initiative coincided with Australian tours of Old Master drawing exhibitions from the Albertina in Vienna and the British Museum, and the British Museum's curator, Nicholas Turner, offered Adelaide advice on purchasing. The most impressive British drawings acquired then were a robust Gainsborough landscape bought in 1978 with funds from the Friends of the Gallery and a Flaxman drawing bought in 1980, *Arcana Cœlestia: Novitiate spirits surrounded by a heavenly sphere*. Another oil painting was acquired in 1982 when a George Romney portrait, *Colonel Robert Abercrombie*, appeared unexpectedly at an Adelaide auction. It was from a deceased estate and was secured for only AUS$10,000, far below London market prices. Apart from the Jacob More acquisition there had been no other purchase of an early British oil painting for the previous thirteen years.

The beginning of the 1980s was a time to reassess the collections of early European and Australian art. Near the end of 1980 the present author was appointed Curator of European and Australian Paintings & Sculptures. The Art Gallery of South Australia Foundation was formally established early the following year to celebrate the Gallery's centenary. It was set up to raise larger sums of money especially for 'blue-chip' works of art from the past; the Gallery Foundation would henceforth have more money for its heritage collections. The magazine *Art and Australia* helped celebrate the Gallery centenary by publishing a special edition on the institution and its collections as they stood after a hundred years. In separate essays the collections of European, Australian and Asian art, and of the different media, were summarised and assessed. The Art Gallery of South Australia had much to be proud of in its small and not especially wealthy city. But after this, where was its collection to head in the next hundred years? What were the significant gaps in the collections? Was it now too late to attempt to fill gaps in the early collections? Should the Gallery continue to collect only Australian and European contemporary art as it largely did in the 1970s?

Following advice from the author and supported strongly by the Director David Thomas, it was decided that while continuing to buy contemporary art, gaps in the early Australian collection would be considered a priority. Colonial and early-twentieth-century works were now less frequently available and local art prices were expected to escalate further with the forthcoming celebrations of Victoria's and South Australia's sesquicentenaries (1985 and 1986 respectively) and the bicentenary of Australia in 1988. With the assistance of the newly established Foundation and generous donor Max Carter, in the first half of the 1980s hundreds of colonial and early-twentieth-century Australian works were acquired, helping to make Adelaide's early Australian collection the most balanced in the country. The pre-1850 colonial works acquired were of course strongly influenced by the late-eighteenth- and early-nineteenth-century British artists documented in this publication.

By the mid 1980s, after many major gaps in the early Australian collection had been filled, it seemed timely to return attention to the early European collections. It had become evident that it was still possible with comparatively limited money and careful planning to build a fairly complete British collection, as was then being done systematically with Australian art. The Gallery already owned outstanding Victorian, Edwardian, Camden Town and Bloomsbury works and a good examples of later twentieth-century British art. The collection of British art pre-1850, however, was credible but had many gaps. From its inception the Gallery had always purchased British contemporary art, but both the former Curator of Paintings & Sculptures, Ian North, and the present author regretted that the Gallery had acquired so much British art of all periods at the expense of nineteenth- and twentieth-century French art and contemporary American art. We both had put aside some of the English art and bemoaned the fact that more works from other countries had not been purchased. But those neglected collecting areas were now prohibitively expensive for the Gallery. To represent one nation like Britain well, rather than many inadequately, was now the argument. And Britain, after all, was Australia's European heritage. So British art of all periods and all media began again to be acquired with some enthusiasm. In mid 1985 the Gallery published its first lengthy Acquisitions Policy, written by Director Daniel Thomas with input from Gallery curators. The policy stated under

European art: "An emphasis should be placed on the British School for, although not fully outlined, it is the collection's existing strength in painting and sculpture."

As a consequence, the collection of British (and other European) paintings and drawings before 1850 doubled in the next decade and a half. Weaknesses were addressed, particularly in the early eighteenth and early nineteenth centuries, but works by major artists were acquired in all periods and media from the late sixteenth century onwards. With international travel now regularly possible for curators and faster means of communication, London advisers were no longer considered necessary. Yet at the same time as early British works were bought so too were Continental Old Masters. They were far cheaper than nineteenth- and early-twentieth-century works or American mid-twentieth-century works. As in the past, the acquisition of early British art could not be separated from the desire also to acquire early works from across the Channel.

Up until about 1980 major acquisitions had largely been purchased using the Gallery's invested bequest funds. The oldest were those of Sir Thomas Elder and Morgan Thomas, established as early as 1898 and 1904 respectively. From the mid twentieth century these funds were supplemented from the A. R. Ragless bequest of 1947, the A. M. Ragless bequest of 1953, and the d'Auvergne Boxall bequest of 1954. The inflation of art prices meant that interest from these funds was no longer adequate. It would now be mainly the Art Gallery Foundation and, much more importantly, targeted individual benefactors who would fund the British acquisitions and major works in other heritage areas. The modest State Government grant for acquisitions was seldom used for such purposes as it was needed mostly for the purchase of contemporary art.

In 1984 the purchase at a very reasonable price at auction in London of a beautiful early-seventeenth-century portrait by Cornelius Johnson demonstrated a new determination to fill in the collection's early gaps. It was followed later in the same year by the Gallery's first Elizabethan portrait, a 1590 work by Elizabeth I's painter George Gower. In 1985 came an unexpected gift from a Melbourne donor, Mrs Anne Clemens, of a rare flowerpiece by Jean-Baptiste Monnoyer, probably painted in London in the 1690s. Gifts by Geoffrey O'Halloran Giles and his sister Diana Evans of a Portsmouth view dated 1782 by Dominic Serres, and by Geoffrey B. Angas Parsons of J. F. Herring senior's equine masterpiece *Autumn* (1846), were welcome highlights of local benefaction in the late 1980s. Although most of the Gallery's British acquisitions came directly from London, a number of significant works came from local sources. Interestingly, too, a surprising number of key British paintings were acquired in London indirectly from American collections.[9]

The expansion in the 1990s of the early British collection was the most vigorous in the Gallery's history. In mid 1991 a Ten Year Acquisition Strategy was endorsed by the Board. Unlike the Acquisitions Policy, which was a public document, this detailed document explaining the strengths and weaknesses of the collection and listing specific works needed, was highly confidential; it was a competitive strategy. Gaps in all areas including the early British collection were rigorously targeted. The Strategy stated, "…there are some significant artists, subjects and types of objects which are not yet represented if we are to tell a comprehensive story of British art".

In 1991 the British collection was expanded by an early and fresh oil sketch by Charles Eastlake, a fine early-eighteenth-century portrait by Godfrey Kneller and a very interesting late-seventeenth-century trompe l'œil by Edward Collier, the last a gift of the James & Diana Ramsay Fund. In 1993 possibly the most serious gap in the British and European collection was filled by the purchase of a splendid early double portrait by Anthony van Dyck, the artist who had the greatest influence on British portraiture. It was generously funded by James Fairfax. The Art Gallery of South Australia Foundation raised funds for the acquisition in 1994 of a group portrait by the early-eighteenth-century painter Joseph Highmore of his wife and two children. The painting had been in the artist's family who immigrated to Australia in the nineteenth century and it belonged by the mid twentieth century to Sir Keith and Lady (later Dame Elisabeth) Murdoch. In the same year another very important artist's work was acquired, a rare single portrait by the greatest early-eighteenth-century British painter, William Hogarth. It is one of only two of his paintings held in Australasia. Also in the same period rare drawings by Van Dyck, Thomas Barlow, James Thornhill and Thomas Lawrence were purchased in London, funded mainly from the V. B. F. Young bequest, received in the mid 1980s and used for early works on paper.

The most important donor to the British collection, and indeed to all the Gallery's international collections, was William Bowmore of New South Wales. His gifts of earlier British art began in 1991 with a portrait of an attractive English nun painted in 1729 by the part English-trained French artist Nicolas de Largillierre. In the mid 1990s William Bowmore gave a strikingly imaginative watercolour by William Blake, *St Paul before Felix and Drusilla* (c.1803). His other British gifts in the second half of the decade included distinguished Regency portraits by Thomas Lawrence and Henry Raeburn, and a rare oil landscape by watercolourist John Sell Cotman. His final gift of British art in 2004 was a splendid Gainsborough landscape drawing from the mid 1770s. William Bowmore had purchased most of his works from London dealers and nearly half his gifts of paintings were British, including works from the early twentieth century. Of Middle Eastern heritage, his father had instilled in him a strong interest in British culture and respect for British institutions. In numbers and value of works, William Bowmore has been the most generous single donor of works to the Gallery's international collections.

In 1998 another Elizabethan portrait was acquired with funds from the Gallery's Foundation. It was an elegant and dignified portrait by Robert Peake of *Frances, Lady Reynell of West Ogwell, Devon* (c.1595). (South Australia's Reynell family, who set up the Reynella Winery, the first commercial winery in South Australia, is directly related to the Reynells of Ogwell Hall; Reynella, now an outer suburb of Adelaide, has an Ogwell Street.) In the year 2000 Mary Overton, the Gallery's most generous donor of Continental European Old Masters, funded the purchase of a unique English still-life oil painting by the botanical artist Ferdinand Bauer.

A steady stream of early British works pre-dating 1850 continued unabated into the collection in the first years of the twenty-first century. If anything, the momentum of the previous decade accelerated. In 2001 an updated Ten Year Acquisition Strategy was adopted by the Board. New acquisitions included a major cattlepiece landscape by T. Sidney Cooper, a delightful mid-eighteenth-century portrait by Arthur Devis, both gifts of Dorothy Spry of Sydney, and a remarkable mid-eighteenth-century masterpiece of marine painting by Francis Swaine, owned for two centuries by the Douglas family of Kelso, Roxburghshire, and for the past century held by a South Australian branch. The Gallery's strong portrait collection was strengthened further by an early-nineteenth-century marble bust by John Gibson, a gift of the Foundation Collectors' Club, and a seventeenth-century painting by Britain's first professional female artist Mary Beale, a gift of Helen & John Bowden in memory of John's aunt, the Gallery's great benefactor Mary Overton.

In 2003 the Gallery acquired four 1830s flower studies, representing the seasons, by Louisa Anne Meredith. The artist later emigrated from England to Australia, where she became a significant colonial artist. Also in 2003 a collection of fifteen British drawings by the British–Australian artist John Glover were bequeathed (with other works) by Shirley Cameron Wilson who had had a long association with the Gallery. The Glover drawings had belonged to her great-grandfather, Thomas Wilson, a considerable collector in Regency London who brought the works with him to Adelaide in 1838. (Shirley Cameron Wilson in 1997 had also helped the Gallery to acquire Thomas Wilson's portrait by J. J. Halls.) Four further British subjects by Glover, two fine watercolours and two oils, were given in 2004 and 2005 respectively by Max Carter. Max Carter, the Gallery's most generous donor of nineteenth-century Australian paintings, has for a long time especially admired and collected British and Australian works by Glover for the benefit of the Gallery's collection. His significant gift of seven Australian landscapes painted by Joseph Lycett in Britain in the 1820s from Australian drawings, worked-up for the purpose of engraving, provides an important synergy between British and Australian art. Furthermore Max Carter gave at the same time three English watercolours by William Westall to complement the watercolours and drawings – Australia's first landscapes – executed when Westall accompanied Matthew Flinders on a circumnavigation of Australia in 1800–03. These English works by artists who came and worked in Australia provide the collection with vital clues to the understanding of Australian colonial art before 1850.

In 2004 in preparation for this book, the Gallery improved its representation of British art with a number of strategic works, notably a late-Elizabethan miniature by Isaac Oliver, purchased with the Mary Overton Bequest Fund with the help of the Gallery Foundation, and an early-eighteenth-century miniature by Nathanial Hone purchased with the Helen Bowden gift fund. Miniature painting has long been an integral part of British painting and these examples strengthen and make better sense of the existing miniature collection, most of which dates from the Regency period. Further recent acquisitions include a very arresting portrait by the early-Elizabethan artist Cornelius Ketel. The portrait of haughty young *Richard Goodricke of Ribston* (c.1578) is the finest of the Gallery's Tudor works and strengthens the nation's only collection of this early period in British art. It was funded from the very generous Roy & Marjory Edwards Bequest. The final gift in 2004 was an interesting portrait by the Italian artist Pompeo Batoni of *Edward Weld* (c.1761). Although Italian, Batoni painted many Englishmen in Rome on the Grand Tour and English collections formed then and now abound with his fine portraits. The painting was funded by the Gallery's faithful donor Diana Ramsay.

It is interesting to note here that nearly all the Gallery's early bequest funds and most of the more recent major individual donors have helped build the collection of early British art even if this period was not always the area of their first love. This includes recent donors to other areas like Mary Overton, Helen Bowden, Max Carter, James Fairfax, Tom Phillips, James & Diana Ramsay, and Marjory Edwards.

The Art Gallery of South Australia's collection of British oil paintings, watercolours, drawings and sculptures from 1550 to 1850 is now remarkably representative. There remain a number of gaps, but it is the most balanced in Australasia. Few better balanced British collections – of all media including the decorative arts – exist outside Britain itself. It is true that the National Gallery of Victoria in Melbourne has far grander works from the great moment in the eighteenth and early nineteenth centuries, though it lacks a number of artists of that period that Adelaide represents.[10] But the significant difference is in Adelaide's sixteenth- and seventeenth-century collection which, although not large, covers most of the major British artists of the earlier period and most of them not to be seen elsewhere in Australia, for example the works by Ketel, Gower, Oliver, Peake, Gheeraerts, Johnson, Lely, Beale, Verelst, Barlow, Collier and others. The Art Gallery of South Australia holds one of the very few public collections of Elizabethan and Jacobean works outside Britain. There is some depth to the Gallery's early British collection. Important artists like Van Dyck, Largillierre, Reynolds, Romney, Gainsborough, Wilson, Rowlandson, Lawrence, Turner, Palmer and Prout are represented by more than one work. John Glover, the popular British watercolour and oil painter who immigrated to Tasmania in 1831 aged sixty-four and became Australia's leading early-colonial landscape artist, is represented by a considerable number of both British and Australian works.

As explained at the beginning of this chapter, the collection has been put together carefully, fairly recently and with relatively little money. Many donors from other Australian states have been very generous, especially in recent decades: Gladys Penfold Hyland, Anne Clemens, James Fairfax, Dorothy Spry, and above all William Bowmore. Recently within South Australia there have been Tom

Phillips, Geoffrey O'Halloran Giles and his sister Diana Evans, Geoffrey Angas Parsons, James & Diana Ramsay, James & Ann Douglas, Max Carter, Shirley Cameron Wilson, Mary Overton, John & Helen Bowden, Marjory Edwards, and the Art Gallery of South Australia Foundation. It can be truly said that the community has actively helped build the collection. Adelaide has not had just one very generous bequest fund like Melbourne's renowned Felton Bequest or for that matter the generous historical portrait fund set up for Melbourne by the Everard Studley Miller Bequest. Those bequests enabled the purchase of most of Melbourne's European Old Master pictures. Apart from the Penfold Hyland gifts in 1964, Adelaide's early British paintings have been acquired one by one from different donors.

Most importantly, in a collection that covers a three-hundred-year span of British art from 1550 to 1850 there are many individual works of superb quality. From the sixteenth century there are the Ketel and Peake portraits which have survived in remarkably fine condition. From the seventeenth century there are the fine works by Gheeraerts, Johnson, Van Dyck, the Lely portraits and the flower piece by Monnoyer. From the eighteenth century there are the Largillierre, Romney, Cotes, Kettle, and Gainsborough portraits, but also Wilson's landscapes and Swaine's seascape. From the early nineteenth century the watercolours by Rowlandson, Blake, Turner, De Wint, Palmer and Prout are outstanding. The major early-nineteenth-century oils include those by Lawrence, Cotman, Ward, Herring and Holman Hunt. The Gallery's very fine and broadly representative collection of British art between 1550 and 1850 also serves as a basis for the study and understanding of the Gallery's much larger collection of later British art and the important early-colonial Australian collection of works pre-dating 1850. While the balanced collection of British art helps inform us of the development of British visual culture, even more important is the fine quality of the individual works that make a study of the collection all the more edifying and enjoyable.

**Notes**

1. The early non-British paintings that entered the collection in 1948 were: Unknown fourteenth-century Venetian artist, *St Francis receiving the stigmata*; Bonifazio Veronese, *Rest on the Flight into Egypt* (late 1520s); Michiel van Miereveld, *Portrait of a gentleman* (1614); Jacques Courtois, *Rocky valley* (c.1650s); and Adrian Verboom with Johannes Lingelbach, *Landscape with hunters* (1660s).
2. Kenneth Clark, *The Other Half: A self-portrait*, London, 1977, p. 154.
3. Robert Campbell, letter to H. D. Molesworth, 25 February 1955. AGSA Research Library.
4. H. D. Molesworth, letter to Robert Campbell, 13 October 1959. AGSA Research Library.
5. H. D. Molesworth, letter to Robert Campbell, 22 August 1960. AGSA Research Library.
6. Ron Appleyard, letter to Robert Campbell, 22 August 1964. AGSA Research Library.
7. The three other non-British pictures included in the Penfold Hyland gift were Salomon van Ruysdael, *River landscape with ferry* (1661), Nicholas Maes, *Portrait of a lady* (1670s) and Jan van Os, *Flowers* (c.1780s).
8. Ian North's official title was originally Curator of Paintings. I am grateful to Ian North for much of the information about this period.
9. For instance, the Gallery's Van Dyck portrait was de-accessioned from the financially troubled Detroit Museum of Arts where it had been held for over a hundred years. The Francis Cotes portrait came from the Walter P. Chrysler Collection, Massachusetts; the Hogarth from Earl Newton Brookfield, Ohio; and before 1938 the Gheeraerts formed part of the Otto Kahn Collection, New York. The Thomas Lawrence portrait of *Caroline Matilda Sotheron* was in Frederick Vanderbilt's collection, New York, in the 1950s and William Blake's *St Paul before Felix and Drusilla* was owned by several collectors in New York in the late 1960s to mid 1970s. A number of the Gallery's Continental European Old Masters also came from American collections.
10. For instance the Gallery's collection represents the eighteenth- and early-nineteenth-century artists Thornhill, Hogarth, Hone, Cotes, Kettle, Swaine, Serres, Shee, Rooker, Robson, Wheatley, Flaxman, Bauer, Hills, Halls, Gordon, Gibson, Eastlake and also a few other more minor artists absent from Melbourne. On the other hand, Melbourne's collection represents Stubbs, Wright of Derby, Zoffany, Barret, Dance, Hoppner, Haytley, Constable, Marshall and Owen which Adelaide does not.

# Catalogue

The following is a complete illustrated list of the Art Gallery of South Australia's collection of British paintings, watercolours, drawings and sculptures dating from c.1550–c.1850. Works are listed alphabetically by artist. Measurements are given in centimetres, height before width.

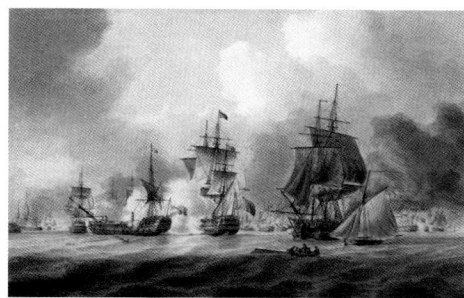

1 **William ANDERSON** 1757–1837
*Battle of Copenhagen*, 1798
watercolour on paper
30.3 x 46.4 cm (sight)
South Australian Government Grant 1955
0.1625

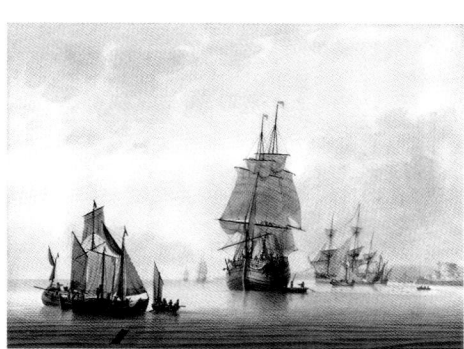

2 **Samuel ATKINS** 1760–1810
*A calm*, c.1790?
watercolour on paper
35.0 x 47.7 cm (sheet)
Elder Bequest Fund and South Australian Government Grant 1955
0.1627

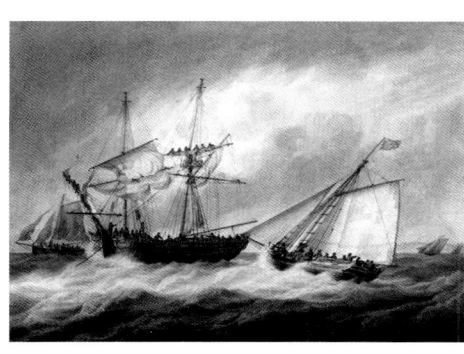

3 **Samuel ATKINS** 1760–1810
*A fresh gale off the foreland and a Brig just come to anchor*, c.1800?
watercolour on paper
27.7 x 38.3 cm (sight)
South Australian Government Grant 1955
0.1631

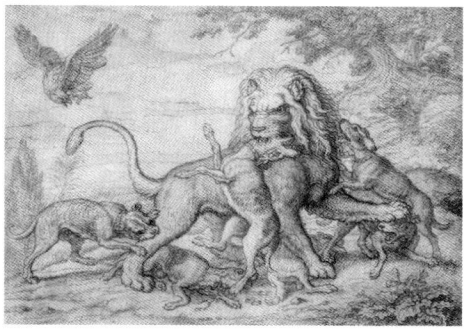

4 **Francis BARLOW** c.1626–1704
*A lion attacked by hounds*, 1694
pen & brown ink, grey wash on paper
14.8 x 20.3 cm (image)
V. M. Stuart Bequest Fund 1991
917D26

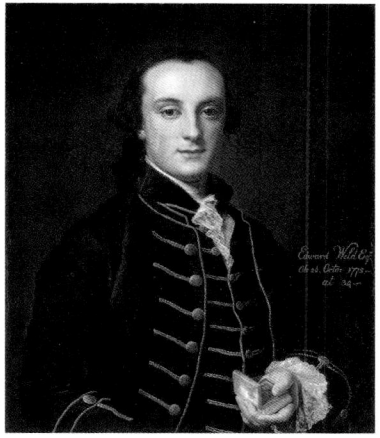

5 **Pompeo BATONI** 1708–1797
*Edward Weld*, c.1761
oil on canvas
75.0 x 62.0 cm
James & Diana Ramsay Fund 2004
20049P83

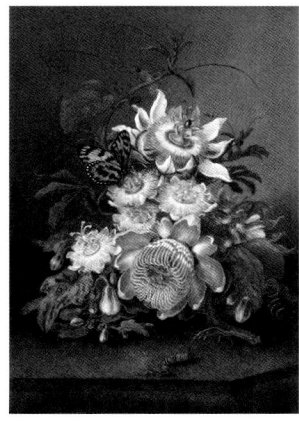

6 **Ferdinand BAUER** 1760–1826
*Passionflowers*, 1812
oil on wood panel
34.3 x 25.0 cm
Mary Overton Gift Fund 2000
20009P38

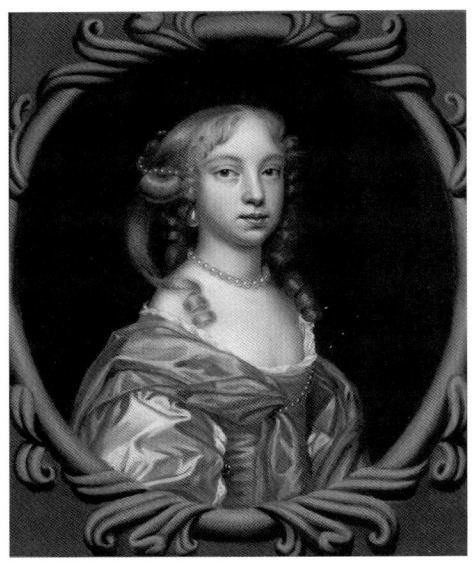

7　**Mary BEALE**　1632–1699
*Mary Wither of Andwell*, early 1670s
oil on canvas
73.0 x 60.0 cm
Gift of Helen & John Bowden in memory
of Mary Overton 2003
20038P59

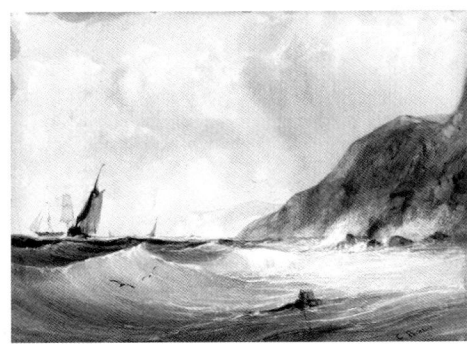

9　**Charles BENTLEY**　1806–1854
*Coastal scene*, c.1840?
watercolour on paper
19.0 x 25.4 cm (sheet)
Morgan Thomas Bequest Fund 1933
0.801

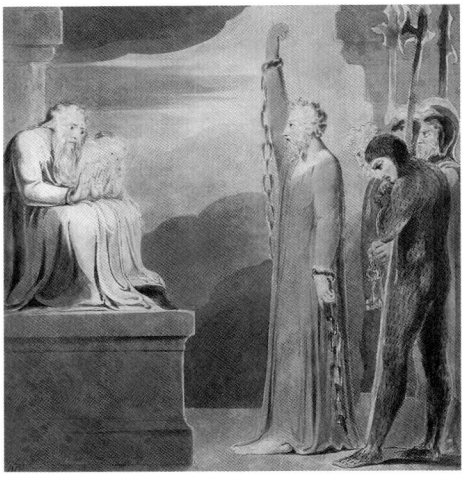

11　**William BLAKE**　1757–1827
*St Paul before Felix and Drusilla*, c.1803
watercolour on paper
37.5 x 35.5 cm (sheet)
Gift of William Bowmore AO OBE
through the Art Gallery of South
Australia Foundation 1995
954P29

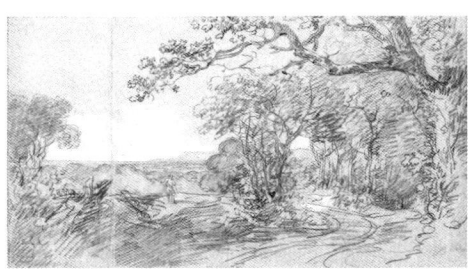

8　**George BEAUMONT**　1753–1827
*Landscape near Ashburnham*, c.1805?
black chalk, ink wash, white chalk on
blue paper
30.5 x 53.3 cm (sheet)
South Australian Government Grant 1965
657D27

The artist, a talented amateur was an
enthusiastic patron of living artists and
collector of European Old Masters. He donated
this distinguished collection to the British
nation in 1823, which formed the basis for the
collection of the National Gallery, London.

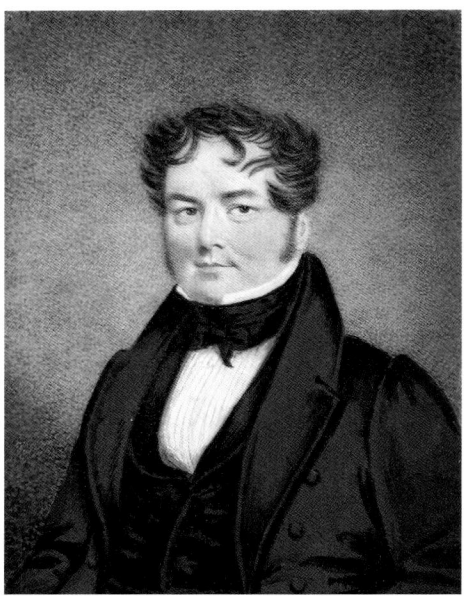

10　**Sarah BIFFIN**　1784–1850
*Portrait of a Gentleman*, 1834
oil on ivory
10.7 x 8.5 cm
Gift of Miss F. H. Little 1949
0.1403

The artist was a famous curiosity in her day
because of her ability to paint fine miniatures
by holding the brush in her mouth, having been
born without hands, arms or feet.

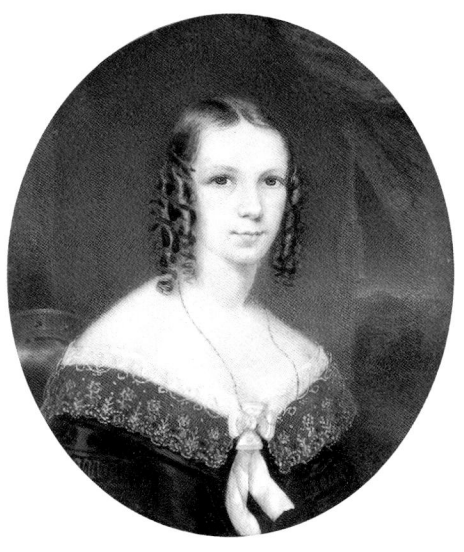

12　**Henry BONE**　1755–1834
*Portrait of a lady,* c.1830
gouache on ivory
7.6 x 6.3 cm
South Australian Government Grant 1907
0.633

This was acquired as a portrait of Queen
Adelaide.

13   **John BROWN**  1749–1787
*Seated woman*, early 1780s
pencil on paper, 17.8 x 14.8 cm (sheet)
South Australian Government Grant 1980
804D7

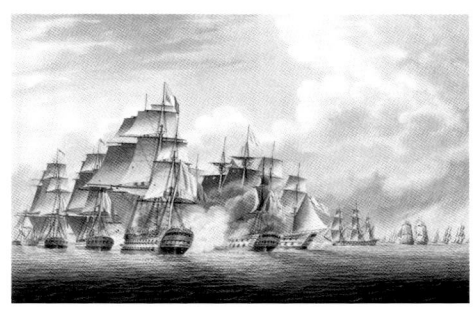

14   **Thomas BUTTERSWORTH**  1768–1842
*China fleet*, 1804
watercolour on paper
31.3 x 46.7 cm (sheet)
South Australian Government Grant 1955
0.1626

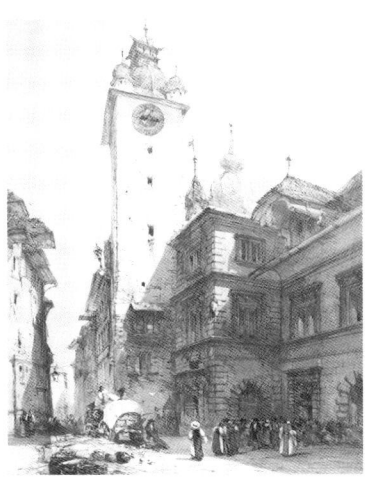

15   **William CALLOW**  1812–1908
*The Rathaus, on the Platz at Lucerne*, 1848
watercolour, gouache on paper
74.6 x 56.8 cm (sheet)
South Australian Government Grant 1955
0.1600

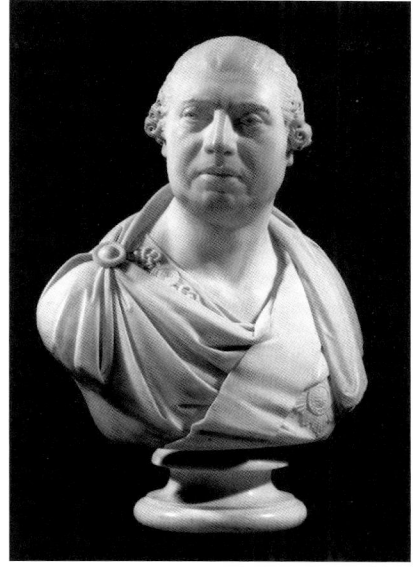

16   **Francis CHANTREY**  1781–1841
*King George III*, 1813
marble, 72.0 x 58.0 x 24.0 cm
Morgan Thomas Bequest Fund 1951
S88

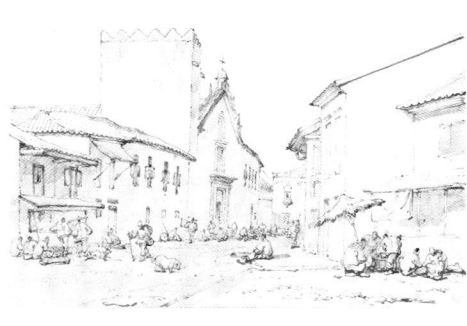

17   **George CHINNERY**  1774–1852
*View in Senate Square, Macao*, 1833
pen & ink, pencil on paper
17.6 x 27.2 cm (sheet)
South Australian Government Grant 1970
707D13

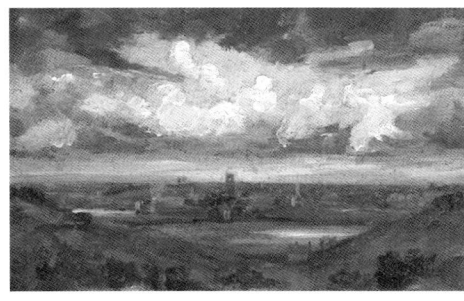

18   **Thomas CHURCHYARD**  1798–1865
*Landscape*, c.1840
oil on paper on wood panel
23.0 x 33.6 cm
South Australian Government Grant 1961
0.1940

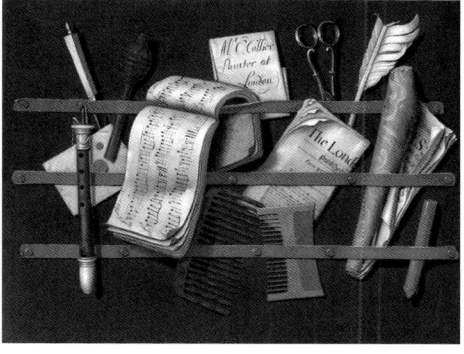

19   **Edward COLLIER**  1640–1710?
*Letter rack*, c.1698
oil on canvas, 48.5 x 61.5 cm
Gift of James & Diana Ramsay and the
James & Diana Ramsay Fund through
the Art Gallery of South Australia
Foundation 1991
909P23

20   style of **John CONSTABLE**  1828–1887
*Sunrise on the Sea*, c.1850?
oil on wood panel, 13.0 x 15.5 cm
Gift of William Bowmore AO OBE
through the Art Gallery of South
Australia Foundation 1996

Purchased by the donor from Agnew's, London, as by John Constable.

21   attributed to **Lionel CONSTABLE**
1828–1887
*A summer sunset*, c.1850
oil on paper on wood panel, 14.0 x 21.0 cm
Gift of Ethel Brookman Kirkpatrick 1959
0.1860

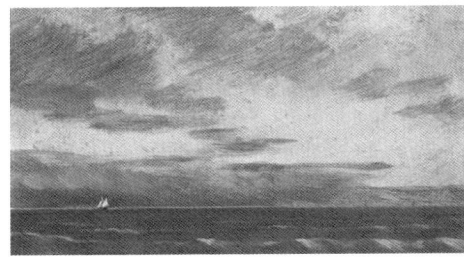

22 attributed to **Lionel CONSTABLE**
1828–1887
*Dawn*, c.1850
oil on paper mounted on canvas
17.4 x 24.7 cm
Gift of Ethel Brookman Kirkpatrick 1959
0.1861

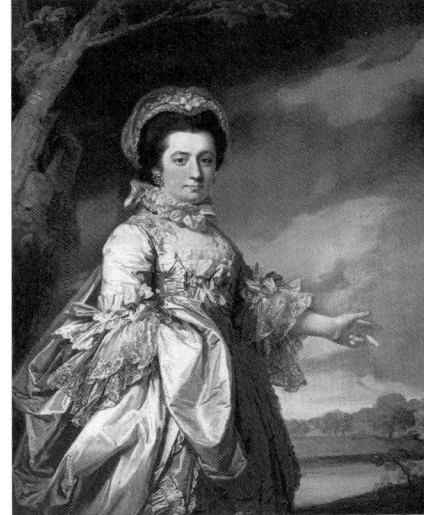

25 **Francis COTES**  1726–1770
*Elizabeth, Lady Jones*, 1769
oil on canvas, 127.0 x 101.6 cm
A. M. Ragless Bequest Fund 1961
0.1942

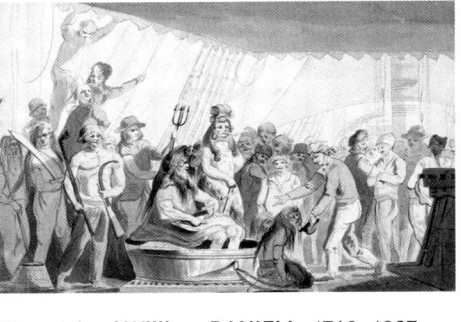

28 style of **William DANIELL**  1769–1837
*Crossing the line*, early 1800s
watercolour on paper
34.6 x 53.3 cm (sheet)
South Australian Government Grant 1955
0.1632

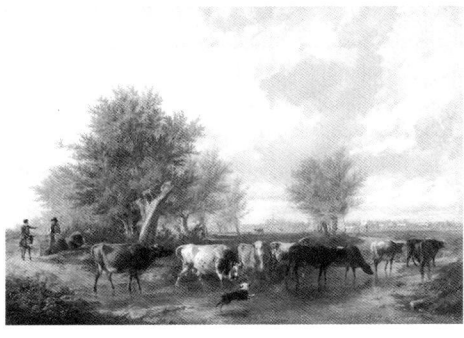

23 **T. Sidney COOPER**  1803–1902
*Fording a brook, suburbs of Canterbury*, 1834
oil on canvas
96.2 x 133.7 cm
Gift of Dorothy Spry 2000
20002P7

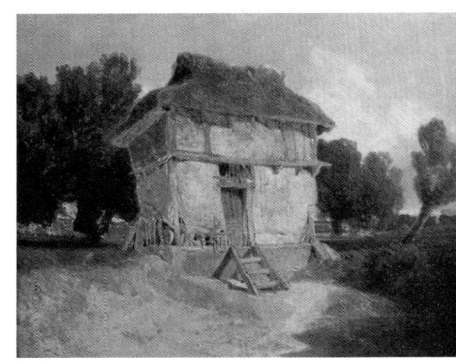

26 **John Sell COTMAN**  1782–1842
*The old pigeon house, Downham Market*, c.1810
oil on canvas, 32.5 x 39.7 cm
Gift of William Bowmore AO OBE through the Art Gallery of South Australia Foundation 1999
993P17

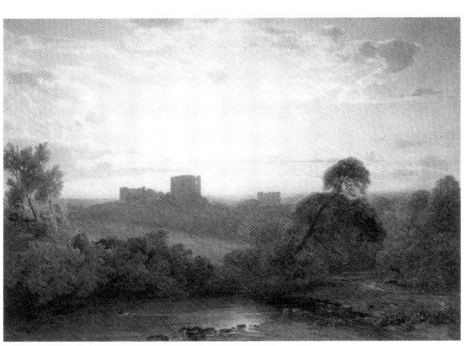

29 **Peter DE WINT**  1784–1849
*Kenilworth Castle*, c.1827
watercolour on paper
51.4 x 70.0 cm (sheet)
South Australian Government Grant 1955
0.1599

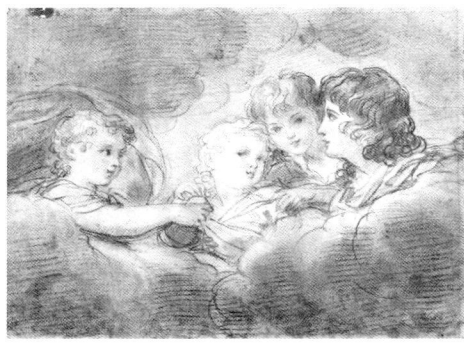

24 attributed to **Richard COSWAY** 1742–1821
*Study of children's heads*, 1790s?
black & red chalk, ink wash on paper
19.4 x 27.3 cm (sheet)
Elder Bequest Fund 1941
4111D4

Purchased as a work by Joshua Reynolds.

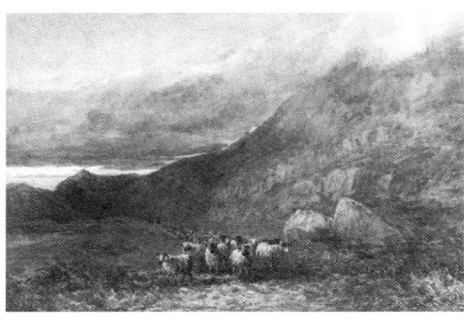

27 **David COX**  1783–1859
*Mountain pass and sheep near Snowdon*, c.1852
watercolour on paper, 41.9 x 62.8 cm
Gift of F. J. Nettlefold 1948
0.1390

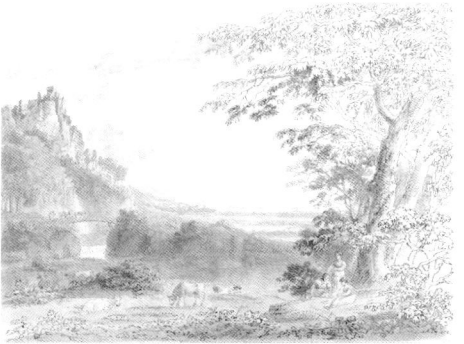

30 **Anthony DEVIS**  1729–1816
*Landscape*, 1808
pen & ink, watercolour on paper
32.4 x 41.5 cm (sheet)
South Australian Government Grant 1960
0.1891

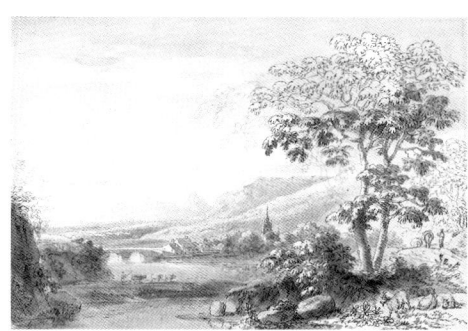

31   **Anthony DEVIS**   1729–1816
*Landscape with village*, c.1808
pen & ink, watercolour on paper
30.4 x 43.4 cm (image)
South Australian Government Grant 1956
0.1668

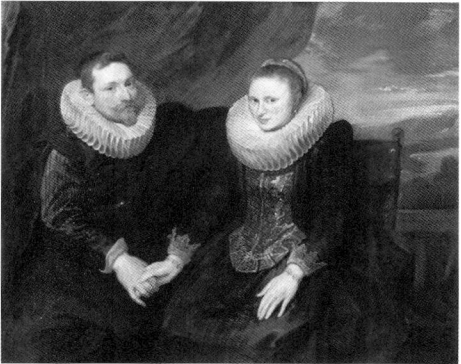

34   **Anthony van DYCK**   1599–1641
*A married couple*, c.1620
oil on canvas, 120.0 x 154.0 cm
Gift of James Fairfax assisted by the Art
Gallery of South Australia Foundation 1993
938P81

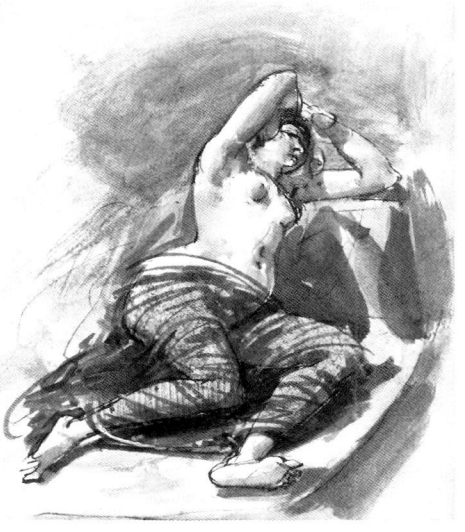

37   attributed to **William ETTY**   1787–1849
*Reclining figure*, c.1830s
pen & ink, brush & wash on paper
10.5 x 8.9 cm (sheet)
Bequest of V. K. Burmeister 1957
573D2

W. E. Frost is another possibility for the artist.

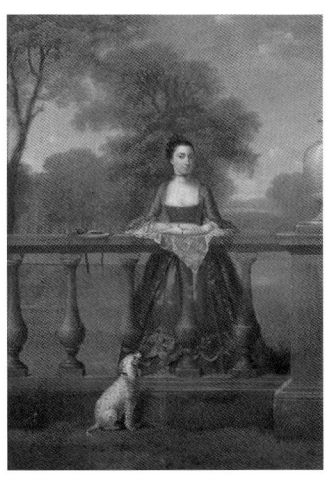

32   **Arthur DEVIS**   1712–1787
*Portrait of a lady with a dog*, c.1755
oil on canvas, 61.2 x 41.3 cm
Gift of Dorothy Spry 2002
20023P14

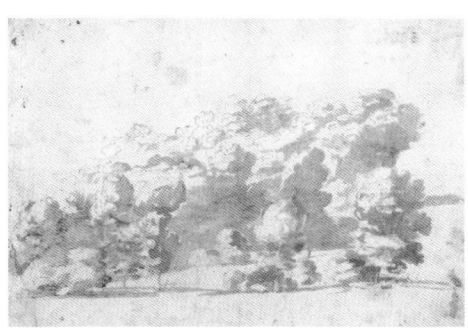

35   **Anthony van DYCK**   1599–1641
*A wooded ridge*, mid 1630s
pen & brown ink, brown ink wash on paper
20.6 x 29.8 cm (sheet)
V. B. F. Young Bequest Fund 1989
893D3

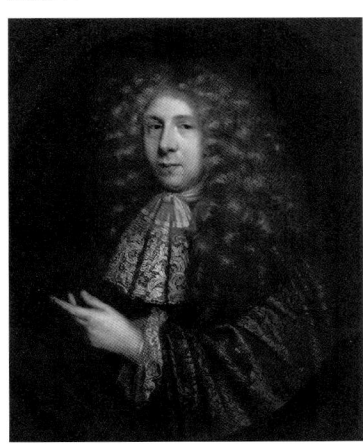

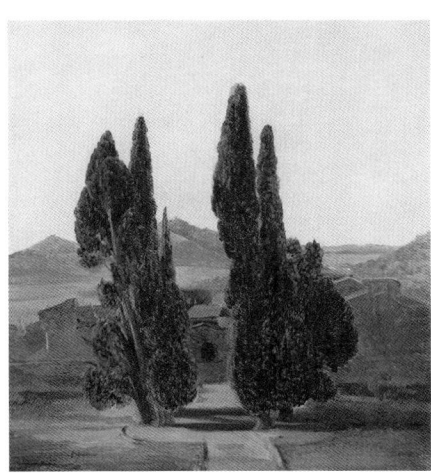

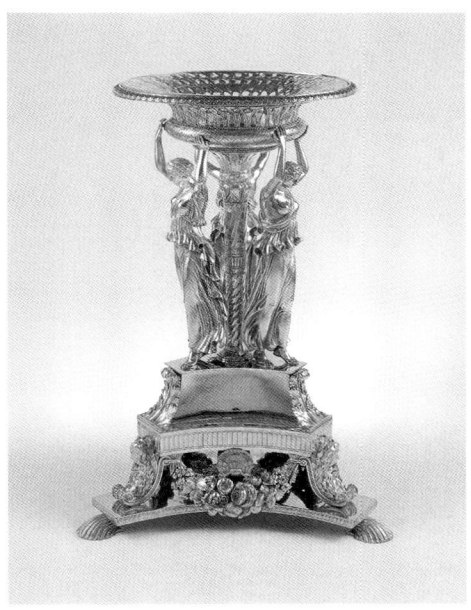

33   attributed to **Matthew DIXON**
1640s?–1710
*Portrait of a man*, 1670s
oil on canvas, 76.2 x 63.5 cm
Gift of Mr A. Cowell 1952
0.1498

36   **Charles EASTLAKE**   1793–1865
*Cypress trees at the Villa d'Este*, 1817
oil on card, 26.0 x 24.2 cm
d'Auvergne Boxall Bequest Fund and
South Australian Government Grant 1990
907P21

38   **John FLAXMAN**   1755–1826,
designer/sculptor
**Paul STORR**   1771–1844, silversmith
*Dessert stand*, 1812/13
silver gilt, glass
62.0 x 38.0 x 38.0 cm
Mr & Mrs J. H. Borthwick and family fund
assisted by the Art Gallery of South
Australia Foundation 1993
932A23

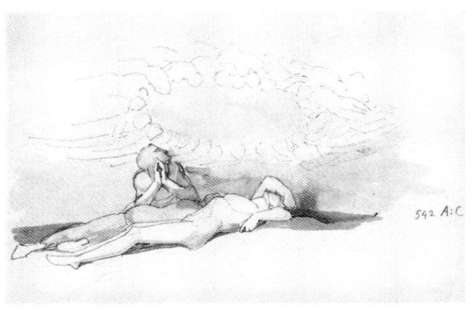

39  **John FLAXMAN** 1755–1826
*Arcana Cœlestia: Novitiate spirits surrounded by a heavenly sphere*, late 1790s?
pen & wash, ink wash, pencil on paper
13.2 x 20.2 cm (sheet)
South Australian Government Grant 1980
804D8

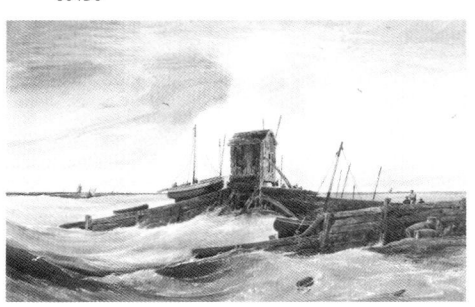

40  **François Thomas Louis FRANCIA** 1772–1839
*A sea piece – Brighton beach*, c.1830?
watercolour on paper, 40.6 x 64.4 cm (sight)
South Australian Government Grant 1934
0.838

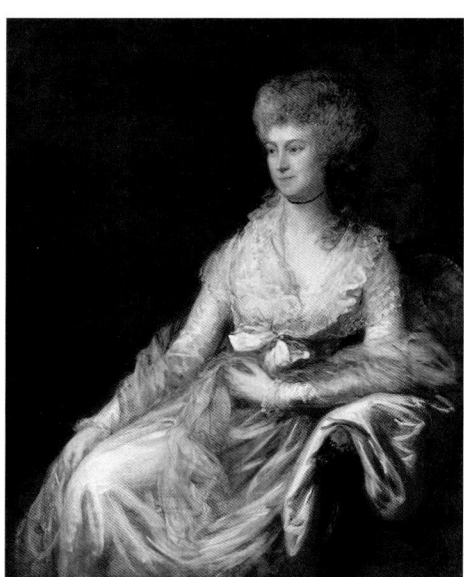

41  **Thomas GAINSBOROUGH** 1727–1788
*Madame Lebrun*, 1780
oil on canvas, 127.0 x 102.6 cm
Gift of Gladys Penfold Hyland in memory of her husband Frank 1964
0.2025

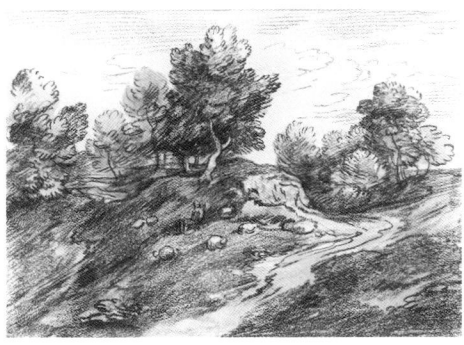

42  **Thomas GAINSBOROUGH** 1727–1788
*Wooded upland landscape with shepherd and sheep and track winding around a knoll*, mid 1780s
black and white chalk, ink wash on paper
28.0 x 37.0 cm (sheet)
Gift of the Friends of the Art Gallery of South Australia 1978
791D1

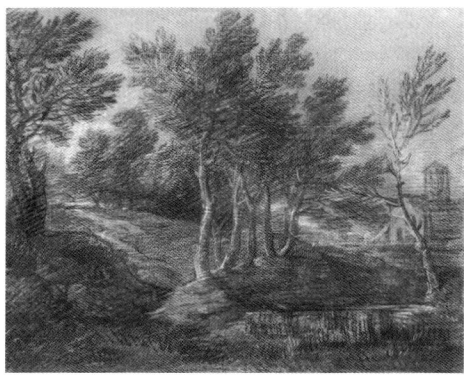

43  **Thomas GAINSBOROUGH** 1727–1788
*Wooded landscape with a building and pool*, mid-late 1770s
black, red, cream and white chalks on blue paper, 25.9 x 31.6 cm (sheet)
Gift of William Bowmore AO OBE through the Art Gallery of South Australia Foundation 2004
20047D4

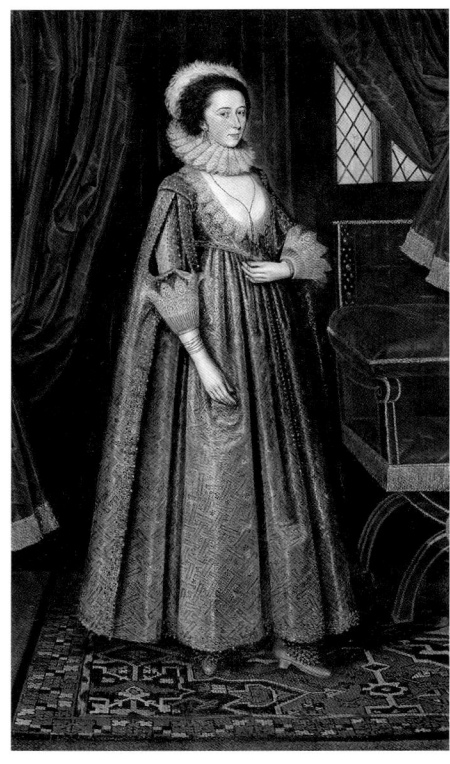

44  attributed to **Marcus GHEERAERTS the Younger and studio** 1561/62–1636
*Magdalen Poultney, later Lady Aston*, c.1620
oil on canvas, 231.7 x 136.0 cm
Morgan Thomas Bequest Fund 1948
0.1366

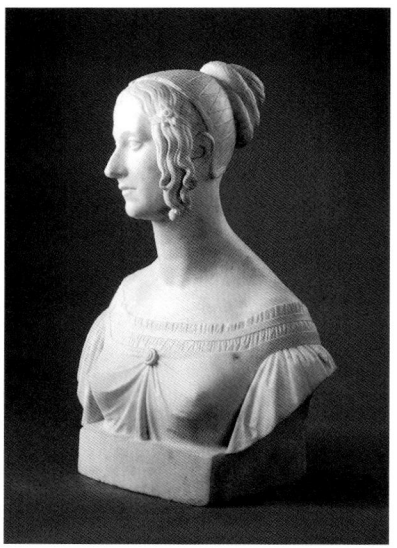

45  **John GIBSON** 1790–1866
*Portrait of a woman*, c.1840
marble, 63.5 x 49.5 x 22.9 cm
Gift of Max Carter, Geoffrey Hackett-Jones, Delcie Norton and Lady Porter through the Art Gallery of South Australia Foundation Collectors' Club 2002
20028S8

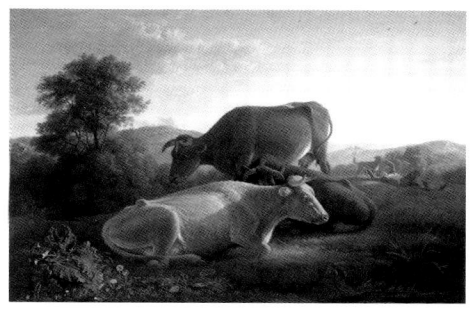

46  **John GLOVER**  1767–1849
*Cattle. The last Gleam of the Setting Sun*,
1816
oil on canvas, 163.0 x 246.0 cm
Given to honour the achievements of
Ron Radford as Curator and Director of the
Art Gallery of South Australia (1980–2004)
M. J. M. Carter Collection 2005

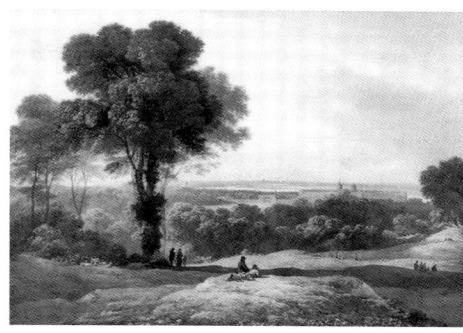

48  **John GLOVER**  1767–1849
*Greenwich*, c.1812
watercolour, pencil, gouache on paper
41.5 x 57.5 cm (sight)
Gift of M. J. M. Carter through the Art
Gallery of South Australia Foundation 2004
20044P56

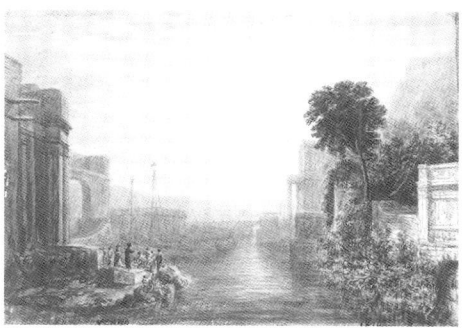

51  **John GLOVER**  1767–1849
*Dido building Carthage
(after J. M. W. Turner)*, c.1817
watercolour on paper
11.0 x 15.0 cm (sheet)
J. C. Earl Bequest Fund 1987
879P32

The composition of this painting is derived
from Turner's famous oil painting, *Dido building
Carthage*, 1815, now held in the National
Gallery, London.

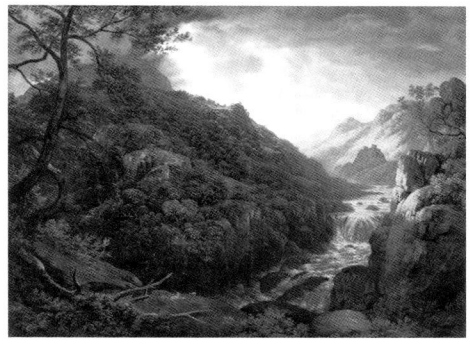

47  **John GLOVER**  1767–1849
*Kilgarren Castle, South Wales*, c.1820
oil on canvas, 76.2 x 101.6 cm
Gift of M. J. M. Carter through the
Art Gallery of South Australia Foundation
2005

The Huntington Library, San Marino, California
holds a sketchbook which includes drawings
by John Glover of the South of Wales. There is
one drawing inscribed "Kilgarren Castle", which
could be a preparatory sketch for part of this
painting.

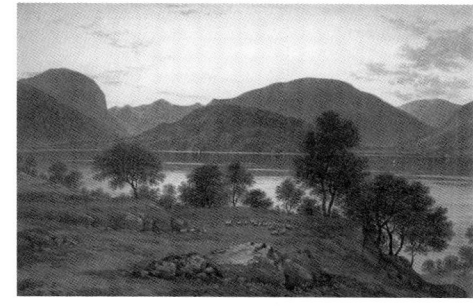

49  **John GLOVER**  1767–1849
*Twilight, Ullswater*, mid 1820s
watercolour on paper
27.5 x 41.5 cm (sheet)
J. C. Earl Bequest Fund 1986
864P16

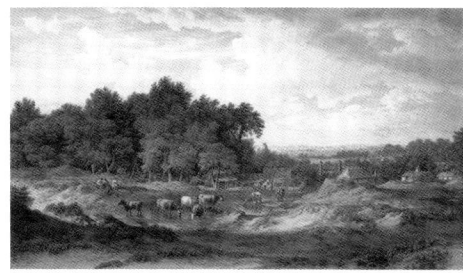

50  **John GLOVER**  1767–1849
*North End, Hampstead Heath*, c.1826
watercolour on paper
22.5 x 38.5 cm (sight)
Gift of M. J. M. Carter through the Art
Gallery of South Australia Foundation
2004
20044P55

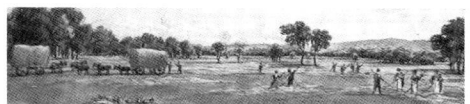

52  **John GLOVER**  1767–1849
*Haymaking*, c.1817
watercolour on paper
4.2 x 15.0 cm (sheet)
J. C. Earl Bequest Fund 1987
879P35

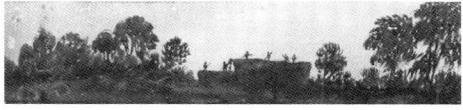

53  **John GLOVER**  1767–1849
*The harvest moon*, c.1817
watercolour on paper
4.3 x 16.0 cm (sheet)
J. C. Earl Bequest Fund 1987
879P34

The two tiny watercolours above relate to
Glover's oil painting, *Hayfield near Primrose Hill*,
1817.

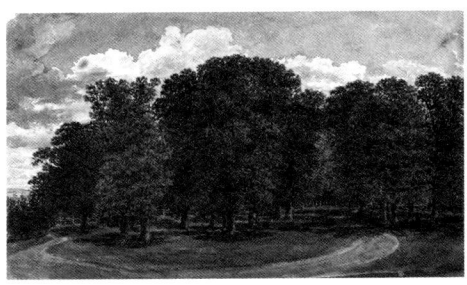

**54  John GLOVER** 1767–1849
*The copse*, c.1817
watercolour on paper
10.0 x 16.5 cm (sheet)
J. C. Earl Bequest Fund 1987
879P33

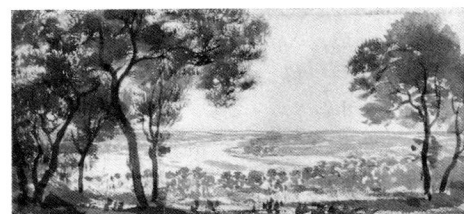

**57  John GLOVER** 1767–1849
*Near Richmond/The Thames*, 1800-1820
brush & ink, wash on paper
5.4 x 11.6 cm (sheet)
Bequest of Shirley Cameron Wilson 2003
20037D22

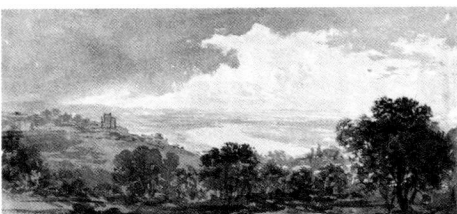

**60  John GLOVER** 1767–1849
*Landscape*, c.1800s
brush & ink, wash on paper
5.7 x 11.3 cm (sheet)
Bequest of Shirley Cameron Wilson 2003
20037D20

It is believed that the four watercolours above (nos 51-54), and certainly the fifteen wash drawings below (nos 55-69) belonged to Thomas Wilson who arrived in South Australia, with his art collection in 1838. This collection included nearly one hundred works on paper by Glover, (who emigrated to Tasmania in 1831), and were probably the first works by the artist to come to the mainland.

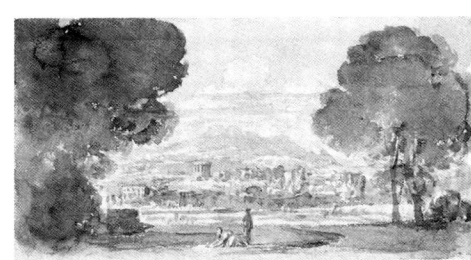

**55  John GLOVER** 1767–1849
*Landscape*, c.1800-1820
brush & ink, wash on paper
6.8 x 11.0 cm (sheet)
Bequest of Shirley Cameron Wilson 2003
20037D21

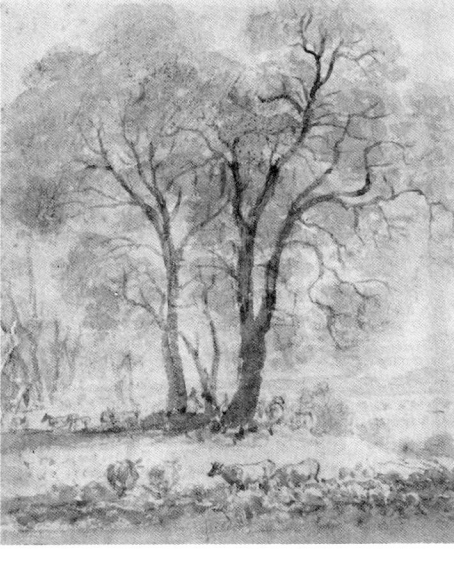

**58  John GLOVER** 1767–1849
*Richmond Park*, c.1800-1820
brush & ink, wash on paper
9.2 x 7.3 cm (sheet)
Bequest of Shirley Cameron Wilson 2003
20037D25

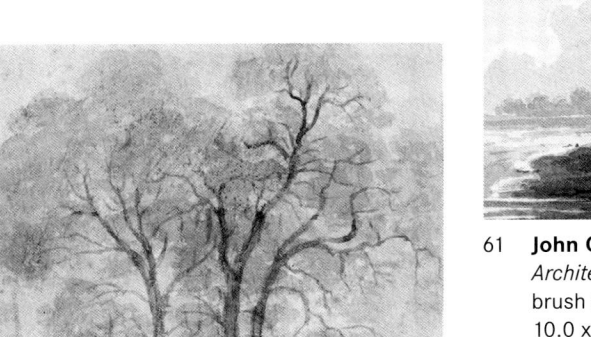

**61  John GLOVER** 1767–1849
*Architectural ruin*, c.1810s
brush & ink, wash on paper
10.0 x 15.5 cm (sheet)
Bequest of Shirley Cameron Wilson 2003
20037D26

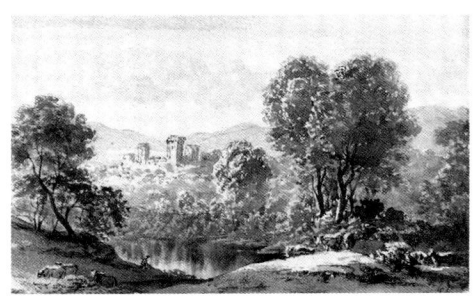

**62  John GLOVER** 1767–1849
*Landscape*, c.1810s
brush & ink, wash on paper
5.5 x 11.7 cm (sheet)
Bequest of Shirley Cameron Wilson 2003
20037D18

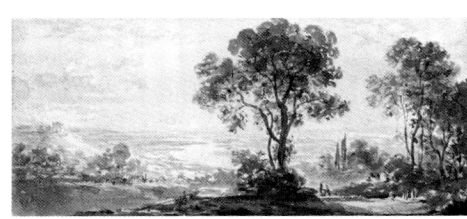

**56  John GLOVER** 1767–1849
*Richmond*, c.1800-1820
brush & ink, wash on paper
5.2 x 11.5 cm (sheet)
Bequest of Shirley Cameron Wilson 2003
20037D23

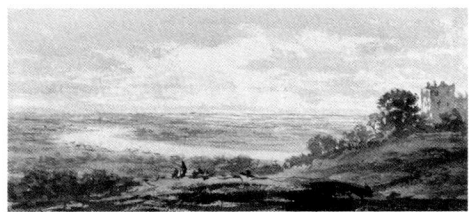

**59  John GLOVER** 1767–1849
*Richmond*, c.1800-1820
brush & ink, wash on paper
5.4 x 11.5 cm (sheet)
Bequest of Shirley Cameron Wilson 2003
20037D24

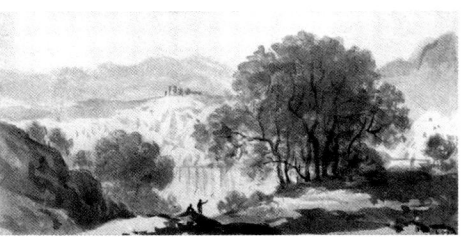

**63  John GLOVER** 1767–1849
*Landscape*, c.1818
brush & ink wash on paper
5.8 x 11.6 cm (sheet)
Bequest of Shirley Cameron Wilson 2003
20037D19

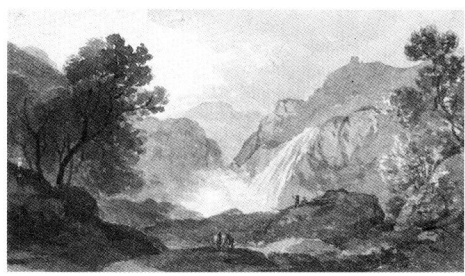

64   **John GLOVER**   1767–1849
*Waterfall in the landscape,* c.1818
brush & ink, wash on paper
6.5 x 10.7 cm (sheet)
Bequest of Shirley Cameron Wilson 2003
20037D28

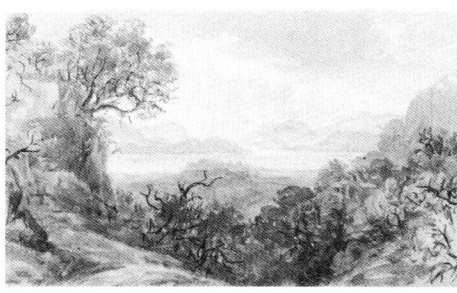

68   **John GLOVER**   1767–1849
*Ullswater*, c.1820s
brush & ink, wash on paper
6.1 x 11.4 cm (sheet)
Bequest of Shirley Cameron Wilson 2003
20037D30

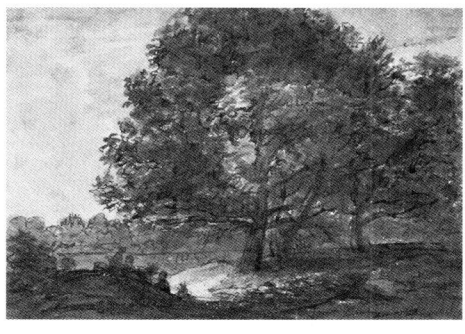

71   **John GLOVER**   1767–1849
*Landscape with oak trees*, c.1790s
pen & brown ink, wash on paper
7.2 x 10.1 cm (sheet)
South Australian Government Grant 1982
825D25

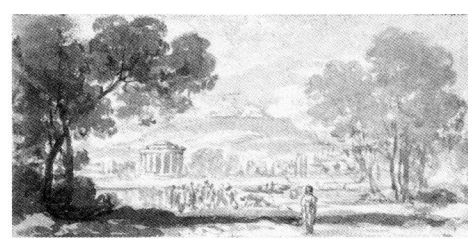

65   **John GLOVER**   1767–1849
*Temple in the landscape*, c.1810–20
brush & ink, wash on paper
5.6 x 11.1 cm (sheet)
Bequest of Shirley Cameron Wilson 2003
20037D27

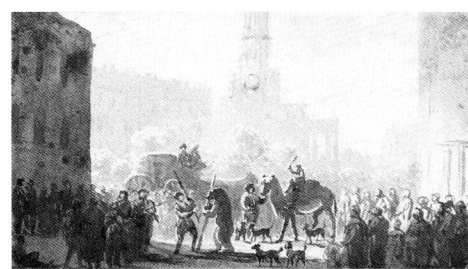

69   **John GLOVER**   1767–1849
*Dancing Bear, Hanover Square*, c.1829
brush & ink, wash on paper
6.4 x 11.0 cm (sheet)
Bequest of Shirley Cameron Wilson 2003
20037D17

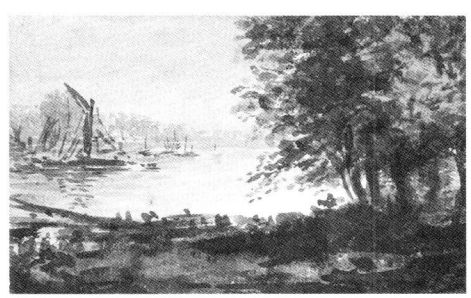

72   **John GLOVER**   1767–1849
*Millbank*, c.1790s
brush & ink, wash on paper
5.7 x 8.8 cm (sheet)
South Australian Government Grant 1982
825D27

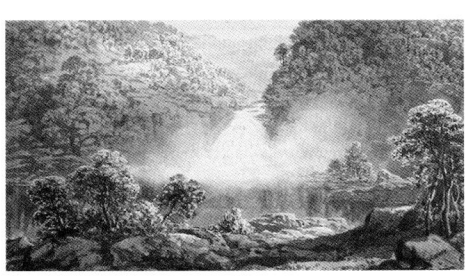

66   **John GLOVER**   1767–1849
*Wales*, c.1810–1830
brush & ink, wash on paper
8.2 x 14.9 cm (sheet)
Bequest of Shirley Cameron Wilson 2003
20037D31

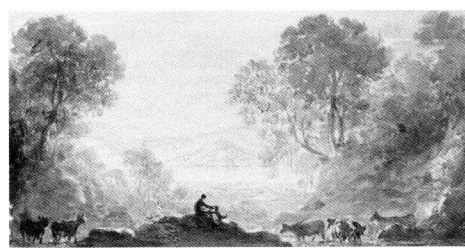

67   **John GLOVER**   1767–1849
*Ullswater*, c.1820s
brush & ink, wash on paper
5.2 x 8.3 cm (sheet)
Bequest of Shirley Cameron Wilson 2003
20037D29

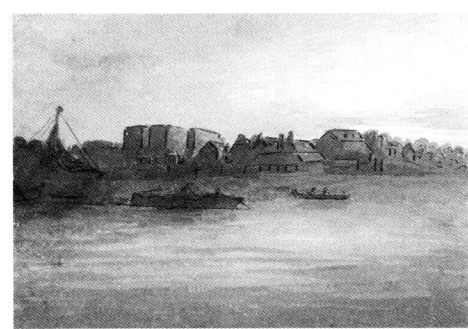

70   **John GLOVER**   1767–1849
*The Thames, Millbank*, c.1790s
pen & ink, wash on paper
8.5 x 11.8 cm (sheet)
South Australian Government Grant 1982
825D26

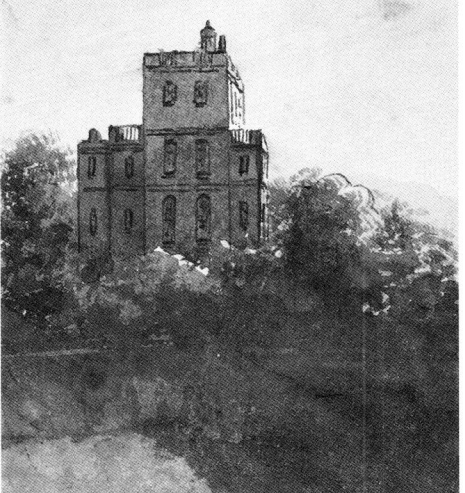

73   **John GLOVER**   1767–1849
*Near Islington*, c.1790s
pen & ink, wash on paper
9.6 x 7.9 cm (sheet)
South Australian Government Grant 1982
825D28

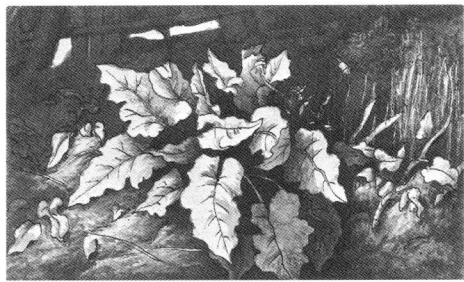

74 **John GLOVER** 1767–1849
*Botanical study of a dock*, c.1797
pen & ink, wash on paper
8.3 x 13.1 cm (sheet)
South Australian Government Grant 1982
825D30

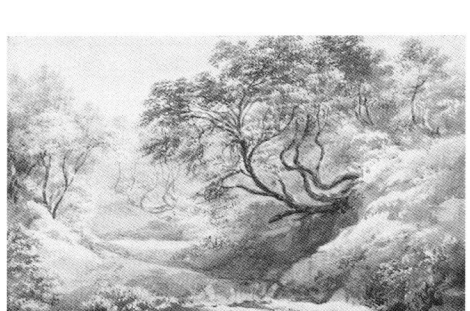

75 **John GLOVER** 1767–1849
*Landscape*, c.1800–1810
brush & ink, wash on card
11.4 x 17.9 cm (sheet)
South Australian Government Grant 1984
844D10

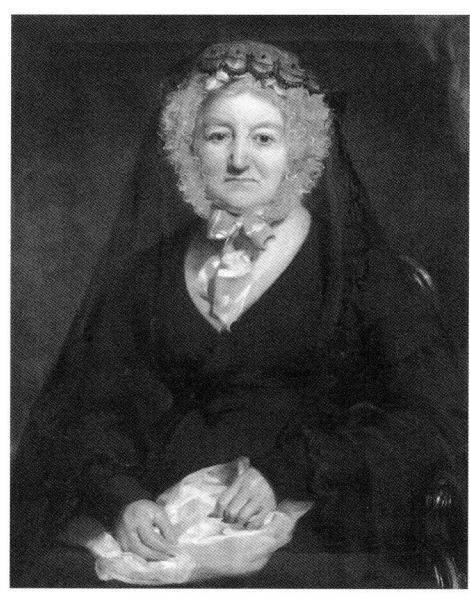

76 **John Watson GORDON** 1790–1864
*Elizabeth Grey*, c.1820s
oil on canvas, 88.9 x 69.1 cm
Gift of Alexander Melrose 1930
0.758

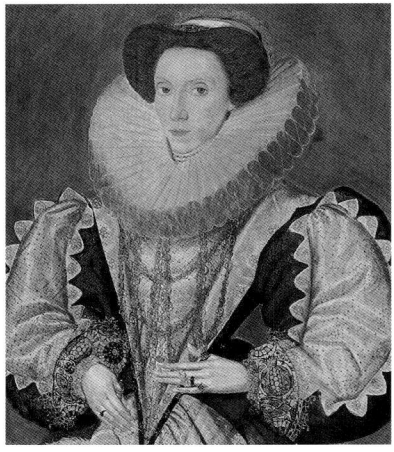

77 **George GOWER** c.1540–1596
*Portrait of a lady*, c.1590
oil on wood panel, 78.1 x 64.7 cm
South Australian Government Grant 1984
849P32

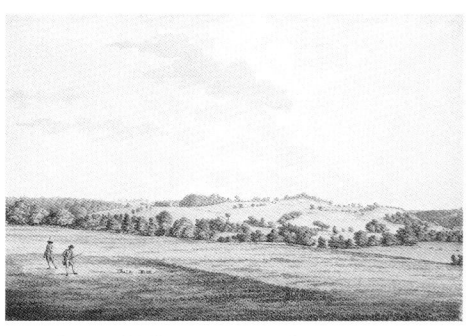

78 **Samuel Hieronymous GRIMM**
1733–1794
*The Grange Hall, Horne Farm and Woolley Wood*, 1781
watercolour on cream paper
38.0 x 54.6 cm (sheet)
South Australian Government Grant 1956
0.1651

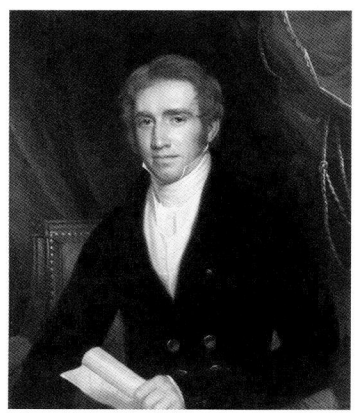

79 **J. J. HALLS** 1776–1834
*Thomas Wilson*, c.1823
oil on canvas, 76.8 x 64.4 cm
J. C. Earl Bequest Fund assisted by Honor and Shirley Cameron Wilson 1997
974P21

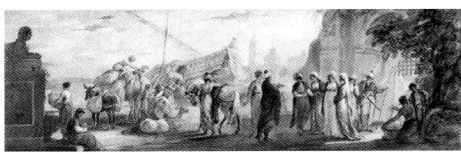

80 **William HAMILTON** 1751–1801
*Middle Eastern port*, c.1780s
watercolour, pen & ink on paper
16.0 x 51.5 cm (sheet)
South Australian Government Grant 1960
0.1887

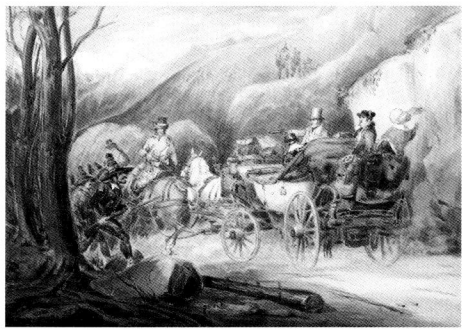

81 **C. Cooper HENDERSON** 1803–1877
*Post-Chaise attacked by Brigands*, c.1840?
watercolour on paper
25.4 x 34.4 cm (sheet)
J. T. Mortlock Bequest Fund 1960
0.1890

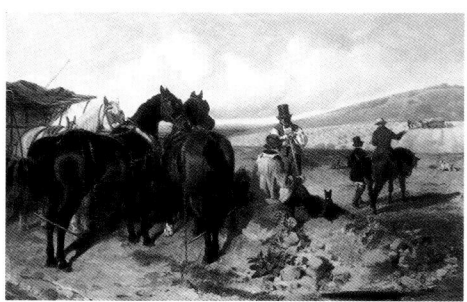

82 **J. F. HERRING senior** 1795–1865
*Autumn*, 1846
oil on canvas, 45.5 x 70.5 cm
Gift of Geoffrey B. Angas Parsons through the Art Gallery of South Australia Foundation 1984
8410P35

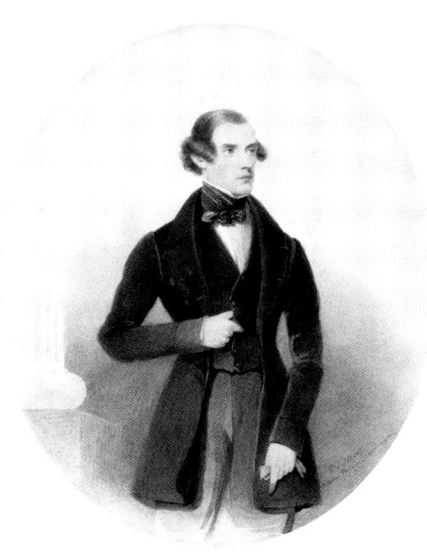

83 **C. S. HERVÉ** fl. 1828–1858
*Major General Sir Joseph O'Halloran*, c.1840?
watercolour on paper
23.9 x 20.0 cm (irreg. oval)
C. V. Michell Fund 1988
891P1

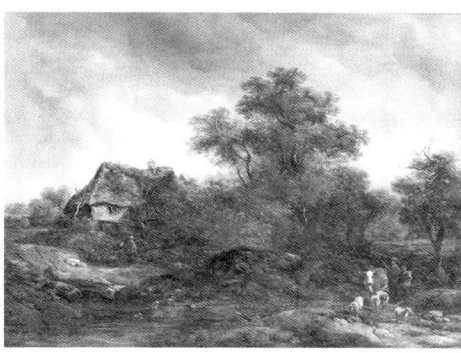

85 **Richard HILDER** 1813–1851
*Landscape*, c.1840s
oil on wood panel, 30.0 x 50.4 cm
Bequest of Sir Samuel Way 1916
0.570

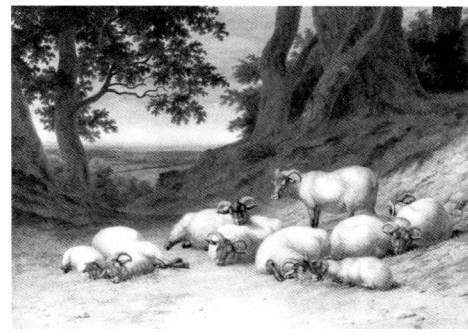

86 **Robert HILLS** 1769–1844
*Soay sheep in a landscape*, c.1805
watercolour on paper
32.4 x 43.8 cm (sheet)
Mortlock Bequest Fund 1957
0.1704

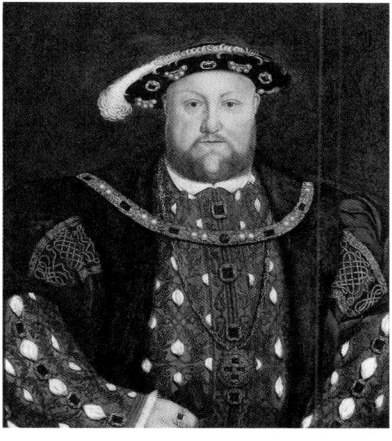

88 **Follower of Hans HOLBEIN the Younger**
1497–1543
*King Henry VIII*, c.1540s
oil on wood panel, 65.0 x 57.5 cm
A. M. & A. R. Ragless Bequest Funds 1965
0.2049

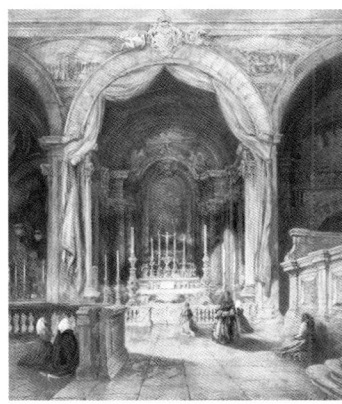

89 **James HOLLAND** 1800–1870
*Chapel of St John the Baptist in the Church of St Rocque, Lisbon*, 1841
watercolour on paper
59.5 x 49.6 cm (sheet)
South Australian Government Grant 1955
0.1622

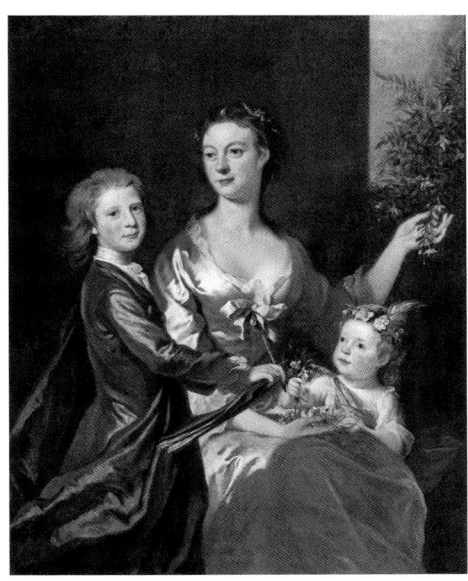

84 **Joseph HIGHMORE** 1692–1780
*The artist's wife Susanna, son Anthony and daughter Susanna*, c.1728
oil on canvas, 126.0 x 101.7 cm
Gift of the Art Gallery of South Australia Foundation 1994
945P65

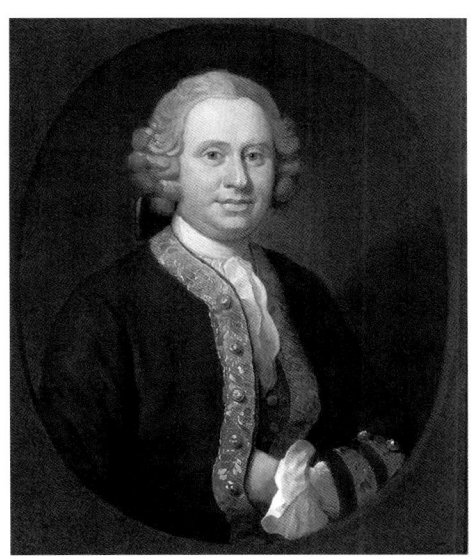

87 **William HOGARTH** 1697–1764
*William FitzHerbert*, early 1740s
oil on canvas, 62.3 x 75.0 cm
F. G. Halloran Bequest Fund 1994
947P74

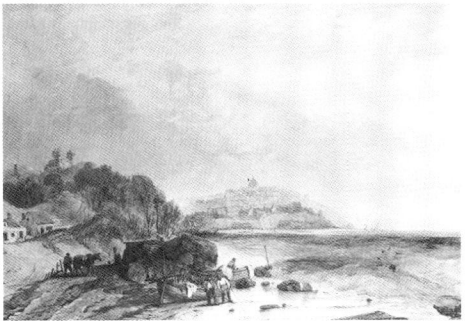

90 **James HOLLAND** 1800–1870
*A view of Rye, Sussex, from the sea*, 1840s?
watercolour, gouache on paper
60.0 x 49.5 cm (sheet)
Elder Bequest Fund 1962
0.1948

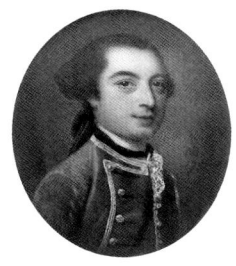

91  **Nathaniel HONE**  1717–1784
*Naval Officer*, 1758
enamel on copper, 3.5 x 3.0 cm
Helen Bowden Gift Fund 2004
20048P78

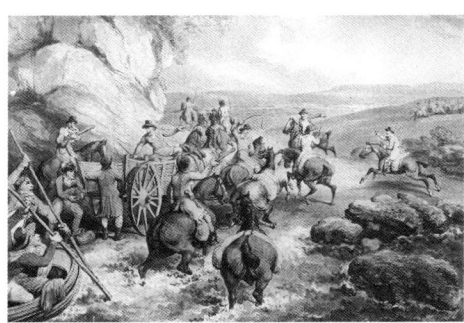

92  **Samuel HOWITT**  1756–1822
*Smugglers alarmed by excise men*, c.1794
watercolour on paper
26.0 x 37.4 cm (sheet)
South Australian Government Grant 1962
0.1947

Probably the painting of the same title exhibited at the Royal Academy in 1794.

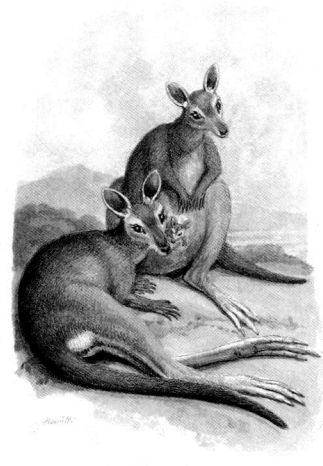

93  **Samuel HOWITT**  1756–1822
*Kangaroos (Didelphis Gigantia)*, c.1818
watercolour on paper
24.7 x 18.4 cm (sheet)
South Australian Government Grant 1955
0.1624

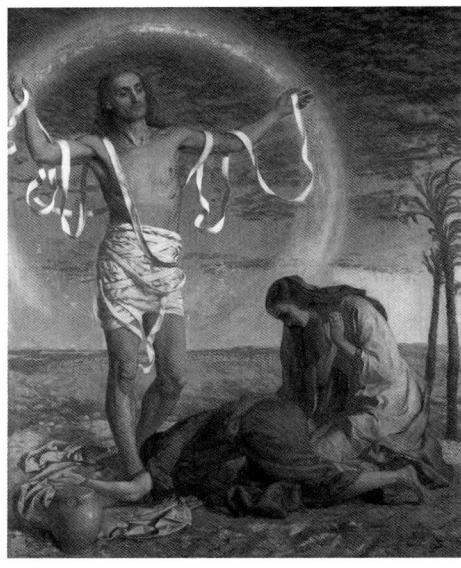

94  **William Holman HUNT**  1827–1910
*Christ and the Two Marys*, 1847 & 1897
oil on canvas over wood panel
117.5 x 94.0 cm
d'Auvergne Boxall Bequest Fund 1964
0.2044

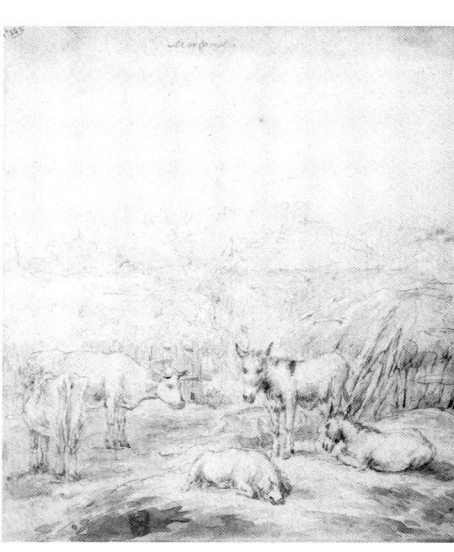

95  attributed to **Julius Caesar IBBETSON**
1759–1817
*Farmyard*, c.1800?
pencil and watercolour on paper
26.2 x 23.5 cm (sheet)
Gift of Miss Smith 1907
0.563

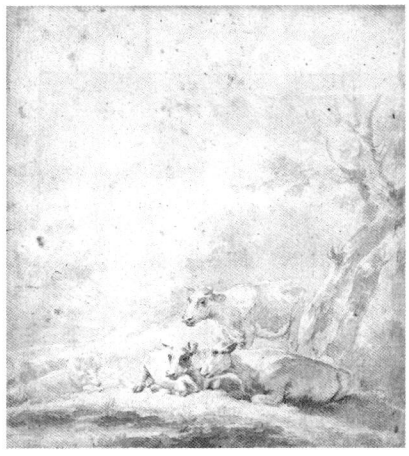

96  attributed to **Julius Caesar IBBETSON**
1759–1817
*Landscape with cattle*, c.1800?
pencil and watercolour on paper
30.0 x 26.0 cm (sheet)
Gift of Miss Smith 1907
0.562

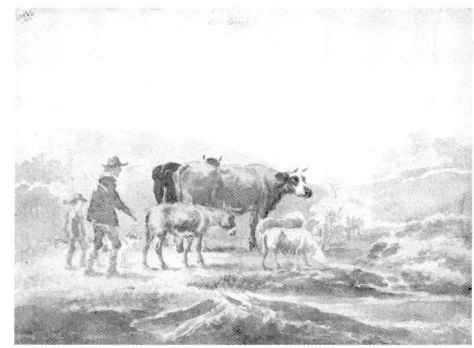

97  attributed to **Julius Caesar IBBETSON**
1759–1817
*Figures with cattle and sheep*, c.1800?
watercolour on paper, 23.4 x 30.7 cm (sheet)
Gift of Miss Smith 1907
0.564

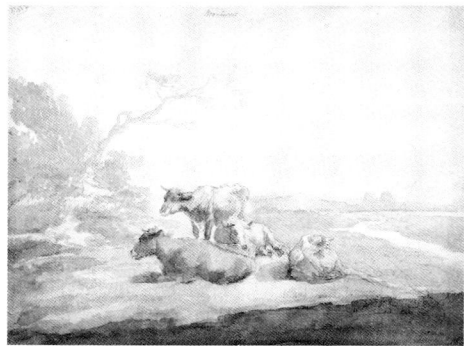

98  attributed to **Julius Caesar IBBETSON**
1759–1817
*Landscape with a group of cattle*, c.1800?
pencil & watercolour on paper
23.4 x 30.9 cm (sheet)
Gift of Miss Smith 1907
0.565

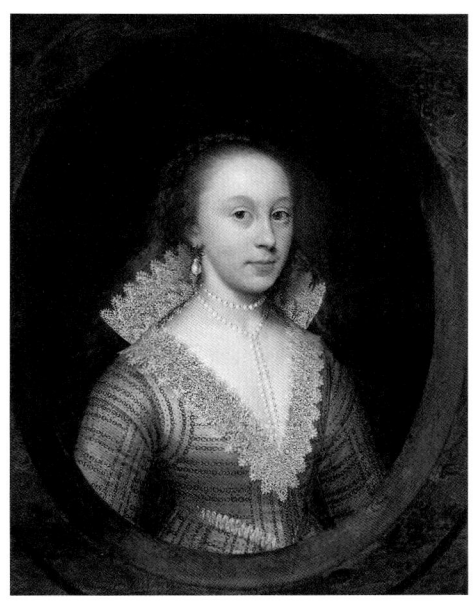

99 **Cornelius JOHNSON** 1593–1661
*A lady, thought to be Catherine Fenn*, 1623
oil on wood panel
77.0 x 60.0 cm
South Australian Government Grant 1984
848P28

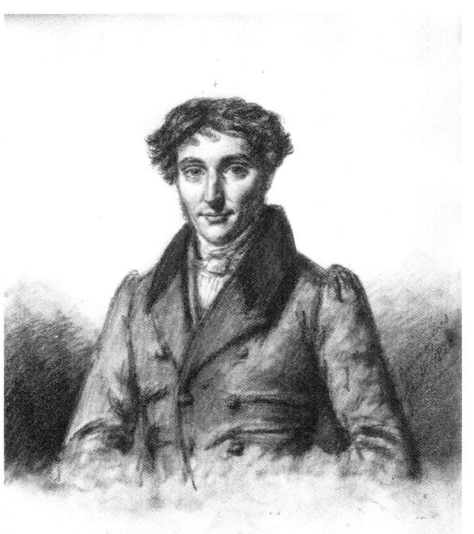

101 **Emma E. JONES** 1813–1842
*Portrait of Joseph Lang*, 1828
charcoal on paper
23.9 x 19.2 cm (sheet)
Gift of Mrs C. Yeatman 1966
669D7

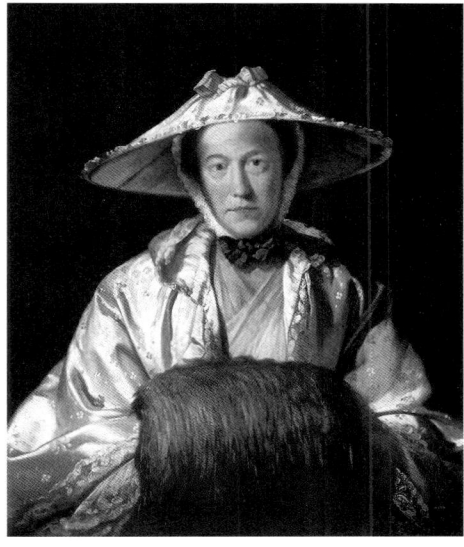

103 **Tilly KETTLE** 1734/35–1786
*Woman with a muff*, early 1760s
oil on canvas
77.0 x 63.6 cm
South Australian Government Grant 1969
703P1

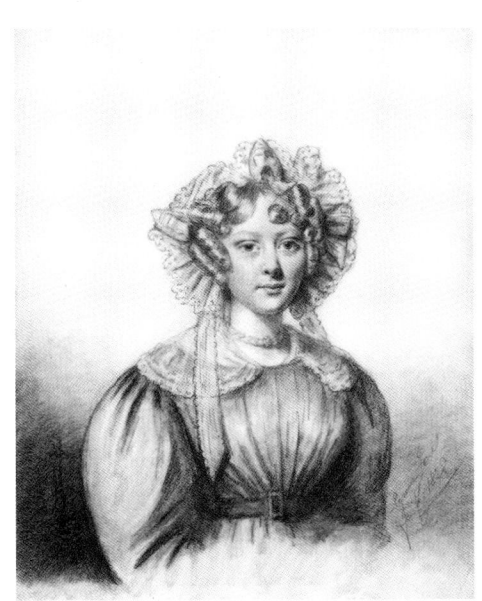

100 **Emma E. JONES** 1813–1842
*Portrait of a woman, possibly Eliza Lang (née Purdey)*, 1828
charcoal on paper
24.0 x 19.2 cm (sheet)
Gift of Mrs C. Yeatman 1966
669D8

Emma Elizabeth Jones was also known as Emma Elizabeth Soyer.

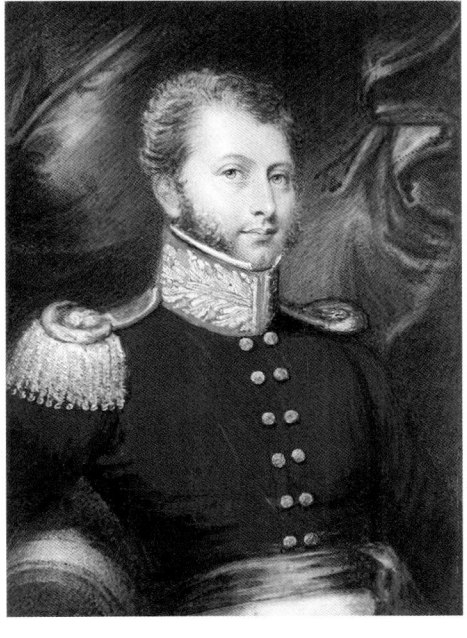

102 **Emma Eleanor KENDRICK** 1788–1871
*Portrait of a gentleman*, c.1815?
gouache on ivory
11.4 x 7.6 cm
Purchased 1907
0.667

Once thought to be a portrait of the navigator and explorer Captain Matthew Flinders.

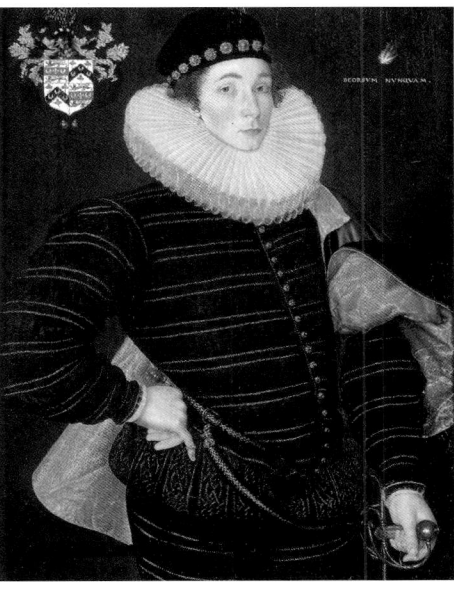

104 **Cornelius KETEL** 1548–1616
*Richard Goodricke of Ribston, Yorkshire*, c.1578
oil on oak panel
106.0 x 81.0 cm
Roy & Marjory Edwards Bequest Fund 2004
20049P85

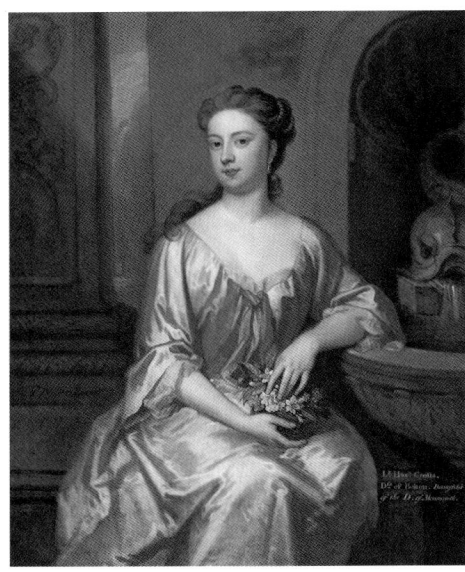

105 **Godfrey KNELLER** 1646–1723
*Lady Henrietta Crofts, Duchess of Bolton*,
c.1715
oil on canvas, 127.0 x 102.0 cm
Elder Bequest Fund 1991
914P4

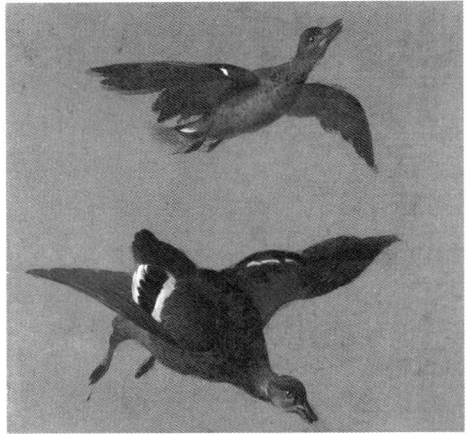

107 **Edwin LANDSEER** 1802–1873
*Wild duck in flight*, c.1842?
oil on canvas laid on pulpboard
21.5 x 22.5 cm
South Australian Government Grant 1957
0.1708

This oil sketch could have been part of the artist's preparatory work (not used) for his painting *The Sanctuary*, 1842 (collection of Her Majesty, Queen Elizabeth II) which shows a stag which has disturbed a flock of ducks.

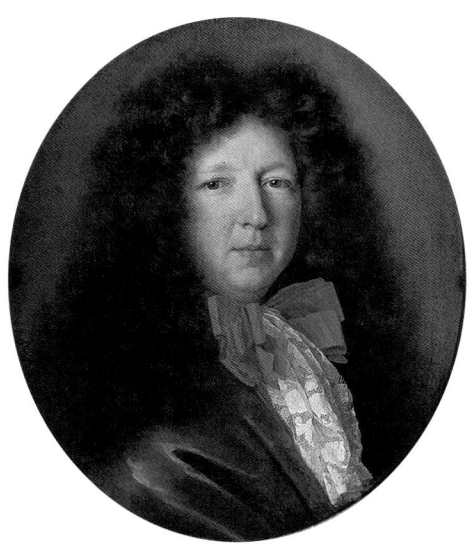

109 attributed to **Nicolas de LARGILLIERRE**
1656–1746
*Portrait of a Frenchman*, c.1678?
oil on canvas
61.0 x 50.8 cm
Bequest of V. K. Burmeister 1957
0.1684

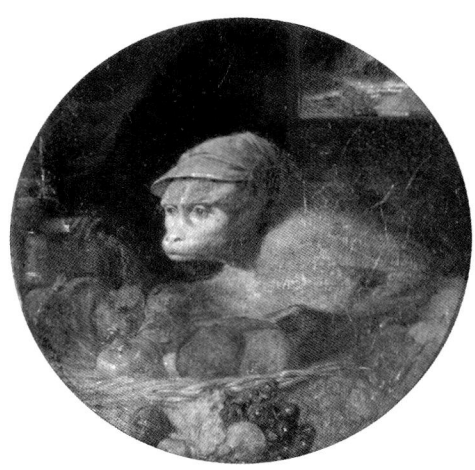

106 **George LANCE** 1883–1901
*The Red Cap*, c.1847
oil on wood panel, 18 cm (diam.)
Gift of Elma S. Gerny 1987
871P5

This is the central detail of the artists' version of the painting of the same title, held by the Tate Gallery, London.

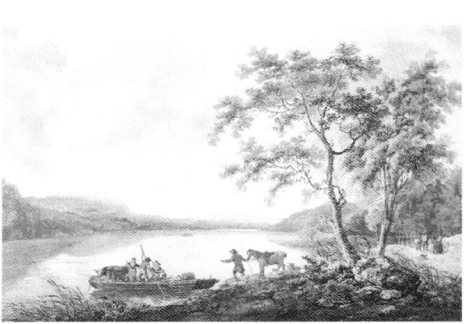

108 **John LAPORTE** 1761–1839
*Lake Windermere*, c.1800?
gouache on paper
42.2 x 62.7 cm (sheet)
South Australian Government Grant 1955
0.1602

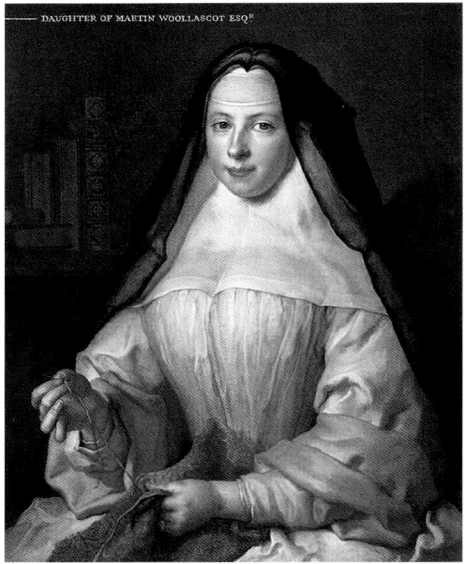

110 **Nicolas de LARGILLIERRE** 1656–1746
*Frances Wollascot, an Augustinian Nun*,
1729
oil on canvas, 80.6 x 65.4 cm
Gift of William Bowmore AO OBE through the Art Gallery of South Australia Foundation 1991
915P12

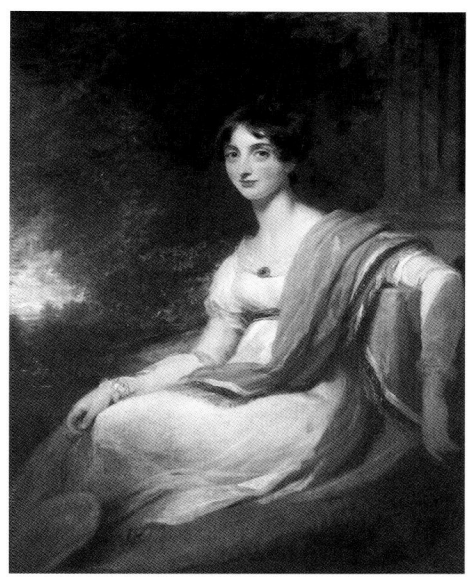

111 **Thomas LAWRENCE** 1769–1830
*Caroline Matilda Sotheron*, c.1808
oil on canvas, 126.7 x 101.1 cm
Gift of William Bowmore AO OBE through
the Art Gallery of South Australia
Foundation 1998
984P25

113 **Thomas LAWRENCE** 1769–1830
*The son of Countess Meerveldt*, 1819
pencil, black, red & blue chalks, grey wash
on paper, 46.8 x 33.5 cm (sheet)
V. B. F. Young Bequest Fund 1993
931D1

116 **Peter LELY** 1618–1680
*Portrait of a man, thought to be George
Booth, Lord Delamere*, c.1660
oil on canvas, 91.2 x 76.2 cm
A. M. & A. R. Ragless Bequest Funds 1957
0.1700

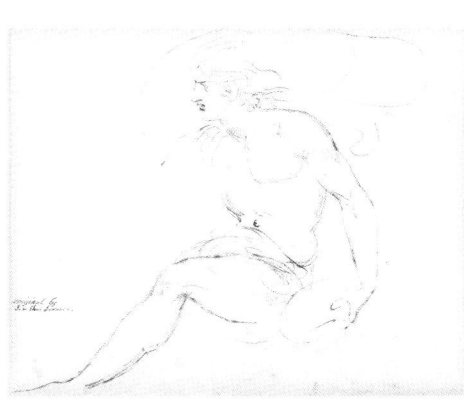

112 **Thomas LAWRENCE** 1769–1830
*Male nude study*, c.1788
pen & brown ink on paper
20.6 x 25.4 cm (sheet)
Gift of Miss E. Bloxam 1931
31D15

Possibly a preparatory drawing for a reclining
nude figure in the Tate Gallery's early painting
by the artist, *Homer reciting his poems*, c.1788.
The model for the figure is thought to be
Jackson the pugilist. The Adelaide donor was a
direct descendent of the artist's sister.

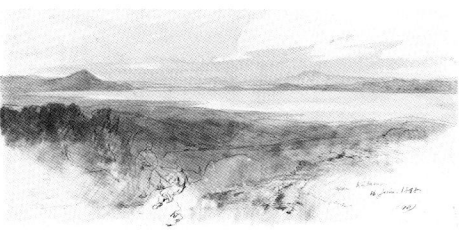

114 **Edward LEAR** 1812–1888
*Near Kalamos*, 1848
pen & sepia ink, wash, pencil on paper
27.3 x 53.0 cm (sheet)
South Australian Government 1970
707D12

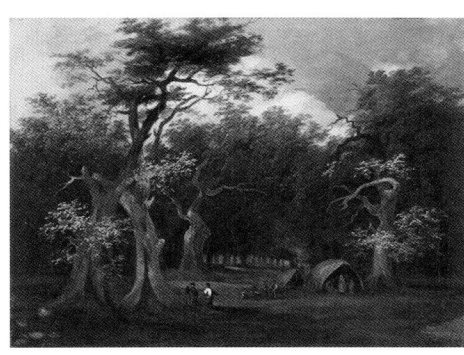

115 **F. R. LEE** 1798–1879
*Forest landscape with campers*, c.1850?
oil on canvas, 28.6 x 39.4 cm
Gift of Miss L. K. Symon 1966
0.2069

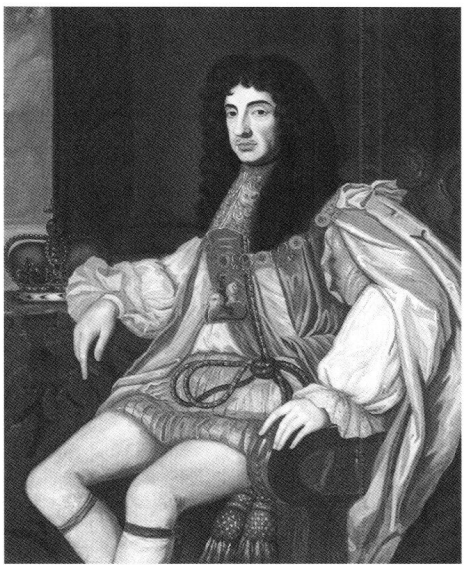

117 after **Peter LELY** 1618–1680
*King Charles II*, c.1690?
oil on canvas, 125.0 x 100.0 cm
Acquired before 1925
0.584

A three-quarter-length copy after Lely's original
of c.1675 now held by The Duke of Grafton,
Euston Hall, Suffolk.

118 **School of Peter LELY** 1618–1680
*Sir Edward Seymour*, mid 1670s?
oil on canvas, 75.5 x 63.2 cm
Gift of Alexander Melrose 1930
0.757

Sir Edward Seymour (1633–1708) was Lord High Treasurer and commissioner of the Treasury of England in 1690. Mary Beale painted similar copies of portraits after Lely.

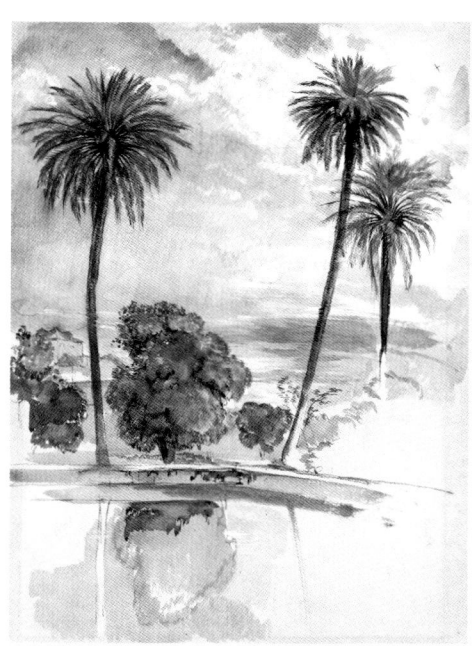

119 **John Frederick LEWIS** 1805–1876
*Landscape with date palms*, 1832–34
gouache on paper
36.2 x 26.0 cm (sheet)
Gift of Mrs Napier 1908
0.380

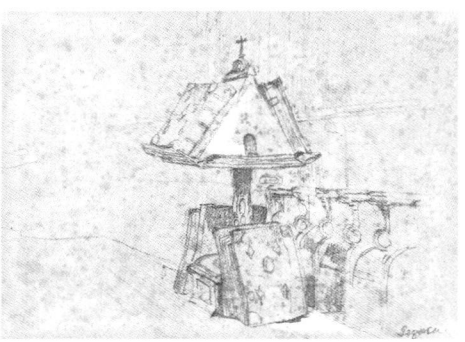

120 **John Frederick LEWIS** 1805–1876
*Bookstand, Segovia*, 1832–34
pencil, white chalk on cream paper
10.6 x 13.9 cm (sheet)
Gift of Mrs Napier 1908
08D4

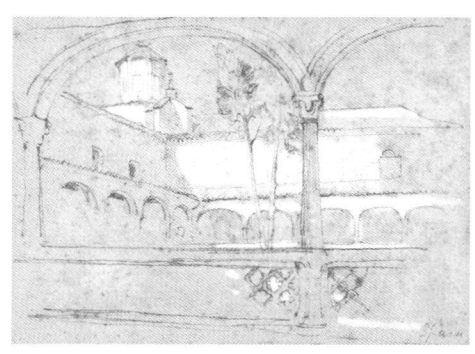

121 **John Frederick LEWIS** 1805–1876
*Cloister, Spain*, 1832–34
pencil, white chalk on cream paper
10.5 x 14.1 cm (sheet)
Gift of Mrs Napier 1908
08D5

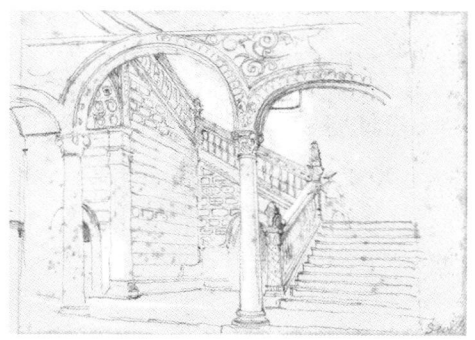

122 **John Frederick LEWIS** 1805–1876
*Architectural sketch, Seville*, 1832–1834
pencil, white chalk on cream paper
10.5 x 13.5 cm (sheet)
Gift of Mrs Napier 1908
08D3

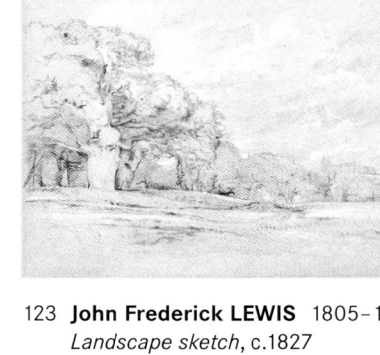

123 **John Frederick LEWIS** 1805–1876
*Landscape sketch*, c.1827
pencil, white chalk on blue-grey paper
25.1 x 36.4 cm (sheet)
Gift of Mrs Napier 1908
08D1

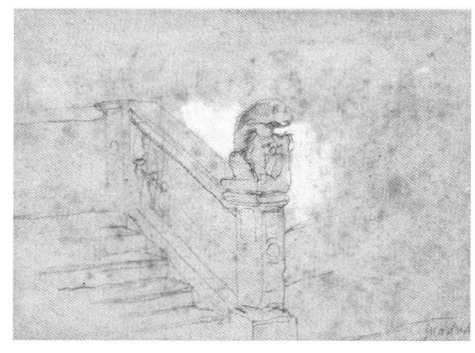

124 **John Frederick LEWIS** 1805–1876
*Balustrade, Madrid*, c.1832–34
pencil, white chalk on cream paper
10.5 x 13.9 cm (sheet)
Gift of Mrs Napier 1908
08D2

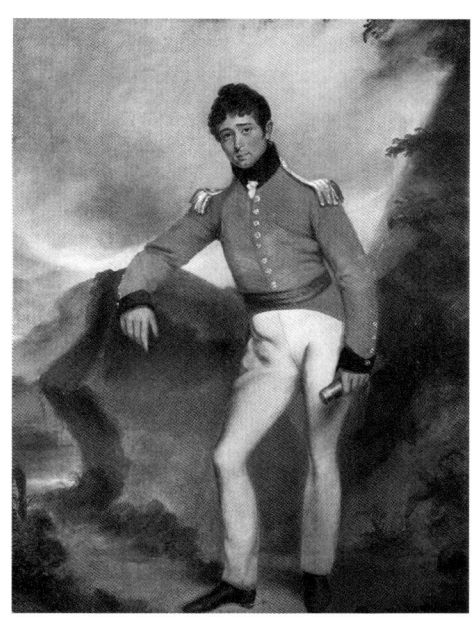

125 **Colonel William LIGHT** 1786–1839
*Self-portrait*, c.1815
oil on canvas mounted on board
83.8 x 61.8 cm
Gift of Standard Chartered Bank Australia Limited to mark its inauguration in South Australia's 150th Anniversary Year 1986 and the Art Gallery of South Australia Foundation
866P21

Colonel Light was an amateur artist and the first Surveyor-General of the colony of South Australia. He chose the site and laid out the plan for the City of Adelaide.

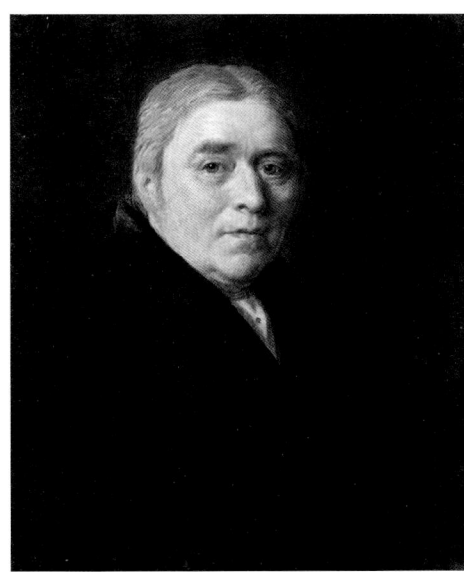

126 **John LINNELL** 1792–1882
*Mr Clare*, 1834
oil on oak panel, 25.2 x 20.2 cm
Public Donations Fund 1983
832P4

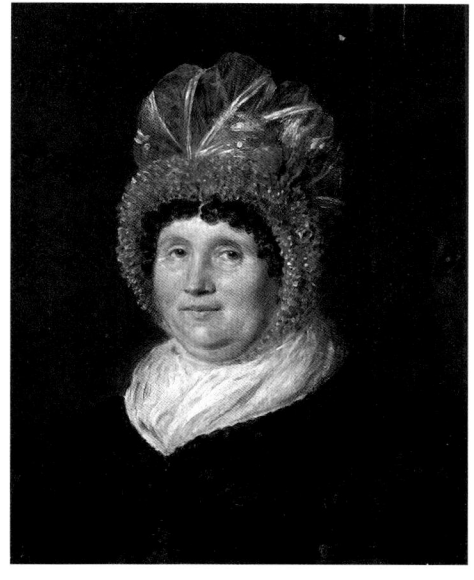

127 **John LINNELL** 1792–1882
*Mrs Clare*, 1834
oil on oak panel, 25.4 x 20.1 cm
Public Donations Fund 1983
832P5

The following eight watercolours (nos 127–134) by the New South Wales convict artist Joseph Lycett of Australian subjects were executed by the artist on his return to Britain. These form part of a series of watercolours that were prepared for his series of hand-coloured prints.

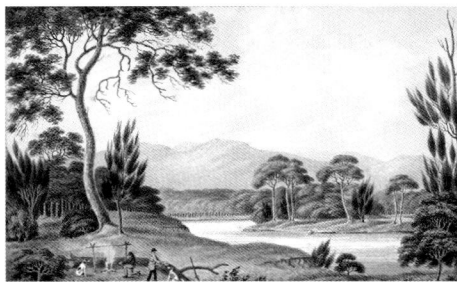

128 **Joseph LYCETT** 1774–1828
*View upon the South Esk River*, c.1824
watercolour on paper
20.6 x 28.6 cm (sheet)
Gift of M. J. M. Carter through the Art Gallery of South Australia Foundation 2004
20044P32

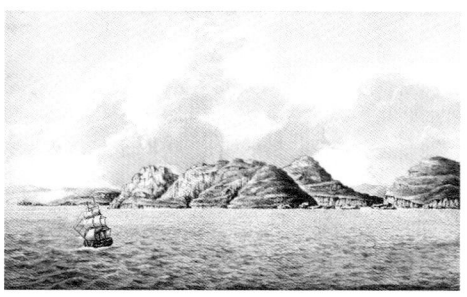

129 **Joseph LYCETT** 1774–1828
*View from the south end of Schouten's Island*, c.1824
watercolour on paper
20.8 x 28.6 cm (sheet)
Gift of M. J. M. Carter through the Art Gallery of South Australia Foundation 2004
20044P31

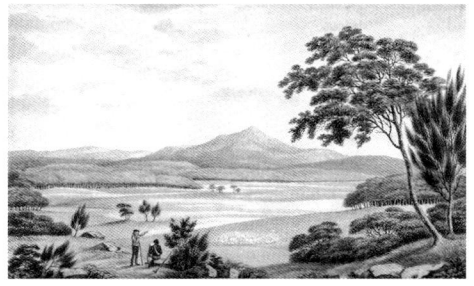

130 **Joseph LYCETT** 1774–1828
*View of Tasman's Peak*, c.1824
watercolour on paper
21.3 x 28.6 cm (sheet)
Gift of M. J. M. Carter through the Art Gallery of South Australia Foundation 2004
20044P33

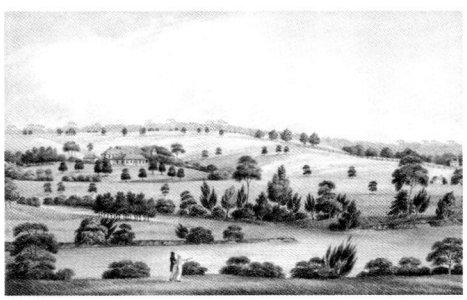

131 **Joseph LYCETT** 1774–1828
*Residence of John Macarthur near Parramatta N.S.W.*, c.1824
watercolour on paper
20.8 x 28.6 cm (sheet)
Gift of M. J. M. Carter through the Art Gallery of South Australia Foundation 2004
20044P29

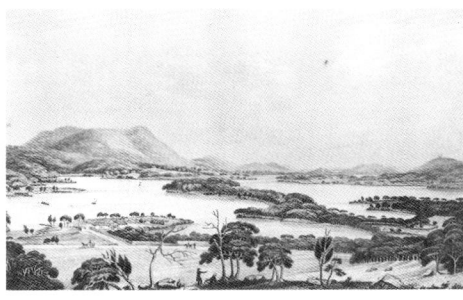

132 **Joseph LYCETT** 1774–1828
*Roseneath Ferry near Hobart Town, Van Diemen's Land*, c.1824
watercolour on paper
17.5 x 27.7 cm (sight)
South Australian Government Grant 1978
787P21

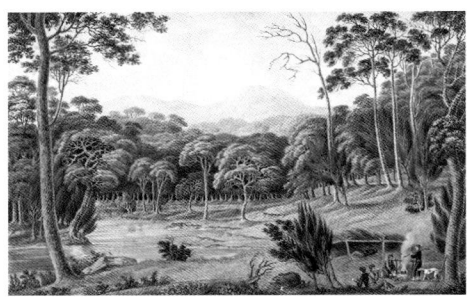

135 **Joseph LYCETT** 1774–1828
*View upon the Nepean River, at the cow pastures, New South Wales*, c.1824
watercolour on paper
20.7 x 28.5 cm (sheet)
Gift of M. J. M. Carter through the Art Gallery of South Australia Foundation 1988
885P23

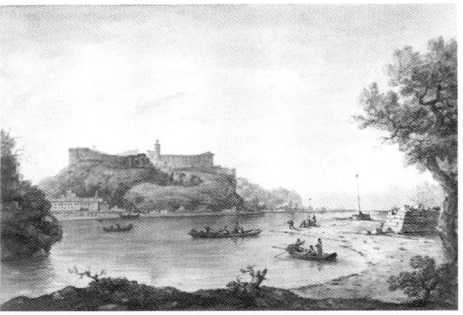

137 **William MARLOW** 1740–1813
*View of the Palais des Papes, Avignon*, c.1790
watercolour on paper
37.8 x 54.0 cm (sheet)
Elder Bequest Fund 1960
0.1875

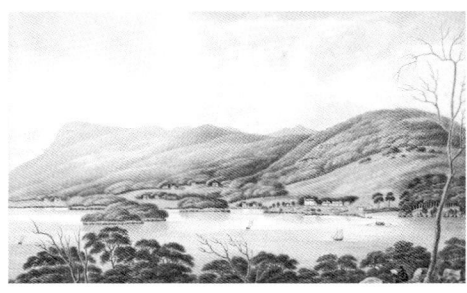

133 **Joseph LYCETT** 1774–1828
*Roseneath Ferry near Hobart Town Van Diemen's Land*, c.1824
watercolour on paper
20.8 x 28.4 cm (sheet)
Gift of M. J. M. Carter through the Art Gallery of South Australia Foundation 2004
20044P30

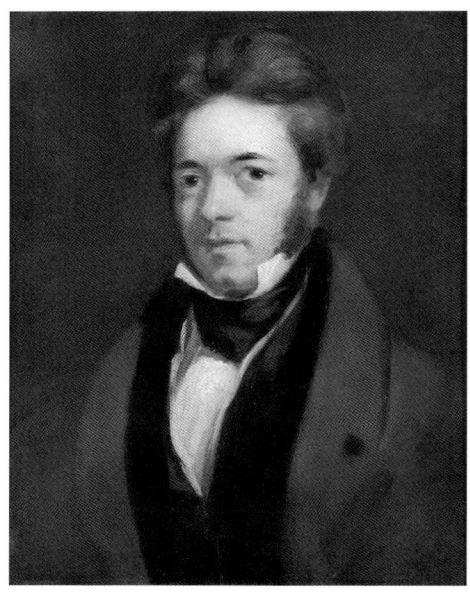

136 **Daniel MacNEE** 1806–1882
*Alexander Murray, M.P., J.P.*, 1828
oil on wood panel, 27.1 x 21.3 cm
Gift of Mrs E. H. McTaggart 1963
0.2004

The following four watercolours (nos 137–140) are from a sketchbook of illustrations and poems, which were painted by the artist before she married her cousin and immigrated to Australia in 1839. They lived in New South Wales before moving shortly after to Van Diemen's Land (Tasmania), the colony with which Meredith became most closely associated.

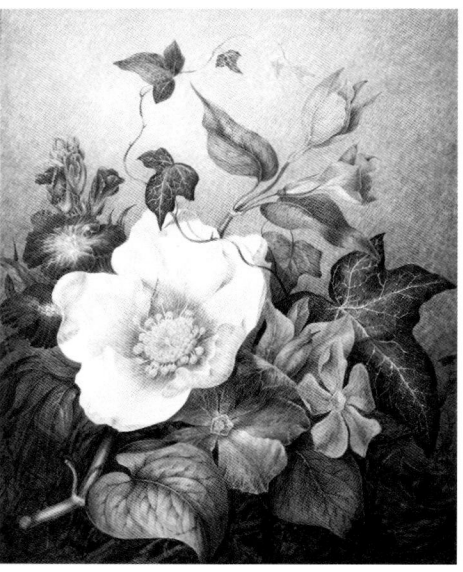

138 **Louisa Anne MEREDITH** 1812–1895
*January*, 1833
watercolour on paper
19.5 x 15.6 cm (image)
J. C. Earl Bequest Fund 2003
20036P18(a)

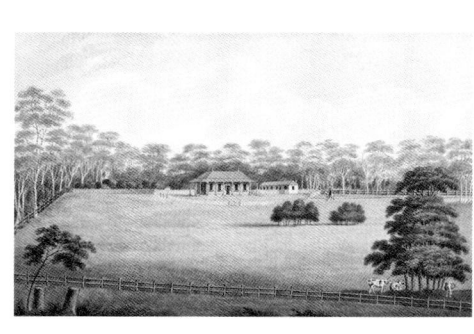

134 **Joseph LYCETT** 1774–1828
*Burwood Villa*, c.1824
watercolour on paper
20.2 x 28.6 cm (sheet)
Gift of M. J. M. Carter through the Art Gallery of South Australia Foundation 1988
885P24

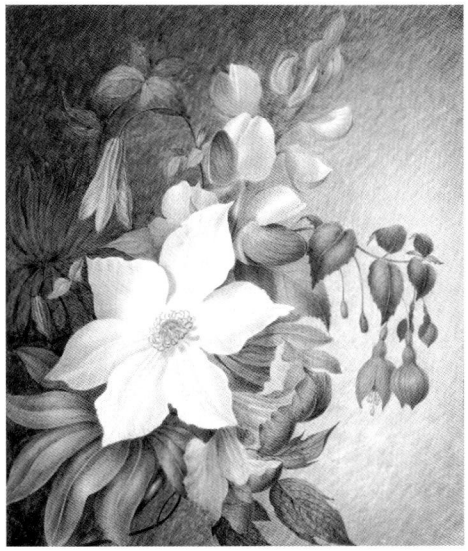

139 **Louisa Anne MEREDITH** 1812–1895
*August*, 1833
watercolour on paper
19.5 x 15.6 cm (image)
J. C. Earl Bequest Fund 2003
20036P18(b)

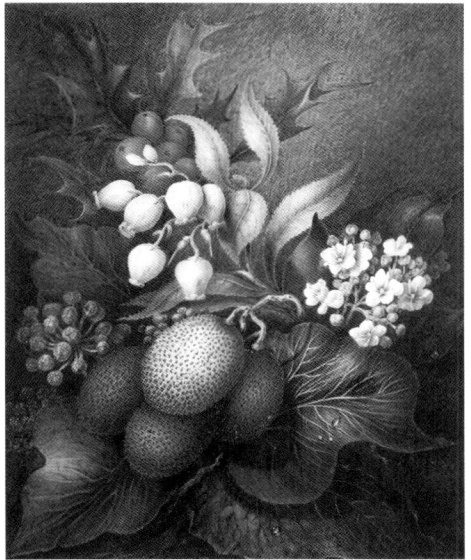

141 **Louisa Anne MEREDITH** 1812–1895
*December*, 1833
watercolour on paper
19.3 x 15.5 cm (image)
J. C. Earl Bequest Fund 2003
20036P18(d)

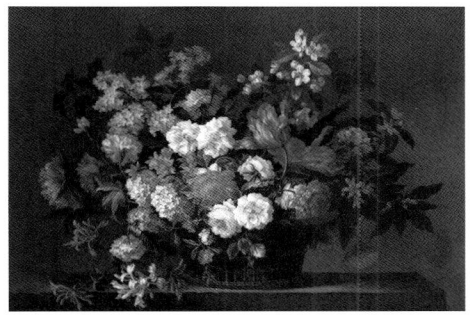

143 **Jean-Baptiste MONNOYER** 1636–1699
*Still-life with basket of flowers*, 1690s
oil on canvas, 73.0 x 103.5 cm
Gift of Anne Clemens 1985
855P13

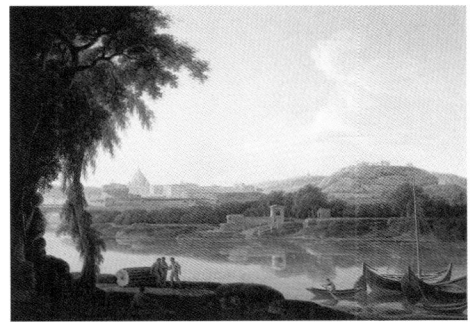

144 **Jacob MORE** 1740–1793
*A distant view of Rome across the Tiber*, c.1774
oil on canvas
78.0 x 106.5 cm
A. M. & A. R. Ragless Bequest Funds 1979
795P10

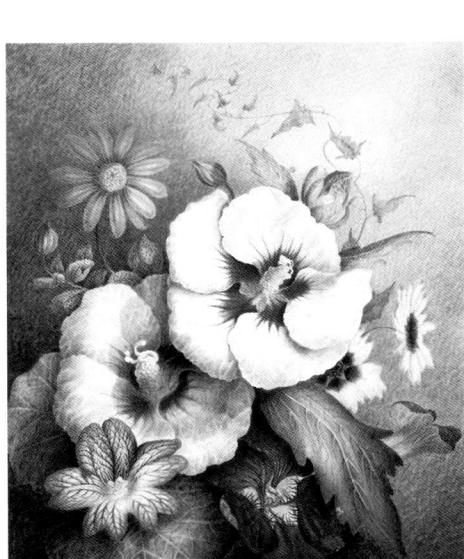

140 **Louisa Anne MEREDITH** 1812–1895
*September*, 1833
watercolour on paper
19.5 x 15.5 cm (image)
J. C. Earl Bequest Fund 2003
20036P18(c)

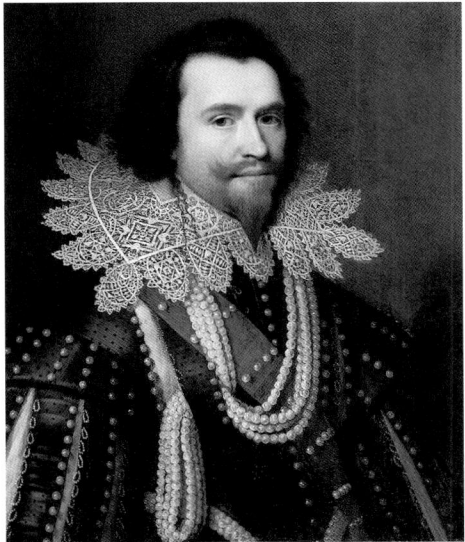

142 **Michiel van MIEREVELD** 1567–1641
*George Villiers, Duke of Buckingham*, 1625/26
oil on wood panel, 69.5 x 57.5 cm
South Australian Government Grant 1967
0.2115

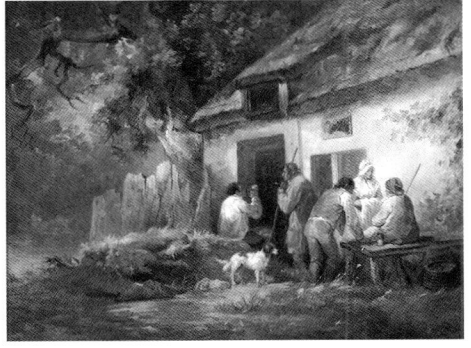

145 **George MORLAND** 1763–1804
*Outside the Bull's Head*, mid 1790s
oil on canvas, 49.2 x 64.8 cm
Gift of Gladys Penfold Hyland in memory of her husband Frank 1964
0.2028

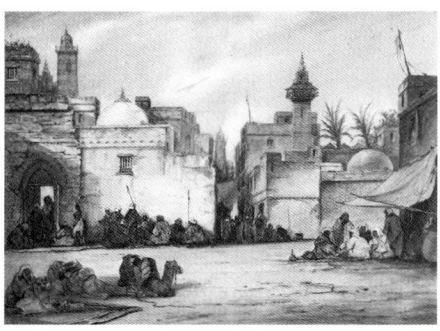

146 **William James MULLER** 1812–1845
*Cairo*, c.1840
watercolour on paper, 35.8 x 50.0 cm (sight)
South Australian Government Grant 1960
0.1883

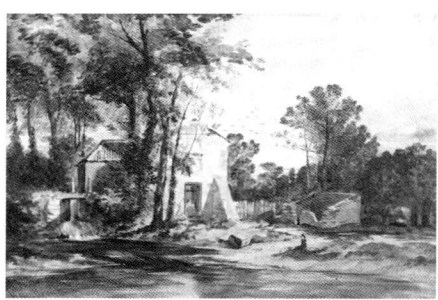

147 **William James MULLER** 1812–1845
*The water mill*, 1835–1845
watercolour on paper, 35.0 x 50.0 cm (sheet)
South Australian Government Grant 1963
0.1995

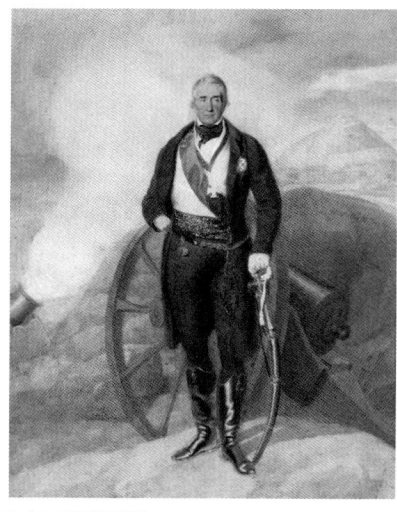

148 **T. MURPHY**
*Thomas Graham, Lord Lyndoch*, 1816
watercolour on paper, 50.3 x 37.3 cm (sheet)
Gift of Lady Morphett 1897
0.677

Colonel Light named the district of Barossa and the township of Lyndoch in South Australia after the Victory of his Commander, Lord Lyndoch, at the Battle of Barossa, Spain. Colonel Light was the first Surveyor-General of the Colony of South Australia.

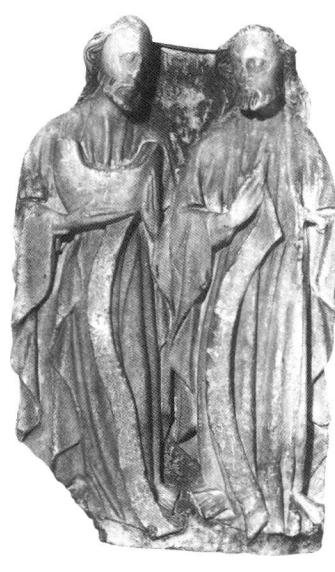

149 **Nottingham workshops**
*Two Apostles, St Matthew and St James (minor)*, mid to late 15th century
Nottingham alabaster with traces of paint
41.0 x 25.0 x 5.0 cm (irreg.)
South Australian Government Grant 1952
S95

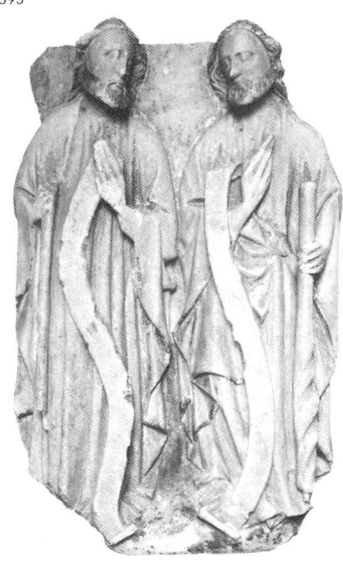

150 **Nottingham workshops**
*Two Apostles, St Simon and St Jude*, mid to late 15th century
Nottingham alabaster with traces of paint
42.0 x 24.5 x 5.0 cm (irreg.)
South Australian Government Grant 1952
S94

These pair of religious figures carved from alabaster quarried near Nottingham in the mid to late fifteenth century, were possibly once part of an altarpiece; only some of the original polychrome surface remains. Easily carved and coloured, small alabasters like these were also exported to Europe in the fifteenth century. Pairs of figures are rare and these are the earliest British works in the Gallery's collection.

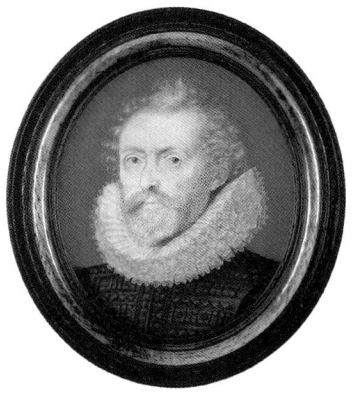

151 **Isaac OLIVER** c.1565–1617
*Man with fair hair and beard*, c.1590
watercolour on vellum backed with ivory
5.1 x 4.2 cm
Mary Overton Bequest Fund assisted by the Art Gallery of South Australia Foundation 2004
20048P74

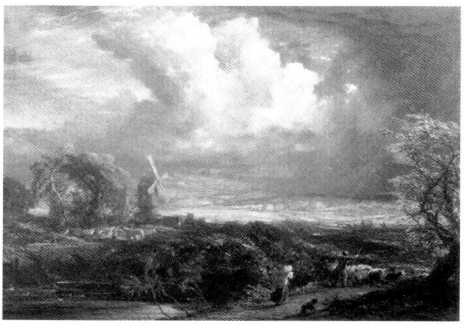

152 **Samuel PALMER** 1805–1881
*Summer storm near Pulborough, Sussex*, c.1851
watercolour, body colour on paper
51.5 x 72.0 cm (sheet)
A. R. Ragless Bequest Fund 1955
0.1619

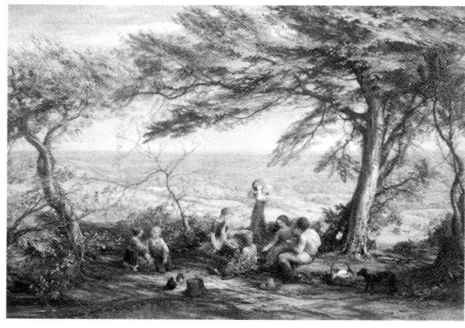

153 **Samuel PALMER** 1805–1881
*The rustic dinner*, c.1853
watercolour, body colour on paper
53.3 x 75.5 cm (sheet)
South Australian Government Grant 1956
0.1654

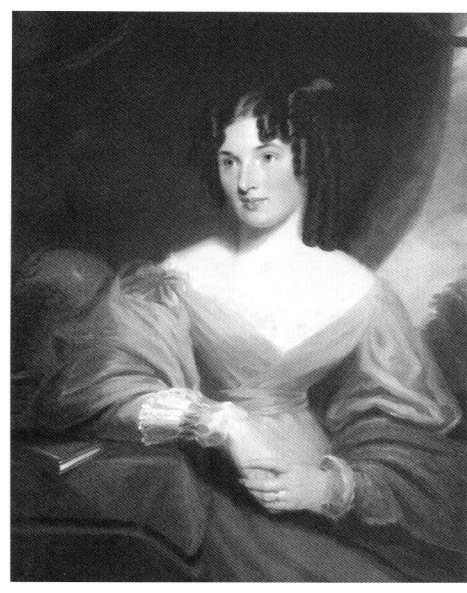

154  attributed to **Mrs PARSONS**
*Portrait of Mrs Caroline Clarke*, c.1830
oil on canvas, 91.5 x 71.0 cm
Gift of Miss Phyllis O. Crompton on behalf of her family 1974
744HP2

The sitter, Caroline Clarke (née Hill), 1800–1877, married Francis Clarke (1789–1853) in 1824, immigrated to Australia, arriving in Adelaide in 1850. The donor was the great-great-granddaughter of the sitter.

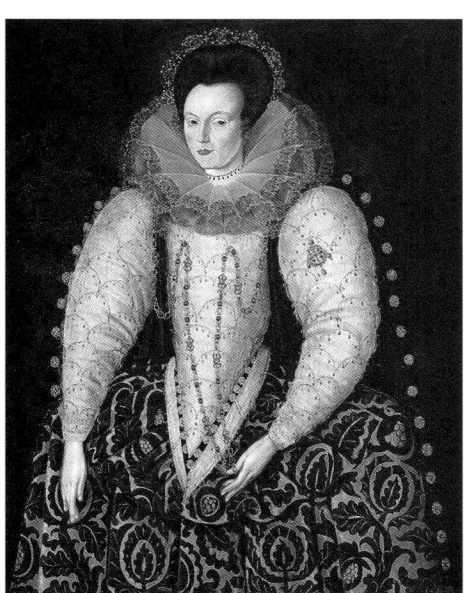

155  **Robert PEAKE**  c.1551–1619
*Frances, Lady Reynell of West Ogwell, Devon*, c.1595
oil on oak panel, 113.5 x 88.5 cm
Gift of the Art Gallery of South Australia Foundation 1998
978P97

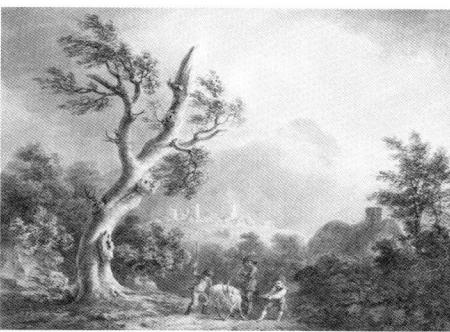

156  **Nicholas POCOCK**  1741–1821
*Grosmont in South Wales*, 1790
watercolour on paper
40.8 x 55.9 cm (sheet)
South Australian Government Grant 1955
0.1623

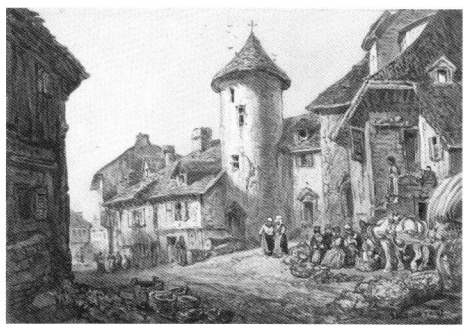

157  **John Skinner PROUT**  1805–1876
*Old European city*, c.1835?
watercolour, gouache on paper
20.5 x 28.0 cm (sheet)
Bequest of Alexander Melrose 1945
0.1302

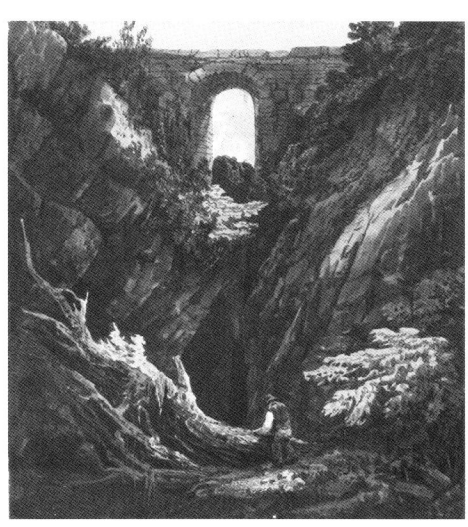

158  **Samuel PROUT**  1783–1852
*Lidford Bridge, Devon*, c.1812?
watercolour on paper
28.7 x 25.5 cm (sheet)
Gift before 1925
0.580

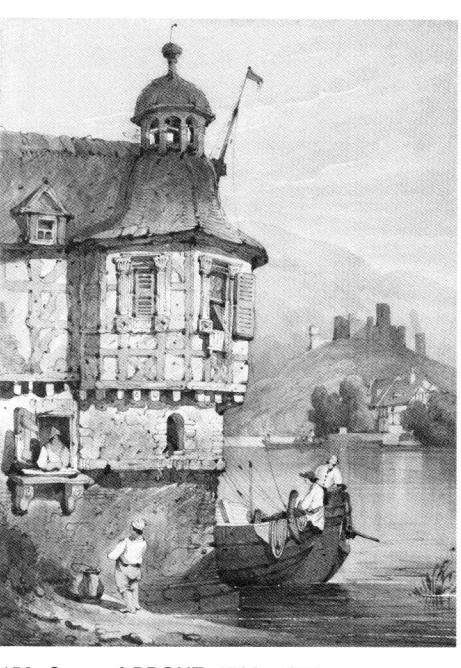

159  **Samuel PROUT**  1783–1852
*Nieder Lahnstein*, c.1825?
watercolour on paper
27.5 x 19.7 cm (sheet)
Bequest of V. K. Burmeister 1957
0.1689

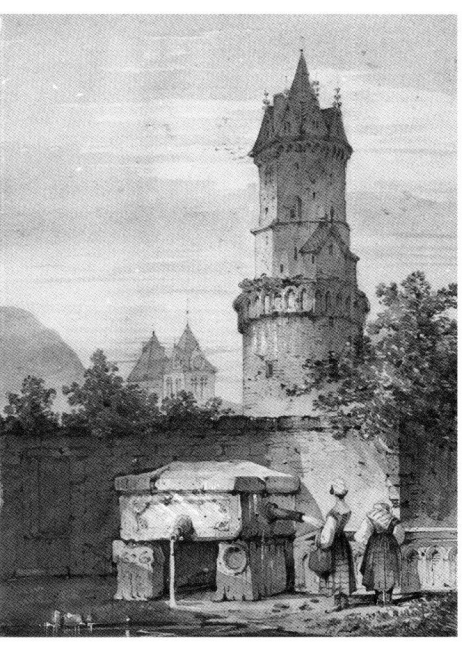

160  **Samuel PROUT**  1783–1852
*Old Tower at Le Havre*, c.1835?
watercolour on paper
36.3 x 26.2 cm (sight)
Colonial Government Grant 1900
0.306

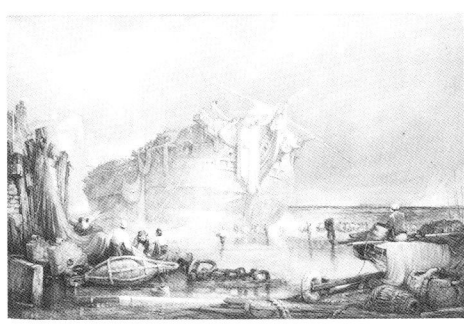

161 **Samuel PROUT** 1783–1852
*Salving from the wreck*, 1848
watercolour on paper
67.2 x 97.5 cm (sheet)
Elder Bequest Fund 1955
0.1620

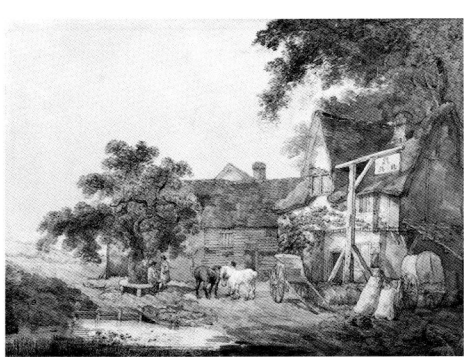

162 **William Henry PYNE** 1769–1843
*Farmyard*, 1794
watercolour on paper
27.4 x 36.1 cm (sheet)
South Australian Government Grant 1960
0.1885

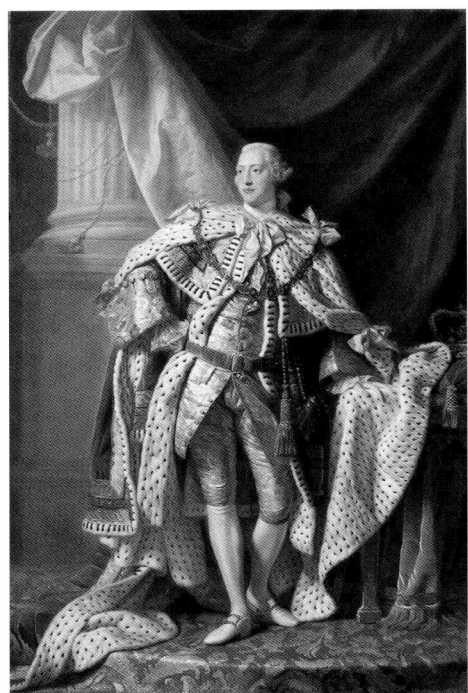

164 **Allan RAMSAY and studio** 1713–1784
*King George III in coronation robes*, c.1765?
oil on canvas
236.2 x 158.7 cm
South Australian Government Grant 1924
0.561

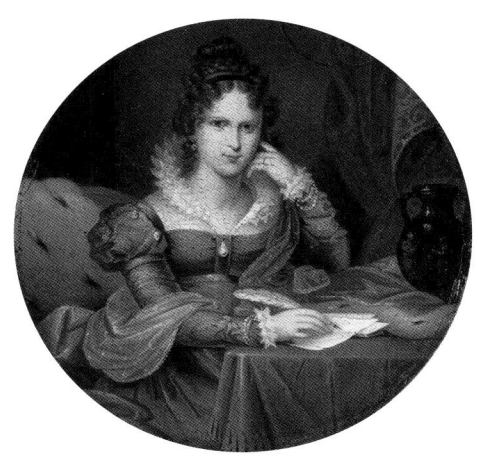

166 **Samuel RAVEN** 1775–1847
after Mary Green, (née Byrne)
*Queen Adelaide as Princess Adelaide*,
c.1818
oil on papier mâché
13.7 cm diam.
Gift of Her Majesty Queen Mary 1946
0.1333

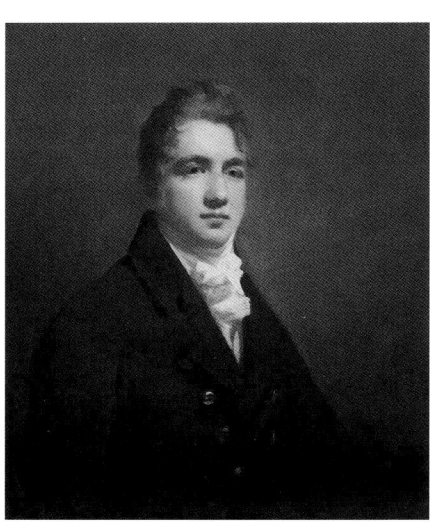

163 **Henry RAEBURN** 1756–1823
*Archibald Trotter of Bush*, 1810
oil on canvas, 76.4 x 63.3 cm
Gift of William Bowmore AO OBE through
the Art Gallery of South Australia
Foundation 1998
984P26

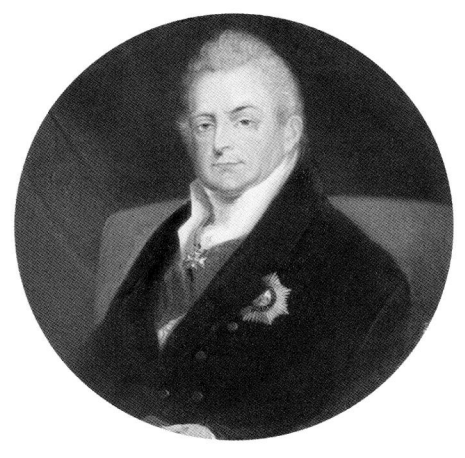

165 **Samuel RAVEN** 1775–1847
after Mary Green (née Byrne)
*King William IV as Prince William,* c.1818
oil on papier mâché, 13.7 cm diam.
Gift of Her Majesty Queen Mary 1946
0.1334

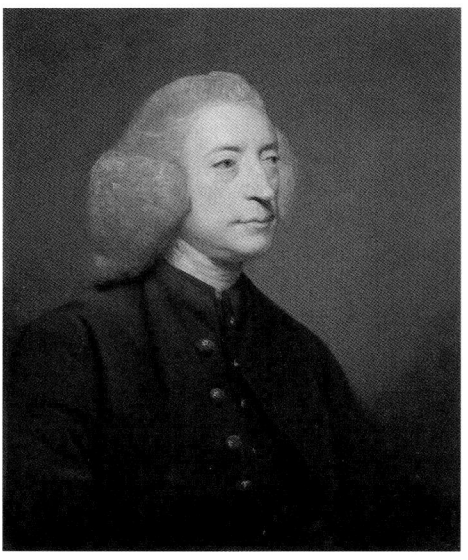

167 **Joshua REYNOLDS** 1723–1792
*Dr John Armstrong*, 1767
oil on canvas
76.0 x 63.5 cm
Morgan Thomas Bequest Fund 1934
0.842

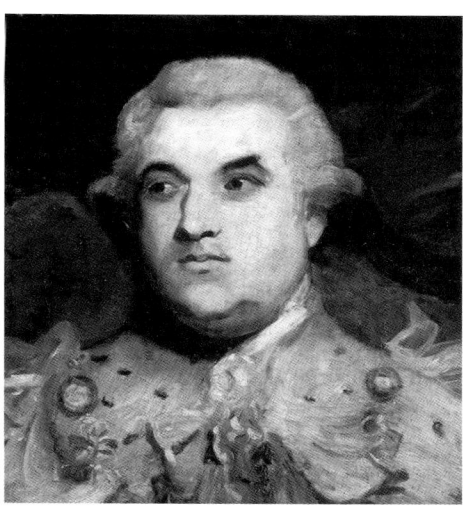

**168 Joshua REYNOLDS** 1723–1792
*Robert Henley, Second Earl of Northington*, 1787
oil on canvas
45.0 x 42.2 cm
A. R. Ragless Bequest Fund 1948
0.1365

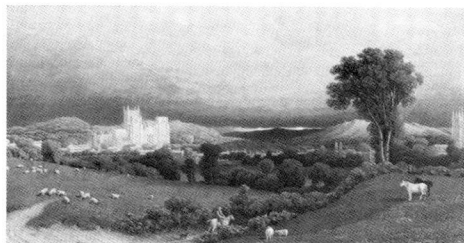

**170 G. F. ROBSON** 1788–1833
*View of City of Wells*, c.1825
watercolour on paper
21.9 x 39.7 cm (sheet)
Bequest of Alexander Melrose 1945
0.1303

This composition was made into an engraving and featured in *Picturesque views of English Cities from Drawings by G. F. Robson*, 1828, engravings by T. Jeanes, p. 23.

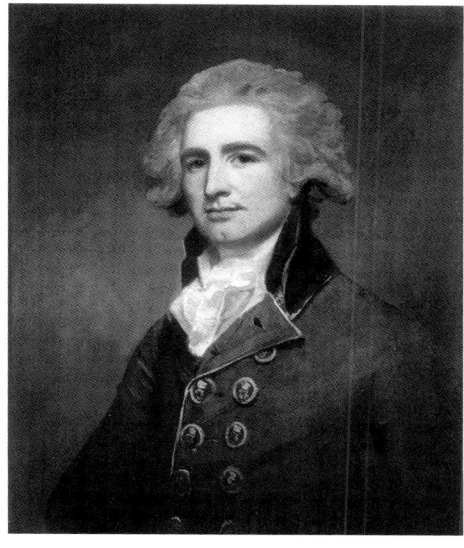

**172 George ROMNEY** 1734–1802
*Colonel Robert Abercrombie*, 1788
oil on canvas, 76.5 x 63.0 cm
Gift of Phillips & Henderson, Adelaide 1982
823P9

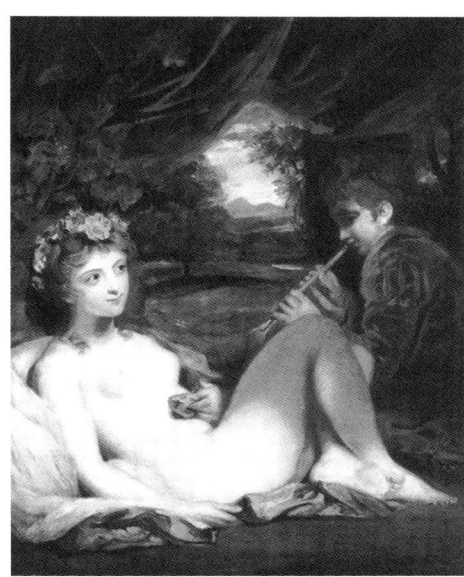

**169 after Joshua REYNOLDS** 1723–1792
*Shepherd piping*, c.1790s
oil on canvas
61.5 x 49.0 cm (sight)
Gift of E. J. Wirell 1881
0.5

After Reynolds's original held at Polesden Lacey, British National Trust (Mannings, no. 2176, p.572). This work was acquired in the first year of the Gallery, making it the first British Old Master painting to enter the collection.

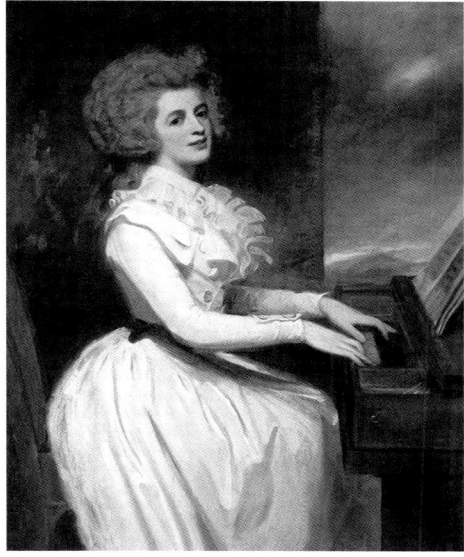

**171 George ROMNEY** 1734–1802
*Charlotte, Mrs Thomas Raikes*, 1787
oil on canvas
125.1 x 99.7 cm
Gift of Gladys Penfold Hyland in memory of her husband Frank 1964
0.2024

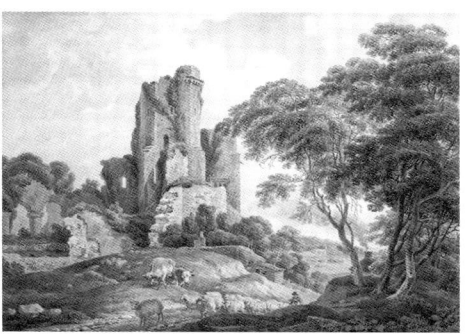

**173 Michael Angelo ROOKER** 1746–1801
*A view of a ruined castle*, c.1798
watercolour on paper
26.4 x 36.4 cm (sheet)
Elder Bequest Fund 1960
0.1866

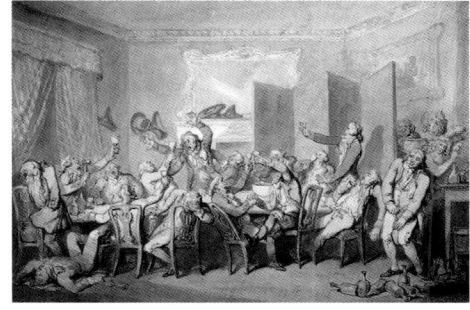

**174 Thomas ROWLANDSON** 1756–1827
*The Brilliants*, c.1801
pen & ink, watercolour, pencil on paper,
30.0 x 44.5 cm (sheet)
A. R. Ragless Bequest Fund 1960
0.1874

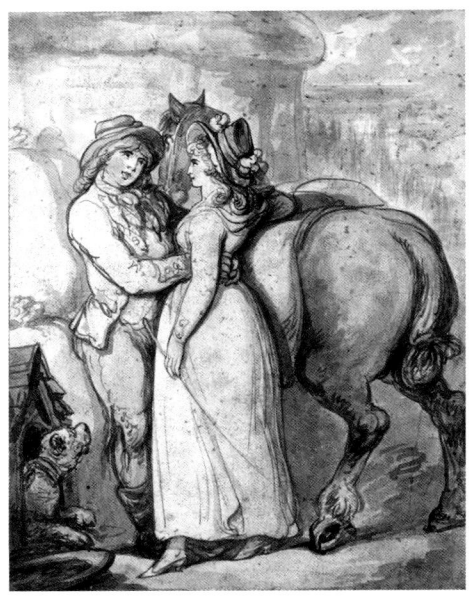

**175 Thomas ROWLANDSON** 1756–1827
*Young couple beside a horse*, c.1785
pen & ink, watercolour on paper
24.2 x 18.4 cm (sheet)
Bequest of David Murray 1908
084D19

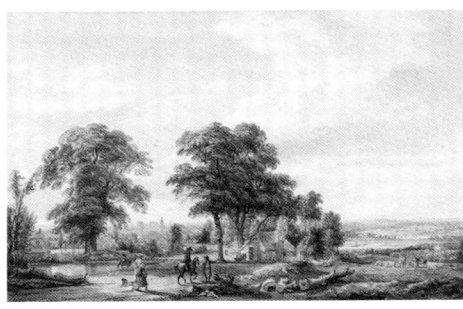

**177 Paul SANDBY** 1731–1809
*Approaching Rochester and the Medway*, 1786
watercolour on paper
36.5 x 54.5 cm (sheet)
Morgan Thomas Bequest Fund 1956
0.1641

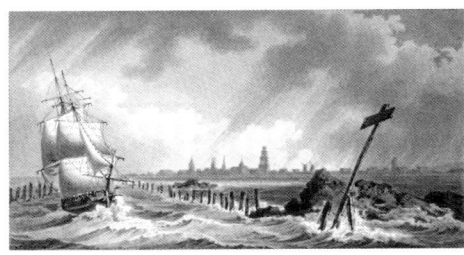

**180 John Thomas SERRES** 1759–1825
*Dunkirk*, c.1810?
watercolour on paper
17.0 x 31.5 cm (sheet)
South Australian Government Grant 1955
0.1629

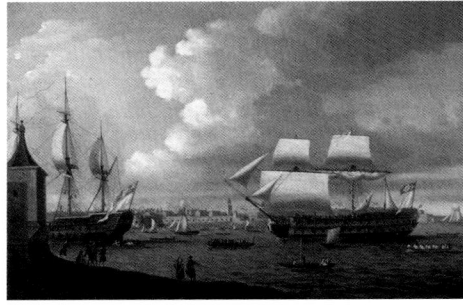

**178 Dominic SERRES** 1722–1793
*Foudroyant and Pégase entering Portsmouth Harbour, 1782*, 1782
oil on canvas
76.8 x 112.3 cm
Gift of Mrs David Evans and Mr Geoffrey O'Halloran Giles in memory of their parents Mr & Mrs Hew O'Halloran Giles 1987
876P16

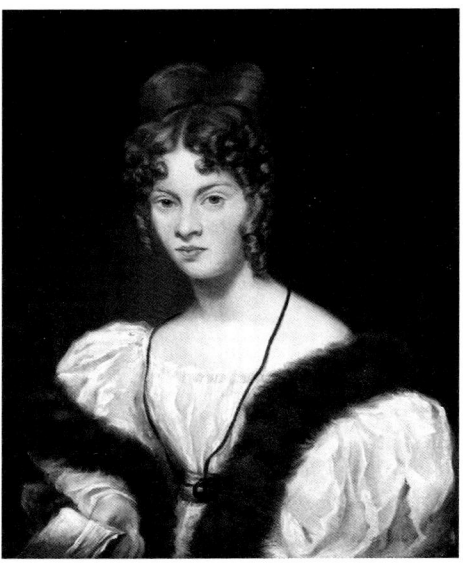

**181 Elizabeth SETCHEL** *fl.* 1832–44
*Dorothea Wilson*, c.1828
oil on canvas, 71.0 x 58.5 cm
Gift of Shirley and Honor Cameron Wilson 1999
991P2

The sitter was the daughter of Adelaide pioneer Thomas Wilson. The donors were Dorothea Wilson's grand-nieces.

**176 Thomas ROWLANDSON** 1756–1827
*An undertaker,* c.1800
pen & sepia wash on cream paper
22.0 x 18.0 cm (sheet)
Gift of George Holman 1947
472D1

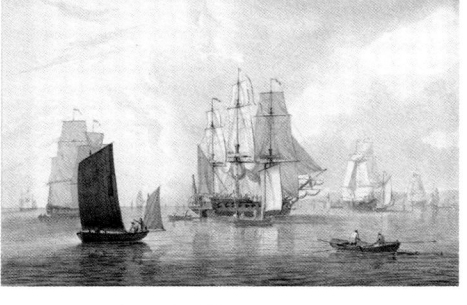

**179 Dominic SERRES** 1722–1793
*Harbour scene*, 1775
watercolour on paper
29.3 x 41.7 cm (sheet)
South Australian Government Grant 1955
0.1630

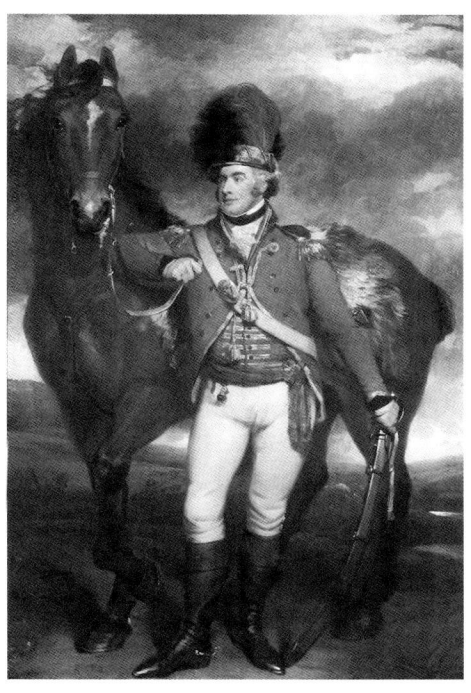

182 **Martin Archer SHEE** 1769–1850
*Major O'Shea of the Loyal Cork Legion*, 1798
oil on canvas, 233.7 x 157.5 cm
Gift of Alexander Melrose 1930
0.756

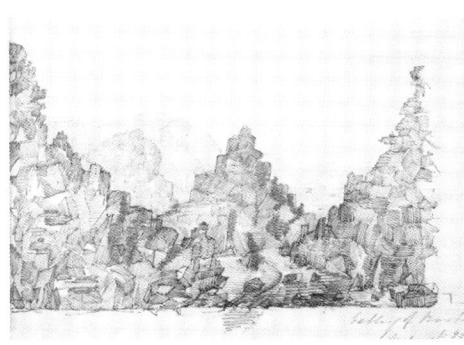

183 **Elizabeth SILLIFANT** working 1820s
*Sketchbook of British landscapes*, 1822–24
pencil on paper
17.9 x 21.9 x 0.9cm (sketchbook)
Gift of the Estate of Kathleen Hilfers 1997
972D15(I-XVI)

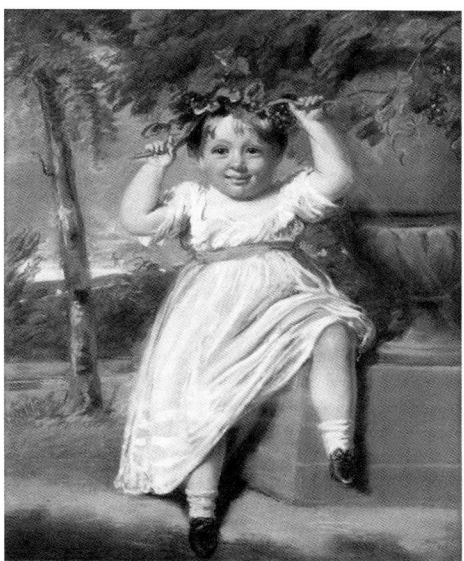

184 **John Raphael SMITH** 1752–1812
*Master Herbert as Bacchus*, c.1805
pastel on paper, 45.5 x 36.5 cm (sheet)
Elder Bequest Fund 1959
0.1850

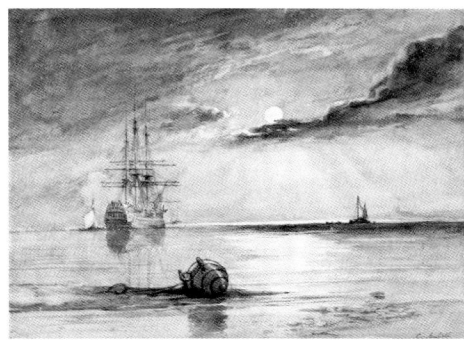

185 **Clarkson STANFIELD** 1793–1867
*The Moon*, c.1830?
watercolour on paper
32.4 x 44.0 cm (sheet)
South Australian Government Grant 1960
0.1884

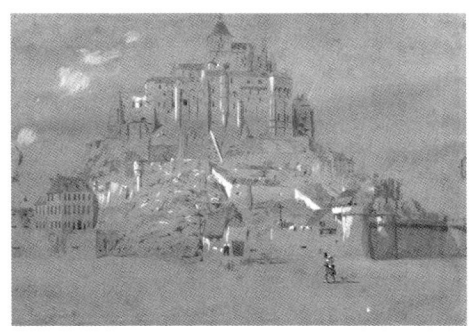

186 **Clarkson STANFIELD** 1793–1867
*Mont St Michel*, 1838/41
pencil, watercolour on brown paper
25.5 x 37.0 cm (sheet)
Bequest of Miss Sarah Crabb 1925
25D6

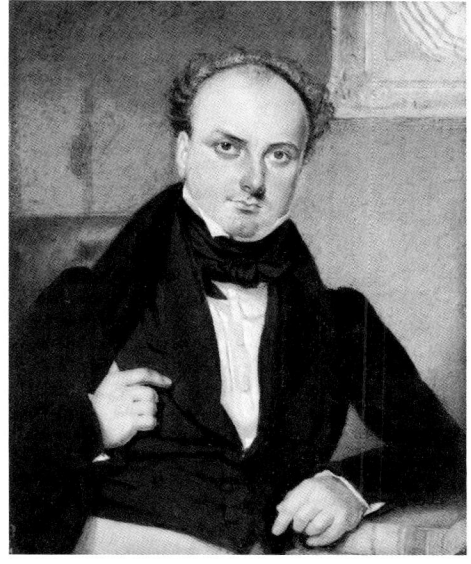

187 **A. STEPHENS** c.1790–after 1838
*Robert Gouger*, 1833
oil on ivory, 12.7 x 10.1 cm
Gift of Miss Gouger 1913
0.682

The sitter was South Australia's first Colonial Secretary, arriving in 1836.

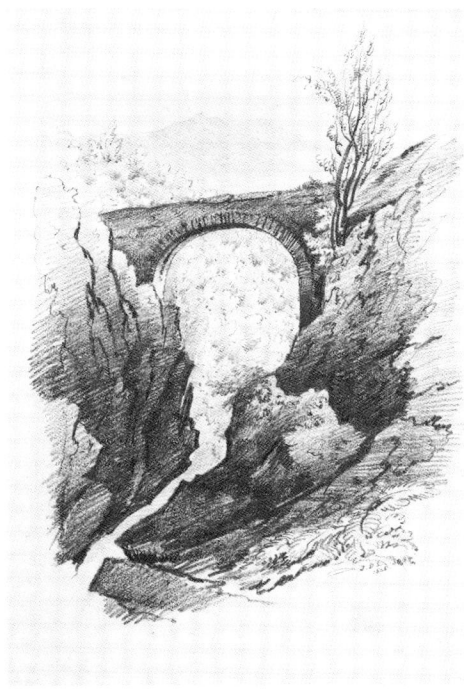

188 **James Doveton STONE** 1831–1908
*The bridge*, 1848
pencil on cream paper
36.4 x 25.5 cm (sheet)
Gift of Miss A. Stone 1936
369D7

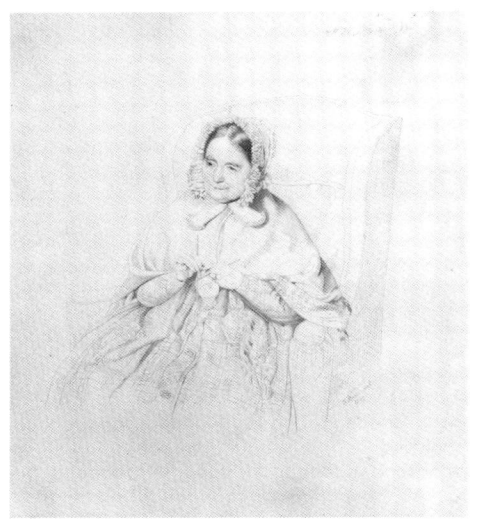

**189 William STRUTT** 1825–1915
*A woman knitting*, 1849
pencil, watercolour on paper
28.7 x 24.5 cm (sheet)
South Australian Government Grant 1984
844D8

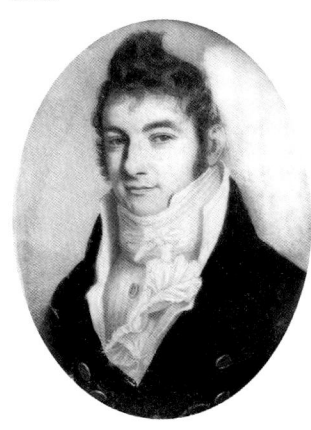

**190 William STURT**
*Miniature of a gentleman*, c.1810
gouache on ivory, 7.6 x 5.7 cm
Gift of Miss Veaitch 1947
0.1339

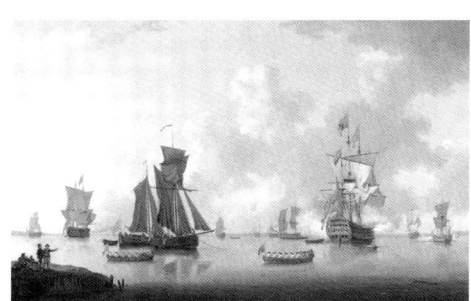

**191 Francis SWAINE** c.1720–1782
*The Landing of the Sailor Prince at Spithead*, 1765
oil on canvas, 106.6 x 167.5 cm
Gift of James & Ann Douglas in memory of Sholto & Alison Douglas 2001
20024P21

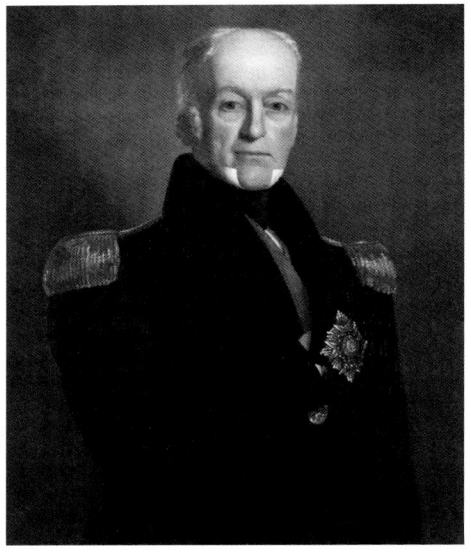

**192 Robert TAIT** *fl.* 1836–75
*Admiral Sir Pulteney Malcolm*, c.1835
oil on canvas, 80.0 x 66.0 cm
Bequest of Sir George Murray 1942
0.1193

This early portrait by Robert Tait is of Welsh-born Pulteney Malcolm (1778–1838) who became a distinguished Admiral. He was active in India, Southeast Asia, Canada, America and the Mediterranean.

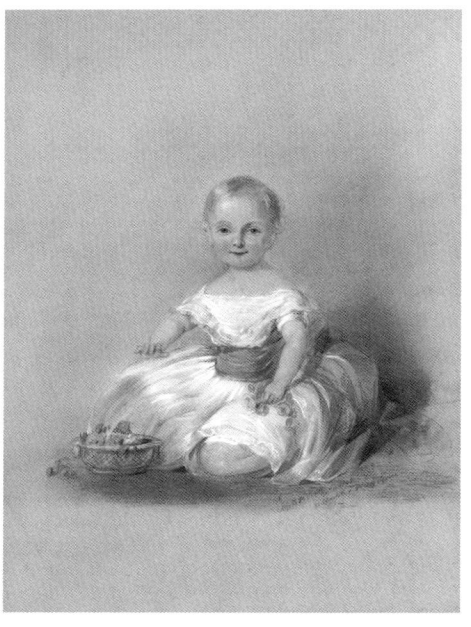

**193 Alfred H. TAYLOR** *fl.* 1838–68
*Young boy*, 1844
pencil, pastel on paper
38.5 x 28.5 cm (sight)
Gift of M. J. M. Carter through the Art Gallery of South Australia Foundation 2004
20044P58

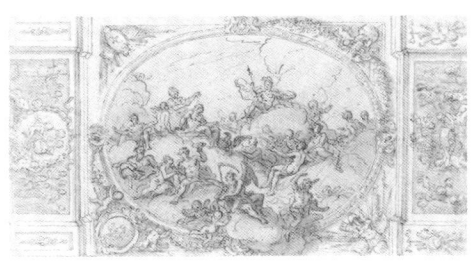

**194 James THORNHILL** 1675–1734
*Minerva and the Gods of Olympus: A design for the hall ceiling at Easton Neston*, c.1712
pen & brown ink, grey wash, black chalk on paper, 25.3 x 46.1 cm (sheet)
V. B. F. Young Bequest Fund 1992
921D1

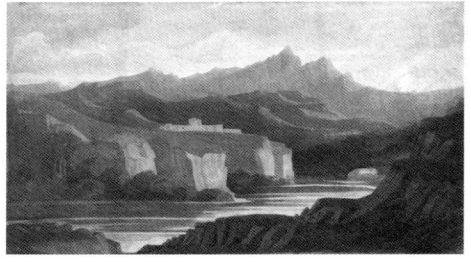

**195 style of Francis TOWNE** c.1739–1816
*Mountainous landscape*, c.1790s?
watercolour on paper
23.5 x 38.7 cm (irreg. sheet)
Gift of L. H. Landseer 1945
0.1319

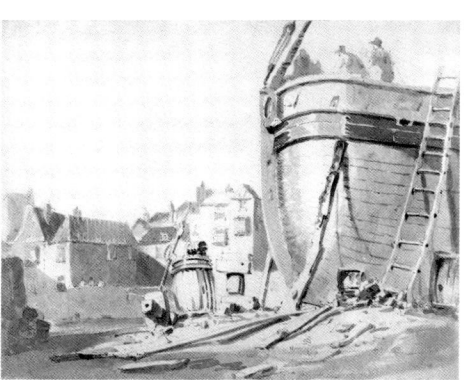

**196 J. M. W. TURNER** 1775–1851
*Dover Harbour*, c.1797
pencil, brush & grey and blue wash on paper, 21.0 x 25.8 cm (sheet)
South Australian Government Grant 1980
804D9

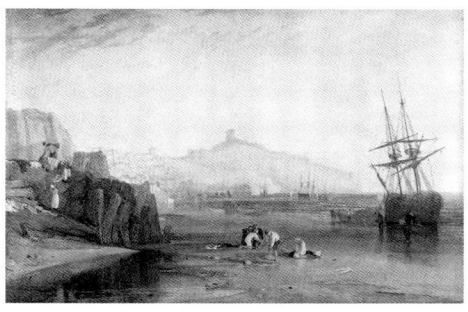

197 **J. M. W. TURNER** 1775–1851
*Scarborough town and castle: morning: boys catching crabs*, c.1810
watercolour on paper
68.5 x 101.5 cm (sheet)
On long-term loan to the Art Gallery of South Australia since 1987
L87CR1

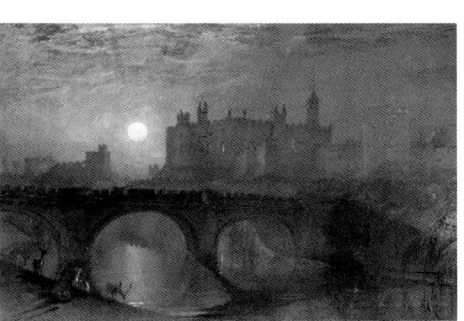

198 **J. M. W. TURNER** 1775–1851
*Alnwick Castle*, c.1829
watercolour on paper
28.2 x 42.2 cm (sight)
South Australian Government Grant 1958
0.1814

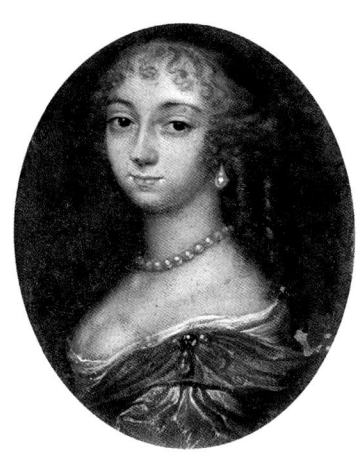

199 **UNKNOWN ARTIST**
*Portrait of a lady*, c.1660s
oil on copper, 7.0 x 5.7 cm
Bequest of G. W. Hawkes 1908
0.546

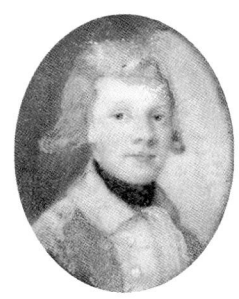

200 **UNKNOWN ARTIST**
*Major-General James Wolfe in his youth*, c.1741
watercolour on ivory
3.6 x 3.0 cm
Bequest of Miss Alice Effie Ferguson 1950
0.1425

Major-General James Wolfe (1729–1759), the supposed sitter, was born in Kent, entered the army aged fourteen in 1741 around the time when this miniature was executed. General Wolfe is best known for his command of the successful military and naval expedition and attack on Québec in 1759, in which he lost his life on the battlefield. It has been suggested that these portraits may have been painted by Joseph Highmore as he was the only artist that Wolfe was known to have sat for.

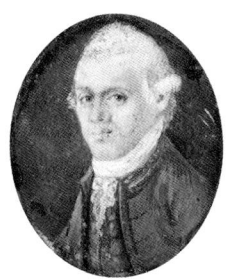

201 **UNKNOWN ARTIST**
*Major-General James Wolfe*, c.1750
watercolour on ivory
3.6 x 3.0 cm
Bequest of Miss Alice Effie Ferguson 1950
0.1424

The same sitter as no. 199.

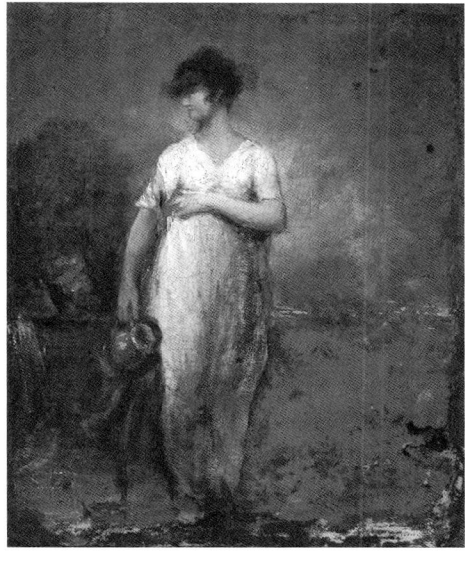

202 **UNKNOWN ARTIST**
*Standing woman*, c.1800
oil on canvas, 30.5 x 25.0 cm
Gift of Mrs B. Hamlyn 1968
686P7

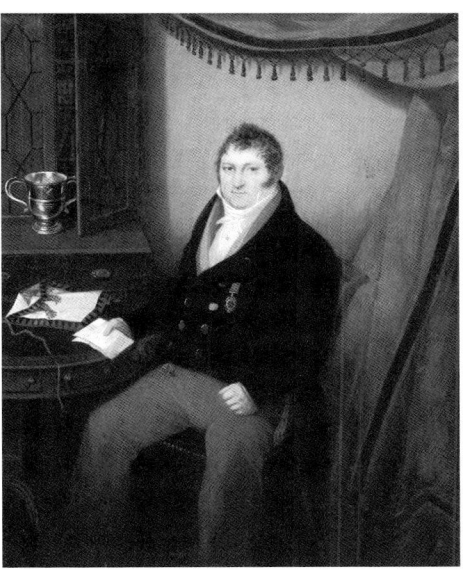

203 **UNKNOWN ARTIST**
*Mr William Thompson*, c.1820
oil on canvas, 44.5 x 34.0 cm
Gift of Miss E. E. Thompson 1969
696P27

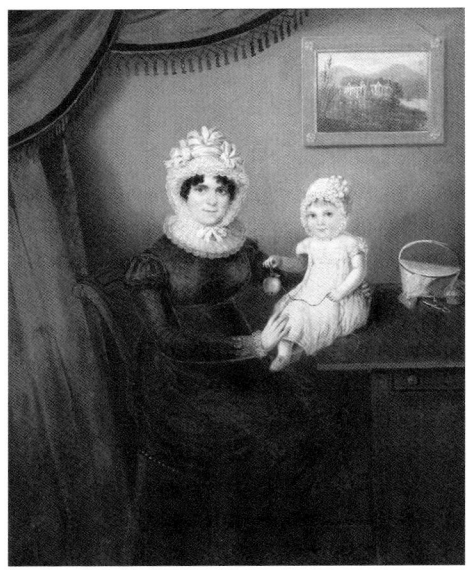

204 **UNKNOWN ARTIST**
*Mrs William Thompson and child*, c.1820
oil on canvas, 63.5 x 50.8 cm
Gift of Miss E. E. Thompson 1969
697P33

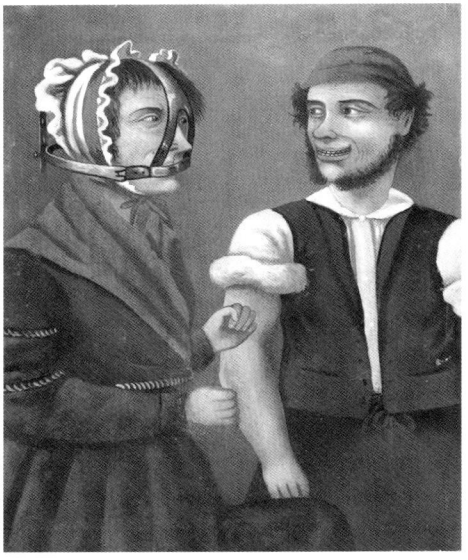

206 **UNKNOWN ARTIST**
*The Scold's Bridle*, c.1830
oil on card
22.7 x 20.3 cm
Gift of Mrs Pearson 1968
6813P24

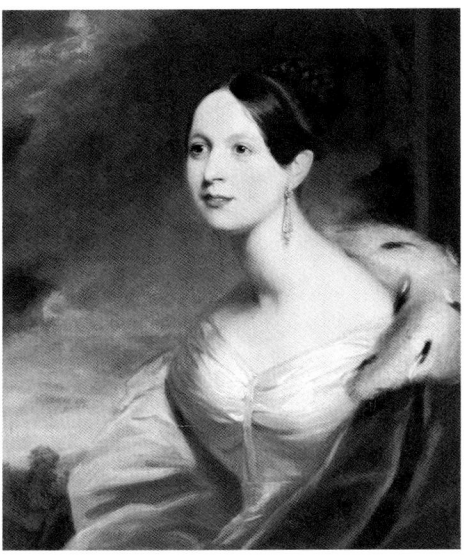

208 **UNKNOWN ARTIST**
*Emily Elizabeth McGeorge Giles*, c.1830
oil on canvas
76.5 x 64.5 cm
Bequest of Mortimer Giles and
Agnes Law-Smith 1980
801HP2

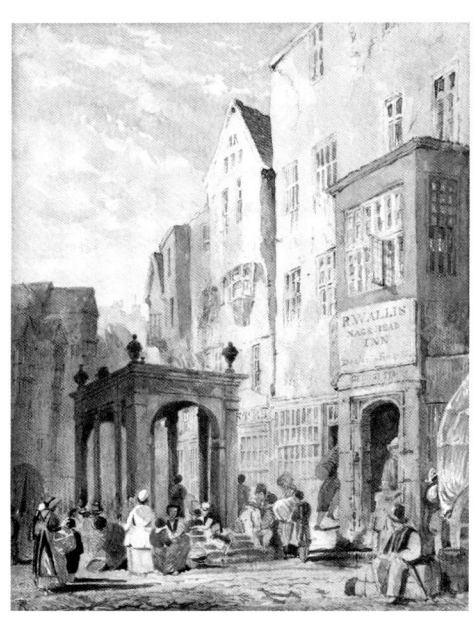

205 **UNKNOWN ARTIST**
*Nag's Head Inn, Newcastle-upon-Tyne*,
1828
watercolour, gouache on paper
22.6 x 17.0 cm (sheet)
Gift of the Misses Kay 1938
0.825

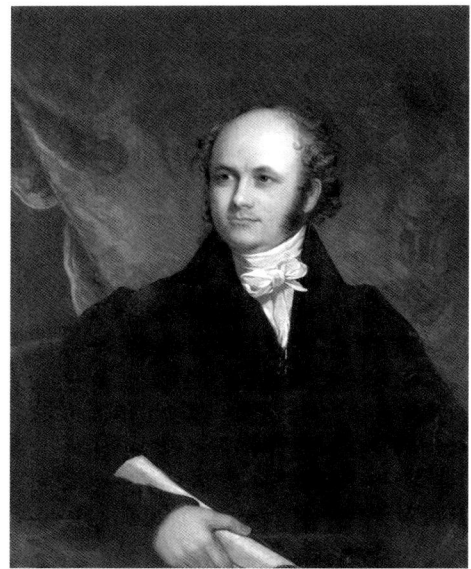

207 **UNKNOWN ARTIST**
*William Giles (1791–1862)*, c.1830
oil on canvas
91.3 x 70.0 cm
Bequest of Mortimer Giles and
Agnes Law-Smith 1980
801HP1

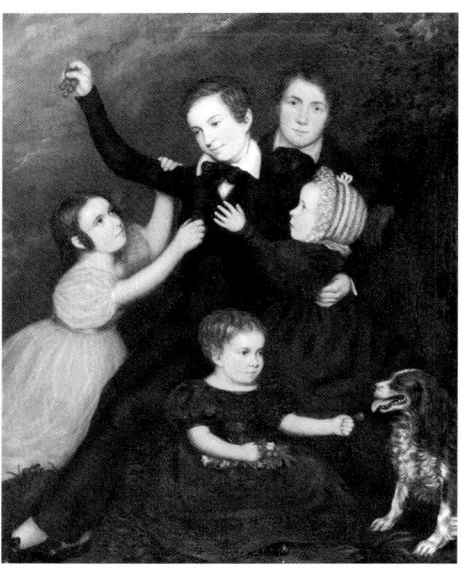

209 **UNKNOWN ARTIST**
*The children of Mr and Mrs Peter Cumming*,
c.1820s
oil on canvas
148.0 x 117.5.0 cm (sight)
Gift of Mrs E. H. McTaggart 1963
0.2007

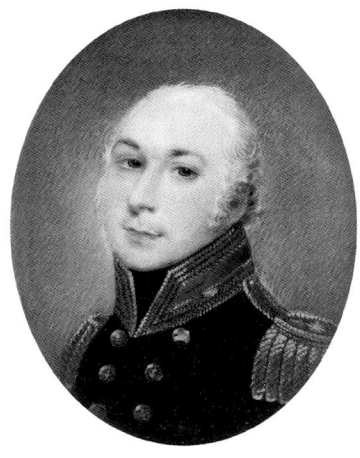

210 **UNKNOWN ARTIST**
*Lt W. Geo. Field*, c.1830s?
oil on ivory
6.3 x 5.0 cm
Gift of Mrs H. S. Field 1882
863P9

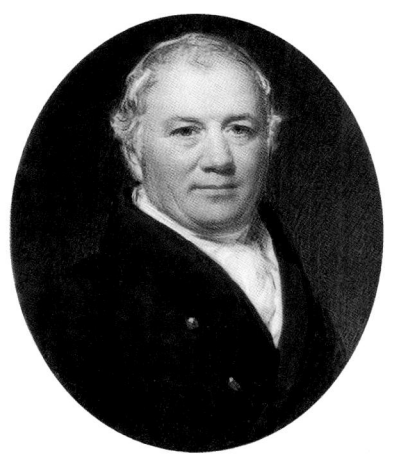

212 **UNKNOWN ARTIST**
*R. W. Elmer*, c.1850
watercolour on ivory
5.0 x 5.7 cm
Gift of Mrs M. G. Elmer 1969
697A23

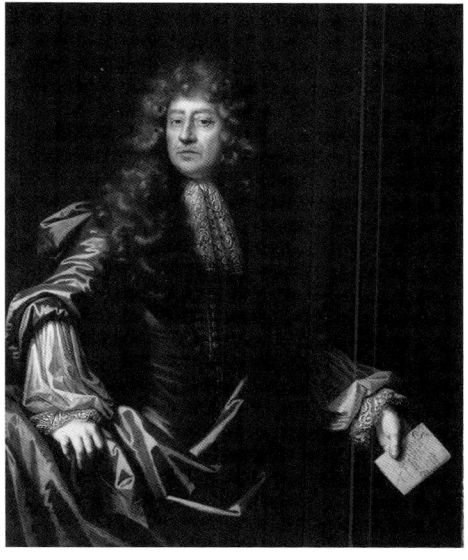

214 **Simon VERELST**  1644–1721?
*Portrait of an Ambassador*, c.1686
oil on canvas
125.1 x 100.9 cm
South Australian Colonial Government Grant 1896
0.113

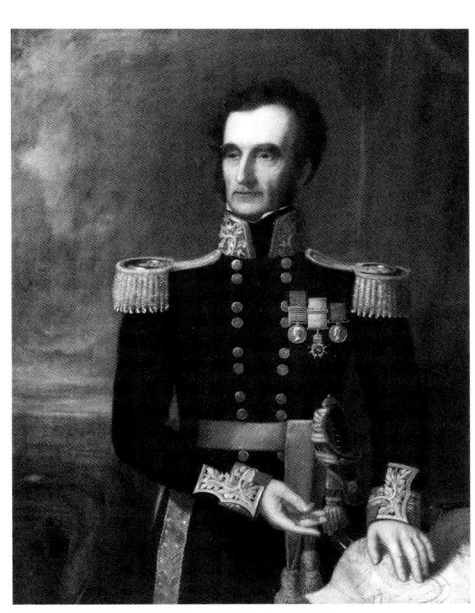

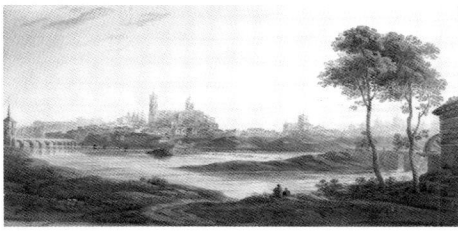

213 **John VARLEY**  1778–1842
*City on a river*, c.1820s?
watercolour on paper
33.3 x 66.3 cm (sheet)
South Australian Government Grant 1955
0.1601

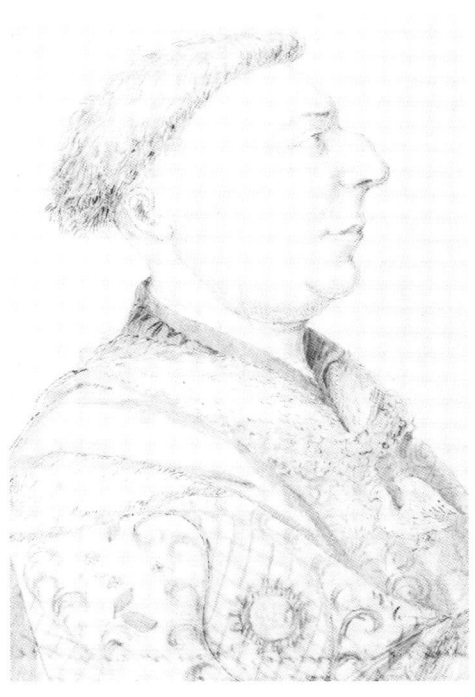

211 **UNKNOWN ARTIST**
*Colonel George Gawler*, c.1845
oil on canvas
120.0 x 90.0 cm
South Australian Government Grant 1981
816HP60

Gawler was the second Governor of South Australia, arriving in Adelaide in 1839 and departing in 1841. This portrait was probably painted soon after his return to England when he was approximately fifty years of age.

215 **George VERTUE**  1684–1756
*John, Duke of Bedford*, c.1747
leadpoint, brush & wash on paper
12.7 x 8.9 cm (sheet)
Bequest of David Murray 1908
084D18

This is a preparatory drawing for an engraving.

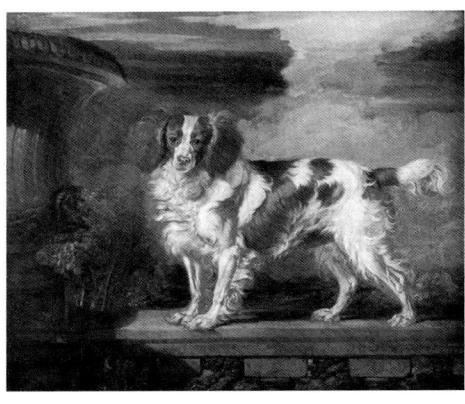

216 **James WARD** 1769–1859
*Portrait of Dash, a Favourite Spaniel, the Property of Lady Frances Vane-Tempest*, 1819
oil on canvas
88.9 x 104.1 cm
South Australian Government Grant 1959
0.1832

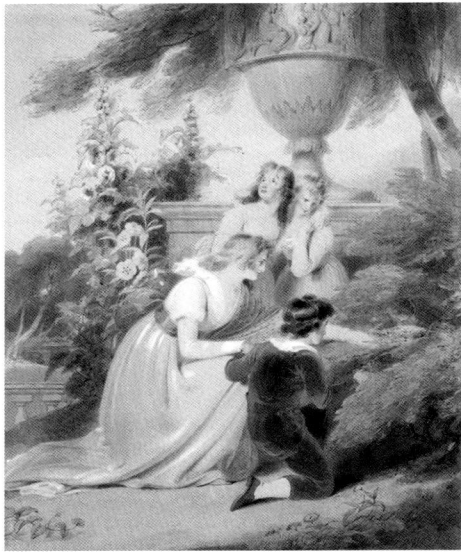

218 **Richard WESTALL** 1765–1836
*The birds' nest*, 1794
watercolour, gouache on paper
44.0 x 35.8 cm (sheet)
South Australian Government Grant 1955
0.1621

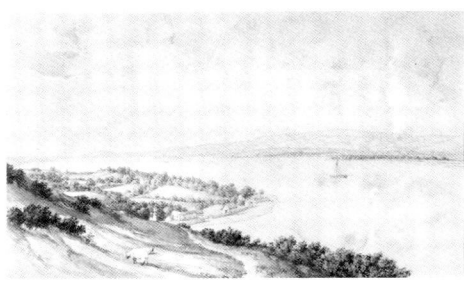

220 **William WESTALL** 1781–1850
*Blyth Estuary*, c.1820
watercolour on paper
20.0 x 31.2 cm (sheet)
Gift of M. J. M. Carter through the Art Gallery of South Australia Foundation 2004
20044P60

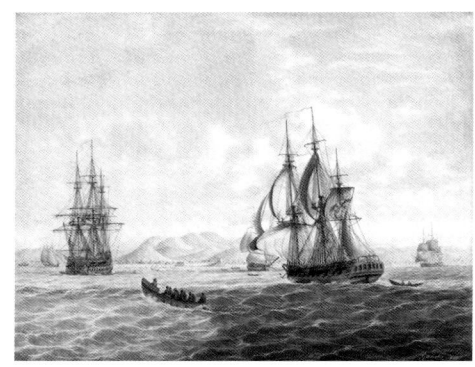

217 **George WEBSTER** *fl.* 1797–1832
*A view from the West Coast of Africa*, 1801
watercolour on paper
37.0 x 47.2 cm (sheet)
South Australian Government Grant 1955
0.1628

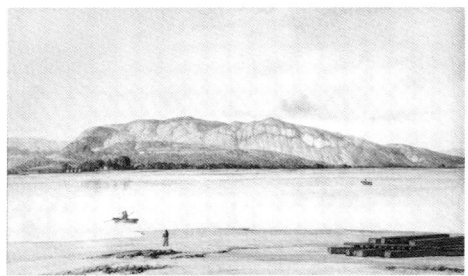

219 **William WESTALL** 1781–1850
*Estuary view*, c.1820
pencil, watercolour on paper, mounted on cardboard
29.8 x 31.6 cm (sheet)
Gift of M. J. M. Carter through the Art Gallery of South Australia Foundation 2004
20044P61

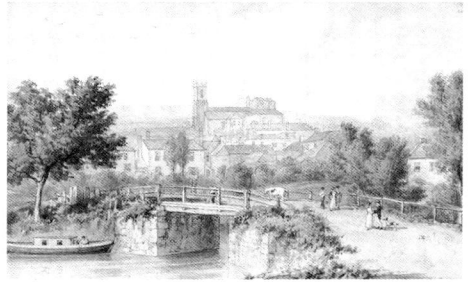

221 **William WESTALL** 1781–1850
*Hythe, Kent: from the canal bridge*, c.1830
watercolour, pencil on paper
9.3 x 14.7 cm (sheet)
Gift of M. J. M. Carter through the Art Gallery of South Australia Foundation 2004
20044P59

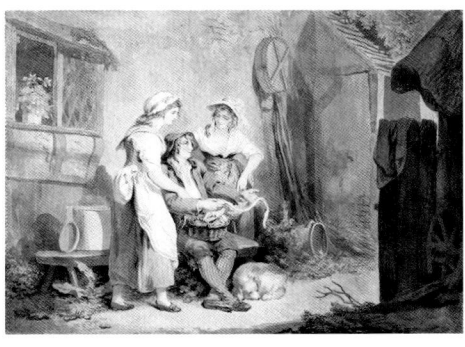
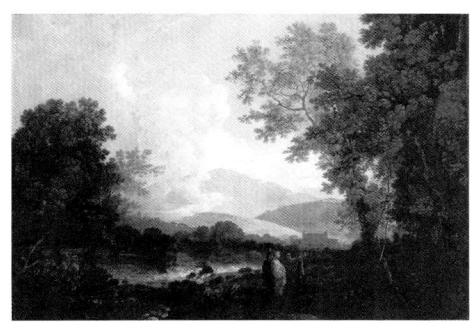

222 **Francis WHEATLEY** 1747–1801
*The blind pedlar*, 1794
watercolour on paper
34.7 x 48.0 cm (sheet)
South Australian Government Grant 1956
0.1648

224 **Richard WILSON** 1713–1782
*Cicero with his friend Atticus and brother Quintus, at his villa at Arpinum*, c.1771–75
oil on canvas
121.8 x 174.5 cm
Morgan Thomas Bequest Fund 1948
0.1371

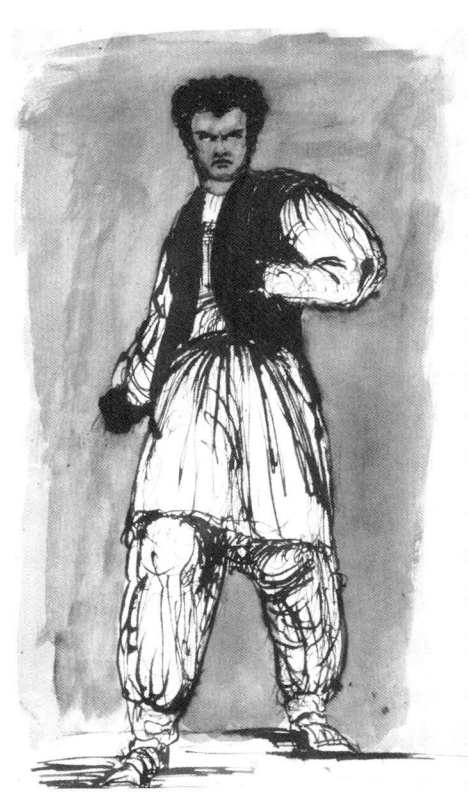
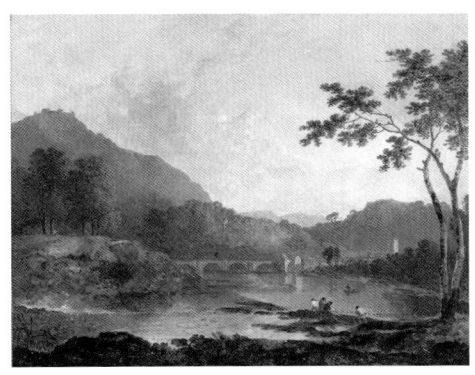

225 **Richard WILSON** 1713–1782
*Dinas Bran from Llangollen*, c.1772–75
oil on canvas
82.5 x 104.1 cm
Gift of Gladys Penfold Hyland in memory of her husband Frank 1964
0.2029

223 **David WILKIE** 1792–1871
*Study of a man in Turkish dress*, c.1840
pen & sepia ink, brush & wash on paper
33.5 x 19.4 cm (sheet)
South Australian Government Grant 1971
714D2

# Select Bibliography

Most references cited in the notes to the individual essays are specific to those essays and are not repeated here. Instead only a few recent or less familiar monographic publications are included, and some general publications on British art. Abbreviations are given for the frequently cited publications of the Art Gallery of South Australia (known until 1967 as the National Gallery of South Australia). Not listed are the standard reference books – dictionaries and encyclopedias of art or biography – that have been drawn upon for the biographical matter. It should be noted that the older standard histories of British art and the British-published recent reference books have the best grip on artists' working names (authorising, for example, "J. F. Herring" in preference to "John Frederick Herring"). We acknowledge the Google search engine into websites for up-to-date and corrected place names.

Andrew, Patricia R. "Jacob More: Biography and a checklist of works." *The Walpole Society 1989/90*, vol. 55, London, 1993.

AGSA *Picture Book* 1972
Art Gallery of South Australia. *Picture Book: Selected works from the collections of the Art Gallery of South Australia*. Adelaide.

AGSA *Master Prints and Drawings* 1978
Carroll, Alison. *Master Prints and Drawings from the Collection of the Art Gallery of South Australia*. Adelaide.

AGSA *1881–1981*
Thomas, David, et al. *Art Gallery of South Australia 1881–1981*. Adelaide, 1981.

AGSA *Hidden Treasures* 1989
Radford, Ron. *Hidden Treasures: South Australia's European Old Master Paintings: Restoration and Re-attributions, and South Australia's European Old Master Drawings*. Adelaide.

AGSA *Selected Works* 1991
Art Gallery of South Australia. *Selected Works from the collections of the Art Gallery of South Australia*. Adelaide.

AGSA *M. J. M. Carter Collection* 1993
Radford, Ron. *19th-Century-Australian Art: M. J. M. Carter Collection: Art Gallery of South Australia*. Adelaide.

AGSA *Treasures* 1998
Radford, Ron, et al. *Treasures from the Art Gallery of South Australia, Adelaide*. Adelaide.

AGSA *The Fine Art of Giving* 1999
Radford, Ron. *The Fine Art of Giving: The William Bowmore Collection: 90 Masterpieces*. Adelaide.

Barber, Tabitha. *Mary Beale: Portrait of a seventeenth century painter, her family and her studio*. [London]: Geffrye Museum, 1999.

Barnes, Susan J., Nora de Poorter, Oliver Millar and Horst Vey. *Van Dyck: A complete catalogue of the paintings*. London: Yale University Press, 2004.

Beckett, Oliver. *J. F. Herring and Sons*. London: Allen, 1981.

Bowness, Alan, et al. *The Pre-Raphaelites*. London: Tate Gallery / Penguin, 1984.

Brooke, Xanthe, and David Crombie. *Henry VIII Revealed: Holbein's portrait and its legacy*. London: Holberton, 2003.

*Bulletin NGSA*
*Bulletin of the National Gallery of South Australia*. Adelaide, March 1939 – October 1967 (quarterly). [Continued from 1968 as *Bulletin of the Art Gallery of South Australia*]

Burke, Joseph. *English Art 1714–1800*. London: OUP, 1976.

Boase, T. S. R. *English Art 1800–1870*. London: OUP, 1959.

Butlin, Martin. *The Paintings and Drawings of William Blake*. New Haven and London: Yale University Press, 1981.

Constable, W. G. *Richard Wilson*. London: Routledge, 1953.

Edmond, M. "Nicolas Dixon, limner: and Matthew Dixon, painter died 1710." *Burlington Magazine*, no. 967, October 1983.

Faigan, Julian. *Paul Sandby Drawings*. Sydney: Australian Gallery Directors' Council, 1981.

Garlick, Kenneth. *Sir Thomas Lawrence: A complete catalogue of the oil paintings*. New York, 1989.

Hansen, David. *John Glover and the Colonial Picturesque*. Hobart: Tasmanian Museum & Art Gallery / Sydney: Art Exhibitions Australia, 2003.

Hayes, John. *The Drawings of Thomas Gainsborough*, London, 1970.

Hayes, John. *The Art of Thomas Rowlandson*. Alexandria, Virginia: Art Services International for Baltimore Museum of Art, 1989.

Hoff, Ursula. *European Paintings before 1800 in the National Gallery of Victoria*. Melbourne: National Gallery of Victoria, 1995.

Keynes, Geoffrey (ed.). *William Blake's Illustrations to the Bible: A catalogue*. Clairvaux, Jura: Trianon Press, 1957.

Kidson, Alex. *George Romney 1734–1802*. London: National Portrait Gallery, 2002.

Larsen, Erik. *The Paintings of Anthony van Dyck*. Freren: Luca Verlag, 1988.

Lister, Raymond. *Catalogue Raisonné of the Works of Samuel Palmer*. Cambridge: CUP, 1988.

Lloyd, Michael (ed.). *Turner*. Canberra: National Gallery of Australia, 1996.

Lockett, Richard. *Samuel Prout (1783–1852)*. London: Batsford, 1985.

Mannings, David. *Sir Joshua Reynolds: A complete catalogue of his paintings*. New Haven and London: Yale University Press, 2000.

Menz *Regency* 1998
Menz, Christopher. *Regency: British Art & Design 1800–1830*. Adelaide: Art Gallery of South Australia.

Millar, Oliver. *The Age of Charles I: Painting in England 1620–1649*. London: Tate Gallery, 1972.

Millar, Oliver. *Sir Peter Lely*. London: National Portrait Gallery, 1978.

Museum of Fine Arts, Montreal. *Largillière and the Eighteenth Century Portrait*. Montreal, 1982.

NGSA *Catalogue* 1940
National Gallery of South Australia. *Catalogue: paintings, pastels, sculpture*. Adelaide.

NGSA *Catalogue* 1946
National Gallery of South Australia. *Catalogue: oil and water colour paintings and pastels with biographical, critical, descriptive and historical notes*. Adelaide, 5th ed.

NGSA *Catalogue* 1960
National Gallery of South Australia. *Catalogue: Oil and water-colour paintings and pastels, with biographical notes*. Adelaide, 6th ed.

NGSA *Picture Book* 1960
National Gallery of South Australia. *Picture Book of selected oil and water-colour paintings and sculpture*. Adelaide.

Paulson, Ronald. *Hogarth: His life, art and times*. New Haven and London: Yale University Press, 1971.

Potts, Alex. *Sir Francis Chantrey 1781–1841: Sculptor of the Great*. London: National Portrait Gallery, 1980.

Preston, Kerrison. *The Blake Collection of W. Graham Robertson, Described by the Collector*. London: Faber, 1952.

Radford, Ron. "Recent Acquisitions at the Art Gallery of South Australia." *Burlington Magazine*, no. CXLV, April 2003.

Roberts, Jane, and Christopher Loyd (eds). *George III and Queen Charlotte: Patronage, collecting and court taste*. London, 2004.

Roding, J. G., E. J. Sluijter, B. Westerweel, M. van der Meij-Tolsma and E. Domela Nieuwenhuis (eds.). *Dutch and Flemish Artists in Britain 1550–1800*. Leiden: Primavera, 2003.

Royalton-Kisch, Martin. *The Light of Nature: Landscape drawings and watercolours by Van Dyck and his contemporaries*. London: British Museum, 1999.

Sartin, Stephen. *Thomas Sidney Cooper, C.V.O., R.A., 1802–1902*. Leigh-on-Sea, Essex, 1976.

Shanes, Eric. *Turner: The Great Watercolours*. London: Royal Academy, 2001.

Smart, Alastair. *Allan Ramsay: Painter, essayist and man of the Enlightenment,* New Haven and London: Yale University Press, 1992.

Smart, Alastair. *Allan Ramsay: A complete catalogue of his paintings*, London: Yale University Press, 1999.

Smith, C. J. *British Mezzotint Portraits* (4 vols). London, 1878–83.

Solkin, David H. *Richard Wilson: The Landscape of Reaction*. London: Tate Gallery, 1982.

Stewart, Brian. *Thomas Sidney Cooper of Canterbury*. Rainham, Kent, 1983.

Stewart, J. Douglas. *Sir Godfrey Kneller and the English Baroque Portrait*. New York: OUP, 1983.

Strong, Roy. *The English Icon: Elizabethan & Jacobean portraiture*. London: Routledge, 1969.

Thomas, Sarah. *The Encounter, 1802: Art of the Flinders and Baudin Voyages*. Adelaide: Art Gallery of South Australia, 2002.

Tomory, Peter, and Robert Gaston. *European Paintings before 1800 in Australian and New Zealand Public Collections*: Summary Catalogue. Sydney: Beagle Press, 1989.

Trumble, Angus, and Christopher Chapman. *Still-life still lives*. Adelaide: Art Gallery of South Australia, 1997.

Waterhouse, Ellis. *Painting in Britain 1530 to 1790*. Harmondsworth, Middlesex: Penguin, 4th ed., 1978.

Waterhouse, Ellis. *Gainsborough*. London: Hulton, 1958.

Whinney, Margaret, and Oliver Millar. *English Art 1625–1714*. London: OUP, 1957.

Wilton, Andrew. *Turner in the British Museum: Drawings and Watercolours*. London, 1974.

Wilton, Andrew. *The Life and Works of J. M. W. Turner*. London, 1979.

Woodall, Mary. *The Letters of Thomas Gainsborough*. London, 1963.

# Index

This index is of names and titles of works of art.
Numbers in italic indicate illustrations.
Numbers in bold indicate main entries.

## A

Abercrombie, Colonel Robert   168, *169*, 284
Ackermann, Rudolph   186, 260
   *The Brilliants*   188
Adelaide, Queen, consort of William IV   2, *2*, 178, 289
Allport, Mary Morton   13
Angas, George French   28
Appleyard, Ron   292
Armstrong, Dr John   20, **130–132**, *131*, *132*, 283, 289
Aston, Sir Thomas   62, 64, 66, *66*
Atticus, Titus Pomponius   140, 142, *143*

## B

Bachelier, Jean-Jacques   96
Baily, John   293
Balen, Hendrik van   56
Banks, Sir Joseph   20, 21, 218, 227
Barlow, Francis   **98–99**, 295
   *A lion attacked by hounds*   99
Barlow, Thomas   20, 238, 294
Barret, George jnr   193
Basire, James   190
Bassano   74
Batoni, Pompeo   20, 295
   *Edward Weld*   7, 8
Bauer, Ferdinand   21, **218–221**, 286, 295
   *Passionflowers*   *219*, 221
Beale, Mary   76, **80–83**, 280, 295
   *Mary Wither of Andwell*   *81*, 83
Beardsley, Aubrey   213
Berkeley, Martha   13
   *Anne Eliza Duff with her daughter Jessie*   13
Bernini, Gianlorenzo   105
Blake, William   26, 164, **190–192**, 213, 242, 251, 266, 285, 294, 296
   *St Paul before Felix and Drusilla*   26, 34, *191*
   *The Destruction of Job's sons*   26
Blocklandt, Anthonie van   42, 72
Bloxam, Miss E.   289
Boccius, Dr Norbert   218
Bock, Thomas   13, 200, 252
Bol, Ferdinand   105
Bologna, Giovanni   74
Bombelli, Sebastiano   105
Bonington, Richard Parkes   226
Booth, George, Lord Delamere   **76–77**, 280

Boucher, François   170
Bowden, Helen & John   295, 296
Bowmore, William   292, 294, 295
Boydell, John   170, 238
Britton, John   260
Brooking, Charles   22, 158
Bruegel, Jan   60
Bruegel, Pieter   60, 256, 266
Butterworth, Thomas   22
Butts, Thomas   190, 192

## C

Calvert, Edward   190
Campbell, Robert   290, 292
Canova, Antonio   222, 254
Cappelle, Jan van de   206
Caravaggio   74
Carpaccio, Vittore   156
Carriera, Rosalba   136
Carroll, Alison   293
Carter, Max   293, 295, 296
Cary, F. S.   264
Champaigne, Philippe de   94
Chantrey, Francis   222–223, 286, 290
   *King George III*   223
Charles I   15, 16, 56, 62, 68, 72, 74, 75, 76, 126
Charles II   16, 18, 22, 76, 80, 84, 88, 105, 122
Charlotte, Queen, consort of George III   126, *128*, 196, 242
Chippendale, Thomas   130
Cicero, Marcus Tullius   140, 142, *143*
Clare, John   245, 251
Clare, Mr and Mrs   **251–253**, 287
Clark, Sir Kenneth   290
Clemens, Anne   294, 295
Cleyn, Francis   98
Clouet, François   46, 50
Colbert, Jean Baptiste   84
Collier, Edward   **100–101**, 294, 295
   *Letter rack*   101
Conder, Charles   218
Constable, Alfred   264
Constable, John   24, 28, 130, 206, 224, 236, 248, 251, 264, 266, 270
Constable, Lionel   **264–265**, 288
   *A summer sunset*   265
   *Dawn*   265
Cook, James   20, 227

Cooper, Thomas Sidney   22, 238, **248–250**, 287, 295
   *Fording a brook, suburbs of Canterbury*   22, *249*
Corot, Jean-Baptiste Camille   30, 204, 226
Correggio, Antonio   72
Cortona, Pietro da   102
Cotes, Francis   20, 119, 130, **136–139**, 164, 178, 283, 290, 296
   *Elizabeth, Lady Jones*   *137*, 139
   *Sir William Jones*   138
Cotman, John Sell   28, **204–205**, 285, 294, 296
   *The Old Pigeon House, Downham*   205
   *The old pigeon house, Downham Market*   205
Courbet, Gustave   30
Cox, David   246
Cozens, J. R.   206
Crabb, Sarah   289
Crane, Walter   213
Creswick, Thomas   248
Critz, John de   16, 52, 62
Crofts, Lady Henrietta, Duchess of Bolton   **105–109**, 281
Crome, John   28
   *Mousehold Heath*   28
Cruikshank, George   18
Cure, William   42
Cuyp, Aelbert   22, 206, 230, 231, 248, 270

## D

d'Auvergne Boxall   294
Davidson, Bessie   54
Da Vinci, Leonardo   72
Davis, John Scarlet   212
   *The Library at Tottenham, the seat of B. G. Windus, Esq.*   212, *212*
Dayes, Edward   206
Deuchar, David   202
Devis, Arthur   18, 23, **116–118**, 240, 282, 295
   *Portrait of a lady with a dog*   18, *117*, 240
De Wint, Peter   26, 28, 182, **245–247**, 251, 287, 290, 296
   *Kenilworth Castle*   26, 182, *247*
   *Kenilworth Castle* (Tate)   246
Dixon, Matthew   33, **78–79**, 280
   *Portrait of a man*   33, *79*

Dobson, William 16
Douglas family 122, 295
Douglas-Hamilton, Hugh 178
Douglas, James & Ann 296
Dowling, Robert 252
Downer, Sir Alexander 292
Drouais, François-Hubert 119
Dughet, Gaspard 24, 140, 144, 148, 154, 206, 224, 234, 236, 266, 270
Dumas, Sir Lloyd 289
Dunstan, Don 293
Dürer, Albrecht 50, 266
Duterrau, Benjamin 176
Dyck, Anthony van 15, 16, 18, 20, **56–61**, 62, 68, 70, 72, 74, 76, 80, 88, 94, 98, 105, 108, 110, 112, 113, 128, 150, 196, 278, 294, 295
   *A hilly landscape with trees and a distant tower* 61
   *A married couple* 15, 17, *57*, 60
   *A married couple* (Budapest) *58*, 58
   *A wooded ridge* 60, *61*
   *Jan Snellinx* 15

## E

Earle, Augustus 218
Eastlake, Charles 204, **224–226**, 286, 294
   *Cypress trees at the Villa d'Este* 204, *225*
   *Lord Bryon's 'Dream'* 226, *226*
Edward VI 36
Edwards, Roy & Marjory 295, 296
Elder, Sir Thomas 294
Elizabeth I 13, 14, *14*, 15, 16, 36, 42, 44, 46, 50, 52, 62, 294
Elizabeth, Queen, consort of Henry VII 12, 36
Evans, Diana 294, 296
Eworth, Hans 16, 41, 62
Eyck, Jan van 58, 272

## F

Fairfax, James 292, 294, 295
Fawkes, Walter 208, 209, 260
Fenn, Catherine **68–71**, 280
FitzHerbert, William **113–115**, *115*, 282
Flatman, Thomas 80
Flaxman, John 26, 164, 190, **213–217**, 254, 286, 293
   *Design for a dessert stand* 214
   *Dessert stand* 213–215, *215*
   *Arcana Cœlestia: Novitiate spirits surrounded by a heavenly sphere* 26, 216, *217*
Flinders, Matthew 21, 218, 295
Fogelberg, Andrew 214
Fragonard, Jean-Honoré 224
Frisbee, William 214
Fuseli, Henry 130, 164, 190, 242, 251

## G

Gainsborough, Thomas 20, 23, 60, 130, 136, **150–157**, 164, 170, 178, 180, 181, 196, 238, 283, 284, 292, 293, 294, 295, 296
   *Edward, 2nd Viscount Ligonier* 180
   *George, Prince of Wales* 180
   *Madam Lebrun* 20, *151*, *153*
   *Study for the portrait of Mrs Siddons* 152
   *Wooded landscape with a building and pool* 156, *157*
   *Wooded upland landscape with shepherd and sheep and track winding around a knoll* 154, *155*
Gambel, Ellis 113
Gaspers, John Baptiste 76
Gentileschi, Orazio 74
George I 18, 105
George II 110, 126
George III 18, 122, **126–129**, 133, 136, 158, 196, **222–223**, 242, 282, 286
George IV 126, 196, 202, 214, 222, 260
George V 2, 289
Gerbier, Balthasar 74
Gheeraerts, Marcus, the Younger 15, 16, 50, 56, 59, **62–67**, 68, 70, 278–279, 289, 295, 296
   *Lady Lucy Reynell* 54
   *Magdalen Poultney, later Lady Aston* 15, *63*, 65, 67
Ghiberti, Lorenzo 213, 216
Gibson, John **254–255**, 287, 295
   *Portrait of a woman* 255
Giles, Geoffrey O'Halloran 294, 296
Gill, H. P. 250
Gill, S. T. 28, 256
Gilliband, James 202
Gillray, James 18
Giordano, Luca 102
Giorgione 74
Girtin, Thomas 24, 206, 245, 292
Glover, John 22, 26, 28, 218, **230–237**, 238, 242, 248, 251, 266, 270, 286–287, 289, 295
   *Cattle: The last Gleam of the Setting Sun* 22, *232–233*
   *North End, Hampstead Heath* 236, *237*
   [*North End, Hampstead Heath*] 237
   *Twilight, Ullswater* 234, *235*
   *View of Mills' Plains* 29
Goltzius, Hendrick 50
Goodricke, Richard 13, *13*, **42–45**, 277
Gordon, John Watson 202, 289
Gott, Joseph 254
Goubau, Antoni 88
Gower, George 14, 16, 42, **46–49**, 54, 56, 70, 277, 294, 295
   *Portrait of a lady* 14, *47*, 49

Gravelot, Hubert 18, 150
Grebber, Frans de 76
Grebber, Pieter de 76
Green, William 234
Greenhill, John 76
Gresse, John Alexander 193
Grimm, Samuel Hieronymus
   *The Grange Hall, Horne Farm and Woolley Wood* 35
Griffith, Thomas 210, 212, 260

## H

Halls, J. J. **242–244**, 295
   *The young haymakers* 244, *244*
   *Thomas Wilson* 243
Harris, J. 256
   *Spring*, from the series *The Seasons* 258
   *Summer*, from the series *The Seasons* 258
   *Winter*, from the series *The Seasons* 258
   *Autumn*, from the series *The Seasons* 258
Hawker, Thomas 76
Haydon, Benjamin Robert 224, 260
Hayley, William 164
Hayman, Francis 150
Hearne, Thomas 206, 260
Heere, Lucas de 62
Hendy, Sir Philip 289
Henley, Robert, Second Earl of Northington 133, *134*, *135*, 283
Henry VII 12, 36
Henry VIII 12, *12*, 13, **36–41**, *37*, *38*, *39*, *40*, *41*, 46, 48, 277, 292
Herring, J. F. 21, 238, **256–259**, 287, 294, 296
   *Autumn* 21, *257*, *259*
Heysen, Hans 289
Highmore, Joseph 18, 105, 108, **110–112**, 281, 294
   *Self portrait* 110
   *The artist's wife Susanna, son Anthony and daughter Susanna* 111
Hilliard, Nicholas 13, 16, 46, 50, 52, 62
Hills, Robert 22, **193–195**, 234, 238, 285
   *Soay sheep in a landscape* 195
Hilton, William 245
Hobbema, Meindert 150, 236
Hogarth, William 18, 102, 105, 108, 110, **113–115**, 122, 126, 150, 186, 188, 282, 294
   *Simon, Lord Lovat* 19
   *The quarrel with her Jew protector* 19
   *William FitzHerbert* 18, *115*

Holbein, Hans, the Younger  12, 13, 15, **36–41**, 42, 44, 46, 72, 113, 277, 292
   *Henry VII and Henry VIII*  40
   *Henry VIII* (Palazzo Barberini)  38
   *Henry VIII* (The Walker)  40
   *King Henry VIII*  37, 39, 41
Hollar, Wenceslaus  16
Hone, Nathaniel  13, 295
   *Naval Officer*  13
Honthorst, Gerrit van  74
Hoppner  178, 242, 244
Horenbout, Lucas  13, 16, 41, 50
Howitt, James  18
Howitt, Samuel  **227–229**, 238, 286
   *Kangaroos (Didelphis Gigantia)*  229
   *Sketchbook of Samuel Howitt*  228
Hudson, Thomas  132, 133
Hunt, William Henry  251
Hunt, William Holman  30, **272–276**, 288, 292, 296
   *Christ and the Two Marys*  30, *31, 273, 275*
   *The shadow of death*  274, *274, 276*
Hyland, Gladys Penfold & Frank Penfold  292, 295, 296
Hysing, Hans  126

## I

Imperiali, Francesco  126

## J

Jacquin, Nikolaus Joseph von  218
James I  15, 16, 50, 52, 56, 62, 72
James II  76, 80, 84, 88, *90*, 91, 160, 289
James, Richard  254
Johnson, Cornelius  15, 16, 59, 62, **68–71**, 72, 280, 294, 295, 296
   *A lady, thought to be Catherine Fenn*  69, *71*
   *Catherine Fenn*  70
Jones, Elizabeth  **136–139**, *137, 139,* 283
Jones, Sir William  136, *138*

## K

Ketel, Cornelius  13, 16, **42–45**, 277, 293, 295, 296
   *Richard Goodricke of Ribston, Yorkshire*  13, *43, 44, 45*
Kettle, Tilly  20, 119–121, 282, 296
   *Portrait of Anne Howard-Vyse*  120
   *Woman with a muff*  121
Knapton, George  136
Kneller, Godfrey  16, 18, 20, 96, 102, **105–109**, 110, 281, 294
   *Lady Henrietta Crofts, Duchess of Bolton*  *107, 109*, 110
   *Women's head* (British Museum)  106
   *Women's head* (V & A)  106

## L

Laguerre, Louis  102
Lambert, George  266
Lamerie, Paul de  130
Landseer, Edwin  22, 238
Largillierre, Nicolas de  33, **88–95**, 96, 100, 281, 294, 295, 296
   *Ann Throckmorton*  92
   *Elizabeth Throckmorton*  92
   *Frances Wollascot, an Augustinian nun*  93, 95
   *James II*  90
   *Portrait of a Frenchman*  33, *89*
   *Sir Robert Throckmorton*  92
Larkin, William  16, 74
Lawrence, Thomas  12, 20, 28, 130, 164, 172, 178, **196–201**, 242, 244, 251, 285, 289, 294, 295, 296
   *Admiral Frank Sotheron*  198
   *Caroline Matilda Sotheron*  20, *197, 199*
   *The son of Countess Meerveldt*  201
Lebrun, Madam Franzisca  **150–153**, 284, *151, 153*
Lee, F. R.  248
Legé, F. A.  254
Lely, Peter  16, 18, **76–77**, 80, 82, 84, 88, 105, 110, 113, 280, 290, 295, 296
   *Portrait of a man, thought to be George Booth, Lord Delamere*  16, *77*
Leslie, C. R.  222
Lewin, John  98
Leyden, Lucas van  266
Light, Colonel William  245
Linnell, John  190, 236, **251–253**, 266, 270, 287
   *Mr Clare* and *Mrs Clare*  253
   *Study for the paintings "Mr Clare" and "Mrs Clare"*  252
Liotard, Jean-Étienne  136
Loo, Jean-Baptiste van  18, 113
Lorrain, Claude  24, 140, 144, 148, 206, 212, 224, 230, 231, 234, 236, 246, 251, 266
Louis XIV  96
Lucas, David
   *A summerland*  25
   *Hadleigh Castle near the Nore*  25
Lycett, Joseph  23, 295

## M

Macdonald, Lawrence  254
Major, Thomas  242
Malton, Thomas  206
Manfredi, Bartolommeo  74
Maratta, Carlo  105
Marchi, Giuseppe  119
Marshall, William Calder  254
Martens, Conrad  28
Martin, David  128, 202
Mary I  36
Mary, Queen, consort of George V  2, 18, 289
McArdell, James  119
   *Anne (Day), Lady Fenoulhet*  120
McCubbin, Louis  289
Melrose, Alexander  289
Mercier, Philip  18, 116
Meredith, Louise Anne  295
Michelangelo  72, 190
Miereveld, Michiel van  15, 20, 33, 59, 68, **72–75**, 280, 292
   *George Villiers, Duke of Buckingham*  33, *73*
Millais, John Everett  272, 274
Molesworth, H. D.  290, 292
Monamy, Peter  22, 122
   *The first-rate ship* Royal Sovereign, *stern quarter view, in a calm*  124
Monnoyer, Jean-Baptiste  80, 84, **96–97**, 100, 281, 294, 296
   *Still-life with basket of flowers*  5, *97*
Monro, Dr Thomas  24, 206, 245, 251
More, Jacob  24, **148–149**, 283, 293
   *A distant view of Rome, across the Tiber*  24, *149*
Morgan, Sir Edward  289
Morland, George  174, **176–177**, 238, 284, 292
   *Outside the Bull's Head*  177
   *The public house door*  177
Mortimer, John Hamilton  186
Muller, William James  292
Mulready, William  236, 251
Murdoch, Sir Keith & Lady (later Dame Elisabeth)  294
Murray, David  289
Mytens, Daniel  16, 62, 68, 72, 74, 75
   *George Villiers, Duke of Buckingham*  74
Mytens, Jan  15

## N

Nash, John  213
Nattes, John Claude  193
Nollekens, Joseph  242
Norie, Robert  148
North, Ian  293
Nottingham workshops
*Two Apostles, St Simon and St Jude*  30

## O

Ogilby, John  98
Oliver, Isaac  13, 16, **50–51**, 62, 74, 277, 295
   *Man with fair hair and beard*  51

O'Shea, Major George · **178–181**, *179*, 284
Oudry, Jean Baptiste 91
Overton, Mary 295, 296

## P

Palmer, Samuel 26, 28, 190, 251, **266–271**, 288, 290, 295, 296
- *Hastings to Covert: A threatening rain storm* 271
- *Landscape with windmill, figures and cattle* 271
- *Summer storm near Pulborough, Sussex* 26, *268–269*, 270, *271*
- *The rustic dinner* 266, *267*

Palser, Thomas 260
Parker, James 190
Parsons, Geoffrey B. Angas 294, 296
Passe, Crispijn de, the Elder
- *Elizabeth, Queen of England* 14

Payne, William 230
Peake, Robert 14, 16, **52–55**, 56, 70, 74, 277, 294, 295, 296
- *Frances, Lady Reynell of West Ogwell, Devon* 14, *53*, *55*

Phillips, Tom 295, 296
Poelenburgh, Cornelis van 76
Potter, Paulus 230, 231, 248
Poultney, Magdalen **62–67**
Pourbus, Frans 62
Poussin, Nicolas 140, 206, 256, 266, 270
Prout, John Skinner 28, 224, 260, 289
Prout, Samuel 28, 210, 224, 226, **260–263**, 288, 290, 295, 296
- *An East Indiaman Ashore* 261
- *Salving from the wreck* 262–263

Pyne, William H. 193

## R

Raeburn, Henry **202–203**, 244, 285, 294
- *Archibald Trotter of Bush* 203

Ragless, A. M. 294
Ragless, A. R. 294
Raikes, Charlotte 164, *165*, 166, *167*, 168, 284
Raikes, Thomas 164, 166, *166*
Ramsay, Allan 18, 20, 24, 108, 119, **126–129**, 130, 136, 150, 196, 202, 222, 282, 289
- *King George III in coronation robes* 127, *129*
- *Queen Charlotte in coronation robes* 128

Ramsay, James & Diana 294, 295, 296
Ramsay, Robert 222
Raphael 30, 72, 94, 164, 224, 272
Raven, Samuel 2, 289
- *Queen Adelaide as Princess Adelaide* 2

Read, Richard, jnr 13
Read, Richard, snr 13
Reinagle, Philip 128
Rembrandt 105, 132, 206, 242, 270
Reni, Guido 74
Reynell, Gladys 54
Reynell, John 54
Reynell, Lady Frances **52–55**, *53*, *55*
Reynell, Lady Lucy 54
Reynell, Sir Richard 52, *54*
Reynolds, Joshua 20, 24, 105, 110, 119, 126, **130–135**, 136, 150, 152, 164, 178, 180, 190, 196, 200, 222, 224, 238, 240, 260, 283, 289, 290, 292, 295
- *Dr John Armstong* 131
- *Robert Henley, Second Earl of Northington* 135
- *Robert Henley, Second Earl of Northington (Dublin)* 134
- *Robert Henley, Second Earl of Northington (Carlisle)* 134
- *Robert Henley, Second Earl of Northington (Paris)* 134

Richard III 36
Richardson, Samuel 110
Richmond, George 190, 251
Rigaud, Hyacinthe 88, 96
Riley, John 105
Robson, G. F. 193, 289
Romney, George 20, 133, 150, **164–169**, 178, 196, 284, 292, 293, 295, 296
- *Charlotte, Mrs Thomas Raikes* 165, *167*, 168
- *Colonel Robert Abercrombie* 168, *169*
- *Thomas Raikes* 166

Rooker, Michael Angelo **182–185**, 246, 285, 290
- *A view of a ruined castle* 183, *185*
- *Castle at Newport on Usk, South Wales* 182, *184*

Rosa, Salvator 234, 240, 266
Rossetti, Dante Gabriel 272, 274
Rowlandson, Thomas 18, 26, **186–189**, 227, 228, 285, 290, 295, 296
- *Come live with me and be my love* 19
- *The Brilliants* 26, *187*, 189

Rubens, Peter Paul 15, 56, 58, 59, 60, 74, 108, 110, 238
- *George Villiers, Duke of Buckingham* 75

Ruisdael, Jacob van 150, 206, 236, 270
Runciman, Alexander 148, 202
Rundell, Bridge & Rundell 213, 214
Ruskin, John 260, 272
Russell, John 166
Ruysdael, Salomon van 150, 162, 248

## S

Sandby, Paul 24, 144, **162–163**, 182, 284, 290
- *Approaching Rochester and the Medway* 163

Serres, Dominic 22, 33, **158–161**, 284, 294
- *Foudroyant and Pégase entering Portsmouth Harbour* 33, *159*, *161*

Serres, John Thomas 158, 160
Seymour, Jane 12, 36
Shee, Martin Archer **178–181**, 284, 289
- *Major O'Shea of the Loyal Cork Legion* *179*, *181*

Shelley, Samuel 193
Sheppard, William 98
Sheraton, Thomas 130
Sibthorp, John 218
Siddons, Sarah 150, *152*, 152
Smith, John 105
- *Lady Henrietta Crofts, Duchess of Bolton* 106

Smith, John Raphael 181, 238
Smith, John Warwick 230
Solimena, Francesco 126
Somer, Paul van 15, 16, 62, 68, 72, 74
Sothern, Caroline Matilda **196–199**, *198*, *199*, 285
Sotheron, Frank 196, *198*
Souch, John 64
- *Sir Thomas Aston at the deathbed of his wife* 66

Spry, Dorothy 295
Stanfield, Clarkson 22, 292
Steele, Christopher 164
Storr, Paul 213–215
Stothard, Thomas 190, 214
Stuart, Gilbert 178
Stubbs, George 20, 227, 230, 238
- *A lion devouring a horse* 20, *21*

Swaine, Francis 22, 33, **122–125**, 282, 295, 296
- *The Landing of the Sailor Prince at Spithead* 33, *123*, *125*

Swaine, Monamy 122
Swedenborg, Emanuel 216

## T

Tatham, Frederick 190
Theed, William 213
Thomas, Daniel 293
Thomas, David 293
Thomas, Morgan 294

Thornhill, James  18, **102–104**, 110, 113, 281, 294
    *Marriage of Jupiter and Juno*  104, *104*
    *Minerva and the Gods of Olympus: A design for the hall ceiling at Easton Neston*  *103*
Thornycroft, Mary  254
Thorvaldsen, Bertel  254
Tillemans, Peter  116
Timbrell, Henry  254
Tintoretto, Jacopo  58, 59, 74
Titian  15, 21, 56, 59, 60, 74, 105, 164, 240
Trotter, Archibald  202, *203*
Turner, J. M. W.  22, 23, 24, 26, 28, 130, 182, **206–212**, 242, 245, 246, 248, 260, 261, 264, 266, 270, 285–286, 290, 292, 295, 296
    *Alnwick Castle*  26, 182, 210, *211*, 246, 261
    *Alnwick Castle and Bridge from the North-West*  210
    *Scarborough*  208
    *Scarborough Castle: Boys crab fishing*  209
    *Scarborough town and castle: morning: boys catching crabs*  10–11, 26, 34, *207*, 210, 246, 260
Turner, Nicholas  293

## V

Vane-Tempest, Lady Frances  238, 240
Varley, Cornelius  236
Varley, John  236, 245, 251
    *Frognal, Hampstead*  236, *237*
Velázquez, Diego  132, 202
Velde, Willem van de, the Elder  22, 122
Velde, Willem van de, the Younger  22, 122, 158, 206
    *Coast scene*  23
Verboeckhoven, Eugène  248
Verelst, Simon  33, **84–87**, 96, 100, 280–281, 289, 295
    *Portrait of an Ambassador*  33, *85*, *87*
Vernet, Joseph  140, 148, 158
Veronese  56, 59, 74
Verrio, Antonio  88, 102
Vertue, George  78, 91
    *King Henry VIII*  *12*
Victoria, Queen  21, 26, 126, 178, 222, 248, 254
Villiers, George, Duke of Buckingham  52, 56, **72–75**, 280, 292
Vos, Cornelis de  56

## W

Wainewright, Thomas Griffiths  200
Wakefield, Edward Gibbon  289
Walker, Robert  80
Walpole, Horace  84
Walpole, Sir Robert  23
Ward, James  21, 176, 193, 194, 230, **238–241**, 246, 287, 290, 296
    *Portrait of Dash, a Favourite Spaniel, the Property of Lady Frances Vane-Tempest*  21, *239*, *241*
Ward, William  238
Wate, William  266
Watson, James
    *Anne, Duchess of Cumberland*  20
Watteau, Antoine  156
Wedgwood, Josiah  130, 213
Weld, Edward  *7*, *8*
West, Benjamin  196, 260
Westall, Richard  26, **172–175**, 284
    *The birds' nest*  26, *173*, *175*
Westall, William  295
Wheatley, Francis  26, **170–171**, 174, 176, 238
    *A travelling potter with his wares outside a cottage*  *170*
    *The blind pedlar*  26, *171*
White, Christopher  292
Whitlam, Gough  293
Wijnants, Jan  231
Wilkie, David  242
William IV  2, 122, 178, 222, 289
Williams-Wynn, Sir Watkin  142, 144, 162
Willemsz, Willem  72
Willmore, J. T.  210
    *Alnwick Castle*  210
Wilson, Richard  24, 130, **140–147**, 148, 230, 283, 289, 292, 295, 296
    *Cicero with his friend Atticus and brother Quintus, at his villa at Arpinum*  *141*, 230, 283
    *Cicero with his two friends, Atticus and Quintus, at his Villa at Arpinum*  *143*
    *Dinas Bran Castle, near Llangollen* (Yale)  *146*
    *Dinas Bran from Llangollen*  24, 144, *145*, *147*, 283
    *Dinas Bran from Llangollen* (Yale)  *146*
Wilson, Shirley Cameron  295, 296
Wilson, Thomas  **242–244**, 287, 295
Wissing, Willem  76
Wither, Mary  **80–83**, 280
Wollascot, Frances  **91–95**, 281
Woollett, William
    *Cicero at his villa*  *143*
Woolner, Thomas  204
Wright, Harold  289
Wright, John  196
    *Caroline Matilda Barker, Mrs Frank Sotheron*  198
Wright, Joseph  130
Wright, Thomas  140

## Y

Young, V. B. F.  294

## Z

Zoffany, Johann  136
Zuccarelli, Francesco  140

*Island to Empire: 300 Years of British Art 1550–1850* was published to coincide with the exhibition of the same title, 11 March – 13 June 2005.

Exhibition and book by Ron Radford

Edited by Daniel Thomas
Designed and produced by Antonietta Itropico
Photography of AGSA works by Saul Steed

Printed on Daltons Paper Ikono Silk 170gsm
Film by van Gastel Graphics Pty Ltd, Adelaide, Australia
Print by van Gastel Printing Pty Ltd, Adelaide, Australia

Distributed in Australia and New Zealand by Thames & Hudson Australia
11 Central Boulevard, Fishermans Bend, Victoria, Australia 3207
telephone (03) 9646 7788  facs (03) 9646 8790

Distributed in North America by Antique Collectors' Club / Woodstocker Books
116 Pleasant Street, suite 60B, Easthampton, MA 01027
toll-free in U.S. (800) 252 5231  facs (413) 529 0862

National Library Cataloguing-in-Publication data

  Radford, Ron, 1949– .
    Island to empire : 300 years of British art : 1550–1850,
    paintings, watercolours, drawings, sculptures from the
    collection of the Art Gallery of South Australia, Adelaide.

    Bibliography.
    Includes index.
    ISBN 0 7308 3014 4.

    1. Art Gallery of South Australia. 2. Art, British. 3.
    Art – South Australia – Adelaide. I. Art Gallery of South
    Australia. II. Title.

  708.994231

front cover detail: Peter De Wint, 1784–1849, *Kenilworth Castle*, c.1827, watercolour on paper, 51.4 x 70.0 cm (sheet). South Australian Government Grant 1955

back cover detail: Robert Peake, c.1551–1619, *Frances, Lady Reynell of West Ogwell, Devon*, c.1595, oil on oak panel, 113.5 x 88.5 cm. Gift of the Art Gallery of South Australia Foundation 1998

© Ron Radford and the Art Gallery of South Australia 2005

All rights reserved. No part of this publication may be reproduced, stored in a retrieval system, or transmitted, in any form or by any means, electronic, photocopying or otherwise, without the prior permission of the copyright owners.

# Art Gallery of South Australia

North Terrace  Adelaide  South Australia
tel: 61 8 8207 7000   facs: 61 8 8207 7070   www.artgallery.sa.gov.au